The Cambridge Companion to Medieval Music

From the emergence of plainsong to the end of the fourteenth century, this *Companion* covers all the key aspects of medieval music. Divided into three main sections, the book first of all discusses repertory, styles and techniques – the key areas of traditional music histories; next takes a topographical view of the subject – from Italy, German-speaking lands, and the Iberian peninsula; and concludes with chapters on such issues as liturgy, vernacular poetry and reception. Rather than presenting merely a chronological view of the history of medieval music, the volume instead focuses on technical and cultural aspects of the subject. In nineteen chapters, seventeen world-leading scholars give a perspective on the music of the Middle Ages that will serve as a point of orientation for the informed listener and reader; the book is a must-have guide for anyone with an interest in listening to and understanding medieval music.

MARK EVERIST is Professor of Music and Associate Dean in The Faculty of Humanities at the University of Southampton. His research focuses on the music of western Europe in the period 1150–1330, French opera in the first half of the nineteenth century, Mozart, reception theory, and historiography. He is the author of *Polyphonic Music in Thirteenth-Century France* (1989), *French Motets in the Thirteenth Century* (1994), *Music Drama at the Paris Odéon, 1824–1828* (2002), and *Giacomo Meyerbeer and Music Drama in Nineteenth-Century Paris* (2005) as well as editor of three volumes of the *Magnus Liber Organi* (2001–3).

The Cambridge Companion to

MEDIEVAL
MUSIC

. . . .

EDITED BY
Mark Everist
University of Southampton

CAMBRIDGE
UNIVERSITY PRESS

CAMBRIDGE UNIVERSITY PRESS
Cambridge, New York, Melbourne, Madrid, Cape Town, Singapore,
São Paulo, Delhi, Dubai, Tokyo, Mexico City

Cambridge University Press
The Edinburgh Building, Cambridge CB2 8RU, UK

Published in the United States of America by Cambridge University Press, New York

www.cambridge.org
Information on this title: www.cambridge.org/9780521608619

First published 2011

Printed in the United Kingdom at the University Press, Cambridge

A catalogue record for this publication is available from the British Library

Library of Congress Cataloguing in Publication data
The Cambridge companion to medieval music / edited by Mark Everist.
p.   cm. – (Cambridge companions to music)
Includes bibliographical references and index.
ISBN 978-0-521-84619-6 (hardback)
1. Music – 500–1400 – History and criticism.   I. Everist, Mark.   II. Title.   III. Series.
ML172.C32   2010
780.9'02 – dc22   2010019928

ISBN 978-0-521-84619-6 Hardback
ISBN 978-0-521-60861-9 Paperback

In memoriam Samantha Jane Verschueren
25 August 1985–22 August 2009

Contents

Illustrations

Music examples

Notes on contributors

Rebecca A. Baltzer is Professor *emerita* at the University of Texas at Austin. Her published work includes an edition of Notre Dame clausulae and articles on the sources of Notre Dame polyphony, the early motet, and the liturgical context of medieval polyphony.

Sam Barrett is Lecturer in music at the University of Cambridge, co-editor of *Music and Letters* and a board member of *Early Music History*. He has published several articles in the field of early medieval Latin song, culminating in a recent edition with Francesco Stella (*Corpus rhythmorum musicum saec. iv–ix*). He is currently finishing an edition and commentary on notated *metra* from Boethius's *De consolatione philosophiae*.

Nicolas Bell is Curator of Music Manuscripts at the British Library, London. His publications include a commentary to the facsimile edition of the Las Huelgas Codex. He is reviews editor of the journal *Plainsong & Medieval Music* and Secretary of the Henry Bradshaw Society.

Susan Boynton, Associate Professor of Historical Musicology at Columbia University, works on medieval Western liturgy, chant, monasticism, music drama, prayer, the history of childhood, and troubadour song. She is the author of *Shaping a Monastic Identity: Liturgy and History at the Imperial Abbey of Farfa, 1000–1125* (2006)

Ardis Butterfield is Professor of English at University College London. Her books include *Poetry and Music in Medieval France from Jean Renart to Guillaume de Machaut* (Cambridge University Press, 2002). She has recently been awarded a Major Leverhulme Research Fellowship (2008–11) to work on the origins of English song.

Robert Curry is principal of the Conservatorium High School and Honorary Senior Lecturer in the Centre for Medieval Studies, University of Sydney. His research focuses on music and monasticism in Central Europe. He is co-editor of *Variations on the Canon: Essays on Music from Bach to Boulez in Honor of Charles Rosen* and author of *Ars antiqua Music and the Clarist Order in Central Europe* (forthcoming)

Emma Dillon is Associate Professor of Music at the University of Pennsylvania. She is a specialist on French medieval music and manuscripts, and author of *Medieval Music-Making and the Roman de Fauvel*.

Lawrence Earp is Professor of Music at the University of Wisconsin-Madison. He is the author of *Guillaume de Machaut: A Guide to Research* (1995). His published articles focus on music in late medieval France.

Mark Everist is Professor of Music and Associate Dean in The Faculty of Humanities at the University of Southampton and has written on the Middle Ages, nineteenth-century opera in France, and Mozart reception. He is the editor of the two-part organa from the *Magnus liber organi*, 3 vols. (2001–3).

Sarah Fuller is Professor of Music at Stony Brook University, New York. Her research focuses on medieval music theory and analysis of early music. Her succinct conspectus of organum, discant and *contrapunctus* theory from the ninth to the fifteenth century appears in *The Cambridge History of Western Music Theory.*

Marco Gozzi is Associate Professor of Musicology and Music History in the Facoltà di Lettere e Filosofia at Trento University. He has published widely on late medieval music, cantus fractus, and liturgical books, and is also an active performer.

Leofranc Holford-Strevens is Consultant Scholar-Editor at Oxford University Press. A classicist by training, he has written on a wide range of topics, classical, medieval, humanistic, calendrical and musicological, this last especially with regard to texts that composers have set.

Elizabeth Eva Leach is University Lecturer in Music at the University of Oxford and a Fellow of St Hugh's College. She has published widely on the music and poetry of Guillaume de Machaut as well as on issues in fourteenth-century music theory. Her book *Sung Birds: Music, Nature, and Poetry in the Later Middle Ages* was published in 2007; her monograph on Machaut is forthcoming.

Peter M. Lefferts is Professor of Music History in the School of Music at the University of Nebraska-Lincoln. His work in medieval music has concentrated on English polyphony, mensural notation, tonal behaviour, and music theory.

Michael McGrade is a musicologist with interests in medieval music, opera, and music in the late eighteenth century. He was a member of the faculty at Brandeis University and Williams College, and is currently Director of Graduate Admissions at Worcester Polytechnic Institute, Massachusetts.

Christopher Page is Reader in Medieval Music and Literature in the University of Cambridge and Vice-Master of Sidney Sussex College. The founder of the acclaimed ensemble Gothic Voices, he has written numerous books and articles on aspects of medieval music. His major study *The Christian West and Its Singers: The First Thousand Years* is published in 2010.

Dolores Pesce is Professor of Musicology at Washington University in St Louis. Her medieval publications focus on pitch theory and thirteenth-century motets. She also writes about the music and life of Franz Liszt.

Chronology

ca150	Justin Martyr's account of a Sunday community meal at Rome with gospel reading and homily
313	Emperor Constantine's legalization of Christianity in the Edict of Milan
330	Constantine moves the imperial capital from Rome to Byzantium, refounded as Constantinople
347–420	Saint Jerome
354–430	Saint Augustine
395	Permanent political division between the Eastern and Western Roman Empire
first half of 5th century	Martianus Capella fl.
410	Fall of Rome to the Visigoths under Alaric
480–524	Boethius fl.
485–580	Cassiodorus fl.; codifies scheme of seven liberal arts
ca540	Rule drawn up by Saint Benedict of Nursia for the monks of Monte Cassino
559–636	Isidore of Seville fl.
late 7th century	Consolidation of Roman schola cantorum (?)
early 8th century	*Ordo Romanus I*
711	Arab and Berber invasion of the Iberian peninsula
28 July 754	Pépin, king of the Franks, consecrated by Pope Stephen II at St Denis
760s	Simeon, member of the Roman schola cantorum, teaches Frankish singers in Rouen
784–91	Arrival at the Frankish court of the Gregorian Sacramentary (*Hadrianum*) sent to Charlemagne by Pope Hadrian I
789	*Admonitio generalis* instructs Frankish clergy to learn Roman chant in conformity with Pépin's suppression of Gallican chant. First Viking invasion of British Isles
Christmas Day 800	Coronation of Charlemagne as Emperor of the Romans by Pope Leo III

ca800	Earliest unnotated mass antiphoners. Antiphoner of Mt Blandin instructs singers to add *sequentiae* to alleluias
ca810–15	Supplement to the *Hadrianum* composed by ?Benedict of Aniane
816	Council of Aachen enjoins observance of the Benedictine Rule in all Frankish monasteries
ca830	Amalarius of Metz describes the *neuma triplex*
ca835	*Psalle modulamina* – perhaps the earliest example of neumatic notation
840–50	Aurelian fl.
ca840–930	Hucbald introduces the tetrachord of the finals *D, E, F, G* as the primary building block of the medieval gamut
843	Treaty of Verdun. Division of Carolingian Empire into three kingdoms
848	The Council of Meaux condemns the performance of prosulae, Gloria tropes and 'other creations'
870	Treaty of Meersen. Old Carolingian Empire now two kingdoms, roughly corresponding to modern-day France and Germany
ca877	First notated *sequentiae* found in Antiphoner of Compiègne
end of the 9th century	*Musica enchiriadis* and *Scolica enchiriadis* provide the earliest instruction in improvising organum or polyphony. First notated *cantatoria* and graduals
ca900	Sequences, singly or in small groups, first appear in manuscripts
ca900	*Alia musica* presents an early attempt to link medieval modes with Greek tribal names and their associated octave species
910	Foundation of monastery at Cluny
923–4	Earliest extant notated troper: Paris, Bibliothèque nationale, fonds lat. 1240
ca925–50	Expansion of trope repertory at St Gall begins; earliest extant tropers from East Francia (?)
ca930	Expansion of trope repertory in Aquitania begins

after 933	Revival of the abbey of Gorze by Bishop Adalbero of Metz
ca950	Romano-German Pontifical first appears in Germany
ca950	Large collections of sequences first appear; earliest extant copies of Notker's *Liber hymnorum*
962	Coronation of Otto I as Holy Roman Emperor
970s	Composition of Bishop Aethelwold of Winchester's *Regularis Concordia* for English Benedictines
late 10th century	*Dialogus de musica* codifies A B C D E F G with octave duplication as standard nomenclature
ca1000–ca1050	Winchester Organa (GB-Ccc MS 473)
ca1030	Guido of Arezzo devises staff notation; writes four treatises including *Micrologus*
ca1050	Appearance of 'transitional' sequences; Eastern and Western practices of notating sequences begin to converge
1054	Schism between Eastern and Western churches
1058	Pope Stephen IX forbids the singing of Beneventan chant at Monte Cassino
1066	Norman invasion of British Isles
1071	Earliest surviving manuscript of Old Roman chant
1071–1126	Guillaume IX, Duke of Aquitaine, first known troubadour
1079	Murder of Archbishop Stanislaus in Cracow Cathedral
1081 or 1083	Monks of Glastonbury rebel against Thurstan of Caen's imposition of chant from Normandy
1085	Alfonso VI of Castile and León, encouraged by Pope Gregory VII, suppresses the Old Hispanic rite
1096–9	Copying of Paris, Bibliothèque nationale de France, fonds latin 1139, containing liturgical drama

1098	Foundation of Cîteaux, the mother house of the Cistercian Order
1100	Johannes Affligemensis fl.
ca1100	Tropes have been replaced by versus as a medium of liturgical expression in southern France.
ca1100	First surviving written version of single Occitan religious song
ca1100	*Ad organum faciendum*
ca1100	Early MSS of Aquitanian polyphony
before 1107	Adam is precentor of Paris
1108	Abbey of St Victor founded by William of Champeaux
1125–48	Jaufre Raudel fl.
1147–70	Bernart de Ventadorn fl.
ca1150	Codex Calixtinus
1158	Foundation of University of Bologna
1159	John of Salisbury, *Policraticus*
ca1160	Cathedral of Notre Dame de Paris under construction
1160–1200	Leoninus fl.
ca1160–after 1213	Gace Brulé
ca1160–26 December 1236	Philip the Chancellor
1177	Completion of choir of Notre Dame de Paris
ca1177–1236	Gautier de Coinci, *Les Miracles de Nostre Dame*
1180–1220	Perotinus fl.
1182	Dedication of high altar of Notre Dame de Paris
1198 and 1199	Bishop Odo of Sully regulates use of polyphony and other liturgical matters at Notre Dame de Paris
Before ca1200	Repertory of Victorine sequences carefully revised and organized to express an Augustinian theology
ca1200	Walther von der Vogelweide fl.
early 13th century	Old Ordinal and Consuetudinary of Salisbury Use drawn up under Richard Poore
1203	Death of Gui, Châtelain de Couci
1208	Foundation of University of Paris
1209	Saint Francis of Assisi gives his followers their first rule

1213–16	Pope Innocent III's revision of mass and office of the papal court
ca1220	First texting of clausula to create motet
1220–1	Formal constitution of the Dominican order of friars
1220–30	Assembly of *Carmina Burana*
1223	Franciscans adopt the Use of the papal court
ca1230	Copying of Wolfenbüttel, Herzog August Bibliothek 628 (677)
1231	Agnes of Prague founds first Clarist monastery in Bohemia. Foundation of University of Oxford
1245–55	Copying of Florence, Biblioteca Medicea Laurenziana, Plut. 29.1
mid 13th century	Johannes de Garlandia, *De mensurabili musica*, discusses the rhythmic modes underlying Notre Dame polyphony
1248 and 1252	Papal authorizations for the use of the Slavic liturgy
1250	Four Dominican brothers commissioned to visit Metz to draw up a standard liturgy for the Dominican Order
ca1250	Copying of Wolfenbüttel, Herzog August Bibliothek 1099 (1206)
ca1250	Revision of the Roman liturgy by Haymo of Faversham, General of the Franciscan Order
1250–75	Copying of Madrid, Biblioteca Nacional de España 20846
ca1250–88	Adam de la Halle
1250–92	Guiraut Riquier fl.
ca1260–after 1330	Jacobus of Liège
before 1265	Composition of 'Sumer is icumen in'
1267	Pope Clement IV approves the revision of the Dominican liturgy by Humbert of Romans
ca1270	Copying of the majority of music in the Worcester Fragments
1270s	Copying of the majority of chansonniers. Copying of the Montpellier Codex = Montpellier, Université Montpellier 1, Bibliothèque de la Faculté de Médecine, H.196 (with additions into the early 1300s)

after 1272	Anonymous 4, an English witness to Parisian polyphony
1275–1300	Copying of first section of Bamberg, Staatsbibliothek, lit. 115
1279	St Emmeram Anonymous
after 1279	Franco of Cologne, *Ars cantus mensurabilis* codifies mensural notation
after 1279	Hieronymus de Moravia, untitled treatise
ca1290–1328	Nicole de Margival's *Dit de la panthère d'amours*
ca1290– after 1344	Johannes de Muris
1291–5	Pontifical of William of Durandus
1291–1361	Philippe de Vitry
1298–1316	Walter Odington fl.
end 13th century	Copying of Paris, Bibliothèque nationale de France, fonds français 25566
early 14th century	Copying of Oxford, Bodleian Library, Douce 308
ca1300	Copying of main part of Burgos, Monasterio de Las Huelgas 9
ca1300	Jakemès, *Le Roman du castelain de Couci*
ca1300	Johannes de Grocheio, untitled treatise
ca1300–77	Guillaume de Machaut
1303–5	Dante, *De vulgari eloquentia*
1317 or 1318	Marchetto da Padova, *Lucidarium*
after May 1317	Copying of Paris, Bibliothèque nationale de France, fonds français 146
1319–21	Johannes de Muris, *Notitia artis musicae*
ca1320	*Ars nova*, formerly attributed to de Vitry
1326–7	Copying of Paris, Bibliothèque nationale de France, fonds français 571
after 1330	Jacobus of Liège, *Speculum musice*, largest surviving medieval treatise on music
1332	Jehan Acart de Hesdin's *La Prise Amoureuse*
1344	Prague raised to status of archbishopric
1348	Foundation of the Charles University, Prague
1350–6	Copying of Paris, Bibliothèque nationale de France, fonds français 1586
mid 14th century	New Ordinal of Salisbury Use
1364	Foundation of the Jagellonian University, Cracow

ca1370	Philippus de Caserta, *Tractatus de diversis figuris*, describes *ars subtilior* music and its notation
1370–2	Copying of Kansas City, Private Collection of Elizabeth J. and James E. Ferrell, MS without shelfmark currently on loan to Cambridge, Corpus Christi College (*Mach Vg*)
1392	Eustache Deschamps *L'Art de Dictier*
late 14th century	Berkeley Manuscript
ca1410	Copying of Modena, Biblioteca Estense, α.M.5.24 (olim Lat. 568)
1410–20	Copying of Chantilly, Bibliothèque du Musée Condé 564 (formerly 1047)
1435–42	Copying of second, third and fourth parts of Aosta, Biblioteca del Seminario Maggiore, 15 (olim A1 D 19)
1440–50	Copying of Modena, Biblioteca Estense, α.X.1.11 (olim Lat. 471)

Manuscripts and their abbreviations

By location

Aosta, Biblioteca del Seminario Maggiore 13	*I-AO* 13
Aosta, Biblioteca del Seminario Maggiore 15	*I-AO* 15
Arezzo, Museo Diocesano, s.n., C.216	*I-AR* s.n. C.216
Assisi, Biblioteca Comunale, MS 338	*I-Ac* 338
Bamberg, Staatsbibliothek, lit. 115 (*Ba*)	*D-BAs* lit. 115
Barcelona, Arxiu Eclesistic de Vic 105	*E-VI* 105
Benevento, Biblioteca Capitolare 34	*I-BV* 34
Benevento, Biblioteca Capitolare 38	*I-BV* 38
Benevento, Biblioteca Capitolare 39	*I-BV* 39
Benevento, Biblioteca Capitolare 40	*I-BV* 40
Berkeley Castle, Select Roll 55	*GB-BER* sel. 55
Berkeley, University of California, Music Library 744 (olim Phillipps 4450)	*US-BEm* 744 (olim Phillipps 4450)
Bologna, Biblioteca Universitaria 2216	*I-Bu* 2216
Bologna, Museo Internazionale e Biblioteca della Musica Q15	*I-Bc* Q15
Bratislava, Archív mesta Bratislavy 33	*SK-BRm* 33
Bratislava, Univerzitná knižnica 318	*SK-BRu* 318
Brussels, Bibliothèque Royale de Belgique/Koninklijke Bibliotheek van België 10127–10144	*B-Br* 10127–10144
Brussels, Conservatoire Royal/Koninklijk Conservatorium X 27.935	*B-Bc* X 27.935
Burgos, Monasterio de Las Huelgas 9 (*Hu*)	*E-BUlh* 9
Cambridge, Corpus Christi College 473	*GB-Ccc* 473
Cambridge, Gonville & Caius College 512/543	*GB-Cgc* 512/543
Cambridge, University Library, additional 710 (Dublin Troper)	*GB-Cu* Add.710
Cambridge, University Library, Hh. vi. 11	*GB-Cu* Hh. Vi. II
Chantilly, Bibliothèque du Musée Condé 564 (formerly 1047)	*F-CH* 564
Cividale del Friuli, Museo Archeologico Nazionale, Biblioteca 35	*I-CFm* 35
Cividale del Friuli, Museo Archeologico Nazionale, Biblioteca 58	*I-CFm* 58
Cividale del Friuli, Museo Archeologico Nazionale, Biblioteca 79	*I-CFm* 79
Cleveland, Museum of Art 21140	*US-CLm* 21140
Cortona, Biblioteca Comunale e dell'Accademia Etrusca 91	*I-CT* 91
Cracow, Uniwersytet Jagielloński, Biblioteka Jagiellońska 257	*PL-Kj* 257

Cracow, Uniwersytet Jagielloński, Biblioteka Jagiellońska 40098	*PL-Kj* 40098
Dendermonde, Sint-Pieter- en Paulusabdij Codex 9	*B-DEa* cod. 9
Einsiedeln, Kloster Einsiedeln, Musikbibliothek 121 (1151)	*CH-E* 121 (1151)
Faenza, Biblioteca Comunale MS 117 (Codex Faenza)	*I-FZc* 117
Florence, Archivio di Stato, Notarile Antecosimiano, n. 17879	*I-Fas* n. 17879
Florence, Biblioteca Medicea Laurenziana, Archivio Capitolare di San Lorenzo 2211	*I-Fl* 2211
Florence, Biblioteca Medicea Laurenziana, Palatino 87 (Squarcialupi Codex)	*I-Fl* Palatino 87
Florence, Biblioteca Medicea Laurenziana, Plut. 29.1 (*F*)	*I-Fl* Plut. 29.1
Florence, Biblioteca Nazionale Centrale, Banco Rari 18	*I-Fn* Banco Rari 18
Florence, Biblioteca Nazionale Centrale, Banco Rari 20	*I-Fn* Banco Rari 20
Florence, Biblioteca Nazionale Centrale, Panciatichiano 26	*I-Fn* Panciatichiano 26
Foligno, Archivio di Stato, MS without shelfmark	*I-FOLas*
Gorizia, Seminario Teologico Centrale, Biblioteca, H, c. 274	*I-GO* H c. 274
Grottaferrata, Badia Greca, Biblioteca, collocazione provvisoria 197	*I-GR* 187
Gubbio, Archivio di Stato, Fondo S. Domenico, Corale O	*I-GUBa* Corale O
Hradec Kralové, Statní vedecka knihovna II A 7	*CZ-HK* II A 7
Ivrea, Biblioteca Capitolare, 115	*I-IV* 115
Kansas City, Private Collection of Elizabeth J. and James E. Ferrell, MS without shelfmark (*Mach Vg*; Ferrell-Vogüé Manuscript) currently on loan to Cambridge, Corpus Christi College	*US-KAferrell* on loan to *GB-Ccc*
London, British Library, Additional 16975	*GB-Lbl* add. 16975
London, British Library, Additional 28598	*GB-Lbl* add. 28598
London, British Library, Additional 29987	*GB-Lbl* add. 29987
London, British Library, Additional 36881	*GB-Lbl* add. 36881
London, British Library, Additional 57950 (Old Hall Manuscript)	*GB-Lbl* add. 57950
London, British Library, Cotton Vespasian B. VI	*GB-Lbl* Cotton Vesp. B. VI
London, British Library, Egerton 2615 (*LoA*)	*GB-Lbl* Egerton 2615
London, British Library, Harley 3965	*GB-Lbl* Harley 3965
Lucca, Archivio di Stato 184	*I-La* 184
Lucca, Biblioteca Statale 1061	*I-Lg* 1061
Madrid, Biblioteca Nacional de España 10029 (Azagra Codex)	*E-Mn* 10029
Madrid, Biblioteca Nacional de España 10069 (*Cantigas de Santa Maria*)	*E-Mn* 10069
Madrid, Biblioteca Nacional de España 20486 (*Ma*)	*E-Mn* 20486
Madrid, Real Academia de la Historia, Biblioteca, Aemil. 56	*E-Mh* Aemil. 56

Milan, Biblioteca Ambrosiana, Tesoro della Basilica di S. Giovanni, Cod. CIX	*I-Ma* Cod. CIX
Modena, Biblioteca Estense, α.X.1.11 (olim. Lat. 471)	*I-MOe* α.X.1.11
Modena, Biblioteca Estense, α.M.5.24 (olim. Lat. 586)	*I-MOe* α.M.5.24
Modena, Biblioteca Estense, α.R.I.6	*I-MOe* α.R.I.6
Montefiore dell'Aso, Francesco Egidi, private collection	*I-MDAegidi*
Montpellier, Université Montpellier 1, Bibliothèque de la Faculté de Médecine, H.159 (Tonary of St Bénigne of Dijon)	*F-MOf* H.159
Montpellier, Université Montpellier 1, Bibliothèque de la Faculté de Médecine, H.196 (*Mo*; The Montpellier Codex)	*F-MOf* H.196
Montserrat, Biblioteca de l'Abadia de Montserrat 1 (Llibre Vermell)	*E-MO* 1
Monza, Basilica di S. Giovanni Battista, Biblioteca Capitolare e Tesoro L 12	*I-MZ* L12
Monza, Basilica di S. Giovanni Battista, Biblioteca Capitolare e Tesoro L 13	*I-MZ* L13
Monza, Basilica di S. Giovanni Battista, Biblioteca Capitolare e Tesoro CIX	*I-MZ* CIX
Munich, Bayerische Staatsbibliothek, clm 4660	*D-Mbs* clm 4660
Munich, Bayerische Staatsbibliothek, clm 9543	*D-Mbs* clm 9543
New York, Pierpont Morgan Library M.979	*US-NYpm* M.979
Orléans, Bibliothèque Municipale 201	*F-O* 201
Ostiglia, Opera pia Greggiati, Biblioteca 201	*I-OS* 201
Ostiglia, Opera pia Greggiati, Biblioteca E.46	*I-OS* E.46
Ostiglia, Opera pia Greggiati, Biblioteca, rari 35	*I-OS* rari 35
Oxford, Bodleian Library, Bodley 775	*GB-Ob* Bodley 775
Oxford, Bodleian Library, Canonici misc. 213	*GB-Ob* Can. misc. 213
Oxford, Bodleian Library, Douce 308	*GB-Ob* Douce 308
Oxford, Bodleian Library, Rawlinson G. 22	*GB-Ob* Rawl. G. 22
Padua, Duomo, Biblioteca Capitolare C 56	*I-Pc* C. 56
Padua, Duomo, Biblioteca Capitolare, Curia Vescovile, A.20	*I-Pc* A.20
Paris, Bibliothèque de l'Arsenal 1169	*F-Pa* 1169
Paris, Bibliothèque de l'Arsenal 5198 (Chansonnier de l'Arsenal)	*F-Pa* 5198
Paris, Bibliothèque nationale de France, fonds français 146 (*Fauv*; Roman de Fauvel)	*F-Pn* fonds fr. 146
Paris, Bibliothèque nationale de France, fonds français 571	*F-Pn* fonds fr. 571
Paris, Bibliothèque nationale de France, fonds français 844 (Chansonnier du Roi)	*F-Pn* fonds fr. 844
Paris, Bibliothèque nationale de France, fonds français 845	*F-Pn* fonds fr. 845
Paris, Bibliothèque nationale de France, fonds français 846 (Chansonnier Cangé)	*F-Pn* fonds fr. 846
Paris, Bibliothèque nationale de France, fonds français 847	*F-Pn* fonds fr. 847

Paris, Bibliothèque nationale de France, fonds français 1050 (Chansonnier de Clairambault)	*F-Pn* fonds fr. 1050
Paris, Bibliothèque nationale de France, fonds français 1584 (*MachA*)	*F-Pn* fonds fr. 1584
Paris, Bibliothèque nationale de France, fonds français 1585 (*MachB*)	*F-Pn* fonds fr. 1585
Paris, Bibliothèque nationale de France, fonds français 1586 (*MachC*)	*F-Pn* fonds fr. 1586
Paris, Bibliothèque nationale de France, fonds français 9221 (*MachE*)	*F-Pn* fonds fr. 9221
Paris, Bibliothèque nationale de France, fonds français 12615 (Chansonnier de Noailles)	*F-Pn* fonds fr. 12615
Paris, Bibliothèque nationale de France, fonds français 22543	*F-Pn* fonds fr. 22543
Paris, Bibliothèque nationale de France, fonds français 22545 (*MachF*)	*F-Pn* fonds fr. 22545
Paris, Bibliothèque nationale de France, fonds français 22546 (*MachG*)	*F-Pn* fonds fr. 22546
Paris, Bibliothèque nationale de France, fonds français 25566 (Chansonnier of Adam de la Halle)	*F-Pn* fonds fr. 25566
Paris, Bibliothèque nationale de France, fonds italien 568 (*Pit*)	*F-Pn* fonds italien 568
Paris, Bibliothèque nationale de France, fonds latin 112	*F-Pn* fonds lat. 112
Paris, Bibliothèque nationale de France, fonds latin 1139	*F-Pn* fonds lat. 1139
Paris, Bibliothèque nationale de France, fonds latin 1240	*F-Pn* fonds lat. 1240
Paris, Bibliothèque nationale de France, fonds latin 1337	*F-Pn* fonds lat. 1337
Paris, Bibliothèque nationale de France, fonds latin 3343	*F-Pn* fonds lat. 3343
Paris, Bibliothèque nationale de France, fonds latin 3549	*F-Pn* fonds lat. 3549
Paris, Bibliothèque nationale de France, fonds latin 3791	*F-Pn* fonds lat. 3791
Paris, Bibliothèque nationale de France, fonds latin 10587	*F-Pn* fonds lat. 10587
Paris, Bibliothèque nationale de France, fonds latin 12044	*F-Pn* fonds lat. 12044
Paris, Bibliothèque nationale de France, fonds latin 13159 (Tonary of St Riquier)	*F-Pn* fonds lat. 13159
Paris, Bibliothèque nationale de France, fonds latin 14817	*F-Pn* fonds lat. 14817
Paris, Bibliothèque nationale de France, nouvelles acquisitions françaises 1050 (Chansonnier de Clairambault)	F-Pn n.a.f. 1050
Paris, Bibliothèque nationale de France, nouvelles acquisitions françaises 6771 (Codex Reina)	*F-Pn* n.a.f. 6771
Paris, Bibliothèque nationale de France, nouvelles acquisitions françaises 13521 (La Clayette Manuscript)	*F-Pn* n.a.f. 13521
Parma, Duomo, Archivio Capitolare con Archivio della Fabbriceria F-09	*I-PAac* F-09

Vyšší Brod, Knihovna cisterciackého klaštera 42	*CZ-VB* 42
Warsaw, Biblioteka Narodowa, Lat.F.I.378	*PL-Wn* 378
Warsaw, Biblioteka Narodowa 8054	*PL-Wn* 8054
Wiesbaden, Hessische Landesbibliothek MS 2 (*Riesenkodex*)	*D-WIl* 2
Wolfenbüttel, Herzog August Bibliothek 628 (677) (*W₁*)	*D-W* 628
Wolfenbüttel, Herzog August Bibliothek 1062	*D-W* 1062
Wolfenbüttel, Herzog August Bibliothek 1099 (1206) (*W₂*)	*D-W* 1099

By siglum

B-Bc X 27.935	Brussels, Conservatoire Royal/Koninklijk Conservatorium X 27.935
B-Br 10127–10144	Brussels, Bibliothèque Royale de Belgique/Koninklijke Bibliotheek van België 10127–10144
B-DEa cod. 9	Dendermonde, Sint-Pieter- en Paulusabdij Codex 9
Ba	Bamberg, Staatsbibliothek, lit. 115 (*D-BAs* lit. 115)
CH-E 121 (1151)	Einsiedeln, Kloster Einsiedeln, Musikbibliothek 121 (1151)
CH-SGs 359	St Gall, Stiftsbibliothek 359
CH-SGs 378	St Gall, Stiftsbibliothek 378
CH-SGs 381	St Gall, Stiftsbibliothek 381
CH-SGs 383	St Gall, Stiftsbibliothek 383
CH-SGs 390–391	St Gall, Stiftsbibliothek 390 (Hartker Antiphonal)
CH-SGs 484	St Gall, Stiftsbibliothek 484
CH-SGv 317	St Gall, Kantonsbibliothek (Vadiana) 317
CZ-HK II A 7	Hradec Kralové, Statní vedecka knihovna II A 7
CZ-Pnm II C 7	Prague, Narodní muzeum – Muzeum České hudby, hudební archiv II C 7
CZ-VB 42	Vyšší Brod, Knihovna cisterciackého klaštera 42
D-BAs lit. 115	Bamberg, Staatsbibliothek, lit. 115 (Ba)
D-Mbs clm 4660	Munich, Bayerische Staatsbibliothek, clm 4660
D-Mbs clm 9543	Munich, Bayerische Staatsbibliothek, clm 9543
D-WIl 2	Wiesbaden, Hessische Landesbibliothek MS 2 (*Riesenkodex*)
D-W 628	Wolfenbüttel, Herzog August Bibliothek 628 (677) (*W₁*)
D-W 1062	Wolfenbüttel, Herzog August Bibliothek 1062
D-W 1099	Wolfenbüttel, Herzog August Bibliothek 1099 (1206) (*W₂*)
E-BUlh 9	Burgos, Monasterio de Las Huelgas 9 (*Hu*)
E-E b.I.2 (j.b.2)	San Lorenzo de El Escorial, Biblioteca del Real Monasterio, b.I.2 (j.b.2) (*Cantigas de Santa Maria*)
	San Millán de la Cogolla, Rioja, MS without shelfmark
E-E T.I.1	San Lorenzo de El Escorial, Biblioteca del Real Monasterio, T.I.1 (*Cantigas de Santa Maria*)
E-Mh Aemil. 56	Madrid, Real Academia de la Historia, Biblioteca, Aemil. 56
E-Mn 10029	Madrid, Biblioteca Nacional de España 10029 (Azagra Codex)

E-Mn 10069	Madrid, Biblioteca Nacional de España 10069 (*Cantigas de Santa Maria*)
E-Mn 20486	Madrid, Biblioteca Nacional de España 20486 (*Ma*)
E-MO 1	Montserrat, Biblioteca de l'Abadia de Montserrat 1 (Llibre Vermell)
E-SC Codex Calixtinus	Santiago de Compostela, Catedral Metropolitana (Codex Calixtinus)
E-SI 4	Santo Domingo de Silos, Archivo Musical de la Abadía 4
E-VI 105	Barcelona, Arxiu Eclesistic de Vic 105
F	Florence, Biblioteca Medicea Laurenziana, Plut. 29.1
Fauv	Paris, Bibliothèque nationale de France, fonds français 146 (*F-Pn* fonds fr. 146; *Le Roman de Fauvel*)
F-CH 564	Chantilly, Bibliothèque du Musée Condé 564 (formerly 1047)
F-MOf H.159	Montpellier, Université Montpellier 1, Bibliothèque de la Faculté de Médecine, H.159 (Tonary of St Bénigne of Dijon)
F-MOf H.196	Montpellier, Université Montpellier 1, Bibliothèque de la Faculté de Médecine, H.196 (*Mo*; The Montpellier Codex)
F-O 201	Orléans, Bibliothèque Municipale 201
F-Pa 1169	Paris, Bibliothèque de l'Arsenal 1169
F-Pa 5198	Paris, Bibliothèque de l'Arsenal 5198 (Chansonnier de l'Arsenal)
F-Pn n.a.f. 1050	Paris, Bibliothèque nationale de France, nouvelles acquisitions françaises 1050 (Chansonnier de Clairambault)
F-Pn fonds fr. 146	Paris, Bibliothèque nationale de France, fonds français 146 (*Fauv*; Roman de Fauvel)
F-Pn fonds fr. 571	Paris, Bibliothèque nationale de France, fonds français 571
F-Pn fonds fr. 844	Paris, Bibliothèque nationale de France, fonds français 844 (Chansonnier du Roi)
F-Pn fonds fr. 845	Paris, Bibliothèque nationale de France, fonds français 845
F-Pn fonds fr. 846	Paris, Bibliothèque nationale de France, fonds français 846 (Chansonnier Cangé)
F-Pn fonds fr. 847	Paris, Bibliothèque nationale de France, fonds français 847
F-Pn fonds fr. 1050	Paris, Bibliothèque nationale de France, fonds français 1050 (Chansonnier de Clairambault)
F-Pn fonds fr. 1584	Paris, Bibliothèque nationale de France, fonds français 1584 (*MachA*)
F-Pn fonds fr. 1585	Paris, Bibliothèque nationale de France, fonds français 1585 (*MachB*)
F-Pn fonds fr. 1586	Paris, Bibliothèque nationale de France, fonds français 1586 (*MachC*)
F-Pn fonds fr. 9221	Paris, Bibliothèque nationale de France, fonds français 9221 (*MachE*)

F-Pn fonds fr. 12615	Paris, Bibliothèque nationale de France, fonds français 12615 (Chansonnier de Noailles)
F-Pn fonds fr. 22543	Paris, Bibliothèque nationale de France, fonds français 22543
F-Pn fonds fr. 22545	Paris, Bibliothèque nationale de France, fonds français 22545 (*MachF*)
F-Pn fonds fr. 22546	Paris, Bibliothèque nationale de France, fonds français 22546 (*MachG*)
F-Pn fonds fr. 25566	Paris, Bibliothèque nationale de France, fonds français 25566 (Chansonnier of Adam de la Halle)
F-Pn fonds italien 568	Paris, Bibliothèque nationale de France, fonds italien 568 (*Pit*)
F-Pn fonds lat. 112	Paris, Bibliothèque nationale de France, fonds latin 112
F-Pn fonds lat. 1139	Paris, Bibliothèque nationale de France, fonds latin 1139
F-Pn fonds lat. 1240	Paris, Bibliothèque nationale de France, fonds latin 1240
F-Pn fonds lat. 1337	Paris, Bibliothèque nationale de France, fonds latin 1337
F-Pn fonds lat. 3343	Paris, Bibliothèque nationale de France, fonds latin 3343
F-Pn fonds lat. 3549	Paris, Bibliothèque nationale de France, fonds latin 3549
F-Pn fonds lat. 3791	Paris, Bibliothèque nationale de France, fonds latin 3791
F-Pn fonds lat. 10587	Paris, Bibliothèque nationale de France, fonds latin 10587
F-Pn fonds lat. 12044	Paris, Bibliothèque nationale de France, fonds latin 12044
F-Pn fonds lat. 13159	Paris, Bibliothèque nationale de France, fonds latin 13159 (Tonary of St Riquier)
F-Pn fonds lat. 14817	Paris, Bibliothèque nationale de France, fonds latin 14817
F-Pn n.a.f. 6771	Paris, Bibliothèque nationale de France, nouvelles acquisitions françaises 6771 (Codex Reina)
F-Pn n.a.f. 13521	Paris, Bibliothèque nationale de France, nouvelles acquisitions françaises 13521 (La Clayette Manuscript)
GB-BER sel. 55	Berkeley Castle, Select Roll 55
GB-Ccc 473	Cambridge, Corpus Christi College 473
GB-Cgc 512/543	Caius College 512/543 & Cambridge, Gonville
GB-Cu Add.710	Cambridge, University Library, additional 710 (Dublin Troper)
GB-Cu Hh. Vi. II	Cambridge, University Library, Hh. vi. 11
GB-Lbl add. 16975	London, British Library, Additional 16975
GB-Lbl add. 28598	London, British Library, Additional 28598
GB-Lbl add. 29987	London, British Library, Additional 29987
GB-Lbl add. 36881	London, British Library, Additional 36881
GB-Lbl add. 57950	London, British Library, Additional 57950 (Old Hall Manuscript)
GB-Lbl Cotton Vesp. B. VI	London, British Library, Cotton Vespasian B. VI
GB-Lbl Egerton 2615	London, British Library, Egerton 2615 (*LoA*)

GB-Lbl Harley 3965	London, British Library, Harley 3965
GB-Ob Bodley 775	Oxford, Bodleian Library, Bodley 775
GB-Ob Can. misc. 213	Oxford, Bodleian Library, Canonici misc. 213
GB-Ob Douce 308	Oxford, Bodleian Library, Douce 308
GB-Ob Rawl. G. 22	Oxford, Bodleian Library, Rawlinson G. 22
Hu	Burgos, Monastario de Las Huelgas, 9 (*E-BUlh* 9)
I-Ac 338	Assisi, Biblioteca Comunale, MS 338
I-AO 13	Aosta, Biblioteca del Seminario Maggiore 13
I-AO 15	Aosta, Biblioteca del Seminario Maggiore 15
I-AR s.n. C.216	Arezzo, Museo Diocesano, s.n., C.216
I-Bc Q15	Bologna, Museo Internazionale e Biblioteca della Musica Q15
I-Bu 2216	Bologna, Biblioteca Universitaria 2216
I-BV 34	Benevento, Biblioteca Capitolare 34
I-BV 38	Benevento, Biblioteca Capitolare 38
I-BV 39	Benevento, Biblioteca Capitolare 39
I-BV 40	Benevento, Biblioteca Capitolare 40
I-CFm 35	Cividale del Friuli, Museo Archeologico Nazionale, Biblioteca 35
I-CFm 58	Cividale del Friuli, Museo Archeologico Nazionale, Biblioteca 58
I-CFm 79	Cividale del Friuli, Museo Archeologico Nazionale, Biblioteca 79
I-CT 91	Cortona, Biblioteca Comunale e dell'Accademia Etrusca 91
I-Fas n. 17879	Florence, Archivio di Stato, Notarile Antecosimiano, n. 17879
I-Fl 2211	Florence, Biblioteca Medicea Laurenziana, Archivio Capitolare di San Lorenzo 2211
I-Fl Palatino 87	Florence, Biblioteca Medicea Laurenziana, Palatino 87 (Squarcialupi Codex)
I-Fl Plut. 29.1	Florence, Biblioteca Medicea Laurenziana, Plut. 29.1 (*F*)
I-Fn Banco Rari 18	Florence, Biblioteca Nazionale Centrale, Banco Rari 18
I-Fn Banco Rari 20	Florence, Biblioteca Nazionale Centrale, Banco Rari 20
I-Fn Panciatichiano 26	Florence, Biblioteca Nazionale Centrale, Panciatichiano 26
I-FOLas	Foligno, Archivio di Stato, MS without shelfmark
I-FZc 117	Faenza, Biblioteca Comunale MS 117 (Codex Faenza)
I-GO H c. 274	Gorizia, Seminario Teologico Centrale, Biblioteca, H, c. 274
I-GR 187	Grottaferrata, Badia Greca, Biblioteca, collocazione provvisoria 197
I-GUBa Corale O	Gubbio, Archivio di Stato, Fondo S. Domenico, Corale O
I-IV 115	Ivrea, Biblioteca Capitolare, 115
I-La 184	Lucca, Archivio di Stato 184
I-Lg 1061	Lucca, Biblioteca Statale 1061
I-Ma Cod. CIX	Milan, Biblioteca Ambrosiana, Tesoro della Basilica di S. Giovanni, Cod. CIX

I-MDAegidi	Montefiore dell'Aso, Francesco Egidi, private collection
I-MOe α.M.5.24	Modena, Biblioteca Estense, α.M.5.24 (olim. Lat. 586)
I-MOe α.R.I.6	Modena, Biblioteca Estense, α.R.I.6
I-MOe α.X.1.11	Modena, Biblioteca Estense, α.X.1.11 (olim. Lat. 471)
I-MZ CIX	Monza, Basilica di S. Giovanni Battista, Biblioteca Capitolare e Tesoro CIX
I-MZ L12	Monza, Basilica di S. Giovanni Battista, Biblioteca Capitolare e Tesoro L 12
I-MZ L13	Monza, Basilica di S. Giovanni Battista, Biblioteca Capitolare e Tesoro L 13
I-OS 201	Ostiglia, Opera pia Greggiati, Biblioteca 201
I-OS E.46	Ostiglia, Opera pia Greggiati, Biblioteca E.46
I-OS rari 35	Ostiglia, Opera pia Greggiati, Biblioteca, rari 35
I-PAac F-09	Parma, Duomo, Archivio Capitolare con Archivio della Fabbriceria F-09
I-PCd 65	Piacenza, Biblioteca e Archivio Capitolare 65
I-PCd 285	Piacenza, Biblioteca e Archivio Capitolare 285
I-PCd 302	Piacenza, Biblioteca e Archivio Capitolare 302
I-Pc A.20	Padua, Duomo, Biblioteca Capitolare, Curia Vescovile, A.20
I-Pc C. 56	Padua, Duomo, Biblioteca Capitolare C 56
I-PEc 3065	Perugia, Biblioteca Comunale Augusta 3065
I-PS C.102	Pistoia, Biblioteca dell'Archivio Capitolare C.102
I-REas Mischiati Fragment	Reggio Emilia, Archivio di Stato, Mischiati Fragment
I-Rvat ASP B 79	Rome, Biblioteca Apostolica Vaticana, Archivio San Pietro B 79
I-Rvat Barb. lat. 560	Rome, Biblioteca Apostolica Vaticana, Barb. lat. 560
I-Rvat Barb. lat. 657	Rome, Biblioteca Apostolica Vaticana, Barb. lat. 657
I-Rvat Reg. lat. 1490	Rome, Biblioteca Apostolica Vaticana, Reg. lat. 1490
I-Rvat Rossi 215	Rome, Biblioteca Apostolica Vaticana, Rossi 215 (Rossi Codex)
I-Rvat Vat. lat. 10654	Rome, Biblioteca Apostolica Vaticana, Vat. lat. 10654
I-Rvat Vat. lat. 4770	Rome, Biblioteca Apostolica Vaticana, Vat. lat. 4770
I-Tn T. III. 2	Turin, Biblioteca Nazionale Universitaria, T. III. 2
I-TOD 73	Todi, Biblioteca Comunale Lorenzo Leonj 73
I-TRsf 310	Trento, Biblioteca dei Padri Francescani di S. Bernardino 310
I-Tr Vari 42	Turin, Biblioteca Reale, Vari 42
I-UD 10	Udine, Duomo, Archivio Capitolare 10
I-UD 27	Udine, Duomo, Archivio Capitolare 27
I-VEcap 89	Verona, Biblioteca Capitolare 89
LoA	London, British Library, Egerton 2615 (*GB-Lbl* Egerton 2615)
Ma	Madrid, Biblioteca Nacional de España, 20486 (*E-Mn* 20486)
Mach A	Paris, Bibliothèque nationale de France, fonds français 1548 (*F-Pn* fonds fr. 1548)

Mach B	Paris, Bibliothèque nationale de France, fonds français 1585 (*F-Pn* fonds fr. 1585)
Mach C	Paris, Bibliothèque nationale de France, fonds français 1586 (*F-Pn* fonds fr. 1586)
Mach E	Paris, Bibliothèque nationale de France, fonds français 9221 (*F-Pn* fonds fr. 9221)
Mach F	Paris, Bibliothèque nationale de France, fonds français 22545 (*F-Pn* fonds fr. 22545)
Mach G	Paris, Bibliothèque nationale de France, fonds français 22546 (*F-Pn* fonds fr. 22546)
Mach Vg	Kansas City, Private Collection of Elizabeth J. and James E. Ferrell, MS without shelfmark (Ferrell-Vogüé Manuscript) currently on loan to Cambridge, Corpus Christi College (*US-KAferrell* on loan to *GB-Ccc*)
Pit	Paris, Bibliothèque nationale de France, fonds italien 568 (*F-Pn* fonds italien 568)
PL-Kj 257	Cracow, Uniwersytet Jagielloński, Biblioteka Jagiellońska 257
PL-Kj 40098	Cracow, Uniwersytet Jagielloński, Biblioteka Jagiellońska 40098
PL-Pu 7022	Poznań, Biblioteka Uniwersytecka, Sekcja Zbiorów Muzycznych w Oddziale Zbiorów Specjalnych 7022
PL-STk 2	Stary Sącz, Biblioteka Klasztoru Sióstr Klarysek pod wezwaniem św.Kingi.
PL-Wn 8054	Warsaw, Biblioteka Narodowa 8054
PL-Wn 378	Warsaw,Biblioteka Narodowa, Lat.F.I.378
S-Uu c.233	Uppsala, Universitetsbiblioteket, c.233
SK-BRm 33	Bratislava, Archív mesta Bratislavy 33
SK-BRu 318	Bratislava, Univerzitná knižnica 318
US-BEm 744 (olim Phillipps 4450)	Berkeley, University of California, Music Library 744 (olim Phillipps 4450)
US-CLm 21140	Cleveland, Museum of Art 21140
US-KAferrell on loan to *GB-Ccc*	Kansas City, Private Collection of Elizabeth J. and James E. Ferrell, MS without shelfmark (*Mach Vg*; Ferrell-Vogüé Manuscript) currently on loan to Cambridge, Corpus Christi College
US-NYpm M.979	New York, Pierpont Morgan Library M.979
W_1	Wolfenbüttel, Herzog August Bibliothek, 628 (677) (*D-W* 628 (677))
W_2	Wolfenbüttel, Herzog August Bibliothek, 1099 (1206) (*D-W* 1099 (1206))

Introduction

MARK EVERIST

'O sing unto the Lord a new song' is the text introduced by the initial on the cover of *The Cambridge Companion to Medieval Music*. But our two Austin canons pictured in the initial stand with their mouths resolutely closed. Furthermore, it is difficult to square the elaborate ligatures on the roll before which the two Augustinians stand with any sort of psalmody; at the very least the music looks more like a melisma from a gradual, alleluia or responsory; the more optimistic modern gaze might even see the tenor of a polyphonic work there. And while the cleric on the right is pointing to the notation on the roll, there is very little doubt that the one on the left is indicating solmization syllables on his hand (although never described by Guido d'Arezzo, this practice was known throughout the Middle Ages as the Guidonian Hand). In many ways, then, the initial that adorns this book addresses issues raised by its contents: monophony and polyphony, psalmody and composed chant, written and unwritten, codex and *rotulus*, musical literacy, cheironomy, silence and sound.

The component parts of our 'Cantate' initial are very much the concerns of the contributors to *The Cambridge Companion to Medieval Music*. We are interested, of course, in following the path of music history from the middle of the first millennium to around 1400, but we are also interested in the ways in which plainsong and polyphony interact: there is always the risk in any book of this sort of treating monophony – liturgical, sacred and vernacular – as something that stopped as soon as someone sang a fifth above a fundamental, and our accounts, for example, of the role of plainsong in trecento Italy or in Parisian organum of the twelfth century, or the weight given to Machaut's monophonic songs will make clear our reluctance to fall prey to this sort of reasoning. The friction between theory and practice – perfectly dramatized by our two Austin canons – lies at the heart of much of the volume, and our chapters on liturgy and institution take us right to the centre of the question of when and when not music was composed, performed and consumed.

The Cambridge Companion to Medieval Music is a totally different proposition to almost every other volume in the Cambridge Companions series. Whereas *The Cambridge Companion to Stainer* or *The Cambridge Companion to the Ocarina*, when they are written, will have their scope relatively straightforwardly defined by their subject matter, our attempt to assemble a companion to a body of music that spans the best part of a millennium, and most of what is now considered Europe, is an exercise fraught with ambiguity and uncertainty. So while *The Cambridge Companion to Mozart* and *The Cambridge Companion to Rossini* treat the life, works and contexts of their respective subjects in clearly different ways, there is little doubt as to how many concert arias the former wrote or how long the latter spent in Naples. Furthermore, in companions with such clearly defined limits, the scope for the examination and analysis of, say, Mozart's *Requiem* or Rossini's *Guillaume Tell* is broad; by contrast, the luxury of more than a handful of exemplary analyses to support general points would have made *The Cambridge Companion to Medieval Music* significantly longer than it already is. We focus, then, on repertories and their contexts rather than on groups of works defined by composer.

'Composer' is of course a highly contested term. In a post-Romantic age that professionalizes the composer in a way largely unknown before the past two hundred years, it is helpful to return to the idea of composition as something that went hand in hand with singing, instruction and theorizing. In particular, coming back to the idea of composition as the placing together – as its etymology (*componere*) suggests – gives a context to the common medieval practices of reworking text and music sometimes over a period of centuries. This is no less a process of composition than the one portrayed in the images of Beethoven composing the 'Pastoral' Symphony or of Haydn composing in his best clothes. Time and time again in the pages that follow, the question of composition and authorship will surface in very different ways, and our understanding and enjoyment of medieval music will be impoverished if reworking and embellishment are treated as something on a lower plane than what we understand today as 'composition'. There is a sense then that the *canticum novum* sung by our Austin Canons might allude to almost any part of the music of the Middle Ages: all could be considered old, and all could also be counted as new.

What are the Middle Ages, and what should a *Companion to Medieval Music* include? Both beginnings and endings are severely problematic, to say nothing of the general question of periodization. One could speculate on what the successor to this volume might be called: *The Cambridge Companion to Music of the Early Modern Period* – in acknowledgement of the unease that the terms Renaissance and Reformation have generated? An answer to this question might assist with finding an end point for our study. But at the beginning of the period treated by this volume, the problem can be articulated through a number of questions: how does the formulation 'late antiquity' play into the history of music? Is there a place for the concept of the Dark Ages? What criteria might one use for answering such questions? Yet at the end of the period, there are almost more answers than questions:

the fall of Constantinople (1453), the end of the Wars of the Roses (1485), the beginnings of the colonization of America (1492) or the beginnings of the Reformation (1517). But as these examples show, decisions about periodization are largely formed along disciplinary lines: different fields of study prefer different solutions (European history, English history, the history of colonization, and so on). And if such divisions are marked by events that are deemed of significance in individual subject areas, it might seem, there should be little difficulty in doing the same for music, although even here there are significant differences even between different areas of study: Du Fay seems fairly placed in the 'Renaissance' whereas arguments are made for considering Dunstaple 'medieval', although Reese's *Music in the Middle Ages* was unique in including the composer. Looking further afield – and this is the case in Robert Curry's chapter on medieval music east of the Rhine – the points of change may be even more marked. It of course goes without saying that Lawrence Earp's chapter on the modern reception of medieval music largely begins where the rest of the book leaves off.

It is easy to subject the question of periodization to endless interrogation and to overlook the equally important issues of geography and topography. In this regard, *The Cambridge Companion to Medieval Music* is simultaneously conservative and path-breaking: conservative in its conventional distinction – made by the choices of chapter and author in Part II – between England, Italy, the Iberian peninsula and Eastern Europe, but path-breaking in the synoptic view of the Middle Ages provided by Christopher Page, which, among other things, looks back to third-century Carthage as the origins of the gradual, in the context of what he calls 'circuits of communication'. There is an important counterpoint in the volume between the disciplining of musical repertories that are given in Part II and an account of modes of musical transmission found in Page's chapter.

Needless to say, such an organization – regional studies in Part II and a chronological account of musical repertories in Part I – opens up the unattractive prospect of a *Hauptcorpus* identified with French mainstream repertories in Part I and subsidiary *corpora* in Part II, coupled to the implication that the French music that forms the basis of the chapters in Part I somehow represents a centre to which the music discussed in Part II is a periphery. Such a view is of course as pernicious as the analogous one that holds Austro-German music of later periods a centre with other repertories as 'national' – as if there were little or no national importance to Austro-German music or that non-Austro-German repertories had no role to play east of the Rhine. Page's chapter goes a long way towards blurring the boundaries between centre and periphery, but it would be a wilfully blind editor who denied that any volume such as this is to a degree a prisoner of its disciplinary and scholarly past.

And in other ways, *The Cambridge Companion to Medieval Music* differs from previous studies in its attempts to control the music of the Middle Ages. While questions of performance, instrumental music and iconography are treated in those chapters where they belong, rather than being selected for special attention, Part III deploys the knowledge gained from Parts I and II to give a synoptic view on such subjects as the liturgy, institutions, poetry, composition, manuscripts and music theory. Thus, some repertories will appear both in Part III and in either Part I or II. This bifocal view enables the reader constantly to balance a view of the subject based both on repertories and on musical cultures.

There is always an irony about writing about music: the one thing that characterizes music – its sonic quality, whether in modern recorded sound or *musica instrumentalis* – is absent, and the closed mouths of the Austin canons in our 'Cantate' initial bear eloquent testimony here. There is a further irony in writing about medieval music in that almost the only witnesses that come down to us are essentially visual, whether in terms of the manuscripts that preserve musical repertories or those that record theoretical and other writings about music (again our initial is emblematic). And while this irony has only recently been acknowledged in literary studies in the wake of the so-called New Philology, in music the importance of the visual – the manuscript evidence – has always been paramount. Nowhere is this more clear than in the dozens of published facsimiles of medieval music manuscripts that grace library shelves, both public and private. Hardly surprisingly, then, contributors have made regular reference to the particular wealth of visual material also available to readers of *The Cambridge Companion to Medieval Music*. Useful collections of facsimiles are also in print (all listed in the bibliography), and may well be viewed as addenda to this volume. Particularly useful are Cullin's *L'image musique*, Besseler's *Schriftbild der mehrstimmigen Musik*, Bell's *Music in Medieval Manuscripts*, and, more important perhaps, the online *Digital Image Archive of Medieval Music* (www.diamm.ac.uk/index.html) where some of the material discussed in this volume is presented in high-quality colour images. Such initiatives are certain to continue with individual libraries presenting treasures of their own in an open-access digital format; major sources from St Gall and Montpellier have been made available during the final stages of work on this project, and more will certainly have emerged by the time of the book's publication.

Acknowledgements in a multi-authored volume such as this, beyond the editor's thanks to his contributors, are probably superfluous; each contributor recognizes the debts, both acknowledged and unacknowledged, to the giants on whose shoulders we sit. I am however personally grateful to Penny Souster who first broached the idea of this project, and to Vicki Cooper who has supported it with such enthusiasm. Thanks must also go to Rebecca Taylor, Laura Davey and Jodie Barnes at Cambridge University Press who have made our typescript such a beautiful and accurate object. Antonio Cascelli translated chapters 7 and 8, and prepared the index. The chronology was prepared by Samantha Verscheuren, the list of manuscripts by Amy Williamson and the music examples by David Bretherton. And finally, the editor thanks British Airways for cancelling flight BA 329 to Baltimore Washington International Airport in April 2008; had the editor travelled on that flight, Chapter 18 would not have figured in the volume.

PART ONE

Repertory, styles and techniques

1 Plainsong

SUSAN BOYNTON

After the introduction of public Christian worship services in the fourth and fifth centuries, chant genres of varying styles developed gradually as the parts of the services sung by the congregation became distinguished from those performed by a soloist and choir. Already in the fourth century, responsorial psalmody, performed by a soloist with congregational responses, followed the readings in the first part of the mass. Descriptions of Western liturgical practice in the fourth and fifth centuries suggest an emerging repertory of chant along the lines of the full annual cycle that was established in the Jerusalem liturgy by the middle of the fifth century.[1] Patristic writings such as the sermons of Saint Augustine and Pope Leo I refer to commentary by the celebrant at mass on a psalm verse just performed, but at first the liturgical assignments of these verses were not entirely fixed.[2] The emphasis of early writers on the psalms in the liturgy is part of a broader intellectual movement in late antiquity that made the Book of Psalms central to Christian liturgy and exegesis; as early as Augustine and Cassiodorus, commentary traditions present the psalms as prophetic texts, and allegorical readings of the psalms profoundly shaped the choice of those psalm verses that were used as chant texts.[3]

The principal scriptural influence on the shape of the annual liturgical cycle was the gospel reading at mass. The Roman cycle of gospel readings for the Sundays and principal feast days of the liturgical year was established by the end of the sixth century.[4] The gospel reading reflected the event commemorated on that day or occupied a place in a series that emerged from the continuous reading of the gospels over the course of the year. The theme of the gospel often shaped the texts of the liturgy for the day as a whole.

Another important consideration governing the selection of chants for the liturgy was the difference between proper texts, which change according the liturgical occasion, and common texts, which remain essentially unchanged (throughout the year, during a liturgical season, or on the same day of every week). Over the course of the Middle Ages, the number of propers increased with the introduction of new feasts and cults of saints.

Patristic writings suggest that the responsorial proper chants of the mass were already florid, virtuosic pieces. However, liturgical books from the period before 900 provide only the texts for the chant repertory, and even with the development of Western musical notations in the ninth and tenth centuries, the unheighted neumes of Latin chant must still be interpreted in light of sources with staff lines. Each genre of plainsong had a particular musical style and liturgical function. In the divine office, the focus of individual hours on the communal chanting of psalms and canticles seems to have fostered musical settings that are fairly unadorned except in some of the antiphons for the canticles, and in the great responsories of matins and vespers. In the mass, the ritual focus on the Eucharist and the diverse responsibilities of the ministers involved in this celebration engendered both a wider range of styles than in the office and a more complex distribution of musical roles. The liturgy included many different forms of musically heightened declamation that correspond to various points on a continuum between song and the spoken word. Readings were sung to reciting tones that varied from place to place and also by occasion, with the most elaborate tones reserved for major feasts.[5] The psalms pervaded the Latin liturgy both as the source for the texts of individual chants in practically all the genres of plainsong (except for the ordinary of the mass and the office hymn), and in the form of entire psalms, which comprised the foundation of the eight daily services of the divine office.

Chant in the office

By the early Middle Ages the singing of psalms in the daily office followed a particular ordering which distributed the totality of the psalter over the hours of the day and the days of the week; the distribution employed in monastic churches, found in the Benedictine Rule, differed from that in collegiate or cathedral churches, where services employed fewer psalms.[6] Certain feast days had particular series of psalms, which like the ferial psalm series differed slightly in monastic and secular churches.

The psalms of the office were sung to tones consisting of melodic formulas employed in the syllabic chanting of a psalm verse on a single pitch; each formula had its own melody for the intonation and intermediary pause in the middle of the verse. The conclusion of a psalm verse was sung to a cadential termination formula known as a differentia; each psalm tone had several different possible differentiae.[7] The lesser doxology (*Gloria Patri et filio et spiritui sancto sicut erat in principio et nunc et semper et in secula seculorum amen*) was performed at the end of a psalm or a group of psalms. In many chant manuscripts the vowels of the last two words in the doxology (*e u o u a e*) are written below the melodies of the differentiae as a guide to singers.

The performance practice of psalms in the monastic office changed over time from responsorial singing in late antiquity to antiphonal singing in the Carolingian period.[8] Beginning in the ninth century, the psalm tones were linked to the modes; each mode was represented by one psalm tone, and the psalm tone and possible cadences of each mode were listed in tonaries (catalogues of chants by mode). Other texts in the divine office that were sung to recitation tones were the New Testament canticles at vespers (the Magnificat) and lauds (the Benedictus).[9] Over the course of the Middle Ages, the modality of chants came to be categorized in reference to the characteristics associated with these tones.[10]

The office genre with the largest repertory is the antiphon, a brief chant of relatively simple style sung chorally in alternation with psalms. Antiphons were performed before and after each psalm or group of psalms (and in the early Middle Ages, the antiphon seems to have been sung after each psalm verse). Antiphons for the daily office had texts drawn from the psalms with which they alternated; greater textual variety characterizes the antiphons for feast days. The mode of an office antiphon determined the choice of the psalm-tone cadence so as to ensure that the termination of the psalm was in the same mode as the melody of the antiphon. Antiphons for the psalms illustrate the relationship between mode and formulaic structure; most antiphons in mode 1 exhibit similar turns of phrase, such as a minor third from D to F and a leap of a fifth between D and A.[11] These gestures combine in a melodic contour that reflects the characteristics associated with the mode. Consequently, many different antiphon texts have similar or nearly identical melodies. Longer and often more complex than the psalm antiphons are those sung with the Magnificat at vespers and the Benedictus at lauds. These chants (known as gospel antiphons because the Magnificat and Benedictus originated in the gospels) usually have texts from the gospel reading of the day's mass. Still more elaborate antiphons are those sung at the beginning of matins with the invitatory psalm (Psalm 94, *Venite exultemus*), and repeated after each verse. Even antiphons that are not part of such a cohesive group draw upon similar melodic conventions. Nevertheless, the medieval repertory of office antiphons, which numbers in the thousands, exhibits enough diversity that more study is required to achieve an adequate description of the whole.

Two further antiphon types are distinct from the rest of the repertory in that they were sung independently, without psalms. Processional antiphons were performed during the processions on major feasts of the church year such as Palm Sunday, Christmas, and the Rogation Days. Another genre of independent antiphon was the Marian antiphon, which emerged in the twelfth century for use in devotions to the Virgin, including the procession after compline that concluded with the performance of a Marian antiphon in front of an image of the Virgin.

Each hour of the divine office also included a hymn, sung to a melody (usually strophic) in strophic form.[12] Hymns were introduced into the office as early as the fifth century, but their melodies were rarely recorded before the eleventh.[13] Another syllabic genre was the brief responsory, which consisted of a respond sung by a soloist and repeated by the choir, followed by a solo verse, a choral repeat of the respond, a solo doxology, and a second choral repeat of the respond. The simplest genres of the divine office were those texts chanted to recitation tones: besides the psalms, these comprised the readings, prayers, and versicles and responses (sung in dialogue by choir and presider) that opened and closed each service.

The great responsories of matins, much lengthier and more ornate than the brief responsories, employ a wide variety of melodic formulas.[14] Great responsories are proper chants; their texts are often related to the lessons that precede them. The office of matins included three sets of chants organized in units called nocturns, each one comprised of antiphons and psalms followed by lessons and responsories (nine in secular uses, twelve in monastic use).[15] The verses of great responsories were often formulaic tones (one was associated with each mode), although newly composed verses are not unusual, especially in the later repertory. The performance practice for great responsories varied somewhat from place to place, but it essentially followed the alternation of choir and soloist just described for the brief responsory. The repeat of the respond was usually abbreviated to only its second half; many manuscripts contain cues indicating where the repeat should begin. According to the Benedictine Rule, the doxology should be sung only with the last responsory of each nocturn, and in the Middle Ages the custom was to perform only the first half of the doxology (the words *Gloria patri et filio et spiritui sancto*).[16] Example 1.1, a transcription of the final responsory in the monastic office of St Benedict as found in an eleventh-century antiphoner from the Parisian abbey of St-Maur-des-Fossés, demonstrates the repetition of the second half of the respond and the performance of the doxology. The verse of this responsory is newly composed, not one of the traditional responsory verse tones.

Chant in the mass

Whereas the great responsories were the only musically elaborate element of the divine office, the liturgy of the mass included several different complex genres of plainsong (see Table 1.1).[17] Mass began with the introit, a proper chant composed of an antiphon with psalm sung by the choir during the

Example 1.1 *Gloria Christe tuo tibi personat in benedicto*, twelfth responsory for matins of St Benedict in an eleventh-century antiphoner from St-Maur-des-Fossés (*F-Pn* fonds lat. 12044, fol. 63r)

procession of the clergy into the church. The style of the introit was comparable to office psalmody, but the tones used for the psalm verses in introits were slightly more elaborate. The communion, also a proper chant, similarly included a psalm verse chanted to a formulaic tone. The length of the introit could vary according to the amount of ceremonial accompanying the

Example 1.1 (*cont.*)

entrance of the clergy; apparently its length would be extended by performing multiple verses of the psalm. On major feasts, tropes could introduce
the introit and alternate with its phrases (see Chapter 2).

The introit was followed by the Kyrie, an ordinary chant with an invari-
able Greek text (*Kyrie eleison, Christe eleison, Kyrie eleison*, each performed
three times). Introduced into the Latin mass in the fifth century, the Kyrie
was employed as an invocation in many different liturgical contexts. It was
originally a congregational chant, but by the eighth century was sung by
the choir, as stated in the early-eighth-century description of the papal
mass known as *Ordo Romanus* I. Kyrie melodies seem to have originated
in the same period as this change of performance practice; they can be
fairly ornate, exhibiting a variety of patterns of repetition and contrast.[18]
Already in the earliest manuscripts containing notated Kyries, which were
copied in the tenth century, many compositions include Latin verses

Table 1.1 *Outline of the mass in the central Middle Ages*

introit (proper)
Kyrie (ordinary)
Gloria (proper)
epistle (first scriptural reading)
gradual (proper)
alleluia (proper; replaced by tract in penitential seasons)
sequence (proper)
gospel (second scriptural reading)
Credo (ordinary; not sung at every mass)
offertory (proper)
preface (celebrant's prayer)
Sanctus and Benedictus (ordinary)
canon of the Mass
Lord's Prayer
versicle and response (Peace)
Agnus Dei (ordinary)
rite of peace
communion (proper)
post-communion (prayer)
Ite Missa Est (ordinary)

that seem to be original to the chants; recent research suggests that they were not interpolated as tropes into pre-existing Kyrie melodies (see also Chapter 2).[19]

The Kyrie was followed by the Gloria, which was introduced by Pope Symmachus (498–514) as a congregational chant for Sundays and saints' feasts, but eventually came to be performed by clergy. The repertory encompasses a range of styles from simple recitation to more ornate, through-composed melodies. After the reading of the epistle came the gradual, a responsorial chant performed by a soloist in alternation with the choir, like the great responsory. Graduals, the oldest genre in the mass proper, take their origin from the performance of a responsorial psalm in the first part of the mass; in the core repertory of 105 graduals, all but eleven have texts from the psalms. More than half the graduals in the Gregorian repertory are based on two model melodies.

The next part of the mass was the alleluia, a responsorial proper chant consisting of a melismatic vocalization on the word 'Alleluia' followed by a verse (usually taken from the psalms); the lengthy melisma (the jubilus) that concludes the initial Alleluia recurs at the conclusion of the verse. The performance practice of the alleluia was not everywhere the same in the Middle Ages, but generally outlined a three-part form. The first part (just the Alleluia, or the Alleluia and jubilus) was sung by the cantor and repeated by the choir, after which the cantor sang the verse, and finally the choir repeated the opening Alleluia with the jubilus. Example 1.2, the *Alleluia. Ascendens Christus*, illustrates the characteristic style and structure of this

Example 1.2 *Alleluia. Ascendens Christus*, in a thirteenth- or fourteenth-century Parisian gradual (*F-Pn* fonds lat. 1337, fol. 158v)

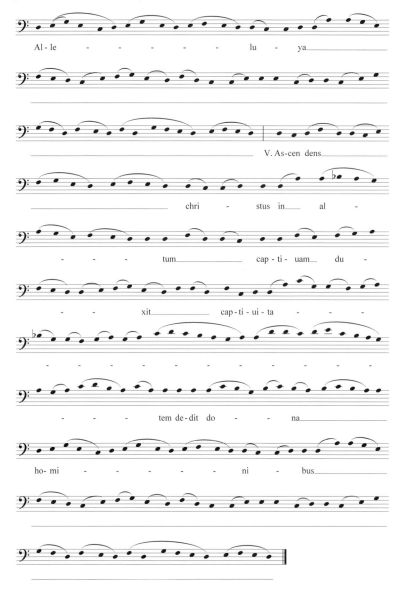

genre; the word 'hominibus' at the conclusion of the verse is sung to the same music as the initial word 'alleluya'. Much of the melody's ornate circular movement remains within the span of a fifth from D to A; in the verse, the melisma on the penultimate syllable of 'captivitatem' explores the fourth from A to D and repeats the pitch on A, both features characteristic of the first mode. The alleluia was interpreted by medieval writers as angelic song, an image explored in prosulae (see Chapter 2), sequences, and liturgical commentary.

Because of its associations with rejoicing, the Alleluia was not performed during penitential seasons such as Advent and Lent; it was replaced by the tract, a lengthy proper chant performed by a soloist. Tracts constitute one of the most formulaic genres, both in their overall structure and in their use of individual melodic gestures. The construction of tracts is closely bound to their modality; all tracts are either in mode 2 or mode 8, and those in the same mode are so similar to one another that they can be described as realizations of the same compositional template.[20]

The alleluia and the sequence (see Chapter 2) were followed by the chanting of the gospel reading of the day, then by the Credo, an ordinary chant with a small repertory of mostly syllabic melodies. The next proper chant was the offertory, which like the gradual is a responsorial chant with formulaic melodies set to texts mostly taken from the psalms. As it accompanied the liturgical action of carrying gifts to the altar, it originally included multiple verses, but over time the number of verses was reduced to one or at most two. Unlike the verses of the introit, which are related to office psalmody, the verses of offertories are ornate compositions.[21]

The Sanctus and Agnus Dei are chants of the ordinary that in the early church are thought to have been performed by the congregation (in the case of the Agnus Dei, along with the clergy); numerous melodies for these chants are preserved beginning in the eleventh century. Many feature repetitive phrases with melismas that are narrower in range than those found in the mass propers. The communion, the final chant of the mass proper, is generally less melismatic in style than the responsorial genres, and bears some resemblance to the introit in its structure of antiphon with verse.

In addition to liturgical books, valuable information on plainsong can be found in theological or homiletic writings, commentaries on the liturgy, and prescriptive texts (such as monastic rules and ordinals). For instance, the Benedictine Rule, written in the sixth century and diffused in much of Europe beginning in the ninth and tenth, states unequivocally that no activity in a monastery should ever take precedence over the divine office.[22] The lengthy section on the performance of the office concludes with a passage that indicates the theological significance of the liturgy: 'therefore we should consider how one should be in the sight of the divinity and his angels, and let us stand to sing the psalms in such a way that our mind be in concord with our voice'.[23]

The origins of Gregorian chant

Although the liturgy developed in response to the church calendar and the annual cycles of feasts, liturgical assignments were formalized or codified at different times. In the early Middle Ages certain elements (such as the choice and number of verses in some responsorial chants) might be left to the discretion of the soloist or choirmaster, which could account for some of the differences between early manuscripts. The question of who composed the early mass proper chants and determined their liturgical assignments has no single answer. James McKinnon argues that the *schola cantorum* at Rome in the seventh century collectively composed the mass propers in cycles by genre, while Peter Jeffery maintains that the early mass proper chants instead cluster around liturgical occasion.[24] New feasts introduced in the seventh and eighth centuries employed chants that were borrowed from already existing feasts, suggesting that a process of new chant composition had come to an end. In the Carolingian period a legend emerged attributing to Pope Gregory I the formidable corpus that had come into existence by that time, but there is no historical basis for applying the name 'Gregorian' to a repertory that formed gradually, in the eighth and ninth centuries. Beginning with Pépin's consecration by Pope Stephen II in 754, the political relationship between the Frankish kings and the Holy See fostered the introduction of Roman chant in the Frankish kingdom. This tendency became a systematic programme of liturgical reform under Charlemagne and Louis the Pious. From a long-term process of assimilation came a new, hybrid repertory which would more accurately be called 'Romano-Frankish', although the misnomer 'Gregorian' remains standard (and is used here for that reason).

The earliest books of Gregorian chant represent the products of reception and adaptation described in ninth- and tenth-century historical narratives that recount (from both northern European and Italian points of view) the Franks' importation of chant from Rome.[25] Even the earliest extant manuscripts containing notated cycles of Gregorian chant for the proper of the mass, which date from the tenth century, preserve a relatively uniform melodic tradition; thereafter, chants tend to have similar contours in mass books from different places. A quite different transmission pattern appears in the manuscripts of the divine office, which attest to considerable variation in the selection, ordering, assignments, and melodies of chants. Even in the first notated office books, the repertory was much less stable than the mass and more local in character.[26]

The coherence of the mass repertory witnessed by the earliest notated sources is particularly remarkable given that most of the musical information had to be preserved in the oral tradition. Singers had to learn from one another rather than from books, for the early forms of neumatic notation used at this time indicated general contour and phrasing, but not pitch or intervallic content. Scholars have put forth various explanations for this phenomenon. If the earliest extant notated manuscripts are chance survivals of a longer manuscript tradition, they may represent vestiges of earlier written exemplars that would have made it possible for the melodies to be widely distributed in essentially the same form. Such melodic uniformity in earlier manuscripts now lost would suggest that the melodies were precisely fixed in singers' memories for generations before they were written down. On the other hand, the relationship between notation and performance may have been more indirect; scribes copying chants could have relied primarily on what they remembered aurally instead of mechanically reproducing the neumes in the exemplar.[27]

Part of the mystery surrounding the origins of the Gregorian chant resides in the difficulty of recovering what came before. The Gallican chant practised in Gaul before the Carolingian importation of the Roman liturgy seems to have been almost completely effaced by the Gregorian repertory.[28] The earliest extant notated sources from Rome with mass and office chants were produced in the eleventh and twelfth centuries, long after the transmission of Roman chant to the north. Many scholars believe that the Roman chant repertory was preserved in the oral tradition until that time, but we cannot be certain that the earliest Roman chant manuscripts preserve what was sung in earlier centuries.[29] The melodies in these 'Old Roman' manuscripts exhibit a recognizable relationship to the melodies transmitted with the same texts and liturgical functions in manuscripts of Gregorian chants. In many cases the deep structures of the Old Roman and Gregorian versions are comparable, but the chants employ different melodic formulas and ways of deploying them.[30] Many Old Roman chant melodies are more ornamental and repetitive than their Gregorian counterparts, as can be seen from the comparison of a Gregorian melody with an Old Roman melody for the first antiphon of lauds on Holy Saturday in Example 1.3. Many Old Roman chants also exhibit an archaic tonal organization apparently predating the eight-mode system, which developed in eighth-century Jerusalem and was received in the West in the ninth century.[31]

Other early Latin chant traditions differ notably from both the Roman and the Gregorian chant repertories in genre, form and style. Most of these regional traditions were largely supplanted by the Gregorian chant as a result of reforms promoted by eleventh-century popes who sought to impose the Roman rite throughout the Latin West. Practically the only corpus of Latin chant to survive this period besides the Gregorian is the Ambrosian rite, the ancient liturgy of the diocese of Milan named after Saint Ambrose (Bishop of Milan from 374 to 397). The Old Hispanic chant, which originated in the Visigothic period, was replaced in the Iberian peninsula by the Gregorian chant beginning in the late eleventh century. At the time of the suppression of the Old Spanish rite, almost none of the melodies were written down in staff notation, so the adiastematic neumes in which they are recorded

Example 1.3 Comparison of the Gregorian and Old Roman melodies for the antiphon *O mors ero mors tua* in *F-Pn* fonds lat. 12044, fol. 99r and *I-RVat* ASP B 79, fol. 102v

have not yet been deciphered (on the Iberian peninsula, see Chapter 9 by Nicolas Bell).

The native south Italian repertory known as the Beneventan chant was also suppressed, but some of it survives in manuscripts of Gregorian chant copied in the region.[32] One of the most widespread of these survivals is the Beneventan version of the Exultet, a lengthy late-antique text performed by the deacon to accompany the lighting of the paschal candle during the Easter Vigil on Holy Saturday. The Beneventan Exultet had a distinctive text and melody and was performed from a scroll; several illuminated examples of such Exultet rolls have survived.[33]

In England, where the texts and chants brought from Rome in the early Middle Ages blended with local repertories, the Norman Conquest and the subsequent introduction of usages from France led to a radical transformation of liturgy and chant not unlike what had taken place in those parts of Europe where the Gregorian chant replaced earlier traditions. Comparison of the few extant pre-Conquest liturgical manuscripts with later books suggests that the Anglo-Saxon chant tradition did not entirely disappear, but the melodies are difficult to recover because they are written in unheighted staffless neumes. Syncretism in the post-Conquest period fostered the development of local English cathedral repertories such as the Salisbury rite, as well as particularly insular usages among the religious orders.

Notation and performance

With the widespread reception and adaptation of the Gregorian chant in the eleventh and twelfth centuries, the melodies came to be written down more frequently. The development of staff notation in this period

Figure 1.1 Aquitanian neumes in a late-eleventh-century antiphoner (collection of author): antiphons and psalm incipits for the office of lauds on the Tuesday of Holy Week

enables us to transcribe chant melodies and to compare them with the contours outlined less precisely by earlier unheighted staffless neumes.[34] Not all staffless neumes were unheighted, however: in Aquitanian notation, drypoint lines provided an axis around which pitches could be oriented with great precision (see Figure 1.1).

In the 1020s or 1030s, the north Italian monk Guido of Arezzo devised a system of staff notation with a red line indicating F and a yellow line indicating C, the type seen in Figure 1.2. In the course of the eleventh century, analogous systems using one or two lines were introduced in much of western Europe. The wide variety of neumatic notations that had existed in

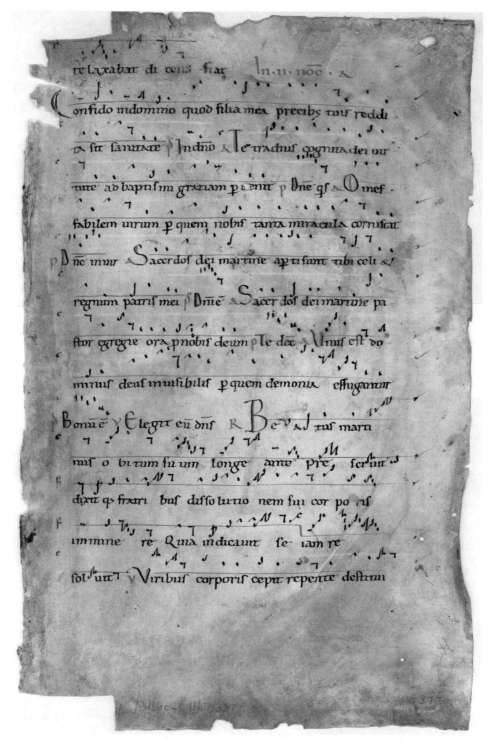

Figure 1.2 Central Italian neumes in a twelfth-century antiphoner (collection of author): responsories, antiphons and psalm incipits for matins on the feast of St Martin

chant manuscripts gradually gave way, in many places, to a more uniform type known as 'square' notation (based on solid black squares). Staff notation and square notation lack most of the nuances and idiosyncrasies that are such a prominent feature of the earlier neumatic notations. Some of the performance indications that gradually fell away include the significative letters in tenth- and eleventh-century manuscripts, principally from the areas that now comprise Germany and eastern France, but also Aquitaine, Winchester and the Iberian peninsula. These letters signify directions for pitch and rhythm, instructing performers to sing higher, lower, or at the same pitch, to speed up or to slow down, and so on. Such information would have been useful because the early neumes do not indicate precise pitches, intervals or durations. Other features of early notation that all but disappeared in the high Middle Ages were the distinctive neume forms signalling ornaments or changes of vocal production. Their precise meanings are not fully understood. Notational diversity was not lost altogether, however. In some regions, particularly in Germanic areas, the Netherlands and Bohemia, neumes were used well into the thirteenth century and later, often written on staff lines. Even square notation can manifest regional particularities.

Late chant composition

The performance and composition of chant continued throughout the Middle Ages and beyond. Chant composition met a variety of needs, such as providing music for the celebration of new feasts, or creating a repertory of proper chants specifically tailored to a particular occasion. Although some of the most prominent manifestations of this compositional activity are tropes and sequences (see Chapter 2), the same historical context gave rise to thousands of new chants for the mass and office. Late chant resembles the earlier layers of Gregorian chant in many ways, but tends to use melodic formulas and conventions even more consistently. In a few rare cases one can study the work of individuals who created new services by composing new chants and compiling existing ones.[35]

Following a trend initiated in the tenth century, many new office chants had texts in verse (sometimes in quantitative metres); for a number of saints, entirely new versified offices were composed.[36] In late offices, the antiphons and responsories were often arranged in modal order, so that a chant in mode 1 would be followed by one in mode 2.[37] The earliest examples of such organization are the offices attributed to Bishop Stephen of Liège (ruled 901–20).[38] Modal ordering was not a universal feature of new offices, but it was common enough to indicate that from the tenth century onwards, composers of chant consciously deployed the eight modes as they are described by theorists of the period, emphasizing the final pitch and the species of tetrachord (fourth) and pentachord (fifth) that, in combination, comprise the typical range of each mode. By the eleventh century, each mode was associated with certain melodic gestures that pervade the corpus of late chant. Both old and new office antiphons embody these features, whereas office responsories present a wider range of possibilities. For the verses of great responsories, composers employed the traditional melodic formulas associated with the modes, adapted the existing tones for the verses, or composed entirely new music for them. Each office presents its own combination of tradition and innovation.[39]

With the spread of new religious orders across Europe came a heightened production of offices celebrating their most important saints.[40] To name just a few, the cults of saints particularly venerated by the Franciscans, Dominicans and Carmelites engendered works that led to the creation of a new form of archetype: for instance, the office for Saint Francis of Assisi provided a model for later offices of the Franciscan saints Clare, Louis of Anjou and Elizabeth of Hungary. Contrafacts (settings of new texts to existing melodies) reflect the composer's coordination of the new melody with the poetic structure of the original text, but in some cases the new office entirely reworks the underlying textual and musical structure.[41]

Religious reformers also transformed entire chant repertories. In the eleventh and twelfth centuries, monasteries reformed by the abbey of Cluny sometimes adopted its chant repertory, in whole or in part.[42] The Cistercian revision aimed to produce a more authentic version of the Gregorian antiphoner.[43] The Carmelites introduced new feasts particular to the cults of their order.[44] The Dominicans diffused exemplars from which to copy liturgical books so as to ensure uniformity throughout the order.[45] The Franciscans shaped the late medieval liturgy of the Roman curia.[46]

Throughout the high and late Middle Ages, European ecclesiastical centres continually produced new chant books and new compositions. Brussels, Florence and Toledo are but three of the major cities whose long chant traditions have been explored in recent years.[47] In the fifteenth century, plainsong remained the central component of religious services, even as vocal polyphony flourished. The Hussite movement in Bohemia produced liturgical chants with Czech texts (both translations of Latin chants and new vernacular compositions).[48] Guillaume Du Fay, a composer best known today for his polyphony, created a collection of chants for feasts of the Virgin Mary that offers insight into a late medieval composer's approach to chant.[49] The proliferation of devotional and liturgical performances at different locations in a single church characterized the late Middle Ages, when commemorations founded by individuals created numerous services in addition to the principal ones at the high altar.[50]

The performance and composition of plainsong continued to flourish in the sixteenth, seventeenth and eighteenth centuries, responding to reforms and liturgical needs.[51] Revised versions of plainsong can be heard in a few churches today (albeit rarely since the Second Vatican Council), but medieval chant now reaches listeners most often through concert performances and recordings. The increasing availability of such resources will enable the readers of this volume to explore the rich and varied legacy of plainsong more easily than ever before.

2 Enriching the Gregorian heritage

MICHAEL McGRADE

New music in Francia

In 843, Charlemagne's descendants met at the city of Verdun and divided the Carolingian empire into three kingdoms. By this time churches and monasteries from Aquitania to Saxony were, for the most part, observing a common liturgy based on Roman practices.[1] The stability of this Gregorian rite, its ability to survive the political division of the empire, rests on the success of the educational programmes Charlemagne established in the late eighth century. The Carolingian emphasis on literacy, musicianship and the accurate reproduction of books all provided a solid foundation for the new liturgy, and the ninth-century canons and monks who inherited the newly forged rite developed a wide variety of tools – tonaries, theory treatises, and musical notation itself – to preserve and pass down this legacy.

The division of the Carolingian empire in 843 had important consequences for the history of music. The Treaty of Verdun polarized the European continent, creating Eastern and Western realms divided roughly by the Rhine river. The geographic division is reflected in the emergence and development of two musical traditions. Whereas chants that entered the liturgy before the early 840s appear in books across the European continent with substantial fixity, melodies that were composed later, in the late ninth, tenth, and eleventh centuries, tend to appear exclusively in sources either east or west of the Rhine. After about 1100, the boundary between East and West became more permeable, and the wide dissemination of chant once again became common.[2]

The educational strategies the Carolingians developed to preserve the Gregorian chant also offered a set of principles for the invention and notation of new works, stylistically distinct from the Gregorian repertory. Some scholars refer to these newer compositions as 'medieval' or 'Frankish' chant.[3] The two most important genres of Frankish chant emerged and flourished late in the ninth century and early in the tenth: the trope and the sequence.

Two monastic houses are particularly important to our understanding of these new genres, the monastery of St Gall in the East Frankish kingdom, and the monastery of St Martial in the heart of the Aquitaine region of

West Francia. Their libraries preserve the largest collections of early tropes and sequences; their books are the foundation of our knowledge about this music before 1100.[4]

Only two years after the meeting at Verdun, Charles the Bald, ruler of the West Frankish kingdom, assembled an ecclesiastical synod at Meaux, just outside of Paris. The delegates voiced concern over the deterioration of church services, and they took steps to improve discipline and promote orthodox observances among the clergy. In one statute, the council denounced the practice of adding new compositions and new words to the Gregorian music:

> ... we decree that no member of the clergy [and] no monk may presume to undertake, interpose, recite, murmur, or sing any compositions which they call *prosas*, or any other creations [*uel ullas fictiones*], during the angelic hymn, that is *Gloria in excelsis deo*, or during the *sequentiae*, which are usually sung after the Alleluia. If one will have been made, throw it out.[5]

For many singers, no doubt, the imperative to preserve the chant had cultivated an impulse to enrich it. Here that enrichment seems confined to the addition of new texts to melismatic passages, but the prohibition of 'other creations' suggests that adding words to melismas was not the only outlet for creative singers. The council also documents the performance of sequentiae, long melismatic passages added to the alleluia, but it is not the earliest witness of that practice. Indeed, neither of these activities – the addition of text or melismas – was new in 845. Both must have been sufficiently common to warrant such condemnation.

Melismas

Evidence that singers were adding new music to Gregorian chant appears in one of the earliest of all chant books – in fact, it is the first book to call the newly collected mass propers 'Gregorian' – the unnotated gradual from the abbey of Mont-Blandin near Ghent, copied around the year 800.[6] Six alleluias in this book are marked with a rubric that instructed performers to add an extensive melisma, known as a sequentia, to the chant.[7] The sequentia replaced or extended the usual melisma, known as the *jubilus*, when the Alleluia was repeated after the verse. A performance could follow this scheme:

> Alleluia. Alleluia + jubilus
> psalm verse
> Alleluia. Alleluia + sequentia

About a generation after the Mont-Blandin gradual was copied, Amalarius of Metz, in his allegorical commentaries on the liturgy, described the singing not only of sequentiae, but also of the ornate *neuma triplex*, a three-part melisma appended to the last office responsory on the feasts of Christmas and St John the Evangelist.[8]

Sequentiae and the neuma triplex were lengthy melodies, but more modest melismatic additions can be found as well. For example, the introit for the feast of St Gall, *Sacerdotes tui domine*, was drawn from the *commune sanctorum*, a pool of generic chants that commemorated a saint according to his or her classification as a confessor, martyr, virgin, bishop and so on. The text of the introit, drawn from Psalm 132, is:

> [Introit:] Sacerdotes tui domine, induant iustitiam, et sancti tui exsultent: propter David servum tuum, non avertas faciem Christi tui. Alleluia, alleluia.
>   V[erse]: Memento domine David: et omnes mansuetudinis eius

> Let your priests, O Lord, be clothed with justice, and let your faithful rejoice; for your servant David's sake do not turn away the face of your anointed one. Alleluia, alleluia.
>   V: Remember, O Lord, David and all his mildness

The monks at the monastery of St Gall composed two sets of melismatic additions for this chant. Like most musical embellishments of this kind, the placement of the new melismas is identified in the sources only by cues provided by the scribes, so in the manuscript St Gall, Stiftsbibliothek 484, we find melismas appended to the following words (Figure 2.1):[9]

> Sacerd[otes] D[omi]ne
>   Iustitiam
>   Exultent
>   Tuum   [fa]ciem

A comparison of these cues with the psalm text above shows that they highlight breaks in the syntax of the text. Both sets of melismatic additions in St Gall 484 use the same words as cues.

New texts

Adding a new melisma was just one way in which a singer could ornament a chant. It was also common for singers to add words to lengthy, untexted melodies. The earliest notated example of this practice appears in a book from the abbey of St Emmeram in Regensburg. This book contains a reading of the chant *Alleluia. Christus resurgens* in which a text beginning with the words 'Psalle modulamina' has been added to the melismatic verse; such a

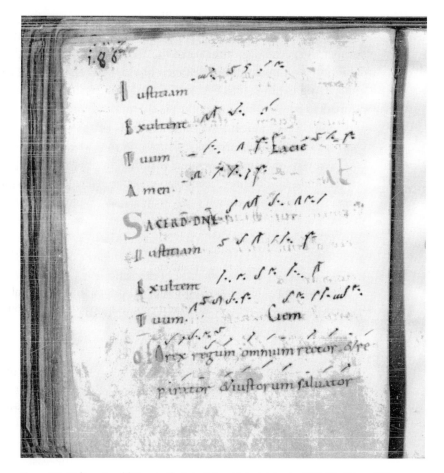

Figure 2.1 Melismatic additions to the introit *Sacerdotes tui domine* (*CH-SGs* 484, p. 186)

text is known as a *prosula*.[10] The St Emmeram copy of the *Psalle modulamina* may be the earliest surviving example of neumatic notation, dating perhaps as far back as the third or fourth decade of the ninth century.[11]

Tropes

Like so many medieval terms, the word 'trope' has the irritating property of meaning both less and more than modern scholars would like it to mean, and our notions of what it should mean has led to confusion.[12] In modern scholarship, the word 'trope' frequently refers to three practices: the addition of new music to a chant, the addition of text to a melisma, and the addition of newly composed words and music to pre-existing chant.[13]

When used as a generic category in the Middle Ages, the term had a narrow scope: it referred to newly composed words and music in a small number of specific liturgical contexts.[14] The disadvantage of the modern definition is its tendency to subsume a broad spectrum of musical activities under a single rubric, thus encumbering our efforts to study those activities sympathetically. Nevertheless, the modern use is convenient, entrenched, and unlikely to change; thoughtful students of the period should avoid confusing it with the more specific medieval meaning.

One body of music associated with the Kyrie eleison highlights this terminological problem.[15] Compositions often referred to in modern literature as 'Kyrie tropes' are not really tropes at all. Typically, any Kyrie chant that includes more than the Greek words of the acclamation – 'Kyrie eleison, Christe eleison, Kyrie eleison' – has been called a trope. But because there is no evidence that the Latin texts were not part of the original composition, it is more accurate to think of these compositions as Latin-texted Kyries. In other words, there is no indication that *Kyrie Cunctipotens genitor* or *Kyrie Te Christe* ever existed in an untexted (or 'untroped') form, and that generically their history is distinct from that of tropes in the specific, medieval sense. These texted Kyries were almost certainly original compositions, not melismatic chants with prosulae added later.

One further argument against thinking of Latin-texted Kyries as tropes is the existence of true Kyrie tropes, which are newly composed phrases of text and music that introduce the Kyrie chant and appear between its acclamations.

We return to the introit *Sacerdotes tui domine* and the feast of St Gall for a nice example of a trope in the narrow sense. It appears in the manuscript St Gall, Stiftsbibliothek 381, dating from the early to mid tenth century.[16] In the transcription below, the boldfaced words belong to the introit, the italicized words and syllables, also part of the introit, mark the placement of added melismas. The phrases written in plain text indicate the newly composed tropes. As in St Gall 484, only cues for the introit are provided.

Hodie sanctissimi patroni nostri Galli anima choris supernis iuncta iubilat quapropter et nos exultemus canentes.
Sacerdotes tui domine Qui es verus sacerdos et rex summus atque immensus. *Domine*
Iustitiam Ut tibi placere possint sanctis meritis. *Tiam*
Exultent In exultatione sempiternae trinitatis. *Tent*
Tuum Que exultasti de pastore in regem *Tuum*
Memento. Eius Quique consueverat spiritu

Today the spirit of our most holy patron Gallus, joined to the choirs above, shouts with joy, and for this reason we rejoice, singing:

> **Let your priests, O Lord,** [you] who are the true priest and the highest, fathomless king
> **Be clothed with justice,** so that they might please you with holy actions
> **And let your saints rejoice,** in praise of the everlasting trinity
> **For the sake of your servant David,** who leapt from shepherd to king,
> **Do not turn away the face of your anointed one.**
> V: **O Lord, remember David and all his meekness,** and each person who had become accustomed to the spirit

Each new line is itself a trope, sometimes called a trope verse or a trope element. The introductory line and all of the interpolations constitute a set of tropes.[17] This particular set includes an element for the psalm verse, a relatively uncommon feature.

Scribes notated the music for this set of tropes with staffless neumes. This is the case for all of the early books from St Gall, so it is difficult to draw any conclusions about the nature of the early trope melodies composed there. The earliest St Gall manuscripts with diastematic notation – notation that provides pitch information – date from the late twelfth century. The melodies from West Frankish institutions are more accessible, and, unlike many Gregorian melodies, they tend to be strongly rooted in the modal system. The individual elements also tend to reflect a sensitivity to musical phrasing to coordinate with the Gregorian phrases, sometimes through unresolved cadences, sometimes not.[18]

Tropes were appealing because they made generic chants serve specific purposes. The introit *Sacerdotes tui domine* was used for confessor-saints at many religious houses. By adding a set of tropes to this chant, the monks at the monastery of St Gall drew attention to his special status as patron of their community. Because the introit was the chant that began the mass, it was the best place to focus attention on the special relevance of a given feast. It is not surprising, then, that of all types of trope (by any definition), those for the introit are the most numerous.

Aquitanian versus

Some time in the eleventh century, tropes began to lose their appeal. The trend is most clearly documented in the Aquitanian sources, where tropes are recorded in smaller and smaller numbers through the eleventh century.[19] They were replaced by a new type of song, notable for its poetic sensitivity and grace, the versus. Versus (the word is both singular and plural) were usually strophic, and their melodies bore a close syntactic relationship with the verse forms they set. There was no standard form, so the versus invited experimentation and novelty. This sense of innovation and play also characterizes the polyphonic settings of these works.[20]

Versus commonly begin with a repeated note, syllabically setting the opening words of the poem. Following this simple declamation, the tune usually unfolds in a series of phrases that vary in length. The melodies move within the confines of the various octave species and have a clear tonal focus. Aquitanian composers paid increasing attention to the pitches on which individual phrases came to rest. Short phrase units are often coordinated with the sense of the text, and the ends of lines or other important syntactic breaks are frequently punctuated with melismas, some extravagant in their length.[21]

The versus had a counterpart in northern France in the conductus. While many aspects of the two genres differ, they share important features, among them a freedom of verse forms, the originality of the melodies, the delicate coordination of text and music, and a magnetic appeal to polyphonists.

The early sequence: Notker's *Liber hymnorum*

Interest in the versus had diminished by the end of the twelfth century, and the conductus began to decline in the second quarter of the thirteenth. The liturgical sequence, on the other hand, experienced a resurgence in the twelfth century.

Sequences first appeared late in the ninth century. They were new chants composed for specific feasts and they sound very different from the Gregorian propers, Frankish ordinaries, and tropes of the period. They were usually sung during the mass after the alleluia; occasionally they were melodically related to the alleluia that preceded them. Sequences were composed for many centuries, with new ones joining the liturgy until the middle of the sixteenth century, when all but five were banned by the Council of Trent (1546–65).

Sequences are characterized by a simple design principle. Lines of text are composed in pairs. A melody is composed for the first member of the pair and repeated for the second. Each new pair of lines receives a new repeating melody, as follows:

> Melody: AA BB CC etc.
> Text: ab cd ef etc.

Sometimes a single line of text begins and ends the composition, and occasionally an unmatched line will appear in the middle of a work, especially in the early repertory, but the scheme above can be considered a model of the form despite this variance.

The first document that refers to the liturgical sequence unambiguously is the preface to the earliest known collection of these pieces, the *Liber hymnorum* (Book of Hymns) by Notker of St Gall (ca840–912).[22] The *Liber hymnorum* was probably completed around 884. Notker begins his preface with the complaint that the very long *melodiae*, melismas known elsewhere as sequentiae, easily escaped his memory. But when he inspected the contents of an antiphoner from the Abbey of Jumièges – the book was carried to St Gall by a Norman monk fleeing the Vikings – he found a solution to his mnemonic troubles. The antiphoner contained examples of the liturgical alloy condemned by the Council of Meaux: the Jumiégeois monks had added words to sequentiae.

Adding text to a sequentia does not make a sequence, but many of these long melismas have internal phrases that repeat, and such a structure could have suggested to Notker the double cursus that characterizes the sequence. Notker himself tells us that the *exempla* he found in the antiphoner were disappointing, but that they inspired him to compose his own works, which he developed further with the advice of his teacher and abbot. A small number of early sequences have a clear melodic relationship to an alleluia, but such relationships are not an essential feature of the genre. Once he had completed several sequences, Notker assembled them in his *Liber hymnorum* and presented the collection to the Bishop of Vercelli.

A fragment of the original *Liber hymnorum* may survive in the monastery of St Gall. Susan Rankin has persuasively shown that the manuscript St Gall, Kantonsbibliothek (Vadiana) 317 is a kind of master copy from which presentation copies of the *Liber hymnorum* were prepared.[23] Nearly all other copies of the *Liber hymnorum* appear about a century after Notker's death.

Early manuscripts: the two traditions

Notker's *Liber hymnorum* formed the heart of the sequence repertory in the East Frankish lands, but this was not the case in the West. In fact, the East and West Frankish sequence repertories are almost completely exclusive. When a melody appears both east and west of the Rhine, its texts are almost always different. The separation of Eastern and Western sequences is reflected not only in the content of the repertories, but also in the material record, in the structure of the books.[24]

The notation of eastern books differs from that used by West Frankish scribes in significant ways. Eastern scribes copied sequence texts in a way that draws attention to the paired lines of the text. They began each new line of verse at the left margin and highlighted the opening word with a capital letter. The melodies were then notated as melismas in the margins.

In some later East Frankish books neumes were placed over the syllables of text, but these supplemented the marginal notation; they did not replace it. Each melody is also usually identified by a name. For example, the melody for the sequence honouring St Gall, *Dilecte deo Galle perenni*, is *Iustus ut palma minor*, perhaps reflecting the melodic incipit the sequence shared with the alleluia that preceded it.

In the West, scribes did little to represent the structure of the text on the page. Instead, the lines of the chant were laid out continuously, like sentences in a paragraph, with the first word of each new versicle marked with a capital letter. Sometimes neumes were placed above the text, but West Frankish scribes never wrote melismas in the margins. Instead, they often wrote out entire untexted sequence melodies in separate fascicles. The beginning of an untexted sequence melody was usually indicated by the word 'Alleluia' (or some abbreviation of it) written under the first musical phrase. Subsequent phrases were sometimes introduced with the letter 'a', and the ends of phrases were often marked with a letter or some other sign. A rubric giving the opening words of the sequence often follows the complete tune, but the melodic names found in the East Frankish books are absent. Figures 2.2a and 2.2b show pages from East and West Frankish books respectively.

Also marking the division between East and West Frankish traditions is the relatively small body of partially texted sequences (the modern designation is misleading – they are not sequences, but rather partially texted sequentiae). These works appear only in West Frankish books, chiefly from England and France. Partially texted sequences begin like a typical alleluia, but continue with extensive melismas, some of which are constructed to form a series of repeated melodic phrases. Selected phrases in the melisma – most typically the fifth, eighth or ninth, and eleventh or thirteenth – are then provided with words.[25]

Finally, terminological differences separate the East and West Frankish traditions. In the East, *sequentia* refers to the liturgical chant we now call a sequence; the word *prosa* was not used in Germanic sources. In the West, *sequentia* was either a textless melody, or a partially texted sequence, while *prosa* was the term analogous to the modern sequence. Some writers have argued that this difference in terminology may indicate differences in performance practice and perhaps even musical conception.[26]

Notker's Pentecost sequence

Notker's Pentecost sequence *Sancti spiritus assit nobis gratia* is one of the few East Frankish sequences to find a home in the West Frankish realm.

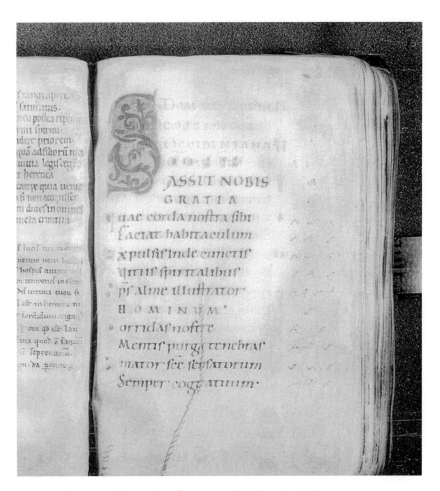

Figure 2.2(a) East Frankish notation of a sequence (*CH-SGs* 378, p. 223)

Ulrich von Zell, writing in the late eleventh century, noted that Eastern and Western tastes differed, but that this one sequence appealed to musical sensibilities on both sides of the Rhine:

> ... although not all the French care very much for the proses of the Germans, nevertheless, the blessed father Odilo, being pressed and then allying himself with our countrymen, maintained that this one only, *Sancti spiritus adsit gratia*, might be sung on this day in our place [i.e., Cluny].[27]

The two opening versicles illustrate Notker's style nicely (Example 2.1):[28]

1	Sancti spiritus adsit nobis gratia,	May the grace of the Holy Spirit be with us,
2a	Quae corda nostra sibi faciat habitaculum,	and make our hearts its dwelling place,
2b	Expulsis inde cunctis vitiis spiritalibus.	having driven out all spiritual vices from them.[29]

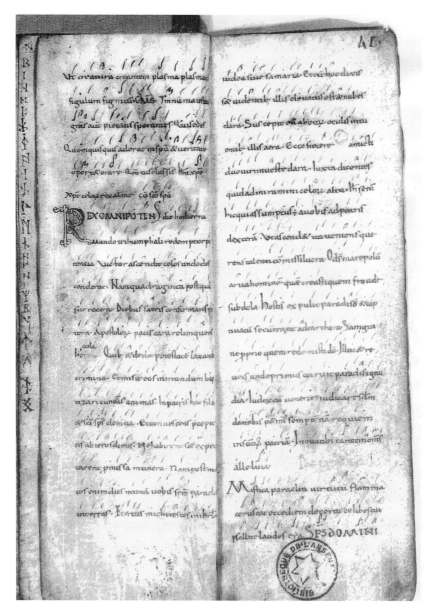

Figure 2.2(b) West Frankish notation of a sequence (*F-Pa* 1169, fols. 40v–41r)

Notker's melodies have direction, and his sequences reflect a sensitivity
to the overall shape of the piece. His melodies tend to lie within the ambitus
of the various octave species, with individual phrases and versicles moving
thoughtfully, often dramatically, within the constituent fourths and fifths of
each mode. The opening versicle, for example, establishes the fourth from
G to C, with a lower neighbour to the final, F. The A–G–F–G–G cadence, a
figure that punctuates each of the phrases, is also established in this opening

Example 2.1 Opening of *Sancti Spiritus adsit nobis gratia* (*CH-SGs* 383, p. 85)

phrase. The second versicle expands the tonal space to the fifth pitch above the final. In the third phrase, the melody descends; now that the fifth above the final has been established, the fourth below is explored here and in the next versicle. By the end of the fourth versicle, the plagal form of the G mode has been confirmed, and the fifth and sixth phrases confine themselves, for the most part, to the fifth above the final.

The number of syllables changes from line to line in early sequences; in *Sancti spiritus assit nobis gratia* the first versicle has twelve syllables, the second, fifteen. Often the line lengths grow progressively longer until they reach a point of climax. Consider, for example, the sixth and seventh versicles (Example 2.2):

6a	Ut videri supremus genitor possit a nobis,	That the Father on high may be seen by us,
6b	Mundi cordis quem soli cernere possunt oculi.	Whom only the eyes of the pure heart may see.
7a	Prophetas tu inspirasti, ut praeconia Christi praecinuissent inclita:	Thou didst inspire the prophets to proclaim their glorious foretellings of Christ;
7b	Apostolos confortasti, uti tropheum Christi per totum mundi veherent.	Thou didst strengthen the apostles to convey Christ's trophy throughout the world

In the seventh versicle, by far the longest thus far, the melody for the first time traverses both the lower fourth and the upper fifth of the plagal mode

Example 2.2 Sixth and seventh versicles of *Sancti Spiritus adsit nobis gratia* (*CH-SGs* 383, pp. 86–7)

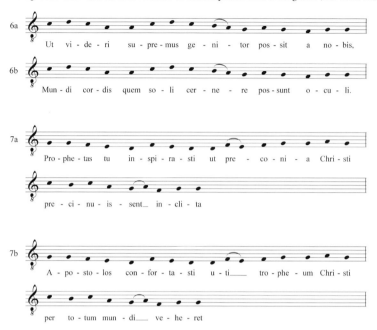

on G. The length of this versicle, combined with the greater range of the melody, mark it as an important turning point, one that is supported by the structure of the text.

The seventh versicle also shows how the lines of text tend to follow the same syntactic plan, so caesurae and other breaks in the sense of the text are coordinated with the shape of the melody; an example appears in lines 7a and 7b after 'inspirasti' and 'confortasti.' Note also the alignment of the word 'Christi' in each line of the seventh versicle, as well as the words 'possit' and 'possunt' in the sixth versicle. In addition to these verbal patterns, the texts are constructed so that word boundaries and vowel sounds are often preserved from line to line.

Notker's sequences have a declamatory freedom that sets them apart from the liturgical poetry of the period. This is due in part to the variation in line lengths, as well as the variety of phrasing within each individual line. The lines themselves seem to reflect an awareness of their artfulness; they are invigorated by the spirit of poetry, yet tempered by the decorum of classical oratory. The melodies, with their calculated phrasing and attention to a large-scale plan, also seem indebted to the rhetorical principles of antiquity.

After 1050, as noted above, the imaginary boundary between East and West became more permeable and the systems of writing down sequences began to converge. In the East, the names of the melodies gradually disappeared and the preferred method of notation placed neumes above the individual syllables of text. In the West, sequence melodies were no longer collected and notated without their texts. Furthermore, a small collection of approximately a dozen new sequences, sometimes labelled 'transitional' works, began to appear throughout Europe. The patterns of dissemination that governed the earlier East and West Frankish sequences did not apply to these new compositions. They are characterized by more florid melodies and the introduction of rhyme, metre, and other poetic devices into what was formerly art prose. The link between text and melody also seems stronger in the transitional sequence. When new texts were composed for these late-eleventh- and early-twelfth-century sequence melodies, they often referred to the original text, drawing attention to it by similar word choice and syntax.[30] These transitional works do not form a repertory; rather, they were at first copied and preserved *ad hoc* in collections that retained a strong Eastern or Western orientation; later, after 1050, the sources themselves became more cosmopolitan, reflecting the performance of Eastern and Western compositions under one roof.[31]

Parisian sequences

The sequence underwent a significant change in the first quarter of the twelfth century. The most obvious manifestation of this change was the adoption of a strict poetic structure: the number of syllables, poetic metre, and rhyme scheme became standardized. From the early twelfth century onwards the typical sequence followed a verse form in which lines of text were broken into 8 + 8 + 7 syllables. For example:

Templum cordis adornemus	Let us adorn the temple of the heart
Novo corde renovemus	Let us renew with new heart
Novum senis gaudium;	The new joy of the old man:
Quod dum ulnis amplexatur,	While he embraces it with his arms
Sic longevi recreatur	Thus is fulfilled the long-standing desire
Longum desiderium.	Of the aged man.[32]

As the form of the sequence verse changed, so too did the content. Twelfth-century sequences tend to align themselves with the traditions of liturgical commentary and exegesis rather than the conventions of hagiography and hymnody that influenced earlier generations of the genre.[33] The centre for this shift was twelfth-century Paris, a city where theology, poetry and music flourished with new vigour.

Twelfth-century sequences are more allegorical than those of the past, no doubt a reflection of the influence of Saint Augustine, who, in his *De doctrina christiana*, argued that sacred texts were to be read in multiple ways, and that literal, historical truth was only one of several truths contained in scripture. He pointed the way towards seeing the events of the Old Testament as prefigurations of the events in the New.[34] Augustine prompted readers to ask what symbolic meaning a text held (the allegorical mode of interpretation) and what lessons might be drawn from it (the tropological mode). He offered a vision of reading and explication that the Parisian students and masters took up with gusto.

The chief poet and musician associated with the new sequence was Adam of St Victor (d. 1146). Adam was precentor at the cathedral of Notre Dame in Paris by about 1107, and he advocated reforming the clergy according to principles of religious living derived from the writings of Saint Augustine.[35] He moved to the Abbey of St Victor in Paris around 1133, where he was a colleague of the great theologian Hugh (ca1096–1141). Adam composed texts and melodies for numerous sequences in the new style. More than 100 of the new sequences survive in Parisian books, with a core of approximately 40 shared by both Notre Dame and St Victor, but it was almost certainly the canons at St Victor who led in the creation of these new works. The exegetical teachings of Hugh are clear in the texts, as is a strong Augustinian bias, both of which point to the abbey as the centre of composition.[36]

Later in the century, probably sometime between 1150 and 1175, the canons at St Victor began to edit and rearrange the works of Adam. New texts were composed, others were excised and replaced. The canons of St Victor, having perhaps inherited the West Frankish tendency to associate and preserve the relationship between specific feasts and specific sequence melodies, began to construct an intricate genealogy of sequences by fitting new texts to pre-existing sequences, a process known as contrafacting. Contrafacting differs from simple texting in that contrafacted words replace a text already in place. The practice was far from new, but the Victorine canons actuated its exegetical power like none before them. The new texts addressed and developed complex theological themes, and the common ground occupied by these texts was emphasized by the melodies they shared.[37]

The sequence for the ritual purification of Mary provides a fine example of the Victorine sequence. The depth and intricacy of this work is too complicated to explore here, but a few points will highlight some features of the new style. The rhyming, poetic text immediately sets the work apart from the compositions of Notker, his contemporaries, and his followers. Individual melodic phrases are uniformly periodic, standing in sharp contrast to the ebb and flow of line lengths and caesurae in the early sequence. The orderly structure of the Victorine text is further emphasized by the trochaic

Example 2.3 Opening of *Templum cordis adornemus* (*F-Pn* fonds lat. 14817, fol. 60r).

metre, a feature that may have contributed to the development of rhythm in twelfth-century Parisian polyphony.[38]

The texture of the Parisian sequence, the approach to text setting, also differs from earlier works. Notker's melodies are more regularly syllabic than the Parisian compositions. The melody of the first versicle of *Templum cordis adornemus* clearly shows this stylistic difference when compared to the opening of Notker's Pentecost sequence. Only one syllable in Notker's setting is supplied with more than one pitch, and that is the first syllable of the composition. There are a few instances of two-notes-per-syllable later in the work, but they are exceptional. The setting of *Templum cordis adornemus*, on the other hand, does not strictly follow a one-note-per-syllable rule, as the opening versicle shows (Example 2.3), and this melodic richness is typical of the late style.

The melody of *Templum cordis* is shared by five other texts, all of which, arguably, have a Marian theme. The model for this melody was the well-known Marian hymn *Ave maris stella*, and this association would have given the sequence an unmistakable Marian connotation, one that would have been recognized by the singers of the day.[39]

Liturgical drama

Along with tropes and sequences, the oldest notated books also contain brief musical dialogues that are the earliest surviving examples of an abundant, diverse genre known as liturgical drama.[40] In the earliest dialogues or plays, phrases of direct speech were performed by two or more singers who represented the speakers in a biblical story. There was no effort to impersonate a character in the modern sense; rather, these exchanges drew attention to the rhetorical status of the text as speech. As Susan Rankin has pointed out, these works were foils for celebrating the message of the Resurrection or the Incarnation in the present.[41]

The earliest liturgical dialogue, the *Quem queritis*, recounted the New Testament scene in which the three Marys met a (single) angel at Christ's tomb (Mark 16:1–7).[42] In its most simple form it has only three lines:

[Angels'] Question:	Whom do you seek in the tomb, devotees of Christ?
[Marys'] Answer:	Jesus of Nazareth who was crucified, O creatures of heaven.
[Angels]:	He is not here; he has risen as he foretold. Go forth, tell that he has risen from the tomb.[43]

The *Quem queritis* dialogue survives in a wide variety of forms. Nearly all share these three lines, but the large number of antiphons, hymns and other chants that were added to them suggest that the play was a favourite vehicle for the creativity of medieval singers. Its wide dissemination and preservation in both East and West Frankish books, along with the clearly Frankish melodic style, point to a date of origin in the ninth century.[44]

Just as the complement of chants making up the *Quem queritis* dialogue varied, likewise the liturgical position of the play changed from place to place.[45] In some locales *Quem queritis* served as a trope to the Easter introit *Resurrexi*, in others it was incorporated into a procession before the Easter mass. Most typically it was performed after the third responsory of the matins service for Easter. It was in this liturgical position that the singers elaborated and developed the dialogue to the greatest degree. Modern scholars refer to these more complex versions of the dialogue as *Visitatio sepulchri* plays.[46]

The earliest example of the *Visitatio sepulchri* is preserved in the first source to provide information on its performance, the *Regularis Concordia*. In this work, a handbook on monastic life copied around 970 by Bishop Ethelwold of Winchester, singers are told when to dress for the play, where to stand, how to behave ('to move about as though they are seeking something', *velut erraneos ac aliquid quaerentes*), and how to sing ('with a sweet voice', *dulcisone voce*).[47] Later plays also contain performance instructions of this type.

Quem queritis served as a model for a Christmas play that first appears in sources from the middle of the eleventh century. The play is a trope in dialogue form for the introit *Puer natus est*. It borrows some of the language of the Easter model and also replicates the dramatic situation: this time shepherds are seeking the newborn Jesus in the manger. Similarly, the more elaborate *Visitatio sepulchri* finds a counterpart in the *Adoration of the Magi*, an expanded Christmas drama that was performed during the matins service.

The late eleventh century marks the beginning of a new epoch in the history of liturgical drama. New topics received dramatic treatment – a wider range of biblical scenes as well as episodes from the lives of the saints – and the preference for verse composition that we observed in the late sequence and the versus began to express itself in the lines of liturgical plays.

The ten works collected in the Fleury Playbook (Orléans, Bibliothèque Municipale, Ms 201) provide an excellent example of the diversity found in later liturgical plays. Bound as a group in a larger codex containing sermons and other religious writings, the plays were probably copied in the second half of the twelfth century. Four dramatize a series of miracles by Saint Nicholas, five draw on scenes from the life of Jesus, and one takes the conversion of Saint Paul as its subject. Some mix original melodies with traditional antiphons and other liturgical songs, while others are newly composed in their entirety.[48]

The Fleury plays possess a richness of dramatic representation that sets them apart from the earlier dialogues. Works such as the *Play of Herod*, the *Play of the Innocents*, and the *Visitatio* introduce a mild element of struggle or conflict not otherwise encountered in medieval religious observances.[49] These dramatic struggles are engendered in part by the depiction of emotions such as the anger of Herod or the sorrow of Rachel. Although the melodies attenuated anything we might call 'personal expression', the texts, the performance rubrics and perhaps the singing itself nudged these plays towards theatre.[50] In fact, the twelfth-century writers Gerhoh of Reichersberg and Herrad of Landsberg, both leaders of monastic communities, identified and condemned a drift away from ritual propriety in liturgical drama.[51] Nowhere was the lapse into theatrical entertainment more evident than in the Beauvais *Play of Daniel*.[52] After *The Play of Daniel*, that is, after the early thirteenth century, the composition of new Latin liturgical plays declined steadily, and the tradition of religious drama found expression in the vernacular mystery plays of the fourteenth and fifteenth centuries.

Performance

We have seen that liturgical plays were sometimes appointed with rubrics for their performance, but how did canons and monks perform a sequence like *Templum cordis* or a set of tropes like *Hodie sanctissimi*? Very few sources from the ninth or tenth centuries can answer this question directly, but later books known as *ordinals* provide detailed information about liturgical observances from the twelfth century onwards. Ordinals vary from church to church. They describe the correct execution of the various feasts of the year. Most commonly they reminded the celebrant of the chants that were to be sung and the personnel who were assigned to sing them. The description of some rites remained stable for many generations, changing little from one book to another copied many centuries later. Changes in the architecture of a church, the accumulation of relics, and the adoption of new feasts, or the wholesale reform of a liturgical tradition, often prompted the composition of a new ordinal with new instructions.[53] Within any given ordinal, the instructions for the performance of a chant could vary from feast to feast.

An ordinal from the cathedral of Metz, copied in the late thirteenth century, shows us how the performance of the sequence varied over the course of the year. For the feast of the Ascension, we are told

> This sequence is sung: *Rex omnipotens* . . . the first verse should be sung by two canons in the middle of the choir, the second [verse] by the right part, the third by the left, and in this way the others.[54]

In other instances, the cantor was given the option of choosing the chant. At the second mass for the Holy Innocents, the *ordo* reads: 'This sequence is sung: *Hac clara die* or another which will please [the cantor].'[55]

An unusual set of instructions appears in the *ordo* for the mass commemorating the Invention of St Stephen (3 August), the patron saint of Metz cathedral:

> The aforementioned monks [. . .] should sing *Alleluia Iudicant sancti*. The nuns should sing the words of the sequence, namely: *Congaudent angelorum*, the canons, on the other hand, should sing the notes next to the words.[56]

Aside from the surprising participation of the nuns in this service, there is no mention of *alternatim* performance here. Rather, the *ordo* seems to ask for parallel performances of the chant, one with words and one without; perhaps it dictates a performance of organum. Another possibility is the alternation of texted and untexted phrases of the chant. Earlier in the same service, a Latin-texted Kyrie was performed in the same way:

> One of the cantors should take the little books which are called *Tropier* and give them to the nuns for the singing of the *Kyrie Fons* or *Cunctipotens* or *Te Christe supplices exoramus*. For the nuns should sing the words, the canons, on the other hand, the notes next to the words.[57]

A more straightforward *ordo* for the feast of St Stephen (26 December) lends support to the idea that one group sang the chant with text, while another only a melisma. The *ordo* for mass on that day says simply: '*Kyrie eleison* is sung alongside [*cantatur iuxta*] *Kyrie fons bonitatis*.'[58] Like early copies of West Frankish sequences, Latin-texted Kyries often appear in two forms in the earliest manuscript sources: once in a melismatic version, and once texted. This common notational ground may point to common performance practices, and perhaps even a common conceptual foundation.

Information about performance can also be inferred from polyphonic settings of chants. The Winchester tropers, for example, contain a large body of polyphony from the late tenth and eleventh centuries. Polyphony was only performed by skilled soloists, and in this collection we find polyphonic settings of trope elements, as well as the soloists' parts in Gregorian chant. This distinction between music for soloists and music for the choir is preserved in the *ordo* for Epiphany at Metz:

> Once terce has been sung, all the bells are rung together at mass. Three or four subdeacons standing in the middle of the choir begin: [the trope] *Nos respectu gratie* and they sing the whole first verse. When the verse is finished, the chorus begins [the introit antiphon] *Ecce advenit Dominator Dominus*, after this [the subdeacons] sing another [trope] verse: *Cuius stellam*. The chorus begins: *et regnum in manu eius*. [etc.][59]

Descriptions of tropes in later ordinals are rare because they occupied a very small place in the liturgy after about 1100, but this case agrees with what we would expect based on the Winchester books.

Ordinals often dictate when bells are to be used during the ceremony, as the excerpt from the Epiphany *ordo* shows. Bells were commonly tolled during the sequence. In his *Decretals*, Lanfranc writes that 'two large bells are tolled during the sequence'; in the 1230s at Bury St Edmunds, 'two large bells [were] tolled in the choir during the sequence'; an early-fourteenth-century *ordo* for Christmas from St Mary's Abbey in York prescribed the performance of the sequence *Nato canunt* 'at which, as always when the sequence is sung, two or three bells are rung'.[60]

The Council of Meaux, like so many reform efforts, did little to arrest the blossoming musical creativity of medieval monks, canons and nuns. The Carolingian campaign to standardize liturgical observances by improving musicianship and literacy stimulated interest in musical expression generally. The inventiveness of the Carolingian musicians and their heirs found utterance in a rich variety of new songs. The chants composed in East and West Francia were, for many centuries, no less orthodox, no less a part of the Latin liturgy and no less inspiring to later composers than the Gregorian propers themselves.

3 Early polyphony to circa 1200

SARAH FULLER

Some surface aspects of musical art for the adornment of ecclesiastical songs have been outlined here.[1]

Here begin mellifluous songs of organum upon the sweetest praises of heaven.[2]

But in whatever way it is done . . . in producing diaphony the precentor must harmoniously sing in praise of the creator.[3]

As the above quotations suggest, early Western polyphony was broadly viewed as a way of elaborating and adorning monophonic chant, was heard as beautiful and sweet in sound, and was considered an appropriate means of religious praise. The close connection with religious worship is not surprising, given that the extant written record – both theoretical descriptions and musical notations – of polyphony stems from literate ecclesiastical and monastic spheres. But that record is decidedly incomplete and radically discontinuous. This is because early polyphony was 'produced' or 'made', not 'composed' in the present-day sense of 'composition': it was in the first instance sounded, not notated. Polyphony arose and continued as a performance practice, a way of elaborating a known monophonic melody with a second line that was produced according to accepted conventions.[4] Polyphonic singing enhanced worship through amplification of mono- phonic song. The earliest treatise to describe the phenomenon, the *Musica Enchiriadis* from *circa* 850, treats it as a familiar extempore practice, one known under two names: diaphony and organum. These alternative terms (the latter characterized as 'customary'), refer to different core facets of polyphony: *diaphonia* to the dual sounds produced between two voices, the sounding-apart of the pair; *organum* to the perfect consonances or *sympho- niae* (fourth, fifth, octave) that controlled the relationship between voices.[5] Guido of Arezzo's formulation in Chapter 18 of *Micrologus* (ca1030) was widely read and often quoted or paraphrased by later theorists: 'Diaphony sounds as a disjunction of pitches [or lines] which we call organum since these differentiated pitches/lines both sound separately in concord and concord in their separate sounding.'[6] Diaphony remained a two-part phe- nomenon through the mid twelfth century, although in the most basic types attested in the earliest treatises (and still practised into the fourteenth century) either voice or both might be doubled at the octave.

From a present-day historical perspective, 'early' medieval polyphony is generally understood to span a time period of roughly three centuries, from the mid ninth century, when the first written descriptions of the phenomenon appear, to around the mid twelfth century, when polyphonic repertories preceding the advent of Parisian polyphony were notated. Parisian polyphony (sometimes designated 'Notre Dame' polyphony, after the famous cathedral) is considered a prominent articulation point in the history of polyphony because of many factors: the magnitude of its notated repertory, transmission of that music in multiple sources, an innovative technology of rhythmic notation, its status as a foundation for later developments in polyphony (pieces for 3–4 voices, the thirteenth-century motet), the extensive theoretical literature that accrued around it. This chapter deals principally with what can be discerned about diaphony or organum up to the advent of the Parisian repertory. Although ca1160 is a rough cut-off point for this survey, basic techniques for generating polyphony engendered in this 'early' period persisted for decades beyond the 1100s.

Broadly speaking, our knowledge of early polyphony stems from two sorts of material traces: instructions in theoretical treatises and notations of organum in musical neumes. The two are decidedly different in nature: the former essentially didactic and verbal in expression, the latter 'practical' representations of pieces in musical notation that directly evoke sound. Because they are generally cast as basic training for novices or summary digests of simple principles, the theoretical dicta must not be taken as assured guides to the actual practices of skilled organum singers. Indeed comparison between theorists' precepts and collateral notated repertory invariably shows discrepancies (a situation hardly unique to this material and time period).[7] But because the notations transmitting the repertory are all indeterminate to varying degrees, and because the active interpretative traditions that informed those notations evaporated centuries ago, any modern reconstructions of the music (in editions or in performances) require historical grounding in theoretical precepts contemporary with the notations.[8]

Music historians generally parse pre-Parisian polyphony in three phases (see Figure 3.1). The earliest is organum based on the concept of parallelism with a pre-existent chant. This is attested by the oldest treatises of the ninth into the eleventh century and is manifested in the Winchester organa of ca1000. The middle phase, described by theorists towards the end of the eleventh century, is a more freely associative organum in which the added line is melodically independent from the principal melody. The final phase is a florid organum characterized by decorative figures in the organal voice and frequent contrary motion between the lines. The twelfth-century repertories of Aquitanian and Compostelan polyphony exemplify this individual and elaborate organum. But such 'phases' are not to be viewed as stages in

	Position of voices	Primary Intervals	Rhythm	Representative Sources
1	ov below pv	Focus on 4th or 5th; octave doublings of ov or pv or both; 2 types: 1) strictly parallel, 2) freely parallel with boundary tones and unison convergences (occursus).	ov observes rhythm of pv	*Musica Enchiriadis* and related treatises, Guido's *Micrologus*, Winchester organum repertory
2	ov above pv	Mix of 4th, 5th, 8ve, u.	ov observes rhythm of pv	*Ad organum faciendum* and related treatises, John's *Musica*
3	ov above pv, voice-crossings	Mix of 4th, 5th, 8ve, u; ov figural elaborations with diverse intervals	ov independent rhythmically from pv	Aquitanian polyphony, Compostelan polyphony; late phase 2 treatises and interval-progression treatises

Figure 3.1 Cumulative phases of early organum production
(ov = organal voice; pv = principal voice; u = unison)

which one practice supplants the previous one; rather, each practice simply adds another strand to accrued possibilities. Earlier practices continue actively alongside later ones, as we know from fourteenth-century theorists who describe how to produce 'simple' parallel polyphony, and from late medieval notations of polyphony in retrospective styles.[9] This continued vitality of early traditions for producing diaphony may be traced both to regional habits and to the level of musical competency available in local situations.[10]

The changing course of new protocols for realizing polyphony is more apparent in the pedagogical treatises – of which there is a fairly steady (if chronologically blurred) record – than in the substantial notated repertories where there is a considerable gap between the Winchester organa of ca1000 and the emergence of Aquitanian polyphony around 1100. But the treatises, limited as they are to giving compact directions for improvising music in two parts, offer only partial guidance to actual practices and would all have required considerable amplification by a seasoned singing master. The *Musica Enchiriadis* author admits to providing only a surface view of polyphonic adornment, while a later author, coping with a situation in which the organal voice exercises considerable choice relative to the cantus, simply acknowledges the inadequacy of written precepts: 'All this is better revealed through the practice of organum singers than through rules.'[11] The repertories, along with sporadic notations of individual polyphonic pieces, not only manifest creative musical facets that extend well beyond didactic formulations, but also provide essential (if partial) insight into ritual contexts for polyphony. Polyphonic examples in the earliest treatises, such as the *Musica Enchiriadis* and Guido's *Micrologus*, are largely isolated phrases drawn from recitation tones and office antiphons – brief, elementary illustrations accessible to novice singers. In contrast, the Winchester repertory presents a strikingly rich image of liturgical contexts for early polyphony, including as it does organum for core chants of the mass and offices (alleluias, proses, Kyries, responsories, etc.) collected in liturgically ordered groups and preserved as complete pieces. This record of intense polyphonic activity around 1000 at Winchester Cathedral constitutes our best glimpse of the possible scope of organum singing in major European churches and monasteries as the first millennium drew to a close.[12] Treatises within the second phase characteristically offer only capsule illustrations, some on an alleluia incipit, but some abstract exempla with no liturgical association. The twelfth-century Aquitanian polyphonic repertory, however, manifests a new forum for polyphonic production, one removed from the formal liturgy, centred instead on rhymed, often strophic religious poetry or versus.[13] The mixture of two-voice liturgical settings and devotional versus in the coeval Compostelan repertory indicates that polyphonic adornment spanned a broad spectrum of worship and celebration (formal and informal) at the Compostela shrine. Although limited in its focus on veneration of a single saint, the Compostelan repertory evidences a breadth of polyphonic activity congruent with that registered in the far more extensive collections of Parisian organa and conductus.

Partial and incomplete though they are, the written traces of early polyphonic practice constitute the foundation for any account of Western polyphonic production from the ninth into the mid twelfth century that tracks the striking changes in idiom that transpired over that time period. The following account of key way stations, which follows a loosely chronological path, should be read with due awareness of the condition of polyphony as an extempore (and characteristically ephemeral) means of sonic elaboration practised in ecclesiastical spheres and of the persistence of the earliest protocols for generating organum alongside more complex procedures.

The earliest layer of organum teaching extends from the *Musica Enchiriadis* (ca850) to Guido's *Micrologus* (ca1030), and includes various affiliates and adaptations (of indeterminate date) of these core texts. Although differing in specific formulations and explanations, the treatises largely concur on general procedures.[14] The singers start with a pre-existent chant (designated the principal voice) and supply to it a complementary organal voice. This voice lies below the principal chant, relates to it through the perfect consonances or *symphoniae* of fifth and fourth, and mainly matches it note for note in rhythmic synchronization (see Examples 3.1a and 3.1b). Two procedures are taught. In one, a strict organum, the second singer parallels the principal voice consistently at the fifth below. In the other, a flexible organum, he follows it loosely at the fourth below. The *Musica Enchiriadis* theorist differentiates these two types of organum according to the primary

Example 3.1a *Musica Enchiriadis*, Chapter 15, *Sit gloria Domini*, diaphony at the fifth with octave doublings

Example 3.1b Guido of Arezzo, *Micrologus*, Chapter 19, *Ipsi soli*, flexible diaphony at the fourth

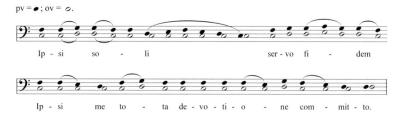

interval of coupling, fifth or fourth respectively, while Guido, in *Micrologus*, distinguishes them as *durus*, or strict, and *mollis*, or flexible.[15]

Diaphony at the fifth is strictly parallel, as is evident in Example 3.1a where the organal voice persistently shadows the principal chant at the fifth below.[16] Either voice (or both) may be doubled at the octave (above or below) to amplify the aural effect.

Flexible organum at the fourth is more complex and entails more decisions by the organum singer (Example 3.1b). Depending on factors of mode, linear path, and register of the parent chant, the organal voice may parallel the chant at the fourth, remain stationary on a lower boundary tone, or join it in unison at a phrase ending, an action Guido calls *occursus*. Articulating moments of occursus are determined by textual units in conjunction with the chant's phrasing. Guido's presentation of the D-mode antiphon *Ipsi soli* shows the organal voice observing a mandatory *tritus* boundary within each phrase and varying its phrase endings according to context.[17] For this melody, unison occursus is strategically located only at the ends of the first and final phrases, with the last the sole close on the modal final. The non-consonant seconds and thirds introduced by the boundary tone convention, along with unison occursus, impart to flexible organum a sound palette considerably more varied than that of the consistently parallel strict organum.

Beyond technical aspects of how to produce appropriately consonant organum, the early treatises provide some informative comments on general performance aspects of early diaphony. Several mention doubling either voice or both at the octave or double octave, and associate this with boys and men singing together. That organum should be sung at a moderate tempo and with due attentiveness is another recurring theme. One teacher specifically remarks that this kind of music is so weighty and deliberate that the usual rhythmic ratios of chant cannot be observed.[18] The importance of textual articulations, of musically observing units of text syntax (phrase, clause, sentence), is often mentioned, especially in conjunction with flexible organum and decisions about occursus. In addition to extolling diaphony as an appropriate means of praising God, the theorists call attention to its beauty of sound: 'Truly, delivered with restrained care, which is most proper to it, and attentive management of concords, the sweetness of the song will be most beautiful.'[19] This appreciation of beautiful sound is also manifested by the scribe of the Winchester organa, who variously characterizes the organa he copies as 'melliflua', 'pulcherrima', 'iocunda'.[20]

The remarkable collection of Winchester organa, preserved uniquely in the manuscript Cambridge, Corpus Christi College 473, manifests practices much richer and more diverse than those promulgated in the elementary teaching manuals. Although the organal voices are notated separately from their companion chants, and in non-diastematic neumes, the nature of this polyphony has been well established.[21] In general, the organa manifest traits characteristic of flexible diaphony at the fourth. The organal voice mainly operates below the principal one, matches it rhythmically note for note, and responds to it with a mix of parallel motion, sustained boundary pitches, and unison convergence. But compared with the theoretical expositions, the Winchester pieces show more open choice of reiterated boundary tones, more frequent occursus and provision of an extra tone or two in the organal voice, freedom occasionally for the added line to rise above the principal voice, and overall sensitivity to the text syntax and structure of a complete chant.[22] Marginal annotations in the manuscript not only point toward actual performance of the repertory, but also indicate a willingness to alter or vary passages in the organal voices originally notated. The *Alleluia. Ascendens Christus*, one in a major cycle of 53 polyphonic alleluias, clearly ranges beyond the usual short theoretical examples in complexity and variety of organal voice movement (Example 3.2).[23] The principal voice, a second-mode melody, is narrow in range, circling within the fourth d–g, with c as a frequent lower neighbour to the final, d. Only twice in this excerpt does it rise to the fifth above the final, once at the beginning

Example 3.2 Winchester organum, *Alleluia. Ascendens Christus* through first phrase of verse (Principal voice, *GB-Ob* Bodley 775, fol. 79v; organal voice, *GB-Ccc* 473, fol. 167r)

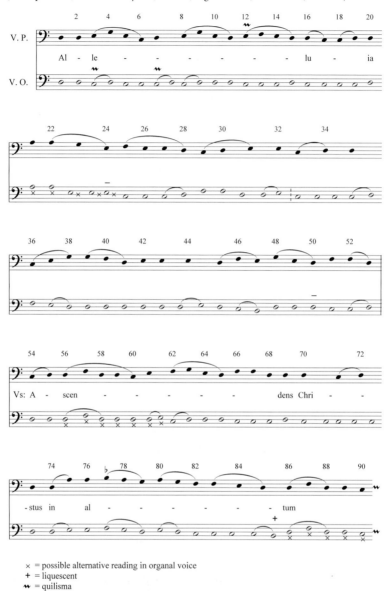

× = possible alternative reading in organal voice
+ = liquescent
♩ = quilisma
‒ = extended duration

of the jubilus and once at the suggestive words 'in altum' (on high). The organal voice accordingly remains in a low register, often reciting on the sub-final, c, or the final, d (notes 12–19, 38–44, 66–73). It joins the principal voice in unison at the end of basic text units and of the jubilus (notes 20, 52, 69, 73, 90) and also converges at numerous points within melismas (e.g. notes 11, 28). Although the organum sometimes sounds at the fourth (notably when the chant rises, notes 75–82), it liberally intermixes seconds, thirds and unisons. Seconds are quite frequent, not only at occursus (notes 10–11, 31–35) but also elsewhere (notes 42–3, 54, 70). The overall sound quality is hardly that of theoretically mandated *symphonia* of the fourth, although more descents to the tetrachord zone below the final would have increased the consonant sound quality.[24] Sometimes the notation indicates a momentary position above the chant (notes 29–30, 36), sometimes the two voices sing in unison (notes 55–9, 86–90), and sometimes extra notes in the organum enhance the effect of a convergence (notes 32–5, 44, 70–3). In its liberal approach to flexible organum, this alleluia setting is representative of the Winchester repertory as a whole, and hints at abundant creativity in the actual practice of organum around 1000. The few extant notations of early Continental polyphony manifest a similarly inventive approach to producing flexible organum at the fourth.[25]

Guido's elementary teaching about strict and flexible organum in the *Micrologus* dates from around 1030. By the end of the eleventh century, theorists are describing a very different sort of organum practice, such that the *Ad organum faciendum* theorist prefaces his exposition of the new way of generating organum with the remark that Guido's teachings are 'worthless' and 'scarcely to be esteemed'.[26] The *symphoniae* remain central to the concept of organum, but now fourths and fifths may be intermingled and are joined by octaves and unisons not just as intervals of doubling and occursus respectively, but as fully participating vertical sonorities. The older notion of boundary tones has disappeared. Remarkably, the organal voice has shifted its standard position from below the principal chant to above it. In contrast to the first-phase teaching, which stipulates but one or two appropriate organal responses to a given cantus, this second-phase pedagogy provides for, even encourages, a multiplicity of possible organa against a cantus. *Ad organum faciendum* organizes its teaching neatly in terms of five modes or types of producing organum, and illustrates each with a uniform cantus, the opening twelve-note phrase of the *Alleluia. Justus ut palma* (Example 3.3a).[27] Each type entails a different disposition of perfect consonances and unisons within the phrase. For example, the first two types feature different opening gambits, the first beginning conjunctly with the first cantus note (here at the octave), the second beginning disjunctly (here at the fourth) (Example 3.3a, I, II). The third type intermingles disjunct intervals and unisons in its middle passages (Example 3.3a, III). In a fifth category – one that bears important implications for the emergence of florid organum – the organal voice sings multiple notes against a cantus tone, a tactic here strategically located at phrase end (Example 3.3a, V). A longer example, the beginning of this Alleluia's verse, shows how the procedures of the preceding exercises can be freely combined in a series of phrases

Example 3.3a *Ad organum faciendum*, modes of organum I, II, III and V on incipit of *Alleluia.*
Justus ut palma

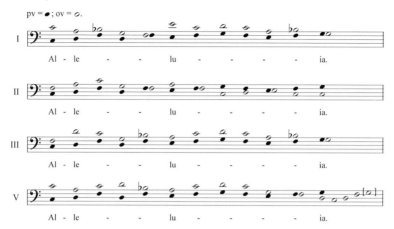

Example 3.3b *Ad organum faciendum*, beginning of verse, *Alleluia. Justus ut palma*

1) Low C-A in one source.

(Example 3.3b).[28] The absence of boundary tones coupled with acceptance of octave intervals above the cantus give this manner of producing organum a more consistently consonant quality than that of earlier flexible organum (compare Examples 3.3a, 3.3b with Example 3.2). In distinguishing among inceptions, medial passages, and terminations (arrivals on unison or octave termed *copula* by some teachers), the *Ad organum faciendum* pedagogue and his associates foster in the novice singer functional awareness of constituent phrase units within the music. The open choices for intervallic successions and for ranging either above or below the given line afford the late-eleventh-century organal singer considerable scope for individuality in responding to a cantus.

The verse treatise that follows *Ad organum faciendum* in its principal source advances similar teaching but is more colloquial in expression and more informative about cultural attitudes than its technically oriented companion. Its characterizations of the relationship between the two parts announce a new, dominant status for the organal voice. The opening introduces a metaphor of friendship between the voices, figurative language that may emanate from the notion of 'affinity' between the note pairings in organum.[29] But by the end of the treatise, the metaphor has shifted to serve a vigorous assertion of the superiority of the organal voice. It is described as running 'like a very strong soldier, most gratifyingly' and 'breaking up pitches like a prince', a likely reference to florid elaboration in the organal line, even though the proffered examples do not show this.[30] More than *Ad organum faciendum*, this verse treatise encourages and illustrates contrary motion between the parts. Comments on sweetness of sound (lines 66, 85–6, 138, 140) promote genuine aesthetic appreciation for organum and mesh with similar comments from the first stage of organum theory.[31] Other brief treatises conventionally grouped with *Ad organum faciendum* extend explicit recognition to thirds and even sixths as acceptable organal intervals, and increasingly draw attention to contrary motion between the voices. John's treatise on *Musica* from around 1100 even goes so far as to advocate contrary motion between cantus and organal voice as the 'simplest' procedure.[32] John also encourages multi-note elaboration in the organal part. Concerning a short example in which an organal part is paired strictly note to note with a syllabic cantus, he remarks that the organal singer could well 'double or triple' or otherwise competently accumulate notes in the sparse line provided.[33]

A subsequent state of organum pedagogy (perhaps emergent around the mid twelfth century) switches perspective radically to focus on standard binary interval progressions between organal voice and cantus.[34] The interval-progression treatises value octaves, fifths and unisons (fourths in some strata) and feature exercises of the type, 'If the organum is an octave above the cantus and the cantus ascends a whole-step, let the organum descend a third to be at the fifth.' Such teaching in terms of discrete two-note segments departs from the phrase-based approach of earlier organum pedagogy, but still fits with extempore production of polyphony through the act of singing. Under this training, singers practise and internalize in ear and memory standard voice-leading moves that they can then string together to produce appropriate organum rendered through approved perfect consonances above a cantus.[35] Although contrary motion is the rule in such treatises, some include formulas with similar or parallel motion, while a very few describe a mode of production based on parallel fifths.[36] But the theoretical discussions are brief and abstract in nature; for a sense of actual production and cutting-edge trends in polyphony during the twelfth century, one must turn to notated music.

The Aquitanian repertory of polyphony manifests a full spectrum of practices that are sporadically attested in the later 'second phase' theoretical documents and are generally compatible with early interval-progression

pedagogy. The designator 'Aquitanian' comes from the type of chant notation in which this repertory is preserved, a notation practised in the area
of southwestern France known as Aquitania in Carolingian times.[37] This
polyphony, which seems to have flourished from around the 1090s into
the second half of the 1100s, contrasts sharply with that of Winchester, not
just in musical idiom but with respect to texts, religious functions, and
manuscript transmission. Rather than adhering to the formal liturgy, Aquitanian polyphony comprises versus, some versus-like Benedicamus Domino
tropes, and a few liturgical proses – with versus the predominant genre.
Versus are settings of devotional poetry, poems that are newly created and
express contemporary religious sensibilities, particularly veneration of Jesus
and of Mary. Typical subjects celebrate the birth of Jesus, the motherhood
of Mary, the miracle of the Virgin Birth, the union of the divine and human
in the Incarnation. Such songs could be inserted into ceremonial offices, but
could also have been sung on more informal occasions.[38] This polyphony
is preserved in nine small to medium-sized pamphlets (libelli) that transmit both monophonic and polyphonic songs. Each source is an individual
collection with its own independent selection and ordering of pieces; from
among some seventy polyphonic settings, only four pieces appear in as many
as three sources, and only one appears in four sources.[39] It is likely that individual poet-singers, or their followers, copied these songs for personal use.
Important beyond the history of polyphony, the Aquitanian versus repertory manifests a remarkable creative outpouring of devotional Latin song
by twelfth-century poets and singers in southwestern Europe.

The turn to newly created poetic texts means that the polyphonic Aquitanian versus were not necessarily based on a pre-existent melody – indeed,
rarely is a monophonic ancestor documented for a polyphonic versus. Some
versus music may well have been conceived as polyphony from the start,
a conclusion fortified by extended melismas in which the two voices are
so intertwined as to be an inseparable pair. Such concurrent conception
would represent a facility of invention beyond that expressed in organum
pedagogy, which regularly postulates a given cantus, even if that is reduced
to a two-note element. The thirteen proses in the Aquitanian repertory are
based on pre-existent chants, as are a few combinations of a Benedicamus
versicle with a superimposed versus. To avoid the assumption of a given
cantus, I will here designate the voices as upper and lower, a reflection of
the manuscript notation and prevailing registral positions (although some
voice-crossing does occur).[40]

Like their monophonic siblings, polyphonic versus settings are shaped
on the one hand by poetic versification and syntax, on the other by melodic
norms, tonal centring, and matrices (horizontal and vertical) of perfect
consonances and unisons. Other musical resources coordinated with text

1a	Per partum virginis/ dei et hominis/ sunt juncta federa.
1b	Vita tribuitur/ culpa diluitur/ que clausit ethera.
2a	Verbum, lumen dei patris/ sumpta carne alvo matris/ in hac die claruit.
2b	Verus deus verus homo/ est de Jesse natus domo/ ut propheta docuit.
3a	Sub carnis tegmine/ homo pro homine/ sol verus latuit.
3b	Felix puerpera/ que nos et supera/ unire potuit.
4a	Quam miranda quam laudanda/ quam ditanda celebranda/ dei est clemencia.
4b	Qui pro nobis fit mortalis/ ante manens immortalis/ omni dignus gloria.
5	Immortalis/ fit mortalis/ sola tactus gratia.

1a Through a virgin's childbirth, God and man are joined in alliance.
1b Life is granted, sin is dissolved that made heaven inaccessible.
2a The Word, the light of God the father, having taken on flesh in the womb of the mother, shines forth in this day.
2b True God, true man is born of the house of Jesse, as the prophet declared.
3a Under a covering of flesh, a man for the sake of mankind, the true sun was hidden.
3b Happy the childbirth, that was able to unite us with the heavens.
4a How wonderful, how praiseworthy, how richly to be celebrated is God's mercy.
4b He who became mortal for us, remaining immortal from before, is worthy of all glory.
5 The immortal one became mortal solely through grace.

Figure 3.2a Text and translation of *Per partum virginis*

Music Phrases	Text Line	Syllables/rhyme	Accent
a	1a	6a 6a 6b	dactylic
b	1b	6c 6c 6b	
c	2a	8d 8d 7e	trochaic
d	2b	8f 8f 7e	
e	3a	6g 6g 6e	dactylic
f	3b	6h 6h 6e	
g	4a	8i 8i 7k	trochaic
g	4b	8m 8m 7k	
h	5	4m 4m 7k	trochaic

Figure 3.2b Text structure and musical phrases in *Per partum virginis*

structure include texture and manner of text declamation.[41] As can be seen in *Per partum virginis*, versus poetry exhibits periodic regularities of syllable count, rhyme and line groupings in either couplets or stanzas (see Figures 3.2a and 3.2b). The sequence or prose texts also observe regular, periodicity, the parallel couplets typical of the genre. The periodicities of poetic structure constitute a framework respected and delineated by the musicians, as can be seen in a representative polyphonic versus, *Per partum virginis*.[42] The poem celebrates the birth of Jesus, his mother Mary's virginal childbearing, and the positive consequences for humankind. It is cast in couplets whose clear boundaries (outlined in Figure 3.2b) are created through syllable count, rhyme, accent and syntax. Each line falls into three segments, the first two sharing a common rhyme, the last rhyming with its partner within the couplet. Odd- and even-numbered couplets are differentiated by syllable count within the lines and by verse accent, with couplets 1 and 3 dactylic, 2 and 4 and the single final line trochaic.

Example 3.4a Aquitanian versus *Per partum virginis,* first couplet (*GB-Lbl* add. 36881, fol. 4r)

+ = liquescent | = a syllable stroke in the upper voice   ¦ = a line break

1) MS: c-a. Reading from *F-Pn* fonds lat. 3719, fol. 65.

Example 3.4b Aquitanian versus *Per partum virginis*, last couplet and final verse (*F-Pn* fonds lat. 3549, fol. 151v)

UV

1 3 5 7 9 11 13 15

LV

4a] Quam mi - ran - da quam lau - dan - da quam di - tan - da ce - le - bran - da
4b] Qui pro no - bis fit mor - ta - lis an - te ma - nens im - mor - ta - lis

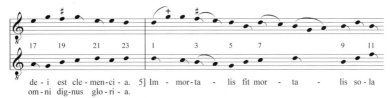

17 19 21 23 1 3 5 7 9 11

de - i est cle - men - ci - a. 5] Im - mor - ta - lis fit mor - ta - lis so - la
om - ni dig - nus glo - ri - a.

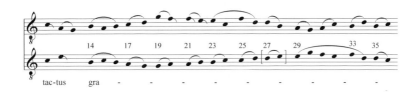

14 17 19 21 23 25 27 29 33 35

tac - tus gra -

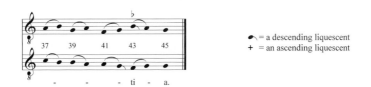

37 39 41 43 45

- - - ti - a.

↘ = a descending liquescent
+ = an ascending liquescent

The musical structure aligns with that of the poetry on many levels from the principal sectional units to phrase and motivic elements (see Examples 3.4a and 3.4b and the left-hand column of Figure 3.2b).[43] In this musical setting, the couplets are through-composed except for the fourth (4ab) where repeated music audibly underscores the verse pairing.[44] Extended terminal melismas with the voices yoked together articulate the ends of the first two lines and the final line.[45] Changes in texture demarcate sectional units. Line 1a maintains a florid upper voice up to the terminal melisma, while line 1b begins with the voices note against note, then intermixes such synchrony with florid figures in the top part. The final couplet and final line offer a sharp contrast to the opening in their very plain note-for-note texture. The rhyme words internal to poetic lines also receive their due. This is particularly clear in line 1a where a sweeping downward scale figure (distinguished in scope from the other ornamental figures) associates *virginis* with *hominis*. Such explicit association of internal rhymes does not continue in the rest of the setting, but the main rhymes are punctuated with stable arrivals on perfect consonances and on the modal final or its close associate.

Per partum virginis is tonally focused on g with the lower voice beginning and ending on that pitch, and returning often to it at the end of text segments. The first two lines are anchored on a g final that is supported in the upper voice with the upper fifth and octave, and often reinforced by an upper-voice descent to g when the lower one rises to the fifth or octave above. At the most stable phrase endings – the end of the first couplet (*ethera*) and the conclusion of the piece (*gratia*) – the voices unite on a unison g final. Together the two voices present a unified tonal profile that mainly projects a g–d^1–g^1 matrix in coordination with the primary text units. The fourth couplet (Example 3.4b) offers tonal contrast in its orientation towards the fourth and fifth above the final, a shift that gives special impact to the restoration of g centring in the final line.

In keeping with their tonal compatibility, the two lines are anchored, both horizontally and vertically, on perfect consonances and unisons. A background of fifths, octaves and unisons can easily be discerned behind the elaborative figures in the upper voice, as, for instance, in the very first text line, shown in a voice-leading reduction in Example 3.5a. Such a spare background calls to mind John's invitation to the organum singer (quoted above) to proliferate notes within a foundational note-against-note context. Less consonant, or even quite dissonant, intervals sometimes enhance the motion towards a stable interval, as on the very first syllable (*Per*, from fourth to fifth) or in line 1b with seconds on *diluitur* and *que*.

Starting with the earliest organum treatises and continuing through John's *Musica* and the interval-progression treatises, voice-leading stands alongside intervallic proprieties as a primary pedagogic concern. Reflecting an accumulation of possibilities, voice-leading in polyphonic Aquitanian versus intermixes contrary, oblique and parallel motion, the latter commonly involving parallel fifths that are sometimes overt, sometimes covered by upper-voice figures.[46] The voice notated in the upper position generally sounds above the notated lower voice, but sometimes crosses below, particularly when the lower voice rises in register.[47] The most striking and characteristic voice-leading routines appear in the long terminal melismas constructed in a mosaic fashion from figures that converge and diverge in contrary motion. Verses 1a and 1b both end with melismas built from two-voice figures that characteristically pivot on a unison b and diverge out to the g–d^1 fifth (see Example 3.4a). The very last melisma of the versus has a more complex, tonally diverse structure that can be parsed in a series of contrary motion elements: octave, fifth, fourth and third converging into unisons, unisons expanding out to a fifth or fourth

Example 3.5a Consonance reduction, first phrase, *Per partum virginis* (see Example 3.4a)

la] Per par - tum vir - gi - nis de - i et ho - mi - nis
Intervals: 5   5   5   4 - 1   5   8 - 5   1   1 - 5   1   8 - 5 8 - 5 3 - 3   5

sunt vic - ta fe - - - - - - - de ra
5 - 1 5   5   5* - 1   5 - 1   4 - 1 - 5   5 - 1   5 - 1 - 4 - 1   1 - 5   5   5

Example 3.5b Consonance reduction, final melisma of *Per partum virginis* (see Example 3.4b)

gra - - - - - -
Intervals: 1   5   8   4   1   4   1   1   4   5   8   3   5*   1   3 - 1

- - - - ti - a
3 - 1   3 - 1   3 - 1   4*   2   1

Basic intervals are indicated below the staff. An underscore (5) indicates that the upper voice has crossed below the lower one. The symbol ∗ marks a diminished fifth or augmented fourth that might or might not have been adjusted. Lower-voice note count appears above the staff.

(see reduction, Example 3.5b).[48] These figures decorate a dramatic scalar arch in the lower voice that rises through the g octave and then descends directly to the final. Such intertwining convergent/divergent figures, common in melismas of the polyphonic Aquitanian versus, appear to have been standard routines, easily produced extempore, adaptable to texted phrases as well.

The three notated versions of *Per partum virginis* – like notations of other versus inscribed in more than one source – indicate some fluidity in how singers might realize a song. Typical differences, seen in the two versions of line 1a aligned in Example 3.6, are details of upper-voice figures and scribal indications of vocal timbre and alignment between the parts.[49] Variants in the upper-voice (the initial c^1–d^1 gesture, the first and last syllables of *virginis*) indicate flexibility in realizing elaborative figures. The 'B' scribe more often indicates special vocal production, such as liquescence or extension of a pitch. Alignment between the parts is variable (and a problematic issue). Whereas the 'D' scribe supplies many vertical strokes to specify syllable coordination, the 'B' scribe scarcely indicates syllable boundaries and is fairly cavalier about depicting vertical alignment through

Example 3.6 First line, *Per partum virginis*, two versions (B = *F-Pn* fonds lat. 3549, fol. 150v; D = *GB-Lbl* add. 36881, fol. 4r)

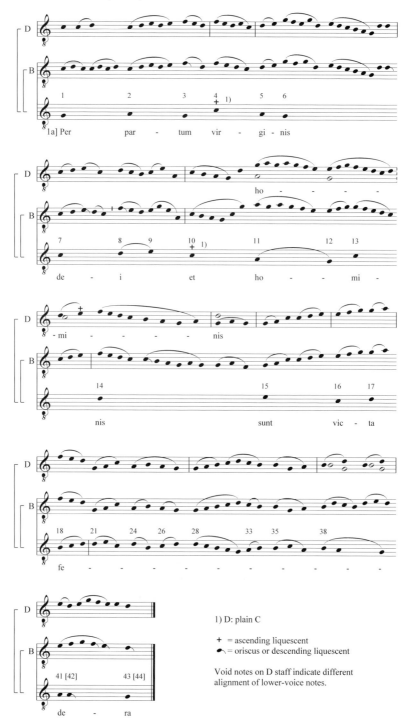

1) D: plain C

+ = ascending liquescent

= oriscus or descending liquescent

Void notes on D staff indicate different alignment of lower-voice notes.

physical spacing. Still, ligature groupings and a few syllable strokes in 'B' do point to some alignments divergent from 'D', as on *hominis*.[50] Each notated version, indeed, seems to represent a somewhat individual view of 'how the piece goes' in keeping with a fluid, improvisational approach to producing polyphony. Still there are passages involving uncharacteristic dissonances in which one source attests a scribal mistake in another, as on *et* (no. 10 in Example 3.6), where the 'D' scribe apparently wrote the last note in the upper-voice figure a step too high.

Another, less extensive, polyphonic repertory contemporary with the later Aquitanian sources is contained in the Codex Calixtinus, a substantial book dedicated to promulgation and celebration of the cult of Saint James at the pilgrimage shrine in Santiago de Compostela.[51] The collection of polyphony appears in a supplement positioned after the formal five books of the Codex Calixtinus.[52] Of the 20 pieces copied there, half occur monophonically in Book I, which transmits special divine offices for the saint's feast. As already noted, Compostelan polyphony comprises both settings of devotional poems, rubricated as 'conductus' or (as appropriate) 'Benedicamus' in Book I, and liturgical chants: matins responsories, a responsory prosa, mass gradual and alleluia, two troped Kyries and three Benedicamus Domino versicles. A cultural context distinct from that of the Aquitanian sources is manifested both in the formal presentation of the polyphony within a carefully designed codex and in the combination of fixed liturgical items and *ad hoc* devotional poems. Insofar as the Codex Calixtinus has been associated with compilers in the region of Burgundy and with Cluniac interests, its polyphonic component would seem to reflect northern traditions.[53]

Like their Aquitanian counterparts, conductus/versus in the Compostela repertory are songs on devotional poetic texts, but their consistent theme is veneration of Saint James. Musically, they resemble their Aquitanian cousins; indeed two of the polyphonic conductus are contrafacta of Aquitanian versus.[54] In both repertories, musical phrases and formal design conform to poetic versification, the voices are tonally coordinated and linked through perfect consonances and unisons, and texture varies from single-note coupling of the voices to florid decoration in the upper voice. One difference is a lack of extended note-against-note melismas except in the two imports from Aquitania.

The liturgical polyphonic settings, all based on a pre-existent chant, adopt florid textures with figures of three to nine notes in the upper voice decorating perfect consonances above individual cantus tones. In contrast with the conductus, there is little voice-crossing in these settings. The upper voice tends to stay above the cantus, or to join it in unison when the cantus rises or settles on the modal final.[55] Although the able scribe provides division strokes to indicate segmental coincidence between the voices, the chant neumes do not permit specification of pitch alignment within those segments. The first segment of the responsory *O adjutor*, for example, combines two two-note neumes in the cantus with six neumes in the upper voice (see Example 3.7a). We do not know how much leeway twelfth-century Compostelan singers would have had to combine the voices rhythmically within a segment, but in any event the alignment (along with relative temporal delivery) is now a matter of informed conjecture.[56]

The polyphonic settings of the responsories and the mass gradual and alleluia involve only the soloist's portions of the chant: the opening phrase of the initial section and the major part of the verse. The remainder of the chant is sung monophonically, as occurs in Parisian settings of responsorial chants. A glance at two passages from a typical responsory, *O adjutor* (Examples 3.7a, 3.7b), shows the upper voice coupled with the D-mode chant through transparent consonances of octave, fifth and unison. Some of these intervals seem locked in place relative to pivotal cantus pitches: a primary octave always surmounts the fourth and the step below the final (A and c), a unison or (occasionally) upper fifth sounds with the fifth above the final (a). In contrast, the d final offers more intervallic choices and is variously paired with its octave, upper fifth, or unison.

The upper-voice melody proceeds conjunctly by step or third, with larger intervals of fourth or fifth generally limited to occasions when the cantus repeats a pitch. Its elaborative figures, varied in length and lineaments, display inventive ways of elaborating a vertical interval or moving through a linear space. Immediate repetition of figures is rare (one occurs in the verse on *mari*), and even separated recurrences are not conspicuous. A seven-note figure in the third segment of the respond recurs a fifth higher at the beginning of the verse (see brackets, Examples 3.7a, 3.7b). The elaborating voice moves through scalar space in varied ways. The motion from c^1 down to d in the first segment is gapped. That in the third segment (on *adjutor*) turns gracefully in its path, while the stepwise descent on *subvenis* in the third segment of the verse is elegantly protracted through reiteration of successive notes in a series of two-note neumes (clivis). This last figure notationally and aurally resembles some figures in the Vatican Organum Treatise, one of the few interval-progression manuals to transmit decorated upper voices.[57] Background voice-leading relative to the cantus is a mixture of contrary and parallel motion, with the former predominating. The second segment in the verse is essentially a series of parallel octaves (g–f–e–d), but that parallelism is masked by ornamental figures in which the upper voice approaches the octave from below as the cantus descends by step. The voices typically reach unison convergences from different directions.

Example 3.7a Codex Calixtinus, opening of matins responsory *O adjutor* (*E-SC*, fol. 217r/188r). Plainchant continuation, fol. 110v.

Lines through the upper voice only indicate syllable strokes in that part.
Lines through both staves correspond with grouping strokes in the manuscript.

Example 3.7b Codex Calixtinus, first part of verse, responsory *O adjutor* (*E-SC*, fols. 217v/188v)

Thus, although from a condensed and selective historical perspective the significance of Aquitanian and Compostelan polyphony may seem to reside in setting the stage for Parisian polyphony, the level of complexity and musical invention manifested in these repertories, as in earlier ones, represents a considerable artistic accomplishment in its own terms and within indigenous local contexts.

That the above survey has concentrated on changes over approximately three hundred years should not obscure the considerable consistencies that existed within this span of Western polyphonic practice. By way of conclusion, these basic consistencies are summarized below.

- Beginning around the mid ninth century, church musicians cultivated standard procedures for generating polyphony extemporaneously; the practice of extemporization persisted even after notation of polyphony became more usual.
- The scope and diversity of these generative procedures increased over the course of the ninth to the twelfth century, although relatively simple procedures, such as singing in parallel fifths, continued in currency into the fourteenth century.
- The perfect consonances (fourth, fifth and octave) along with the unison are fundamental to all early polyphonic practices, oral and written. They anchor the conceptual relationship between the voices and ensure a sound quality perceived as harmonious and beautiful.
- A combination of textual factors (syntactic units, versification in the case of poetic texts) and musical units of the primary melody (whether pre-existent or newly composed) guided organum production from its earliest cultivation.
- Whereas at first the organal voice was regarded as subordinate 'follower' of the principal voice, in the more complex procedures emergent in the late eleventh century the organal voice becomes the prominent line, the focus of aural attention.
- As possibilities for the organal voice became more diverse, the teaching became more generalized and abstract, and notated repertories (which increased in number) became even more central as indicators of concrete practices and applications in song and liturgy.
- In all practices (save for strictly parallel organum) occursus or copula – the joining of the two voices on unison or octave – is a key means of musical articulation and of securing closure.

4 The thirteenth century

MARK EVERIST

Scope and context

Garry Trudeau begins my favourite Doonesbury cartoon with three frames each bearing a date: (1) a hooded figure tries to escape a stoning: '1205 – A plague-stricken calligrapher is driven from Gunbad-I-Qabus'; (2) a mendicant fanatic prepares a burning at the stake: '1233 – A heretic perishes in Castile'; (3) a severed head hangs by its hair from the branch of a tree: '1276 – On the Malaysian archipelago, a gruesome trophy swings in a lagoon.' The fourth frame cuts to Trudeau's ex-Hollywood starlet, Barbara Ann Boopstein, on a beach with a soda in her hand as she muses 'Sometimes it seemed the 13th century would never end!'[1] To turn abruptly to the music of the thirteenth century – although calligraphers and mendicant fanatics have their place there – is to feel some sympathy with Boopsie's ruminations. Not only did the 'long' thirteenth century never quite seem to end, but its beginnings were not quite obvious either. And although no one ever seems to argue for a 'short' century, the claims for thinking about the music of the thirteenth century from around 1170 up to ca1320 are strong. The blurred distinction between versus and conductus is as much geographical as chronological (between north and south as much as early and late twelfth century), and the emergence of a consistent style of Parisian organa is usually assumed to fall somewhere in the last quarter of the twelfth century. Yet these are the staple genres of the thirteenth century, with works copied and recopied at least as late as 1300, and the motet – although probably not surfacing before 1200 – retains its links with the thirteenth century well into the fourteenth alongside works of what might be thought to represent the avant-garde.

The scope of this chapter is largely limited to the genres of conductus, organum and motet. The chapter touches on vernacular monophony (treated in Chapter 12) only tangentially, and it centres on the northern French experience (those of other centres are discussed in chapters 6–10). Although much of the context for organum, and a significant part of the background of the motet, is liturgical, and much important liturgical development took place in the thirteenth century, plainsong and liturgy are explained elsewhere in this volume (chapters 1 and 11). And in its focus on conductus, organum and motet, this chapter challenges one of the fundamental questions of medieval music: the problem of its context and function. Up to around 1300, we have a fairly clear idea of the contexts for the composition, cultivation and consumption of music that was written down: plainsong and its offshoots can be locked into a broadly liturgical environment, and vernacular monophony into those of the aristocratic courts. Even Aquitanian versus, although occasionally suggesting less formal contexts, had a significant liturgical dimension. The massive growth of the northern counterpart of versus – the conductus – exacerbated the range of possible contexts for the genre. And although organum, as a result of its origins and compositional dynamic, could never be shaken from its liturgical context, the emergence of the motet poses problems of function – who composed? who listened? and who appreciated? – at almost every stage of the century.

Conductus

The most striking continuity between the Aquitanian and related repertories and the Parisian music of the later twelfth and thirteenth centuries lies in the versus and conductus.[2] At some points, the two terms almost coexist, and if they are thought to refer to monophonic or polyphonic settings of rhythmic texts in musical styles that do not depend on the use of borrowed material, this brings both categories into a very close alignment. Indeed, monophonic conductus copied well into the thirteenth century could resemble versus of a hundred years earlier.

The conductus is the only genre found consistently in all the major manuscript sources of the thirteenth century, and it exists in great numbers.[3] The largest collections are found in *I-Fl* Plut. 29.1 where 83 monophonic conductus, 130 two-part, 59 three-part and 3 four-part conductus are preserved.[4] They constitute key parts of the organization of the volume, with separate fascicles dedicated to each type and a separate fascicle given over to 60 monophonic conductus in rondellus form.[5] Parisian conductus appear to have been composed as early as 1160 and continued to be copied throughout the thirteenth century. The latest datable event in the text of a conductus is from the 1230s which might suggest a tailing-off in composition towards the mid century;[6] although conductus continued to be copied in the second half of the century, however, sources from around 1300 subject the music to significant editorial change.

Conductus, like versus, are settings of Latin texts with an immense range of subject matter: poems alluding to political events rub shoulders with homiletic verse, and references to classical antiquity sit alongside settings of liturgical texts.[7] This wide range, while testifying to the far-reaching

Example 4.1 Two-part conductus *sine caudis*, *Virtus moritur*, 1–20. (*I-Fl* Plut. 29.1, fols. 322r–322v)

Vir - tus   mo - ri - tur   Vi - vit   vi - ti - um   Fi - des   tru - di - tur   In   ex - il - i - um.

intellectual ambitions of their authors, creates significant difficulties in assigning any function to the genre of the conductus. It seems reasonable to assume that the range of textual reference implies a similar range of function, from a substitute for the Benedicamus Domino or *Sursum corda* to largely recreational contexts that would admit the satirical and the hortatory. There is, furthermore, no apparent mapping of number of voices onto particular types of text.[8]

Polyphonic conductus exist in one of two forms described by contemporary theory: *cum* and *sine caudis*.[9] The presence or absence of such 'tails' (caudae) provides one of the clearest generic markers in the repertory. The conductus *sine caudis* is the simpler of the two types, and consists of a neumatic (note against note or neume against neume) setting of the poetic text. The notation of this music *cum littera* (texted) is invariably unmeasured in the earliest sources, and its rhythm is the subject of debate, with some advocating a metrical approach based on the framework of the rhythmic modes, and others proffering non-metrical rhythms, as here. *Virtus moritur* is a good example of a two-part conductus *sine caudis* (Example 4.1).[10] Much of the piece is purely syllabic, with occasional moments where a ligature of two notes sets the syllable (*moritur* and *vitium*), and there are occasional instances where three notes (but always in ligature) set a single syllable.[11]

Virtus moritur is a simple work, and rather rare in *I-Fl* Plut. 29.1. The conductus *cum caudis* is a more common but more complex proposition. Much of the setting of the poem is in the same *cum littera* style as the conductus *sine caudis* just described, but the composition is embellished by caudae; these are untexted (*sine littera*) melismas that take the note-against-note melismas of Aquitanian versus and subject them to the discipline of the rhythmic modes. Conductus *cum caudis* therefore play *musica cum littera* and *musica sine littera* off against each other in the same composition. The beginning of *Luget Rachel iterum*, in two parts (duplum and tenor), demonstrates how the two discursive modes (*musica cum* and *sine littera*) interact (Example 4.2).[12]

The work opens with a cauda in the first rhythmic mode that uses both *fractio* (duplum 3 and 7; tenor 3) and *reductio modi* (tenor 1, 2, and 5–8).

Example 4.2 Two-part conductus *cum caudis*, *Luget Rachel iterum*, 1–68 (*I-Fl* Plut. 29.1, fols. 359v–360)

Example 4.3 *Luget Rachel iterum*. Text, translation and analysis

1.	*Lu*get Rachel iterum	7pp(a)	Rachel weeps again
2.	Cuius dampnat uterum	7pp(a)	Whose womb is condemned
3.	Filiorum orbitas	7pp(b)	By the loss of her sons.
4.	*Lap*so tabernaculo	7pp(c)	The temple having fallen;
5.	Quondam plena populo	7pp(c)	Once full of people,
6.	Sola sedet civi*tas*	7pp(b)	The city sits solitary.
7.	*Lan*guent Syon filie	7pp(d)	The daughters of Syon mourn
8.	Cotidie	4pp(d)	Daily,
9.	Affligentes animam	7pp(e)	Afflicting their spirits,
10.	Cum non sit qui faciat	7pp(f)	Because none will act
11.	Nec veniat	4pp(f)	Or come
12.	Ad paschalem *vic*timam	7pp(e)	To the paschal victim.

The first three lines of the poem are then declaimed in a simple neumatic style (although note the rhythmic complications in 28–31 that betray the genre's origins in Aquitanian versus), and are followed by another cauda (32–9) that introduces the *cum littera* setting of lines 4–6 of the poem; this closes with a third cauda (61–8). Example 4.2 gives slightly less than half the work, but the structure of the entire composition can be seen in an annotated edition and translation of the poetry (Example 4.3). The three caudae begin the first and fourth lines with similar morphemes, *lu*get and *lap*so, and close the sixth (civi*tas*) (the caudae are shown in italics in the example); the example also shows how the seventh line begins with a cauda and how the entire composition ends similarly.

Whatever disagreement there might be concerning the rhythm of the *cum littera* sections of the conductus, there is no doubt that the caudae (*sine littera*) are notated using the ligature patterns of the rhythmic modes and are therefore measurable. With this in mind, it is striking that the first three caudae of *Luget Rachel iterum* are all of exactly the same length (eight perfections), and this is the case no matter how the notation is transcribed, and no matter where one sets the boundaries of music *cum* and *sine littera*. These three caudae of identical length stand in contrast to the two others, one of six perfections (on *Lan*guent) and the other of no less than 26 perfections (on *vic*timam). At one level, the emphasis given these particular words – 'weep', 'fall', 'city', 'mourn' and 'victim' – picks out the key elements in a text that exploits a wide range of biblical and patristic imagery and that may relate to the fall of Jerusalem in 1187 (although the text is unlikely to predate that event, both the poetry and the music could have been composed later). But at another, more purely musical, level, the particular compositional organization of the caudae generates a set of symmetries in the first half of the piece that are deliberately denied in the second.

Organum

Continuities in liturgical music with the previous generations are less easy to identify. Parisian organum embodies the types of embellishment of plainchant that are strikingly absent from the Aquitanian repertory. However, to glance at the Compostelan chant settings is to witness some strong continuities with the Parisian repertory in terms of liturgical type selected for polyphonic treatment. Both concentrate on responsorial chants: responsories, graduals, alleluias and Benedicamus Domino. The only type found in Compostela and not in the Parisian repertory is the troped Kyrie. This preference explodes into a two-part repertory (as preserved in its most extensive source, *I-Fl* Plut. 29.1) of 34 items for the office (almost all responsories), 10 Benedicamus Domino settings, and 59 mass items (18 graduals; 41 alleluias).[13] The repertory stands in a tradition of composition for the liturgical year that encompasses the *Choralis Constantinus* and Bach's Church Cantatas. In addition to this two-part music is a smaller repertory of three- and four-part compositions (organa *tripla* and organa *quadrupla*); of the latter, the graduals for Christmas and St Stephen, *Viderunt omnes* and *Sederunt principes*, have achieved celebrity through modern recording.[14]

The chronology of Parisian organum is problematic. If we can be reasonably certain that the Compostelan repertory was complete by 1173, the beginnings of the Parisian repertory are shrouded in mystery. The theorist known as Anonymous IV, writing around a century after the event, identified the four-part *Viderunt omnes* and *Sederunt principes* as works by Perotinus Magnus, and pointed to a predecessor of Perotinus, Leoninus, whom Anonymous IV credited with the creation of the 'magnu[s] lib[er] organi de gradali et antifonario pro servitio divino multiplicando' ('the great book of organum from the gradual and antiphonary to elaborate the divine service'). Perotinus was also credited with having '*abbreviavit*' the *Magnus liber organi* ('abbreviavit' could have meant anything from 'shortened', to 'edited', or even just 'written down').[15] Perotinus's two four-part organa were cited in Parisian episcopal edicts in 1198 and 1199 in a context that meant that the works were known in the city at those dates. While the documents provide a fixed chronological point, a blizzard of scholarly debate has interpreted and reinterpreted their implications: either the two organa *quadrupla* represented the final point of 'development' of the work of both Leoninus and Perotinus (in which case the entire project of Parisian organum was complete before the end of the twelfth century) or there are identifiable aspects of the 'Perotinian' repertory that could not have preceded the composition of the two datable works.[16] Arguments on both sides are fraught with teleological difficulties, and no clear answer can be given for the opening and closing dates for the composition of Parisian organum. The earliest manuscript of this repertory is *D-W* 628 which dates from no earlier than the 1230s, with other sources spanning the next half-century.[17] Attempts to delineate continuity and change in musical practice in this repertory, and to identify how long a period of time such a delineation covers, with the present state of knowledge, seem problematic. It almost goes without saying that the music preserved in the surviving sources, its notational style and what may be inferred from it may bear little relation to what had been composed perhaps sixty years previously.

In contrast to its chronology, the function of organa is clear: as partial settings of plainsongs, Parisian organa simply replace those sections of plainsong that they set. Settings survive for most of the major feasts in the liturgical year. *Annuale* feasts were provided with organa for the gradual and alleluia for the day itself and for the days of the octave (Christmas, Easter, Pentecost and the Assumption of the Blessed Virgin Mary); lesser feasts, of *duplex* rank, were provided with organa for the gradual and alleluia of the feast day itself only (for example, St Stephen, St John the Baptist and the Ascension); and *semiduplex* feasts were provided with an alleluia only (Finding of the Holy Cross and St Michael, for example). In addition to music directed towards one specific occasion, and partly to provide compositions for some feasts of duplex and semiduplex rank, the *Magnus liber organi* contains a substantial number of compositions for the Common.[18]

Parisian organum is consistent in its selection of the solo sections of plainsong for treatment in polyphony. In terms of a work, then, a Parisian organum consists of sections newly composed by Leoninus, Perotinus or their contemporaries, and of sections in plainsong filtered through twelfth-century Parisian chant traditions. Example 4.4 gives the text of the entire gradual for the mass at the feast of Sts Peter and Paul (29 June), 'Constitues eos V. Pro patribus'.[19] This shows clearly how the division between the sections of the chant for soloists and the rest of the choir (*schola*) results in different structures for the respond (where only the first two words of the

Example 4.4 Text of gradual *Constitues eos. V. Pro patribus*

Constitues eos principes super omnem terram memores erunt nominis tui domine.

V. *Pro patribus tuis nati sunt tibi filii propterea populi* confitebuntur tibi.

Constitues eos etc.

plainsong are set) and the verse (where all but the last two words are set); plainsong is in roman type, polyphony in italics (Example 4.4).

Different balances between solo and choral portions of the chant result in different structures in alleluias, responsories and Benedicamus Domino settings.

Within the polyphonic sections of Parisian organum are two principal stylistic divisions with a third subsidiary one. Terminological issues are problematic here, but a distinction may be drawn between *organum per se* and discantus. Both are visible in the verse of *Constitues eos* (Example 4.5). *Organum per se* takes the notes of the chant and disposes them in long values in the tenor, above which is composed a voice part that creates largely perfect and imperfect consonances. The notation of both parts is unmeasured, and – as in the case of the *cum littera* sections of conductus – there is significant debate about the extent to which metre governs the rhythm of this music.[20] *Organum per se* occupies 1–12, 19–29 and 62–5 of Example 4.5. These sections, where musical imagination is given a rhythmically free rein, are contrasted with sections in discantus known as clausulae. Here (30–61), the notes of the tenor are organized rhythmically according to one of the rhythmic modes (here mode 1), and may be repeated (as they are here; 45–61). This gives a series of repeating patterns – *ordines* – for one or more cursus.[21] The final note of the last *ordo* of the first cursus (45) is the first note of the second cursus, so even though the *ordines* of the second cursus are the same as the first, the musical results are different, with pitch and rhythm being displaced so that what fell on a longa in the first cursus falls on a *brevis* in the second, and vice versa. Above this tenor is composed a duplum that in this case follows the same rhythmic mode. Phrases may overlap or may cadence simultaneously, as is the case here. As in the case of *organum per se*, cadences are planned around perfect and imperfect consonances. The verse of *Constitues eos* also includes an instance of copula. Alongside *organum per se* and discantus, copula is a third discursive mode in organum; it seeks to impart the metre of discantus to the duplum only, and it may be identified by the fact that the highly varied ligature patterns that characterize *organum per se* in general give way to the patterns (here 3+2+2; 3+2+2) of modal rhythm. Copulae will also exhibit periodic phraseology, usually antecedent–consequent patterns, and also melodic sequence, as the copula in Example 4.5 suggests (13–17).[22]

Example 4.5 Two-part organum, *Constitues eos. V. Pro patribus*, V. 1–65 (*I-Fl* Plut. 29.1, fols. 121v–122r)

With an understanding of the various compositional discourses in play, organa emerge as complex and unique structures that play off plainsong and polyphony in ways that are entirely dictated by the liturgical structure of the original plainsong, and that creatively juxtapose *organum per se*, discantus

Example 4.5 (*cont.*)

and copula within the polyphonic sections. *Constitues eos* again shows how this works. Example 4.4 shows how the polyphonic verse includes no less than six clausulae, alternating with seven passages in *organum per se*. As in the case of the *musica sine littera* in the conductus *cum caudis*, there is clearly some sense of balance in the composition and distribution of the clausulae: the second and fourth are of the same length, while the first is twice the length of the second and fourth; by contrast, the third, fifth and sixth are of eleven, ten and twelve perfections respectively.

A key feature of the repertory of organum duplum is the different selection of polyphonic material in different sources. In the case of *Constitues eos*, the polyphonic material for the respond is largely the same in the two sources (*I-Fl* Plut. 29.1 [also known as *F*], which forms the basis of examples 4.4 and 4.5, and *D-W* 1099 [also known as W_2]) that preserve the piece. But in the case of the verse, there are three sections that are entirely different, and all three affect the clausulae on '*patribus*', '*nati*' and '*filii*'. In the case of 'nati', the clausula is replaced in *D-W* 1099 by *organum per se*. Although the first clausula (32 perfections in *I-Fl* Plut. 29.1) is replaced with one of 28 perfections in *D-W* 1099, the clausula on 'filii' in both manuscripts is of identical length, thus preserving the symmetry with the clausula on 'tuis'.[23]

Three- and four-part organa adhere to most of the principles that obtain for organa dupla with the key exception that the upper voices in the sustained-tone sections are subject to modal rhythm and are notated in modal notation. The aural difference is striking, especially in the four-part works: in the sustained-tone style, three voices are in modal rhythm and one not, but in discantus all four voices are in modal rhythm; the shift in sonority is nothing like as great as from *organum per se* to discantus in two-part works, and the change from one musical discourse to another is not as sharply etched. Furthermore, the repertory of organa tripla and organa quadrupla is much smaller, and the opportunities for swapping clausulae around are that much more reduced.

Motet

The interchangeability of sections of organum, especially in the two-part repertory, led to an autonomous existence for the clausula, and collections of short fragments of discantus were features of some of the manuscripts preserving the repertory as a whole. The clausula began to take on a life of its own, a life that was responsible for the creation of the motet.[24]

The emergence of the motet, which has been dated anywhere between 1200 and 1220, problematizes the relationship between words, notes and notation.[25] Put very simply, the motet was created by adding words to a free-standing clausula as examples 4.6a and 4.6b show.

Both the motet *Immolata paschali victima / Latus* and its source clausula share a tenor that is identical in almost all respects.[26] In addition, it is easy to see how each of the notes of the ligatures in the clausula now carries a single syllable of the motet's text; this, however, does some violence to the melodic integrity of the clausula's duplum. Although the first two perfections text

Example 4.6a Two-part clausula *[Immo]latus est*, 1–39 (*I-Fl* Plut. 29.1, fol. 158r)

Example 4.6b Two-part motet *Immolata paschali victima / Latus*, 1–39 (*I-Fl* Plut. 29.1, fols. 411r–411v)

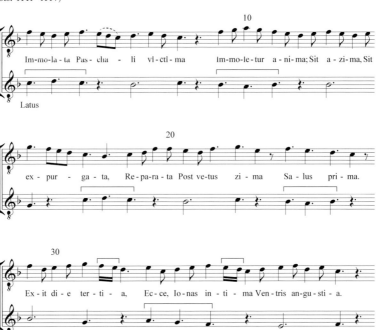

Example 4.7 *Immolata paschali victima / Latus.* Analysis of motetus text

	Line	Rhyme	Phrase End
1. *Immolata*	4p	a	
2. *Paschali* victima	6pp	a	x
3. *Immoletur* anima;	7pp	a	
4. Sit azima,	4pp	a	
5. Sit expurgata,	5p	a	
6. Reparata	4p	a	
7. Post vetus zima	5p	a	x
8. Salus prima.	4p	a	x
9. Exit die tertia,	6pp	a	
10. Ecce, Ionas intima	8pp	a	
11. Ventris angustia.	6pp	a	x
12. Fera Ioseph pessima	7pp	a	x
13. Devorata gelima	7pp	a	
14. Adoratur fraterna;	7p	a	x
15. Post tres dies infima	7pp	a	x
16. Exit de cisterna.	6p	a	
17. Ignea	3pp	a	
18. Remota romphea	6pp	a	
19. Claustra siderea	6pp	a	x
20. Aperit parte *latus*	7p	b	
21. Perforatus,	4p	b	x
22. Ut fenestratus	5p	b	
23. Celo sit meatus.	6p	b	x

the clausula exactly, the third and fourth not only carry two syllables but they also modify the clausula's original rhythm. Similar modifications may be found at perfections 31 and 35.

To a degree, the structure of the motet poem is determined by the phrase lengths of the clausula, but there is significant licence: over the course of two perfections, either two, three or four syllables may be deployed, and several lines of poetry are set to a single musical phrase (Example 4.7).

The text exhibits a wide range of line lengths, ranging from three to eight syllables, and there is no correlation between phrase ends and paroxytones or proparoxytones; nor does there appear to be any logical relationship between musical phrase length and poetic line length. In short, there seems to be a lack of interest in what are conventionally considered text–music relations. What is, however, largely consistent is rhyme. A single rhyme dominates most of the motet, and changes only for the last 4 lines of the 23-line lyric. This is a critical point in the poem and in the motet, since the word that triggers the change of rhyme, 'latus' (the side [of Christ]), assonates with the word of the plainsong from which the tenor is taken: 'immolatus'.

Such correspondences suggest a relationship between the text of the poem and its host plainsong. The plainsong from which the clausula is ultimately taken is 'Alleluia. V. Pascha nostrum immolatus est Christus', and this furnishes much of the text of the first few lines of the poem. Going one step further to the rest of the Easter Day liturgy, from which *Alleluia. V. Pascha nostrum* is taken, shows that 'victima' is the first word of the sequence for the mass, *Victimae paschali laudes*, and that the references to 'azima' derive from the communion chant for the mass on Easter Day, *Pascha nostrum immolatus*, which includes the line 'itaque epulemur in azimis'. The rest of the poem depends on Old Testament analogies – Jonah and the whale, Joseph and the Fiery Furnace – that point to other incarcerations followed by resurrections, which are then made to return to the side ('latus') of Christ.[27]

The close relationships between the text of the motet, its host plainsong and the background liturgy or the mass of Easter Day strongly suggest some sort of liturgical or paraliturgical context for the motet. One possibility is that the clausula should be texted when it forms part of a performance of the entire organum in which it is found; in other words, motets found in manuscript collections should be reinstated in their parent organa.[28] While such a suggestion is entirely plausible, it does not account for motets whose texts are polemical, hortatory or otherwise unrelated to the liturgy in the way that *Immolata paschali victima* is. The problems of function are here analogous to those of much of the conductus repertory, and may be just as varied.[29]

The relationship between clausula and the early motet brought into play two related phenomena: (1) the idea that musicians might compose multiple works (clausulae or motets) for the same context and expect them to be swapped around over time by those who sang them; and (2) the idea that texts could be added to melismatic music. It was a small step to the further practice that characterizes the motet in the thirteenth century: the addition of new voice-parts – a triplum to a two-part work for example – and the replacement of one text with another. Coupled to the possibility of using vernacular texts, these ideas created a potential kaleidoscope of musical and literary practices that were exploited with enthusiasm throughout the thirteenth century and into the fourteenth. With the simple two-part motet (motetus and tenor) being possibly the oldest product of these practices, almost every combination of text and music was exploited during the course of the thirteenth century: voice-parts could be piled up so that not only did a triplum appear but so too could a quadruplum be added to a three-part work (sometimes confusingly called a 'double motet') to create a motet in four parts. French and Latin texts could coexist in the same work (known as a 'bilingual motet').[30]

Simply describing the complexities of the relationships between surviving thirteenth-century motets is a serious barrier to understanding; trying to explain how musicians acted as they reworked musical and poetic material is even more challenging.[31] A sense of how the repertory worked in the second half of the thirteenth century may be gained from looking at a single group of compositions that shares the same musical material:

> a two-part motet *Hec dies leticie / Hec dies*[32]
> a two-part motet *Au commencement d'este / Hec dies* (which shares the same music)[33]
> a three-part French motet *Lonctens ai mi se m'entent / Au commencement d'este / Hec dies* (lower two parts the same music as the first two works; triplum newly added)[34]
> a three-part Latin motet *Salve, virgo Katherina / Sicut solis radium / Hec dies* (music the same as all three parts of the previous work to which new Latin texts are added.[35]

There is no clausula on which this collection of works is based, and it might be reasonably argued that the two-part Latin motet – with a motetus text that cites the text of the plainsong and is therefore closely allied to a liturgical context in the same way as *Immolata paschali victima* – is the first link in this complex chain. But deciphering compositional priority beyond that point becomes very difficult. From the sources in which they are found, it could be argued that the two-part French motet is the second stage in the process – a simple contrafactum of the Latin motet – and that the three-part 'French double motet' arises out of adding a newly composed triplum and poem. But the dates of the manuscripts for both compositions are not sufficiently differentiated to be certain, and it is entirely possible that a musician could have taken *Hec dies leticie / Hec dies* – added a triplum directly and two new French texts, and that the two-part French motet is simply a reduction created by dropping the triplum and its text. What does seem more likely is that the three-part Latin motet *Salve, virgo Katherina / Sicut solis radium / Hec dies* is a further contrafactum of the French double motet.[36]

One way of making sense of the wide range of motet types found in the thirteenth century is to look at the way in which thirteenth-century musicians tried to organize their understanding: to look at the way in which manuscripts were organized. The best-known source for the thirteenth-century motet is the so-called Montpellier Codex, *F-MOf* H 196. In its earliest form (it was added to at least twice later) from around 1270, it divided its contents into four-part motets, three-part bilingual motets (texts in Latin and French), three-part Latin motets, three-part French motets, and two-part French motets. The critical principles of organization and identification for whoever planned the structure of this book were the number of voice parts and the language of the poetry.

For the repertory of French motets, in two and three parts, the position is even more complex as they create intertextual links between the repertory of secular monophonic song, medieval romance and other literature via the sharing of *refrains*.[37] A *refrain* is a short phrase of poetry that re-appears in more than one literary or musical context; the intertextuality may relate to the poetry or to the poetry and music together. A simple example is the motet *Amis, vostre demoree / Pro patribus*, which is found in the sixth fascicle of *F-MOf* H 196.[38] The end of the motet shares its text and music with a secular monophonic song and a treatise on love by Gerard of Liège, the *Quinque incitamenta ad deum amandum ardenter* (examples 4.8a and 4.8b).[39]

The song by Moniot d'Arras (fl. 1213–39) is a *chanson à refrain*, where the *refrain* appears at the end of each stanza; apart from a few ornamental melodic variants and some slight lexical changes the *refrain* is identical to the end of the motetus of *Amis, vostre demoree*.[40] The notation in the two sources for the song, *F-Pn* Fr. 844 and 12615, is unmeasured, whereas – as is always the case in *F-MOf* H 196 – the notation of the motet is measured, and this difference is retained in the example.[41] Such simple cases are outnumbered by far more complex intertextualities where more than one *refrain* is in play in a single motet, where the *refrain* is broken up, where the music of the *refrain* is retexted within the motet within which it is found, etc.[42]

Throughout the creation of all these complex musical and literary networks, some things remained constant: plainsongs were still the source for tenors, and – with the new notation that differentiated graphically between *longae* and *breves* – modal rhythms could be expressed, and the system largely continued to dictate the rhythmic structure of the music and the declamation of the poetry. Towards the end of the thirteenth century, two of these constants were subject to change. The first innovation was the inclusion of vernacular songs as sources for tenors, and the second was a key change to the rhythmic profile of the music. While French tenors form

Example 4.8a Two-part motet *Amis vostre demoree / Pro patribus*, 26–46 (*F-MOf* H. 196, fol. 249r)

Example 4.8b Monophonic song: Moniot d'Arras, *Amours me fait renvoisier et chanter, refrain*
(*F-Pn* fonds fr. 844, fol. 118v)

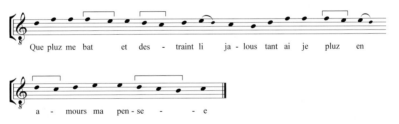

a small part of the overall repertory of motets, in the manuscripts in which they are found they have a proportionally higher profile (seventh and eighth fascicles of *F-MOf* H 196 and *I-Tr* vari 42).[43] Secular songs have a much higher incidence of repetition than plainsong, and in some cases composers experimented with matching the repetitions in the upper voices with results that – musically at least – came to look like the polyphonic songs that would become so important in the fourteenth century.[44]

The second major change to the profile of the motet at the end of the thirteenth century was the end of the relationship between rhythmic structure and declamation. Examples 4.7 and 4.8 show compositions where the declamation of the text largely follows the rhythmic mode of the piece. Towards 1300, not only did the *brevis* – which up till now had never been divided into

Example 4.9 Three-part motet *Aucun ont trouvé chant par usage / Lonctans me sui tenu / Annun[tiantes]*, 1–16 (*F-MOf* H. 196, fols. 273r–274r)

more than three *semibreves* – become divided into much larger numbers, but syllables of the poetry were declaimed at a similar rate (Example 4.9).

The two lower parts of *Aucun ont trouvé chant par usage / Lonctans me sui tenu / Annun[tiantes]* behave very much like any mid-thirteenth-century motet, but the triplum exhibits divisions of the *brevis* into three *semibreves* (which, although found in the motetus, never carry more than one syllable), five, six and seven *breves* in the space of a dozen perfections.[45] More than anything, this particular change in the motet repertory marked an audible change to the texture of the work, and a shift in aesthetic focus.[46]

If the function of non-liturgical Latin motets is unclear, the environment in which motets with French texts were cultivated is even more opaque. Two pieces of evidence may be brought to bear on the question. The theorist Johannes de Grocheo wrote enticingly about how the motet should 'not . . . be propagated among the vulgar, since they do not understand its subtlety nor do they delight in hearing it, but it should be performed for the learned and those who seek after the subtleties of the arts. And it is normally performed in their feasts for their beautification . . .'[47] Johannes's comments are in the context of what he calls *musica canonica*, in other words the music of clerics, and raise as many questions as they provide answers. They do however clearly locate the motet within an educated domain in which the motet's complexity is valued as much as its sonority or style. The second piece of evidence concerns the career paths of the singers at Notre Dame and some of the criticisms levelled at them: many of the key musicians at Notre Dame were forced to resign each year; they may or may not have been re-employed. Moves from an ecclesiastical position to others were therefore more than possible, and these might well have included more courtly environments in which vernacular poetry was more the norm. The collision, then, between musicians trained to sing and perhaps compose (or at least modify) organa and clausulae and a vernacular culture may well have triggered the earliest motets with French texts. Coupled to comments such as those of Robert de Courson, who criticized those who employed the *magistri organici* for their 'scurrilous and effeminate things', these observations might lead one to the same courts that gave room to trouvères and their musicians in a search for the origins of the French motet.[48]

Towards the fourteenth century

Older histories of thirteenth-century music suggest that organum ceased around 1220, conductus around 1240 and that the motet occupied most of the rest of the century until it itself was supplanted by what used to be called the isorhythmic motet around 1300. This seems far too simple a view when the longevity of both organum and conductus is considered: both genres seem to have coexisted with the motet – and were performed throughout the century and beyond. But such coexistence came at a price. The rhythmic and notational changes that were triggered by the changes in motet composition in the middle of the century had an immense impact on both organum and conductus. In both cases, it was the sections that were preserved in an unmeasured notation – *organum per se* and *musica cum littera* respectively – that were subject to change. Theoretical writings from the later thirteenth century try to explain organum and conductus in terms not only of mensural notation but also of a sophisticated mensural notation as found in such treatises as *Ars cantus mensurabilis* or the treatise of Anonymous IV.[49]

Musical sources for both conductus and organum from around 1300 exhibit the same sorts of trends: recasting the notation of *organum per se* and *musica sine littera* in mensural notation. There used to be a time when scholars would extrapolate backwards from these sources to argue that their notation represented the original rhythmic delivery of these sections, but viewing these sources as products of changing views of notation and rhythm – as part of the reception of organum and conductus – probably does greater justice to the complexity of thirteenth-century musical history.[50] The consequences were far-reaching for polyphonic music in general: whereas both organum and conductus (especially the conductus *cum caudis*) exploited contrasting musical discourses that were characterized by the relationship between words and notes and by their rhythmic profile, the motet exploited a single musical discourse – preferring to exploit the vertical complexity of polytextuality and multiple voices. Around 1300, this difference was not quite entirely effaced but significantly weakened: in organum, the difference between *organum per se* and discantus remained in terms of the relationship between voices and in the conductus between syllabic and melismatic settings of the text. But the rhythmic differences that underpinned these differences were completely eradicated in the sources that were copied around 1300 and which presumably bear witness to a style of performance then current.

5 The fourteenth century

ELIZABETH EVA LEACH

Although a famous popular history book's subtitle glossed the fourteenth century as 'calamitous', a consideration of its music would probably see the period as a triumph.[1] In part this is because the chief technology that gives us access to the past – writing – became more widely used for record keeping by this time. In particular, the special kind of writing used to record musical sounds – musical notation – reached a new level of prescription, describing relative pitches and rhythms more fully than before. As the fourteenth century paid more cultural attention to writing things down in the first place, more music books survive from this period than from any earlier centuries, and their contents seem tantalizingly decipherable.

The detailed social and political history of the fourteenth century is complex and beyond the scope of this chapter. However, some of its aspects will be mentioned here, not in order to give a comprehensive history, but in order to suggest ways in which larger historical changes affected musical culture.

The later fourteenth century saw a deep division of the Western Christian church, a problem partly caused by the refusal of successive popes to reside in Rome after the French pope Clement V moved the papal court to Avignon (France) in 1309. The often lavish papal court was responsible for employing a large number of expert singers, many of whom we know to have also been composers because pieces by them survive.[2] Avignon was especially important as a centre for musical activity during the reign of the 'humanist' pope Clement VI (b.1291–2, elected 1342, d.1352), whose circle included the music theorist and scientist Johannes de Muris, as well as the composer Philippe de Vitry, whom several later writers saw as key in the practical deployment of the new notational style of the Ars Nova within motets and secular songs.[3] Despite Avignon's status as an ecclesiastical court, musical activity there included the composition and performance not only of sacred music, but also of secular songs and political motets. Vitry's motet *Petre Clemens / Lugentium siccentur*, for instance, was written for the visit to Avignon in January 1343 of the Ambassadors of the Roman citizens, who tried (unsuccessfully) to tempt the newly elected Clement VI back to Rome.[4] The balades *Courtois et sages* (by Magister Egidius), *Par les bons* (by Philippus de Caserta) and *Inclite flos* (by Matteus de Sante Johanne) were all written for the Avignon 'anti-pope' Clement VII (1378–94), whose election initiated the Western schism that dominated the church until its resolution at the Council of Constance in 1417. In 1378 Gregory XI returned the papacy to Rome, dying there shortly after his arrival. Under threat of violence from the citizens of Rome, the cardinals – including the future anti-pope Clement VII (Robert of Geneva) – elected the Italian archbishop Bartolomeo Prignano of Bari as Pope Urban VI on 8 April 1378. Five months later, however, under the pretext that election under such duress was invalid, another election saw Robert himself elected, acknowledged by Aragon, Castile, Denmark, France, Navarre, Norway, Portugal, Savoy, Scotland and some German states.[5] The Italians continued to support Urban VI; Clement VII returned his papal court to Avignon. Two (and later three) popes then reigned simultaneously until the church was reunified with the election of Martin V in 1417, who finally and unequivocally returned the papacy to Rome.

The fourteenth century also saw much of the so-called Hundred Years War (actually a series of conflicts lasting from roughly 1337 to 1453) between England and France.[6] Although war might be thought a negative influence on culture, medieval warfare differed from modern warfare in scale and process, allowing a far greater role for ceremonial, parleys and other forums. At one point the French king and his entire court were in captivity in England, where they engaged in courtly activities – hunting and performances of poetry and music – similar to those they would have undertaken at home. Music and musicians played important roles in international diplomacy and propaganda.[7]

The schism and war were not the only factors that fed an ever-present late-medieval eschatology – a preoccupation with the Last Things and the Day of Judgement. A European population that since 1250 had expanded to levels not seen again in some states until the middle of the nineteenth century was struck first by a serious famine (1315–22) and then by epidemic disease.[8] The first large-scale occurrence of the so-called Black Death, which contemporaries referred to as the 'Great Mortality', swept Europe between 1347 and 1350, killing an estimated one third of the population.[9] On the other hand the size of court retinues continued to rise during this period, with noblemen and princes employing ever more functionaries.[10] Such large retinues could not be paid merely in kind (with food, lodging, clothes and so on), but required monetary salaries and pensions, accounts of which were more carefully kept than before (in turn necessitating the service of increased numbers of literate clerks, who were often also chapel functionaries).[11] The increase in households and courts saw a concomitant increase in the number of musicians, singers and scribes employed (not least in the capacity of secretary, a post held by the poet-composer Guillaume de Machaut at the court of Jean of Luxembourg, for example). As mentioned above, the rise in the levels of record keeping also affected the amount of music written down.

The other cultural change that affected music in the fourteenth century was bound up with music's continued place within the basic university training of the Middle Ages, the arts degree.[12] *Musica* – a subject whose definition encompassed far more than just sounding music in performance – was one of the mathematical subjects of the quadrivium. The fourteenth century witnessed a revolution in mathematical thinking which broadly shifted from an arithmetical mathematics based on fixed points and which sharply distinguished qualities from quantities, to a geometric mathematics based on movement and allowing for the quantification of quality through estimation and approximation.[13] It seems likely that this had some impact on the conceptual changes in the basis of musical notation, especially as one of the chief music theorists, Johannes de Muris, also wrote on advanced mathematics.[14] Music also received a boost that connected university and court in the shape of the translation of Aristotle's *Politics* from its late-thirteenth-century Latin version into French by Nicole Oresme.[15] Book VIII argues strongly for music's propriety for noblemen not just as an abstract intellectual discipline (as Boethius's treatise implies) but as a leisured pursuit and appropriate for relaxation.

The fourteenth century is often discussed in terms of the rise of the composer; it certainly is the case that we know the names of more composers from this period than from previous centuries, and importantly we know the names of composers of polyphonic music, in stark contrast to the general situation with the polyphony of the thirteenth century. However, the manuscripts of troubadour and trouvère song are often organized by composer, a trait that can be seen as late as the retrospective anthology of trecento song in the Squarcialupi Codex. And we know the names of those who put together (*componere*) chant offices for local saints from as early as the tenth century.[16] It can be seen that musicology has tended to make 'composer' stand for 'composer of polyphony' in a way that is one of many aspects of medieval studies that say more about the preoccupations of latter-day musicologists than about the Middle Ages.[17]

Motets

Certain forms in use in the thirteenth century continued to flourish in the fourteenth. The motet in particular retained its importance, but where formerly whole collections were dedicated to it, in the fourteenth century motets tend instead to be copied within song collections, indicating their migration even further from the liturgical sphere. The formal developments in motet composition in fourteenth-century France – the main place where the form was cultivated – show a reduction from the variety of types practised in the thirteenth century but a greater variety within the remaining type than was explored hitherto.[18] The tenor is a numerical scheme underlying the whole piece and is rhythmically differentiated from the much faster-moving top voices. The uppermost voice – the triplum – moves fastest of all, the motetus a bit slower, and the rigidly patterned tenor slowest of all. The tenor patterns of pitch (*color*) and rhythm (*talea*) can be coterminous or can overlap.[19] The new numerical possibilities of the motet lent themselves to the exploration of numerical symbolism and other inaudible but meaningful features.[20] The large five-section motet *Rota versatilis*, composed in England before 1320, has sections in the proportions 12:8:4:9:6, which symbolize the fundamental musical proportions commonly found in elementary music theory, where they are said to have been discovered by Pythagoras.[21]

Whether or not the upper voices reflect the patterning of the tenor varies. Scholars have traditionally seen a movement from having barely any reflection of the tenor in the upper voices (as in most thirteenth-century motets from the old corpus of Montpellier, for example), to what has been termed 'pan-isorhythm', where the tenor's repeating structure is reflected in all the upper parts. Perhaps composers experienced an increased need to articulate the motet's structure in this readily audible way when its sheer scale expanded to the grand proportions of the fourteenth century. The net effect was that the motet became almost strophic in form.

The upper voices of the fourteenth-century motet began to adopt regular versification, in contrast to the more playful rhymes and metrical schemes which typify the upper voices of earlier motets. The polytextuality of the upper voices continued, and the possibility for intertextual play between each upper voice and both with the tenor was expanded as composers exercised a freer choice of tenor melismas, no longer restricting their choice to those clausula-derived segments of chant that typically group the thirteenth-century motet into tenor families. Machaut, for example, chooses short emblematic words from chants that are not used as the basis for motets at all in the thirteenth century.[22] This freedom of authorial choice probably reflects a complete disengagement of the performance situation of motets from liturgical or para-liturgical use and their newer association with courtly activities. However, this does not necessarily remove the intertextual resonance of the liturgical situation 'cued' by the tenor; as with thirteenth-century motets, those of the fourteenth century can be read as exploring analogical overlap (and difference) between devotional practices of different kinds (sacred and courtly-secular).[23] The situation with English motets differs in this respect from the French repertory. Although most of the 100 or so motets, mainly in three parts with two upper voices texted in Latin, that survive from early-fourteenth-century England are fragmentary, they not only show a far greater formal variety than the French motets of the period but often have more explicitly devotional upper-voice texts.[24]

Songs

Arguably the most important musical innovations of the fourteenth century occurred in the field of secular song. The combination of polyphonic musical textures with a number of refrain forms, known today as the *formes fixes*, whose texts were predominantly high-style courtly poetry, at once broke with the types of song current in the thirteenth century (in which courtly refrain forms tended to be courtly-popular danced poems, high-style poems tended to lack refrains, and neither were polyphonic) and set a standard for the next century and a half.[25] The overwhelming presence attested by the sources is that of Guillaume de Machaut, a major French poet for whom music-writing – especially as facilitated and made precise by the new notation of the Ars Nova – was just a further element in the performance of his poetry over which he could exert his considerable authorial control.

Machaut's thematization of himself as an author, as a controlling presence behind his book, in conjunction with his own training as a secretary and his interest in making books, mean that the source situation for this composer is strongly atypical. His works are preserved in no fewer than six large manuscripts from the second half of the century, that are dedicated entirely to them. A few of his musical works also crop up in other song-books, and his lyrics and narrative poems also appear in other text-only poetry sources. Nevertheless, the weight of authority that accrues to the six so-called Machaut manuscripts is powerful: it enables us to trace a life and works for this composer far more detailed than those of any of his contemporaries. By contrast, his equally famous colleague Philippe de Vitry – a poet-composer perhaps better regarded by those contemporaries who rated their own learning – has no such 'collected works' source. Vitry's works are transmitted in the way in which musical works of this period are generally found: in collections of pieces by a number of different composers, often anonymous, and without the extreme care in presentation that we find in Machaut's richly illuminated books. Although we have a number of motets that can be linked with Vitry, unless they are contained in the interpolated version of the poem *Fauvel* found in *F-Pn* fr. 146, his notated songs are lost. We have only the word of the anonymous author of a poetry treatise dating from 1405–32 that Vitry 'invented' the writing of balades, lais, and simple rondeaux.[26]

Rondels to rondeaux

Of the *formes fixes*, the one that most clearly carries on a form present in the thirteenth century is the rondeau. Musically, the rondeau is perhaps the simplest of the fixed forms as it has two musical sections of roughly equal length. These sections A and B are sung in the pattern AB aA ab AB in which the upper-case letters represent the sections carrying the text of the refrain, and lower-case letters represent new text each time they occur. The first section of music (A and a) is thus heard five times, compared to the three times that the second section of music (B and b) is heard. In terms of the poetic form, the two musical sections can each carry one or more lines of text, and it is not necessary for them each to carry the same number of lines (even though they split the refrain text between them). The simplest rondeau poem has one line per musical section giving a total of eight lines: two refrain lines (one sung three times and one sung twice) and three other lines (a single line that goes with the first refrain line and a couplet). An eleven-line rondeau would have one line of poetry in the first musical section and two in the second; a thirteen-line rondeau would have two lines of poetry in the A section and one in the B section. A sixteen-line rondeau would have two lines in each musical section and so on.

A poet would have to consider that the part of the refrain in the first musical section would have to stand alone in between the two new text segments that surround it in the middle of the piece; a composer would have to ensure that the first musical section makes as much sense going on to the second as it would going straight back to repeat the first section again with new words. In addition, the poet can make links between the musical sections in forms that have eleven, thirteen, sixteen or more lines by interlacing rhymes so that the same rhyme types occur in both sections.

The balade–virelai matrix

The forms that have least to do with the preceding century and that go on to dominate polyphonic song until the end of the fifteenth century belong to what Christopher Page has termed 'the balade–virelai matrix'.[27] The similarity between these two song forms is evident also in their nomenclature. The word 'balade' refers to dancing, while the word 'virelai' suggests the turning (in a circle) that accompanied such dances. Machaut tends to call the virelai the 'chanson baladée' (danced song), and the equivalent form with Italian text is the 'ballata'. Texts of these two forms are mixed together in the section of lyrics in *GB-Ob* Douce 308, which dates from the first half of the fourteenth century.[28] In both balade and virelai types there are a pair of verses which take the same music – perhaps with its endings tonally differentiated to give first an open and then a more closed feel; then there is new text set to music different from that used for the verses, and finally there is a refrain. In the virelai, the refrain (It. 'ripresa') is also performed at the very opening as well, and the music of the latter part of the new text – the 'tierce' or 'volta' – is the same as that of the refrain. In the balade the form opens with the pair of verses sung to the same music (with open and closed endings); the new section of text and music – the 'oultrepasse', or B section – is different from that of the refrain. Subsequent stanzas in both forms repeat the musical form from the first of the verses.

| Virelai / ballata | R | Io | Ic | II 'tierce' / 'volta' (music of R) | R |
| Balade | - | Io | Ic | II 'oultrepasse' | R |

In the first half of the fourteenth century the differentiation between these two forms was widened by their musicalization. Most virelais in Machaut's output are monophonic and syllabic and thus could still be danced to, while being sung by the dancers themselves. An illustration in a mid-century copy of his *Remede de Fortune*, which exemplifies all the *formes fixes* within its narrative, shows exactly this, and this is the only song type to accompany group social activity in the story.[29] Machaut's balades are, with one late exception, all polyphonic and increasingly move towards a standard three-part texture with long melismatic passages. These are now stylized dance songs, akin to the suites of Bach in being removed from actual dancing, yet having assimilated dance forms, rhythms and gestures. Later, the virelai too moved away from syllabic monophony and was regularly sung in three parts; its popular-style dance elements were sometimes transmuted into the singing of non-musical sounds: birdsong, drums, trumpets etc., found more usually in hocket sections of the Italian *caccia*.[30]

The lai

The word 'lai' has a number of etymological resonances, most of which link it to song. The Irish word *loîd* (or *laîd*), meaning 'blackbird's song' has been linked to a supposed Irish origin for the form, but whether this can be linked with the musical lai that appeared in France around 1200 is not certain. The lai can be narrative or lyric, and not everything that calls itself a lai fits the non-strophic developmental form that usually characterizes it. Conversely, lai-like features can be found in songs that are variously called descort, leich, nota/notula, estampie, ductia, garip, sequence, prose, conductus, or versus.[31]

Throughout the fourteenth century poetry remains an 'art de bouche' (oral practice); the human voice emits sounds on a seamless continuum from speech to singing. It is likely that narrative lays, like the *chansons de geste*, were intoned to a simple melodic formula. Like the refrain forms, the lai saw a trend towards greater regularity in the fourteenth century. Lais became longer; in the work of Machaut there is a standard pattern of

12 stanzas with the first and last having the same rhymes and the same melody, usually transposed a fifth higher for the final stanza.[32] Each stanza has a so-called double versicle set-up, so that it divides into two equally structured halves that can be sung to the same music used twice through. In this it resembles the sequence, which seems to have had an influence on the later fourteenth-century lai, rather than affecting its initial development – the thirteenth-century lyric lai is fairly freely structured, often heterometric (having lines of different lengths), and irregular in its rhyme schemes.[33] Because they are not strophic, the lai and sequence are primarily musical in their formal concept, as opposed to the metrical formal concept that dominates the strophic *formes fixes*.[34] Despite not being usually polyphonic (although Machaut wrote some that could be performed canonically in three parts), the lai is arguably a greater musical and poetic challenge to the composer than the other forms.[35]

The madrigal

Despite the greater modern familiarity with the madrigal of the sixteenth century, the first use of this term to denote a musico-poetic genre is by Francesco da Barberino around 1313. In 1334 Antonio da Tempo lists two types – with and without a ritornello. Although da Tempo mentions monodic madrigals, *The New Grove Dictionary of Music and Musicians* estimates that 90 per cent of the 190 surviving examples are for two voices (the rest are for three).[36] The earliest surviving examples, from northern Italy and dating probably from the 1320s, appear in *I-Rvat* Rossi 215. Despite both voices being texted in this source, the uppermost voice predominates, often melismatically, while the lower voice moves slower, emphasizing consonances. By the 1340s the madrigal had reached its final fourteenth-century form, comprising two or three three-line stanzas (with the same rhyme pattern but usually different rhyme types) set to the same music, followed by a one- or two-line terminating ritornello, often in a different mensuration. The individual heptasyllabic or hendecasyllabic lines are separated cadentially in the style found in the works of Magister Piero, Giovanni da Cascia and Jacopo da Bologna (fl. 1340–60). Jacopo also offers the first three-voice settings. The madrigal genre continued to be popular, especially in Florence, until around 1415, although from the 1360s onwards it was rivalled by the newly polyphonic ballata (see above). The final phase of the trecento madrigal saw a move away from the pastoral and courtly poetry that characterizes its early-century incarnation and towards its use as a vehicle for authorial presence in autobiographical pieces such as Landini's *Musica son*, as well as moralizing poetry and occasional or symbolic poems.

Liturgical music

The repertory of polyphonic French settings of texts from the ordinary of the mass was very widely transmitted, with pieces existing in multiple copies and a variety of different versions. The French mass style was highly influential, for example, on mass settings by Italian composers, although England was unique (as far as can be told by source survival) in setting mass propers polyphonically. Of the repertory's known composers, at least five can be associated with the papal court at Avignon. This perhaps explains the wide dissemination of the repertory, since Avignon was a magnet for the most internationally mobile and influential people of the period. In general, liturgical music is in three parts, although the number of voices texted varies from piece to piece and, sometimes, from source to source.[37]

Music for the mass had previously been copied in generic groups, keeping items of the same kind together (Kyries, Glorias etc.). The earliest cyclic groupings – where a set of the different items of the ordinary that would be performed sequentially are placed together in the manuscript – occur in the fourteenth century. The earliest example is the so-called Tournai Mass, which sets the six ordinary texts of the mass: Kyrie, Gloria, Credo, Sanctus, Agnus and Ite Missa Est. The polyphonic setting of the last of these seems only to have been common in the fourteenth century; here it is presented as a three-voice motet also known independently from other fourteenth-century sources.[38] This harks back to the earlier liturgical function of motets as a form of troping, a trait associated with the beginnings of motet composition.[39] One Credo setting appears as part of two different cycles in manuscripts from Toulouse and Barcelona. In the Toulouse Mass the Credo seems related to the Ite, and the Kyrie and Sanctus also seem to form a pair (there is no Gloria). But in the Barcelona Mass the Credo does not seem similar to any of the highly contrasted items: only the Kyrie and Agnus might possibly be related.[40] These cycles were scribal compilations rather than compositionally intended cycles. This does not, however, invalidate their cyclicity – the manuscript layout suggests that they were used as a cycle and would have been heard as a cycle even if they were not composed as one. The expectation of unifying compositional cyclism is one that stems from hindsight and in particular reflects the nineteenth-century musicologists' desire to find a medieval parallel for the unified symphony, whose movements were not only all the product of the same composer, but were also thematically, motivically, and/or tonally linked.[41] In this spirit much has been made of the first complete single-author cycle of the mass ordinary by Guillaume de Machaut, composed in the early 1360s for use in Marian devotions at a side altar in his home cathedral of Reims.[42] Although this seems a further way in which Machaut stands out as a central figure in fourteenth-century music history, it should be remembered that the 'rise of the cyclic Mass' was not a foregone conclusion at this point in music history.

Understanding the music of the fourteenth century

Studying the music of the fourteenth century still poses a number of key questions concerning historical method. How fourteenth-century music is studied is affected by how music is defined (its definition was somewhat broader then than now), how the sources are interpreted, what other materials are thought to bear on their interpretation, and how they are deemed to be relevant. There are inevitable limits in terms of what the predominantly written, predominantly clerical sources for this period can and cannot tell us. Depending on one's scholarly perspective this limitation is either a great frustration – how can we really know anything? – or a fantastic opportunity to make creative interpretative readings that best fit with the available (partial) evidence. We tend to ask questions of this music and the period that its historical actors – the people who made and heard its music, or taught and learned *musica* – did not need to ask. Their writings are unlikely to answer such questions directly. Among these modern concerns three stand out: the issue of the basic social context for music from this period, the issues surrounding its performance, and the issue of how to construct a chronology – a diachronic history – of music and musical culture across this period.

Social context

For sacred music, the liturgy gives at least some indication of the context in which it would have been performed. The mass is a particular kind of social and religious ritual event, well understood even if we do not know for any given piece the specifics for which particular service(s) in which particular year(s) it was used. Sometimes the texts of other pieces, especially motets, make political points that help connect them with particular occasions. However, this connection usually gives only a date that they must be later than (a *terminus post quem*), rather than actually offering a performance situation; Margaret Bent has cautioned against 'over-literal dating according to . . . topical references' of the political motets in the *F-Pn* fr. 146 version of the *Roman de Fauvel* – musical pieces are not newspaper reports.[43] Even when a specific event is being commemorated – the wedding of Jean of Berry and Jeanne of Boulogne in balades by Trebor and Egidius,[44] or the installation of a specific bishop for Machaut's motet *Bone pastor / Bone pastor / Bone pastor* (M18) – a later adaptation or repetition of specially written music is not inconceivable.[45]

For most of the song repertory, the problem of performance context is particularly acute. Who wrote, performed and listened to late medieval songs? The manuscript evidence is difficult to interpret: we often do not know precisely when or where manuscripts were compiled, how long before this the songs were written, how widely they circulated, who would have had the competence to perform them, when they would be performed, how often, who would listen, or what the listeners would make of them. Evidence for all these questions has to be sought from within the songs, whose texts are often highly stylized courtly love songs that seem opaquely general. A little more information is available for the works of Machaut since his narrative poems offer a first-person narrative persona (Guillaume) who is the alter ego of the poet-composer. Suitable caution must be exercised, however, because even when the songs purport to tell of the doings of real historical figures these are not historical accounts but literary works; nevertheless, they can point us to certain contexts. Machaut's *Remede de Fortune*, a long narrative poem with seven inserted musical items – one in each of the *formes fixes* – gives some information about the ideal(ized) use of this kind of musical poetry at court. The action is initiated when the Lady discovers an unascribed written copy of Guillaume's lai and asks him to sing it to her. The poem laments the fact that its *je* loves a lady but cannot tell her. When Guillaume has sung it to her, she asks if he knows who it is by; he flees in terror from revealing that it is his own song. Rehabilitated through more music and singing in a garden by the allegorical figure of Lady Hope (*Esperance*), Guillaume returns to court fortified to withstand the vagaries of unstable Fortune in love by remaining hopeful of gaining the lady's love. He provides social music for a court dance (the virelai *Dame en vous* [V33], see above) and is able to reveal his love to the lady, although there is no happy outcome. In effect, love of Hope (which is within the lover and thus at his control) replaces love of the Lady (who is out of his control and might cause him sorrow). This gives a clear path to happiness based on an abstract spiritual quality, maintained within the loving subject. There is a clear parallel between this kind of courtly love, sublimated as endless hope, and the kind of hope that animates the Christian believer in the Middle Ages. Hope of an eventual reward that might not be in this life can keep one happy only if one loves the act of hoping rather than the presence of the reward.

Machaut's ostensibly secular courtly love motet texts can also be read through the lens of this allegory by means of their sacred plainchant tenor segments. It has even been argued that the ordered cycle of motets in the manuscripts represents a step-by-step journey from unhappiness and sin to union with the divine Beloved (Christ).[46] This is parallel to the *Remede*'s step-by-step journey, except that as in all the Machaut *dits* there is no final union with the earthly beloved lady, perhaps underscoring the point that although the feelings are meant to be of a similar strength in the two journeys, the outcome of only the spiritual journey is secure. Trusting in earthly happiness and earthly (i.e. sexual) love will not give the same guaranteed result of having that love returned as spiritual devotion will give to the surety of God's love.[47] Medieval courtiers took religion seriously, and women among them in particular needed consolation for the frustrations and perhaps boredom of court life by means of a form of entertainment that would not jeopardize social values. Making love poetry into a sublimation of natural sexual urges – shifting loving subjects into inaction, mental self-absorption and analogical understanding of their feelings as misplaced or displaced yearning for union with the divine – was an efficient and convenient way of managing the inevitable human and sexual tensions that would have arisen at court.[48]

When poetry was combined in performance with the sweet sounds of polyphonic singing, its effectiveness increased even further according to the new status of music as an Aristotelian 'leisured pursuit'.[49] Some of the precepts which apply to the music's suitability as a form of virtuous princely relaxation are already present in the work of Augustine and Isidore, but after the translation of Aristotle's ethical works in the later thirteenth century, music-theoretical arguments fairly soon incorporated more strongly worded justifications of music's virtuous power.[50] While Plato and Aristotle exhibit remarkably similar views on the proper ends of music and its role in education and politics, their main difference concerns their emphasis on music's pleasurable qualities.[51] The consoling effect of poetry is heightened and increased through the newly legitimate pleasure of music. In the long text of Gace de la Buigne's mid-fourteenth-century poem *Le roman des Deduis*, the character speaking in favour of falconry cites two Ars Nova pieces – Vitry's motet *Douce playsance / Garison / Neuma* and the chace *Se je chant* by Denis le Grant – ostensibly to prove that a good falconer never flies his birds in high wind or excessive heat. However, Gace's poem is a magnificent hybrid mirror-of-princes advice book, part a battle of the Vices and Virtues drawing on Prudentius' *Psychomachia*, part *jugement* debate poem, both parts linked by the noble theme of hunting. When read as a whole, Gace's poem proposes musical poetry as a consoling antidote to the ills that it might narrate – the heat of excessive amorous desire in *Douce / Garison / Neuma*, or the indulgent time-wasting of a day's hunting in *Se je chant*.[52]

Performance issues

Just as we know relatively little about specifically where and when these songs were performed, we know only small amounts about how these songs were performed. For liturgical music the defined context gives slightly clearer evidence suggesting all-vocal performance, perhaps accompanied or *alternatim* with an organ; with songs, lack of information about performance context connotes lack of information about performance practice.[53] Much of the musicological discussion of medieval performance practice has focused on the issue of performing forces, asking whether the top voice of a song was accompanied by instruments or by other voices.[54] This question is perhaps unduly distracting, since more important issues concern aspects of a piece to which we might in fact be able to get closer: the pronunciation of the text, the correct understanding of its relative pitches and rhythms, and a basic stylistic competence that enables us to make it clear where the music drives forward and where it hangs back, where it fulfils expectations and where it frustrates or surprises them. This would then go some way to offering a route to make a modern performance that was closer in its effects or representation (which can be analysed) rather than necessarily closer in sound (which is unknowable).[55] Our understanding of the rhythmic notation of the fourteenth century is rather good, deriving from fairly clear contemporary theoretical writings.[56] The understanding of relative pitch – there is no single absolute pitch standard for music at this period, so the notational level only guides the general placement of the overall ensemble within that particular group's performable pitches – has been more fraught, especially over the issue of accidental inflections and *musica ficta*.[57] The disagreements of scholars centre on whether sharpening the pitch of one voice in certain situations is at the discretion of the performer or was determined by the composer; whether the sonic product implied by the notation was always the same or whether there was scope for variation between different performances of the same piece; whether the practice is confined to cadences in the modern sense (in which they close a phrase) or in the medieval sense (of *cadentia*, a term which just describes a particular succession of sonorities which can and do occur at the beginning, in the middle and at the ends of phrases). From my own perspective, the cadential progression – for which I prefer to use Sarah Fuller's term 'the directed progression' because I do not see it reserved exclusively for closural syntax – is a defining feature of fourteenth-century musical style.[58] Neither before nor after does it seem to be so pervasive in the musical texture. The marker of the 'modern' style of Guillaume Du Fay in the early fifteenth century seems to be its more sparing use, and a greater reliance on extended phrases of 'imperfect' sonorities (sixths and thirds) in support of a less angular, even smooth, melodic line.

Chronology

Arriving at any clear chronology for the works that have survived from the fourteenth century is more than moderately difficult. Scholars have tended to talk about an 'Ars Nova' (new art) succeeding the 'Ars Antiqua' (old art) some time around 1320, being brought to maturity in the works of Philippe de Vitry and Guillaume de Machaut before being succeeded by a mannerist 'Ars Subtilior' (more subtle art) after the latter's death in 1377.[59] This in turn supposedly gives way to the modern style of Du Fay and his contemporaries in the early fifteenth century. These divisions wrest circular reasoning from stylistic features in combination with evidence from notational change. Ars Antiqua notation is that which is pre-minim and pre-duple time divisions. The Ars Nova incorporates the invention of the minim (whose value was previously expressed by a series of semibreves of which the minim really is the *semibrevis minima*, but the value now has its own graphic indication in the form of an upstem added to the notehead). The Ars Subtilior sees not only the division of this minim value but also the deployment of 'avant-garde' canonic techniques, proportional note values (4 against 3 and more), texts that refer to their own musical performance, plus picture music such as the circular maze within which is copied the famous anonymous balade *En la maison Dedalus*.[60] The situation in Italy is treated as if parallel, with a pure period of Italian trecento notation being followed by a hybrid Italian–French phrase before the mutual accommodation of Italian elements within the ultimately triumphant French notation in the Ars Subtilior.

These tripartite schemes probably owe much to other similar ones in music historiography, notably the three compositional periods of Beethoven.[61] Philippe de Vitry's treatise *Ars nova* is, according to Sarah Fuller, nothing more than a retrospective writing up of what was most likely student lecture notes; certainly Vitry's involvement is indirect in this regard.[62] The Ars Subtilior – a term coined in the twentieth century – according to Elizabeth Randell Upton is the result of undue emphasis on the relatively small number of pieces that make a deliberate essay into notational complexity;[63] the term arguably says more about twentieth-century modernism and the lure of the avant-garde than it does about the music to which it refers. Nevertheless 'subtlety' is a term frequently used for music from 1300 onwards as a guarded kind of praise – the refined thread of a fabric, but perhaps for its detractors signalling unnecessarily recondite and self-aggrandizing compositional practice. However, it seems likely that this usage derives from a topos of ambivalence towards the subtlety of the moderns conventional from at least the twelfth century.[64]

En la maison Dedalus (Figure 5.1) is copied in a single manuscript now housed in the Jean Gray Hargrove Music Library, University of California, Berkeley.[65] The other contents of this source are a music theory

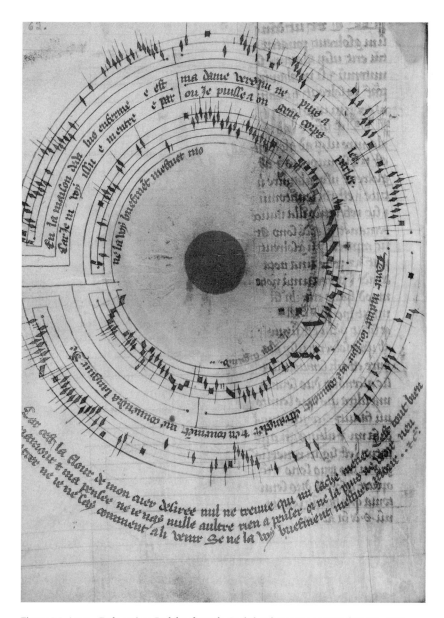

Figure 5.1 Anon., *En la maison Dedalus*, from the Berkeley theory manuscript (*US-BEm* 744, fol. 31v)

treatise completed in 1377, which covers modes, discant and mensuration, speculative theory, and tuning of semitones (including advanced *musica ficta*). The balade makes visual use of a circular maze that symbolizes the 'house of Dedalus', that is, the maze that Dedalus designed and built for the Minotaur. The poem compares this to the path to the lady, who is at the heart of a maze with no entry or exit. The musical staves form the tracks of an 11-course labyrinth, which has been drawn with a pair of compasses. The top voice negotiates its way through the maze by singing the song; the two lower parts are notated as one part, sung in canon – the contratenor chasing after the tenor through the maze. The pair of compasses is to the architect of the maze what the composition of the canon is to the composer – a 'symbol of complex artistry, super-human craftsmanship'. The path of the maze is difficult to follow yet 'it cleverly leads both to the centre and to a successful performance of the music'.[66] Aside from the use of the circular format, the other aspects of this song's complexity can be found already in the music of Machaut. His rondeau *Ma fin* (R14) also has a canon, drawn attention to by the visual aspect of the notation (upside down text), and its text voices the commands of the song telling the singer how to sing it (something that *En la maison* does not do, but which is common in several other so-called Ars Subtilior songs).[67] Machaut also projects the same kind of strong authorial persona, which claims his craft as his own and as a feat of art. In fact *En la maison* cites from other balades by Machaut: its line 1.5 is line 2.3 of his *Nes qu'on porroit* (B33), its line 1.2 is similar to B33's 2.1, and the refrain is very similar to that of Machaut's poem without music *Trop de peinne* (Lo164). The composer clearly knew Machaut's piece and perhaps elevates his own creativity by remaking something of Machaut, the great Dedalus of book, song and music.

One of the biggest problems in the standard periodization of the fourteenth century is that it depends on a teleological narrative not only of notation but also of style. Moreover, the relation between style and chronology is circular. All written musical collections are by definition retrospective and often transmit several decades of musical repertory. For the combination of their pristine sources and sheer numbers, Machaut's works provide a particular point of reference, although the assumption that the ordering of the manuscript represents chronology seems questionable given Machaut's interest in order for other, more aesthetic and semiotic purposes.[68] The style of other secular pieces has generally been assessed by comparison to Machaut's work, with songs of similar style dated to his lifetime. However, the criteria for stylistic features tend to be interdependent on the notational features mentioned above, which does not allow for the notational updating of pieces (a feature that certainly occurred in the Italian tradition), nor for the deliberate use of older styles. It imposes a notational teleology that certainly is hard to sustain outside the central French tradition.[69]

The role of the poetry in dating is not particularly straightforward either. Viewed as a whole, the tendency during the fourteenth century is towards standardization, especially in the production of isometric balade stanzas.[70] But as a trend, this feature is not precise enough to allow dating of individual instances; there is also evidence that some poems considerably predate their settings.[71]

Arguably the greatest chronological challenge that the fourteenth century suffers is to be regarded as the last of the Middle Ages, rather than an early Renaissance. Certain scholars have questioned this historiographical pigeonholing and its detrimental effect on attitudes. Vitry has been praised for his humanism, his early reading of Dante and his friendship with Petrarch.[72] Machaut has been embraced as the first 'writerly' author figure for musical culture, the first vernacular *poète*, and the first poet-composer to have an elegy in words and polyphonic music composed for his death.[73] Christopher Page has laid out the innovations of the thirteenth and fourteenth centuries to claim that it is 'all Renaissance' from 1200 onwards.[74] Other musicologists have looked back to the earliest coverage of the music of this period in standard textbooks to show that it is only a historical accident that music textbooks picked a later date than comparable disciplines.[75] Certainly in terms of a concern with the human and with classical antiquity, Vitry's motet texts seem obvious candidates for an earlier musical Renaissance, but the 'medievalist' interest in the eschatological, the ethical, and the afterlife continued well into the fifteenth century and beyond.

PART TWO

Topography

6 England

PETER M. LEFFERTS

English musical life in the Middle Ages is often treated in standard text-book surveys as peripheral to that of France and Italy. This approach has several causes, but is rooted especially in musicology's preoccupation over the past 150 years of scholarship with medieval France. Noteworthy also in this negligence is the pairing of France and Italy late in the era in the emergence of polyphonic refrain songs as the chief new artefacts of secular high music culture in the 1300s, an attractive trend with no contemporary English-language counterpart. Musicology's paradigmatic narrative of English entrance onto the international stage, through its sacred polyphonic music, once began the story only in the second quarter of the fifteenth century.

What emerges, however, from more extended examination of medieval musical life is that modern political, geographic, linguistic and cultural boundaries are not relevant – for high culture, anyway – in the musical affairs of those parts of northwestern Europe we nowadays identify as France and England. And until this essentially homogeneous Anglo-French cultural sphere began to develop some marked regional differentiations in the thirteenth century, the elite and hermetic worlds both of courtly troubadour and trouvère song, and of the chant and polyphony of the church, spanned the English Channel effortlessly. The English were not latecomers to a game already being played elsewhere.[1]

Further, a burst of research after the Second World War has provided specialists with a much different and expanded sense of the dimensions, vigour and creativity of medieval English musical life in the thirteenth and fourteenth centuries as it diverged from shared Anglo-French practice. This discovery has been mirrored in recent decades by the extraordinary amount of attention lavished on medieval English music in concerts and recordings by leading ensembles of the Early Music movement in Europe and North America.[2]

To gain a perspective on the English contribution to medieval music, it will be helpful to refer to the standard threefold division of music and music making that distinguishes between classical, popular and folk music realms. This categorization is admittedly a very simple one, and it is a means of isolating activities that can deeply interpenetrate one another. Nonetheless it is sturdy enough to be of value. For the nearest equivalent to classical music, we can ask where across the soundscape of medieval Europe there was music that was elite, esoteric, demanding, rigorous and prestigious, requiring not only skill to perform but training to create and an education in taste to appreciate. This is music that was deliberately preserved over time in memory and written record. One such body of music is the plainchant and polyphony of the Western church. Another is secular art songs in Latin and the vernacular, the music of learned clerics and aristocratic high culture.

Popular music is a repertory of more immediate appeal, accessible to listeners across a wider range of social classes and available to hear in less exclusive venues. An entertainment music subject to rapid turnover and without the formation of any permanent written canon of favourites, popular music of any age showcases the performer and is a performer's repertoire. This would have been the most common offering of medieval minstrels, whether in residence in some nobleman's court, working as the local professional in a village or town, or belonging to the itinerant minstrel population.

Folk or traditional music encompasses those songs and dance tunes known by most members of a society. It is the communal repertory carried in memory, preserved for generations, accessible to amateurs, and not necessarily created or performed for profit – thus encompassing but by no means limited to metrical charms and incantations, mothers' lullabies, children's play songs, tunes that lightened the repetitive labour of farmers and the marching of soldiers, and fiddle tunes that quickened the feet. Folk, popular and classical music are not synonymous with lower-, middle- and upper-class music, but while all classes had contact with folk and popular music, the music of the social and educational elite was not as readily available to the lower orders of society.

Accepting the threefold division just outlined, one can move directly to a major point: medieval English folk and popular music do not survive. The ample testimony in documentary archives, in literature and in visual imagery for this kind of music making is not balanced by extant lyrics and melodies. The reason for such a regrettable loss is clear. Although surely known to the literate classes of society, folk and popular music were not preserved by or for that class; those individuals competent to notate such texts and tunes were never given a mandate to do so. We can rail against the literate snobs, but more is at work here that also needs to be acknowledged. For one, literacy meant an education in Latin and an embedded set of biases about what would or would not be committed to writing. Further, from 1066 until the fifteenth century the English upper classes were French-speakers by birth or necessity. Popular and folk musics of medieval England were mainly the province of English speakers, creating a cultural divide not often crossed. Folk musicians in an oral tradition, moreover, would not have needed notation, and one can imagine that minstrels might even have resisted it, as a threat to the trade secrets of their guild.

Finally, a broader perspective. In the twentieth century the West's popular music, commercialized and commodified, became the world's shared music, but this was not always the case. The secular culture shared across linguistic and geographic boundaries used to be high culture, while folk and popular culture were at once less universal, more varied, less transportable. In medieval England most folk and popular music, like dialect, diet, dress, dance steps and recipes for ale, reflected local custom and taste. There was no demand for it elsewhere, and no compelling need to write it down in order to preserve it for others in the present, or for posterity.

The little scraps of medieval folk and popular music that come down to us from the British Isles are to be found in various odd corners, and mainly give us glimpses of texts, not tunes. Beginning in the thirteenth century, for example, Franciscan sermons cite titles and quote lyric fragments and refrains from the kinds of less-refined vernacular songs they assumed their audiences would be familiar with. And a fourteenth-century English Bishop of Ossory in Ireland, Richard Ledrede, wrote new sacred Latin texts to a large number of vernacular songs in English and Anglo-Norman, identifying the original tune with a text tag and preserving for us in the Latin, something like a dinosaur's footprint, the poetic form and stress patterns of the originals. In addition, English motets of the later thirteenth and early fourteenth centuries, like their Continental counterparts, sometimes build up their superstructure of new melodies and texts over a pre-existing foundational melody – the tenor – that is a Middle English or Anglo-Norman song instead of a plainchant fragment (*Dou way Robin; Wynter; A definement d'este lerray*); some of these may be popular songs or folksongs. Quodlibets that stitch together the musical street cries of London vendors survive from the late sixteenth century, and comparable French street cries already are found incorporated in late-thirteenth- and fourteenth-century Continental polyphony, so it may be that the Elizabethan snatches can be fairly heard as echoes from earlier English days.[3]

Another temptation is to hear in the tunefulness, tonal cogency, symmetry and metrical bounce of thirteenth-century polyphonic songs in Middle English and Latin such as *Sumer is icumen in, Edi beo thu hevene quene*, and *Angelus ad virginem* the hallmarks of a British popular or folk style. The temptation is equally strong to see otherwise hidden vernacular idioms as the basis for the language of the few instrumental dances to have been captured in notation.[4] And it is hard to doubt that the foursquare fifteenth-century partsong *Tappster, drinker, fille another ale* is meant to evoke a hearty popular vein of tavern songs of which no authentic examples survive. Tuneful simplicity and harmonic directness remain attractive features of the indigenous English partsongs of Cornysh and others up through the early Tudor period.[5]

Of course, some of the literary monuments of high culture, from the corpus of Old English poetry to the lengthy metrical romances in Anglo-Norman and Middle English and the shorter Middle English ballads, have their roots in an oral tradition of popular songs. Although now stripped of melody and standing at some remove from performance as later finished products of a bookish environment, they surely retain some of the flavour of their lost lyrical predecessors. It is equally likely that some of the lower registers of courtly art song, such as the pastourelle, deliberately invoke the metrical and melodic idioms of popular and folk music, especially the communal dance songs, the karoles. But it is beyond our present powers to distinguish a music thought appropriate for playing at being shepherds and shepherdesses from music truly of the rural peasantry.

Concerning the elite art music of Britain's learned and noble classes, a number of observations demand priority. Above all, this music was song, primarily solo song, and often unaccompanied. And the rich and educated were often themselves the wordsmiths and tunesmiths, while performers were of the lower classes. Lyrical and narrative poetry comprise its texts, and these texts most often survive in anthologies copied without any musical notation. Thus they have become grist for the modern mill of literary studies, with the presence of music underappreciated or forgotten. We need to be reminded, for example, that while some genres of Old English poetry may have been intended from the outset to be merely spoken out loud, the central body of eulogistic and epic narratives known to us was to be sung in public performance. Drawing models for narrative melody from ethnomusicogical examples found outside Western Europe, as well as from medieval examples from France, Germany and the Latin liturgy, modern Early Music singers now offer large swatches of *Beowulf* to paying audiences, trusting that the Old English text of this famous epic in its surviving form is not too many steps removed from its sung version in an oral tradition.[6]

A second principal observation is that the texts of elite art songs varied across a wide range of topics and registers of discourse. One might turn elegant phrases in praise of some lady's virtue while another lauded the joys of clear, red wine or described the amorous advances of Robin upon Marion. And some were surely intended exclusively for listening, while others were participatory dance songs. Elite songs of low register are not folk or popular music, however, although their texts and tunes may have been enriched with the turns of phrase of more mundane genres, as surmised above.

The role of the performer can be informative in regard to song registers and song audiences.[7] In Anglo-Saxon England, the *gleoman* was the professional entertainer, paid for individual performances, who not only sang but harped and piped, juggled, clowned and danced. The *scop*, on the other hand, was a serious and respected individual attached to a court or noble household who made and performed heroic, epic narrative poetry on ceremonial occasions. After the Norman Conquest, a single term, 'minstrel', dominates in British records, but the word clearly had a number of meanings encompassing a variety of duties and spheres of activities. Royal or noble minstrels attached to a court or household had very different duties and occasions for performance than did town musicians, or those travelling professionals perpetually on the go between courts, villages, festivals and fairs. A minstrel who straddled both worlds, called to court one night and playing in an alehouse the next, knew his role and repertory in both spheres.

A third principal observation about the elite secular song repertory of medieval England is that it was polylingual. In Anglo-Saxon times that meant Latin and Old English. After the Norman Conquest, that meant Latin, Anglo-Norman French, and Middle English. The least important of these for over three centuries – until the days of Chaucer and his contemporaries and successors – were the art songs in English. (The ribbon for the least appreciated and most seldom read of these lyrics nowadays would have to go to Latin, of course.) The pattern for survival in the British Isles of later medieval songs of high culture is the same whether they are in Latin, French or English: there are major insular sources of lyrics, mostly copied without music or any accommodation for musical notation, and a much smaller number of sources with empty staves or notated melodies.

Latin lyrics, whether from the international tradition or local products composed in Anglo-Latin, and whether scribbled onto flyleaves or copied into large anthologies, constitute an important and numerous body of medieval British song texts. Their range of subject matter and tone is impressive, from love poetry, humorous stories, and drinking songs to historical narratives and sacred, devotional, philosophical and moral-satirical topics. This was music for the study and recreation of Latinate clerics, bureaucrats, and scholars and students.

Vernacular songs with musical notation are particularly scarce. From before ca1400 there are merely some twenty-odd such songs extant in English and and a similar number in Anglo-Norman. But well-known anthology manuscripts assemble a very much greater number of lyrics and narrative poems intended for singing. These songs, secular or religious, vary widely in topic and tone. The most striking difference between the corpus in each language is the absence of English courtly love lyrics until the fifteenth century, while courtly love is a strong thematic presence in the French songs.[8]

Forces on the Continent propelled the collection of troubadour and trouvère songs into chansonniers in the second half of the thirteenth century – only at the very end of that tradition and almost two centuries after its beginnings. This anthologizing project, with its retrospective, preservationist and monumentalizing overtones, is clearly reflected in major British text collections of the same era. For those who coveted these books, whether as prize trophies or as reading material, the song texts evidently were a much higher priority than their tunes. Very few of the surviving Continental anthologies contain music, a loss felt particularly acutely in the case of the trouvère chanson, for which ten times as many lyrics survive as melodies. From the British Isles, only one scrappy flyleaf of this era (Oxford, Bodleian Library, Rawlinson G. 22), with all or part of two songs in Anglo-Norman and one in Middle English, may have originated in a substantial secular chansonnier that was notated with music. The loss of melodies that did not make it from memory into written record must have been considerable. It is not so clear that we have lost many songbooks copied for noble English patrons.

The making of books of art songs needs to be understood as an enterprise related to but not synonymous with the making of music by and for medieval England's secular high culture. And, as a corollary point, historians of English culture cannot make do with only what was created on English soil or what survives in codices of English manufacture. During the twelfth-century reign of Henry II and Eleanor of Aquitaine the English court was often on the Continent for long periods, and the rich outpouring of literary products for this court, including verse chronicles, epics, romances, lais, fables and lyric poetry in French and Latin, was copied and appreciated across western Europe. The domestic and dynastic struggles of the Plantagenets inspired songs in Latin, Provençal, French and Italian. The son of Henry and Eleanor, Richard I ('the Lionheart'), was himself a poet-musician, writing in French; two of his poems survive, one with music, in troubadour and trouvère sources.

As late as the mid fourteenth century the court was still intensely francophile, most importantly through the circle of Continental artists and men of letters around Philippa of Hainaut, queen of Edward III. No monumental codices or collected works of individual composers survive from this environment, perhaps because there was no one dominating musician approaching the stature enjoyed by Machaut in France (and he himself had to supervise several editions of his own collected works). But bits and scraps of musical sources hint at a repertory of courtly polyphonic art song in French, just as we would expect.

By the turn into the fifteenth century, courtly songs by English musicians, surviving in insular and Continental sources in increasing numbers, show them to be setting secular love lyrics in English and French in the fixed forms of the rondeau, virelai and ballade, and then beginning to favour rime royal. John Dunstable, John Bedingham, Robertus de Anglia, Robert Morton and Walter Frye are representative composers of such songs. The polyphonic English devotional carol in English and Latin is an important indigenous product of the same era that did not circulate abroad. Not the music of the noble courts but not the music of the people either, the carol appears to have been a repertory primarily for recreational use at Christmas and Eastertime in the world of the scholars, fellows and singing-men of schools, colleges and major ecclesiastical choral establishments.[9]

It may strike some initially as odd that Christian service music counts as high culture, since it is functional material not created or performed for entertainment's sake and was nominally available to be heard in church by all classes of society. But important qualifiers need to be put upon the latter points. Although functional, it is yet a complex, artful and esoteric body of music, preserved in writing since the ninth century. And although in later medieval England there were more than 10,000 parish churches and many hundreds of major churches and religious houses, as well as eventually seventeen cathedrals, only a fraction had the wealth and trained manpower to support the full sung daily liturgy at regular intervals around the clock, and to undertake the complexities of florid organum and mensural polyphony.

The endless cycle of the liturgy, moreover, was undertaken on behalf of the populace, rather than for an attentive worshipping congregation. That is, secure in the knowledge that they were being prayed for, the laity seldom stepped into sacred precincts on a regular basis until the very end of our era. And the physical enclosure of the choir, a later medieval development creating a building within a building beyond the rood screen in the transept or east end of the church, cut visitors off from the sight and sound of the high mass and canonical offices. In this respect, the Early Music movement does us a disservice by popularizing concerts and recordings of chant and church polyphony in the resonant, bare stone caverns that surviving medieval churches, especially the large abbeys and cathedrals, have become.

In overview, the history of the liturgy and music of the medieval Christian church in the British Isles is best grasped as a series of overlapping waves of practices and influences.[10] These begin with the separate introduction of early Christianity by Celts and Romans in the second century. About their services and music we know nothing, and the invasions of the pagan Anglo-Saxons in the mid 400s, after the withdrawal of the Romans, extinguished Romano-British Christianity. The church survived in Celtic Britain, however, and missionaries from Gaul were found proselytizing among the Anglo-Saxons when Pope Gregory sent Saint Augustine to Kent in 597. Over the next century Roman customs were established and some form of Roman chanting was disseminated throughout England, but it is undoubtedly the case that local liturgy and chant dialects varied considerably, drifting and evolving away from Rome during this era just as did the Gallican rite in France, the Mozarabic rite in Iberia or the Milanese (Ambrosian) rite in northern Italy. The process is entirely analogous to the early development of Romance languages out of regional dialects of Latin.

Whatever the nature of early Anglo-Saxon liturgy and chanting, it was virtually wiped out in the catastrophic waves of Danish invasion in the mid 800s. The revival of both the secular church and monastic communities initiated under King Alfred at the end of the ninth century, which culminated with the efforts of church leaders such as Dunstan and Ethelwold a century later, relied on northern French missionaries who brought in the customs and music of the religious houses at Cluny, Fleury, Corbie and St Denis. The liturgy they promulgated was mainly a modern Roman liturgy for its day in respect to texts and customs, but the chant dialect in which it was sung was not from the South. It had originated in the later 700s and early 800s in Carolingian Gaul, and its melodies were in the Romano-Frankish or Romano-Gallican hybrid we call Gregorian chant. Thus later Anglo-Saxon England became one of the first regions outside Gaul to adopt the melodic corpus that would by the thirteenth century supplant local chant-families all across Europe, eventually even displacing papal and local Roman urban chant. Textual sources document the later Anglo-Saxon liturgy reasonably well and reveal many small divergences in detail from Roman practices. These older Gallicanisms and indigenous customs would have been sung to older, local, non-Gregorian plainsong.

The core repertory of Gregorian chant comprised simple formulaic tones for prayers and readings, and melodies for antiphonal and responsorial psalmody. In addition to holdovers from older local practices, this body of plainsong was enriched wherever it took hold by new local accretions, which in time became a vast and diverse body of later medieval plainchant for mass and office, including proses in the office and sequences at mass, mass ordinary melodies, new hymns and hymn melodies, Marian and other votive antiphons, processional antiphons, sung liturgical dramas, and much more. English church musicians enthusiastically contributed to these and other categories of later chant composition right up to the reign of Henry VIII and the establishment of the Church of England.

In respect to later medieval chant, the word 'trope' is sometimes used to identify all additions to the Gregorian nucleus. Trope has a narrower meaning, however, when referring just to short musical-textual versicles added later as introductions to lines of Gregorian chant and other pre-existing plainsong. A large Anglo-Saxon repertory of these chant expansions survives in manuscripts of the late tenth and eleventh centuries that were copied at Winchester and Canterbury; the trope melodies cannot be read, but their Latin texts show hallmarks of the Latinity of late Anglo-Saxon authors, and a good number may be the work of one individual, Wulfstan of Winchester.[11]

New saints and new feasts, whether of local or universal celebration, were added prolifically to church calendars throughout the later Middle Ages. These additions might be marked by as little as a single chanted item such as a collect, antiphon, hymn or sequence, but many were provided with a complete set of new texts and melodies for all the Proper chants for daily offices and mass. This body of material could total fifty or more substantial compositions. Anglo-Saxon poet-composers poured significant creativity and energy into offices for local saints, including those for Alphege, Birinus, Cuthbert, Edmund, Guthlac and Swithun.[12]

A different means of elaborating the Gregorian core that was instituted or revived in the tenth-century English church was the singing of two-part polyphony (called organum, pl. organa) by ornamenting a liturgical plainsong with a note-against-note counterpoint. A large corpus of 173 organa survives from pre-Conquest Winchester and may also be primarily the work of Wulfstan of Winchester. They constitute the only major body of European polyphony to survive from before the mid twelfth century. Due to difficulties interpreting the insular chant notation, transcription of this music into modern notation is difficult, but it is not impossible, granting us a modicum of insight into the versions of the underlying chants that were used, and the procedures and aesthetics of making organa circa 1000.[13]

In the wake of the Conquest, Norman clerics took control of the English church, overlaying Norman chants and melodic dialect (in effect just a slightly different flavour of Gregorian) over earlier traditions and purging its liturgy of unfamiliar saints and customs, a process resisted by English clergy in some quarters for many years. Every religious community developed its own distinctive rules for the conduct of its liturgical and non-liturgical routines; these were known as its 'use'. In England, post-Conquest changes were consolidated into uses for the major secular cathedrals over the course of the twelfth century. Of these, the use of Salisbury cathedral rose to pre-eminence. It eventually displaced the local use at many other cathedrals, was adopted in chantries, colleges and private chapels, and even spread abroad into dioceses from Portugal to Scandinavia. The ritual and music of Salisbury (or Sarum, an abbreviated nickname current since the Middle Ages) were essentially Roman and Gregorian, with an admixture of local elements. The ritual's attractiveness and success were due not to its chant versions *per se*, but rather to its perceived authority, splendour, elaboration, comprehensiveness and full documentation.[14]

A softening of Norman attitudes eventually permitted the retention of many Anglo-Saxon saints in British church calendars alongside Norman and Angevin saints. The further admission of new local or universal saints, and of feasts such as Corpus Christi, the Transfiguration and the Holy Name of Jesus, continued right down to the very end of the Middle Ages. These new feasts provided one of the most important impulses for new chant composition (a phenomenon by no means limited to England) and stimulated a creative musical outpouring that has not yet been fully appreciated, much less catalogued or studied. The most important of the slew of new British offices was the celebrated rhymed office for Thomas of Canterbury, composed in the last quarter of the twelfth century by Abbot Benedict of Peterborough. This office travelled over the whole of Continental Europe, where it became the model for perhaps hundreds of later offices.

A number of religious ceremonies falling mainly outside the canonical daily round of high mass and offices and in some cases performed outside of the high choir, although not necessarily unique to late medieval England were of particular importance there. They became the locus not only of ritual elaboration but of the composition of new chants and the performance of polyphony. Processions are one such class of ceremonies. On Sundays, major feast days and other special occasions, processions wound a circuitous route through the church, or out onto the grounds, or out into town to a neighbouring church and back, and they generated a special repertory of processional refrain hymns, antiphons and responsories. Another set of ceremonies, for Holy Week and Easter, included not only major processions but also the singing of the biblical Passion narratives during mass as the New Testament gospel on Palm Sunday and Good Friday. Missals of the Salisbury Use carefully indicate a dramatic approach and separation of character roles for the reading of the Passion texts, and polyphonic English passions are the earliest in a prominent and long-standing European tradition. In many locales, moreover, there was the performance of two fully sung Latin liturgical dramas – the *Visitatio sepulchri* at the end of matins early on Easter Sunday morning and the *Officium peregrinorum* at vespers that evening. Music was also a significant element in the primarily spoken Middle English vernacular dramas of Eastertide and Corpus Christi.[15]

A final set of additional devotions – commemorations and votive services, memorials and votive antiphons – rose to be of the greatest musical importance. By the late Middle Ages they could overshadow or even replace most of the standard daily ritual and music in institutions committed to the fullest expression of the liturgy.[16] Memorials were short services said in the morning after lauds or in the evening after vespers in honour of a saint or other particular occasions. A memorial consisted simply of one principal musical item – an antiphon – plus a versicle, response and collect;

a number of such memorials might be said in a row. A votive antiphon could be sung by itself, usually in the evening after compline outside the high choir at a side altar. The most popular votive antiphons were Marian, and by the mid thirteenth century the post-compline antiphon had been absorbed into a full-fledged Marian memorial often referred to as the Salve service, after the Marian votive antiphon *Salve regina.* The Salve service was incorporated in the customs of many new secular choral foundations of the late fourteenth and fifteenth centuries and was frequently required by the legislation of the most elaborately endowed private chantries, while its polyphonic Marian antiphon became one of the grandest musical forms of late medieval England.

Commemorations were complete sets of office hours and in some cases a full mass, too, that were said weekly in choir on a specified day for the Virgin Mary or Holy Cross or some particular saint (such as the patron saint of the church), replacing the ordinary daily round of services and transposable to another day if in conflict with a significant feast. By the fifteenth century some churches had a commemoration for every day of the week. By long and universal custom, Saturday was Mary's special day, and her weekly commemoration was thus observed vastly more often than any of her feasts. It was enriched in English service books by a great deal of supplementary or alternative plainsong, including many new sequences for example, and also attracted polyphony.

Instead of replacing the daily liturgy, as in the case of commemorations, the services called votive masses and offices were additions to it. The Little Hours of the Virgin, for example, came to be sung after each of the regular hours (and provided the nucleus of texts found in the medieval Book of Hours). Eventually of even greater importance for music and ceremony was the daily votive Marian mass (the Lady Mass), usually celebrated outside of choir as a morning mass for devout layfolk around the time of prime. This service was nearly universal in major English ecclesiastical institutions by the early thirteenth century. Not only did it attract a great deal of new plainsong (including tropes, and series of alternative melodies for the Sequence, Offertory, and Sanctus), but it was for Lady Mass that most or all of the surviving insular polyphonic settings of the mass ordinary from circa 1200 to 1400 (and a large proportion of the settings composed afterwards) were written. It is likely the case, moreover, that the fourteenth-century French adoption of the custom of setting mass ordinary texts polyphonically for votive Marian masses (as in the Missa Tournai and the Mass of Machaut) is modelled on English practice.

Two late medieval developments eventually brought the liturgy back to the eyes and ears of the laity. One was the cult of the Virgin Mary, as expressed in the services described above. From the mid twelfth century onwards Mary not only inspired new services, new chants, and polyphony, but also new architectural spaces in which to house those services, which were often deliberately made accessible to lay audiences. England led the way in these regards. The daily morning Lady Mass and evening Salve service, performed outside of choir, usually in a purpose-built hall extending off the church called the Lady Chapel, became the most important occasions for regular attendance at church by the lay public, especially devout women.

The other development increasing lay exposure to the liturgy and to complex polyphony was the rise of new choral musical establishments outside of churches and monasteries.[17] Their model in Britain was the Royal Household Chapel, an itinerant body always in attendance on the king, which spawned a vogue of personal chapels for the great magnates of the land in the fourteenth and fifteenth centuries. Similar choirs, but of fixed abode, were founded by aristocratic patronage in chantry chapels, in larger metropolitan churches and in the colleges at Oxford and Cambridge, especially during the fifteenth century. Their services, inside or outside of choir, would have had a small but select and appreciative audience. Again, polyphonic Marian antiphons and mass ordinary settings were a staple for these new professional choirs on those private and public occasions requiring their most ostentatious efforts.

The uniformity of the Anglo-French high culture of sophisticated church music began to erode in the thirteenth century with the emergence of a clear differentiation in genres, musical style and notation on opposite sides of the Channel, primarily in polyphony. This drift apart is mirrored as well in politics, and in a variety of trends such as in the shift of the Anglo-Norman dialect away from mainland French, in features of Gothic cathedral architecture, and in various specialized intellectual disciplines at the universities. In terms of musical style the trend towards a distinctive insular musical dialect in church polyphony can probably best be explained as a concentration upon certain elements already present in the international repertory of polyphonic conductus and organum of the later twelfth and early thirteenth centuries. It may well be (and it is certainly an attractive hypothesis) that these new preferences derive from an awareness by elite English church musicians of the language of the popular and traditional music of the British Isles, and their growing desire to play up these indigenous features in more sophisticated music.

This new polyphonic dialect was distinguished by a preference for imperfect consonances (thirds, sixths and tenths) as harmonies, for voice-leading in parallel counterpoint, for trochaic rhythms in ternary metres, for chordal textures and homogeneity of rhythmic activity, for smoothly stepwise melodies projecting a strong sense of tonality, and for balanced, four-square

melodic phrases. By the late thirteenth century an English motet or conductus sounded different and behaved palpably differently from its French
counterpart. Another marked feature of the emerging English idiom was
a fascination with constructivist devices involving repetition and exchange
of music. In simplest form this could be no more than a *rota* or round, a
perpetual canon at the unison, of which the Sumer canon (*Sumer is icumen in*, ca1250) is the most famous example. Voice exchange proceeds in
a series of modules within which a foundational voice (the tenor) states
and repeats a melody, over which two upper parts sing, and then exchange
and sing again, two harmonious counterpointing lines. In a *rondellus* all
three voices participate in the exchange, so that in the module each contrapuntal unit must be stated three times (with swapping of parts) before
moving on to fresh material. Modules of voice exchange and rondellus can
be found in conductus, in motets and in troped chant settings, which are
the three most important compositional genres of late-thirteenth-century
English polyphony; modules of voice exchange and rondellus also stand on
their own in independent compositions that are kin to both conductus and
motet.[18]

The notation of polyphonic music evolved across the thirteenth and
fourteenth centuries towards a fully mensural system with fixed rhythmic
values for each note shape and the means to represent a variety of time
signatures. An aspect of the differentiation of practice between England and
the Continent was the development of an idiosyncratic English Mensural
Notation in the thirteenth century and of several families of notation that
accommodated different means and rationales for the multiplication and
subdivisions of the *brevis* in the first half of the fourteenth century, in
parallel with developments in France and Italy. English theorists engaged
with their Continental counterparts as early as the 1310s in the development
of what is called Ars Nova notation, particularly via *gradus* theory, and
made interesting proposals for the notation and cancellation of chromatic
alterations. Not only was their work cited by French and Italian theorists,
but entire theory treatises (in Latin) by Englishmen circulated abroad, and
English theorists travelled abroad to teach and to copy important treatises
up to the late fifteenth century.[19]

Fourteenth- and fifteenth-century English sacred polyphonic genres
included the motet, votive antiphon, cantilena with hymn or sequence-
style text, and settings of mass ordinary texts.[20] The motet eventually shook
free of the constructivist devices described above, but its composers continued to explore a number of indigenous motet types until deep in the
fourteenth century. Their growing fascination with the numerical disposition of phrase structures and the proportioning of section lengths may have
had a direct influence on the nascent continental isorhythmic motet in the

1310s and 1320s. English isorhythmic motets flourished into the mid 1400s in the hands of composers including Dunstaple, Forest and Benet.

The other sacred genres at first shared two compositional approaches: 'cantilena-style' free composition in two to four voices, and English discant, a three-voice technique of adding two counterpointing lines to a chant. Then composers began to develop approaches for mass ordinary settings that borrowed from contemporaneous techniques for motets and polyphonic secular songs to create more elaborate works. Large-scale mass ordinary settings, whether freely composed or based on a cantus firmus, began to be written in pairs and longer cycles in the early decades of the fifteenth century, resulting in the five-movement English mass in three and then in four voices, with its movements linked by common musical material, most especially by the same tenor cantus firmus.

English cyclic masses, isorhythmic motets, and large-scale antiphons – the polyphonic repertory of its most elite and up-to-date chapels and churches – came to be enormously popular and influential in mainland Europe by 1450. This music was enjoyed, and exerted great influence, in that similarly small, elite world of Continental listeners capable of appreciating its beauty and of Continental choirs equipped to tackle its complexity.

7 Italy to 1300

MARCO GOZZI

We still know very little about medieval music in Italy: our knowledge of the repertory performed at that time is based on a very small number of surviving sources. Only a minuscule part of the repertory of Christian liturgical chant is documented, and, even then, only partially; there are no in-depth studies about the pieces collected in more recent codices and early printed editions; and the greatest part of music, of so-called 'popular' song and the global 'sound landscape', is beyond investigation. We also know very little about the nature of the creation and transmission of the main kinds of musical practice in the Middle Ages, that is, about the mainly oral tradition of songs, performance practices (both vocal and instrumental) and the occasional recourse to writing (which is a very unusual event in a culture based on memory on account of the scarcity of books).

What follows must, therefore, be read with the awareness that it is a series of necessarily fragmentary observations, which should be considered within a very rich and complex cultural and social frame, furthermore, a frame which does not have, and may never have, well-defined boundaries. Too many cultural connections escape us, too many songs have disappeared forever, and too many musical details of the few sources that do survive are irremediably lost (the kinds of temperament used, the different kinds of pronunciation of Latin and of the vernaculars, the different kinds of vocal technique, the extempore inventions of added voices, the embellishments used by singers, the role of instruments, and so on). Modern readers will not, therefore, satisfy their curiosity to know, for example, what Dante's mother sang to make her son fall asleep or what exactly was played and sung for the dancing at Castel del Monte, in 1249, during the wedding of Violante, natural daughter of Federico II, to Riccardo, count of Caserta.

Liturgical chant

The main institution responsible for the preservation and diffusion of Christian liturgical chant in Europe was the school. In monastic and cathedral schools chant was a fundamental ingredient in the education of boys.

Medieval schools had very different methods from today's, in terms of both curricula and the methods of study, which were mainly mnemonic.[1] School was largely responsible for the way learned people in the Middle Ages experienced knowledge and books. It was in school that students came into contact with liturgical chant not only, and not mainly, as a musical experience, but as a cultural and spiritual experience, in a unity of knowledge and personal feeling unknown to the modern student. Through hymns and sequences, for example, children learned Latin, prosody and theological reflection; they also learned to appreciate poetry, learning by heart (with the help of fine melodies) a great number of poetic texts in Latin, some at a very high level.

Furthermore, the curricula of monastic and cathedral schools in Italy reveal an extraordinary homogeneity with those of schools all over Europe, so that an Italian teacher could teach in England or in Spain without much, if any, difficulty. This kind of formation thus created a supra-national cultural and spiritual community, as well as a shared knowledge that allowed frequent and fruitful exchanges.

The second element which should be observed is the great mobility of the clergy during the Middle Ages: secular clergy, but above all friars and monks, moved very frequently and without being overly concerned about the huge distances involved. This phenomenon created unexpected but deep links between distant parts of Christian Europe, even in the liturgical and musical fields.

The essential features of the history and of the repertory of Christian liturgical chant were thus shared all over Europe and are outlined in chapters 1 and 2 in this volume. To investigate the local peculiarities of liturgical music, one resorts to the study of non-musical manuscripts, such as the ordinals[2] and rituals, both of which still lack sufficient attention from modern editors and analysts. Indeed the evaluation of editions of liturgical books must not be neglected: missals, breviaries, graduals, antiphonaries, psalteries, processionals, ceremonials, rituals, pontificals, *officia* for Holy Week, even though belonging sometimes to the sixteenth century, may transmit very old chants (or only texts of chants) and ritual traditions.

Two important aspects in relation to plainchant are documented by Italian manuscripts and editions: simple polyphony and *cantus fractus*. Italian ordinals have plenty of references to the practice of simple polyphony, that is, to the way of singing, extempore, a *vox organalis* as an addition to the traditional Gregorian melody (*vox principalis*), usually note against note. Only recently has this practice, which scholars first called 'cantus planus binatim' and then 'primitive polyphony', been the object of some attention; it is now called 'simple polyphony'.

Let us consider, for example, this short extract, from the *Liber Ordinarius* of the cathedral of Pistoia, datable to the end of the thirteenth or the first years of the fourteenth century (Pistoia, Biblioteca dell'Archivio Capitolare, C. 102, fol. 66r), in which the concept of accompanying another voice to form an organum, that is, to sing in simple polyphony, is expressed by the verb *succinere*, which recurs very often.

> De Nativitate beate virginis Marie . . . In Vesperis . . . *Regali ex progenie*, cuius responsorii principium succinitur sed non repetitur a choro; versus et *Ora pro nobis sancta Dei genitrix* succinitur; antiphona ad Magnificat *Celeste beneficium*, que prius canitur et post succinitur, et Benedicamus succinitur. Et attende quod hec festivitas sollempniter celebratur, nam *Venite* succinitur, et antiphone in quolibet nocturno ante psalmos cantantur et post succinitur; similiter versus et versiculi et antiphone ad *Ben.* et ad *Magn.* et Benedicamus succinitur. In Missa Kyrie, Sanctus et Agnus Dei succinitur.[3]

> On the Nativity of the Blessed Virgin Mary . . . at vespers . . . *Regali ex progenie*, the beginning of the responsory is sung in simple polyphony and is not repeated by the chorus; the versicle and *Ora pro nobis sancta Dei genitrix* are sung in simple polyphony; the antiphon to the Magnificat *Celeste beneficium* first is sung and is then accompanied by another voice, and the Benedicamus is also sung in simple polyphony. Be sure that the festivity is solemnly celebrated, that the Venite is sung in simple polyphony and the antiphons for each nocturne are sung before the psalms and in the repetition are accompanied; in the same way the verses, versicles, the antiphons to the Benedictus and the Magnificat and the Benedicamus Domino are sung in simple polyphony. In the Mass, the Kyrie, Sanctus and Agnus are sung in simple polyphony.

References to the practice of accompanying the main voice with one or more voices added extempore are, however, found already in two missals from the end of the tenth century (or the beginning of the eleventh) in central Italy, now in the Biblioteca Apostolica Vaticana: Vat. lat. 4770 and Barb. lat. 560. In the latter (fol. 66r), the rubrics regarding the last reading (*Prophetia*) of the Easter vigil mass are as follows:[4]

> ≪*Lectio libri Danihelis prophetae . . . in medio ignis dixerunt*≫, hic muta sonum in cantico ≪*Benedictus es Domine . . . per orbem terrarum*≫, et incipit legere in sono priore: ≪*Et non cessabant qui inmiserant eos . . . nec quicquam molestie intulit*≫. Hic canere incipit clerus cum organis: ≪*Tunc hi tres ex uno ore laudabant . . . superexalate eum in saecula*≫, et respondent omnes in choro: ≪*Amen*≫.

'Reading of the book of the prophet Daniel . . . in the midst of fire they said' [Daniel 3:1–25] – here the melody of the chant changes – 'Blessed be thou, Lord . . . for all the earth' [Daniel 3:26–45], and the main melody begins:

Example 7.1 First part of *Angelorum glorie / Pacem bonis* (Benedicamus trope) (*I-AO* 13, fol. 85r)

'And those who threw them inside did not stop . . . and the fire did not harm them' [Daniel 3:46–50]. Here the clergy start singing in simple polyphony: 'Then those three started to praise in one voice . . . exalt him for ever' [Daniel 3:51–75], and everyone answers in chorus 'Amen.'

Certainly this phenomenon of *amplification* of the Christian chant is very old, considering that already in the seventh century Roman *ordines* mention the 'paraphonistae', that is, those who sing the second voice.[5]

Usually the *vox organalis* is not written down: only in very few codices, often with a didactic use, do examples emerge which may explain the style of this practice.[6] One of these is the trope to the Benedicamus *Angelorum glorie*, which is found in the Aosta Codex, fol. 85r. Example 7.1 shows the first verse.

This is a version of the widespread trope *Verbum Patris* (known also with other texts, like *Stella fulget* etc.), which is found in numerous manuscript and printed sources, almost always with one voice, indicated as *vox principalis* in the example. The technique used here for the polyphonic amplification is shown and described in many medieval music treatises: the ninth-century manual *Musica Enchiriadis*; Guido d'Arezzo's *Micro-logus* (ca.1030); the *Ad organum faciendum* (second half of the eleventh century); the *De musica cum tonario* by Johannes Affligemensis (thirteenth century); the treatise known as 'anonymous of San Marziale' or 'anonymous De La Fage', maybe from the twelfth century but transmitted by fourteenth-century Italian and Spanish manuscripts; the *Expositiones tractatus . . . magistri Johannes de Mauris* by Prosdocimo de Beldemandis (who uses the phrase *cantus planus binatim* to describe the phenomenon); Franchino Gaffurio's *Practica musice*; and Johannes Tinctoris's *Liber de arte contrapuncti.*

Besides ordinals, cantatoría and other theoretical sources, the practice of singing *super librum* (also called *biscantare* or *discantare, organizare, tenere organum, secundare, succinere*) is documented by chronicles and literary sources. One short example is taken from the *Cronica* of Salimbene of Parma; written in the 1280s, it refers to events of the previous fifty years, and gives an idea of the diffusion of the phenomenon in Italy. Salimbene writes:

> Frater Henricus Pisanus . . . de resurrectione Domini fecit sequentiam, litteram et cantum, scilicet *Natus, passus Dominus resurrexit hodie.* Secundum vero cantum, qui ibi est, id est contracantum, fecit frater Vita ex Ordine fratrum Minorum de civitate Lucensi, melior cantor de mundo tempore suo in utroque cantu, scilicet firmo et fracto . . . Hic fecit illam sequentiam: *Ave, mundi spes, Maria,* litteram et cantum. Hic fecit multas cantilenas de cantu melodiato sive fracto, in quibus clerici seculares maxime delectantur. Hic fuit meus magister in cantu in civitate sua Lucensi eo anno quo sol ita horribiliter obscuratus fuit, MCCXXXIX.[7]

> Brother Enrico Pisano . . . composed text and music of a sequence for the Resurrection of the Lord, that is *Natus, passus, Dominus resurrexit hodie.* The second voice, that is the *contracantum*, was composed by brother Vita of the Franciscans in Lucca, the best cantor in the world in his time in chants both liturgical and measured . . . He [brother Vita] composed text and music of the sequence *Ave, mundi spes, Maria.* He composed many measured chants, with which many secular priests find delight. He was my singing teacher in his city, Lucca, during the year of the terrible solar eclipse, 1239.

Salimbene speaks very often of the 'second voice' (or *contracantum*) to be added to the newly composed sequences. Thus, the sequence, even as early as the beginning of the thirteenth century, knew a widespread polyphonic practice, but no manuscript contains, for example, the sequence *Ave mundi spes Maria* (mentioned in the above quotation) for two voices or written with mensural notation, whereas the monodic version is quite widespread.

Even though the ordinals of Padua, Siena, Lucca, Pistoia and Florence document a diffuse practice of simple polyphony, which does not leave any celebration in these cathedrals without amplification through the addition of a second voice, notated examples of this genre, present in the surviving Italian manuscripts, are few: they are mostly the Benedicamus Domino (often with tropes) and sections of the *Ordinarium Missae* (mostly Kyrie, Sanctus and Agnus); sections of the *Proprium Missae* are rare. F. Alberto Gallo has made a pioneering list of Italian manuscripts which transmit simple polyphony.[8]

The second important aspect to stress in the tradition of Christian liturgical chant in Italy is the plentiful presence of examples of compositions written with rhythmic-proportional notation, that is, examples of cantus fractus.

Early on in its history Gregorian chant was performed with proportional values, above all in relation to metric texts (hymns and sequences), but in the first years of the fourteenth century a new kind of repertory appears in southern France. It spreads very quickly all over Italy and Europe: in this period, there are Credo movements with mensural notation, the most important of which are the so-called Credo Cardinalis and the Credo Regis or Apostolorum. The former is rather well known and its melody still appears as Credo IV (but without the original mensural notation) in modern chant books; the latter is less well known but nevertheless worthy of attention.

The so-called Credo Regis, often referred to as the Credo Apostolorum, is made up exclusively of breves and semibreves;[9] of this Credo we even know the author: the King of Sicily, Robert of Anjou (b. 1278, d. Naples, 1343).

The identification with Robert of Anjou is supported by the appellation *Regis* found in various codices, from the rubric of an Italian manuscript of the sixteenth century now in Cleveland (Museum of Art, 21140) which says: 'Patrem cum suo cantu ordinatum per regem Robertum' (fol. 78r) and from another rubric found in Parma, Abbazia of San Giovanni Evangelista MS F (fol. 437v),[10] which for the same Credo gives the author as 'Regis Siciliae'. Above all, however, this attribution is supported by the *Sermone de fortitudine* by Gabio de' Zamorei, Petrarch's friend, who states that King Robert composed a new melody.[11] For five years (1319–24), Robert of Anjou lived in Avignon, and it is likely that it was during these years that he composed the Credo, perhaps in competition with the cardinal who invented the melody of the so-called Credo Cardinalis. Around 1324, then, the Apostolic Constitution *Docta sanctorum* and Robert of Anjou's Credo were both written in Avignon. It is possible that the fortune of the Credo Apostolorum (and of its more famous counterpart, the Credo Cardinalis) is linked to the Constitution, which inveighs against compositions 'in semibreves and minims' or that use hocket (it also criticizes the addition of florid discantus and the use of vernacular texts in simple polyphony). It is clear therefore that the Constitution supported and launched this new and simple style (which was nevertheless in line with tradition), and allowed for its quick diffusion, in Italy and beyond. However, the Constitution would not have had any impact if, around the court at Avignon and around Robert of Anjou, there had not been numbers of musicians, composers and singers, who would go on to spread this new Credo around Europe. It ought to be

Example 7.2 First part of *Credo Regis* (cantus fractus) by Robert of Anjou (*I-PAac* F-09, fols. 140v–148)

remembered that the Neapolitan court of King Robert was an extraordinarily fertile place for music production and consumption, both secular and sacred, and that Marchetto da Padova dedicated his *Pomerium* to King Robert.

Many Italian codices contain King Robert's Credo, among them more than twenty fourteenth- and fifteenth-century manuscripts.[12] But what matters is that the same Credo is handed down in versions for two voices, and thus testifies to the widespread practice of simple polyphony, in the following codices: Rome, Biblioteca Apostolica Vaticana, Barb. Lat. 657, fols. 419v–423; Parma, Duomo, Archivio Capitolare con Archivio della Fabbriceria F-09, fols. 140v–148; and Città del Vaticano, Biblioteca Apostolica Vaticana, Ottoboniano Latino 1969.[13] Music example 7.2 shows the beginning of one of these polyphonic realizations, from the Parma codex.

The *vox principalis*, composed by King Robert, uses only breves and semibreves (crotchets and quavers in the transcription) and is in the high register. The *vox organalis* is in the same range as the *principalis*, it moves homophonically and does not show any contrapuntal refinement: many notes are in unison, at cadential points there are only unisons, fifths and octaves; the voices move mostly in contrary motion, with a few short passages in thirds.

In many Italian churches the series of choir books, still preserved, were renewed in the fifteenth and first years of the sixteenth century. These sets contain antiphonaries and graduals (with appendices of kyriales and prosers), sometimes psalters; the main preserved series (many relating to cathedrals, or collegiate or important convents and monasteries) are listed in the *Iter liturgicum Italicum* by Giacomo Baroffio and can be dated to the fifteenth and sixteenth centuries. It must be stressed that these books were used, in the majority of cases, for more than four centuries. Almost all of them were corrected after the promulgation of the Breviary and of the Missal of Pius V (respectively in 1568 and 1570), with the addition of minor variations introduced by the new official version of the post-conciliar books.[14] To these series also belonged the prosers (or sequentiaries), mostly lost because their use was abandoned after 1570. In many cases during the seventeenth and eighteenth centuries, new choir books were copied containing offices and masses of recently canonized saints, and kyriales, almost always containing masses in cantus fractus. But it is important to highlight that the value of the single music reading transmitted by the books is relative: the practice does not faithfully follow the written sign.[15]

The Credo Cardinalis, the Credo Apostolorum of Robert of Anjou and the later Credo Angelorum in cantus fractus are clearly found in these books; also, the Vatican Credo I – perhaps the only intonation used before the fourteenth century – is often found written in mensural notation. For a picture of liturgical chant on a local scale (comparable, in many aspects, to that of many other Italian cities), see Frank D'Accone's study of Siena, *The Civic Muse*.[16]

The Italian lauda

The work of the troubadours and trouvères arrived very early in Italy; French poetry for music was present in Italian courts in the thirteenth and fourteenth centuries, and the whole of Italian poetic production derived forms, vocabulary, themes, general lines (and presumably musical style too, when sung) from French lyric poetry. Certainly, melodies for love songs and ballatas were composed in Italy, even though only three fragmentary sources with notation of thirteenth-century Italian songs survive. A very common practice (not only in Italy) was that of the contrafactum, that is, the adaptation of a new text to a pre-existing melody not only in secular genres (as in Dante's ballata *Per una ghirlandetta*) but also in the sacred and devotional (Salimbene of Parma, for example, remembers that Brother Enrico Pisano composed the hymn beginning 'Christe Deus / Christe meus / Christe rex et Domine' using the music of a popular song with the words 'E s' tu no cure de me / e' no curarò de te . . . ').

The new Franciscan spirituality revalued natural beauty and embraced the simplicity of the poor; it expressed itself in vernacular religious chant. The manifesto of this new approach to the world, which involved music with a by no means secondary role, is Saint Francis's *Cantico delle creature*, in vernacular Umbrian, composed around 1225 and transmitted by the codex Assisi, Biblioteca Comunale, MS 338, but with the space for the music left blank. The renewal of Christian life, as lived and preached not only by Franciscan friars but also by other mendicant orders (particularly the Dominicans and the Servants of Mary), promoted the formation in many Italian cities of lay confraternities devoted to prayer, song and mutual help, which drew up well-laid-out Statutes and Rules from the thirteenth century on. Some of these confraternities dedicated themselves to singing laude during their meetings and are thus called societies of Laudesi. The laude were strophic and devotional compositions in Italian. Other confraternities which emerged with the Laudesi were those of the Disciplinati, Battuti or Flagellanti; these, too, were lay groups, which met periodically to pray, to sing and to carry out the *disciplina*, that is, the mortification of the body by self-flagellation. The movement (and therefore even the singing) of the Disciplinati was the result of premises different from those of the Laudesi: punishment, mortification, penance and fear of the end of the world were the themes preached by Rainerio Fasani of Perugia, founder of the movement around 1260. Their repertory of laude had as its almost exclusive subject the Passion of Christ, and the intonations were formulaic, similar to the psalm tones: the laude were sung using one of only two melodic schemes – the 'Easter' Scheme and that 'of the Passion'; these are very different from the schemes used by the Laudesi, which are pleasant, singable and varied.

Many manuscripts contain texts (almost two hundred) of the plentiful production of monodic laude, which the Laudesi practised between the thirteenth and the fifteenth centuries; however, only two documents (and a few other fragments) preserve musical notation: (1) the Cortona manuscript Biblioteca Comunale e dell'Accademia Etrusca 91 and (2) the Florence codex Biblioteca Nazionale Centrale, Banco Rari 18 (formerly Magliabechi II.1.122). The oldest and best-known manuscript anthology is the Cortona Laudario, made up of 171 parchment sheets, of a smaller size

(23×17 cm) than the Florence document. It was written towards the end of the thirteenth-century and belonged to the confraternity of Santa Maria della Laude, active in the church of San Francesco in Cortona; it contains forty-six laude with music. The laude have various topics: sixteen have texts in praise of the Virgin, and there are also laude for various liturgical celebrations (of Saint Catherine of Alexandria, Saint Francis, Saint Antony of Padua, Saint Mary Magdalene, Saint Michael, Saint John the Baptist and Saint John the Evangelist). The texts of four laude are signed, in the last strophe, by Garzo (whom some identify, but without valid arguments, with Ser Garzo of the Incisa di Valdarno, a notary and great-grandfather of Petrarch); it is not clear furthermore whether Garzo is also the author of the melodies – it is more likely that he is only the writer of the texts.

The other important collection of laude, preserved at the Biblioteca Nazionale Centrale of Florence, is Banco Rari 18, made up of 153 large parchment sheets, 40×28 cm, richly ornate); it was written in the first half of the fourteenth century for the confraternity of Santa Maria, which had its centre at the Augustinian house of Santo Spirito in Florence (the identification has been possible as a result of study of the decorated letters), and preserves eighty-eight laude with music, eighteen of which can also be found in the Cortona Laudario. Comparison of the two codices reveals many variants; the Florentine codex, in particular, is richer in embellishments. The notation in both sources is square with tetragramma and clefs, very similar to the contemporary notation of plainchant. Only the first strophe of each lauda is written below the musical notation.

When the lauda was born in the thirteenth century, the Latin liturgy had been resounding for more than a millennium, more recently through the use of Gregorian chant and, in the most important churches, even in polyphonic settings. There had been expressions of deep religiosity in the troubadour canso and in the Galician-Portuguese cantiga, but this new and peculiar form of sacred and extra-liturgical song was born and spread in Italy, with a text in vernacular Italian and modelled on the form of the ballata. The form preferred by the anonymous thirteenth-century rhymesters for their laude-ballatas was the so-called *zagialesca* structure, from *zagial*, an Arabic metric form, which some consider the origin of the romance, made up of a ripresa of two lines (the ritornello) and a few strophes of four lines (the most usual rhyme scheme is: *xx, aaax, bbbx,* etc.). In fact it is not necessary to invoke the Arabic-Andalusian zagial, given that this strophic scheme is already found in Middle Latin works, such as the very common sequence *Verbum bonum et suave.*

The lines of the laude usually have eight syllables with frequent variation in number of syllables. The kind of lines and the strophic structure

Example 7.3 Refrain and three stanzas of the lauda *Venite a laudare* (*I-CT* 91, fol. 1r)

Ripresa

Ve - ni - te a lau - da - re, per a - mo - re can - ta - re l'a - mo - ro - sa ver - ge - ne Ma - ri - a.

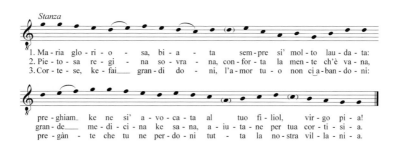

Stanza

1. Ma - ria glo - ri - o - sa, bi - a - ta sem - pre si' mol - to lau - da - ta:
2. Pie - to - sa re - gi - na so - vra - na, con - for - ta la men - te ch'è va - na,
3. Cor - te - se, ke - fai___ gran - di do - ni, l'a - mor tu - o non ci a - ban - do - ni:

pre - ghiam___ ke ne si' a - vo - ca - ta al tuo fi - liol, vir - go pi - a!
gran - de.___ me - di - ci - na ke sa - na, a - iu - ta - ne per tua cor - ti - si - a.
pre - gàn - te che tu ne per - do - ni tut - ta la no - stra vil - la - ni - a.

also suggest a premeditated choice of register and language: not a courtly and formal language, with erudite, literary and rhetorical versification (which usually uses the hendecasyllable and the form of the canzone), but a passionate and simple prayer sung to Christ, the Virgin Mary and the saints with the familiarity and the confidence of those who live the experience of faith through prayer. But where is the matrix of these melodies? There is no doubt that the ancient Gregorian repertory was the model, particularly in the use of modal scales (the eight ecclesiastical modes or tones) and of a few recurrent melodic formulas (for example, the typical first-mode intonation with which *Lauda novella* begins and other formulas derived from the psalm modes); it is also evident that the forms closest to the lauda in terms of their compositional ideas are the monodies with metric text, that is hymns and sequences and, in the secular field, the songs of the troubadours and trouvères. The lauda that opens the Cortona Manuscript (Example 7.3) reveals in the ritornello the meaning of the entire repertory to which it belongs: 'Venite a laudare, per amore cantare l'amorosa Vergene Maria' ('Come to praise, to sing for love the loving Virgin Mary'). The words 'praise' and 'sing' only make sense with 'for love': one does not sing in desperation, and one does not sing for oneself; rather, the invitation 'to sing for love' and praise the Virgin is extended to all people of good will.

The melodic arch which accompanies the ritornello of this lauda has its climax exactly on the tonic syllable of the word 'amore'; the music–text relationship we find here is rare in the intonations of other laude: the modern desire to express the affects of the text through music is foreign to the medieval aesthetic, and even when we find, as in this case, an exact correspondence between word and melody, it may be a mere coincidence and not a purposefully created effect. What the composer looked for in setting these texts to music was merely a beautiful and simple musical phrase which could adapt flexibly to the verse, exactly as happened and was still happening in the composition of hymns and sequences using Latin metric text. The melody could thus sometimes be extended and sung 'cantabile' (as in *Venite a laudare* or in *Altissima luce*) and sometimes in a recitative-like manner (as in *Madonna Santa Maria* and in the strophe of *De la crudel morte di Cristo*), but it was always in the service of the transparency of the text, which is sometimes very long: laude with more than twenty strophes are not uncommon; *Venite a laudare*, for example, has fifteen strophes. The melody without accompaniment, without doubling instruments, does not disturb the prayer; on the contrary it amplifies it, it complies with it, it makes it the experience of the whole human being. The melodic beauty ennobles the word, takes it away from everyday experience, makes it truer and less intellectual; even today, after seven centuries, this simple beauty enchants.

When studying *Venite a laudare* (Example 7.3) another aspect of the intonation of the lauda becomes clear: the ritornello proceeds syllabically (one note for each syllable) in a restricted vocal range and with simple melodic intervals better suited to non-professional singers; the strophe, on the other hand, being reserved for the soloist, shows a wider vocal range and the use of the high register (in other laude, it is possible to find a virtuosic melodic line, rich in melismas and embellishment). See the energetic and joyous attack of the strophe on the words 'Maria, gloriosa, biata', which are given at a higher pitch than in the ritornello: the same effect is found in other laude, such as *Altissima luce, O Maria d'omelia, Regina sovrana, Ave vergene gaudente* and *O divina virgo flore*. The change of register is deliberately created to catch the attention of the audience: there is a time to sing together and there is a time to listen, so that the experience of prayer through beauty is complete and varied and involves participation. There is no risk of making the singing an exhibition for its own sake, or a distraction, because the soloist is the one who can communicate better than others, who can pray better; someone who sings like a member of the congregation would not be capable: the medieval man still lives as a reality the unifying power of shared listening, of shared wonder, of shared emotion of a depth that words cannot reach. Beauty, to be expressed fully, needs competence and professionalism; a noble expression, worthy of prayer through singing, escapes banality and improvisation: it needs work and study. The soloist takes upon himself this most important task: to sing for and with others, to give voice to the splendour of beauty in the name of everyone, then to join once more with the community in the ripresa.

The kind of musical notation used in the two surviving laudarios does not give any indication about the rhythm of these melodies, as is the case with many other monodic compositions from the eleventh to the fifteenth century. Scholars and performers have so far proposed various hypotheses, without formulating a definitive and universally accepted solution.[17] The main problem concerns the most florid laude, which have several notes for each syllable. For example, in the Cortona Laudario there are five notes for each syllable in *Ave donna santissima*, *Ave dei genitrix* and *Ave vergene gaudente*; there are six per syllable in *Cristo è nato*, which is an exuberant lauda in many other aspects as well, but the melodies in the Florence laudario are embellished even more, with up to ten notes per syllable. So far as the music proceeds syllabically, as in the two laude *Altissima luce* and *Regina sovrana* (the latter is sung on a melody derived from the former), almost all hypothetical rhythmic reconstructions concur and lead to a rather convincing result, but in the laude with long embellishments the differences between performances following different kinds of rhythmic interpretation are more notable.

Furthermore, it should be observed that the Cortona codex has a substantial number of notational mistakes (whole phrases transposed a third, missing or wrong clefs, wrong notes, and so on) and may therefore have acted more as a marker of prestige, indicating the opulence of the confraternity, than as a document for reading, given that the choristers would have known the laude by heart. It is thus absolutely necessary that today's performer turns to a good critical edition that rectifies the mistakes and allows a correct alignment of the syllables in the strophes after the first. Liuzzi's pioneering edition, published in 1935, though still a rich source of valuable intuitions, cannot be used for a correct execution of the melodies, and subsequent editions (Ernetti, Terni, Lucchi) still contain many shortcomings. The most recent edition of the laudario, edited by Martin Dürrer, dates back to 1996, but even if this is more accurate, it still does not solve all the problems, and it includes transcriptions only of the first strophe of each lauda.

The istampita

In the seventh and eighth fascicles (from fols. 55v to 63v) of the Florentine codex London, British Library, Additional 29987, there are fifteen monodic instrumental compositions, called *istampite*, which represent the most important extant source of medieval instrumental music. The Italian term *istampita* is synonymous with the French *estampie* and the Provençal *estampida*, whose oldest example is represented by the troubadour *canso*

Kalenda maya (ca1200). The text of this canso, by Raimbaut de Vaqueiras, is adapted to the pre-existing melody of an estampida that the troubadour may have heard performed by two jesters. The compositions in GB-Lbl add. 29987 can be divided into two groups: the first comprises eight long istampite, each with its own title: *Gaetta, Cominciamento di gioia, Isabella, Tre fontane, Belica, Parlamento, In pro* and *Principio di virtù*. The second group comprises seven short pieces, often with names of fast dances: four bear the title *Saltarello* and one *Trotto*. The other two compositions, in binary form, are titled *Lamento di Tristano* and *La manfredina*; they are very similar from the melodic and rhythmic points of view: both are followed by their own *rotta*, that is, by the variation of the first part. The same binary structure (with a *trotto* instead of the *rotta*) is found in a composition titled *Danza amorosa* in a Florentine fragment (Florence, Archivio di Stato, Notarile Antecosimiano, n. 17879), copied by a notary a few years before the London codex was written.[18]

The names of the istampite might suggest a relation with the Neapolitan court of Robert of Anjou (Gaeta is a city near Naples and *La manfredina* might allude to King Manfred of Sicily). The rhythmic character also betrays a possible dating to the first half of the fourteenth century, and this suggests that the istampite may have been originally written using an older notational system: that described by Marchetto da Padova in the *Pomerium* (ca1320).[19] The istampite may have arrived in Florence during the reign of Robert of Anjou himself (1313–22) or that of his son (1325–7). From the formal point of view, the istampite are structured in four or five parts, called *puncta*; each punctum is repeated twice with a different conclusion (x and x': *aperto* and *chiuso*), as in the modern *prima* and *seconda volta*. The conclusion of the first punctum is usually used in the remaining puncta (except for in the istampite *Parlamento* and *In pro*):

Gaeta	ax ax' / bx bx' / b'x b'x' / cx cx'
Cominciamento di gioia	abx abx' / cbx cbx' / dbx dbx' / efx efx' / gfx gfx'
Isabella	abx abx' / cx cx' / dbx dbx' / ex ex'
Tre fontane	abcx abcx' / dbcx dbcx' / ecx ecx' / fx fx'
Belica	abx abx' / cx cx' / dx dx' / efbx efbx' / gfbx gfbx'
Parlamento	abx abx' / cx cx' / dbx dbx' / ey ey' / gy gy'
In pro	ax ax' / bx bx' / cx cx' / dy dy' / ey ey'
Principio di virtù	abx abx' / cbx cbx' / dbx dbx' / ex ex'

In the scheme, the formal divide between puncta is distinguished by a forward slash (/). Usually the first three parts of each piece present both rhythmic and melodic similarities and repetitions, whereas the fourth and the fifth, though similar to each other, are different from the first three.

The other seven pieces are shorter, all notated in folios 62 and 63 of *GB-Lbl* add. 29987; they do not show any separation between the third and fourth puncta:

Salterello	ax ax' / bx bx' / cx cx' / dx dx'
Trotto	ax ax' / bx bx' / cx cx' / dax dax' / eax eax'
Salterello	ax ax' / bx bx' / cx cx' / dcx dcx'
Salterello	ax ax' / bx bx' / cx cx' / dx dx'
Lamento di Tristano	ax ax' / [b]y [b]y' / cx cx'
La rotta	ax ax' / by by' / cy cy'
La manfredina	ax ax' / by bx" / cz cx'
La rotta	ax ax' / by bx" / cz cx'
Salterello	abx abx' / bx bx' / cbx cbx' / dcbx dcbx' / edcbx edcbx' / fedcbx fedcbx'

In all fifteen compositions the melody is highly embellished and there are short recurrent motives, which are varied and developed very often in progression. There are frequent changes of metre, from binary to ternary.

Johannes de Grocheo's description of the *stantipes* and *ductia* forms in his treatise of 1275 coincides with the examples from the London codex. Grocheo states that the stantipes has six or seven puncta, whereas the ductia has only three or four. Another peculiarity of the ductia, according to Grocheo, would be the 'recta percussio'; this expression probably refers to the metric-structural regularity of the puncta and of the ductia as opposed to the greater variety of the stantipes: this would make the *ductia* better suited to dancing.

8 The trecento

MARCO GOZZI

The Italian peninsula in the fourteenth century was divided into a great number of communes, republics (the most important being the Most Serene Republic of Venice) and *signorie* (the Savoia in Piedmont, Scaligeri in Verona, Visconti in Milan, Carraresi in Padua, Malaspina in Lunigiana, Pepoli in Bologna, Gonzaga in Mantua, Este in Ferrara, Manfredi in Faenza, Malatesta in Rimini and Pesaro, Da Polenta in Ravenna, Montefeltro in Urbino, and so on). Every state of some importance had a rich cultural life in which the production and consumption of music played a primary role.

Italian cities were very open at first to Provençal and then to French influence, not only in the Marca Trevigiana (Veneto), in Lombardy (the then name for the western part of north Italy), and in Romagna, but even in the kingdom of Sicily (since the time of Frederick II and then with the Angevin line of Charles I, Charles II, Robert and Joan I). During the time the Holy See was transferred to Avignon (1309–77), exchanges between Rome and France were inevitable. This strong permeability between cultures reveals how Italy was not provincial but an environment open to receive the best European artists of the time. This also partly explains, on the one hand, the lack of surviving musical output in vernacular Italian and, on the other, the reason why numerous codices in Italy contain Provençal songs (two thirds of surviving Provençal song books were written in the Veneto during the thirteenth and fourteenth centuries).

As far as fourteenth-century musical culture is concerned, individual Italian states have not yet been studied in depth; nevertheless the very rich experience of seven cities is evident, cities where both a significant sacred (of which little is preserved) and secular polyphonic practice (called the Italian Ars Nova) developed: Padua, Verona, Bologna, Milan, Florence, Rome and Naples.

Padua

Courtly poetry for music had a long tradition in the Veneto: from the thirteenth century an intensive production in Provençal developed in a few cities. It is likely that in Padua, at the beginning of the fourteenth century, a typical Italian tradition of mensural polyphonic music started, both practical and theoretical. Padua had various links with French cultural milieux, not only through the court but also through the university, which was attended by many students from the other side of the Alps.

The most prominent figure from Padua in the first half of the fourteenth century was the composer and theorist Marchetto da Padova, who was active as a singing teacher in the cathedral of Padua at least between 1305 and 1308. Between 1309 and 1318 he wrote the *Lucidarium in arte musicae planae*, a treatise about church singing started in Cesena and completed in Verona. Between 1321 and 1326, whilst at the court of Rinaldo de Cintis in Cesena, he wrote the *Pomerium in arte musicae mensuratae*, dedicated to the king of Sicily Robert of Anjou. In the *Pomerium* Marchetto describes an Italian notational system, reserved for motets, and which showed many original characteristics, but which shared many features with the French system and the *auctoritas* of Franco of Cologne. The two-voice verses *Quare sic aspicitis, Quis est iste* and *Iste formosus* of the Paduan Office for the Ascension (found in the Processional C 56 of the Biblioteca Capitolare of Padua, fols. 50r–51v) are attributed to Marchetto, as well as three motets: the three-voice *Ave regina coelorum / Mater innocencie* (which was probably written for the inauguration of the Scrovegni Chapel with the Giotto frescos on 25 March 1305 and in which the duplum has the name of the author as an acrostic: *Marcum Paduanum*); the four-voice *Ave corpus sanctum gloriosi Stefani / Adolescens protomartir Domini* (evidently written for Venice between 1329 and 1338, since it contains references to the doge Francesco Dandolo); and the three-voice *Cetus inseraphici / Cetus apostolici* (which appears in the same fragment as *Ave corpus*).

Theoretical discussion of music was conducted at the University of Padua, and the work of Marchetto greatly influenced subsequent theorists; in particular, the mathematician and astronomer from Padua Prosdocimo de Beldemandis (ca1380–1428), teacher at the University of Padua, expressly cites Marchetto's *Pomerium* in one of his eight surviving music treatises, the *Tractatus practice cantus mensurabilis ad modum Italicorum* ('Treatise on the practice of mensural singing according to the Italian method'; first version 1412, second version circa 1427) in an attempt to demonstrate the superiority of Italian over French theory; he states that 'Italici' extol the *ars gallica* as more beautiful, more perfect and more subtle, whereas it is, in his opinion, inferior.

The names of two great composers are also linked to Padua: Bartolino da Padova and Johannes Ciconia.

Bartolino was active in the last quarter of the fourteenth century and was a Carmelite monk. He may perhaps be identified with one of the two monks called Bartholomeus in the Carmelite monastery of Padua in 1376 and 1380. The texts of many of his compositions inform us that he was connected to the Paduan court of Francesco Carrara il Vecchio (1355–88). The ballata *La sacrosanta carità d'amore* has a text by Giovanni Dondi dall'Orologio, medical doctor, philosopher, astronomer and man of letters, who was born in Chioggia in 1330 and was active in Padua until 1383. After Gian Galeazzo Visconti defeated Francesco il Vecchio in 1388, Francesco Novello fled to Florence. It is likely that Bartolino went to Florence with him, together with other exiles from Padua. The texts of Bartolino's compositions *La douce cere*, *La fiera testa* and *L'aurate chiome* are directed against the politics of the Visconti, in perfect agreement with the Florentine attitude of the time. Bartolino also set to music the ballata *Ama chi t'ama*, with a text by Sercambi, who was also a strong opponent to the Visconti. It is not known whether Bartolino survived the catastrophe of the Carraresi: Francesco Novello conquered Padua again in 1404, but he was imprisoned and killed by Venetians in 1406.

After Landini and Niccolò da Perugia, Bartolino is the fourteenth-century Italian author of whom we have the greatest number of surviving compositions: eleven madrigals and twenty-seven ballatas (all found in the Squarcialupi Codex except for the ballata *Serva ciascuno*, found in the Mancini Codex of Lucca).

Johannes Ciconia, a native of Liège, is documented as *custos* (officer) and *cantor* in the cathedral of Padua from 1401 until his death in 1412. Ciconia (the illegitimate son of a canon of Liège Cathedral and born around 1370) came to Italy around 1390 as *clericus cappellae* and *domesticus continuus commensalis* of Cardinal Philippe d'Alençon (titular of the Roman basilica of Santa Maria in Trastevere). He was thus the first of a long series of important Flemish composers who undertook the journey to, and found success in, Italy. Before his arrival in Padua, it is likely that he worked in the chapel of Boniface IX, together with Antonio Zacara da Teramo; it is also possible that he was active in the court of Gian Galeazzo Visconti in Pavia. Of Ciconia the following compositions survive: six glorias and four credos for three or four parts, thirteen motets (two for two voices, six for three and five for four voices), four madrigals (three for two voices, one for three voices), eleven ballatas (five for two voices), two virelais and two canons for three voices with texts in French. At least ten of the motets contain references to famous people: members of the Carrara family, the Paduan Francesco Zabarella, the bishop Pietro Filargo (who became pope with the name of Alexander V), the doge Michele Steno, and the bishops of Padua Albano Michiel and Pietro Marcello. Ciconia was also the author of a theoretical treatise entitled *Nova musica*.

Among the other musicians active in Padua at the end of the fourteenth and during the first years of the fifteenth century the names of Gratioso da Padova and the copyist Rolando from Casale stand out. Rolando, a

Benedictine monk from Santa Giustina, copied many books of polyphony, of which there are several surviving fragments. These musical fragments, together with Ciconia's output, attest to a lively polyphonic practice between 1390 and 1420 in the cathedral of Padua and in the local abbey of Santa Giustina.

The so-called Codex Mancini (Lucca, Archivio di Stato 184 and Perugia, Biblioteca Comunale Augusta 3065), is very likely a codex from Padua, copied around 1395, with successive additions made in Florence (ca1405) and in Lucca (ca1420–30).

Verona and Milan

In the Veronese court of the brothers Mastino II and Alberto della Scala between 1329 and 1351, Giovanni da Cascia, Jacopo da Bologna and possibly Magister Piero were all active: they are the earliest authors of madrigals for two voices and of caccias in vulgar Italian. They wrote together a madrigal cycle about a woman called Anna (possibly Anna della Scala, daughter of Federico), in which a tree (the *perlaro*) and a river are mentioned: *A l'ombra d'un perlaro* and *Sopra un fiume regale* by Piero, *Appress'un fiume chiaro* and *O perlaro gentil* by Giovanni, *O dolce appress'un bel perlaro* and *Un bel perlaro vive sulla riva* by Jacopo all belong to this cycle. These same composers also composed madrigals and caccias in honour of the Visconti; the caccia *Con brachi assai*, composed both by Giovanni and Piero, mentions the river Adda, in Lombardy, which runs through the Viscontis' land; the dog Varino, present in this caccia, is also mentioned in the caccia *Per sparverare* by Jacopo. It is certain that the two families, the Scaligeri and the Visconti, had good relations, as in 1350, Beatrice della Scala, daughter of Mastino II, married Bernabò Visconti (it is possible that Jacopo's madrigal *Fenice fu* celebrates precisely this event).

Piero's madrigal *Ogni diletto e ogni bel piacere* was very probably written in honour of Bernabò Visconti: the first line of the ritornello, 'Soffrir pur voglio ancora', is the translation of Bernabò's French motto, 'Sofri m'estuet'.

Jacopo was already active at the Visconti court in 1346, as two madrigals testify: *O in Italia felice Liguria* (which praises the birth, in that year, of Luchino Visconti's twins Giovanni and Luchino Novello) and *Lo lume vostro* (with the acrostic *Luchinus*, datable to 1341 according to Corsi).

The main codices copied in the Veneto are the so-called Rossi Codex (seven bifolia in Rome, Biblioteca Apostolica Vaticana, Rossi 215, and two bifolia in Ostiglia, Opera Pia Greggiati, Biblioteca, rari 35) and the codex Paris, Bibliothèque nationale de France, nouv. acq. fr. 6771 (Codex Reina). The former is datable to around 1370 and is, therefore, the oldest surviving evidence of Italian polyphony, together with the Mischiati Fragment in the state archive in Reggio Emilia; the latter was copied in the first decade of the fifteenth century.

The caccia *Or qua compagni* of the Rossi Codex, the three caccias of the Mischiati Fragment and the compositions in the tenth fascicle of the codex Florence, Biblioteca Nazionale Centrale Panciatichiano 26 (from fol. 91 to fol. 100, copied from an old northern exemplar) together form a group of pieces from the Visconti milieu.

Florence

Around 1350 the polyphonic practice of northern courts was flourising, and particularly so in Florence. The most important Florentine composers, all clerics, were Bartolo (author of a Credo for two voices much appreciated by the parishioners of Santa Reparata), Gherardello (between 1345 and 1352 chaplain of Santa Reparata, at that time the cathedral of Florence, then, until his death – in 1363 – prior of San Remigio) and Lorenzo da Firenze (canon of San Lorenzo at least from 1348 until his death around 1372). Of the output of Gherardello and Lorenzo there remain a few sections of the mass ordinary, besides ten monodic ballatas, which must be considered examples of those 'canzonette' that Giovanni Boccaccio makes the protagonists of *The Decameron* sing and play. Of both composers, we also have ten madrigals and a caccia each.

The vicissitudes of Italian-language polyphony in Florence were closely linked to the activities of Franco Sacchetti (1332–1400), a poet and short-story writer as well as a businessman and prominent character in Florentine political life. Sacchetti edited a collection of his own rhymes (ballatas, madrigals, caccias and canzonettas), which he arranged chronologically from circa 1354 and in which, beside each text, he indicated the musician who set it to music. The list of the composers contains the names of all the major composers active in Florence at that time: Lorenzo, Gherardello, Giacomo (brother of Gherardello), Niccolò da Perugia (with twelve compositions), Donato da Cascia, Giovanni da Gualdo, Guglielmo of France and Francesco Landini. There is also the name of Ottolino da Brescia, of whom there are no surviving musical compositions, and only four sonnets exchanged with Sacchetti.

Niccolò da Perugia was the son of the Proposto (provost) of Perugia; as a priest, Niccolò was a guest in 1362 in the monastery of Santa Trinità together with his elder colleague Gherardello. It is possible that Niccolò was in touch with his contemporary Bartolino da Padua, since both set to music the madrigal *La fiera testa*, whose text mentions with dislike the coat of arms and the motto of the Visconti. It is not unlikely that this madrigal was composed around 1400, when hostilities between Florence and Milan were in full swing, during which the Visconti governed Perugia for a short time. There are forty-one remaining compositions by Niccolò: sixteen madrigals, four caccias, and twenty-one ballatas. Niccolò, together with Landini, was among the first composers who cultivated the genre of the polyphonic ballata.

The most important Italian composer in the fourteenth century was certainly Francesco Landini, indicated in the Squarcialupi Codex, as *Franciscus cecus orghanista de Florentia* ('the blind organist of Florence') because he had lost his sight as a consequence of smallpox when he was a child. Landini was born around 1330 and many biographical details come from an entire chapter dedicated to him in the *Liber de origine civitatis Florentie et eiusdem famosis civibus* by Filippo Villani (written after 1381, while Francesco was still alive). He was a virtuoso on various instruments besides the organ and the organetto; he sang, recited and wrote poems. He was also a tuner and builder of organs and other instruments: according to Villani he invented a bowed instrument called *serena serenarum* ('the sirene *par excellence*'). The chronicle of Villani and the Dante commentary of Cristoforo Landino remind us of Francesco's philosophical, ethic and astrological interests: a follower of William of Occam's nominalist philosophy, he wrote a long poem in praise of Occamist philosophy; with this work, and the verses *In contumelia Florentinae juventutis effeminatae*, Landini participated in the philosophical, political and religious debates of his time. It is thus very likely that he wrote many of the texts he set to music. It is also possible that Landini sojourned for some time in north Italy before 1370; in support of this hypothesis there are not only the style and the text of some of his madrigals, such as *Non a Narcisso*, but also the text of a motet written for the doge Andrea Contarini (1368–82) of which only one voice survives, and in which the author describes himself as 'Franciscus peregre canens'. The text of his madrigal *Una colomba candida e gentile* most likely refers to the wedding between Gian Galeazzo and Caterina Visconti and can be dated to 1380. The isorhythmic madrigal *Sì dolce non sonò* was maybe written by Landini in 1361 on the death of Philippe de Vitry.

Landini was organist at the monastery of Santa Trinità in 1361 and chaplain, from 1365 until his death in 1397, in the church of San Lorenzo in Florence, the same church where Lorenzo da Firenze (Lorenzo Masini) was canon. A reference letter for Landini written by the chancellor and humanist Coluccio Salutati, dated 10 September 1375 and addressed to the bishop of the city, informs us of the good relationship between Landini and the municipal authorities. From the 1370s Francesco was in close contact with the composers Paolo Tenorista and Andrea dei Servi (Andreas de Florentia).

In 1379 he was called to the Santissima Annunziata to build the new organ and in the same year he was paid by Andrea 'pro quinque motectis'. In 1387 he took part in the design of the new organ of the Florentine cathedral.

A posthumous but vivid representation of Landini's role in the Florentine society of 1389 is offered in *Il Paradiso degli Alberti*, written by Giovanni Gherardi from Prato in the early fifteenth century. The composer is here represented as a skilful singer and performer on the portative organ, who also takes part in erudite conversations and philosophical and political discussions. Francesco died in Florence on 2 September 1397: two days later he was buried in the basilica of San Lorenzo. His tombstone, discovered in Prato during the twentieth century and now once again in the Florentine church (in the second chapel on the right), shows the blind composer with his portative organ, in a setting similar to that in the portrait from the Squarcialupi Codex.

At least 154 compositions can be attributed to Landini: 140 ballatas (91 for two voices and 49 for three), 9 madrigals for two voices and 2 madrigals for three voices, 1 virelai (*Adiu, adiu*), 1 madrigal in canon (*Deh dimmi tu*) and 1 caccia (*Così pensoso*).

A contemporary of Landini, Andrea is described as an organist – *Magister Frater Andreas Horganista de Florentia* – in the Squarcialupi Codex. In the London Codex he is called 'Frate Andrea de' Servi', which allows us to identify him with one Andrea di Giovanni, who entered the order of Servants of Mary in 1375. From 1380 to 1397 he was, with some interruptions, prior of the Florentine monastery of the Santissima Annunziata. In 1393 he was prior in Pistoia and from 1407 to 1410 he was provincial father of the Tuscan Serviti. He was Camerlengo, or Chamberlain, of the commune of Florence several times. Andrea was in close contact with Francesco Landini and worked with him on the construction of the organs of the Santissima Annunziata in 1379 and of the cathedral in 1387. Some of the texts of his ballatas contain quotations of the same female *senhal* (dedication: to Sandra and Cosa) which can also be found in Landini's and Paolo's ballatas. This coincidence suggests that the three of them circulated within the same Florentine milieu. (Note that our Andrea should not be confused with Andrea Stefani.) Andrea died in 1415, and of his output we are left with thirty surviving ballatas (eighteen for two voices and twelve for three voices), of which twenty-nine are to be found in Squarcialupi, plus one ballade in French (*Dame sans per*), in the codex of Modena, of uncertain attribution. His works had little resonance outside Florence, because of their traditional character.

In Florence there were also Egidio and Guglielmo, two French friars and contemporaries of Landini. Sacchetti put at the head of his madrigal *La neve e 'l ghiaccio* (dated 1365), sung by Guglielmo, the information that

Guglielmo was 'frater romitanus' (a brother, that is, of the hermitic order of Saint Augustine) and 'Pariginus' (of Paris); the information is completed by a rubric of the London Codex (at fol. 46v, where there is the same madrigal), which calls the composer 'Frate Guglielmo di Santo Spirito', thus revealing him as an Augustinian belonging to the Florentine monastery of Santo Spirito.

The Modena Codex attributes to 'Magister Egidius' the ballatas *Franchois sunt nobles* and *Curtois et sages,* the latter composed in honour of the antipope Clement VII (r. 1378–94), as the acrostic indicates. Besides the madrigal for two voices *La neve e 'l ghiaccio,* the Squarcialupi Codex contains five ballatas for two voices by Egidio and Guglielmo.

Abbot Paolo da Firenze (Paolo Tenorista) was a well-known and influential figure. His biography is particularly well documented, thanks to the various ecclesiastical offices he held. He was probably born in Florence around 1355 and became a Benedictine monk around 1380. The first documentary evidence relating to him concerns his election in 1401 as abbot of the monastery of San Martino al Pino in the diocese of Arezzo; Paolo held this office till 1428. In 1409 he attended the Council of Pisa, where he presumably came into contact with the musicians of the chapels of the schismatic popes Gregory XII and Alexander V. According to a hypothesis of Nádas, Paolo wrote the madrigal *Girand'un bel falcon* to express the Florentine aversion to Gregory XII. The only composition of Paolo that can be dated with certainty is the madrigal *Godi Firenze,* written to celebrate the Florentine victory over Pisa in 1406.

The numerous compositions by Paolo, contained in the Italian Codex 568 in the National Library of Paris, belonged to the Capponi family and suggest a possible relationship between Paolo and that wealthy family. Considering the personal contact of Paolo with the Florentine monastery of Santa Maria degli Angeli, a renowned school of illuminators, it is possible that Paolo had a decisive role in the writing out of the Squarcialupi Codex. Paolo was also one of the counsellors of the Florentine bishops and ruled the church of the hospital of Orbatello in Florence from 1417 to his death (soon after September 1426). Paolo was one of the most prolific composers of the fourteenth and fifteenth centuries. Of his works there remain thirteen madrigals, more than forty ballatas and two liturgical compositions. Paolo followed Landini's style, developing it according to his own refined and sometimes sophisticated taste: it is a serious loss that the pages reserved for him in the Squarcialupi Codex were never used to copy his music.

The name of Giovanni Mazzuoli (Johannes horghanista de Florentia, 'Gian Toscano') appears in the last section of the Squarcialupi Codex but, as with Paolo, none of his music is to be found there. The reason for the defective copying of his compositions is probably the fact that at the time of the compilation of the codex Giovanni was still alive. He was born in Florence around 1360 and died there in May 1426. He was organist of Orsanmichele in 1376 and again from 1379 to 1412; furthermore he was organist of Santa Felicità from 1385 to 1390, as well as of the cathedral, most likely from 1391 until his death. He was possibly Francesco Landini's pupil and friend, then teacher of the very young Antonio Squarcialupi.

The compositions of the Italian Ars Nova have been transmitted mostly through great anthologies copied in Florence; the oldest codex is the Florence manuscript, Biblioteca Nazionale Centrale, Panciatichiano 26, copied around 1390 (with additions made until 1450) by very competent scribes. Slightly later is the London codex British Library, Additional 29987, which is the last part of a bigger collection: the first section of 97 folios, most likely written in Padua and presumably containing very recent sacred and secular music, was detached and is now lost. The second section, the only one surviving, is almost entirely the work of an amateur Florentine scribe; it contains a mixed secular repertory – partly copied from Paduan sources, partly recovered in Florence – and it was altered soon after copying with the addition of rests, stems and other features, which makes the pieces impossible to perform. The two most important collections (with clear cross-references in their contents) are the Paris codex Bibliothèque nationale de France, fonds italien 568 (*Pit*), copied around 1410, and the very beautiful Squarcialupi Codex, Florence, Biblioteca Medicea Laurenziana, Palatino 87, copied between 1410 and 1415 in the Florentine *scriptorium* of Santa Maria degli Angeli, which contains 352 compositions, of which 150 are *unica*. It is divided into sections, each dedicated to a single composer and introduced by a splendid illuminated page with a portrait of the musicians; the composers are arranged in chronological order: Giovanni da Cascia, Jacopo da Bologna, Gherardello da Firenze, Vincenzo da Rimini, Lorenzo da Firenze (Lorenzo Masini), Paolo da Firenze, Donato da Cascia, Niccolò son of the Proposto of Perugia, Bartolino da Padova, Francesco Landini, Egidio and Guglielmo of France, Antonio Zacara da Teramo, and Andreas de Florentia (Andrea dei Servi) from Florence.

In 1982 Frank D'Accone found a previously lost Florentine manuscript containing polyphonic music from the first years of the fifteenth century, whose 111 sheets of parchment had been completely erased and reused in 1504 as a revenue register of the Chapter of the church of San Lorenzo; this is the Florence palimpsest codex, Biblioteca Medicea Laurenziana, Archivio Capitolare di San Lorenzo 2211, first copied around 1420 by the same scribe who added a Gloria and a Credo among the final leaves of the codex, which is now in London. The original manuscript is very difficult to read, but from what one can see with the help of ultraviolet photographs, it is divided into sections dedicated to the composers following criteria similar to the

Squarcialupi Codex (Giovanni's madrigals have the same order in *I-Fl* 2211 as in the Squarcialupi Codex); the compositions in the sections dedicated to Giovanni Mazzuoli (gatherings 9 and 10), to his son Piero (organist in San Lorenzo from 1403 to 1415, gathering 17) and to Ugolino from Orvieto (booklet 18) are *unica*. The codex also contains French chansons by Machaut, Grimace and Senleches (gathering 15), a booklet of caccias (gathering 16) and one of motets (gathering 19, the last one).

Rome and Naples

John Nádas and Giuliano di Bacco have shed light on the importance of Rome, a place of cross-fertilization between different cultures as the centre of the Holy See, in the creation and spreading of the 'international style' that distinguished much music from the end of the fourteenth century onwards.

Italian musicians and those who, attracted by new possibilities, moved to Rome had the opportunity to get in touch with the ultramontane tradition of Avignon: it was certainly during the first years of the schism (1370–80), for example, that the composer Antonio Zacara da Teramo came to know and developed the practice, derived from the French tradition, of intoning the Gloria and Credo polyphonically. Furthermore, the influence of their Italian sojourn on the musicians who went back with Clement VII, and who very likely took something of Italian styles and techniques back to France, must be thoroughly reconsidered.

The creation and the development of the Italian papal chapel in Rome from 1376 onwards sees a preponderance of foreign singers, arriving in Italy at different times; this phase ends with the papacy of Urban VI (1378–89). From 1390 to 1409, there is an increase in the importance of Italian singers, coming from the areas to the south and east of Rome.

Among the composers who worked in Rome for a long time one must cite at least Antonius Berardi from Teramo, called Antonio Zacara, who is mentioned as a famous singer, copyist and illuminator in a Roman document dated January 1390 and described as *scriptor litterarum apostolicarum* (copyist of the Pope's letters) in the Holy See from 1389 to 1407. Johannes Ciconia was also active in Rome in the same years as Zacara, and many Italian and foreign musicians were active in the sumptuous chapels of the bishops living in Rome.

A few fragments of late-fourteenth-century polyphony (Foligno, Grottaferrata, Cortona, the Egidi fragment and Warsaw 378) have been related to the Roman milieu in the first decades of the Great Schism by John Nádas and Giuliano di Bacco.

The Naples of Charles II (1285–1309) and above all Robert of Anjou (1309–43) paid special attention to liturgical music (both monodic and polyphonic) as well as celebrative and refined courtly polyphony, cultivated in the Angevin court. Robert himself composed a Credo in *cantus fractus* (very common in liturgical manuscripts), and the *Pomerium* by Marchetto da Padova is dedicated to him. Nothing of the chansons and motets composed for Anjou survives, but the interest in music of both Charles and Robert is attested to by their patronage of singers and composers.

During the long reign of Queen Joan of Anjou (1343–81) Naples also enjoyed a rich cultural life, in which music, including polyphony, had a primary role, but this particular aspect of fourteenth-century Neapolitan history still needs to be studied.

A group of singers of the courts of Alexander V and John XXII (1410–15), itinerant between Rome, Florence, Bologna and Constance, loved to test themselves with refined notational and rhythmic complexities, which were intended to compete with French mannerism in a supreme test of technical mastery. Bartolomeo from Bologna, Corrado from Pistoia, Matteo from Perugia and Antonio Zacara from Teramo contributed to this repertory which, made up of ballades on French texts and motets, is also called Ars Subtilior. But the oldest representative of this trend was Filippotto from Caserta, followed by Antonello Marot, also from Caserta; both of them had contact with the Angevins of Naples, but they were active in other places too, maybe in northern Italy. With reference to this, one should remember that three popes during the last part of the fourteenth century and the first years of the fifteenth were from Naples: Urban VI (Bartolomeo Prignani, 1378–89), Boniface IX (Pietro Tomacelli, 1389–1404) and John XXII (Baldassarre Cossa, 1410–15).

Two codices, compiled by Italian scribes in the second decade of the fifteenth century, contain Ars Subtilior repertory: the manuscript Modena, Biblioteca Estense, α.M.5.24 (with one hundred pieces, above all ballades, virelais, rondeaux and sections of the mass ordinary) and the Turin Codex, Biblioteca Nazionale Universitaria, T. III. 2 (a fragment of 15 folios with 16 sections of the ordinary, twenty Italian and French secular pieces and two motets).

The madrigal

The madrigal, mostly for two voices, is the musical-poetic form most used by the first masters of the Italian Ars Nova. The term *madrigale* has an uncertain etymology; it is thought that it might derive from *matricale* ('written in the mother tongue') or from *mandria* ('herd': a *mandriale* would, therefore, be a shepherd's song). There are also other less likely hypotheses: *materialis* from *materia*, that is, 'material' as opposed to spiritual or in the sense of 'without art'; *matricale* from *amatricius* ('love poetry'), and so on.

In any case, the madrigal has a specific poetic form: it has two (rarely three) *terzine* (that is, stanzas with three hendecasyllables each), followed by a final distich (two lines) with rhymes in pairs, called a *ritornello*, always in hendecasyllables. The rhyme scheme can vary; these are Petrarch's schemes:

ABC ABC DD (*Nova angeletta*)
ABA BCB CC (*Non al so amante*)
ABB ACC CDD (*Or vedi, Amor*)
ABA CBC DE DE (*Perch'al viso*, with double ritornello).

The most common scheme in manuscripts with notation is ABB CDD EE. As regards content, the madrigals collected in music codices are courtly love lyrics (not popular) – idyllic or pastoral compositions. They often cite symbolic animals (lamb, leopard, snake, falcon, eagle, phoenix, turtledove etc.) which mostly have a metaphorical and heraldic meaning (they refer to personages or city people). Moralistic, political (celebratory) or didactic themes are not excluded. It is a poetry rich in convention (the same themes and situations recur several times), in symbolism (the use of allegory, metaphor, heraldic symbolism, *senhal* etc.) and in artifice (acrostics, rhyming answers etc.). The final distich, which shows a similarity to the caccia, expresses the gist, the 'moral' or a poignant commentary on the situation described in the three-line verses.

Formally the musical setting follows closely the poetic form: every three-line verse receives the same music (section A), whereas the ritornello has a different melody (section B), treated as a separate section (and often with a mensuration different from the preceding three-line section). It should be noted that the ritornello is not a refrain, that is, it is never repeated; the name possibly derives from the more archaic form, which required the repetition of the ritornello after every three-line verse. In brief: a normal eight-line madrigal (3+3+2) has the structure AAB, whereas an eleven-line madrigal (3+3+3+2) has the structure AAAB. The form of the madrigal is mainly practised by the early composers of the Italian Ars Nova (Piero, Jacopo da Bologna, Giovanni da Cascia, Gherardello, Lorenzo and Vincenzo), whereas in the second half of the fourteenth century (from circa 1370 onwards) the form was progressively abandoned in favour of the ballata: Landini (who died in 1397), for instance, left only 12 madrigals but 140 ballatas.

The musical style of the madrigal shows several constants: the tenor has relatively long values, the higher part (or parts) is embellished with typical

Ars Nova decoration; one scholar has defined it as 'embellished conductus style', in contrast to the polyrhythmic style of contemporary French secular music (Machaut). The same madrigal often appears in different manuscripts with different embellishments in the discantus, maybe proof of a widespread improvisatory practice.

Both voices often have the text in the codices, suggesting a purely vocal performance, but even when the tenor does not show the text, a vocal performance is perfectly legitimate; we also have proofs of solely instrumental performances of madrigals in the form of intavolatura for keyboard notation. The madrigals for three voices, which are the exception, very often have particular features: canonic writing in the higher voices or different texts for all the three voices (as in Landini's *Musica son*).

As an example of a classical madrigal I have chosen Petrarch's *Non al so amante* (*Rerum vulgarium fragmenta*, LII), set to music by Jacopo da Bologna.

This is the text (derived from the version in Paris, Bibliothèque nationale de France, fonds italien 568), with a translation and the rhyme scheme.

Non al so amante più Diana piacque	A	Diana was no more pleasing to her lover
quando per tal ventura tutta nuda	B	when by chance all naked
la vide in mezo delle gelid'acque	A	he saw her in the midst of the cold waters
ch'a me la pasturella alpestra e cruda	B	than was the cruel mountain shepherdess to me,
fissa a bagnare un legiadretto velo	C	intent on dipping in the water a pretty veil
che 'l sole all'aura el vago capel chiuda.	B	which hides her lovely hair from sun and wind
Tal che mi fece quando egli arde 'l cielo	C	So that she made me, when the sun burns the sky,
tutto tremar d'un amoroso gelo.	C	tremble with an icy love.

As we can see, the meaning of the text does not find closure at the end of the first three-line verse, but carries over into the second; this is one of the reasons why the ritornello must not be repeated after every three-line verse, but sung only at the end. In the first terzina there is a reference to Actaeon, the mythological character instructed by the centaur Chiron, who while hunting saw Diana and her companions bathing naked in a little lake; the goddesses, angered, transformed him into a deer and made his own dogs devour him.

The poet sees his lover (Laura), called 'pasturella alpestra e cruda' (rustic and cruel shepherdess: it is the only occurrence of the term *pastorella* in Petrarch's poetry; the humble and rural representation is certainly a homage to the madrigal genre, which, according to the theorists, *must* deal with rural people and things – 'de villanellis'), washing a handkerchief (*velo*) and compares this encounter, to stress the intensity of his love, to that of Actaeon who, by chance, had seen his lover Diana naked while she was bathing in the lake. In the ritornello ('Tal che mi fece quando egli arde 'il cielo / tutto tremar d'un amoroso gelo') he describes his condition at that sight: the burning sun notwithstanding, he trembles 'd'un amoroso gelo'.

Example 8.1 allows us to observe the musical style of the madrigal. Almost every one of the hundred and fifty or so madrigals transmitted by the Italian Ars Nova manuscripts and fragments has a textual and musical structure similar to that of *Non al so amante*, revealing a rather rigid canonization of the form.

As far as the macrostructure of the madrigal *Non al so amante* is concerned, there is total respect, in the music, for the ends of individual lines, as happens in almost all surviving fourteenth-century madrigals. At the end of every hendecasyllable there is a closing cadence, even when there is an enjambment (see the words *piacque, nuda, acque, cielo, gelo* in the transcription); however, when there is an enjambment, the tenor continues the discourse with a linking phrase (see particularly bars 12 and 23–4), creating musical continuity between lines, which, in turn, reflects the continuity of sense. The stereotyped segmentation of each line, which can be observed in many madrigals of the first Ars Nova masters (the same happens in the ballades), is as follows: the first syllable is set to a melisma which ends on the following syllable.

The caccia

This is perhaps the most typical musical-poetic form of the Italian Ars Nova repertory. There are almost thirty examples with music. The text usually presents animated hunting and fishing scenes, or conjures up images of lively markets. The texts have plenty of first-person dialogue, often very agitated (imitating dogs' barks, vendors' calls etc.). There is no fixed metrical scheme; lines of five and seven syllables alternate with hendecasyllables and are variously rhymed.

The musical texture is for three voices, with the two higher voices in strict canonic imitation: the second voice begins six or more breves after the first voice. The two chasing voices are supported by a tenor with long values, almost always without text (but not necessarily destined to be performed instrumentally), which takes no part in the imitation. The short ritornello section, which can also have the two higher voices in canon, follows the rather extended first section.

Example 8.1 Jacopo da Bologna, *Non al so amante* (*F-Pn* fonds italien 568, fols. 4v–5r)

This kind of writing – for three parts with two in canon – has great historic importance because it is the first appearance of a style with a sustaining low part.

Sometimes it can happen that a madrigal with a realistic text is set to music in the form of a caccia. There is an analogous and contemporary

Example 8.1 (*cont.*)

form with a French text: the *chace* (four examples are contained in the Ivrea Codex; there are other examples by Machaut).

The term 'caccia' refers both to the prevailing argument of the text and to the fugue-like procedure in the higher voices, which chase and follow one another: it should be remembered that the term 'caccia' in the fourteenth century indicates the chase of the enemy or the escape from the enemy, as in Dante's use of it in the *Inferno* (XIII, 33) and the *Purgatorio* (VI, 15 and XIII, 119). Even in *Il Fiore* (a collection of late-thirteenth-century sonnets, sometimes attributed to Dante) the phrase 'to put to caccia' means 'to put to flight', 'to drive away' (XIII, 13; LXX, 7; XCIII, 11).

Example 8.2 shows the beginning of a typical Ars Nova caccia, from the Mischiati Fragment in the Reggio Emilia state archive, a bifolio dated circa 1370 and copied in the Po area. This is the text of the caccia:

Nella foresta al cervo caciatore	In the forest the hunter of the deer
'Qua, qua, Lion! Qua, qua, Dragon!' chiamava.	'Here, here, Lion! Here, here, Dragon' called.
'Te, te, te',	'Te, te, te',
dintorno al riço i cani pur baiava:	around the hedgehog the dogs were barking:
'Bauff, bauff, bauff'.	'Bauff, bauff, bauff'.
'Al riço, al riço francho!',	'To the hedgehog, to the hedgehog, free!',
quando lo vide: 'Al riço, al riço stancho.'	when he saw it: 'To the hedgehog, to the tired hedgehog.'
Dicean 'Da, da, da, da'	'Da, da, da, da', said
li chan rendendo baglio.	the dogs making a blunder.
El riço vigoroso in ogni taglio	The hedgehog vigorous in every hedge
rimase senza innoia e senza tedio.	was cool and calm and totally unbothered.

The fact that the rhyme of the last line is unrelated to what precedes it may indicate that the text we have is the first verse of a caccia that originally had two verses, like *Segugi a corta* (which, by the way, has the same rhyme scheme, but whose last line is a seven-syllable line and not a hendecasyllable) and as Corsi hypothesized about Giovanni's caccia *Per larghi prati*.

The text depicts a scene in which the protagonists are hunting dogs which, during a deer beat, are distracted by an encounter with a little hedgehog (*riço* or *riccio*) and stop to bark at it. Rebuked and spurred on by the hunter to continue their chase, they start running again and the hedgehog remains unhurt. It is likely that the text hides a war metaphor and that the hedgehog represents the emblem of a city or of a family: a *condottiere* (that is, a mercenary leader) with expansionist designs (Luchino Visconti?) disregards the conquest of a certain place in order to lead a much more important military campaign elsewhere.

The hedgehog mentioned in the caccia *Nella foresta* could be an allusion to the coat of arms of the Bertacchi, lords of the Rocca Alberti of Garfagnana, a few kilometres from Camporgiano. The Florentine Republic expropriated the Rocca Alberti castle together with other villages and little castles when its armies invaded the upper valley of the Serchio; yet the castle was not touched thanks to the immediate signing of the Treaty of Pietrasanta on

Example 8.2 *Nella foresta* (caccia) (*I-REas* Mischiati Fragment, fol. Av)

Nel - la fo - re-sta al cer-vo_ ca - cia - to - re 'Qua, qua, Li - on! Qua,

Nel -

qua, Dra-gon!' chia-ma-va. 'Tè, tè, tè', din-tor no al ri - ço i ca -

-la fo - re-sta al cer-vo_ ca - cia - to-re 'Qua, qua, Li - on! Qua,qua, Dra-

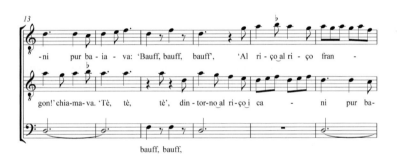

-ni pur ba-ia - va: 'Bauff, bauff, bauff', 'Al ri - ço al ri - ço fran -

gon!' chia-ma-va. 'Tè, tè, tè', din-tor-no al ri-ço i ca - ni pur ba-

bauff, bauff,

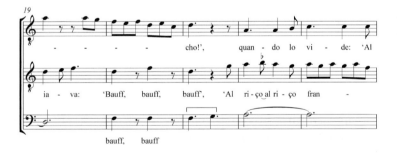

- - - cho!', quan - do lo vi - de: 'Al

ia - va: 'Bauff, bauff, bauff', 'Al ri - ço al ri - ço fran -

bauff, bauff

Example 8.2 (*cont.*)

15 May 1346, which brought peace between the Republic of Florence, Luchino and Galeazzo Visconti on the one hand and the Republic of Pisa on the other. If the identification suggested above is correct, the composition of the caccia would date back to around 1346.

The agitated shouts in the caccia *Nella foresta* create a dense web of textual cross-references with other known caccias:

- 'Da, da' appears in the caccia for the Visconti family *Con bracchi assai*, set to music in competition by Giovanni from Florence and by Magister Piero.
- 'Te, te' occurs in Jacopo's *Per sparverare*, also written for the Visconti (given the presence of the dog Varin), and in Gherardello's *Tosto che l'alba*.
- 'Bauff, bauff', 'Da, da' and the dog Dragon appear in the caccia *Segugi a corta*.
- 'Bauff, bauff', 'Te, te' and the dog Dragon feature in the caccia in the accompanying page of the Mischiati Fragment (*Mirando i pesci*).

There is no ritornello in the text, but the musical setting reserves the typical treatment of the ritornello for the last line (with a change of *divisio* and reduction to two voices), as in the caccia *Segugi a corta*.

The ballata

The ballata is the main musical-poetic form of the Italian Ars Nova; it does not have anything in common with the French ballade, rather it is like the virelai. From the point of view of text, the ballata consists of a ritornello, called ripresa (R), and normally three strophes (S) which alternate with the ritornello: R S_1 R S_2 R S_3 R. It is possible to use the abbreviated form – without repetition of the ripresa – R S_1 S_2 S_3 R. The strophe consists of two *piedi* – feet – (or *mutazioni*), with the same rhyme scheme, and a *volta*, which has the same metric structure as the ripresa. The feet form the *fronte* of the verse, the volta is also called *sirma*. Sometimes the ripresa and each foot are formed of two lines, sometimes the ripresa consists of three lines and the foot of two. The lines are usually hendecasyllables, or seven-syllable lines, or a mixture of seven-syllable lines and hendecasyllables. The following are a few examples of the rhyme schemes used in the ballatas found in music codices; the feet are divided by the comma and between fronte and sirma there is a semicolon:

XX AB, AB; BX (the most common scheme)
XYY ABC, ABC; CYY
XyX AB, AB; ByX
XYY AB, AB; BCY
XyY AbC, AbC; XyY
XyyX AB, AB; BCcX
xYxY AB, AB; bXbX
XyyX AB, AB; BccX
X AB, AB; X

The ballata is the favourite metre of the Stil novo poets and is extensively used by Petrarch. A ballata with more than a verse is called 'ballata vestita' (dressed ballata) or 'ballata replicata' (replicated ballata). When the ballata has a ripresa with more than four lines, it is called 'grande' (great); if the ripresa has three lines, it is called 'mezzana' (medium); it is called 'minore' (minor) if it has two lines, 'piccola' (small) if it has just one hendecasyllable for the ripresa, 'minima' (minimum/smallest) with a seven-syllable line, and 'stravagante' (extravagant) with a ripresa of more than four lines. The ballata usually treats of love, very often with moralizing turns; sometimes it is sententious or imploring.

The music is composed only for the ripresa and the first foot; it is then repeated for the remaining lines in this way:

RIPRESA: A; *PIEDI*: B B; *VOLTA*: A; *RIPRESA*: A, etc.

In modern transcriptions there results the form A BBA, written usually with two sections (A and B) repeated. In the original source only the ripresa and the first foot are written below the notes; the text of the second foot and of the volta are usually written one after the other at the end of the discantus. Unlike in the virelai, the ballata very rarely presents *ouvert* and *clos* endings.

Because of its name, which derives from the verb *ballare* (to dance), it is thought that the ballata was a song accompanying a dance. The choreographic figurations associated with the ballata, sung by the dancers who held each other by the hand, were these: before opening the dance there was an invitation to the youngsters to dance; later, as suggested by Sacchetti's' poem *Così m'aiuti Dio*, the invitation became a simple request, to a young man or girl, to lead the song and the dance. The ripresa, sung by the soloist, was immediately repeated by the chorus; then there followed the verse for solo voice. With perfect correspondence to the poetic-musical structure, the dancers performed a full turn to the right during the ripresa; a half turn to the left and a half turn to the right respectively, corresponding with the first and the second foot; and again a full turn, but this time to the left, during the volta, so that at the end of the verses all the dancers were in the opening position to repeat the turn of the dance from left to right.

Other evidence about ways of performing the ballata is provided by Giovanni del Virgilio, a teacher of rhetoric in Bologna and a friend of Dante, who gives the following description in his *Ekloge diaffonus* (ca1316): after the short opening of a few lines, sung by a cantor and repeated by the chorus (the 'ripresa' or 'recantus'), a group of girls and boys sings the verse with the two feet and the volta; so far no one moves, but the dance of the antistrophe and of the successive verses starts immediately, until the ripresa, sung together by the cantor and the dancers, marks the conclusion. Singing the ripresa and the first verse without choreography allowed the dancers to 'count' the number of steps necessary for the dance, paying great attention to the music; a similar experience is maybe what Dante describes in *Paradiso*, X, 79:

Donne mi parver non da ballo sciolte,	Women seemed to me not freed from dance
ma che s'arrestin tacite, ascoltando	but they stopped in silence, listening
fin che le nove note hanno ricolte.	until they picked up the new notes.

The poetic structure of the ballata can be also found in the *lauda*. As for the ensemble, there have been transmitted to us fourteenth-century ballatas for one, two and three voices. We know ninety-one examples for two voices by Landini and forty-nine for three voices; many of them have one strophe. Of the vast production of monophonic fourteenth-century ballatas, only sixteen pieces and one fragment survive: five anonymous ballatas in the Rossi Codex; eleven ballatas in the Squarcialupi Codex (five by Gherardello, five by Lorenzo Masini, and one by Niccolò da Perugia); and the ripresa and the beginning of the feet of *Da la somma beltà* in the Mischiati Fragment.

Example 8.3 shows one of these monophonic ballatas: *I' vo' bene a chi vol bene a me* with a text by the poet Niccolò Soldanieri. The Squarcialupi Codex contains only the ripresa and the feet of the first verse. The text in the transcriptions is integrated with the versions found in non-music codices, which report this work by Soldanieri.

The transcription in 6/4 underlines the typical metric structure of the monodic ballata, which in the majority of cases is based on the *division duodenaria*. The twelve eighth-notes, which add up to a *brevis* in this Italian

Example 8.3 Gherardello da Firenze, *I' vo' bene* (*I-Fl* Palatino 87, fol. 29r)

mensura (4+4+4), can be divided in 3/4 plus 6/8 (see, for example, bars 3, 6, 7 and 8 of the ripresa in *I' vo' bene*), creating a rhythmic pattern well known to composers and singers. The notation of the Squarcialupi Codex simplifies the original rhythmic patterning (and makes things easier for the singer); thus, the ballata is written using the *senaria perfecta*, whose brevis is half the *duodenaria*; for this reason all modern editors transcribe the ballata in 3/4.

Motets and sacred polyphonic music

Polyphonic pieces with Latin texts (some celebratory, others written for liturgical use) composed for Italian courts and churches in the fourteenth and fifteenth centuries have not yet been thoroughly studied by musicologists. Over the past few years numerous fourteenth-century Italian fragments have been discovered, which considerably enrich our knowledge of this repertory – even though we still await a more complete picture of the size and scope of the phenomenon.[1]

Certainly the French motet is better known and more studied than the Italian, and it is also older and more widespread: many Italian sources contain motets of French origin and it should not be forgotten that the author of the greatest number of Italian celebratory motets (mostly for Paduan bishops or events in the Veneto) is Johannes Ciconia, a composer of Belgian origin.

Among the first Italian examples to consider are the already-mentioned motets of Marchetto da Padova: *Ave regina celorum – Mater innocencie* (1305), *Ave corpus sanctum* (ca1335), and *Cetus inseraphici – Cetus apostolici.*

Two motets by Jacopo da Bologna: *Lux purpurata radiis* and *Laudibus dignis merito laudari* are dedicated to Luchino Visconti (and can be dated, therefore, between 1339 and 1349); in both motets the text of the triplum has the name *Luchinus* as an acrostic.

We do not know how much of the polyphonic mensural repertory in the liturgy was practised in thirteenth-century Italy: the impression is that mensural polyphony in the Franconian style was not widespread and that, on the contrary, the practice of simple polyphony was very common.

The first clear proofs of compositions for the mass ordinary in Italy begin to appear in the fourteenth century: for example, at the end of a manuscript of Tuscan origin – Paris, Bibliothèque nationale de France, fonds italien 568 (*Pit*) – there is a cycle of the ordinary (with the Benedicamus but without the Kyrie), quite likely assembled by the copyist from the work of several famous Florentine authors:[2]

> *Pit*, fols. 131v–133, Gloria by Gherardello of Florence
> *Pit*, fols. 133v–136, Credo by Bartolo of Florence
> *Pit*, fols. 136v–137, Sanctus by Lorenzo of Florence
> *Pit*, fol. 137v, Agnus Dei by Gherardello of Florence
> *Pit*, fol. 138r, Benedicamus Domino by Paolo of Florence

Von Fischer has pointed out the great stylistic differences between these five pieces:[3] first, Bartolo's Credo has an archaic construction, with the two voices in the same range, frequently crossing, and moving mostly in contrary motion; it shows frequent changes of *mensura*. Second, Gherardello's Gloria and Agnus are stylistically similar, formally speaking, to the madrigal; and, third, Lorenzo's Sanctus sets a traditional tenor part against a very florid and sometimes heterophonic *superius*, but the composition does not have the experimentalism of his secular works. The only piece composed on a liturgical cantus firmus (and with equal values in the tenor)[4] is the Benedicamus by Abbot Paolo of Florence.

Table 8.1 *Surviving polyphonic settings of mass movements by four Italian composers*

Composer	Gloria	Credo
Zacara da Teramo	6 Glorias: 'Micinella', 'Rosetta', 'Fior gentil', 'Gloria laus', 'Ad ogne vento', 'Anglicana' (all in *I-Bc* Q15), plus two of uncertain attribution	6 Credos: 'Cursor', 'Scabioso', 'Deus deorum', 'Du vilage' and two untitled (five in *I-Bc* Q15)
Johannes Ciconia	7 Glorias: 'Suscipe trinitatis' plus three more (in *I-Bc* Q15) [untitled]{without appellative}, a fragmentary intonation and two with the Marian trope 'Spiritus et alme'	4 Credos (three in *I-Bc* Q15)
Antonio da Cividale	3 Glorias (in *I-Bc* Q15, *BU2216* and *I-CFm 79*)	1 Credo in *I-Bc* Q15
Matteo da Perugia	7 Glorias (all in Modena, Bibl. Estense, *α*.M.5.24)	2 Credos in *I-MOe α*.M.5.24

In the surviving Italian codices the most commonly found sections of fourteenth- and early-fifteenth-century polyphonic ordinaries are Glorias and Credos (more than fifty examples of the former and almost forty of the latter); there are also seventeen examples of the Sanctus, seven Kyries and only five Agnus Deis.

The relatively plentiful production in this field of four composers active in Italy in the late fourteenth and early fifteenth centuries – Zacara from Teramo, Ciconia from Liège, Antonio from Cividale, and Matteo from Perugia – reveals only settings of Glorias and Credos. Table 8.1 summarizes the data about the surviving production of these movements of the mass.

Since the four authors worked in different places it is evident that the Gloria and the Credo (probably for solemn masses) received privileged treatment. There was already a stable tradition of mensural polyphonic performance of the Credo (*cantus fractus secundatus*), whereas the Gloria needed new solemn settings in more places. However, the polyphonic and mensural setting of the Gloria and Credo had already come into use, and to replace it with compositions for three or four voices of higher artistic quality appeared in line with the liturgical tradition; furthermore, this replacement was not perceived as an extreme novelty or as a break with tradition. The polyphonic settings for the Kyrie, Sanctus and Agnus remained rarer and were reserved for specific festivities. These settings too, particularly if provided with tropes, came to resemble very closely the texts of the Gloria and Credo, and therefore were accepted without problems.

In the setting by Zacara there are the first examples of the 'parody' technique, which consists in the use of polyphonic material from pre-existing compositions; thus – for instance – the Gloria 'Rosetta' is based on the ballata *Rosetta che non cambi mai colore* by the same author. We have to wait until the beginning of the sixteenth century for this practice of using pre-existing compositions to be applied to whole mass cycles.

Certainly the liturgical repertory of Italian polyphony still needs much research in order to clarify the performance contexts of the surviving music, including the role of the organ and of Gregorian chant in solemn liturgical celebrations.

9 The Iberian peninsula

NICOLAS BELL

As with so many other aspects of Hispanic culture in the early Middle Ages, the musical life of the Iberian peninsula was distinct from that of other parts of Europe for many centuries. Though Christianity reached the peninsula as early as the third century, most of the country came under Muslim rule in 711, to be reconquered by Christians in a series of campaigns through the Middle Ages. Not only did this bring Arabic music into Europe, but the Muslims were also uniquely tolerant of the Jews, allowing a Judaeo-Spanish musical tradition to flourish, which has had wide influence elsewhere in later centuries. Until the eleventh century, the church in the Spanish kingdoms remained independent from the Roman rite and employed a separate liturgical structure, with its own musical tradition. The later Middle Ages saw much greater assimilation of musical traditions from the rest of Europe, but the peninsula also developed its own discrete musical genres, particularly in secular music making.

Isidore of Seville and Old Spanish chant

Though some evidence survives for music and dance from the Stone Age onwards,[1] it will be as well to begin this survey after the Visigoths had established a kingdom centred on Toledo and extending across almost the whole of modern-day Spain, Portugal and the south of France, by the end of the sixth century. Isidore, Archbishop of Seville (ca559–636), is a figure of major importance in all branches of learning. He compiled an encyclopaedia, the *Etymologiarum sive originum libri xx*, which enjoyed an extraordinary Europe-wide influence throughout the Middle Ages, surviving today in more than a thousand manuscripts.[2] The *Etymologiae* are largely a synthesis of the writings of various classical authors, and Isidore's definition of music as a discipline concerned with numbers as sounds directly follows Cassiodorus. As well as defining music as a subject of study within the Quadrivium, Isidore provides much information here and in his practical text on the liturgy, *De ecclesiasticis officiis*, on the role of music in the divine office.[3]

Isidore played an important part in the fourth council of Toledo in 633, one of the canons arising from which prescribed a single order of prayer and singing ('orandi atque psallendi') to be kept through all of Spain and Gaul (Gaul here meaning the Roman province centred on Narbonne). Neither his own writings nor the decrees of the fourth council suggest that Isidore himself was directly involved in the composition of the chants for the newly reformed liturgy, but his writings enhance our understanding of the surviving liturgical books, all of which date from later centuries. Isidore and others do, though, mention various composers of chant, including his brother Leander, whom he succeeded as Bishop of Seville and who 'composed many works of sweet sound'.

The liturgy of the Spanish church is often misleadingly referred to as the 'Mozarabic rite', since it is known today from books used by Christians living under Moorish rule, the Mozarabs (from the Arabic 'making oneself an Arab'). The more general term 'Old Spanish' or 'Hispanic' is nowadays preferred, since it is clear that the liturgy was well established before the Muslim invasion in 711, at least from the fourth council of Toledo and probably in some form long before this. It was also used for some time in parts of the Christian north of Spain that never came under Muslim rule, and other parts that returned to Christian rule in intervening years. The rite did not go unchallenged within Christian territories, however: in parts of Catalonia the Roman rite was preferred from a very early date, and a growing desire for liturgical uniformity (and imposition of papal authority) through the tenth and eleventh centuries led eventually to the suppression of the Old Spanish rite in favour of the Roman throughout reconquered Spain in the treaty of Burgos in 1080.[4] Meanwhile the Portuguese territories had used the Roman rite from as early as the sixth century, and the Old Spanish rite was employed for only a somewhat briefer period than in the northern Spanish kingdoms.[5]

Only one liturgical book, an *orationale* written in Tarragona, survives from as early as the time of the Muslim occupation.[6] This does not include any musical notation, but the chant texts it records concur with later sources, confirming that the liturgical prescriptions were broadly fixed by this time. Notation is preserved in more than twenty complete manuscripts of the Old Spanish rite, mainly from the tenth and eleventh centuries, and a further twenty or so fragments.[7] This is a large number when compared with other chant traditions from this time, but because of their early date, almost all of the manuscripts are written in a notation that is not decipherable. The suppression of the rite unfortunately occurred just before pitch-specific notation was becoming common elsewhere. The notation bears some relation to other neumatic systems, but is in many respects quite different, the extravagantly florid style of some complex neumes being unlike any other traditions in western Europe. It may be divided into two broad categories: about one third of the surviving manuscripts employ an oblique, almost horizontal ductus, associated with manuscripts from the school of Toledo, and the remainder use the 'northern' notation especially associated with León and the Rioja, which has a more vertical aspect.[8]

It is a particular shame that no manuscripts survive from the southern half of the country, since those parts which remained under Muslim rule into the fifteenth century might well have continued to use the Old Spanish chant late enough to have notated it on a staff. As it is, we are fortunate that in a single tenth-century manuscript from the monastery of San Millán de la Cogolla (Rioja), the Old Spanish notation of eighteen chants for the Office of the Dead was erased in the eleventh century, to be replaced by heightened – and therefore decipherable – Aquitanian neumes.[9] Similarly, three antiphons for the washing of feet on Maundy Thursday were replaced with Aquitanian notation in MS 4 of San Domingo at Silos, a monastery from where many other important liturgical manuscripts also survive. This may leave us with only twenty-one decipherable melodies out of a complete repertory of many thousands, but scholars have extrapolated from this slender evidence to reveal many general similarities with other Western chant traditions.[10]

The manuscripts preserve a large repertory of antiphons for the mass and office, which Isidore tells us were sung by two choirs alternating, as in the Gregorian tradition. There is no evidence of a structured system of eight modes, but certain formulas are found regularly in particular contexts, which again shows a certain degree of resemblance to other Western chant traditions. The responsory chants are closer in form and structure to their Frankish equivalents, but show a considerable degree of variation in their psalm-tones between sources from the different regions. The various chants for the mass use a separate terminology from their counterparts in other rites, but have broadly similar functions in the service.

The gradual suppression of the Spanish rite in favour of the Roman was generally brought about through new liturgical books using Aquitanian notation, though a few examples survive from the time of transition of manuscripts of the new rite using the old notation.[11] The extent to which Spanish plainchant demonstrated uniformity across the country and remained true to its Roman sources in succeeding centuries is not a subject that has yet received much attention. There were certainly national and local characteristics in particular liturgical forms, some of which are likely to be a legacy from the old rite. For example, though the majority of hymn texts found in the Spanish kingdoms were widely disseminated in other countries, almost two thirds of the melodies are not generally known outside the peninsula. Many of these are likely to be native compositions, and some are probably remnants of the Old Spanish rite.[12]

New musical forms in the church

It seems improbable that tropes or sequences were ever employed in the Old Spanish liturgy.[13] There are references to *prosaria*, a term often used to describe books containing both tropes and proses, in various Catalan documents listing the books required for the Roman liturgy from as early as the mid tenth century, but the earliest trope manuscript to survive from the Iberian peninsula dates from no earlier than the late eleventh century. MS 105 in the Cathedral Archive of Vic (north of Barcelona) contains tropes for the ordinary of the mass, as well as several introit tropes and a large number of sequences.[14] Only around a dozen such manuscripts survive in all from the Iberian peninsula through to the fifteenth century, but it seems likely that the practice of troping was far more widespread than the surviving sources might lead us to believe.[15] In later sources, a far greater number of ordinary tropes are found than of proper, and while the repertory used in Vic appears to have been compiled locally, sources from elsewhere are often derived directly from Aquitanian practice.

A similar pattern of dissemination may be assumed in the case of liturgical drama. A later portion of the same manuscript in Vic, dating from the early twelfth century, includes a play of the three Marys, and similar plays are known from elsewhere in Catalonia from a relatively early date.[16] It is clear that while Catalonia was one of the great centres of creativity in the practice of liturgical drama, these forms of liturgical expression were much less widespread elsewhere in the peninsula. Brief versions of the *Visitatio sepulchri* are found in two eleventh-century manuscripts from the abbey of Silos written in Mozarabic script and notation yet forming part of the Roman rite, but other examples from outside Catalonia are few and far between. It seems that their place was taken by a complementary tradition of vernacular drama on ecclesiastical subjects, beginning in the late twelfth century with the *Auto de los Reyes Magos*, which cannot properly be considered as liturgical drama and for which music does not generally survive.

In Catalonia in the later Middle Ages several dramatic innovations took place in the context of the liturgy. A customary or *consueta* from Girona, dated 1360, describes eight different representational ceremonies, including a particularly sophisticated *Visitatio sepulchri*, the first of three plays to take place at Easter. Though the texts used at Girona do not for the most part survive, this book provides much useful information as to how the plays were enacted. Among the Christmastide representations was one on the martyrdom of Saint Stephen, a theme which appears to have been a Catalan speciality and which extended in Barcelona to a realistic stoning of the protomartyr with imitation stones.[17] In the fourteenth and fifteenth centuries the feast of the Assumption of the Virgin came to be celebrated in ever more elaborate processions, often including dramatic elements sometimes in the vernacular. The most famous of these, the Mystery of Elx (or Elche), is an extended drama in Catalan which is still performed each year. Though the present format and music largely derive from the seventeenth century, it represents a continuous tradition from the end of the Middle Ages.

Another ceremony that sometimes took on a dramatic form in the Spanish church is associated with matins on Christmas morning. The song of the Sibyl, prophesying the Second Coming at the Day of Judgement, has its origins in the first years of Christianity and began to be used in a liturgical context in the twelfth century, as the sixth or ninth lesson of matins for the Nativity, in certain monasteries as well as a few cathedrals. This practice was especially common in the Spanish territories, though examples are also found in France and Italy. The foreboding refrain, 'Iudicii signum: tellus sudore madescet' ('Sign of Judgement: the earth will grow wet with sweat'), is sung in alternation with a series of verses. In some churches the prophecy would be sung by a boy dressed up as the Erythraean pythoness. Some of the Spanish sources from the fifteenth and sixteenth centuries give the words in Catalan or Spanish instead of Latin, thereby making this remarkable chant even more direct and immediate to its audience.[18]

Just as tropes and sequences were unknown in the Old Spanish rite, let alone such dramatic ceremonies as the Sibylline prophecy, so it seems that the practice of polyphony was unknown to the Visigoths and Mozarabs. At the very least we can say that no notated examples survive, nor is there any testimony to the practice in documentary sources. The sparse material that has survived postdates the imposition of the Roman rite by some considerable time, and much of it shows the strong influence of French polyphonic styles.

The earliest significant manuscript in this context was probably made in France, possibly around Vézelay, in the mid twelfth century. It is a compilation of historical, hagiographical and liturgical material connected with Saint James, and was used at his shrine at Santiago de Compostela.[19] At the end of the book are found 21 polyphonic pieces, a mixture of mass chants, responsories, Benedicamus settings and conductus, all in two parts except for one in three parts. Very unusually for this period, the pieces are fictitiously ascribed to various named individuals, all of them French and including several bishops. Even if the manuscript was not created in Spain, its presence at Santiago from such an early date provides important evidence of the practice of polyphony in the Iberian peninsula in the twelfth century.

Our knowledge of polyphony in the Iberian peninsula in the following century derives largely from a diverse range of fragmentary sources from various monastic and secular institutions spread throughout Catalonia and Castile,[20] but in addition to these we are fortunate that two of the principal sources of polyphony prior to the Ars Nova are of Iberian provenance. The origins of the first, the Madrid Codex, are unclear. It was kept in Toledo Cathedral until being transferred in 1869 to the Biblioteca Nacional in Madrid, where it now has the number 20486, but there is no evidence to connect it directly with Toledo before the seventeenth century. It was probably written in northern Spain around 1260, and comprises some 61 conductus and 35 motets, as well as a few other polyphonic compositions, notably including texted and untexted versions of the famous *quadrupla* attributed to Perotinus, *Viderunt omnes* and *Sederunt principes* (some parts of which are now missing).[21] Many of the compositions in the Madrid Codex are also known from Parisian sources, but there are a good number of pieces unique to this manuscript, several of which may reasonably be assumed to be native Iberian compositions.

The second major source of polyphony is the Las Huelgas codex, which is still housed in the Cistercian convent for which it was written towards the end of the first quarter of the fourteenth century, the Monasterio de Santa María la Real de Las Huelgas, outside Burgos.[22] The manuscript is chiefly the work of a single scribe, and presents a substantial repertory of 48 organa (including several ordinary tropes in two or three parts), 31 sequences (eleven of them polyphonic), 58 motets and 29 conductus, to which another nineteen pieces in various genres have been added by eleven later hands.

The singing of polyphony, let alone tropes and sequences, was strictly forbidden by the Cistercian order, but Las Huelgas was in many respects an exceptional convent. It was founded in 1187 by Alfonso VIII and his queen, Eleanor of England, as both a monastic house for noblewomen and a royal mausoleum. It is very likely that this book, which brings together music written throughout the thirteenth and early fourteenth centuries, from France and elsewhere in Europe as well as a large number of Spanish compositions, was intended as a complete repertory of the music required at the convent outside that of the regular liturgical books. It is not certain that the nuns themselves sang the music: the foundation had a large retinue of chaplains who may well have formed a choir.

Unlike several of the major sources of organa and motets from other countries, the Las Huelgas codex is not a beautiful manuscript; it is written on parchment of poor quality and the pages are often heavily and inelegantly corrected. This makes it all the more interesting, as it was clearly intended as a practical manuscript, representing the music exactly as it was performed. The notation appears clumsy and unsystematic when compared with other manuscripts, but in fact shows considerable subtlety and nuance in matters of performance, particularly of rhythm. The repertory of pieces unique to this codex, at least some of which we may assume were specially composed at or for the convent, includes some attractive sequences in honour of the Blessed Virgin, and four *planctus* or songs of mourning for deceased kings and an abbess which show particular melodic extravagance.

As in the thirteenth century, so in the fourteenth various fragments give testimony to the widespread practice of Ars Nova polyphony in the Iberian peninsula, albeit on a less sophisticated scale than is found in other countries. The most famous source from this period is the so-called Llibre Vermell ('red book'), which was compiled in the last years of the fourteenth century as a collection of materials relating to the pilgrimage site of the shrine of the Black Madonna at the abbey of Montserrat in Catalonia, where the manuscript remains to this day. As well as accounts of miracles, homilies and many other miscellaneous texts, seven folios are devoted to ten pieces of music.[23] An annotation makes it clear that these were written not for use in the liturgy but for pilgrims to sing for their own amusement and edification during the night vigil and in the courtyard by day. Four of the pieces are monophonic, two in two parts and four in three parts; eight are in Latin and two in Catalan. All but the last are songs in honour of the Virgin; three are simple canons, and another three are in virelai form.

The Llibre Vermell is an exceptional survival of a fairly simple type of songwriting from the end of the fourteenth century. Evidence for the creative development of liturgical polyphony in the Iberian peninsula in the following century is relatively limited. Simple polyphony is found on occasion in books of predominantly monophonic chant, very probably reflecting a more widespread tradition of improvised polyphony, but surviving polyphonic choirbooks do not demonstrate the degree of contrapuntal sophistication found in the Low Countries and elsewhere at the time. Studies of the rich archives of the Catalano-Aragonese court have shown that music had an important place in the life of the court, both inside and outside the royal chapel, and other archives are now being mined for similar information.[24] However, it was not until after the marriage of Isabella of Castile to Ferdinand of Aragón in 1469, and the subsequent union of the two kingdoms, that we may observe a conscious attempt to bring the latest polyphonic styles from central Europe into the peninsula. At first this was effected more by importing music than by commissioning new works from native composers. An unnumbered manuscript in Segovia Cathedral written in 1495–7 combines many works of such northern composers as Obrecht and Josquin with much simpler native Spanish compositions by Juan de Anchieta and others.[25] But in the early years of the sixteenth century fully fledged northern-style counterpoint came to be done with confidence in the peninsula, and such composers as Peñalosa and Morales may be ranked with the most sophisticated and talented of their contemporaries elsewhere.[26]

Music outside the church

As with liturgical polyphony, our knowledge of secular music in the Iberian peninsula in the Middle Ages depends on a very small number of manuscripts all of which are of immense importance in an international context. A tenth-century manuscript known as the Azagra Codex contains versus some of which are supplied with simple neumes.[27] In subsequent centuries we know that there was a tradition of professional musicians in courtly and perhaps also more lowly circles, but only very few musical fragments survive as testament to this tradition: it was not until the fifteenth century that romances (or ballads) and the increasingly popular genre of the *villancico* came to be written down.[28] A small bifolio now in New York is the sole musical source for six love songs, or *cantigas de amigo*, by a minstrel named Martin Codax, dating from the second half of the thirteenth century.[29] The stories told in the songs are set in Vigo, on the border of Spain and Portugal, and the texts are written in Galician Portuguese. A comparable manuscript fragment was recently discovered with the music of seven Galician love songs by the Portuguese king Dom Dinis (1261–1325).[30]

Among these piecemeal testaments to a widespread tradition of vernacular monophonic song, pride of place goes to the most famous medieval secular song repertory to survive from any country, the *Cantigas de Santa María* of Alfonso X of Castile and León (1221–84), known as Alfonso el Sabio, Alfonso the Wise. Some 420 cantigas survive in four luxurious manuscripts, principal among them codex b.I.2 in the library of El Escorial.[31] The language is again Galician Portuguese, and most of the cantigas tell stories of miracles effected by the Blessed Virgin; every tenth song is a *cantiga de loor* in praise of the Virgin. Whether the king actually composed any of the cantigas himself is open to question: illuminations in the Escorial manuscript show him overseeing its production, and in some of the cantigas the king speaks in the first person, but it is more likely that his responsibility took the form of closely involved patronage.

The context in which this large repertory came into being has been hotly contested. No immediate precursors survive in written form, and it has been suggested that the melodies, which are notated rhythmically, may derive from Spanish folksongs, from the music of French or Spanish troubadours, or even from an Arabic song tradition.[32] Most of the cantigas are in the form of the virelai (ABCCABAB). Only a single melodic line is written, but the manuscripts are richly illuminated with pictures of musicians playing very accurate depictions of various instruments, most probably implying that they should be sung to the accompaniment of one or more instrument, and maybe also with dancers. Many modern reconstructions of medieval instruments have been made on the basis of the illustrations in codex b.I.2. The repertory as a whole is a remarkable survival and has spawned a considerable diversity of modern realizations.

Muslim and Jewish musical life

The Muslim invasion of 711 was driven by a fundamental difference in religion, and yet it seems that Christians living in the Moorish territories (known as al-Andalus) were not severely persecuted. The church naturally lost its administrative authority, many people were converted to Islam and the majority assumed the language and dress of Muslims by becoming Mozarabs, but Christian worship was not proscribed; even some monasteries were allowed to continue to operate. Likewise, if to a lesser extent, the Christian reconquest in subsequent centuries left room for a considerable degree of acculturation between Christian, Muslim and Jew.

No musical manuscripts survive from Muslim Spain, but we know a good deal about music making at court and elsewhere in Moorish society from literary and other documentary sources.[33] The Arab influx brought many new instruments to the peninsula. Several of these, such as the *'ūd* (lute), *rabāb* (rebec) and *naqqāra* (nakers), subsequently enjoyed wider influence throughout Europe. The exceptional skills of Moorish craftsmen were used to full advantage after the reconquest by the Christian rulers; Moorish instrument-makers, as well as players and dancers, enjoyed high status in courtly circles. The cultural achievements of the Muslims were cherished, not spurned.

In the ninth century, a great number of classical Greek texts were translated into Arabic. This gave birth to an Arabic tradition of speculative writing on music which reached a level of great sophistication in its interpretation of the nature of harmony, melody and rhythm, providing an interesting counterpart to the more theologically charged discussions in the Latin West.[34] One of the greatest cultural influences from the Arab world on the reconquered territories came in the twelfth century, when many scientific and philosophical works were translated from Arabic into Latin. These included many musical writings, but also Greek texts which had until then remained unknown to Latin-speaking scholars.[35] Though the Andalusian frontier provided a conduit for the dissemination of these newly available sources throughout Europe, surprisingly little survives in the way of Latin music theory written in the peninsula before the fifteenth century.[36] There is nevertheless enough evidence to suggest that the study of music held a position within the Spanish scholastic tradition comparable with other countries, and the university of Salamanca was the first to have a chair of music, established in 1254 by Alfonso el Sabio.

Like the Muslims, the Jews were finally expelled from the Spanish kingdoms in 1492, when Ferdinand and Isabella's newly combined forces conquered Granada and ended the Muslim rule that had been in place there since 711. In the preceding centuries, the Jews of Spain (known as Sephardi from a Hebrew word interpreted as meaning 'Spain') had actively participated in the musical culture of the peninsula, both Christian and Muslim, incorporating elements of the *villancico* and other secular genres into their own music making.

Though no medieval sources of Jewish music survive from Spain or Portugal (from where the Jews were similarly expelled in 1497), the Jews' musical traditions were maintained in exile, in particular by the Sephardi who settled in North Africa and parts of the Ottoman Empire. Much speculative work has been done to evaluate the extent to which later sources from other countries retain vestiges of Iberian musical practices.[37] The influence of the Castilian ballad, a secular genre that flourished in the fifteenth century, persists to the present day, and though textual similarities with medieval Iberian sources can be shown to exist, it is impossible to say with any conviction that the melodies known from later sources bear any relation to those that may have been sung across the peninsula in the fifteenth century or earlier.[38] Formal vestiges of certain of the Galician cantigas may likewise be found in the texts of some later, post-exile Jewish songs. The close ties between Arabic and Jewish culture brought about new styles of Hebrew verse founded on Arabic models, as well as a developed understanding of the theory of music in Hebrew treatises, again inspired by Arabic rather than Latin sources.

The tremendous diversity to be found in the musical life of the Iberian peninsula in the Middle Ages has perhaps been unduly neglected in the standard histories, which have often seen Spain as a peripheral concern in the context of the wider story of music making in Europe. While it is true that many aspects of the peninsula's musical practices had few ramifications beyond its borders, the numerous innovations and idiosyncrasies that characterize its history are increasingly coming to be understood as an integral part of European cultural history. Spain and Portugal are both countries where important new sources continue to be discovered, and the process of reassessment will continue in years to come.

10 Music east of the Rhine

ROBERT CURRY

National historians of East Central Europe look back to the Middle Ages and early Renaissance as the glory days of their respective countries: to Bohemia-Moravia in the mid fourteenth century under Charles I/IV, King and Emperor; to Hungary in the later fifteenth century under Mátyás Corvinus; and to the Polish-Lithuanian Commonwealth in the sixteenth century under the Jagiellonian kings and their Hungarian-born successor, Stefan Batory. By 1518, the year in which Zygmunt Stary (Sigismund I) married Bona Sforza (Poland's metaphorical embrace of the Renaissance) the vast Jagiełło realm extended from the Baltic to the Black Sea (see Figure 10.1).[1] East Central Europe, the commonly accepted designation for these countries east of the Rhine, conveys no necessary implication of shared cultural identity, although, as we shall see, the musical traditions of medieval Poland, Bohemia-Moravia and Hungary were as interrelated as their aristocratic families. Indeed, for much of the time from 1300 until well into the sixteenth century, two of these countries, and on one occasion all three of them, were ruled by the same monarch.[2]

Powerful though these medieval states once were, their contribution is often treated as peripheral to the broader narrative of European cultural history. This is particularly so in the case of music historiography, which gives short shrift to music east of the Rhine. Factors contributing to this state of affairs are the relatively small amount and inaccessibility of much of the source material, the lack of a synoptic coverage in a western European language, and a teleological view of music history that privileges polyphonic repertoires over monophonic. True, East Central Europe has contributed no big books of florid organum, *libri motetorum* in vernacular languages, or collections of polyphonic chansons. On the other hand, there is abundant evidence of the lively cultivation of late chant genres – sequences, rhymed offices and hymns – and of vernacular adaptation and reworking of Ars Antiqua-type polyphony into distinctive (perhaps hybrid) forms, the most distinctive of which is the cantio.[3]

Figure 10.1 States of East Central Europe, ca1480 (adapted from Paul R. Magocsi, *Historical Atlas of Eastern Europe* [Seattle and London: University of Washington Press, 1993], p. 32)

Plainchant

The earliest liturgical music heard in East Central Europe was Byzantine chant sung in Old Slavonic. Having the Greek liturgy translated into the vernacular language undoubtedly contributed to the success of Saints Cyril and Methodius (863–85) in spreading Orthodox Christianity.[4] The ascendancy of the Latin rite over the Orthodox dates from the conversion of the kings of Poland and Hungary, Mieszko I (966) and István I (1000), and the establishment soon thereafter of archbishoprics in Gniezno (1000), Esztergom (1001) and Kalocsa (1006). A bishopric had existed in Prague since 973, papal approval having been contingent on its adherence to the Latin rite. With the hardening of relations between the Eastern and Western churches that culminated in the Great Schism (1054), the successors of Charlemagne emulated their forebear by employing the liturgy of Rome, in the language of the Roman church, as a powerful tool for furthering their interests in *antemurale christianitatis*, the territories beyond the Empire's eastern border. Centuries after its introduction into East Central Europe, the Latin rite, unlike Orthodox Christianity, remained closely associated with German-speaking clergy. This not always happy state of affairs was exacerbated by the arrival of the Cistercians in the mid twelfth century.

Orthodox Christianity nonetheless maintained a presence in the region, most obviously in sacral art and architecture. Charles I of Bohemia reintroduced the Slavonic rite as a way of asserting cultural identity, importing Benedictine monks from Croatia to the Emmaus monastery near Prague. In 1385 and 1390, monks from this house established two new Slavonic-rite monasteries in Poland, at Oleśnica and Cracow where the rite continued in use up to the fifteenth century. And in April 1440, following the Roman Catholic victory at the Council of Florence, Isidore, Metropolitan of Kiev and All Russia, was invited by Bishop Oleśnicki to celebrate a solemn Orthodox liturgy in Cracow cathedral. Despite the longevity of the legacy of Cyril and Methodius, however, musical evidence of the Slavonic rite is very scanty. One famous remnant is the Old Slavonic litany invocation used in Bohemia, 'Hospodine, pomiluj ny' ('Lord, have mercy on us').[5]

The wealth of late medieval chant sources in East Central Europe has sustained the research of some outstanding scholars, notwithstanding the institutionalized impediments of the Communist period after the Second World War, which restricted publication of translations and facsimile editions.[6] While quality facsimiles of chant manuscripts are few, digitization of a number of important collections is now well under way.[7]

The earliest extant Latin service books, imports from Cologne, Salzburg and Bavaria, date from the late eleventh and early twelfth centuries: the Tyniec Sacramentary (Poland), Codex Albensis (Hungary) and the Bratislava Breviary fragment (Slovakia). They are notated in non-diastematic German neumes and mostly preserve south German musical practice. Over time, certain regional melodic variants and, occasionally, the notational characteristics associated with diocesan centres, started to infiltrate the distinctive plainchant traditions of the monastic and mendicant orders. Cantus fractus, for example, the notational permutations indicating rhythmicization of the chant, can be found in both diocesan and monastic service books.[8] Prevalent throughout the region is the so-called German chant dialect, a melodic inflection that broadens intervals of a second into a minor third, giving the melody a pentatonic flavour – 'a byproduct quite possibly of ears and throats accustomed to an anhemitonic, that is, semitoneless, folk idiom'.[9] Generally speaking, the dialect is transmitted in service books notated in Gothic neumes but mix-ups occasionally occur even in Franciscan and Dominican books that use square notation exclusively (Jerzy Morawski attributes these notational 'mishaps' to the clergy's ignorance of the local language).[10]

As in western Europe, devotions to the Virgin Mary and the cult of saints stimulated composition of new chants. Widely venerated throughout East Central Europe were Vojtěch (Adalbert) and Elizabeth of Thuringia. The latter was an inspiration for women, especially Franciscan Tertiaries and Beguines, while Adalbert, Bishop of Prague and patron of the Polish archdiocese of Gnezno, was literally fought over by the Poles and Czechs.[11] Equal to Adalbert, in terms of the number of compositions inspired by her cult, is Jadwiga (Hedwig), the saintly queen closely associated with Silesia and the Cistercian Order.[12] László [Ladislaus] and István [Stephen] were popular in Hungary, the latter's office being adapted in part from Adalbert's.[13] Stephen's office, in turn, was a source for the office of Stanislaus, the Cracow bishop who met the same fate as Thomas of Canterbury, and with whose office Stanislaus's has textual though not musical connections.[14] Ludmila, Procopius and Václav (Wenceslas) were favourites in Bohemia and Moravia, where the hymn *Svatý Václave* became identified with the coronation of Czech kings.

In his studies of the offices of these last-named Czech saints, Dominique Patier identified musico-poetic attributes which he believes are characteristic of a Bohemian school of chant composition, namely, a pentatonicism similar to that in Hungarian melodies, a tendency to word painting, and disjunct melodic movement that can include leaps of a seventh or an octave.[15] A key figure in this school, the composer of offices for Saint Wenceslas and Saint Ludmila, is Domaslav, a Dominican who lived at the turn of the thirteenth century.[16] The characteristics identified by Patier can be seen in the music of the Prague rite as transmitted in the set of books that were commissioned by Arnestus of Pardubice (1297?–1364) on the occasion of Prague's being raised to the status of archbishopric. Many of the chants in these codices, the tropes to the readings especially, are strikingly original compositions.[17] Another Archbishop of Prague, Jan of Jenštejn

(1348–1400), was a noted composer of hymns and cantiones. The Office of the Visitation of the Virgin, which he introduced into the Prague calendar in 1386 and may himself have composed, combines biblical prose with rhymed poetic texts set in sequential modal order.

Hungary's liturgical tradition was 'of a synthetic nature'. Dobszay's studies have identified Norman and north Italian influences in combination with south German models that preserve a pentatonic dialect. Throughout the country the Esztergom rite was all-pervasive. The traditions of this archdiocese, the first in East Central Europe to have its books in diastematic notation (Messine neumes), were propagated and entrenched by the schooling system and became the norm, the *mos patriae*, throughout Hungary.[18] The contentious question of whether chant in Hungary possessed attributes that might be regarded as constituting a 'national' character has been taken up by Janka Szendrei. Her research into the melodic behaviour of rhymed offices for local saints, for example, reveals that notwithstanding the often high degree of borrowing and reworking of pre-existing chants, these melodies evince within the prevailing *mos patriae* both period style and distinctive individual invention.[19]

By far the greatest variety and largest number of plainchant sources in East Central Europe are to be found in Poland. Attracting the lion's share of research are the hymn and sequence repertories. The latter genre can be divided into three groups: Benedictine-diocesan, Norbertine-Victorine, and Dominican.[20] Sequences in Cistercian sources, a considerable number of which are transmitted without music, fall into the first group; they were taken up progressively from diocesan use in the latter part of the twelfth century as the Cistercian Order started to relax its strict adherence to the 1147 liturgical reform. Original local compositions are most prevalent in the third, Dominican group. Vincent of Kielce (1200–62), the best-known Dominican poet-composer, is author of two *Vitae* of Saint Stanislaus, the sequences *Laeta mundus* and *Jesu Christe rex superne*, and the hymn *Gaude mater polonia.*

The Polish sequence and hymn repertories are differentiated not just formally but also modally: modes 1 and 2 for sequences, 7 for hymns. There are no sequences in modes 7 and 8, and the few score in deuterus and tritus modes can be put down, according to Jerzy Pikulik, to the pervasiveness of the 'German' chant dialect.[21] Antoni Reginek's analyses of hymns associated with the greater Cracow diocese reveal not only the dominance of mode 7 but also the rarity of plagal forms generally and the complete absence of tritus mode. In the hymn repertory, the high degree of concordance between Cracow and northern Hungarian sources around Bratislava testifies to the close political and ecclesiastical connections that existed between these centres in the fifteenth century.[22]

Polyphony

In liturgical books throughout East Central Europe one finds examples of simple polyphony of the type studied in German sources by Geering and Göllner.[23] Seen against the mainstream repertories that define late medieval and Renaissance polyphony, this method of adorning the plainchant appears stylistically 'retrospective' or 'archaic'. As descriptors of polyphonic repertories in East Central Europe these terms are unhelpful for, while stylistic tendencies may well have been generally conservative, polyphonic practices did not simply replicate ossified imported models. Simpler forms of polyphonic writing, deriving perhaps from western European Ars Antiqua practices, enjoyed much greater longevity here than elsewhere in Europe. They gave rise to repertories that find no real match with contemporaneous polyphony in western Europe.[24]

That some connection might have existed between the sorts of polyphony found in East Central Europe and the western European Ars Antiqua and Ars Nova repertories has long fascinated scholars. Fuelling the speculation is some tantalizing but circumstantial evidence: a fragment of a motet by Philippe de Vitry found in Wrocław,[25] references by Guillaume de Machaut to his travelling from Prague to Cracow through various towns in Bohemia and Silesia,[26] a number of Ars Nova treatises found in Bohemia and Poland,[27] and fragments of the *Magnus liber* and related motets in Stary Sącz.[28] This last find is the one that has proved most intriguing.

Binding strips recovered from a thirteenth-century gradual in St Kinga's Poor Clare monastery (founded in 1280) reveal parts of three office organa and snippets of twenty-one Latin two-part motets (Figure 10.2). The fragments were cut from a Parisian manuscript (ca1248), its most unusual feature being a *mise-en-page* for motets which encapsulates the tenors in red circles positioned in the outside margins. Speculation that there might have been some local compositional engagement with the Parisian Ars Antiqua received a measure of support with the recent discovery at St Kinga's of an inexpertly copied new melodic version of Philip the Chancellor's well-known sequence *Ave gloriosa*. This new version can be combined with the standard melody as a *vox secunda* to produce a two-part organal setting of Philip's sequence.[29]

Also found in St Kinga's is a four-voice cantio, *Omnia beneficia*, dating from the fourteenth century. Its first-person confessional tone is characteristic of much of the religious verse associated with the mendicant orders. The Observant Franciscans in particular were adept at contrafacting popular tunes and adapting well-known chant melodies to better spread

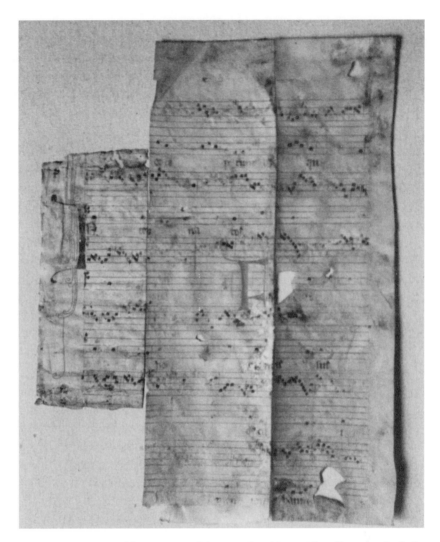

Figure 10.2 Reconstituted fragments containing part of two *Magnus Liber* office organa (end of *Dum complerentur. V. Repleti sunt* and beginning of *Inter natos. V. Fuit homo*) recovered from the binding of a Franciscan gradual at St Kinga's Poor Clare monastery (*PL-STk* 2)

the Word. The many collections of popular devotional texts (*pia dictamina, Leichs* and cantiones) found in Poland and Bohemia attest to the creative energies stirred by *devotio moderna*.[30]

Cantio

The term cantio covers a wide variety of non-liturgical religious songs, mostly strophic and often with refrain, that are found as inserts in service books or gathered together with liturgical items in cantionalia. As applied to East Central European sources the term is something of a catch-all for a range of highly variegated repertories. The topic awaits systematic study. It would appear that early cantiones originated as tropes attached to the Benedicamus Domino and Deo gratias, as interpolations into sequences, and as melodies to accompany religious processions. The major centre of cultivation was Bohemia under the Luxembourgs, Charles (1346–78) and Wenceslas (1378–1419). The wide dissemination of cantiones reworked and translated into the region's vernacular languages suggests that Prague university and the international milieu associated with it might have been a primary centre, if not the the locus, of compositional activity. Similar, conductus-like two-part pieces are found in a source associated with the university milieu in Cracow.[31] Černý sees cantio as a genre embracing a wide range of song styles from simple *Stimmtausch* works (quasi-improvised songs with alternating monophonic/polyphonic sections), to through-composed two-voice compositions akin to conductus in the way they alternate homorhythmic syllabically texted sections (such as *cum littera* conductus) with melismatic sections (such as *sine littera* conductus).[32]

The grandest cantio collection is, somewhat unusually, associated with a monastic establishment, the Cistercian community at Vyšší Brod. Unlike western European Cistercian books, the Vyšebrodský Sborník (1410) uses both Latin and vernacular, employs both chant and mensural notation, and it includes, as do most cantionalia, both monophonic and polyphonic items.[33] Monophonic cantiones are not necessarily the polyphonic version stripped of one voice; rather, they often appear to be a composite of both parts of the polyphonic version. It is a characteristic of the cantio genre that the process of tranmission admits of a high degree of textual and musical reworking. *Ave yerarchia* is a case in point: it appears first as a trope to the *Salve regina* in the Vyšebrodský Sborník; it became a favourite with the Utraquists as *Jesus Christus nostra salus;* it appears in the Środa Śląska Śpiewnik (Neumarkt Cantionale, 1474/84) as *Ave Morgensterne,* and it turned into the Lutheran hymn *Gottes Sohn ist kommen.*[34] And to these versions can be added yet another, its Hungarian-language version *Idvözlégy Istennek szent anyja,* which is found in the Nádor Codex (1508).

If the conductus-like cantio in the fourteenth and fifteenth centuries was, as Černý believes, an adaptation of the Ars Antiqua genre into a vehicle for popular religious expression, then the Bohemian polytextual motet, which also remained current well into the fifteenth century and is transmitted in many of the same sources as are cantiones, might be considered the preferred vehicle for more learned display. Tenor repetition is a feature of these almost exclusively Latin-texted motets but it never develops to the level of structural complexity found in French isorhythmic motets. The harmonic vocabulary of many of the polytextual motets differs little from that of the conductus-type cantiones, although the later motets do start to employ thirds and sixths. Both these genres were cultivated by Petrus Wilhelmi de Grudencz (Piotr z Grudziądza, ca1400–ca1480), one of a handful of fifteenth-century composers from East Central Europe whose reputations extended beyond the region.[35]

Petrus de Grudencz

Although Petrus's works appear in thirty-eight sources (mostly Bohemian), few facts are known of his career.[36] Educated at the Jagiellonian University (receiving an MA in 1430), he held the position of *cappelanus* in Frederick Ill's Imperial chapel through the 1450s during which time, in 1452, he made a trip to Rome. His score or so of authenticated works, almost exclusively cantiones (15) and motets/rotuli (7), are transmitted in various states of reworking and contrafacta in sources as late as the mid sixteenth century. Stylistically, his cantiones and motets keep company with the Bohemian polyphony discussed above, showing few traces of Burgundian influence, notwithstanding his connection with the Imperial chapel and his visit to Rome. In a Bohemia where musical life had been much debilitated by the religious turmoil of the Hussite wars (1419–34), Petrus's works, the cantiones in particular, found favour as quasi-liturgical church music that was sung by schoolboys, there being no money in Catholic and Utraquist churches to maintain professional choirs. Later in the century, the cantio repertory, and Petrus's pieces especially, was taken up by literary confraternities that thrived well into the seventeenth century.[37]

If one can speak of the aesthetics of a religious movement, Hussitism was undoubtedly a conservative force, but it was probably not the 'historical catastrophe', at least not for music, that the Czech historian Zdeněk Nejedlý would have us believe.[38] The exodus of religious orders from Bohemia and of foreign teachers from the Charles University when it fell under Utraquist control no doubt diminished the vigour of intellectual life, but the movement did enrich the repertory of popular religious song and promote congregational singing in the vernacular. The Bible in Czech had been available since before the turn of the century and the Bethlehem Chapel, from its inception (1393), had promoted Czech over Latin as a liturgical language. Translating the plainchant into Czech was a logical next step; the result was the Hymnbook of Jistebnice (1420). In addition to liturgical chant, it contains scores of Latin and Czech songs dealing with contemporary events:

Ó svolánie konstanské ('O Council of Constance'), *Povstaň, povstaň, veliké město Pražské* ('Arise, Great City of Prague'), and the famous battle song, *Ktož jsú boží bojovníci* ('You Who Are God's Warriors').[39]

Polyphonic sources

Hungary is the least fortunate of the East Central European countries in terms of lost sources of medieval polyphony. The court of Mátyás Corvinus (1458–90) and Beatrice of Aragón was a byword for Medicean splendour, and nowhere better exemplified this opulence than the Italianate royal chapel. Under the direction of Johannes de Stokem, a Fleming, its musical achievements were esteemed by the Vatican legate Bishop Bartolomeo de Maraschi as superior even to the papal choir itself.[40] Unfortunately, almost nothing has come down to us in the way of music associated with Corvinus's court.[41] After 150 years of Turkish occupation, the Reformation, and the dissolution of monasteries under Emperor Joseph II, what little remains can be comprehensively surveyed in a short article.[42] It was a probably therefore a kind blow of Fate that Corvinus never lived to take possession of the splendid codex he commissioned for his wife; otherwise the Mellon Chansonnier, too, might have been lost to posterity like the rest of his library treasures.[43]

The most significant polyphonic source so far recovered are the fragments from the Dominican monastery in Košice, in northeastern Slovakia.[44] They date from around 1465. These pastedowns have yielded cantiones, twelve sacred and secular, mostly three-part compositions of both local and external provenance, and Frye's *Missa Ave regina celorum*. The closest repertorial links are with Bohemian-Silesian sources and with the Głogów Songbook, in particular.[45]

From the Silesian town of Żagań in the western part of Corvinus's domain,[46] the region formerly controlled by Bohemia, come the part-books known as the Glogauer Liederbuch. The Augustinian canons of Żagań, thanks perhaps to their Leipzig-educated prior, Martin Rinkenberg, seem to have enjoyed a remarkably wide range of musical styles. This collection of 292 sacred and secular works, mostly three-part, comprises 165 cantus firmus Latin pieces, 65 German songs, and untexted contrafacta, plus a section of standard liturgical works (antiphons, responsories and hymns) which appears at the beginning of the collection. Almost all the Latin works are of local origin; among the untexted items and contrafacta we find pieces by composers of the Ockeghem generation: Busnois (4 works), Caron (3), Hayne van Ghizeghem (2) and Tinctoris (2). The concordance patterns of this international section of the songbook strongly favour Italian sources: Florence, Ferrara and especially Naples. After Corvinus's marriage in 1476 to the daughter of the Aragonese king of Naples, his court came ever more under the influence of Neapolitan tastes in music and the arts. Żagań's musical connections with Italy probably ran through Buda.[47]

The Strahov Codex takes us from the German-speaking parts of Silesia that were in sympathy with the Utraquist Hussites to the Catholic cathedral in Olomouc, the former capital of Moravia.[48] The book, its format that of a Liederbuch or chansonnier, contains some 291 items, the majority of which are three-part works combining liturgical and non-liturgical music: works for the church (mass ordinary, office hymns, Magnificat) and for the archbishop's court (German songs and a chanson). A high proportion of the pieces are of local origin, unconnected with outside repertories but, as with the Głogów Songbook, there are also a number of works by leading early-fifteenth-century composers: Du Fay (two, possibly five works), Walter Frye (3) and Tinctoris (5).

The Codex Speciálník gives a glimpse into the musical fare of the Utraquist Literary Confraternity in Prague.[49] It is primarily but not exclusively a book of sacred music, 'Speciál–' because it is not a traditional service book. First come the proper and ordinary of the Mass (without Agnus Dei which had no place in the Utraquist liturgy), then motets and songs. The repertory, monophonic and polyphonic, includes music from the 1300s to the most up-to-date compositions of the Josquin generation. For the earlier repertory it uses older notation (chant and black mensural) and for the more recent works, white mensural. Into the former category, notated in black, fall the fourteen pieces by Petrus de Grudencz; in the latter, notated in white, come works by his contemporaries, Frye, Bedyngton, Plummer and Barbigant, then composers of the following generation, Busnois, Morton, Tinctoris, and finally the most recent masters, Agricola (4 works), Josquin (4), Isaac (2) and Brumel's *Missa Ut re mi fa sol la*. This last work is probably the most recent inclusion; it, too, reflects Utraquist liturgy: the Agnus Dei is left untexted.[50] The codex reveals the confraternity's remarkable catholicity of taste and high level of musical cultivation. Compositions by local composers (10 by Johannes Touront) take their place with Burgundian and Netherlandish works, some of them being the earliest known transmission of that piece. This evenhandedness was carried over into the mode of production, it would seem, for no less than twenty-seven scribes had a hand in its copying.

The aforementioned sources – the Strahov and Speciálník codices, the Głogów Songbook, and the Košice fragments – were practical collections, the repertory therein reflecting the needs and customs of the group or institution that compiled them.[51] They transmit a variety of genres, employ a variety of notational styles, and were periodically updated with new works. Unlike many of the western European mensural codices of this period that were commissioned as luxury objects for presentation, these manuscripts were in the nature of *libri usuales*, compilations produced by those who would use them. Notwithstanding 'international' influences evident in some of the updates, these sources, all dating from the last quarter of the fifteenth century, attest to the longevity of local, generally conservative compositional traditions. In Bohemia and neighbouring Utraquist enclaves, musical conservatism was a byproduct of the religious–nationalist upheavals that were sparked by the martyrdom of Jan Hus at the Council of Constance (1414–17). But this great international forum that lasted for almost three years also afforded musicians east of the Rhine opportunities to hear advanced musical fare from elsewhere in Europe.

About the career of Mikołaj Radomski (Nicholas of Radom) we know almost nothing. His musical style, however, is readily identifiable as mainstream Italianate fifteenth century.[52] The majority of his pieces, twelve *in toto*, are three-part Latin liturgical works, mostly paired mass movements. Only one of his compositions can be securely dated, the ballata contrafact *Hystorigraphi aciem;* this celebratory chanson-motet was composed to commemorate the birth of Prince Kazimierz Jagiełło in 1426. Radomski's most striking piece is his Magnificat. In technique and style, verses alternating fauxbourdon and chanson format, this work is, as Strohm puts it, indistinguishable from Grossin or Du Fay.[53]

Omitted from this brief coverage of the major sources of fifteenth-century mensural music in East Central Europe are details of repertorial links with regional neighbours, for example, Codex Engelberg 314 and the Trent codices. In a musical sense East Central Europe was part of a larger cultural formation that encompassed the area east of the Rhine and north of the Alps. The foregoing roll call of composers and enumeration of the variegated contents of half a dozen sources cannot mask the great lacunae in musical records from this period, but it does suggest, nevertheless, that across the great expanse of Europe, the realm over which Zygmunt Stary and Bona Sforza presided, there existed in certain cities and regional centres a level of musical cultivation that both esteemed local traditions and appreciated the most advanced musical fare from countries far to the west and south.

PART THREE

Themes, topics and trajectories

11 Music and liturgy

SAM BARRETT

One of the earliest surviving accounts of Christian liturgy is a report of Sunday Eucharist written at Rome around AD 150 by Justin Martyr:[1]

> And on the day named for the sun there is an assembly in one place for all who live in the towns and in the country; and the memoirs of the Apostles and the writings of the Prophets are read as long as time permits. Then when the reader has finished, he who presides speaks, giving admonishment and exhortation to imitate those noble deeds. Then we all stand together and offer prayers. And when, as we said above, we are finished with the prayers, bread is brought, and wine and water, and he who presides likewise offers prayers and thanksgiving, according to his ability, and the people give their assent by exclaiming Amen. And there takes place the distribution to each and partaking of that over which thanksgiving has been said, and it is brought to those not present by the deacon.

A description of a solemn mass as celebrated at Rome some six centuries later runs to several thousand words. The account of the introit, cited here in abbreviated form, is in itself longer than the entirety of Justin Martyr's earlier description.[2]

> Then [the choir] rises up and passes in order before the altar, and the two rows arrange themselves in this manner: the men-singers on either side without the doors [of the presbytery], and the children on each side within. Immediately the precentor begins the anthem for the entry: and when the deacons hear his voice, they at once go to the pontiff in the sacristy. Then the pontiff, rising, gives his right hand to the archdeacon, and his left to the second [deacon], or whoever may be appointed: who, after kissing his hands, walk with him as his supporters . . . After this the pontiff passes on, but before he comes to the choir the bearers of the candlesticks divide, four going to the right and three to the left; and the pontiff passes between them to the upper part of the choir, and bows his head to the altar . . . Then turning towards the precentor, he signs to him to sing, *Glory be to the Father, and to the Son* etc.; and the precentor bows to the pontiff, and begins it . . .

The differences between the two accounts are striking. Justin Martyr gives no explicit indication that music was used as part of the Eucharist, whereas in the later account a separate body of singers is assigned a distinct role within an elaborate ceremony. There is also a marked difference between

Table 11.1 *A comparison of the mass as described by Justin Martyr and in Ordo Romanus I*

Justin Martyr caAD 150	Ordo Romanus I ca700
	Introit chant
	Kyrie eleison
	Gloria in excelsis
	Greeting
	Collect
Readings	Epistle
	Gradual chant
	Alleluia
	Gospel
Homily	
Prayers	Prayers
Kiss of greeting	
Presentation of gifts	Presentation of gifts, with
	Offertory chant
	Prayer over gifts
Eucharistic prayers	Eucharistic prayers, including: Sanctus
	Kiss of Peace
	Agnus Dei
Communion	Communion, with chant
	Postcommunion collect
	Dismissal

an apparent fluidity – according to Justin, readings last 'as long as time permits' – and the detailed prescriptions for all aspects of ceremonial conduct in the later document. It is tempting on the basis of such reports to propose a history of music and liturgy that passed from simplicity to complexity, from fluidity to fixity. The problem with such a linear approach is that the surviving documents from this era present a partial and highly inflected picture of liturgical practice.[3] Justin Martyr's description, for example, occurs within the context of a letter to the Emperor Antoninus Pius in defence of Christianity; the absence of reference to ceremony and vagueness over certain details can be read as much as an attempt to present Christian worship as both sober and reasonable as a summary of the celebration of the Eucharist at that time. There must also remain doubts as to whether Justin Martyr is describing the Eucharist as practised at a specific institution, a standardized pattern abstracted from Roman practice, or a generic outline of Christian custom.

For all their differences, the points of agreement between these two Roman witnesses to the celebration of the Eucharist before the mid eighth century may be taken as a starting point for understanding the ways in which a shared framework was realized under differing conditions.[4] As can be seen from Table 11.1, what is common to the two reports is a basic pattern of readings followed by prayer from the part of the service that has come to be known as the fore-mass or Liturgy of the Word, that is, up to but not including the presentation of gifts. From the Liturgy of the Eucharist, the elements of presentation, Eucharistic prayer, and communion are shared.[5]

There would appear to be little continuity between the two reports concerning music, but when Justin Martyr's account is read alongside other extracts referring to music in the Eucharist during the early centuries of Christianity then a more varied picture emerges. For what may be detected in broad terms is a shift in kind from music as an optional amplification of the word to music as a constituent element of a discrete liturgical act. The difference may be illustrated with respect to the gradual. Clear evidence for a psalm routinely sung in the fore-mass as a discrete liturgical event dates only from the later fourth century; before this time, it is more than likely that one of the readings in the fore-mass could be a psalm that was on occasion intoned in a more or less lyrical manner.[6] A comparable shift can be traced in the expansion at points of liturgical action without words, that is, at the entrance, the presentation of gifts and the distribution of communion. Before the later fourth century, it seems that services began rather abruptly (Justin Martyr, for example, makes no mention of any items of greeting), there is equally hardly any evidence for singing during the presentation of gifts, and only sporadic and late evidence for singing during communion. Yet from this time onwards, Eucharistic celebration was expanded at these points by similar means, the addition of a chant followed by a prayer, resulting in discrete liturgical items with music as a key component, namely introit, offertory and communion chants.[7]

Several factors in the rise of the formalized expansions including music may be highlighted here.[8] With the Emperor Constantine's legalization of Christianity in 313, imperial financial support enabled a significant expansion in the building of public spaces for Christian devotion. Christians adopted a basilican style for their new buildings, which in practice meant the erection of large buildings resembling assembly halls, with a long central nave ending in an apse and with side aisles.[9] The size of such buildings enabled the increasing numbers of those attending worship to be accommodated, while the long naves made provision for the expanding sequence of events at the beginning of the service. Processions between buildings, making use of the public spaces within the city, became increasingly popular after Constantine's edict; in the course of time, the Kyrie, which had been used as a litany accompanying processions between churches, was added to the opening rites within the church, while the Gloria was first added on solemn occasions presided over by the bishop.

A second important factor in the formalized expansion of liturgical action was an enthusiasm for psalm singing that peaked in the late fourth century.[10] The psalms, which were extensively quoted by church fathers of the time, seem to have solved two related problems that faced the early church. Amid the general movement to larger-scale worship and more formalized patterns of ecclesiastical life, the psalms provided an inspired language that retained a personal, expressive appeal through their frequent invocation of first-person experience. Equally, at a time of controversy over core elements of Christian doctrine, and most especially over the nature of the Trinity, the psalms provided canonically approved texts for singing, in direct contrast to the hymns used as vehicles for spreading the ideas of heretical movements. An important consequence of this preference for psalmody was an adoption of the formal possibilities inherent in psalmody, whether direct (singing verses straight through), responsorial (in which a soloist sang the verses and the congregation responded with a refrain usually drawn from the psalm), or antiphonal. In the early centuries of Christianity, the congregational refrain of responsorial psalmody was divided between two choirs, who responded alternately to soloists singing the psalm verses. Through most of the Middle Ages, however, psalm verses were sung antiphonally with successive psalm verses sung by two choirs positioned opposite each other.[11]

A third important factor in the expansion of formalized worship was the transition from lector to *schola* chant.[12] In the early church, psalms were led by lectors, who were adolescent or even younger boys of varied musical training. The relatively low status of these lectors is mirrored by the fact that the choice of psalms for particular days, aside from the recurrence of specific and obvious correlations, appears to have been determined on a largely *ad hoc* basis before at least the later fifth century. By contrast, the development of *scholae* to perform the psalms appears to have been related to the development of cycles of sung texts assigned to specific feasts. The Roman *schola cantorum*, for example, appears to have been founded towards the end of the seventh century, and it is from the same century that there is evidence for a fixing of sung texts across the liturgical year.[13] As for the composition of the Roman schola, the later document quoted above mentions four chief cantors and a further body of male singers and boys. It would seem no coincidence that the same document records a fully elaborated version of solemn mass as found throughout the Middle Ages; in other words, a complex liturgy and the institutional means to perform and sustain it appear to have gone hand in hand.[14]

* * *

> And he directed that same clergy, abundantly instructed in divine law and in
> Roman chant, to follow the custom and ritual order of the Roman church,
> which up to that time had scarcely been done in the church at Metz.[15]

So wrote Paul the Deacon in the first half of the 780s about the achievements
of Chrodegang (Bishop of Metz, 742–66), but what are we to make of this
reported transfer of music and liturgy from Rome to the heartlands of
the Carolingian kingdoms north of the Alps? The underlying motivations,
means and relative success of this cultural transfer have repeatedly been
questioned, and will no doubt continue to fascinate historians of music, if
only because the gap of almost a century before the earliest surviving substantial notated chant sources allows ample room for informed speculation.
Paul the Deacon's account nevertheless directs us to the nub of the matter: a
Frankish clergy instructed in Roman chant (*cantilena romana*) was directed
to observe the custom (*mos*) and ritual order (*ordo*) of the Church of Rome.
In other words, a Roman way of doing liturgy including music was to
be imitated, a manner of celebration for which *cantilena romana* was not
simply central but, as implied by Paul the Deacon's phrasing, a prerequisite.

Several documents shed light on the attempt by both Chrodegang and
his successor to introduce a Roman form of music and liturgy, from which
it would appear that the formation of a *schola cantorum*, an ordered clerical
lifestyle, Roman architectural features and an imitation of the Roman use of
ritual space were all intrinsic to the process of imitation.[16] By the mid ninth
century, a pattern of worship for the mass through the year, revised from
Roman models, is recorded in a sacramentary belonging to Charlemagne's
son, Drogo (Bishop of Metz, 823–55).[17] Sacramentaries, or books recording
the prayers used by the celebrant in the mass, are of crucial importance:
containing the prayers used by the highest-ranking individual at the most
important service, they were taken by the Carolingians as the book that
provided the outline for the liturgical year. Drogo's Sacramentary is something of a special case in so far as it is a collection reserved for ceremonies
presided over by the bishop; in containing texts only for the main feasts, it
provides an ideal introduction to the framework of the liturgical year as it
had developed by the mid ninth century (Table 11.2).

The annual cycle recorded in Drogo's Sacramentary represents not only
the outcome of centuries of development, but also the outline of the pattern
that was to endure through the Middle Ages and beyond. The liturgical
year it records is formed out of two main overlapping cycles celebrating
events in the life of Christ (the Temporale or Temporal cycle) and Saints
(the Sanctorale or Sanctoral cycle). The two main poles of the Temporale are the feasts of Christmas and Easter. By the fourth century, Easter

Table 11.2 *The annual cycle of feasts in Drogo's Sacramentary*

Date	Festal observance	Roman stations
25 Dec.	Christmas	
	Mass in the night	St Mary
	Mass at dawn	St Anastasia
	Mass in the day	St Peter
26 Dec.	St Stephen	
27 Dec.	St John the Evangelist	
28 Dec.	Holy Innocents	
1 Jan.	Octave of Christmas	St Mary
6 Jan.	Epiphany	St Peter
20 Jan.	St Sebastian	
2 Feb.	Purification of the Blessed Virgin Mary	St Mary
	Septuagesima	St Lawrence outside the walls
	Quadragesima	St John in the Lateran
	Palm Sunday	St John
	Maundy Thursday	
	Good Friday	
	Holy Saturday	
	Easter	St Peter
	Octave of Easter	
	Feria II	St Peter
	Feria III	St Paul
	Feria IV	St Lawrence
	Feria V	Holy Apostles
	Feria VI	St Mary
	Sabbato	St John
	First Sunday after Easter	
1 May	Philip and James Apostles	
	Ascension	
	Pentecost	St Peter
	Octave of Pentecost	
	Feria II	[St Peter] in chains
	Feria III	St Anastasia
	Feria IV	St Mary
	Feria VI	Holy Apostles
	Sabbato	
24 June	St John the Baptist	
29 June	SS Peter and Paul	
30 July	St Paul	
10 August	St Lawrence	
15 August	Assumption of the Blessed Virgin Mary	
16 August	St Arnulf	
8 Sep.	Nativity of the Blessed Virgin Mary	
9 Sep.	St Gorgonius	
14 Sep.	Exaltation of the Cross	
(3 May)	Finding of the Cross	
29 Sep.	Dedication of the Basilica of the Holy Archangel Michael	
1 Oct.	St Remigius	
11 Nov.	St Martin	
22 Nov.	St Caecilia	
23 Nov.	St Clement	
30 Nov.	St Andrew	

Note: Since the annual cycle, rather than every service celebrated, is of interest here, vigils (services held the on the eve of a feast) have not been included as a matter of course. Modern English equivalents for certain feasts have been adopted. The feast of the Finding of the Cross is listed immediately after the Exaltation, but is assigned its date in the Roman calendar of 3 May.

was routinely celebrated on a Sunday with a following fifty-day festal season, in which the fiftieth day was associated with the gift of the Spirit (Pentecost) and the fortieth day with Ascension.[18] The celebration of Christmas on 25 December was also established by the fourth century, but only in Rome and North Africa; Christmas was celebrated elsewhere on 6 January. The differing emphasis given to Christmas in these celebrations came to be reconciled as complementary celebrations of the nativity (25 December, Christmas) and the manifestation of Christ (6 January, Epiphany). Preparatory periods to the main feasts of Christmas and Easter are also first attested as widespread phenomena in the fourth century, with the emergence of both a Lenten forty-day fast and a short period of fasting before Christmas known as Advent, which seems to have been developed into a more extended observance sometime during the seventh century. By the mid ninth century, octaves of individual feasts were also celebrated, thus either the week of the feast was celebrated (for example the Easter octave, whose eight days continue through to the following Sunday), or the eighth day of a feast was celebrated in its own right (for example the octave of Christmas on New Year's Day, which was only later established in Rome as the Feast of the Circumcision). Specific days within the week were specified by a mainly numerical system: feria II (Monday, the second day of the week) through to feria VI (Friday), followed by sabbato (Saturday).

The commemoration of individual saints both on the anniversary of the date of their death and at the place of their burial dates back to the mid second century, but such celebrations were necessarily local and, given that under Roman law it was illegal to open graves in order to transfer relics, the spread of cults was inevitably slow. By the time of Drogo's Sacramentary, however, a fully developed Sanctorale was in place, celebrating saints of local importance (e.g. Saint Arnulf of Metz, supposed ancestor of the Carolingians), as well as saints of regional significance (such as Saint Remigius, so-called Apostle of the Franks) alongside widely recognized saints (e.g. Saint Stephen, the first Christian martyr). Material collected together in Drogo's Sacramentary immediately after the Sanctorale represents a further important category of liturgical material, that of the Common. In this section, which is not listed in Table 11.2, were copied prayers for services of dedication and for groups of similar feasts that share texts; thus the commemoration of individual apostles, virgins and martyrs would draw upon general texts for this category of saints in the absence of any specifically composed texts. One final category of information requires explanation, namely the churches listed in association with each feast. A similar listing of churches, otherwise known as stational indications, is also found in the earliest unnotated antiphoners (chant books) dating from ca800 onwards. These refer not to local churches but to churches in Rome and, as is evident from a comparable list that survives for Metz from the late eighth century, the system of celebrating the Eucharist under the bishop at different churches within Rome was translated into a parallel system within Frankish towns and abbeys, with major feasts of the Temporale celebrated in the main churches, and feasts celebrating saints in lesser churches.[19]

The liturgical cycle represented in Drogo's Sacramentary reflects not only Roman practice, but adaptation to Carolingian tastes. In specific terms, the model for this book is the Gregorian Sacramentary as requested by Charlemagne from Pope Hadrian (772–95), which was then revised according to the standards of classical Latin that were taken as normative in the Carolingian renaissance and to which were added texts for specific occasions and other liturgical formulas omitted from the Sacramentary in a supplement prepared by Benedict of Aniane (d. 821).[20] In more general terms, Drogo's book provides an early example of the accommodation between an imported Roman rite and its local implementation that remained a feature of liturgical practice through the Middle Ages. By the late ninth century, the Roman rite had spread across the Carolingian kingdoms, with other rites and their associated chant traditions used outside of this axis: chiefly, the Visigothic rite in what is now central and northern Spain and Portugal, the Ambrosian rite at Milan, the Beneventan rite from the region of Benevento in southern Italy, and the Byzantine rite in areas that once formed the eastern Roman Empire. By the end of the Middle Ages, the Roman rite had become so widespread in the Latin West that only the Visigothic rite as followed in Toledo and the Ambrosian rite used in Milan remained.

In contrast to the mass, the divine office was rooted in the passing hours of the day, marking out the cycle from darkness to light and back again. Since the medieval history of the office is far more complex than that of the mass, only the most general observations will be made here.[21] Crucial for understanding the later development of the office is the fact that, by the fourth century, two separate traditions of daily prayer can be identified in the West: 'cathedral' practice, the normal practice of local Christian churches, and 'monastic' practice, as observed both by individual ascetics and by monks in urban monastic centres.[22] The 'cathedral' office consisted of daily morning and evening worship and was characterized by a selective use of psalms and hymns; the nucleus of morning prayer, for example, was the Laudate psalms (nos. 148–50), which led to the name *lauds* for this service. In addition, a variety of occasional vigils were followed within this tradition. An alternative model of daily prayer was followed in many urban monastic communities, where a fivefold pattern of daily prayer corresponding to the principal divisions of the day in the Roman Empire was the normal pattern, thus morning, third hour, sixth hour, ninth hour and evening. Night prayer was also observed. This 'monastic' practice drew on both the selective approach to psalmody of the 'cathedral' office and the more or less continuous recitation of psalms practised in desert monasticism. Saint Benedict (ca480–550) was not the first to combine these two traditions, but it was his achievement to draw them together in a way that was not only manageable but also lightened previously sober Roman practices through the introduction of hymns.

The pattern of the daily office outlined in Benedict's Rule was initially only one among many patterns encoded in monastic rules, but by virtue of its promotion under the Carolingians it achieved widespread (if not uniform) adoption in the West by the ninth century. For all its combination of traditions, Benedict's pattern nevertheless remained a monastic use distinct from what was known from the twelfth century onwards as 'secular' use, that is, the liturgical pattern followed by clergy not bound by vows to a religious order, such as those serving in collegiate and parish churches. The main difference between the two traditions was that monastic use was more elaborate, especially in the nocturns of Vigils (see below). Both uses nevertheless had their roots in Roman monastic practice and were treated as part of the Roman rite which spread rapidly from the ninth century onwards.

Any attempt to provide a summary of the structure of the office is complicated by the fact that variation was intrinsic to its design. The pattern of worship changed in response not only to the nature of the institution (monastic or secular), but also to the natural cycle with its changing hours of daylight and seasons, and to the many-layered liturgical cycle with its observation of ferial (daily) and festal worship, itself divided into Temporale and Sanctorale, proper and common. When extensive local variation and development over time is added to this mixture, the only way to proceed is to provide a summary based on a single document. Although lacking certain indications and in all probability a combination of varied sources, one of the earliest full accounts of the structure of the office is provided by Amalarius of Metz (ca775–ca850).[23] His outline (given in Table 11.3) combines features from the Rule of Benedict with the Roman (secular) rite, and remained at the core of the pattern of daily offices up to the reforms of the twentieth century.

Certain aspects of Table 11.3 require further elucidation. A versicle is a short dialogue between the minister and those present; antiphons and responsories consist of short texts taken, at least in the Roman tradition, from scripture, sung (respectively) either in conjunction with a psalm or canticle, or after readings. The *Gloria patri* is a Trinitarian doxology (Glory be to the Father) customarily sung at the end of psalms and canticles, and the *preces* are a sequence of prayers later fixed as comprising a lesser litany or Kyrie, the Lord's Prayer, and versicles and responses. Although not always mentioned by Amalarius, each office apart from Vigils ended with a collect or prayer (variable or fixed) and a blessing (Benedicamus

Table 11.3 *An outline of the offices on Sunday according to Amalarius of Metz (ca775–ca850)*

Vigils or Matins			Lauds	Prime	Terce, Sext, None	Vespers	Compline
First Nocturn	Second Nocturn	Third Nocturn					
Opening versicle followed by *Gloria patri*			(Weekdays: opening versicle)	Opening versicle	Opening versicle	Opening versicle	Opening versicle
Psalm 94 with invitatory antiphon 12 psalms without antiphons, grouped by 4s, with *Gloria patri* after each group	3 psalms with antiphons	3 psalms with alleluias	4 psalms with antiphons, Hymn of Three Boys (Canticle of Daniel) with Laudate antiphon, and 3 Laudate psalms (148–50)	Psalm 53 and two sections of Psalm 118 without antiphons	Three sections of Psalm 118 without antiphons	5 psalms with antiphons	4 psalms without antiphon
Versicle	Versicle	Versicle					
3 lessons, each preceded by a blessing and followed by a responsory	3 lessons, each preceded by a blessing and followed by a responsory	3 lessons, each preceded by a blessing and followed by a responsory	Lesson		Lesson, followed by a short responsory with *Gloria patri*	Lesson	
			Versicle	Versicle with *preces*	Versicle with *preces*	Versicle	Versicle
			Canticle (Benedictus) with antiphon			Canticle (Magnificat) with antiphon	Canticle (Nunc dimittis)

Domino). It should also be noted that later developments standardized a difference between monastic nocturns (on Sundays, three nocturns with twelve lessons and responds, with Old Testament canticles replacing psalms in the third nocturn) and secular nocturns (on Sundays, three nocturns with nine lessons and responds), as well as replacing the last response in the final nocturn by a Te Deum.

Leaving to one side the many daily variations on this pattern, what may be appreciated by reading across the columns in Table 11.3 is that the offices observed a basic structure of interspersed singing and reading, concluded by prayers, that is, in the most general of terms, the same elements of worship as seen in the fore-mass. As for the realization of this pattern of worship on any given day, Vigils was held during the night and was followed almost immediately by lauds, which took place at dawn; prime, terce, sext and nones (the Little Hours) took place at the first, third, sixth and ninth hours of the day respectively; vespers was held at dusk and Compline took place before retiring to bed. The distribution of psalms should also be noted: psalms 1 to 108 were assigned to Vigils, while psalms 109 to 150 were reserved for vespers. The complete Psalter could thus be recited through the week at these two services; those psalms with fixed assignments to lauds and the Little Hours were excluded from this cycle.

To appreciate quite how varied the realization of this framework might be, it is worth recalling Amalarius's own trials in trying to bring order to the traditions of chanting the office.[24] A vivid picture of prevailing diversity is painted by his report of a journey to Rome in 831 to compare the antiphoner in use at Metz to the Roman Antiphoner. In Rome, Amalarius was referred to Corbie, to where, several years previously, the antiphoner of Pope Hadrian I was sent as a present for Abbot Wala (the cousin of Charlemagne). Amalarius returned to Corbie, where he compared the two antiphoners and was surprised to find that the two repertories differed in construction, texts, and in the number and order of antiphons and responds. Faced with such diversity, he adopted the approach of a compiler, indicating more recent Roman additions by R, whereas those introduced by Chrodegang to Metz he indicated by M; he also indicated numerous personal options by the letters IC. For all that Amalarius represents an early stage in the history of the office, the difference between two traditions supposedly directly linked and the provision of a number of texts for individuals to choose between remained a feature of the office throughout the Middle Ages.

While the basic structures of worship used throughout the Middle Ages were in place by the end of the ninth century, the subsequent history of medieval music and liturgy was characterized in the most general terms by expansion, most notably in the proper. This was achieved in part through an exponential increase in the number of feasts, especially those commemorating individual saints, to the extent that by the end of the Middle Ages few days in the whole year were without a festal observance in the Roman Missal. New departures of particular interest in this expansion included the elaboration of offices with newly composed texts and music both for individual saints and for particular feasts.[25] Expansion in music for the mass occurred primarily through accretions to existing liturgical items, principally by means of the introduction of tropes and sequences. The addition alongside chant of what were often poetic sung texts, but could also be solely musical interpolations, took place soon after the introduction of Roman chant into the Carolingian kingdoms; indeed, given reported difficulties in learning Roman chant, it is quite possible that these so-called accretions were introduced alongside the formalization of the repertory through the ninth century. While even a short introduction to tropes and sequences lies beyond the scope of this survey, what may be said is that the texts served in general to expound the significance of the feast being celebrated.[26] Many tropes, for example, begin with the word 'Hodie' ('Today'), before making explicit the themes of the day that had often remained implicit in the base chant texts.[27]

Although it is possible to identify an overall tendency to prolixity, the development was by no means linear or uniform, as may be illustrated by two examples from the era of monastic reform, the tenth and eleventh centuries. The Benedictine monastery at Cluny, which lies near Mâcon in Burgundy, was founded near the beginning of the tenth century: while operating independently of any external control, it developed a rich pattern of life and worship, the grandeur of which was symbolized by the abbey church itself, which remained the largest church building in Western Christendom until the sixteenth century. As for its liturgy, the abbey of Cluny and the international network of houses that shared its customs were famed by the eleventh century for a seemingly ceaseless liturgical round, yet the repertory of sung items at Cluny appears to have been conservative for it appears that tropes were scarcely used and that texted sequences were sung only on the highest feasts.[28] Liturgical expansion was realized instead through intercessions offered for specific intentions, whether commemorations of the dead, or the recitation of additional psalms (*psalmi familiares*) at each of the canonical hours for patrons, benefactors and friends, or the requirement for each monk to celebrate mass daily.

A broadly contemporary movement stemming from Gorze was characterized by a full use of tropes and sequences.[29] The abbey of Gorze, which lies some nine miles to the southwest of Metz, had been founded by Bishop Chrodegang as a Benedictine house and was revived by Adalbero (Bishop of Metz, 929–62) with the intent to reclaim the former glory of Metz through a return to strict adherence to the Benedictine Rule and a renewed intent to spread Messine chant. This reform proved so successful that the customs of Gorze spread throughout monastic houses in Lotharingia and the Eastern kingdoms ruled by the Ottonians. A certain degree of uniformity between houses associated with Gorze was ensured by the fact that it was the abbot (who was appointed from outside the community and remained in touch with the major centres of reform), rather than the cantor, who decided which chants were to be sung. Even so, there is little evidence to suggest a centrally coordinated reform of liturgy and chant within any of the monastic reform movements associated with individual houses in the tenth and eleventh centuries.

While musical and liturgical exchange during the tenth and eleventh centuries appears to have occurred largely through individual networks of association, overall development was shaped by a shared concern to seek renewal through a return to the Benedictine Rule, albeit as filtered through the Carolingians, under whose influence manual labour was replaced by increasingly elaborate communal worship. The Cistercian movement of the twelfth century stands out in sharp relief against this background, for the monks who settled at Cîteaux (near Dijon) in the closing years of the eleventh century sought a return to the letter of the earlier Benedict's Rule and thus to a pattern of worship free of the accretions of intervening centuries. Unlike earlier reform movements, there was at the same time a centrally coordinated attempt to revise the melodic repertory by returning to supposedly authentic musical sources, which in practice meant an attempt to reform chant on the basis of a gradual and antiphoner from Metz (whose legend of exemplary Roman practice endured) and a hymnal from Milan (the seat of the father of Latin hymnody, Saint Ambrose).[30] The results, however, were soon found to be unsatisfactory, in no small part because of the inadequate state of the sources used, prompting a second reform in the mid twelfth century based on a different model of authority. In this instance, the emphasis was placed not so much on authentic texts as on an intent to apply *a priori* rules in the reform of chant, namely that authentic and plagal modes should be kept separate, chants should not exceed a ten-note range, B flats were to be avoided in notation, and melismas should be cut down. Despite the apparent severity, it should be remembered not only that Cistercian chant reforms were not applied systematically, but also that the overall aim of Cistercian reform was to promote a simple and sober manner of worship that would encourage both unity and inner devotion.

A growing emphasis on individuals and inner experience can be detected in other movements with their roots in earlier medieval practices that achieved widespread prominence by the twelfth century. The shift can be traced most clearly with respect to the celebration of the mass and can be divided into two related tendencies. The period from the ninth to the twelfth century saw a rapid expansion in 'private masses', in which ceremonial splendour was reduced to a minimum (although it would still seem extensive to many modern observers): these masses, which made little or no use of music, were held by smaller groups in addition to the main community celebration as an act of intercession (often for the departed, or as part of devotion to the Blessed Virgin Mary).[31] In apparent opposition to this movement, there was a parallel tendency to expansion in all aspects of ritual gesture, including genuflexion, kissing the altar, kissing the Gospel, signing the cross and beating the breast. What these two tendencies shared was a growing conception of the mass as an act of piety offered by the priest on behalf of the assembled people, a notion expressed in the increasingly common practice of the priest celebrating facing East and himself reciting all parts of the mass, even when these were duly executed by the proper ministers or the choir. At the same time, physical separation increased between on the one hand the priest and attendant ministers, whose observances mainly took place around the altar in the sanctuary, and on the other hand the people, gathered in the nave, and separated not only by the chancel, in which were seated the choir, but increasingly by choir screens. The main participation open to the laity in such circumstances was through interior devotion, a state of affairs which goes some way towards explaining the growth in popular and affective practices centred on Mary and Jesus from the eleventh century onwards.[32]

A parallel emphasis on both specialized roles for select individuals within worship and an inner devotion that was the counterpart of an ever more elaborate ritual spectacle can be traced in the rapid expansion of polyphony in the liturgy up to the thirteenth century. Polyphony had been cultivated within worship for many centuries previously: indeed, any attempt to speak of an introduction of polyphony into the liturgy has to be tempered by the fact the earliest witnesses to polyphony are of the same date as the earliest notated repertories of monophony, namely the late ninth century. With that said, the polyphony recorded at this date is not a codified liturgical repertory, but examples of performance practice in treatises of music theory. Indeed, there has to be caution in treating these examples as polyphony and drawing a straight line between them and the repertories of the later Middle Ages, for what is recorded in these ninth- and tenth-century treatises is a method for amplifying a single line. As for the liturgical role of polyphony, it is hard to extract a picture of wider practice from the selection of office antiphons, psalm tones and a portion of the Te Deum contained in the earliest theory treatise to include polyphonic examples.[33] In one sense, however, the paradigmatic appearance of polyphony in the earliest treatises is significant in itself, for all the indications are that an earlier multiplicity of performance options only gradually crystallized into discrete items. One of the key features in this development was the elaboration and increased density of compositional rules such as can be seen in the eleventh-century repertories of polyphony from Winchester and Chartres. While both these centres are cathedrals, it should be remembered that polyphony was also sponsored by monasteries: Winchester itself was staffed by Benedictine monks under an abbot-bishop; polyphony was also practised at the substantial Benedictine monasteries of Fleury (reformed via Cluny) and St Maur-des-Fossés in Paris. Rather than being characterized by any divide by personnel or institutional type, polyphonic experimentation, formalization and latterly codification took place at larger institutions associated with the new currents of learning fostered especially in northern France during the eleventh century.

When considered as an element of liturgy, it is the ceremonial grandeur of polyphony that is most impressive. The execution of polyphony by soloists wearing silk copes on major feasts of the liturgical year at Notre Dame in Paris sits easily alongside the use of extra candles, incense and the richest vestments and vessels on such occasions. The element of outward display was further heightened by the use of polyphony originally associated with other liturgical functions (such as alleluias and responsories) in processions. Turning to stylistic developments customarily associated with the twelfth century, the consistent placing of the polyphonic voice above the base chant might also be considered a feature of increased outward display, the prominence of the new line a far cry from monastic prohibition against self-promotion and placing chants too high in the voice. In a related vein, the twelfth century also saw the development of techniques of extension and elaboration in the form both of polyphonic pieces with a highly melismatic voice above a slower-moving plainchant (*organum purum*) and compositions with up to four separate voices, thus announcing a decisive break with the previous insistence on music as a projection of the text akin to reading. At the same time, innovation was announced in polyphonic repertories by an increasingly self-confident distancing from liturgically assigned material, whether in the use of non-liturgical tenors in the Aquitanian repertory or in the increased expansion around the edges of the liturgy in the Parisian repertory in the form of the conductus. As for its underlying motivation, the development of polyphony has frequently been linked to Gothic splendour and a new-found urban self-confidence. Less often mentioned is the extent to which polyphony also served the immediate needs of the church, for liturgical polyphony soon centred on those parts of the chant repertory traditionally reserved for more elaborate singing by soloists (chiefly the verses of graduals, alleluias and responsories), thereby continuing, while also renewing, the functions already established in monophony. Viewed from a different perspective, polyphony served to foster the growing interest in inward and affective devotion, especially among the increasingly distinct and numerous crowd whose place it was to listen. The justification provided for such a new departure was an equally new-found emphasis on the pastoral role of the church, for polyphony was concentrated on those services to which the people of Paris had access and may be interpreted as 'a conscious attempt by the canons to demonstrate their superior abilities, or those of their subordinates, and to heighten the spirituality of the common folk'.[34]

The polyphonic repertory developed at Paris rapidly spread across Europe and remained the most elaborate liturgical music in circulation until the development of the Ars Nova in the early fourteenth century, yet during the same period it was Rome that led developments in liturgy. Symptomatic in this regard is the attitude taken by the new preaching orders in seeking to adopt new liturgies. A century after the Cistercians, the Dominicans turned to Metz in search of an authentic and standardized liturgy; they soon realized, however, that despite the continuance of legends, Metz no longer maintained an authoritative practice. The Dominicans therefore elected to follow Cistercian chant as codified in a master-exemplar of music and liturgy compiled around the mid thirteenth century. At about the same time, the Franciscans turned to a new source of authority in matters of chant and liturgy, namely the revised versions of the Breviary and Missal as drawn up at the papal court or curia in a series of revisions beginning with Pope Innocent III (1198–1216).[35] The return to music and liturgy as practised in Rome by the Franciscans was undoubtedly in part a matter of political expediency, but more fundamentally reflected a renewal of the political authority of the papacy.

The basis of the Roman rite adopted by the Franciscans was the so-called Romano-German Pontifical, a heterogeneous collection of liturgical rites which first appeared in Germany in the late tenth century. Following the coronation in Rome of Otto I as Holy Roman Emperor in 962, the liturgy associated with the Romano-German Pontifical became rapidly established at Rome: in a related process, the chant tradition as developed by the Franks also began to return to Rome, eventually replacing the local tradition now known as Old Roman chant. An attempt to revise and reclaim this received liturgy and music as distinctively Roman received significant impetus under Gregory VII (1073–85), who in attempting to reassert papal authority over territorial rulers claimed that the period of Germanic domination of the church had come to an end. While his desire to restore a pristine Roman liturgy proved idealistic, Gregory's efforts led to a curtailment of other rites, most notably the Visigothic. At the same time, Gregory's insistence on the authority of the priesthood above all laity (including rulers) served to further the developing divide between the clergy, who administered sacraments, and the laity, who were reduced to the role of observers.

The final stage in the spread of Roman liturgy occurred with the adoption of the practices of the curia by the Franciscans. Since the mendicant friars and the clerks of the papal court were both mainly concerned with affairs in the world, what was required was a liturgy that could be performed with the minimum of elaboration, and, crucially for the Franciscans, one that could be reduced into practical and portable collections. The eventual result was the codification of shortened forms of services in the form of a uniform Breviary (for the office) and Missal (for the mass) as regulated by the Ordinal of the Papal Court (ca1213–1216).[36] Again, however, it must be noted that at the same time as movement was taking place towards uniformity, there was an increase in popular devotions, especially those sponsored by the Franciscans, whether the Stations of the Cross in Holy Week, or the singing of simple religious songs in the vernacular (*laude spirituali* or carols).

Although no major liturgical reforms followed from the thirteenth century until the Council of Trent, two developments should not go unmentioned. First, the later Middle Ages saw a spread to the laity of forms of worship developed in monasteries; thus Books of Hours transferred both corporate hours and additional devotions, such as to the Virgin Mary or to the dead, into the sphere of private piety. Second, in the closing years of the thirteenth century a new pontifical was assembled in Avignon by perhaps the most famous liturgical commentator of the later Middle Ages, Bishop William Durandus. This compilation, which represented the clearest arrangements of materials to date, eventually superseded even the Pontifical of the Roman curia to become the model that was used until the Second Vatican Council. However, as Durandus noted in his commentary on the divine office, liturgical diversity persisted despite the spread of a uniform Breviary and full Missal of the Roman rite:[37]

> The reader should not be disturbed if he reads about things in this work which he has not found to be observed in his own particular church, or if he does not find something that is observed there. For we shall not proceed to discuss the peculiar observances of any particular place but the rites that are common and more usual, since we have labored to set forth a universal teaching and not one of particular bearing, nor would it be possible for us to examine thoroughly the peculiar observances of all places.

A striking example of the variety that could occur within the Roman rite is provided by Salisbury (Sarum) Use, not only because the various local uses that constitute Salisbury Use were in themselves highly varied, but also because the ceremonial elaboration within Salisbury Use stands in contrast to the pruning that took place in the Roman rite as observed in the papal chapel in the Lateran.[38] Sarum Use, namely the version of the

Roman rite associated with Salisbury, the earliest surviving documents for which date from the thirteenth century, gradually spread through England, Wales and Ireland so that by the Reformation only the local uses of Bangor, Hereford, Lincoln and York remained. A comparison of the Roman rite of the papal court, as filtered through the order and ceremonial prepared for the Franciscan order in around 1250, with a summary of Salisbury Use highlights several points of difference (Table 11.4).[39] Most notable is the greater use of processions in Salisbury Use, especially before High Mass on Sundays, although it should be recognized that processions were only infrequent in the papal court and places that adopted its use. The grander use of space in Salisbury Use is also apparent in the restriction of the celebration of mass in the papal court to the area around the altar, whereas Salisbury Use raises up certain activities to the height provided by the choir screen. A further difference is the amount of censing of the altar, which in Salisbury Use took place even during lessons at Matins. A final distinction which cannot be appreciated from the tabular comparison is the number of ministers involved: Salisbury Use could feature as many as seven deacons and subdeacons, two thurifers, and two to four priests in copes acting as cantors; the custom of the papal court as codified in Franciscan documents specifies for solemn mass on Sundays only a single priest, deacon, subdeacon and acolyte.

* * *

> For things should not be loved for the sake of places, but places for the sake of good things. Therefore select from each of the Churches whatever things are devout, religious, and right; and when you have bound them, as it were, into a Sheaf, let the minds of the English grow accustomed to it.[40]

These words, attributed to Pope Gregory the Great (590–604) in response to a question from Saint Augustine of Canterbury about the justification for variant local customs, may be taken as a spur for bringing together the strands addressed in this chapter. The importance of the first millennium for establishing the structures that lie at the basis of the medieval liturgy has been stressed, as well as the way in which diverse practices were gradually aligned. Similarly, the importance of Rome as a centre for disseminating a model of practice, yet nevertheless one that not only arose from varied practices, but also allowed different expressions of an established framework, has also been emphasized. The extent to which liturgy was shaped by the identity of individual places (Rome, Metz, Paris), as well as the way in which local places were articulated through a liturgical mapping out of space and formalization of communities, has also been touched upon.

Table 11.4 *An outline of solemn mass on Sundays in the Roman rite as celebrated at the papal chapel and in Salisbury Use*

Papal chapel, ca1250	Salisbury Use ca1400
Prayers – said privately by the celebrant in front of the altar.	Aspersion – and blessing of the altar accompanied by sung antiphon and followed by aspersion of ministers.
Introit	Procession – antiphon or responsory sung as the procession leaves through the north door of the choir and circles the presbytery – the celebrant sprinkles water on altars on the way. Procession continues down the south aisle and returns past the font to the choir screen. Verses sung by soloists at the rood step, followed by bidding prayers. Procession continues into the choir with another antiphon or responsory. Celebrant ends the procession with a versicle at the choir step, before proceeding to the canon's cemetery to sprinkle water and pray for the dead.
Kyrie	Kyrie – sung by choir, recited by celebrant.
Gloria in excelsis	Gloria in excelsis – intoned by celebrant, sung by choir.
Collect	Collect – intoned by celebrant.
Epistle – intoned by subdeacon before the step in front of the altar.	Epistle – intoned by subdeacon from lectern on pulpit.
Gradual – (sung by choir and) read through in their seats by ministers.	Gradual – sung by soloists from lectern on pulpit.
(Alleluia)	Alleluia – sung by soloists in copes, during which, the deacon censes the altar and the procession for the gospel moves to the choir screen.
(Sequence)	Sequence – sung *alternatim* by choir.
Gospel – intoned by deacon, with subdeacon and acolyte with thurible in attendance.	Gospel – intoned by deacon at lectern on the choir screen facing north.
Creed – intoned, but only used on occasion.	Creed – intoned by celebrant.
Offertory – during which, preparation of the table; blessing of incense; censing of cup and altar; censing of priest, deacon, subdeacon and choir.	Offertory – sung by choir, during which, procession of bread and wine, censing of bread and wine, censing of celebrant, ministers and choir, and censing of altar.
(Secret offertory prayer)	Secret – said privately by celebrant, last phrase sung.
Eucharistic prayer – including Sanctus and Benedictus.	Eucharistic prayer – including Sanctus and Benedictus sung by choir and said privately at altar. Bells rung to signal blessing and elevation of host.
Lord's prayer	Lord's prayer
Peace	Peace
Agnus Dei – after which, kiss of peace passed from priest, to deacon, to subdeacon, to acolyte, and to choir.	Agnus Dei – sung by choir, during which, kiss of peace passed from celebrant to deacon to subdeacon to choir.
Communion – taken by priest (with communion chant sung by choir).	Communion – taken by celebrant, with communion chant sung by choir.
Postcommunion collect	Postcommunion collect – intoned by celebrant.
Dismissal	Dismissal – sung by deacon, response by choir.
Blessing – followed by return to vestry.	Recessional – ministers leave, including celebrant, reciting first 14 verses of St John's Gospel.

Told in this way, the story is one of growth and circumscribed diversification, but a less positive evaluation of the spread of practices across the Latin West could also be told. A narrative based on the rise of a coherent historical, cultural and geographic Latin West overlooks not only the practices of different faiths within this domain, but the parallels and exchanges between Eastern and Western practices. While the comparative lack of sources makes it difficult to address Jewish and Islamic worship,[41] increasing awareness of the fundamental discontinuities between even the Latin liturgical sources that survive, as well as increasing suspicion of their witness to current practice, is prompting renewed interest in the stories that have been told about them.[42]

A more general reflection on Gregory's words could begin from his use of the word 'things' to refer to the contents of liturgical exchange. On the one hand, the transfer of material goods is intrinsic to the history of music and liturgy, whether in the form of the paraphernalia needed for worship (fine vestments, vessels, candles, incense, books etc.), or the ongoing supply of wealth needed to maintain institutions (including, centrally, choirs). On the other hand, the terminology is indicative of the fact that, for all that has been said about the relation of music and liturgy up to this point, no single word for 'liturgy' and no clearly separable word for 'music' was in use in the Middle Ages.[43] The customary liturgical distinction between rite (texts or things uttered) and ceremonial (actions or things done) highlights instead the way in which an attempt has been made here to address music as an aspect of ceremonial. In considering music in the liturgy as ceremonial *agenda* or things done, the extraordinary power that it wielded over both the self and others is finally brought into consideration. It is precisely this power that caused the earlier Saint Augustine to hesitate before, in a move indicative of the widespread acceptance that music was later to find in Christian worship, sanctioning its use as divine enchantment:[44]

> I vacillate between the peril of pleasure and the value of the experience, and I am led more – while advocating no irrevocable position – to endorse the custom of singing in church so that by the pleasure of hearing the weaker soul might be elevated to an attitude of devotion.

12 Vernacular poetry and music

ARDIS BUTTERFIELD

Prima la musica, poi le parole: this assertion, the title of an opera by Antonio Salieri, wittily alludes to the conundrum faced by any poetic and musical collaboration. In the story of the opera the music is already written and the harassed poet is told he must write the verse to fit the music in just four days. It is not important, according to the musician, for the music to convey the meaning of the words. But of course this is a joke that works by inverting the usual expectations of any text–music relationship, especially in opera. One of the primary aims of this chapter will be to assess the character of this relationship in its earliest formation in the medieval period. Poetry and music come together in vernacular song to create some of the most subtly exquisite survivals of medieval music. The art of the troubadours in the twelfth century, closely followed by that of the trouvères in the thirteenth, persists in our time as one of the most vividly enduring images, not only of the medieval singer, but also of song *tout court*, and of the Middle Ages in general.

Yet many questions remain about the character of this art. It seems not only paramount but impossible to decide which comes first, the poetry or the music. In communicating so strongly across the centuries, medieval song teases us with the question of *what* it is communicating and whether what we hear or perform as we re-create it bears any relation to what was heard or performed in the Middle Ages. This matters for several reasons. Many editors and performers since the nineteenth century have based their reconstructions of medieval songs on the assumption that the words drive the melody, especially with regard to rhythm.[1] More recently, others have argued that this assumption undervalues the importance of the music (Aubrey, 244) and that 'music's elements follow rules of their own, regardless of which poetic elements are present' (Aubrey, 253). That this debate exists shows how little modern agreement there is about what constitutes the 'poetic' or the 'musical' in the period. It also shows that it is a vital and continuing point of inquiry for any attempt to understand the nature of medieval song. Whether the words or the music have primacy turns out to have powerful consequences for the way we interpret the songs, how we understand them to have been composed, and what their larger function and significance was for medieval poet-composers and their audiences.

The chapter will begin by describing this seminal stage, the age of the troubadours, in the composition of song and trace its origins, character, function and generic variety. It will then give an account of the multiple ways in which the relationship between poetry and music fundamentally changed throughout the thirteenth century and into the fourteenth, most significantly in the development of new genres and new ways of perceiving genre; in the polyphonic motet; and in song's relationship with narrative. The concluding sections will turn to wider questions about the figure of the poet and of the composer and how ideas about poetry and music were articulated, practised and debated.

Vernacular song

Origins

The idea of an origin for vernacular song has haunted many scholars. It remains elusive partly because of the conundrum I have just outlined. The very first example of vernacular song, by definition, is rather like the very first word: we are never going to know when it was uttered and its utterance would have long preceded any thought of writing it down. But in mentioning writing, we have to distinguish the writing down of the words from the writing down of the melody. With just one exception – a song with an Occitan text of around 1100 from St Martial de Limoges – the melodies of vernacular song do not survive in written form until the thirteenth century.[2] Moreover, even when we reach the thirteenth century, only some of the surviving copies of vernacular songs contain music. Of the forty manuscripts (including fragments) of twelfth- and thirteenth-century Occitan literature, ranging from epic and didactic works to over 2,500 lyrics, just two contain music.[3] There are two more that date from the fourteenth century. Immediately, then, we are presented with a view of song that – on the face of it – is highly prejudiced towards the words.

For some scholars, these survival patterns are proof that troubadour songs were appreciated in the thirteenth century for their words rather than for their melodies. Others are quick to point out that the relative paucity of music tells us more about the shortage of skills for copying music (as true in the modern period as it was in the medieval) than about the allegedly 'literary' character of the songs. But the argument goes deeper than this. For instance, there is much debate about whether troubadour song was *meant* to be written down. Since the written versions that we have date from 100 to 150 years after the songs were composed, how can we be sure that they give us an accurate impression of the songs as they were first composed and performed? It seems quite likely that, in a situation rather like the game of consequences, what survives in writing has travelled a long way from its oral genesis. There are several important issues here: one is that the oral version of a song is always going to be different from its written version. This is true even when the act of writing is contemporary with the performance, and the differences are naturally exacerbated when the act of writing postdates the performance by more than a century. It follows that the act of writing down a song probably bears more relation to the act of writing down a play or a piece of poetry than to the activities of singing or speaking. It is the activity of writing itself, in other words, that helps to make a work 'literary'. A second issue concerns the passage of time. It is crucial to bear in mind when we seek to interpret troubadour song that our knowledge of it is shaped by thirteenth- and fourteenth-century writers.[4] We cannot find its origins because it is always already distanced from its own time by having been modernized as well as turned into writing.

Social and literary functions

The functions of the earliest surviving vernacular songs can only be appreciated by knowing something of the social and historical context of their poet-composers. Some 460 troubadours, including a few women known as the *trobairitz*, are known by name over the period from around 1100 to 1300: they lived and worked across a large area of what is now southern France, at first only in Poitiers, Ventadorn and Narbonne, and then more widely into the Auvergne, Limousin, Aquitaine, Gascony and Languedoc and eastwards into Provence. Some were based in the northern Italian courts of Lombardy and Piedmont, and in Catalonia. This very substantial poetic and musical movement ebbed and flowed in successive generations: the first includes Guillaume IX, Duke of Aquitaine (1071–1126), Jaufre Rudel (. . . 1125–48 . . .), and Marcabru (. . . 1130–49 . . .), followed by Bernart de Ventadorn (. . . 1147–70 . . .) and Peire d' Alvernhe (. . . 1149–68). Bernart and Peire are also often viewed as part of the central 'classical' generation, with such other figures as Raimbaut d'Aurenga (. . . 1147–73), Bertran de Born (. . . 1159–95, d. 1215), and Giraut de Bornelh (. . . 1162–1199 . . .). The later, third and fourth generations, include troubadours who worked into the second half of the thirteenth century alongside their northern French counterparts, the trouvères. Perhaps the most well known of these is the so-called last troubadour, Guiraut Riquier (. . . 1250–92), whose musical output – unsurprisingly considering his dates – survives more fully than any other troubadour (48 melodies out of 87 poems). Otherwise, music survives far more patchily: 42 of these 460 authors have songs attributed to them with music, and for most of them just one or a small handful of songs in their total surviving output has music.[5] A single song by a female composer, the 'Comtessa' de Dia (second half of the twelfth century(?)[6] survives with music.[7]

Our knowledge of the social standing of the troubadours is largely provided by short prose mini-biographies and commentaries called *vidas* and *razos* that accompany the songs in several of the manuscripts. A kind of marketing device to advertise and sell the songs and their authors, these are colourfully written with an air of dubious authority. Nonetheless, some of their information seems plausible enough and can sometimes be corroborated or supplemented by documentary records or references in the songs themselves. Many of the troubadours starting with Guillaume, at once ninth Duke of Aquitaine and seventh Count of Poitou, belonged to the nobility: many were minor nobles and younger sons of aristocrat families. Richard I (the Lionheart), eldest son of Guillaume IX's granddaughter Eleanor of Aquitaine and Henry II of England, is the famous example of a king turned poet and composer. Others, however, were of humble or middling origins: several rose to fame from being mere *joglars* or jobbing professional instrumentalists and singers, such as Cercamon and Albertet; others again were from urban or mercantile backgrounds, such as Aimeric de Peguilhan, said to have been the son of a draper; many more are likely to have been clerics who had abandoned their training or livings.

The evidence of such high status for certain troubadours has helped shape the (largely correct) impression we have of a type of music that belonged in exclusive circles. Yet it is an interesting feature of the *vidas* that they often like to create an image for a troubadour of a self-made man pulling himself up out of obscurity.[8] Social mobility was clearly important: many of the song texts develop a pose of detachment, of the clever, mocking outsider to love, which may well have reflected a genuine experience of social exclusion. This needs to be borne in mind when the function of the songs is considered, because it shows that the picture of the songs as being part of a high courtly ethos has more than one dimension. Courtliness, perhaps the key defining term with which to understand troubadour song, may be described as a complex relationship between social, cultural and aesthetic aspiration on the part both of lords and the members of their households.[9] The image of courtliness, in short, was as important as the social reality, and the social reality itself was not so much indulgently self-enclosed as loose, itinerant and profoundly involved with war (frictions between Angevin rulers and the French royalty, the Crusades), trade (burgeoning urban and maritime economies) and religion (the Albigensian heresy). The words and melodies of troubadour song help to define a discourse of courtliness by satirizing it as well as promoting it, by wild exaggeration as well as piercing social comment, by invention as well as description. At the same time, the very fact that many lords were themselves keen to compose indicates that vernacular song was more than a matter of courtly entertainment. It was an aspect of living the courtly life, or at least of ventriloquizing its most potent characteristics.

If there is a single overarching theme that defines courtliness in vernacular song, it is *fin' amors* or, as Gaston Paris termed it in 1884, 'amour courtois' (courtly love).[10] This difficult, richly contentious notion of refined, rarefied, extreme love is the air which many genres of troubadour song breathe. Recent research has greatly deepened and enlarged our knowledge of how love and its associated themes in song, such as adultery, secrecy (*celar*), the imagined power of the lady (*domna*), the role of the *lauzengier* (slanderer) or *gilos* (the jealous ones) relate to the changing social and ecclesiastical representations of love and marriage in the medieval period. It has become possible to see that some of the contradictions in *fin' amors* are part of a wider exploration of cultural fault lines in the portrayal of women as both passive and active in love, as silent and yet dominating, as objects of both worship (*pretz, valor, onor*) and derision. Some of the specific functions of troubadour song thus include the creation of a discourse about women's conflicted roles in an aristocratic household alongside an explicitly male-voiced expression of frustrated desire. Less abstractly, perhaps, the large amount of surviving debate poetry indicates that song was a means of establishing a public forum for brilliantly fast-moving exchanges between lords and the shifting group of people in attendance on them, a platform for public argument about the qualities and values of courtly life.

Genres

Scholars have found many ways of discussing and defining genre in vernacular song. It is often difficult to know whether it is form, genre or style that is under consideration. For an older generation including Friedrich Gennrich and Hans Spanke, followed more recently by Pierre Bec, form was a key perspective, yet subsequent work influenced by literary considerations, by John Stevens and Christopher Page, for example, has preferred a broader notion of genre that includes social context and style. Where form is emphasized, monophonic song can be divided up into different structural types: the *laisse*, the refrain-song, the sequence and the strophic song. This offers an illuminating sense of the fundamental technical choices made by composers, but it provides no means of linking these choices of poetic and melodic arrangement to theme or content, tone, diction and choice of pitch range, register and, more broadly, social meaning. Stevens and Page develop ways of approaching the songs particularly through style, higher and lower, but also through matters of performance (rhythm and the use of instruments) and social history (Parisian music theorists and practitioners, and Cistercian anxieties about dance-song). Perhaps the most interesting newer work by such scholars as Margaret Switten and Elizabeth Aubrey has gone on to ponder how far the music and the texts correspond generically. The widespread use of contrafacta in early vernacular song means that there is no intrinsic connection between a melody and its textual partner, and provokes questions about the kinds of generic expectation carried by melodies, and whether they overlapped with, were independent of, or, conversely, were determined by the texts.

Here there remains a marked gulf between the thinking on genre carried out by literary scholars and that by musicologists. Whereas much research has gone into the literary and social contexts for the texts, in which scholars have developed approaches from psychoanalysis, intertextuality, gender studies, and ecclesiastical and economic history, the melodies have received less attention. In part, this is perhaps because it has seemed hard to talk about the melodies without the words, and harder still to comment on both together. As Switten has rightly remarked, we have yet to find a critical and scholarly language to talk of the relations between music and words. These relationships 'do not constitute a discipline with a distinguishing ideology and approaches sanctified by use. There is even no satisfactory terminology to speak of both [disciplines] at once.'[11] More positively, the lack of a hallowed critical language indicates how far the scope for further research into vernacular poetry and music extends, and its consequent potential as an innovative field of enquiry.

The pre-eminent genre of medieval vernacular song was the strophic troubadour canso, a term used after the 1150s (the earlier, more general term was *vers*) to refer to songs on love.[12] Cansos explore the topic of *fin' amors* in all its variety and complexity, through an equally rich and varied use of versification. The canso had a kind of counter-genre in the *sirventes*, a satirical and moralizing type of poem that became more widespread, and acquired this generic title, at a similar date. It was characterized by often being attached to a borrowed canso melody, as, for example, Bertran de Born's *Un sirventes on motz no falh* which, as he points out, uses a melody by Giraut de Bornelh. Other genres include the *tenso, partimen, joc-partit* or debate songs; *pastorela*, a song that narrates an encounter between a knight and a peasant girl; *dansa*, a song based on a dance; *descort*, a 'discordant' song in which the stanzas (unusually) vary in rhyme, metre, and sometimes language; *enueg*, a canso listing unpleasant subjects; *planh*: a lament on the death of a king or other dignitary; *gap*, a boasting poem.

In mentioning dance, it is worth remarking that there also existed a lively unwritten dance-song tradition. Textual sources from the twelfth century onwards ranging from chronicles, romances and sermons to town records contain many references (some sternly condemnatory) to round dances and processional dancing that clearly involved a lead singer and some kind of chorus response.[13] A vivid illustration in the Oxford Chansonnier, MS Douce 308, placed at the head of the section of *balletes* shows two figures dancing with linked hands in front of a pipe and tabor player. This kind of evidence hints at the much larger world of performance and improvised music that surrounded the relatively meagre written remains that we now possess both of texts and of melodies. Many texts refer, often obliquely, to dance movements, yet cannot be tied to particular surviving tunes, and indeed the song copied next to the picture just described seems to have no particular connection to dance in its text, nor does this chansonnier contain music. As with instrumental music more generally, it is important to be aware that the written sources represent only a fraction of what was played and composed throughout the medieval period.

Moving back from genre to form, we find in troubadour song perhaps the most artful exploitation of sound patterns in any short genre, modern or medieval. Metre (number of syllables per line) and rhyme are used through the careful placing of words to partner pitch, intervallic relationships, motifs, incipits and cadences in the melody. The fundamental structural unit is the strophe, organized in its most general outline for words and music in the form AAB. Within this outline, each song, of five, six or seven stanzas (*coblas*) with one or more shorter envoys (pendant stanzas) or *tornadas*, is crafted to contain sequences of repetition and variation in both words and melody of often dazzling virtuosity. Remarkably, very few songs have the same pattern: over half the poems with extant melodies have a unique rhyme and verse structure.[14] In one of the earliest and most influential analyses of troubadour song, *De vulgari eloquentia* (ca 1303–5), Dante describes the two-part structure of the canso strophe as the frons and the cauda, each frons usually divided into two pedes (singular pes). The distribution of rhymes across the frons and cauda falls into several common patterns: the same rhyme sounds in each strophe (*coblas unissonans*) but with different rhyme words; *coblas doblas* and *coblas ternas* where the rhyme sound changes every two or three stanzas; *coblas capfinidas* where the first line of a stanza repeats a word from the last line of the previous stanza; and *coblas retrogradas* where the rhyme sounds are reordered in a different sequence from stanza to stanza.

When we turn to the music, the language of description immediately becomes less straightforward. It is not so easy to plot patterns of repetition in melodies as it is in texts, or at least the patterns are more open to diverse forms of analysis. Scholars who have worked closely with troubadour texts and music together (Stevens, Switten and Aubrey) have drawn attention to the way that verbal rhyme and musical repetition, while they may be subtly juxtaposed, rarely simply coincide. Their relationship is poised and

Example 12.1 *Can vei la lauzeta* ('When I see the lark') by Bernart de Ventadorn (Hendrik van der Werf and Gerald A. Bond, eds., *The Extant Troubadour Melodies: Transcriptions and Essays for Performers and Scholars* [Rochester, NY: authors, 1984], pp. 62–71)

balanced, intimate yet also independent. Nonetheless, as remarked above, the practice of contrafacta puts a brake on attempts to see a song as necessarily an organic text–music whole. Where individual texts are copied with more than one melody we cannot be sure in any single manuscript version that the same person composed the text and the music, and therefore that there is a single *intentio* governing the operation of words and melody. Or again, a poet-composer may have been more gifted as a musician than as a poet, or vice versa: the vida of Jaufre Rudel somewhat waspishly complains that 'he composed many songs about [his lady] with good tunes and poor words'. A melody by Guiraut de Bornelh reused by Peire Cardenal (Aubrey, 153) suggests further creative possibilities in showing how some troubadours deliberately reworked material.

The celebrated canso *Can vei la lauzeta* ('When I see the lark') by Bernart de Ventadorn well illustrates the interpretative challenges posed by troubadour song (Example 12.1). The challenges arise in the first instance out of the text but then need to be considered alongside the music. The melody of this canso is more widely transmitted than any other troubadour melody and with fewer differences between versions, but this relative stability in musical terms is not matched by the words. As is fairly common among the troubadour repertory as a whole, the seven stanzas plus envoy are arranged in more than one order in the various manuscript copies. For an older generation of text editors, it was a matter of selecting the 'best' order and printing that once, thus creating a fixed song of which three stanzas are given below:

> Can vei la lauzeta mover
> de joi sas alas contral rai,
> que s'oblid'e.s laissa chazer
> per la doussor c'al cor li vai,
> ai! tan grans enveya m'en ve
> de cui qu'eu veya jauzion,
> meravilhas ai, car desse
> lo cor de dezirer no.m fon.
>
> Ai, las! tan cuidava saber
> d'amor, e tan petit en sai!
> car eu d'amar no.m posc tener
> celeis don ja pro non aurai.
> tout m'a mo cor, e tout m'a me,
> e se mezeis e tot lo mon;
> e can se.m tolc, no.m laisset re
> mas dezirer e cor volon.
>
> Anc non agui de me poder
> ni no fui meus de l'or'en sai
> que.m laisset en sos olhs vezer
> en un miralh que mout me plai.
> miralhs, pus me mirei en te,
> m'an mort li sospir de preon,
> c'aissi.m perdei com perdet se
> lo bels Narcisus en la fon.

When I see the young lark moving its wings for joy in the ray of the sun so that it forgets itself and lets itself fall for the sweetness that goes to its heart, alas! such great envy comes to me of anyone whom I may see rejoicing, I wonder that forthwith my heart does not melt with desire.

Alas! so much did I think that I knew about love, and so little do I know, for I cannot abstain from loving her from whom I shall never have reward. She has stolen my heart from me and has stolen myself from me and herself and the whole world. And when she stole herself from me she left me nothing except desire and a heart filled with longing.

> Never did I have control over myself, nor was I my own master from that moment when she let me look into her eyes, into a mirror that pleases me greatly. Mirror, since I beheld myself in you, my deep sighs have slain me, for so did I lose myself as fair Narcissus lost himself in the fountain.[15]

More recent approaches to text editing, by contrast, have encouraged scholars to consider the different text orders as potentially interesting in their own right.[16] Rather than seek a single definitive version of 'the' song, we are now invited to think of *Can vei la lauzeta* as having several possible realizations, perhaps indicative of its being reworked for different audiences and occasions. Thus in one stanza order shared by five manuscripts, two of the stanzas, including the one on Narcissus, come later and two others are shifted earlier.[17] The result in this case is the stark difference between a speaker/singer who is despairing but ultimately reconciled to the nature of love, and one that a recent scholar has called 'an angry and recalcitrant woman-hater'.[18]

What then of the music? In general terms, the strophic melody is characteristic of Bernart's restrained, mellifluous style, moving largely in adjacent steps, with short ornamental passages not so much interrupting as easing the beautifully composed flow of sound. This quiet control in the music is balanced by a similarly restricted palette of rhymes and rhythmic patterns: 8 syllables per line, 8 lines per stanza and only 4 rhyme sounds (although again this varies slightly across the manuscripts). Just one abrupt descent of a whole fifth occurs in the whole melody at the end of the fifth line. Is there a connection here with the text? For instance, it is tempting to argue that this feature, coming just after the mid-point of the strophe, has a structural parity with the singer's declaration in stanza 5 just after the mid-point of the song that he will renounce his destructive lady and leave her forever.[19] But in another version of the song this stanza occurs not fifth but seventh, being the last before the envoy. Clearly the same argument could not be made with the text–music relationship in this version. In part this is a matter of reading each version responsively and individually. But it also speaks more widely of the need for a critical approach to the mutual support of words and music in troubadour song that can take account in some way of the structural asymmetry of a linear text aligned with a strophic melody. It must also take account of the distance as well as the intimacy of text and music in any one song.

The sheer variety of musical devices and compositional features makes it hard to generalize about the music of the troubadours. Yet the attempts by scholars such as Aubrey and Switten to discuss the style and musical language of individual composers have made important steps towards our reaching a sense of the expectations that circulated about song on the part both of the composers themselves and of their audiences.

The changing contexts of song: *grand chant,* motet and narrative

If genre is a multivalent concept for the twelfth century, then it has even greater flexibility and inventiveness in the thirteenth. It is worth recalling that the very first written record of a troubadour song, Jaufre Rudel's *Lanquan li jorn son lonc en may* ('In May when the days are long'), occurs in an early-thirteenth-century romance by Jean Renart known as *Le Roman de la Rose*. Romance is a key resource for vernacular song: Renart's *Le Roman de la Rose* alone contains the first surviving examples and extracts from a range of genres – the *chanson de toile, rondet de carole,* and the independent refrain – and two further genres – the *chanson d'éloge* and *tornoi de dames* – which are unique to the work.[20] Altogether some seventy narratives cite song from the early thirteenth century to the early fifteenth, in several hundred manuscripts. Music is provided in just under a quarter of these copies.[21] If the genre of romance seems an unusual place to start in describing vernacular song then this is an accident of modern scholarly emphases. Recognizing the importance of narrative as a context for the writing down of song throughout the thirteenth century helps us to grasp how broadly song participated in, and contributed to, the increasingly sophisticated explorations of vernacular literacy through the medium of the book.

The trouvère chanson, traditionally seen as the northern cousin of the canso, is equally traditionally described as a kind of appendage to its southern predecessor. It undoubtedly shares much common ground, especially in its treatment of love. However, placing it here in a separate section from the troubadours is a way of emphasizing that in several ways the account needs to be reversed. The trouvères invented the troubadours rather than merely followed after them. Moreover, the work they performed on song was part of a much wider cultural movement that included new prominence given to the vernacular in France through increasingly centralized legal practice, a rapid rise in the production of vernacular books, the growing international importance of the university in Paris, extensive urban expansion and a marked increase in ecclesiastical and monastic institutional activity. In musical terms, there were far-reaching changes in notational practice and an extraordinary proliferation of compositional techniques in which musical material from liturgical sources was juxtaposed with, cut through and transformed by the increasingly widely transmitted secular monophony of both troubadours and trouvères. It was the trouvères who effected these changes, partly by the very process of writing down the songs of their predecessors, and partly by creating many new directions for the relationship between text and music.

In broad terms, the genres practised by the trouvères were similar: the principal kind, comparable to the canso, is the *chanson d'amour* or *grand chant courtois* ('grant chant' is a resonant classifying term used in the late thirteenth-century chansonnier Oxford, Bodleian Library MS Douce 308).[22] Trouvères such as the great Châtelain de Couci (d. 1203) or Gace Brulé (ca1160–after 1213) built on the success of the troubadours by creating through the *grand chant* a powerfully pervasive courtly discourse of text and melody that dominated the thirteenth century and the two centuries following. Yet alongside these heights of refined expression, trouvère writing is distinctively characterized by a fascination with 'lower-style' genres. Apparently humble genres such as the *rondet de carole* (later rondeau), *chanson de toile*, *chanson de femme*, *chanson de mal mariée*, *rotrouenge* and *sotte chanson* are newly recorded from the thirteenth century, and crossover genres taken over from the troubadours such as the *pastourelle* or the *jeu-parti* are greatly expanded. Interspersed among, and to a large extent at the basis of, many of these types is the refrain, a brief formulaic tag of verse and (in many cases) melody cited in thousands of permutations.[23]

The trouvères, in short, were not exclusively interested in creating single poetic–musical artefacts of superlative craft. They were also drawn towards breaking down that creative product into its constituent elements. This can be illustrated by two contrasting pieces. One is a song by the Châtelain de Couci often performed and recorded for modern listeners, the first stanza of which is given in Example 12.2. This song through its music and its words distils all the courtliness one could hope to find in a medieval love song: a limpid spring setting impelling the lover to sing of his intense desire yet also of his pain as he is forced to leave his lady to go 'outremer' or beyond the sea. The haunting melody follows a classic AAB schema, rising in the B section to the highest pitch of the song rapidly followed by the lowest, yet with an unbroken, flowing continuity of melody.[24] At the opposite end of the spectrum of medieval song comes this second example, a short, technically simple exclamation: *Jolietement m'en vois; jolietement* ('Happily I go; happily').[25] This little phrase has an almost cheekily insignificant character when set beside the long, exquisitely expository eroticism of *Li noveaus tanz*. It implies accompanying movement, and for an older generation of scholars was a surviving trace of a world of lost popular dance. Yet what happens to this phrase is revealing of the many changes in focus that take place in the treatment of song during the thirteenth century. We find it cited in four different pieces: a song text in the motets and rondeaux section of the unnotated chansonnier Douce 308; in the tournament romance *Le Tournoi de Chauvency*, also copied in Douce 308; at the end of a stanza in a short strophic narrative, *La Chastelaine de Saint Gille*, again without music;

Example 12.2 *Li noveaus tanz et mai et violette* ('The new season, May, the violet') by the Châtelain de Couci, (*F-Pn* fonds fr. 12615, fol. 155r)

and finally in a notated polyphonic motet (Mo 260) copied into the seventh fascicle of a huge motet compilation, the Montpellier Codex.[26] In each of these contexts it has a different form: in Douce 308 it is split in two around a single-stanza text, with 'Jolietement m'en vois' at the start and 'jolietement' at the end. *La Chastelaine de Saint Gille* simply quotes it 'in full' at the end of the stanza. In the Montpellier motet, by contrast, it is the refrain of a rondeau which has itself become the tenor of the three-voice motet (Example 12.3).

These three views of this song take us into a seemingly very different compositional world from *Li noveaus tanz*. From song as a highly wrought self-contained structure, designed to evoke a specific and thoroughly imagined emotional landscape in which the act of singing such a song is self-consciously a part, we have moved to a much more fragmentary, protean notion of song as a brief yet key motif, able to move readily between genres and function as a complex organizing tool in the creation of the rhythmic and motivic patterns of a polyphonic motet. Rondeau-motets are a relatively small subgenre of the motet, yet they illustrate a much broader general preoccupation with juxtaposing distinct and sometimes seemingly

Example 12.3 *Jolietement m'en vois; jolietement* ('Happily I go; happily') (*The Montpellier Codex*, ed. Hans Tischler, trans. Susan Stakel and Joel C. Relihan, 4 vols., Recent Researches in the Music of the Middle Ages and Early Renaissance 2–8 [Madison, WI: A-R Editions, 1978–85]; hereafter *Mo*; *Mo* 260, vol. III, pp. 78–9)

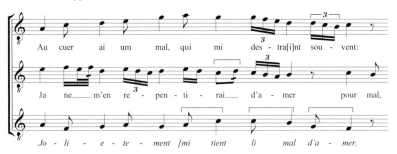

incompatible registers, styles and genres. Modern distinctions between song and narrative, strophic and non-strophic, and sacred and secular often do not seem adequate ways of describing the pleasure in dissonance and hybridity so evident in thirteenth-century song composition. 'Song' is overturned in these explorations and reinvented as a set of smaller elements, ready to be recombined, grafted, strung in sequence cento-style or layered polytextually and polymusically in ways that often seem more interested in disruption than in communication.

A motet that seems to make lack of communication a central theme of its comic textual and musical manipulations occurs within a cluster of Robin and Marion motets from fascicle 7 of the Montpellier Codex. These motets draw on texts taken from the pastourelle genre in which the feelings felt by an attractive shepherdess for her sturdy but not over-bright peasant lover are threatened by an adventuring chevalier. *En mai, quant rosier sont flouri / L'autre jour, par un matin / Hé, resvelle toi [Robin]* ('In May with rose bushes blooming / The other day, in morningtide / Hey, wake up Robin'), *Mo* 269, is unusual in bringing together three texts of this type, not just in the upper two voices but in the tenor as well (Examples 12.4a, 12.4b). For instead of the more usual Latin chant extract, the tenor is here a refrain:

Example 12.4a and 12.4b *En mai, quant rosier sont flouri / L'autre jour, par un matin / Hé, resvelle toi [Robin]* ('In May with rose bushes blooming / The other day, in morningtide / Hey, wake up Robin') (*Mo* 269, vol. III, pp. 93–5)

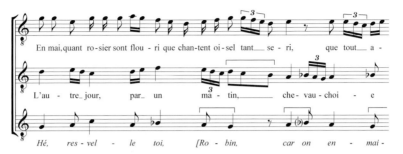

En mai, quant ro-sier sont flou - ri que chan-tent oi-sel tant_ se - ri,   que tout_ a -

L'au - tre_ jour,   par_ un   ma - tin,___   che - vau - choi - e

Hé,   res - vel - le   toi,   [Ro - bin,   car   on   en - mai -

mant sont res - bau - di en-con-tre   le dous tans jo- li,___   par un ma - tin me le-vai,

lés   un___ pré;   re - gar-dai   en mon   che-min si

ne   Ma - rot,   car   on   en - mai - ne Ma - rot.]

//

et di- soit: "Ay - mi,___ Ro - bin, mi-se___ m'a - vés_ en___ ou - bli

et   di - soit: "Ay - mi!   Quant ven-

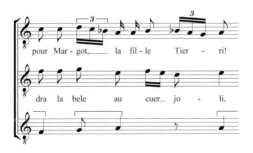

pour Mar - got,___ la fil - le Tier - ri!

dra la bele   au   cuer_ jo - li,

Hé, resvelle toi [Robin],
Car on enmaine Marot,
Car on enmaine Marot.

[Hey, wake up Robin, for someone is taking Marot away, for someone is taking Marot away!]

Like several of the other Robin and Marion motets, *Mo* 269 has a link with the Arras poet and composer, Adam de la Halle: in this case the refrain also occurs with both text and music in Adam's *Le jeu de Robin et de Marion.*

It is worth looking more closely at the context of this refrain in Adam's *Le jeu de Robin et de Marion* because it provides insight into the cleverly allusive practices of the motet's composer, who may even have been Adam himself. First, we may appreciate the comic timing of the juxtaposition of the two main texts. The triplum (the second texted upper voice above the tenor), given like nearly all pastourelle narratives from the perspective of the chevalier, recounts that Marion is sitting near a wood lamenting that Robin has abandoned her for Margot, 'la fille Tierri' (Tierri's daughter). But as soon as her lament is uttered, Robin, who has overheard it, comes running up and takes her away to play. In a neat reversal, the motetus (the first texted upper voice above the tenor) has the chevalier see Robin sighing for Marion, who then, having likewise overheard *him*, runs up quickly and assures him that he has 'conquered' her love. Musically, the two texts interwine to play off each character's self-enclosed (and, as we learn retrospectively, misguided) misery, most comically when first Marion and then Robin sings 'Aymi!' The composer places the identical words 'et disoit: "Aymi"' in direct succession across the two parts, so that just as Marion is complaining in the triplum that 'Robin, mise m'avés en oubli' (Robin, you have forgotten me), Robin is simultaneously exclaiming 'Aymi! Quant vendra la bele au cuer joli?' (Alas, when will she come, the fair one with the gay heart), each cry reinforced sonically by the chiming 'i' rhymes. At their most self-enclosed, in short, the composer brings the two characters into tight musical and verbal congruence.

The refrain adds a further comic layer, indeed layers, to the situation being played out in the upper voices. *Hé, resvelle toi Robin! / car on enmaine Marot* is sung in Adam's *Le jeu de Robin et Marion* by Robin's cousin Gautier whose warning that the chevalier has carried Marion off comes somewhat gratuitously since poor Robin has just been thoroughly beaten up in his attempt to stop this from happening. Adam presents Robin throughout as bested not only by the chevalier but also by Marion, who briskly rescues herself straight afterwards. So it is appropriate that the tenor of the motet should keep reiterating that Robin should wake up. But the refrain has a further, darker context in another pastourelle text 'Hier main quant je chevauchoie' ('Yesterday morning when I was riding') (attributed to Huitace de Fontaine).[27] In this song, Marion is alone and in a remote place – 'pres de bois et loing de gent' (near a wood and far from any people; line 4). She anxiously sings 'Dex, trop demeure; quant vendra? / loing est, entroubliee m'a' ('God he is too long; when will he return? He is far away, I am anxious'; lines 9–10). But Robin is asleep, and does not awake even when Marion screams as loudly as she can: *Hé! resveille toi, Robin! / car on en maine Marot.* He only appears in the final strophe after she has been raped by the chevalier. If the composer of *Mo* 269 had this pastourelle in mind then the repetitions of *Hé, resvelle toi Robin!* would have a redoubled intensity, mocking Robin for his somnolent failure to break out of his textual trap. In this artful piece, the composer seems to use the overlapping motet voice structure to draw attention to the verbal miscomprehension it promotes: the characters overhear each other singing within each text, yet caught in simultaneously uttered voice parts they can neither understand what each other is expressing nor communicate with each other. It is in spite of their efforts rather than because of them that the motet ends happily, with a song of triumph ('Robins, conquis avés l'amour de mi' ['Robin, you have conquered my love']) and a silvan frolic ('au bois sont alé pour deporter' ['they went off to the woods to play']).

These contexts for song, motet and narrative were of crucial importance to the fundamental changes that occurred as the thirteenth century moved into the fourteenth. The high point of monophonic song in the art of the troubadours and trouvères passed, and polyphony assumed in vernacular song composition the kind of importance it already had in sacred contexts. At the same time, the relatively lowly genres associated with dance, rondeau, ballade and virelai, by a mysterious alchemy became elite courtly fare. Two factors may be singled out here, both of which are central to modern scholarly questions about these changes: rhythm and textuality. The celebrated *Roman de Fauvel* manuscript, *F-Pn* fonds fr. 146, exemplifies both. It contains a unique 1316–18 revision of this satiric narrative, in which 169 pieces of music were interpolated.[28] No other medieval narrative contains such a remarkable number and range of musical pieces. They are of particular interest to music historians for being a mélange of disparate genres, some newly recorded, others known from older sources and traditions but recorded here with updated notation in the newer style, old genres reworked into unusual forms, old texts given a new language or context. The manuscript provides substantial evidence of change, yet in terms that are hard to understand without a much more detailed context than we possess from other surviving sources. The challenge for current scholars is to bring together detailed work on such evidence that does exist, principally the notated and unnotated motets and other song forms from the Montpellier Codex and the Douce 308 chansonnier, together with the work of such turn-of-the-century authors of song and narrative as Adam de la Halle, Jehan de Lescurel, Nicole de Margival and Watriquet de Couvin.[29]

In all these sources questions of rhythm and textuality are at once intensely problematic and intertwined. It is one thing to recognize that a sea-change occurs in high-style song, from the largely unmeasured notation of a *chanson courtoise* to an intricately measured polyphonic ballade by Guillaume de Machaut, but another to track the practical, creative and cultural reasons for this change. Scholars have drawn attention to several factors: the importance of urbanization, of increasing literacy and awareness of the creative potential of writing for musical transmission and composition, the new first-person love narrative, and the rise of the *puys* or cultural societies in northern French-speaking towns which encouraged competitive song production in a spirit of bourgeois social solidarity. One of the most unexpected symbols, perhaps causes of change in the character of song is the refrain, an example of which would be set as the basis for an annual compositional lyric challenge for members of *puys*. On the edges of strophes, creating changes of rhythmic mode in motets, marking divisions in a narrative, refrains are a connecting thread between genres, styles and registers. They liaise between orality and literacy, and between the languages of music and poetry.

By being so pervasive, refrains are part of the very fabric of thirteenth-century textuality. The key generating elements of works from so many different genres, they are the core materials of courtly discourse. Tracing the course of refrain citation across different generic contexts is like seeing the raw material of courtly speech and song being shaped, divided, combined, amplified and structured before one's eyes. Refrains are the ultimate examples of literate songs: their citation makes a song part of a larger textual whole, just as it also makes a text confront or absorb song.[30]

Poets and composers

Voice and authority

That the new love narratives of the early fourteenth century, such as Nicole de Margival's *Dit de la panthère d'amours* and Jehan Acart de Hesdin's *La Prise amoureuse*, are the first surviving locations for the new *formes fixes* is worth further comment. It alerts us to the importance of narrative as a means of framing song throughout the later Middle Ages. In this final section I want briefly to outline some of the ways in which the relationship between words and music in medieval vernacular song was influenced by narrative practices. One of the earliest trouvères, Chrétien de Troyes, who was a master of Arthurian narrative as well as a composer of chansons, reminds us that the two genres were closely connected and, indeed, that narrative was the earliest source in the early thirteenth century for both secular and sacred vernacular song: in the *Roman de la Rose* by Jean Renart and the *Miracles de Nostre Dame* of Gautier de Coinci. By being set into narrative, song gained a certain visibility and distinctiveness: the practice stimulated and was no doubt itself provoked by a desire to promote authorship. Perhaps the most explicit example of authorial promotion is the *Roman du castelain de Couci* by Jakemès (ca1300) in which the Châtelain de Couci's songs are woven into a biographical romance that tells the story of the love affair allegedly expressed in the songs.

In these decades at the end of the thirteenth century and into the four-teenth, song authorship gradually became once more a matter of self-proclaimed courtly and aesthetic status as it had been for the troubadours. But where trouvère poet-composers tended to look back or sideways for models of vernacular authorship, the early-fourteenth-century love poets put forward their own compositions and their material representation of them in specially produced books as evidence of an authoritative approach to the art of love. To cite a song in a larger narrative frame is to assign it a voice, and many subtleties are available to the composer of a song who wishes to appropriate another's poetic voice in the service of his own authorial identity.

Citation

Citation was a key technique in the development of new approaches to song and authorial power. We can see this in a key transitional composer, Adam de la Halle. Associated primarily with Arras, but also with Paris and Naples, Adam's surviving works exhibit great versatility: he wrote *grands chants*, motets, polyphonic rondeaux, *jeux-partis*, two dramatic *jeux* – *Le Jeu de Robin et Marion* and *Le Jeu de la Feuillée* (a third is attributed to him, *Le Jeu du Pelerin*, that may have been posthumous) – an incomplete *chanson de geste* in *laisses* – *Le Roi du Sicile* – and a strophic *congé*. All of these compositions except the last two survive with music; in the case of the *jeux*, both for the refrains and for the dramatic songs. Adam's work is marked by widespread citation, not only of well-known refrain material but also of his own texts and melodies, including his own reworkings of refrain material. Motet 279 from the Montpellier Codex, for example, contains refrains from his polyphonic rondeaux (*Dieus, coument porroie* ['God, how could I'], vdB, refr.496, and *De ma dame vient* ['From my lady comes'], vdB, refr.477), as well as one that is sung in *Le Jeu de la Feuillée*.[31] This master of citation became noted as a figure of authority: his chansons are cited with respect by the narrator of Nicole de Margival's *Dit de la panthère*. It was a short step from here to the work of Guillaume de Machaut in which the practice of auto-citation received eloquent expression, most notably in his sequence of set-piece songs in the *Remede de Fortune* and in *Le Voir Dit*. Adam is evidence of the public importance attached to citation in the period, and also of the continuities of practice across the border of the centuries. New research into the nature and uses of citation from the thirteenth to the fifteenth centuries is already producing a substantial body of information about the intensive cross-referencing of poetic and melodic phrases among song composers throughout that period.[32]

Music and literature

It is often remarked that the arts of music and poetry start to diverge in the late fourteenth century. It cannot be denied that after Machaut, perhaps the last great trouvère, no single author appears to have a comparable control over music and text together. And even Machaut has a bulkier poetic than musical output. But what continues into the fifteenth century is an increasing interest in the textuality of music as well as the musicality of the text. The production of commentaries and handbooks on the art of song from Eustache Deschamps's *L'Art de Dictier* (1392) to the *Arts de seconde rhétorique* (fifteenth century) testifies to a desire to give song an ever greater specificity of textual control. Books of music paradoxically give music more transmissive freedom than ever: through being written down and in due course printed a song can be known, remembered and reworked across a wider audience rather than being confined to a relatively narrow life as a performance. The transformation of the scribe into the poet, and of poetry into literature, gave music yet more reason to find rhetorical heights in the art of song.

13 Latin poetry and music

LEOFRANC HOLFORD-STREVENS

The Latin poetry set to music during the Middle Ages and discussed in this chapter may be divided into two main types, *metra*, based on syllabic quantity, and *rhythmi* (in the Middle Ages often spelt *rithmi* or the like), based on accent and syllable count, but from the fourteenth century often on the latter alone.[1] Not regarded are psalms and other texts of like form such as the Te Deum, based on paired phrases of parallel or quasi-parallel but unregulated structure.

The term 'verse' will be used throughout as a synonym of 'line', not of 'stanza', though 'verse-form' will be used to accommodate both the measures of single verses and their combinations into stanzas as a single concept. To avoid confusion, only quantitative measures will be called 'metres'.

It is on verse-forms that primary emphasis will be laid, the better to assist study of the relation, or lack of relation, between words and music. Some literary criticism will be offered, principally of motet texts, since these have been neglected by students of literature and only of late considered by musicologists. (This neglect is not only modern: the state of many texts in our manuscripts indicates that music copyists did not always take much interest in them; sometimes it was already a corrupt text that the composer set.)

Ancient and medieval *metra*

Although some surviving classical Latin poetry was written to be sung, notably the *cantica* of early Roman drama and the *Carmen Saeculare* of Horace (performed at a state occasion in 17 BC), and some dramatic passages were apparently delivered in recitative, we have no information about the music beyond for certain Plautine comedies the name of the slave who composed it. We are left to make inferences from metre, which as in Greek was based on syllabic quantity, that is to say the distinction between long and short syllables. The basic rule is that a syllable containing a long vowel or a diphthong is itself long 'by nature'; if the vowel is short, the syllable is nevertheless long 'by position' if the vowel is followed by two or more consonants, otherwise short. For this purpose *x* counts as two consonants ('makes position'), as does Greek *z* within a word (initially it ceased to do so around AD 100) but not *qu*; *tr* and some similar groups do not always make position (hardly ever at the start of a word). Initial *s* + consonant does not make position in the early poets but does in Catullus; the Augustans and their successors, disliking both scansions, avoid placing such groups after a short final vowel, but they return in medieval (and Renaissance) writers, generally not making position. A final vowel, diphthong, or vowel + *m* is elided when it precedes an initial vowel, diphthong, or *h*; this was a feature of the spoken language at all levels, as it still is of Spanish and Italian. (Early medieval writers sometimes treat *h* as a consonant, especially in Germanic names.)

By the end of classical antiquity, vocalic quantity had ceased to be a feature even of educated speech; which vowels were long and which were short had to be learnt. Nevertheless, quantitative verse continued to be written with a greater or lesser degree of correctness. For the Middle Ages the most important metres are the dactylic hexameter, the dactylic pentameter, and the sapphic stanza; these and a few others are explained below. Note that – represents a long syllable, ◡ a short syllable, × an *anceps* position, where either is allowed, ◡◡ two short syllables that may be replaced by a long, ×̆ an *anceps* also admitting two short syllables, and that the final position of any verse, though counted as long, may be occupied by a short syllable.

The structures of the main metres are set out below.

Hexameter

$$- \overline{\smile\smile} - \overline{\smile\smile} - \overline{\smile\smile} - \overline{\smile\smile} - \smile\smile - -$$

In the tenth position ◡◡ is occasionally replaced by –. There must be a word-break (caesura) in at least one of three places: after the fifth position, after the seventh, or between the two short syllables of the sixth position, in this case commonly supported by breaks after the third and seventh. Short syllables ending in a consonant are occasionally admitted instead of long, mostly at the caesura; this licence is abused in the Middle Ages, and even extended to short vowels ending the word. There is a preference, which by Augustan times is a rule, that save in satire, or for special effects, the last two feet of a verse should have a word-break either between or after the short syllables of the tenth position, or two word-breaks if a monosyllable in ninth position is followed by two disyllables; monosyllabic prepositions and conjunctions count as one with the following word. Not all medieval writers respect this rule, though it was known.

Pentameter

$$- \overline{\smile\smile} - \overline{\smile\smile} - \mid - \smile\smile - \smile\smile -$$

The pentameter regularly follows a hexameter to form an 'elegiac couplet'. In classical poets the syllable before the caesura tends to be long by nature, though this is far from a rule; by contrast, medieval writers admit short syllables – even those ending in a vowel. In Augustan poets the last word of the verse is usually a disyllable, or failing that, almost always comprises four or more syllables. Ovid rarely allows the verse to end in short *a* not followed by a consonant.

Sapphic stanza
This comprises three sapphic hendecasyllables (eleven-syllable lines of the form – ᴗ – – – ᴗ ᴗ – ᴗ – –) and an adonic (– ᴗ ᴗ – –). After Horace, the stanza is self-contained, and the hendecasyllable regularly has word-breaks after the third and fifth syllables. This is the metre, for example, of Paul the Deacon's *Ut queant laxis*; occasionally, as in verse 49 of that poem, 'Gloria Patri genitaeque proli' ('Glory be to the Father and the begotten offspring'), medieval poets adopt the licence of short syllable for long.

Iambic dimeter
(This is the metre of Saint Ambrose's hymns and of Venantius Fortunatus's *Vexilla regis prodeunt*.)

$$\overset{\smile\smile}{\times} - \cup - \overset{\smile\smile}{\times} - \cup -$$

Iambic trimeter

$$\overset{\smile\smile}{\times} - \cup - \overset{\smile\smile}{\times} - \cup - \overset{\smile\smile}{\times} - \cup -$$

There is a caesura after the fifth or seventh positions; when the ninth position is the last syllable of a word, it is usually long (in contrast to Greek practice).

Trochaic tetrameter catalectic
(This is used as such in Venantius Fortunatus's *Pange lingua*):

$$- \cup - \times - \cup - \times \mid - \cup - \times - \cup -$$

In classical poetry, –, except in the last position, may be replaced by ᴗᴗ; in Venantius's hymn, the only possible instance, *pretium*, which would also be the only instance of initial ᴗᴗ in *Vexilla regis prodeunt*, is probably to be pronounced *pretsjum*.[2]

In addition there is a metre known to ancient metrists but not attested in Latin poetry before the fifth century:

$$- - - \cup \cup - \mid - \cup \cup - -$$

Since this metre was used in several hymns ascribed or attributed to Hucbald of St-Amand,[3] it may be called the hucbaldian in preference to its technical description of minor asclepiad catalectic. It regularly appears in four-line stanzas on the analogy of Horace's lyric metres (some of which are also used in chant). In the fifth century too we find 'stichic' pentameters (that is, pentameters used by themselves without hexameters), and likewise stichic adonics.

Although rhyme between neighbouring verses occasionally happens in classical poetry by accident or for special effect, it is not a structural principle; despite a few appearances in Christian poetry of earlier date it does not become a frequent feature until the sixth century, and is extremely rare in *metra* till the ninth. It then becomes frequent both between and within hexameters, or within both lines of the elegiac couplet; these internal rhymes are called 'leonine'. A precedent was found in Ovid's famous line 'Quot caelum stellas, tot habet tua Roma puellas' (*Ars amatoria* 1. 59: 'As many stars as the heaven, so many girls has your Rome'), which when originally written was less blatant because the *e* of *stellas* was long and closed (phonetically [e:]), that of *puellas* short and open (phonetically [ɛ]). Rhymed hexameters and pentameters are particularly frequent during the eleventh century, but continued in use throughout the Middle Ages. Rhyme may be monosyllabic (of final syllables only), disyllabic (of the last two syllables), or even trisyllabic (of the last three). Since Latin is not a difficult language to rhyme in (especially since distinctions of quantity are ignored), the requirement is rarely onerous.

Certain passages of classical and late antique poetry (for example, from Vergil, Horace, Martianus Capella, and Boethius) are notated for music in medieval manuscripts; the choice of texts often suggests educational purposes, as does the musical setting of a prose calendrical table that Bede, *De temporum ratione*, chapter 22 proposed for memorizing and reciting, but there is no overlap between the Horatian odes selected for setting and those included in anthologies.[4] However, whereas in antiquity the quantitative distinctions of *metra* were carried over into musical rhythm, and attempts were made to do so in the Renaissance, in the Middle Ages no such effort was made either in plainchant or in polyphony; at most, strong positions may be represented by higher pitches, but there is no uniform practice, either in this or in the treatment of elision, which (as later in vernacular texts) is sometimes respected by the setting and sometimes undone.[5]

In Vergil and his classical followers, the individual hexameter need not be the self-contained expression of a single idea; rather verses are combined as it were into paragraphs, with frequent enjambment from line to line and constant variation in the placing of sense pauses; this feature is not always replicated by medieval poets, but when it is it may induce medieval composers to override their normal practice of respecting verse-structure in preference to sense. The most striking example is afforded by the six hexameters of *Alma redemptoris mater*, broken in the chant into four main parts (divided by vertical lines below) of which the first two end in mid-verse:

> Alma redemptoris mater, quae pervia caeli
> porta manes,| et stella maris, succurre cadenti,
> surgere qui curat, populo.| Tu quae peperisti,
> Natura mirante, tuum sanctum genitorem,|
> virgo prius ac posterius, Gabrielis ab ore
> sumens illud Ave, peccatorum miserere.[6]

> Hail, mother of the Redeemer, who remainest the open gate of heaven, and star of the sea, aid the falling people that wishes to rise. Thou that, as Nature gazed in wonderment, borest thy holy begetter, a virgin before and afterwards, taking that famous 'Hail' from Gabriel's mouth, have mercy on sinners.

Medieval and even Renaissance polyphonic settings regularly follow the chant rather than the verse-structure; a striking exception is that for four voices by the apparently Coimbra-based composer Aires Fernandez (fl. ca1550), in which the top voice or *tipre* clearly marks the verse ends even where the chant does not.[7]

Syllabo-clausular *rhythmi*

In Latin, unlike Greek, verbal accent is regulated by syllabic quantity: if the penultimate syllable is long it is stressed, otherwise the stress falls on the antepenultimate; in consequence, according as words end at one place or another in the verse the accent will either coincide or conflict with strong positions in the metre. Accent, which inscriptions show to have been far more perceptible to uneducated ears than quantity, displaced it in poems written by (or for) persons without a literary schooling; such verses were known as *rhythmi*, first distinguished from *metra* by grammarians who assigned 'rhythm without metre' to the 'songs of low-class poets' (*cantica vulgarium poetarum*).[8]

Saint Ambrose's hymns soon inspired imitation by writers who no longer knew their quantities; after some irregularities, a standard accentual adaptation of the iambic dimeter was developed comprising eight syllables of which the sixth is stressed; such lines are notated 8pp, where 'pp' stands for *proparoxytone*, 'accented on the antepenultimate'. Compared with their metrical antecedents, these verses admit long syllables in place of short and vice versa, but exclude the resolution of one long into two short syllables that Ambrose still freely used. A hymn in praise of Saint Patrick (*Audite omnes amantes Deum*) attributed to the Irish saint Sechnall (d. 447), but at any rate no later than the early seventh century, transforms the trochaic tetrameter into a fifteen-syllable verse divided by caesura into eight syllables with an accent on the seventh and seven syllables with an accent on the fifth (the thirteenth of the line); this is notated 8p + 7pp, where 'p' stands for *paroxytone*, 'accented on the penultimate'.[9] These four lines are grouped into quatrains beginning with all 23 letters of the alphabet in turn, affording an early Latin example of the 'alphabetic hymn' ultimately derived from Hebrew.

Although grammarians continued to parrot the reference to low-class poets, the *rhythmus* was not confined to them; moreover, even before the Carolingian reforms established a sharp distinction between the popular *lingua Romana* and the educated *lingua Latina*, the emergence of a reading pronunciation in which every word formed a unit by itself – and final *m*, now silent in the living language, was artificially rendered as a full consonant – is demonstrated by the rarity in *rhythmi* of elision, which remained the norm in *metra*, even though it undoubtedly continued to be a feature of everyday speech. (The exception that proves the rule is an 8p + 8p *rhythmus* in semi-popular language and pronunciation by Saint Augustine, the *Psalmus contra partem Donati*, in which elision is as freely and regularly used as in any classical poet.) When elision is found, it is almost always with identical vowels (*monstra te esse matrem* as 6p in the hymn *Ave maris stella*);[10] usually either the two syllables are left to stand in hiatus, or the collocation is avoided altogether.

Accentual *rhythmi* should be distinguished from quantitative *metra* with the occasional false quantity (e.g. *patībulo* in *Vexilla regis prodeunt*, verse 4); in the better-educated writers false quantities are mostly found in Greek words (*cātholicus, ecclĕsia*), though they are not unknown in Latin words, especially those not familiar from Vergil and Ovid. Errors in accentuation, though not unknown, are rare, since whereas quantity had by the end of antiquity to be learnt from books, the position of the stress was apprehended orally (even in France, an attempt was made to realize it by pitch);[11] nevertheless, some words acquired new stresses (*muliéres, erádicans*), and Greek words sometimes retained the Greek accent in defiance of Latin rules (*paráclitus, Iácobus*) but sometimes took a stress justifiable by neither criterion (*charáctere, epitríta*).

The earliest *rhythmi* showed no regularity of accent until the cadence; this freedom remains characteristic of the 8pp line, despite a tendency towards iambic rhythm with stress on the fourth and often the second syllable, but 8p from the seventh century onwards shows a strong tendency towards trochaic rhythm, being divided by internal caesura into 4p + 4p or occasionally 5pp + 3p, relieved only by 3p + 5p; likewise 7pp, though freely admitting 3p + 4pp besides 4p + 3pp and 3pp + 4pp, generally eschews 4pp + 3pp, and 6p admits 3p + 3p but not 4pp + 2p. This is not to deny occasional exceptions, such as in the conductus *Mundus vergens* the 7pp line *quod explicit explicat*, admitted for wordplay's sake, or in *Gedeonis area* the 8p lines *radiat absque calore* and *liquitur petra liquore*, both 3pp 2p 3p.[12]

Other *rhythmi* include 12pp, divided either 5p + 7pp in imitation of the iambic trimeter or 6pp + 6pp, and accentual sapphics; these do not mimic the quantitative structure of the *metrum* but preserve the normal distribution of the stresses. The hendecasyllables thus become 5p + 6p, with an iambic pulse varied only by the possibility of stressing the first syllable of the line instead of the second; the adonic becomes 5p, with the same initial option:

> Aures ad nostras deitatis preces,
> Deus, inclina pietate sola;
> supplicum vota suscipe, precamur
>   famuli tui.[13]

God, bend thy divine ears to our prayers in pure pity; receive the vows of suppliants, we thy servants beg thee.

This last verse-form apart, rhyme steadily becomes the norm in *rhythmi* during the early Middle Ages; in paroxytone lines it is regularly disyllabic, and from the twelfth century in proparoxytone lines too, though trisyllabic rhyme is sometimes achieved.

Far from suppressing *rhythmi* as the Renaissance would do, the classicizing movement of the twelfth century raised them to the same literary level as classicizing *metra* (Hildebert of Lavardin is a master of both) and a comparably disciplined technique; instructions are given in manuals either of poetics or of *dictamen*, which emphasize that – as hymns, sequences, and conductus bear out – *rhythmi* are especially suitable for setting to music. Many are written in regular six-, eight- or ten-line double stanzas comprising two lengths of line (in particular 8p and 7pp, or 7pp and 6p) and three rhymes distributed *aabccb*, *aaabcccb* or *aaaabccccb*, the *b* rhymes being the shorter lines. We also find monorhymed tercets and quatrains, characteristically 8pp or 8p + 7pp; but the most important monorhymed quatrain is the 'goliardic stanza' (*Vagantenstrophe*) comprising four 'goliardics' (*Vagantenzeilen*) of 7pp + 6p.[14] Despite the names, suggestive of wandering scholars and disreputable foolery, many writers in this verse-form were settled and respectable, including such eminent men as Walter of Châtillon and Philip the Chancellor; but they were scholars, who even when writing in satirical vein or with less than total seriousness display their learning: a variant form of the goliardic stanza consists of *versus cum auctoritate* ('verses with an authoritative statement'), three goliardic lines preceded or followed by a hexameter (often from a classical or other prior poet) rhyming with them.[15] This principle was later extended to other verse-forms.

The goliardic, in which the 7pp elements do not rhyme, should be distingished from combinations of independent 7pp and 6p lines, for example in the conductus *Novus miles sequitur*, which is a ten-line stanza 7pp 6p 7pp 6p 7pp 7pp 6p 7pp 7pp 6p rhyming *ababccdeed*.[16] There also appear a 10pp line with caesura at the fourth syllable (usually 4p, but 4pp is not excluded), which is a Latinization of the French *décasyllabe* (and therefore not to be read with the iambic rhythm natural to English or German), and an 11pp line divided 4p + 7pp. This does not exhaust the verse-forms attested, and more irregular stanzas are found, for instance in the *Carmina Burana*. Likewise, there is a wide variety of rhyme patterns, often demonstrating the poet's ingenuity, for example in constructing long runs of lines on a single rhyme, or in the use of internal rhymes; short rhymed lines seem especially prominent in verses meant for singing.

Two points should be noted here. First, this versification, whatever the origin of individual verse-forms, is international; English-speakers accept the initial 3p inversions of stress that disrupt the trochaic flow, and good French authors respect the Latin accent. Second, musical setting takes no account of verbal accent either melodically or rhythmically.

It is difficult to correlate verse-form with poetic level: although goliardics are often used for light or satirical verse, John Pecham could employ them for his Passion meditation *Philomena praevia temporis amoeni*,[17] frequently ascribed to Saint Bonaventure; conversely the grandest of classical *metra*, the hexameter, could as in Roman times be used for poems less than serious. Many conductus (whose authors overlap with those responsible for goliardic poems) are preserved for their literary quality in poetical as well as musical manuscripts; most such texts concern religious or other serious themes, but there are exceptions such as *Consequens antecedente*,[18] a satire on venality that purports to be a lesson in logic:

Consequens antecedente	8p	*a*
destructo destruitur,	7pp	*b*
bene namque sequitur	7pp	*b*
nemine contradicente	8p	*a*
quod si dabis dabitur;	7pp	*b*
sed si primum tollitur	7pp	*b*
non cures de consequente,	8p	*a*
quoniam negabitur	7pp	*b*
si non approbabitur	7pp	*b*
auro viam faciente.	8p	*a*

> Once the antecedent has been refuted, the consequent is refuted; for it
> properly follows, with no one gainsaying, that if you give, it shall be given;
> but if the first is taken away, do not worry about the consequent, since it will
> be denied [*or* your request will be refused], if it is not supported with gold
> making the way.

In the conditional proposition 'if the first then the second' or 'if *p* then *q*',
p is called the antecedent, *q* the consequent; from it one may validly infer
'but *p*, therefore *q*' (the *modus ponens*, 'putting-there mode') or 'but not
q, therefore not *p*' (the *modus tollens*, 'taking-away mode'). However, the
text offers the inference 'but not *p*, therefore not *q*', which is invalid, since
q may still be true: if Socrates is walking, he is awake; but even if he is not
walking, that does not mean he is not awake. Written by the educated for the
educated, *Consequens antecedente* wittily contrasts the manifest fallacy of
the logical contention with the undeniable truth of its practical application:
if you do not pay bribes you will get nothing. The same lightness of touch
may explain the loose rhythm of the first two 8p lines, which do not conform
to the regular patterns noted above.

In the *Carmina Burana*, we find a wide range of stylistic levels even in
erotic poetry, from macaronic texts and such Latinized vernacular as *domi-
cella* (meaning 'damsel', not 'little house')[19] to goliardic parody of Scripture, liturgy, scholastic philosophy, and devotional address to the Mother
of God:[20]

> Si linguis angelicis loquar et humanis . . .
>
> Pange lingua igitur causas et causatum . . .
>
> Ave formosissima, gemma pretiosa.
> ave decus virginum, virgo gloriosa,
> ave lumen luminum, ave mundi rosa,
> Blanziflôr et Helena, Venus generosa.
>
> Though I should speak with angelic and human tongues [cf. 1 Cor. 13:
> 1] . . . Therefore recount, my tongue, the causes and the effect . . . Hail most
> beauteous one, precious jewel, hail ornament of virgins, virgin glorious, hail
> light of lights, hail rose of the world, Blanchefleur [heroine of romance] and
> Helen, noble Venus.

Syllabic verse

Besides quantitative and accentual verse, there is a third type governed
purely by syllable count. This is found, with rhyming final syllables, in
sixth- and seventh-century Irish Latin; but modern writers also reckon
under this heading the texts composed from the ninth century onwards

for sequences, known as *prosae* because they originated as art prose. The main body of a *prosa* consisted of successive couplets comprising two lines with the same number of syllables and set to the same melody. Accent and quantity played no part, nor in principle did rhyme, though many West Frankish *prosae* affected a final *-a* or *-ia* (as in *alleluia*) at the end of every couplet, all too often at the expense of syntax and sense. Such texts, more grandiloquent than coherent, contrast sharply with the elegant, complex and rational unrhymed diction of Notker Balbulus at St Gall. (Since prosae were sometimes sung as melismas, the term *prosa* was loosely extended to the *prosula*, a text composed to match a chant melisma syllable for note.) From ca1000 onwards, however, sequence texts moved in the direction of verse, becoming more regular in scansion and/or adopting rhyme; by the twelfth century most sequences are stanzaic *rhythmi*, though the form of the stanza may change in the course of the poem.

In the thirteenth century, the practice of adding texts to melismas in subordination to their phrase structure gave way to the addition of one, two, or even three texts over a tenor; the resulting composition is known as a motet ('little word').[21] At first these texts, mostly in the vernacular (outside England) but sometimes in Latin, were no more regular in their syllabic count than *prosulae*; an example is the following motet – a tour de force of rhyming – on the tenor 'et gaudebit', from the alleluia for the Sunday after Ascension:[22]

Non orphanum	4pp	*a*
te deseram,	4pp	*b*
sed efferam	4pp	*b*
sicut libanum,	5pp	*a*
sicut clibanum,	5pp	*a*
ponam te virtutis,	6p	*c*
sicut tympanum	5pp	*a*
et organum	4pp	*a*
leticie	4pp	*d*
et salutis;	4p	*c*
auferam	3pp	*b*
Egyptie	4pp	*d*
iugum servitutis,	6p	*c*
conferam	3pp	*b*
me secutis	4p	*c*
post lacrimas gaudium,	7pp	*e*
premium	3pp	*e*
post laboris tedium;	7pp	*e*
cum iero veniam,	7pp	*f*
subveniam,	4pp	*f*
per graciam	4pp	*f*

tribuam veniam,	6pp	*f*
celestium	4pp	*e*
civium	3pp	*e*
gloriam,	3pp	*f*
mentem puram	4p	*g*
et securam	4p	*g*
efficiam,	4pp	*f*
carnis curam	4p	*g*
et pressuram	4p	*g*
seculi reiciam.	7pp	*f*
Inclitus	3pp	*h*
Paraclitus	4pp	*h*
divinitus	4pp	*h*
tuum cor docebit,	6p	*i*
et radicitus	5pp	*h*
tuus spiritus	5pp	*h*
Domino sic herebit	7p	*i*
tuus ut introitus	7pp	*h*
tutus sit et exitus;	7pp	*h*
cor penitus	4pp	*h*
gaudebit.	3p	*i*

I shall not abandon you to be an orphan, but exalt you like incense-smoke (?); like an oven of virtue shall I make you [cf. Psalms 20:10 Vulgate], like a drum and *organum* [in medieval Latin this may be a stringed or a wind instrument] of happiness and salvation; I shall take away the yoke of Egyptian bondage, I shall bestow on those who have followed me joy after tears, the reward after the weariness of toil; when I have gone I shall come, I shall assist, by my grace I shall grant mercy, the glory of heaven's citizens, I shall make your mind pure and free from worry, I shall throw back the care of the flesh and the oppression of the world. The renowned Paraclete in his divine wisdom will instruct your heart [= mind], and your spirit will be so rooted in the Lord that your going in and going out shall be safe; your heart will rejoice through and through.

This motet already has a degree of independence from the clausula – found also by itself – that serves as its tenor, since the setting is not entirely syllabic; in the Las Huelgas manuscript the music is so heavily reworked as no longer to fit the tenor, which is omitted. The same clausula is also used for a vernacular pastourelle, *El mois de mai*, which again does not match it syllabically but is also written in lines of varying length with insistent rhymes; a triplum, *Quant florist la violete*, of similar type is found with both the Latin and the French motetus.[23]

By the end of the thirteenth century, irregular versification had lost its charms and motet texts were subjected to the laws of measured verse just like other forms of poetry. When written in Latin, they are generally written in *rhythmi*, in particular the decasyllable and the octosyllable, though in Italy we also find the native *endecasillabo*, an 11p verse with stress on the fourth and/or sixth syllable.

In both the irregular and the regular manners, French poets pay less heed to the distinction between p and pp than in the conductus; from successive centuries we find such rhymes as *trína* with *máchina* in the irregular motet *Benigna celi regina / Beata es, Maria / In veritate*,[24] *nóbilis* with *puerílis* in the decasyllables of *Servant regem / O Philippe / Rex regum*,[25] and *probarétur* with *pátitur* in the octosyllabic portion of Du Fay's *Iuvenis qui puellam*.[26] This is but one sign that French-speakers were finding the effort of reproducing Latin stress too great, along with monosyllabic rhymes such as *dixistis* ~ *honestatis, arguo* ~ *eo* ~ *unico* ~ *titulo* in the last text,[27] and irregular rhythms within the line such as *dum ángelo credidísti* and *inimicísque destrúctis* in the triplum of Machaut's motet *Felix virgo / Inviolata genitrix / Ad te suspiramus gementes et flentes*.[28] This is the versification not of Philip the Chancellor but of Baudelaire.[29]

Although some motets use pre-existing texts, the majority of texts appear to be newly written for the occasion, either by the composer or by someone else, who may be named at the end of the motetus as in *Argi vices Poliphemus / Cum Pilemon rebus paucis* (written in or after 1410 for the conciliar Pope John XXIII):[30] 'William wrote these words as a favour to Nicholas, who sang them, in order for the work to be complete.' Since composers are not necessarily any better as poets than poets as composers, the quality of the texts they write varies widely: some simply cannot be construed as rational human discourse, such as *Apta caro* (the triplum to a straightforward motetus, *Flos virginum*),[31] whose first five lines,

> Apta caro plumis ingenii
> desidie barrum et studii,
> laborisque foco mollicies
> et coniuga centro segnicies
> que pigrescit, plumbum consumito,

typical of the entire text, would have to be translated something like 'Let flesh fit for feathers consume the elephant of idleness of intellect and fervour, and let softness at the hearth of labour, and laziness conjugate with the centre, which grows sluggish, consume lead.' On the other hand Machaut, poet and musician, writes as fluently in Latin as in French; and texts of Philippe de Vitry's motets are found in literary manuscripts, one in a sermon collection from Avignon in the late 1340s, others in fifteenth-century humanistic anthologies compiled by German scholars who had been in Italy.[32] This is a testimony to his relationship with Petrarch, who called him 'now the only poet of the Gauls'; his poetry certainly cannot be described as humanistic (though a few specimens are in metre), but they are ambitious, abound in classical and biblical allusions, and show considerable power of rhetoric. Some of Vitry's verse, as well as his music, may reside in the expanded recension of the *Roman de Fauvel*, some texts in which adopt the initial or closing *auctoritas*, and exploit classical quotations in a way that suggests knowledge of their context, rather than reliance on a florilegium.

Some motet texts praise music, or the musicians of the day, listed at length, a genre still practised by Compère in the fifteenth century and Moulu in the sixteenth. A widely disseminated example is Bernard de Cluny's motet *Apollinis eclipsatur / Zodiacum signis lustrantibus / In omnem terram*. The duplum is written in octosyllables forming five enjambed sestets with the rhyme scheme *aabccb ddeffe gghiih jjkllj mmnoon*:[33]

Apollinis eclipsatur	
nunquam lux, cum peragatur	
signorum ministerio	
bis sex, quibus armonica	
fulget arte basilica	5
musicorum collegio	
multiformibus figuris:	
e quo nitet I. de Muris	
modo colorum vario;	
Philippus de Vitriaco,	10
acta plura vernant a quo	
ordine multiphario;	
noscit Henricus Helene	
tonorum tenorem bene;	
Magni cum Dionisio	15
Regnaudus de Tiramonte	
Orpheyco potus fonte;	
Robertus de Palatio	
actubus petulancia;	
fungens gaudet poetria	20
Guilhermus de Mascaudio;	
Egidius de Morino	
baritonans cum Garino,	
quem cognoscat Suessio;	
Arnaldus Martini, iugis	25
philomena, P. de Brugis,	
Gaufridus de Barilio;	
vox quorum mundi climata	
penetrat ad algamata,	
doxe fruantur bravio!	30

(In verse 11 *a quo* in French pronunciation = *aco*, and hence makes the requisite double rhyme with *Vitriaco.*) The sense is not always clear, but a tentative translation might be:

> Apollo's light is never eclipsed, since it is achieved by the service of twice six signs, whereby the church gleams with the harmonic art through the company of musicians in note-shapes of many forms, from which [company] shines Jean des Murs, with his varied manner of colours; Philippe de Vitry, several deeds by whom flourish in many kinds of order; Henri d'Hélène, who well knows the course of notes; with Denys le Grant, Regnaud de Tirlemont, who has drunk of Orpheus' fount; Robert of Aix, with actions and forwardness; Guillaume de Machaut rejoices when exercising poetry; Gilles de la Thérouanne, singing low with Guarin, whom may Soissons know; Arnaud de St-Martin-du-Ré, a perpetual nightingale, Pierre de Bruges, Godefroy de Baralle; may they whose voice pierces the zones of the worlds to the high places enjoy the reward of glory!

The contratenor (which describes the above text as the triplum), in decasyllables rhyming *aab aab bba bba*, also refers to music, and to these musicians;

> Zodiacum signis lustrantibus
> armonia Phebi fulgentibus
> musicali palam sinergia,
> Pictagore numerus ter quibus
> adequatur preradiantibus   5
> Boetii basis solercia,
> B. de Cluni nitens energia
> artis pratice cum theoria
> recommendans se subdit omnibus
> presentia per salutaria;   10
> musicorum tripli materia
> noticiam dat de nominibus.

Again, translation is at times uncertain:

> While the signs light up the zodiac and gleam with Phoebus's harmony, openly through musical cooperation – to which most radiant signs Pythagoras's number, taken thrice, is made equal by the ingenuity of Boethius's basis – Bernard de Cluny, illustrious as a practical musician who also understands the theory, humbly recommends himself to all by these present wholesome words; the subject matter of the triplum gives information on the musicians' names.

Much recent scholarship has sought to make all it can of thematic, verbal and numerical relations between the texts of a motet, and to relate the tenor phrase with its textual and liturgical context to them. Such an analysis would find, in the case of Bernard's motet, that the first word of the duplum text, *Apollinis*, begins with *A*, that of the contratenor, *Zodiacum*, with *Z*; but each text alludes to the other, for the duplum speaks of 'twice six signs' in the zodiac (cf. *Zodiacum*), and the contratenor of 'Pythagoras's number, taken thrice', which matches the signs that light up the zodiac and shine with Phoebus's harmony (cf. *Apollinis*). Pythagoras's number was 10, but called the *tetractys* as being the fourth triangular number; hence we have both 3 × 4, the number of musicians mentioned in the triplum, and 3 × 10, the number of verses. The duplum, in 30 octosyllables, contains twice as many syllables as the contratenor, in 12 decasyllables; together they comprise 360 syllables, which corresponds to the number of days in twelve 30-day months (as in the Egyptian calendar); the full year requires another five days, supplied by the five syllables of the tenor incipit, *In omnem terram*. This comes from Psalms 18:5 Vulgate. 'In omnem terram exivit sonus eorum, et in fines terrae verba eorum', 'Their sound hath gone forth into all the earth, and their words unto the ends of the earth' (Reims–Douay–Challoner version), which is obviously appropriate for renowned musicians, some of whom were also theorists or poets; since this text furnishes the first antiphon at matins for the common of apostles, it might be thought to pick up on the number twelve as being that of the first apostles, and suggest that as all apostles, not merely the original twelve, ought to be venerated, so ought all musicians, not merely those mentioned in the triplum.

Such subtleties are, alas, compatible with ungrammatical or hypercontorted diction. They are also imperceptible to the listeners, though the singers may appreciate them if they pay attention to the sense of the words that not only they but also their fellows are singing; how far the fact should inhibit the analysis of the written texts is a matter of dispute, since poets and composers were and are capable of building in features that only they, and God, would notice. Moreover, echoes from one motet to another (such as the phrase *musicorum collegio*, which begins the triplum of another musician motet)[34] suggest that (as in the case of the Fauvel manuscript) we are dealing not so much with an elite (a term that darkens counsel) as with an in-group of persons who knew each other's work and competed to better it.

By contrast, it is evident that composers sometimes took care to match sound or indeed sense at certain places (particularly the beginning and the end) in simultaneous voice-parts, with an effect that even the untrained modern ear can recognize; thus in one anonymous motet of the thirteeth century not only do quadruplum, triplum and motetus all begin *Mors* ('Death'), but the word forms the tenor incipit (if indeed that was sung); every line but one ends in the vowel *o*, sung simultaneously in three voices on eleven occasions and in two on thirteen, five of them against a mid-word *o* in the third voice – including the close, where the triplum ends with the words 'O Mors'.[35] In Vitry's *Vos quid admiramini / Gratissima / Gaude gloriosa*, the words *hec regina* ('this is my queen') in the triplum dovetail with *O regina* ('O queen', meaning the Virgin) in the motetus, set to the same music a fourth below.[36] Such effects, however, pertain to poetical technique only if planned before the texts were written, since they could be achieved by the judicious selection of existing poems.

On the road to the Renaissance

Vitry's motet *O canenda / Rex quem / Contratenor / Rex regum*[37] has a triplum in decasyllables but a motetus in hexameters; the setting respects the verse-ends even at the one place where the sense continues. In the mid-fourteenth-century motet *Degentis vita / Cum vix artidici / Vera pudicitia*[38] both triplum and motetus are written in what the poet fondly imagined to be hexameters with the occasional pentameter; the setting largely ignores line ends, but pays some heed to rhymes; hexameters of no better quality form the motetus of *Inter densas deserti meditans / Imbribus irriguis / Admirabile est nomen Domini*,[39] in which the composer respects the line ends both of the hexameters and of the decasyllables in the triplum.

 Metra become commoner in the fifteenth century, not least in Italian ceremonial motets, though even there they do not oust the *rhythmi* with which the northern composers were familiar; Ciconia, despite the classical pretensions of his theoretical writings, sets only one metrical text, and that not faultless: *Ut te per omnes celitus / Ingens alumnus Padue* in Ambrosian iambic dimeters marred by false quantities.[40] For composers, and those who wrote their texts, *metra* were no more than another resource; thus Du Fay's Latin motets exhibit hexameters varying from the frankly medieval to the would-be classical, elegiac couplets, stichic leonine pentameters, and quatrains of stichic sapphic hendecasyllables, but also *rhythmi* of greater or less regularity, syllabic verses of various measures (including *endecasillabi*), irregular rhymed verse, and prose.[41] None of the classicizing texts approaches the correctness and elegance of the elegiacs set by Ockeghem, *Intemerata Dei mater*;[42] however, Du Fay's settings show respect for line endings even when the text is enjambed ('quamque | egregios', 'and how | excellent').[43] Towards the end of the fifteenth century we begin to find settings of classical poetry, which may be regarded as pertaining to the Renaissance.[44]

14 Compositional trajectories

PETER M. LEFFERTS

This chapter is intended to operate as a complement to the survey of musical theory presented in Chapter 16. Here, to illuminate a small set of issues in respect to style and compositional practice, we will approach the medieval composer via specific repertory, namely, some sacred chants and some two-voice polyphony.

A persistent conviction of many relative newcomers to medieval music is that all chant sounds the same – melodically vague, undifferentiable, hypnotic and slightly 'New Age' – and that it is governed by a universal, monolithic, standard medieval 'theory of the modes'. Neither of these points is true, but one needs to gain a broad familiarity with some very large bodies of melodies, and the histories of their genres, to be able to come to grips with chant's diversity in all its dimensions, and it is equally important to learn some individual melodies very well.

The plainchant of the medieval Western church was, in fact, highly varied in musical language. There were different dialects, including Roman, Gallican, Mozarabic, Beneventan and Ambrosian, before and after the hegemonic rise of Gregorian chant circa 800. There are strong generic or functional fault lines within the Gregorian core itself (distinguishing prayer and reading tones, antiphonal psalmody, responsorial psalmody), and variant idioms emerged within the later Gregorian universe (e.g. the German chant tradition). On top of that, many different stylistic strands developed in all the newly composed, later medieval plainsong from the ninth century forward – melodies which over time far outdistanced the Gregorian core in sheer numbers.

And as to mode, both in theory and in practice in respect to medieval melody, the term has a rich and varied multi-dimensional history of meaning and influence. The earliest trace of modal thinking in the West dates to the very late eighth and early ninth centuries. In this era Carolingian musicians were struggling to stabilize, learn and teach the vast body of melodies in the hybrid Roman-Gallican chant dialect that became known as 'Gregorian chant'. Influenced by a recent eightfold system of classification developed by contemporary Byzantine Greeks, the Franks worked out a similar system to sort and classify liturgical melodies by two significant markers: the very last note (the final) and the range (distinguishing those melodies lying above the final and those lying around the final as authentic and plagal, respectively). In their early tonaries, which were books listing chants by musical characteristics, the Franks then went another step, further subdividing chant groups by a third powerful marker, the initial melodic gesture.

This process of classification worked well because Western chant was fundamentally diatonic. Indeed, a diatonic backbone is an underlying feature of most sacred and secular bodies of melody from northern Europe, the Mediterranean basin, and East Asia going back thousands of years. For medieval church musicians, the recognition that the myriad melodies of Gregorian chant each ended on just one or another of four different finals and could be conceptualized in notation along a single scale was a hard-won discovery. It was, in fact, one of the signal triumphs of Frankish music theorists in the late 700s and early 800s. The frequent addition of B flat into the white-note scale was one small concession to problems in the process of conceptualization and classification, and some early notations may be attempting to convey microtonal nuances of performance practice as well.[1]

Tonaries allowed Frankish musicians (and us) to look at Gregorian melodies of this or that mode and derive from them further observations about the character of Gregorian melodies generally, the characteristics specific to a given mode, or features specific to distinctive subcategories of chants in that mode. In a small number of cases the three markers – final, range and initial gesture – could be ambiguous or in open conflict, because of a chant's lack of consistent diatonicism or the conflict of assignment between a chant's beginning and end. Furthermore, some chants assigned to different modes share a common vocabulary of interior gestures and phrases. The discrepancies between real melodies and the Frankish *a posteriori* method of classification shows us that mode did not originally govern the composition of these melodies, and, moreover, that some chants were – how shall we say it? – not well-behaved.

The discussions by theorists of chants whose modal assignment was problematic offer us additional insights into the character of Gregorian chant and the earliest conception of modality. Their proposals for resolving difficulties in classification included transposition to unusual finals, using accidentals beyond B flat, and, of course, outright amendment of the shape of the non-conforming melody.

In later developments of the theory of the melodic modes that were pursued from the ninth century down to the end of the Middle Ages, theorists turned their attention from simple classification towards an effort to account more abstractly and methodically for the characteristics of the repertoire. They derived their concepts from two principal sources: much earlier Hellenistic Greek theory as found in authors of late classical antiquity and the Early Christian era, especially Boethius, and additional empirical features of the Gregorian corpus and later medieval chants. Hellenistic notions of scales generated by adjacent and overlapping tetrachords, of mode as scale, and especially of mode as octave species comprised of species of fourths and fifths – a body of concepts that the Franks did not fully understand – eventually dominated the standard explanation of mode in the later Middle Ages. The pseudo-Greek modal descriptions also absorbed empirical features such as reciting tones, and theorists attempted to make accommodation for problem children such as melodies of extremely wide range and those that cadenced to a non-standard final. However, later medieval theories of mode, whether derived empirically from melodies of the Western church or prescriptively from Hellenistic models, still do not account for all tonal features of Gregorian chant melodies.

In composing post-Gregorian chants, some composers looked back to Gregorian idioms and turns of phrase. In other cases, composers struck out in a direction reflecting local or regional melodic languages of their own day, whether within the ecclesiastical realm or drawing on secular or personal idioms. Some chant was directly affected by theory, including both new melodies whose composers were constrained from the outset by schoolroom doctrines, and older melodies that were re-edited to fit the mould of theory, such as took place in the twelfth-century reform of Cistercian chant. Pseudo-Greek modal constraints on melody also began to influence secular melodies, but not until a relatively late date; the central role of the fourth below the final and of the fifth and octave above are an especially distinctive feature, for example, in the French chansons of Du Fay written in the 1400s.

Medieval musicians were virtuosos of the diatonic, sensitized to the subtle differences of weight and role of the various scale degrees and the intervals between them, especially the semitones. They were accustomed to locating themselves in tonal space by means of the final note of the melody, from which they could assess the characteristic kernel of tones and semitones around it, the melody's range in respect to the final, and many other tonal features. Tonal weight and role manifest themselves through where individual phrases and whole melodies begin and end, what notes most often appear or are directly repeated, what notes form the upper and lower boundaries of melodic contours, what notes are constantly returned to from above or below, what notes are approached or left by leap or step, and so forth.

Two additional kinds of information are also valuable. The relationship of text to music can hold clues to the tonal hierarchy by means of how individual syllables, words, and larger syntactical and structural units are set in tones. And in rhythmically measured music, especially in metrical music, the length of a note and its weak or strong metrical position also convey powerful tonal information. If we knew them, the dance steps for dance songs and instrumentally accompanied dances would also help us to understand the roles of the tones in their tunes. But most medieval sacred monophony was either not measured or lost its rhythmic nuances over time, becoming in simple terms 'plain chant' by the twelfth century.

To pursue mode in a musical and scholarly way beyond the simplest classification schemes into subtler issues of melodic behaviour immediately requires limits to be defined that are generic, chronological and geographical. Poised on the brink of that potentially vast effort, the work of many books, a few examples will serve here briefly to lay some groundwork. To begin, let us take the approaches just suggested for reading the tonal language of a melody and put them to work on two medieval plainchants. One, *Exsurge domine*, is Gregorian, thus a Roman chant of ca 700 preserved in a Frankish melodic dialect of ca 800, and the other, *In principio*, is later medieval German chant of the mid twelfth century. To make a pointed comparison, they are both in mode 3. Modes 3 and 4 have E as their final, and here, the third mode is the authentic member of the pair, which means that these melodies both move primarily above the final (rather than around and below it).

To penetrate any farther into their melodic languages, an approach through the text is essential. *Exsurge domine* is the respond of a gradual. In most medieval service books it was performed at mass on the third Sunday of Lent (see Example 14.1).[2] Its prose-like text is one verse from the Latin Psalter (Vulgate Psalm 9:20). Graduals are highly formulaic chants, and *Exsurge domine* shares with chants in its family of mode-3 graduals many specific formulaic gestures of melody. These gestures are most frequently found at points of formal text articulation, so laying out the text following its structure and syntax allows many features of the melody to come rapidly into focus.[3]

The psalm verse is comprised of two half verses, each of two subphrases, so we may speak of it in terms of four lines. Their music is rich in mode-3 clichés. The music of line 1a begins with what we know to be a common initial formula, which is centred on F (the final, E, has a very minor role to play here). Lines 1b, 2a and 2b share a subsidiary opening gesture for interior lines that rises from G to C and then falls to A. Lines 1a and 2a end with the same cadence, a formula for the mid-point of half verses that elaborates A and then falls through B flat and G to F and, from there, on to a cadential goal a minor third lower on D. This particular formula, known in mode-3 chants but even more a standard half-cadence in mode 4, ends with a figure that is also typical of cadences in mode 1. Line 1b ends with a formula for the close of half verses, rising and falling from D and then swirling

Example **14.1** Anon., respond of *Exsurge domine*, a Gregorian gradual of ca800

repeatedly around F before the cadential fall back to D once more. And line 2b ends with a formula for the close of the entire verse, twice rising to C and then falling through B flat and G to F in a variation of the formula that closes lines 1a and 2a. Only from there does it quickly move to the ultimate final by reiterating G before falling to the cadential goal a minor third lower on E.

The overall range of *Exsurge domine* is an octave and a step, the ninth from C up to D, and thus does not even explore the full E to E octave. The pitch collection is reducible to a white-note diatonic scale plus B flat, where B natural is used in ascents to C, and B flat is used as the crest of an arc (F–A–Bb–G–F) in a cadential formula. The melody spends most of its time in the fifth between F and C before regularly falling to a frequent lower boundary point and cadential goal on low D. The D an octave above appears as upper neighbour to C, and C itself is frequently an upper boundary tone and repeated pitch, just as we would expect from its status as the Gregorian 'reciting tone' in this mode.[4] *Exsurge domine*'s wavelike rising and falling

Example 14.2 Hildegard of Bingen, beginning of *In principio*, 1140s figures, reiterations of individual pitches, and insistent spinning around single notes and intervals of a third, are typical of the most elaborate kind of Gregorian idiom. Weighing the role of pitches, D–F–A–C emerge as a central collection, pitted against a secondary set including E–G–B♭. Thus it should come as no surprise that *Exurge domine* shares many of its turns of phrase with D-final chants. Its own final, E, is an infrequent and weak secondary pitch.

Our other third-mode chant, *In principio*, is the last number, a chorus, in *Ordo virtutum*, a sacred music drama or sung morality play of the 1140s by Hildegard of Bingen (1098–1179) (see Example 14.2).[5] In its lyrics a narrative introduction and conclusion frame the direct speech of Christ. Hildegard writes a kind of heightened and occasionally rhymed prose that can be parsed as a series of sentences. These are lines of irregular syllable and word count that are syntactic units mainly ended by a verb. In setting her text Hildegard employs a very personal non-Gregorian melodic language. With only a few exceptions, each sentence unfolds as a free, florid variation on the same melodic arc, beginning with an ascent from E to B, spinning around B in the upper register, and cadencing via a descent from C, D or E down to low E.

Here in *In principio* mode 3 is represented with very different pitch language than that of *Exurge domine*. The melody is broader, extending from the C below low E to the G above octave E, for the unusually wide total span of a twelfth, though it principally unfolds within the E–E octave. Most striking, the note E plays a very different and more central role here than in the gradual. Low E begins and ends the chant, and it begins and ends almost every text line, and high E is an important pitch, too, as a frequently occurring upper boundary tone. The next most important pitch to E is B natural, which is similarly emphasized. (There is no place for B flat in this idiom.) Sentences, phrases, subphrases and individual words begin and end on E or B, and most melodic gestures either spin around E or B, or rise or fall through the fifth or fourth from one to the other. The central melodic role of these two pitches, and the very minor role for C, is the basis of a melodic language very unlike that of mode-3 Gregorian melodies. Instead, it is a personal idiom consistent with other florid E pieces by Hildegard, and at the same time it reveals Hildegard to be well-schooled in the prescriptive Germanic modal theory of her era (species theory), with its strong roots in quasi-Hellenistic notions of species of octave, fourth and fifth.

Taken in sum, the melodic and tonal languages of *Exsurge domine* and *In principio*, two florid chants classifiable in the same mode by final and range, exploit their tonal space in very distinct ways. The differences are not those of two different melodies by the same composer or by two contemporaries,

Example 14.3 Anon., sequence *Fulgens preclara*, ninth century

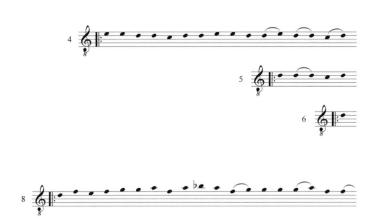

but are representative of the differences one finds between melodies in bodies of plainchant written over 400 years apart in different geographical regions by musicians with very different schooling and different ideas about the roles of the tones in a high-lying E-final chant.

Two other post-Gregorian plainchants, *Fulgens preclara* and *Ortum floris*, introduce issues having to do with consistency of tonal behaviour. *Fulgens preclara* is a an early Frankish sequence of the ninth century for Easter Sunday Mass (see Example 14.3).[6] Its text has the typical couplet form of the sequence, that is, a chain of paired text lines, in which each pair of lines is set syllabically to a melody and its immediate repetition (with some permissible irregularity at the start and finish of the chant). This sprawling melody is interesting in the first place because of its unusually wide

Example 14.3 (*cont.*)

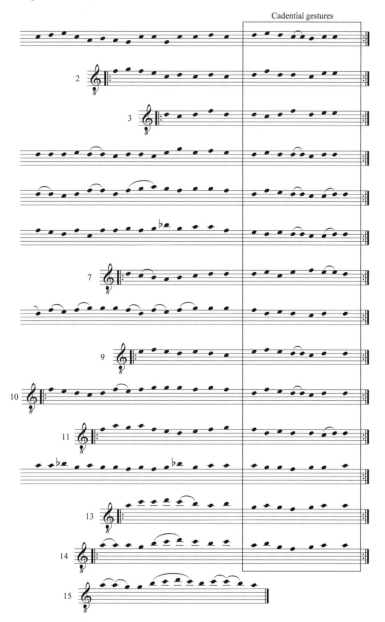

range – from G to the D a twelfth above. The span is not, however, articulated as a single central octave that occasionally is breached, as Hildegard handles it in *In principio*. Nor do we find it to be a modal octave articulated into species of fifth and fourth, and then extended by a fourth or fifth above or below, as one might expect in a melody governed by Hellenistic modal theory (e.g., G–D–G with an extra fifth above to D, or D–A–D with an extra fourth below to A). So it is not a melody ping-ponging between boundary tones of the fifths and fourths, and cadencing to one of the boundary tones. Rather, the melody rises through pitch regions best defined in terms of ascending registers and successive pitch centres (cadential goals) around which individual phrases and sections spin.

Fulgens preclara starts its fifteen arcs of melody in its lowest register, the region from G to C, for couplet 1 (lines 1, 2), then shifts to E for couplets 2 and 3 (lines 3–6) before settling around D for the next eight couplets (lines 7–22). While cadencing to D, the melodic lines open up a higher register in contours first reaching G, then A, then B flat. The last three couplets and closing singlet (lines 23–9) move upward again to centre around and cadence on high A (via material first introduced in couplet 6).

The *Fulgens preclara* melody is highly motivic, with motives that are closely word-bound, and it is repetitive both on a local scale and across couplets. Most markedly, all couplets, in all pitch registers, present close variants of a single cadential gesture. The tonal region around high A shares figures with the phrases cadencing to D, especially in initial gestures (now up a fifth), and with the phrases cadencing to E, especially at the cadence itself (now up a fourth). Well-behaved and coherent in its own terms, *Fulgens preclara* is not conventionally well-behaved either in textbook modal terms or in respect to the empirical features of earlier Gregorian chants. Its melodic language, not surprisingly, is most akin to other new Frankish compositions of the ninth century.

Ortum floris is a non-liturgical Latin devotional song – a versus – probably of the later twelfth century, in four stanzas set strophically (see Example 14.4).[7] As is typical for versus poetry, the text is rigorously governed by an elaborate and strict scheme of versification, which, in turn, is tightly reflected in the melody's repetitions of motive and phrase. It unfolds in the relatively narrow range of a sixth, mostly above the final, in a tonal realm with G as the final and a signature B flat. These features allow it to be classified as a transposed first-mode chant. But the usefulness of that classification is to be doubted. This song's distinctive melody, alien to the language of Gregorian first-mode chants, is cut from the cloth of a popular G-major/G-minor idiom employed in many Anglo-French sequences, lais, planctus, conductus and versus that were newly composed in the twelfth century.[8]

The pitch collection of *Ortum floris* is diatonic with the addition of B flat, but the B-flat/B-natural inflection is handled in a recurrent way that strikingly challenges one of the most prominent musical features of first mode, namely the minor third above the final, and defines what is best explained as two alternating pitch sets or tonal areas, one primary and one

Example 14.4 Anon., versus *Ortum floris*, twelfth century

secondary. To grasp the alternation, let us formulize the melody as XYZY, or in more detail, reflecting the versification, as

$$XX\ Y^1Y^2\ ZZY^3\ Y^1Y^2$$

The first of the two pitch sets, the primary material, is the opening G material in section X spanning the fourth F to B flat (i.e., from a tone below G through the tone and a semitone above). It returns at section Z in a recognizable extension opening up the fifth from G to D. The contrasting or secondary pitch set, in section Y, functions as a realm 'away from home'. Spanning the fifth from F to C, it is centred not on the lowest pitch, F, but on A, moving a minor third above to C (by tone and semitone, with B natural) and a major third below to F. Y^1 and Y^2 are an open and closed melodic pair (and the melodic phrase Y^3 is a variant of Y^1). Closure in Y^2 is accomplished by a return to the original G pitch set via the cadential reintroduction of B flat and the B♭–A–G descent. If the two pitch sets are condensed to scales, we have F–**G**–A–B♭–C–D systematically contrasted with F–G–**A**–B♮–C, with very different weights for the individual pitches in each set.

To practised throats and ears, the four chants discussed above emerge as representatives of very different tonal idioms and formal types. Each is unique, yet is related to a larger repertory, grounded in a particular time and place, with which it holds many features of style in common. Growing in familiarity, and thus in individuality, all four chants resist being packaged as New Age background music and reduced to the status of aural wallpaper. Medieval chant is far from homogeneous, and its distinct idioms are there to be savoured by the virtuosos (and connoisseurs) of the diatonic.

The medieval polyphony surviving in musical notation floats atop a vast unwritten substrate whose roots undoubtedly go back for millennia before a significant amount of evidence begins to turn up for it in the ninth century. Procedures for making polyphony differ both chronologically and geographically, and depend on the performance milieu as well. And it would not be surprising if the elite practices of professional singers at cathedral and court bore some kinship to local folk polyphony, though this escapes proof for now.

As one secure point of departure for some basic considerations of polyphony, we may safely say that a very high percentage of all medieval polyphony is for just two voice parts. This is true historically, generically and geographically well into the fourteenth century. It is true for ecclesiastical organa, for conductus and versus, for simple polyphony including psalm and lesson tones, for secular and sacred motets from France, for secular songs in French, Italian and English, and for polyphonic instrumental dances. Moreover, most of the three- and four-voiced polyphony from the end of this epoch is based on two-part counterpoint, with two voices clearly working as a structural duet to which one or more additional parts have been added.

Questions of ultimate origins always lead scholars onto dangerous ground, but it seems intuitively likely that two-voice polyphony began in the decoration of unison performance, so that the discantus, the second ('dis') melodic line ('cantus'), may be understood as splitting off from the first and ranging alongside it through the same tonal space.

The calculated addition of a second voice to a complete, previously existing melody, whether the new musical line is added in precisely the same register or lies generally higher or lower, seems plausibly to be a next step (beyond splitting off and returning) in exploring the potential of the effect. If instead the process of composition is more simultaneous in the composing together of two entirely new voices (a way of making artful polyphony from scratch that is new in the West in the twelfth century), then we still normally assume, and can usually detect after the fact, the priority of one voice over the other in the act of composition.

A basic observation, therefore, concerns the degree of entanglement or separation of voices, the most fundamental and deliberate conception under which composers and performers are operating. The new part may be added above or below the original, or be deliberately entwined – that is, sharing range and frequently crossing the given voice. We tend to find that the crossing of voices is usually either welcomed or shunned. If mainly unfolding in distinct registers, the two voices may stay free of all contact, just touch on unisons, or cross occasionally.

The setting may be note-against-note (strictly or very nearly so), or more florid. If more florid, it is most often the second part that will have more notes than the original, as long as it is not merely adding some kind of drone. The relationship may be to set many new notes against one in the original or, in some cases, to set a larger number of notes in the added voice against a smaller cluster of original notes. In the latter case, just how to align the notes for a modern edition or performance can be a knotty conundrum.

In the resulting polyphony, the original voice may retain its primacy, or instead become a background element, a foundational *tenor* or *cantus firmus*. Looked at from the other direction, we may ask of the second part whether it remains subordinate or whether it emerges to an important degree as independent, acquiring the characteristics of a cogent, coherent, idiomatic melody. It may move entirely into the foreground, or have its independence but still be subordinate, which is for example how we would characterize the tenor of a Machaut chanson of the mid 1300s.

We further will want to know what constraints or rules are apparent for the defining of consonance and dissonance, and for the handling of voice-leading and cadences, and what is their effect on the independence and tonal features of the new part. Under these constraints, how do the tonal and melodic features of the new voice compare to those of the original? And what is the stylistic relationship of the new line to contemporary idioms for new monophonic songs, or in comparable polyphony?

The commonest simple form of polyphony is parallelism – a thickening or doubling by mirroring the contour of the original a few steps away. Whether flexibly or strictly applied, parallelism effectively preserves the identity of the original melody. The two voices may move out and back from unison to the interval of parallel motion – thus starting as one, then splitting and rejoining. Alternatively, the discanting voice may be set from the outset at the desired interval and remain always at that distance, or fall back into a unison at cadences. Note-against-note parallelism appears to be a strong norm in the earliest practices of which we have any record, for example ecclesiastical organum of the ninth to eleventh centuries, and thereafter in what scholars call simple polyphony, meaning the most rudimentary and widespread practice of extemporized polyphonic adornment of a chant. Some elementary written examples barely go beyond it.

Example 14.5a Guido, modified parallel organum at the fourth below from *Micrologus*, ca1025

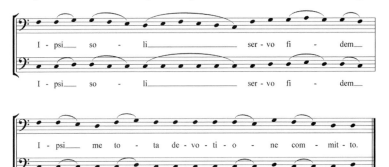

Example 14.5b Anon., reciting tone for a Christmas matins lesson, ca1300

Example 14.5c Burgos, Monasterio de Las Huelgas 9, fol. 54v, from the sequence *Victime paschali laudes*

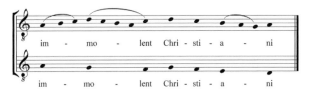

Example 14.5d London, British Library, Additional 16975, fol. 166, from the hymn *Conditor alme siderum*

From the medieval West there are examples in two voices of parallel seconds, third, fourths, fifths and sixths. Not all possibilities for these intervals sounding above or below are found, however, and some preferences demonstrably unfold on geographical or chronological axes. For example, parallel fourths lying beneath the chant are the predominant language of

Example 14.6a Anon., *Nobilis humilis*

No - bi - lis   hu - mi - lis   Ma - gne   mar - tyr   sta - bi - lis

No - bi - lis   hu - mi - lis   Ma - gne   mar - tyr   sta - bi - lis

Example 14.6b Anon., *Laudes deo*, troped lesson from Christmas midnight mass, mid fourteenth century

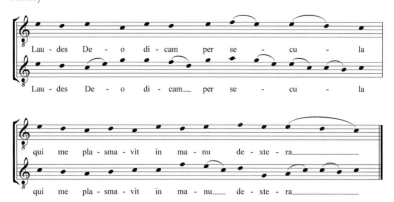

Lau - des   De - o   di - cam   per   se - cu - la

Lau - des   De - o   di - cam___   per   se - cu - la

qui   me   pla - sma - vit   in   ma - nu   de - xte - ra____

qui   me   pla - sma - vit   in   ma - nu___   de - xte - ra____

ecclesiastical organum in Anglo-French theory and practice from the ninth to the eleventh centuries (see Example 14.5a).

The status and role of the fourth, and of the location of the added voice, then change in an extraordinary and epochal paradigm shift. By the twelfth and thirteenth centuries, in organum, clausula and motet, the counterpointing voice is conceived as lying above the original melody, and the preferred interval for parallel voice-leading is at the fifth above (see Examples 14.5b, 14.5c, 14.5d).[9] Parallel fourths disappear in two-voice writing, and the fourth is treated more and more as a harmonic dissonance. A great sea-change in taste has occurred.

A different sonorous image emerges at the same time in some elite polyphony in the British Isles, where thirds and sixths are often used harmonically as consonances and in parallel voice-leading. We believe that this very different sound world reflects folk practices and is a regional preference that extends into Scandinavia and Iceland. English discant treatises allow parallel imperfect consonances and acknowledge discanting below as well as above the given voice. In practice, in two voices, thirds are found in parallel above and below, as well as twining around the original voice, and sixths are found below (see Examples 14.6a, 14.6b, 14.6c).[10]

Example 14.6c Anon., *Ave celi regina virginum*

Example 14.7 Anon., clausula on *Nostrum*, early thirteenth century

Far to the south, parallel seconds are attested in some Milanese funeral music, where note-against-note polyphony follows beneath the chant in a mixture of parallel seconds and parallel fourths.[11]

Elements of the parallel style often remain detectable in more elaborate works, in particular where a counterpoint of varied harmonic intervals and voice-leading can be read as the florid expansion upon a simpler substrate. In a large number of two-voice Parisian conductus and discant clausulae of the later twelfth and thirteenth centuries, for example, harmony is governed by fifths sounding above the principal voice at the beginning and the end, at the outset and conclusion of most important interior phrases and sections, and in metrically strong positions more locally. Although the two voices may cross, an underlying scenario of splitting and rejoining is not at work here; rather, the rule is greater distance, independence, and equality of the parts (see Example 14.7).[12]

The two-voice French and English ecclesiastical organa of the later tenth century, such as are preserved in a Winchester repertory, are composed

Example 14.8 Guillaume de Machaut, refrain of virelai *Se je souspir*, mid fourteenth century

'from the top down', with the discanting line ranging beneath the given chant, while organa of the twelfth century are composed 'from the bottom up'. Reversing field again, composing 'from the top down' defines the compositional strategy in fourteenth- and fifteenth-century polyphonic French refrain songs, where the tenor is added around or below the principal melodic line, the *cantus*. Machaut and his contemporaries and successors explored various possibilities for the relationship of the cantus and the tenor in respect to cadences and the width of counterpoint, and on occasion they will cross the voices.[13]

The tightly interwoven cantus and tenor of the refrain of Machaut's virelai *Se je souspir* show one possibility (see Example 14.8).[14] In this song the text is sung only by the upper voice, whose tune is a well-shaped melody lying above and below its final on F. This melody in all likelihood was composed in its entirety before the tenor was added to it. The tenor is closely related, yet subordinate, helping to propel rhythmic activity within the phrase by off-beat accents, and to sustain sound and motion across the phrase rests in the cantus. It is, in respect to range, not a lower-lying part but tightly intertwined with the cantus in the same plagal register around the final; the voices share the ninth C to D, to which the cantus adds one higher step (E); they cross regularly, and cadence to a unison. The two parts sound mainly thirds and fifths together, with occasionally unisons, seconds and fourths, while rarely separating to sixths and octaves, and once a tenth; contrary motion between the voices predominates. In other polyphonic French chansons we see composers explore different

Example **14.9** Giovanni da Firenze, first text line of madrigal *Nel meço*, mid fourteenth century

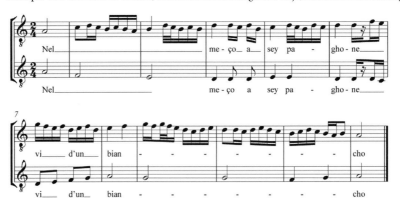

possibilities for the relationship of the two voices in respect to width of counterpoint, especially with the duo lying further apart on average. In effect
this means that the tenor lies more consistently beneath, or further beneath
(rather than entwined around) the cantus. By later in the fourteenth century the tenor most often sounds the octave beneath the cantus at structural
cadences.[15]

Early Italian trecento two-voice madrigals articulate a different concept
of polyphonic duo. Characteristically they begin and end on a unison and are
fully texted in both voices, with simultaneous declamation of syllables and
no crossing of parts. The conception is of two equal voices singing the text
together that split, keep their distance, and then rejoin. The duo is decidely
not entwining, however. The upper part is generally more rhythmically
active, while the lower has more long-sustained notes, especially in the
melismas that open and close the setting of each line of text; upper-voice
rhythmic diminutions usually decorate one tone or a simple progression
over the longer-held lower note. As a rule the upper voice here, too, as
in the French chanson, has precedence in the structural duet, and the
typical prevalence of harmonic fifths, and of parallel fifths in the underlying
contrapuntal motion suggest the conceptual origin of the style in modified
'underfifth' parallelism. The setting of the first text line of Giovanni da
Firenze's madrigal *Nel meço a sey paghone* exemplifies these features of the
earliest two-voiced trecento duet songs (see Example 14.9).[16]

In two-voice polyphony that polyphonically elaborates a chant or chant
excerpt, tonality is ultimately governed by the behaviour of the chant.
In freely composed polyphony (free, that is, in the sense of lacking the
constraint of a pre-existing melody) of the later twelfth century and beyond,
the possibility exists for the deliberate juxtaposition of contrasting tonal
areas. As in monophonic chants, we may find temporary internal shifts and

Example 14.10 Anon., conductus *Soli nitorem*, early thirteenth century

also permanent shifts of tonal language and behaviour. One final example, a two-voice Notre Dame era conductus, *Soli nitorem*, will introduce us to some of the possibilities (see Example 14.10).[17]

The two voices of *Soli nitorem* are tightly entwined equal partners in their duet. The overall tonal centre of the conductus is G, which is indeed the

Example 14.10 (*cont.*)

tonal centre of about 60 per cent of the polyphonic versus and conductus of the Aquitanian and Notre Dame repertories. Here, both voices move primarily in the G to G octave, though the lower descends occasionally to the D below lower G, and they hold a great deal of motivic material in common. In the repertory to which *Soli nitorem* belongs, there are G pieces with B natural and G pieces with signature B flat, but a very high percentage, curiously, actually employ both B natural and B flat, changing from one

Example 14.10 (*cont.*)

to the other in a structural way. *Soli nitorem* shows just this alternation.
(*Ortum floris*, the tonally fluctuating chant discussed above, originates in
the same milieu.)

This conductus explores a total of three tonal areas, which are aligned
with its formal architecture and with the poetry's verse structure. An initial
cauda, none of whose musical material is later reused, is on G with signed

B flat. Then follow the first four lines of the conductus text, written as two couplets. Each couplet is set with declamation on double longs for its first line, moves to declamation on single longs (fifth mode) for its second line, and is followed by a first-mode cauda that concludes with a short point of sustained-tone organum. Tonally, the text couplets are set on G with B natural; each musical section begins at the octave and concludes at the unison.

In the second half of the poem, however, the poet shifts versification and syntax, and the composer has matched this textual shift with a shift of tonal material, now emphasizing the fifth A to E with C as central pitch axis and (local) final. Closure is achieved in a final cauda that revisits the musical material of the previous first-mode caudae, thus moving back to a tonal centre on G with B natural, though the cauda material is now recast into a rhythmically broader fifth mode before the final sustained-tone flourish.

A move into a discussion of three- and four-voice writing, as it emerges at the very end of the Middle Ages, would not be out of place at this moment, but space does not permit it. I will simply emphasize that most fundamental considerations are the same as for two-voice writing. We may ask if a pre-existing melody is being garlanded with additional parts unfolding together with it, or is the entire polyphonic complex of new composition? If new, does one voice have priority? Or now is there perhaps a structural duet of two counterpointing voices that has conceptual or chronological priority? Can we speak of the work having been composed from the bottom up or from the top down? And is its tonal language consistent or deliberately varied? From these points of departure, our trajectory of inquiry must move back into the theory treatises, to generate from their dicta a set of queries involving the grammar and vocabulary of consonance and dissonance, and of voice-leading and cadencing. Furthermore, the unfolding of constructive principles in three and four parts is more diverse, and even more contingent on genre (motet, chanson, conductus) and geography (for instance, the fourteenth-century motet in Italy, England, and France) than previously. But these must be topics and questions for another day.

15 Ecclesiastical foundations and secular institutions

REBECCA A. BALTZER

After the fall of Rome and the disappearance of the Roman Empire in the late fifth century, the sixth and seventh centuries are considered to represent the low point of medieval civilization in the West, when Roman administrative and political systems had crumbled and there was little to take their place. The Christian church was scattered, fragmentary and unable to exert any universal authority. As society became largely rural again under the control of local lords, and as towns and cities declined, the light of classical learning came close to being entirely snuffed out.

In Frankish territory, the sixth and seventh centuries are referred to as the Merovingian period, after the Merovingian kings. By the eighth century the Merovingian kings had become such ineffectual figureheads that the real ruler/administrator was the Mayor of the Palace, supposedly the king's chief assistant. The Carolingian dynasty stemmed from two Mayors of the Palace – Charles Martel (r. 714–41) and Pépin III the Short (r. 741–68), the father of Charlemagne (r. 768–814). Pépin enquired of the pope if the person who ruled as king of the Franks ought not to be called King of the Franks, and the pope agreed. Thus in 751, with papal sanction, Pépin deposed the last Merovingian king, sent him off to a monastery, and assumed the throne in name as well as in fact.

In the Carolingian world of the eighth and ninth centuries, there were three 'orders' of society: the regular clergy, the secular clergy, and the laity. The regular clergy, who lived apart from the world under a rule (*regula* in Latin) such as the Rule of St Benedict, included monks, nuns and a few others. The secular clergy, who lived in the world (*secula* in Latin), were those who staffed cathedrals and parish churches. The laity comprised the complete spectrum of non-clerical society, from the poorest peasant to the richest lord. Because life was still primarily rural, many members of the nobility were more powerful than the churchmen in their territory and in fact controlled the appointment of bishops and priests in their domains. Except for the top ranks of the regular and secular clergy and the lay nobility, the majority of society was largely illiterate.[1] Many parish priests had little education and could barely stumble through the liturgy in Latin. It was primarily the regular clergy (monks) who copied manuscripts and preserved what remained of the classical and early Christian written heritage; their schools, too, were more capable and more stable than cathedral schools at this time, since the few cathedral schools often depended on a single teacher who could not guarantee the school's continuity. In the ninth century, the largest monastic libraries were at Lorsch, which had some six hundred manuscripts, and Fulda, which had nearly a thousand.

Early in his rule, Charlemagne perceived that to have the three orders of society functioning as they should, a more educated and literate clergy was needed. He depended on a partnership with the church to carry out his political and educational goals; he sought to have the clergy function as extensions of his government who could help to keep independent-minded and rebellious lords in check and who could ensure the Christian salvation of his people. For this, they needed more education. Not only did Charlemagne establish his palace school, run from 782 to 796 by the well-educated Englishman Alcuin of York (ca730–804), but he encouraged the establishment of other schools throughout his realms. He appointed men who had been educated at his palace school as bishops to go and do likewise.[2]

Charlemagne's biographer Einhard (d. 840), a son of noble parents who was educated at the monastery of Fulda, was sent by his abbot to Charlemagne's palace school, and there he was a first-hand observer of the last two decades of Charlemagne's life. He reports in his *Vita Caroli* interesting details of this life that shed light on music and the arts at court.[3] For example, Charlemagne wanted all his children, both boys and girls, to be instructed in the liberal arts. The sons also learned horsemanship, hunting and battle, while the daughters learned spinning, weaving and cloth-making. He took his children with him on journeys, and he always wanted them present at meals. At the dinner table, it was his custom to listen to readings or to music[4] – the readings were about 'the stories and deeds of olden time: he was fond, too, of Saint Augustine's books, and especially of the one entitled *The City of God*'.[5] Einhard adds that Charlemagne 'also had the old rude songs that celebrate the deeds and wars of the ancient kings [*chansons de geste*] written out for transmission to posterity', and that he even began a grammar of his native language.[6]

Einhard reports that Charlemagne not only had an excellent command of his native tongue (Frankish) but also could speak Latin as eloquently as though it were his first language. He could understand Greek, too, but was less adept at speaking it. Einhard adds:

> He most zealously cultivated the liberal arts, held those who taught them in great esteem, and conferred great honors upon them. He took lessons in grammar of the deacon Peter of Pisa, at that time an aged man. Another

deacon, Albin of Britain, surnamed Alcuin, a man of Saxon extraction, who was the greatest scholar of the day, was his teacher in other branches of learning. The King spent much time and labor with him studying rhetoric, dialectics, and especially astronomy; he learned to reckon, and used to investigate the motions of the heavenly bodies most curiously, with an intelligent scrutiny. He also tried to write, and used to keep tablets and blanks in bed under his pillow, that at leisure hours he might accustom his hand to form the letters; however, as he did not begin his efforts in due season, but late in life, they met with ill success.[7]

He cherished with the greatest fervor and devotion the principles of the Christian religion, which had been instilled into him from infancy. Hence it was that he built the beautiful basilica at Aix-la-Chapelle [Aachen], which he adorned with gold and silver and lamps, and with rails and doors of solid brass. He had the columns and marbles for this structure brought from Rome and Ravenna, for he could not find such as were suitable elsewhere.[8] He was a constant worshipper at this church as long as his health permitted, going morning and evening, even after nightfall, besides attending mass; and he took care that all the services there conducted should be administered with the utmost possible propriety ... He was at great pains to improve the church reading and psalmody, for he was well skilled in both although he neither read in public nor sang, except in a low tone and with others.[9]

Charlemagne had a sincere high regard for the holy places in Rome and for the pope; he saw himself as the protector of the pope and the church, and he wanted Frankish churches to do as the Roman church did, insofar as it was possible. Over time, his revival of learning, his interest in a well-ordered liturgy performed by well-educated clerics, and his interest in building and maintaining churches led to a true renaissance of education and the arts as they functioned to serve the church.[10] This Carolingian renaissance saw in music the development of the ecclesiastical modal system; the beginnings of musical notation; the rise of tropes, prosulae, sequences and liturgical drama; and the beginnings of polyphony.

Charlemagne's palace school included as students not only Charlemagne himself but his entire family and his courtiers, as well as various scholars attracted by Alcuin. Under Alcuin's direction, the palace school focused upon the verbal arts of the Trivium (grammar, rhetoric and dialectic), with selections from the mathematical arts of the Quadrivium (arithmetic, geometry, music and astronomy) included, all for the purpose of producing a more educated Christian society. Alcuin himself wrote treatises on the arts of the Trivium – grammar, rhetoric and the virtues, and dialectic. A very short treatise on music, known as the *Musica Albini* ('the *Musica* of Albinus'), dating from the end of the eighth century, has also been ascribed to him. It is the first extant writing on music to mention the medieval church modes. For much of the twentieth century, scholars believed that the attribution of this little work to Alcuin was not true, but Hartmut Möller has convincingly argued that this attribution is correct.[11]

Only four paragraphs long, the treatise says nothing about precise pitches or how the modes differ from one another, except that the plagals are lower than the authentics; it basically just reports that an eightfold classification of Romano/Frankish (that is, Gregorian) chant was being made by the Franks.[12] Similarly, the earliest surviving tonary, the so-called Tonary of St Riquier, is a late-eighth-century fragmentary source that classifies chants by mode, comprising a list of various chants in each mode.[13] These two documents indicate that the Carolingian interest in things Byzantine (in this case the Byzantine *octoechos*) together with the Frankish passion for order had already combined, before the beginning of the ninth century, to begin modally classifying the large repertory of Gregorian chant.

Charlemagne's *Admonitio generalis*, issued in 789,[14] contains a provision listing the feasts of the liturgical year which should be universally observed in churches: Christmas, St Stephen, St John the Evangelist, Holy Innocents, the octave of Christmas, Epiphany, the octave of Epiphany, the Purification of the Virgin, Easter week, the Major Litany, Ascension, Pentecost, St John the Baptist, Sts Peter and Paul, St Martin, and St Andrew. It specifically left open the question of the Assumption of the Virgin, which several centuries later had become one of the most important saints' feasts in the liturgical calendar.

Despite the important courts of Charlemagne and his successors, especially that of his grandson Charles the Bald, who ruled 840–77, monasteries remained the primary centres of learning in the ninth to the eleventh centuries. During this time, of special significance for music was the south German monastery of St Gall, today in Switzerland.[15] Founded by Irish monks, St Gall for several centuries had a very active scriptorium which produced beautiful and important manuscripts, and a portion of its medieval library still survives there today, with many codices now digitally available online.[16] The earliest surviving liturgical book expressly designed to include musical notation comes from St Gall – Stiftsbibliothek MS 359, copied in the very early tenth century: it is a *cantatorium* that provides neumes only for the soloistic chants of the mass (graduals, alleluias, and tracts).[17] Other notated Sangallian chantbooks – graduals, the Hartker Antiphonal, and several tropers – stem from the second quarter of the tenth century into the twelfth. The tropers include works by Notker Balbulus (d. 912) and Tuotilo (d. 915), both monks at the abbey. Notker's *Liber hymnorum* (in Stiftsbibliothek MS 381) is justly famous for its establishment of the East

Frankish liturgical sequence based on West Frankish models. Notker wrote some forty eloquent sequence texts to improve upon those brought with their West Frankish melodies to the abbey by a monk from Jumièges in Normandy who was fleeing the Norman invasions; Tuotilo left us a number of tropes for which he composed both text and music. In both cases, the melodies are unquestionably from the ninth century.[18]

By the later tenth century a monastic revival was under way in England. The Wessex king Edgar appointed his mentor Ethelwold (b. ca908) to be Bishop of Winchester (963–84), and there Ethelwold removed the secular canons and established a community of Benedictine monks to staff the Old Minster.[19] The multitude of new English monastic foundations led abbots and abbesses to meet the king in circa 970 to formulate a universal customary to regulate monastic life. The result was the *Regularis Concordia*, drawn up by Bishop Ethelwold. It includes his well-known account of the *Visitatio sepulchri* or Easter liturgical drama as performed by monks at the Old Minster.[20] Ethelwold thus provides the earliest description of the widespread Easter dialogue trope *Quem queritis* performed as a drama at the end of Easter matins. In this version the original introit trope has already been expanded by the addition of several antiphons with appropriate texts from elsewhere in the liturgy.

Within a period of about eighty years (circa 970–1050), the monks at Winchester became renowned not only for the practice of troping the liturgy but also for the creation of sequences for the mass and a large body of liturgical polyphony, all preserved with Anglo-Saxon staffless neumes in the two Winchester tropers: Oxford, Bodleian Library, MS Bodley 775, and Cambridge, Corpus Christi College, MS 473. The tropers contain both proper and ordinary tropes plus the largest repertory of early sequences west of the Rhine and north of the Loire.[21] And the Corpus Christi troper contains the earliest collection of polyphony intended for performance in the liturgy – that is, polyphony not found simply as examples in a theoretical treatise. In the back of the book (fols. 135–190v) are organal voices for more than 170 chants: Kyries, Glorias, alleluias, tracts (unique in medieval polyphony), sequences, great responsories for vespers and matins, and a few miscellaneous items.[22] A difficulty for modern editors and performers, however, is how to combine the staffless neumes of the organal voices, which do not exist in more precisely pitched later copies, with the chant voices elsewhere in the tropers; most efforts have followed the rules of contemporary theoretical treatments of organum such as those of Guido of Arezzo.

Overall, the monastic musicians at Winchester exhibited their liturgical creativity on all available compositional fronts – tropes, prosulae, sequences, polyphony, and liturgical drama, with significant interactions in the first four categories such as troped polyphonic ordinary chants and polyphonic settings of sequences. A major feast day at Winchester Cathedral in the first half of the eleventh century, with the liturgy troped and embellished with polyphony to the maximum extent possible, was no doubt a lengthy but splendidly impressive occasion, one not immediately replicable anywhere else at that time.

In the twelfth century we can witness the lives and effects on music of two singularly important women who could hardly be more different: Eleanor of Aquitaine (1124?–1204) and Hildegard of Bingen (1098–1179). Eleanor, who inherited the duchy of Aquitaine and the county of Poitou from her father in 1137, soon became queen of France as the wife of Louis VII; she later became duchess of Normandy and queen of England as the wife of Henry II, and subsequently mother of two kings of England, Richard the Lionheart and John. Over time she became a consummate political figure who was not afraid to exercise her considerable power and influence on behalf of her goals, even when they ran counter to her husband's.[23]

Undeterred by gender or motherhood, in 1147 Eleanor went with Louis VII on the Second Crusade to retake the Holy Land. But as the marriage produced only two daughters and grew increasingly cold, in the course of a few weeks in 1152 Eleanor transferred control of huge territories in the south of France from one kingdom to another when she left Louis and married Henry, who became king of England in 1154. She bore him at least eight children, but only two outlived her.

Eleanor was the granddaughter of one of the first troubadours (Guillaume IX of Aquitaine), and her patronage in courtly life and secular song may be glimpsed in the troubadour songs – more than 40 cansos on themes of *fin' amors* – of Bernart de Ventadorn, whose posthumous vida placed him at her court and even suggested a fanciful romantic involvement between the two.[24] Also the romances of the earliest known trouvère poet–composer, Chrétien de Troyes, who was associated with Eleanor's Capetian daughter Marie, Countess of Champagne, give a vivid picture of music at court, and we may assume that this picture reflects Eleanor's court as well as her daughters', since they were often held together. Such gatherings were important sites of musical mingling between south and north, troubadours and trouvères, in the second half of the twelfth century. *Erec et Enide*, the first of Chrétien's romances, dates from ca1165–1170. Whenever a royal wedding, coronation, or other joyous occasion is described, music takes an important part in the proceedings. For instance, we find that after the wedding of Erec and Enide,

Quant la corz fu tote asanblee,	When the court was all assembled,
n'ot menestrel an la contree	there was not a minstrel in the countryside
qui rien seüst de nul deduit,	with pleasing accomplishment
qui a la cort ne fussent tuit.	that did not come to the court.
An la sale molt grant joie ot;	In the great hall there was much joy,
chascuns servi de ce qu'il sot;	each one contributing what he could:
cil saut, cil tunbe, cil anchante,	one jumps, one tumbles, one does magic;
li uns sifle, li autres chante,	one whistles, another sings,
cil flaute, cil chalemele,	one plays the flute, one the shawm,
cil gigue, li autres viele;	one the gigue, another the vielle.
puceles querolent et dancent;	Maidens carole and dance,
trestuit de joie fere tancent.	and outdo each other in merrymaking.
Riens n'est qui joie puisse fere	Nothing which can give joy
ne cuer d'ome a leesce trere,	and incline the heart to gladness
qui as noces ne fust le jor.	was left undone at the wedding that day.
Sonent tinbre, sonent tabor,	There is playing of timbrel, tabor,
muses, estives et freteles,	bagpipes, panpipes,
et buisines et chalemeles.[25]	buisines, and shawms.

On another joyous occasion at court it is mentioned that

Harpes, vieles, i resonent,	Harps, vielles, gigues, psaltery,
gigues, sautier et sinphonies,	and organistrums resound,
et trestotes les armonies	and all the other hurdy-gurdies
qu'an porroit dire ne nomer.[26]	that one could name.

Eleanor's incalculable influence on political and dynastic events continued on through her grandchildren and their children during most of the thirteenth century. She personally chose her granddaughter Blanche of Castile to marry Louis VIII of France; their heir, her great-grandson Louis IX (1226–70), became a saint. She was also the great-grandmother of the most prolific trouvère in the thirteenth century, Thibaut IV (1201–53), Count of Champagne and '*roi de Navarre*', who holds the place of honour under this title at the beginning of several thirteenth-century chansonniers.[27] Another of her descendants in the same generation was Alfonso X ('El Sabio'), king of Castile and León, at whose court in the mid thirteenth century the collections of more than 400 *Cantigas de Santa Maria* were produced, a rich mine of music and folklore.[28]

In contrast to Eleanor's political, dynastic and courtly visibility, Hildegard of Bingen, the tenth child of noble parents, was given at an early age as a tithe to the church and spent her long life as a cloistered nun in areas along the middle Rhine. But Hildegard was unusual in the range of her spiritual and intellectual activity, for which she became known as 'the Sibyl of the Rhine'. Over a period of some thirty years, around 1140–70, she produced three books of her mystical visions and revelations, a treatise on natural history and another on medical treatments, lives of the German saints Disibod and Rupert, and more than 300 extant letters to contemporaries who range from popes and kings to other monastics and to ordinary lay folk. During this same time, Hildegard's spiritual and mystical life inspired her to compose both sacred poetry and music – some 77 works collected into her *Symphonia armonie celestium revelationum*, extant in two musical manuscripts from the 1170s and 1180s with German neumes.[29]

Though her musical style is distinctively different from the inherited plainsong of her day, Hildegard nonetheless functionally labelled her compositions as antiphons, responds, sequences, hymns, a Kyrie and an alleluia. They tend to have a wide ambitus (pitch range) extending through both the authentic and plagal dimensions of a church mode, and they make frequent use of recurring melodic formulas, including broad leaps of a fifth, that coalesce to create a sense of ecstatic spirituality. We can only assume that her compositions were included wherever appropriate in the liturgy of the nuns under her spiritual care, since a particular use that they followed has never been firmly identified. Hildegard also composed the earliest extant dramatic morality play, the *Ordo virtutum*.[30] Using more than eighty formulaic melodies, it is sung throughout by personified virtues and the soul, except for the part of the devil, who cannot sing and only speaks. Whether Hildegard's music was ever heard beyond her convent walls during her lifetime we cannot know, but it is evident that she considered sacred music to be both an individual and a communal way of approaching God.

By the third quarter of the twelfth century, the new Gothic cathedral of Notre Dame in Paris was under construction to replace an earlier church, and with this building flowered a new creativity in sacred and liturgical polyphony, designed to embellish the most important occasions of the church year in this new ecclesiastical space. Notre Dame of Paris is a pre-eminent example of a cathedral staffed by a chapter of secular canons, presided over by a bishop. The hierarchy of secular clerical orders included priests, deacons, subdeacons, acolytes, and tonsured clerks. The chapter at Notre Dame was composed of 51 canons plus the dean. At the top were the eight dignitaries – the dean (the spiritual and administrative head of the chapter), the cantor or precentor (in charge of the music, liturgical books, and basic education of the singers), three archdeacons (each in charge of the lesser clergy in approximately one third of the diocese of Paris), the succentor (the cantor's chief assistant), the chancellor (in charge of the legal work and the library of the chapter, and later, the head of the University of Paris as well), and the penitentiarius (the bishop's chaplain, who substituted for him when necessary).[31] Next in rank were the 28 beneficed clerks, each of whom held a benefice or prebend that paid his living; these clerks were the performers of the daily services of the *opus dei.* Twenty of the clerks were canons (either priests, deacons, or subdeacons), while the other eight were known as the 'great vicars' of Notre Dame; they served vicariously for the dignitaries of the chapter, whose administrative duties frequently kept them away from the choir. Though canons of the chapter did not live under a monastic rule, most lived within the cloister to the north of the cathedral; some were required to do so by virtue of their offices.

Below the beneficed clerks of the chapter were sixteen unbeneficed clerks, known as the clerks of matins or *pauperes clerici.* Since they did not have endowed positions, they were dependent on the charity of those who did. While they might function as household help for the canons who lived in the cloister, they also played a major role in the performance of the liturgy: the six most senior clerks of matins, known as the *machicoti,* were the soloists and singers of polyphony, who took special pride in their distinctive repertory and musical skills. All the unbeneficed clerks were annually required to submit their resignations to the chapter, who could refuse to reappoint them if their work or behaviour had been inappropriate. Below the clerks of matins in the thirteenth century were as many as fourteen choirboys; they had specific singing assignments in the liturgy during vespers, matins, and mass and were schooled in the cloister, with the hope that in due time they might grow up to become canons.

The cathedral also employed four priests and four laymen as *marguilliers* (*matricularii*) or sextons, who had responsibility for the security of the building and the furnishings and people inside. One was required to sleep in the cathedral every night, and at least two had to be present during the day. They made sure that the right liturgical objects were in the right places for the services; they replenished the candles; they put away the vessels and utensils after a service; and they literally decked the halls (with banners etc.) on important feast days. Not the least of their duties was bell-ringing to signal the start of services and other important events in the life of the chapter and the cathedral.[32]

Except for the area immediately surrounding the main altar, the cathedral belonged to the chapter of canons, and the bishop needed their permission to enter and approach his space at the altar to officiate at a service. The chapter answered directly to the Holy See or to the papal legate, not to the bishop, though the bishop had certain strings of power that he could pull. For example, he appointed to office seven of the eight dignitaries of the chapter – all but the dean, who was elected by the chapter; naturally, the bishop would appoint officials who were sympathetic to his views.

In the liturgy at Notre Dame, polyphony could be heard on the most important feast days at vespers, matins, mass and certain processions (a procession at vespers or the procession after terce). The great responsory and

Benedicamus Domino at first vespers; the third, sixth and ninth responsories of matins (one of which might be the same as the vespers responsory);
the gradual and alleluia in the mass; and the verses of processional responsories are the customary polyphonic items found in the *Magnus liber organi*.
More than a hundred days per year with sufficient rank for polyphony had
at least one organum available. On the four most important annual feasts
– Christmas, Easter, Pentecost and the Assumption of the Virgin, liturgical
books specify that the full complement of six soloists from the clerks of
matins sang polyphony. At the next level below (for example, St Stephen,
Epiphany, the Purification, Sts Peter and Paul), four soloists were required.
Feasts that minimally qualified for polyphony would have two soloists and
most likely only the gradual or the alleluia in the mass set in polyphony,
while the feast of the Assumption of the Virgin – the most important saint's
feast at Notre Dame – included opportunities for as many as eight organa,
counting the vigil mass on the eve of the day. Thus the amount of polyphony
on a given feast, like the number and weight of candles specified to light
the cathedral, was an immediate indication of liturgical rank and significance – and, more indirectly, an indication of cost to the cathedral and its
staff.

   Both the bishop and the chapter owned large amounts of property –
their temporal, as opposed to their spiritual, authority – which produced
revenues for their respective operations. Overseeing the administration
and civil jurisdicition of those properties and supervising the collection
of revenues were very time-consuming obligations for the bishop's men
and for the dignitaries of the chapter, but both employed a corps of civil
servants to administer them. The chapter even had its own 'bar of justice'
where disputes were settled, and its own jail. These were needed because
living under its temporal jurisdiction were some 2,000 serfs who simply
belonged to the chapter, and during the years between the mid twelfth and
the mid thirteenth century the chapter imposed one 'head tax' after another
on the poor serfs. This was, of course, a very good source of income for the
building of the cathedral, and it was employed with shameless frequency –
several times in a given decade, on more than one occasion.

   But a serf could pay a certain sum of money to the chapter – a ransom,
in effect – and free himself from the feudal obligation of serfdom, though
he was probably then indebted to a moneylender for the rest of his life.
The cost varied from 15 to 90 livres, and this 'manumission' of serfs, as it
was known, was another source of enormous income to the chapter. Great
numbers of serfs obtained their manumission in the 1230s and 1240s, for
instance, and it was during this same period that at least a dozen feasts were
either newly added or increased in rank in the cathedral calendar, doubtless
funded unawares by the freed serfs.

Adding a new feast to the calendar or elevating in rank a feast already present required the agreement of both the chapter and the bishop; each had to commit the necessary funds on an annual basis to pay for candles and for those who participated at the altar or in choir in the services, extra pay being an incentive to encourage fulfilment of their liturgical duties. In the 1240s, for instance, ordinary members of the choir received two deniers for attending mass, but singers who 'organized' the alleluia were paid six deniers each.[33] Endowments for a specific feast were welcomed, but sometimes new feasts were funded out of general revenues of the bishop and chapter. With its vast properties and administrative operations, a secular cathedral such as Notre Dame of Paris in the early thirteenth century was probably the nearest thing in financial and management complexity to the headquarters of a large multinational company in today's world.

With increasing frequency during the course of the thirteenth century, royalty took an interest in commissioning and owning beautifully produced manuscript books.[34] Large psalters with full-page miniatures of Biblical scenes were perhaps the earliest type of personal book, giving way by the end of the thirteenth century to smaller, lavishly illuminated books of hours, but others of particular musical interest do make their appearance. The two most heavily illuminated Parisian manuscripts of thirteenth-century polyphony could well have been royal books. The Florence manuscript of Notre Dame polyphony – illuminated, pristine, and lacking corrections and other signs of use as a perfomance copy – has recently been posited as a royal book made for Louis IX.[35] And the Montpellier motet manuscript, the most beautifully decorated and largest collection of thirteenth-century motets, was in its Old Corpus (fascicles 2–6) very likely also a royal commission from the time of Philip III's second wife, Marie de Brabant, queen of France 1275–85, who brought with her from the north to the royal household a taste for secular music and culture, a notable change after the more austere years of Louis IX's reign.[36] Made near the end of the second decade of the fourteenth century, another Paris manuscript with royal connections is the earliest musical monument of the French Ars Nova – the distinctively different musical manuscript of the *Roman de Fauvel* (*F-Pn* fonds fr. 146). Unusual were its large three-column format, *ad hoc* insertion of miniatures and musical compositions, use of the cursive chancery script rather than the more formal and elegant Gothic bookhand, and scarcely veiled criticism of the king and his ministers as well as the hierarchy of the church. Although it was a book made in the royal chancery, its intended recipient is not known.[37]

An exquisitely elegant book most certainly produced for royalty in the 1340s is the first of Guillaume de Machaut's 'complete works' manuscripts, known informally as Machaut MS 'C' (*F-Pn* fonds fr. 1586). It is thought to have been begun for Bonne of Luxembourg, daughter of John of Luxembourg, King of Bohemia, Machaut's earliest patron in the 1320s and 1330s. Bonne was the wife of the Duke of Normandy, who subsequently became King John II of France (r. 1350–64), but she died unexpectedly of the plague in 1349 before the manuscript was completed. In the next decade it was probably finished for her husband. Although Machaut had more than 25 years of compositional activity still ahead of him, this first 'complete works' manuscript gives us an early look at almost all the musical genres to which he contributed, including motets and secular fixed-form pieces; only the mass and the 'David' hocket were yet to come.

As though it were an entertaining primer of instruction on courtly behaviour, Machaut's narrative poem *Remede de Fortune* from the 1340s – composed with Bonne of Luxembourg as both the model lady and the intended recipient – included in MS 'C' notated examples of all the secular fixed-form types of his day – the lai, the complainte, the chant royal, the baladelle, the ballade, the virelai (or chanson balladée), and the rondeau – as well as indications of their social setting. The virelai, for example, was most likely to be monophonic, danceable, and syllabic in text setting; in MS 'C', the noted monophonic virelai in the *Remede de Fortune* is illustrated with a miniature (No. 27) showing elegantly dressed courtiers, both men and women, holding hands while dancing in a circle and singing, without any instrumental accompaniment.[38] On the other hand, the rondeau was polyphonic from the beginning in Machaut's oeuvre, since both the example in the *Remede de Fortune*, which is the earliest rondeau in MS 'C', and his subsequent rondeaux all have three, two, or even four voice-parts. Here we should recall that polyphonic three-voice rondeaux first appeared in the later thirteenth century in the works of Adam de la Halle, and thus in this instance Machaut inherited the tradition. Similarly, it is evident that Machaut's musical composition began in the 1320s with isorhythmic motets and those of Philippe de Vitry as his model, yet once Machaut turned to fixed-form pieces in the 1340s, he ceased composing motets with French texts on themes of love, though he later turned briefly to 'occasional' motets with Latin texts.[39]

After Machaut became a canon at Reims Cathedral around 1340, according to the tax rolls he had a large house outside the cloister of the canons, and it was evidently a place hospitable to noble guests. We know that in 1361 the future King Charles V stayed with Machaut when he came to settle a dispute between the Archbishop of Reims and the city officials. Charles and his brothers John, Duke of Berry, and Philip, Duke of Burgundy, had grown up knowing Machaut in the household of their mother Bonne and their grandfather John of Luxembourg. Machaut composed several works apparently intended for Charles V – a rondeau for his wedding in 1350, the

Latin motet no. 22 in 1358, and the 'David' hocket for Charles's coronation in 1364. In his semi-autobiographical late poem the *Voir Dit* ('True Story'), Machaut refers to Charles repeatedly as 'Monseigneur', and it is possible that Machaut MS 'A' (*F-Pn* fonds fr. 1584) was intended for Charles. It is certain that more than a decade after Machaut's death in 1377, John of Berry commissioned the copying of Machaut MS 'E' (*F-Pn* fonds fr. 9221) in the 1390s as a book for himself.[40] All three brothers were great bibliophiles and amassed significant libraries.

Ownership of important musical manuscripts in the later thirteenth and fourteenth centuries is one signal that musical patronage was changing along with other features of society. Courts of royalty and the nobility across Europe began to employ musicians for their households and/or 'chapels', whether these chapels were peripatetic or stationary, in increasing variety. Whereas most earlier composers of polyphony had their livelihoods in the church, Machaut enjoyed support from both royalty and Reims Cathedral. At times in the latter part of his life, this secular and sacred patronage was simultaneous. When courts in the fourteenth century retained musicians, their duties tended to involve a mix of sacred and secular music; this was even true of the Avignon papacy which, despite its sacred mission, was noted for its lively patronage of secular music. A special example of courtly patronage is that of the brilliant and learned Gaston Fébus (or Phoebus), third Count of Foix (1331–91), himself a musician of substance.[41] But churchly support for musicians expanded, also, with such foundations as collegiate chapels[42] and even nunneries giving evidence of polyphonic performance.[43] Ultimately, despite the devastating ravages of the Black Death and the Hundred Years War in the fourteenth and early fifteenth centuries, the landscape of institutions offering support to musicians began to broaden significantly as the humanistic outlook of the Renaissance took root and began to flower.

16 Theory and notation

DOLORES PESCE

An overview of medieval theory involves three primary content areas: pitch, rhythm and counterpoint. Two far-reaching concerns of medieval theory surface time and again in this overview: early theorists continually attempted to understand an inherited repertory, chant, in terms of an evolving theory, and they tried to bring their own theory into congruence with venerated ancient Greek theory. Not unrelated, the writers searched for a satisfactory notation, both letters and music symbols, to transmit their repertory and theory about it. As we read these theorists' exposés, differences emerge in how they formulate and present their ideas. With respect to audience, teaching in the Middle Ages shifted increasingly from monastic settings to cathedral school and university settings. We also witness certain differences in genre presentation, including dialogues and compendia. Finally, it is useful to think of early theoretical writings in terms of categories set up by Claude Palisca: precompositional, compositional, executive (performance) and critical.[1] That is, theorists could engage in theory largely for its own sake, prescribe how to compose and perform, and describe/critique the music they were hearing in their respective societies.

Early Middle Ages

The writer who unquestionably exerted the greatest influence on medieval theorists was Boethius (AD 480–524). In *De institutione musica*,[2] one of four treatises he devoted to the quadrivium or the four mathematical disciplines, Boethius foregrounded an understanding of music in terms of numerical ratios: he interpreted musical intervals as consonant or dissonant in accordance with the simplicity of their ratios. Through Boethius the emphasis on unison, octave, fifth and fourth as perfect consonances entered the consciousness of the medieval mind.

Although Boethius had taken his harmonic science from the Greek writer Nicomachus (first–second century), he contributed his own thoughts on the classification of music and the definition of a musician. He divided music into three types: *musica mundana, musica humana* and *musica instrumentalis*. Thus, music determines planet movements and other natural cycles, harmonizes the body and soul, and is created by man through his voice or an instrument. Music, in essence, is a microcosmic reflection of the macrocosmic experience. Boethius also emphasized music's potential ethical power to influence human behaviour, an idea he had inherited from Plato. As to the *musicus* or musician, Boethius asserted that this individual (as opposed to one who composed or performed) applied his knowledge of music's principles to judging music compositions and performances – in short, the *musicus* exercised critical judgement. Although many medieval theorists passed on Boethius's definition of a musician, some challenged the elevated status of the *musicus* as opposed to a singer or *cantor* whose practical musical skills aided in the Christian act of worship.

The final aspects of Boethius's theory that affected medieval theory concerned letter notation and scales. Using a monochord to derive his tonal system, Boethius designated points on the string with the letters A to P; although he may have intended these letters in a theoretical sense only, some tenth- and eleventh-century manuscripts actually notated chant using A to P. Boethius also explained the Greek *tonoi*, or transpositions of the entire two-octave tonal system, each of which carried a Greek name such as Dorian, Phrygian, Lydian. Later writers appropriated these tribal names as designations for the medieval modes.

Three other pre-ninth-century writers deserve mention. Martianus Capella (first part of the fifth century) predates Boethius; his significance rests in having supplied a widely read allegory about the seven liberal arts, in which music was included.[3] Cassiodorus (ca485–580) was pivotal, with Martianus, in establishing the number of liberal arts as seven; he also argued that music theory could be founded on a quadrivial approach yet remain applicable to Christian practice.[4] Isidore of Seville (559–636) provided an account of musical terminology in his encyclopaedia on all branches of knowledge. Most important, he described music in the divine office, offering us a glimpse of musical practice at a very early date.[5]

From the seventh to the ninth century no new music theory appeared. Beginning in the ninth century manuscripts with some music notation survive. Charlemagne's politically driven educational and ecclesiastical reforms are discussed in Chapter 15, but the reforms' importance must be reiterated in a discussion of how music theory grew and notation took shape around this time. To guarantee that his kingdom would be strong, Charlemagne followed on Alcuin's late-eighth-century educational initiative, and furthermore promoted a unified liturgy, both textually and musically. Charlemagne wanted to disseminate throughout the Frankish kingdom the chant heard by his emissaries in Rome, the so-called Gregorian chant, whose development was credited to Pope Gregory I (590–604). Hence among the Franks the impetus grew to develop a musical notation and theory through which singers could be trained to read and sing the all-important music of the church.

As we turn to the ninth-century treatises, we recognize that none of the specific notational solutions they proposed was widely adopted. But some surviving ninth- and tenth-century manuscripts reveal a first step in notational standardization: they use musical symbols called neumes, probably derived from the Greek system of accents, indicating from one to usually four notes; the neumes themselves may be diastematic, that is, they indicate the pitch of notes by their vertical placing on the page (in the absence of ruled horizontal lines), or non-diastematic (which requires the singer to remember the relative directional movement from one neume to another). A handful of manuscripts from the St Gall monastery uniquely preserve neumes with performance nuances such as lengthening of note values, microtonal inflections, acceleration, etcetera Surviving chant manuscripts in general reveal a fair amount of uniformity in their pitch content, despite the regional notational dialects that emerged.[6]

Aurelian (fl. ?840), one of several ninth-century Frankish theorists, provides a view of plainchant repertory and its performance at this time. Unfortunately, he did not possess the nomenclature to describe with any accuracy what he experienced, so his treatise *Musica disciplina* is of limited use when we attempt to re-create his examples of modes, psalm formulas, and office and mass chants.[7] The slightly later anonymous *Alia musica* (ca900) deserves mention: it associated the medieval modes with the Greek tribal names and their associated octave species.[8] For some time, this appropriation was an isolated case, but use of the Greek tribal names eventually became the norm once a scalar understanding of mode took hold.

The third ninth-century writer is Hucbald (ca840–930), who wrote his *Musica* as a handbook for training young monks in psalmody.[9] *Musica* is organized in a cyclical manner, going through its subjects three times, each time elaborating them and compensating for the lack of a dedicated medieval music nomenclature: he asked the reader to recall chant melodies which illustrated his points; he referred to Boethius's A–P notation and even suggested adding some of the letters, in lower-case form, to neumes to pinpoint some pitches; and he proposed a kind of graphic notation in which syllables of chants would be placed between lines on a six-line staff, to which tone (T) and semitone (S) would be attached in the manner of clefs. Most important, Hucbald fruitfully began the process of discussing the tonal system that lay behind the chant repertory; provided with such a vocabulary, the singers could learn the chants more quickly. In essence, he introduced the idea of the tetrachord of the finals D, E, F, G as the primary building block of the medieval gamut, explaining it by reference to the Greek division of their tonal system by a different tetrachord; the medieval gamut is thus divided into 4 tetrachords whose pitches are separated by tone–semitone–tone (Hucbald's Greek names for letters are given below in their modern equivalent):

T	S	T	T	S	T	T	T	S	T	T	S	T	T
A	B	c	d	e	f	g	a	b	c'	d'	e'	f'	g'	a'

The final relevant ninth-century treatises are known as *Musica enchiriadis* and *Scolica enchiriadis* (reaching their standard form by the end of the century).[10] Both treatises serve as handbooks for training singers (hence *enchiriadis*), while the *Scolica* additionally presents the quadrivial rudiments. The *Scolica* was written as a dialogue between master and pupil, modelled after Augustine's *De musica*. The *Enchiriadis* treatises provided the earliest instruction in improvising organum or polyphony: organum consisted of a *vox organalis* moving in parallel movement with the chant or *vox principalis*, at the perfect intervals of an octave, fifth or fourth. A second type of organum grew from the practice of sounding a drone under the chant: the vox *organalis*, at first stationary (that is, in oblique motion), moves into parallel motion with the chant, then reaches a unison with the chant at the end. The *Enchiriadis* treatises presented their exposés using a variation of the notation Hucbald had proposed, namely, text syllables are placed in between lines. But in this case, the lines are prefaced by a system of clefs derived from manipulations of the *daseia* of ancient Greek prosody, hence the term *Daseian* notation. While the concept of a staff, albeit with notes on the lines and spaces, was to become standard, the *Daseian* symbols presented orthographic difficulties that prevented their widespread adoption.

Medieval music theory experienced a breakthrough in the late tenth century with the treatise known as *Dialogus de musica*, most likely written in the province of Milan by an anonymous monk.[11] Presented as a dialogue between master and pupil, the *Dialogus* codified the letters A B C D E F G with octave duplication as the standard nomenclature for the medieval gamut; the next octave was designated by lower-case a–g, culminating in aa to complete the two-octave span (below A lay Γ, hence the word 'gamut'). The tone b was inflected: it could appear as 'square' or 'hard' b (♮) and 'round' or 'soft' b (♭). One of the writer's pedagogical innovations was to promote the use of the monochord, whereby a singer could learn a chant quickly by imitating its intervals sounded on the monochord. Significantly, he contributed to the classification of chants according to mode, which also helped singers master the vast repertory. Following on Hucbald's ideas about the importance of the finals D E F G within the gamut, the *Dialogus* author identified their importance for modal recognition in the first clear definition of mode: 'A tone, or mode, is a rule which classes every melody according to its final.' That is, the final of a chant identifies its mode. Each of the finals is designated by a Greek number, as shown in column 2 of Table 16.1,

Table 16.1 *Finals and their modes*

		Alternative naming system
D	*protus*	modes 1 and 2
E	*deuterus*	modes 3 and 4
F	*tritus*	modes 5 and 6
G	*tetrardus*	modes 7 and 8

and each numerical modal category in turn can be subdivided into authentic and plagal, depending on the range of the melody: specifically, an authentic melody usually does not ascend more than an octave above and one tone below the final, while a plagal melody usually does not ascend more than a fifth, sometimes a sixth above, and a fifth below the final. (An alternative naming system shown in Table 16.1 simply assigned two numbers in order to each final for its authentic and plagal form.) Despite his spelling out of the ranges as quasi-octaves in order to distinguish authentic and plagal, the *Dialogus* author was not proposing a scalar concept of mode; clearly, a final could identify a melody's mode only by virtue of its distinguishing intervallic movement around that final tone: D *protus* moves a tone and a semitone up, a tone down; E *deuterus* moves a semitone and a tone up, a tone down; F *tritus* moves two tones up, a semitone down; G *tetrardus* moves two tones up, a tone down.

Often accompanied by the *Dialogus de musica*, Guido d'Arezzo's treatises (1026–33) were the most widely circulated music writings of the Middle Ages.[12] Since Guido devoted his writings to his thoughts on how to train a choir, probably in Arezzo, his works have little quadrivial content. The wide-ranging topics of his *Micrologus* include an introduction to the emotional qualities of the modes, a method for composing chant, the rhythmic performance of neumes, and a brief overview of organum. The latter suggests he witnessed the parallel organum described in the *Enchiriadis* treatises, but also a freer sort of parallel organum into which a higher degree of oblique motion had infiltrated.

The *Micrologus* also extended the discussion begun by Hucbald about the gamut's construction; although Guido did not use tetrachord terminology, he recognized that the interval set of the finals D E F G (tone–semitone–tone) was replicated at the fifth above on a ♭ c d and fourth below on A B C D, a relationship he referred to as *affinitas*. Guido recognized a practical aspect of this theory by stating that these related tones can serve as alternative finals or *affinales* (at least for a ♭ c) since they share the same configuration of surrounding intervals as the finals. In his *Epistola ad Michahelem*, Guido presented what is now a well-known pedagogical tool to aid singing, the hymn *Ut queant laxis*, whose lines' opening syllables are *ut re mi fa sol la*, matching up with the pitches C D E F G a. Although Guido did not discuss a second site at a ♭ c d e f, one can assume that he recognized it, since the core of these two six-note segments are, respectively, the four finals and the four affinales or *cofinales*, whose relationship he did acknowledge. Eventually, the two segments came to be known as the natural and hard hexachords, while a third segment with b flat, F G a ♭ c d, was called the soft hexachord. *Mi–fa* signalled the semitone in any of the three locations. The fundamental importance of the hexachordal concept in medieval musicians' thinking is reflected in the fact that from 1270 onward, some theorists, in discussing the mode of a chant, referred to a modal final by its pitch or by its *vox* or syllable, so that *re* signalled *protus*, *mi deuterus*, *fa tritus*, and *sol tetrardus*.[13]

Guido's final pedagogical contribution involved notation. By the late tenth century some scribes had begun to scratch onto the parchment a single line in relationship to which neumes could be arranged diastematically. What Guido seems to have promoted for the first time was multiple lines separated by a third. He also prescribed using letter clefs before certain lines or spaces, but a surviving manuscript from Dijon suggests that letter clefs (without lines) may have predated 1031. His third suggestion, unique to his writings, involved adding coloured lines to certain lines or spaces, notably those signifying C and F, the two notes in the gamut distinguishable by the semitone that falls below them. This last innovation manifested itself in European manuscripts from the eleventh to fourteenth centuries. Of course, the multiple-line staff based on the separating interval of a third has continued to the present day.

Two non-Italian theorists deserve some mention in this overview of early theory. A contemporary of Guido, Hermannus Contractus (1013–54) was a Benedictine monk associated with Reichenau. Hermannus mentioned the principle of *affinitas* as he knew it through Guido as well as his own interpretation, which grew from an eleventh-century Germanic emphasis on species of fourth, fifth and octaves as basic building blocks of the tonal system: that is, D E F G and a ♭ c d are identical tetrachords, an identity retained when one extends the core by one tone in either direction, yielding two identical six-note segments.[14]

The other non-Italian was Johannes Affligemensis (fl. 1100), most likely from southern Germany or northeast Switzerland. Johannes's *De musica*, essentially a reworking and expansion of Guido's *Micrologus*, diverged in its prescription for writing organum: Johannes favoured contrary motion in the newly composed voice.[15] Examples of free organum survive from the late eleventh century and became the norm in the twelfth century.

Early polyphony and mensural music

Whereas how to discuss, notate, and teach chant dominated Carolingian music writings, twelfth- and thirteenth-century theoretical writings turned to polyphony – how to improvise it, compose it and notate its rhythm. The theoretical endeavours were initially centred in Paris, whose cathedral of Notre Dame spawned a renowned body of polyphony and whose university attracted scholars and students to ponder man's achievements, music included. The scholasticism of Parisian thinkers at the time affected the cast of some music theoretical writings.

The music of the cathedral of Notre Dame survives in three main sources dating from considerably later than the repertory's conception between the 1150s and ca1200: W_1 (1230s), F (1245–55), W_2 (ca1260).[16] This gap between conception and transmission allows that the notation does not necessarily represent what was current at the time of conception. When we turn to the theorists for clarification, particularly of the rhythm, a similar disconnect occurs, since they too – Johannes de Garlandia (second quarter of the thirteenth century), the St Emmeram Anonymous (1279), Franco of Cologne (after 1279), Anonymous 4 (after 1279) – were looking retrospectively at the Notre Dame repertory.

Until recently Garlandia was thought to have written *De musica plana* and *De mensurabili musica*[17] as texts for the University of Paris; the most recent scholarship suggests they were probably the work of another, nameless author active about the middle of the thirteenth century.[18] Following the scholastic tendency to create classification schemata, this anonymous author presented a new consonance theory with three subdivisions: perfect (unison and octave); intermediate (fourth and fifth); imperfect (major and minor thirds). Dissonances too were imperfect (major sixth, minor seventh); intermediate (whole tone, minor sixth); perfect (semitone, tritone, major seventh). A similar classifying tendency led the author to present an elaborate working out of the rhythmic modes that underlay Notre Dame polyphony. The rhythmic modes, particularly relevant to the subspecies of polyphony called discant (where both voices are measured), were based on a common unit called the *tempus*. The *tempus* could appear singly (a short or *breve*), in a note twice its length (a long or *longus*), or three times its length (an extended long). Assuming a *tempus* of ♪, the six rhythmic modes were:

mode 1 ♩ ♪   mode 4 ♪ ♩ ♩.
mode 2 ♪ ♩   mode 5 ♩. ♩.
mode 3 ♩. ♪ ♩   mode 6 ♫♪

A discant in a given mode reiterates the succession of values proper to that mode. A glimpse at the Notre Dame sources does not in fact reveal all of the modes nor all of the variations on them that the author proposed.[19]

This same author explained the notational concept that underlay the rhythmic modes: the modal pattern is not shown primarily by individual note shapes, but instead by a combination of ligatures (neumes) and single notes of the 'square' plainchant notation that developed in France during the twelfth century. Each mode was identified by a particular succession of ligatures and single notes, as follows: first mode: 3–2–2 . . . 2; second mode: 2–2–2 . . . 3; third mode: 1–3–3 . . . 3; etc.[20] This notation relying on ligature patterns was appropriate only for melismatic passages. Even then, the author recognized its ambiguity, particularly for more complicated rhythmic substitutions, and made some innovative suggestions. But these were codified and applied more generally only through the influence of Franco of Cologne's *Ars cantus mensurabilis*,[21] hence the expression Franconian notation. Franconian notation specified a distinct note shape for a short value and the various forms of a long, presented rules for ligatures in standard and modified form, and created a set of graphics for rests. Thus mensural notation provided a reasonably unambiguous way to present rhythm in syllabic contexts. Once such unequivocal symbols were available, composers could move outside the confines of the rhythmic modes and their underlying adherence to triple metre. But most music continued for some time to be written under the influence of the rhythmic modes, as witnessed by the primary motet manuscripts from the later part of the thirteenth and early fourteenth centuries: Montpellier, Bamberg, La Clayette and Las Huelgas.[22]

Mention of the motet links back to the issue of polyphonic genres and styles. The writing previously attributed to Garlandia described *organum per se*, copula, and discant, three styles that coexist within a two-part organum (still the generic term for polyphony in the thirteenth century). Whereas discant is measured in both voices, copula has sustained tones in the lower voice (tenor) presenting the chant, while the upper organal voice uses the rhythmic modes; *organum per se* is distinguished by sustained notes in the tenor and a rhythm not strictly modal (*modus non rectus*) in the upper part (that is, the modal ligature patterns appear sometimes, but not always). *Organum per se* is thus not measured in the regular way that discant and copula are, and the treatise offered three not always compatible rules for distinguishing long and short notes in this species: they included judging the length of a note by its relative consonance with the tenor, and attending to its note shape. The explanations for interpreting *organum per se* given by the St Emmeram Anonymous[23] and Franco of Cologne are no less ambiguous. Consequently, the rhythm of these sections in Notre Dame polyphony remains conjectural in modern-day performances. Some scholars argue that a flexible approach is consistent with the rise of Notre Dame polyphony from an improvisatory tradition.

The three main Notre Dame sources contain conductus and motets, in addition to organum. Franco of Cologne referred to the conductus as the one type of liturgical music that was not based on a pre-existing melody. He mentioned the motet without defining it; in short, it is a genre that arose from texting the upper voice(s) of discant sections of organum, while the lower voice (the chant-based tenor) remained untexted. Conductus notation is problematic in that this syllabic genre required the use of single notes, whose as yet unstandardized shapes could not convey an unequivocal rhythmic meaning. The few comments offered by the theorists, together with a verse analysis of the poetic text, make it possible to come up with reasonable guidelines for rhythmic interpretation of the genre. Similar problems plague the early motets transmitted in the Notre Dame sources, but the genre attained clarity through the use of Franconian notation to varying degrees in the main motet manuscripts from the end of the thirteenth and early fourteenth centuries.

One final rhythmic development of the thirteenth century concerned shorter note values. Franco extended the basic relationship that governed the *long* (◼) and *breve* (◼) to the *breve* (◼) and *semibreve* (◆), that is, the principle of ternary mensuration. Petrus de Cruce (fl. ca1290) took the next step of introducing a notation that could allow other subdivisions of the *breve*: he accepted up to seven ◆ within the *breve*, subdivisions that could be shown by placing a dot of division (*punctus divisionis*) on either side of the grouping.[24]

Finally, the thirteenth-century treatise by Hieronymus de Moravia, written shortly after 1272, represents a new genre: a compilation made up of excerpts and a few entire treatises, ranging from Boethius to Hieronymus's contemporaries. Hieronymus was a member of the Dominican order, believed to have been active in Paris at the order's convent on the rue St-Jacques. He apparently compiled the work to help his fellow Dominicans to judge, compose and perform chant and polyphony, but he also addressed some precompositional concerns of quadrivial writers, including the science of harmonics. In Hieronymus's four *positiones* or theses on polyphony, he transmitted the mensural treatise formerly attributed to Johannes de Garlandia uniquely with chapters on three- and four-voice writing.[25]

The fourteenth century

France and England

Fourteenth-century theorists confronted two main challenges: how to expand the notational system to accommodate duple as well as triple metres and note values shorter than the *semibreve*, and how to contextualize the increasing number of accidental pitches appearing in polyphony. The latter concern at times took them into highly speculative realms, in which they expanded on the mathematical calculations of their Greek forebears. Some theorists also provided a critical, quasi-historiographical view of earlier music which was still being performed even as new repertory emerged.

The primary name associated with fourteenth-century rhythmic theory is Philippe de Vitry (b. ?Champagne, 31 October 1291; d. 9 June 1361), a composer and bishop who travelled in royal and princely circles from the 1320s onward. Although de Vitry was long considered the author of a treatise known as *Ars nova*, scholars now agree that while its teaching may be associated with Vitry and with the innovations of his compositions, its connection with him as author is tenuous. The treatise can be dated to around 1320 based on comparisons of its contents with other dated treatises.[26]

While the thirteenth-century motet repertory offered some isolated examples of duple metre, the fourteenth century witnessed its full-blown acceptance on an equal level with triple metre. This change in rhythmic profile is acknowledged by both the *Ars nova* and Johannes de Muris (b. diocese of Lisieux, ca1290–95; d. after 1344), the latter in his *Notitia artis musicae* of 1319–21.[27] The French notational system now contained four graphically distinct values: *long* (◗), *breve* (■), *semibreve* (◆), and *minim* (♦). The relationship of *long* to *breve* was termed *modus*, of *breve* to *semibreve* *tempus*, and of *semibreve* to *minim* *prolatio*. Each of these relationships could be ternary (perfect or major) or binary (imperfect or minor) and their combinations came to be known as mensurations. The signs for the four combinations of *tempus* and *prolatio* were attributed to de Vitry:

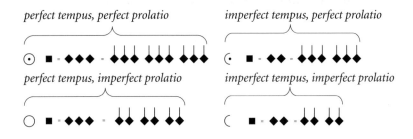

perfect tempus, perfect prolatio

imperfect tempus, perfect prolatio

perfect tempus, imperfect prolatio

imperfect tempus, imperfect prolatio

These signs did not attain much currency until late in the century. While the L had been the basic unit of the musical measure in the thirteenth century, the B took that role in the fourteenth century. Most upper-voice parts moved in a combination of *tempus* and *prolatio* as shown above, while lower-voice parts used *modus* and *tempus*.

The other notational innovation of the *Ars nova* treatise was the use of red colour to indicate a number of rhythmic changes. Where black notes were perfect, red signalled imperfect *modus* or imperfect *modus* and *tempus*; the roles of black and red could also be reversed. Furthermore, red could be used to prevent individual notes from being perfect or altered (that is, to fix their value regardless of context). Later fourteenth-century treatises begin to discuss dots: dots of division on either side of a group of notes indicated how many fell within the *breve*, while a dot of addition added half again to the value of an imperfect note, a usage it retains to the present.

Outside the realm of rhythmic concerns, several fourteenth-century treatises deserve mention. Walter Odington and Jacobus de Liège wrote significant compendia. The Benedictine monk Odington (fl. 1298–1316), an English theorist and scientist, dedicated part of his *Summa de speculatione musice*[28] to the quadrivial aspects of music theory, then turned to the practising musician, including sections on chant, a tonary, discant theory and notation, and a discussion of polyphonic genres. The *Summa* continued to be copied into the fifteenth century. Jacobus of Liège (born ca1260; died after 1330), a Franco-Flemish theorist, wrote his principal work, the *Speculum musice*,[29] probably in Liège, not before 1330, after he had spent most of his life in Paris. The *Speculum* is the largest surviving medieval treatise on music, containing 521 chapters arranged in seven books, of which the first five treat speculative music largely according to Boethius; the sixth deals with ecclesiastical chant, and the seventh discant. In the seventh, Jacobus defended 'ancient' practice according to Franco of Cologne versus the more modern rhythmic and notational usages he was witnessing. He commented specifically on how there had been a slowing of performance tempo to accommodate the smaller note values (*minims*) employed by the 'moderns', and he also weighed the relative perfection, subtlety, freedom and stability of the older and newer styles. Like Odington, Jacobus discussed various categories of polyphonic composition.

The issue of genres brings us another theorist who contributed a great deal to our understanding of medieval music and its performance contexts, Johannes de Grocheio (fl. ca1300) in his *De musica*.[30] Grocheio is linked to Paris both because his observations focused most pointedly on the practices of that city and because he showed a deep knowledge of Aristotelian thinking, which may have been garnered while he was a Parisian master. Grocheio's significance lies in his abandonment of the Boethian taxonomy of music that had been handed down for centuries. First, he rejected celestial music (Boethius's *musica mundana*), then set out his own classifications for Paris: *musica civilis* (music for laymen), *musica canonica* (music for clerics) and *musica ecclesiastica* (chants of the mass and offices). He rejected the dichotomy between measured and unmeasured music, saying that all music is measured to some degree. Whereas *musica canonica* included precisely measured polyphonic music such as the motet to be performed before individuals who could appreciate subtleties in the arts, *musica civilis* included a variety of monophonic music such as trouvère songs, rondeaux, epics, dances, and instrumental genres. Interestingly, when Grocheio described chants, he compared them to secular genres, perhaps suggesting the 'affective power of plainchant over the minds of clergy and laity alike'.[31] By applying to his generic taxonomy the Aristotelian practice of describing each subject three times, Grocheio offered a highly detailed and perceptive account of musical experience in his time.

Italy

Marchetto da Padova wrote his *Lucidarium* in 1317 or 1318 and the *Pomerium* shortly thereafter but no later than 1319.[32] Marchetto is a valuable source of information on the rhythm not only of Italian music of the early fourteenth century but of contemporaneous French music as well. The earliest surviving Italian manuscripts date from the mid to late fourteenth century: Rossi/Ostiglia and Panciatichi[33].

Italians based their notational system on a *breve* which could encompass 8 *divisiones* as follows, wherein the first option is to divide the *breve* into 2 or 3 *semibreves*:

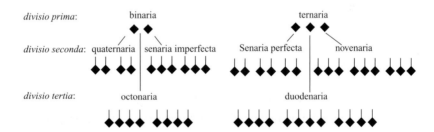

On the level of the *divisiones secunda* and *tertia*, the *semibrevis* carried an upward stem (we would call it a *minim*). A given grouping of notes within one *divisio* was marked with a dot on either side, a feature suggesting that Italian notation was related to Petronian usage. In some manuscripts, a piece's *divisio* was indicated at the outset by an abbreviation: .*q*.: *quaternaria*; .*i*.: *senaria imperfecta*; .*p*.: *senaria perfecta*; .*n*.: *novenaria*; .*o*.: *octonaria*; .*d*.: *duodenaria*.

This notational system was responsive to the fluid, melodic character of Italian music, characterized by chains of short note values, often in sequential patterns. It also allowed for adjustments and variations within a *divisio*, both through additional note shapes and contextual rules such as *via naturae* (when less than the full complement of notes are present in a *divisio*, long notes appear at the end of a group) versus *via artis* (larger values at the beginning or middle of the group, indicated by an altered *semibreve* shape). On the other hand, the system basically precluded syncopation across the *breve* unit. Perhaps because of this feature and because of Italian contact with contemporary French music which showed a predilection for syncopation, a hybrid notation developed. It combined French and Italian features, which scholars today call 'mixed' notation. In fact, many of the surviving Italian manuscripts that preserve fourteenth-century repertory are primarily in mixed notation.

Marchetto da Padova deserves further mention because he developed an influential extended theory of mode for plainchant. According to Marchetto, a mode is either perfect, imperfect, pluperfect or mixed, depending on whether its range is respectively normal, narrow, wide in the direction away from the mode's authentic or plagal partner, or wide in the direction of that of the partner. A further term, 'mingled' (*commixtus*), was applied when the mode in question showed qualities of a mode other than its authentic or plagal partner. In addition, Marchetto tackled the problem of explaining the increasing number of inflected pitches in Italian pieces by devising a division of the Pythagorean whole tone into five equal parts. His thinking represented a highly innovative, speculative extension of what had been passed down from the Greeks, and it opened the way to experiments in tuning and temperament in centuries to come.

The late fourteenth century

The end of the fourteenth century witnessed an extraordinarily complicated music and notation that has come to be known as mannered or Ars Subtilior, based on Philippus de Caserta's *Tractatus de diversis figuris* (ca1370), which referred to composers moving away from the style of the Ars Nova motets 'post modum subtiliorem comparantes' and developing an 'artem magis subtiliter';[34] similarly Egidius de Murino (uncertain dating) referred to composition 'per viam subtilitatis' in his *Tractatus cantus mensurabilis*.[35] The musical style demanded greater rhythmic complexities, primarily of syncopation and proportional relationships, to which end the two primary manuscript transmitters, Chantilly and Modena,[36] are filled with new note shapes, many of which have varied meanings from piece to piece and even within a piece. Red coloration, both filled and void, is used generously, and a beautifully decorated circle and heart convey the technique of canon.

This striking style developed in the secular courts of southern France, Aragon and Cyprus during the period known as the Great Schism. From 1309 to 1377 the papacy had been exiled to Avignon, but now the schism (1378–1417) produced rival popes in Avignon and Rome. The creative impetus in the realm of sacred music first associated with the papal chapel and rival cardinals' chapels now transferred to secular courts, which had available to them virtuosic singers and an intellectually sophisticated audience who were amused by both the notational and sounding complexities. The Ars Subtilior manuscripts include works by both French and Italian composers.

Mode and *musica ficta*

The theory of the eight church modes (*protus, deuterus, tritus, tetrardus*, each with an authentic and plagal member), conceived for plainchant, was regularly appended to medieval discant treatises although most did not establish any definitive link between composing counterpoint and modal theory. A continuous tradition applying mode to polyphony began only in 1476 with Tinctoris,[37] who worked with Marchetto's extended theory of mode. Tinctoris touted the tenor as establishing the mode for the polyphonic complex as a whole, though scholars interpret this to mean the soprano–tenor pair which together form most of the principal cadences. As for polyphonic music before Tinctoris, often one or two tonal foci inherent in the pre-existing tenor may be emphasized as a piece unfolds.[38] Sarah Fuller holds that a composer such as Machaut chose tenors not for their modal coherence, but for their distinctive tonal traits that could be developed through harmonic and linear means.[39] One can describe many thirteenth- and fourteenth-century pieces not so much as being 'in a mode', but rather as having certain tonal emphases.

Modern scholars refer to the issue of pitch inflections in medieval music as *musica ficta*. As explained earlier, the medieval gamut, allowed for the inflection of the tone b as hard b (♮) and soft b (♭). The entire gamut, including the inflected b, came to be known as *musica vera* or *recta*. From the ninth century onward, medieval theorists began to discuss tones they could not notate within their tonal system, at first referring to them as semitones outside the gamut, in the thirteenth century as *musica falsa*, and in the fourteenth century as *musica ficta* or *coniuncta*. Such tones could arise in plainchant, but theorists tended to concentrate on their occurrence in polyphony where they were essential to consonant contrapuntal writing;

this was particularly true in the fourteenth century when theorists placed greater stress on contrary motion and a controlled succession of imperfect to perfect intervals. A perfect interval is approached by a third or sixth, with a semitone movement in one part; thus, at cadences, an octave is preceded by a major sixth, a unison by a minor third, and a perfect fifth by a major third. Theorists linked ficta notes to producing such correct interval successions; for example, when the sixth B–G progresses to the octave A–A, either B or G would move to A by a semitone, requiring that one of them be inflected.

A few theorists from ca1300 onward distinguished the reasons for using semitones as *causa necessitatis* and *causa pulchritudinis*; the former apparently referred to the essential correcting of vertical perfect consonances (for example, making a diminished fifth perfect) while the latter referred to the 'colour of beauty' that resulted when a tone was inflected in the imperfect to perfect progression.[40] Beginning with the treatise formerly attributed to Johannes de Garlandia, the latter inflected tones are described as melodic 'leading notes' a semitone from their destination. More detail comes from Johannes de Muris who stated that lower returning notes (e.g. in the progression G–F–G) should be raised (G–F♯–G); and that leading notes approached by any other means (for example, by leap) should be raised. This concept of leading tones in imperfect to perfect progressions resulted in double leading-tone cadences in fourteenth-century manuscripts; in essence, two interval progressions are combined: a sixth to octave and a third to fifth, each with inflected tone.[41]

Medieval manuscripts do not always show pitch inflections in the very situations theorists described as requiring them. Most scholars accept that inflections were and should be applied according to a partly or largely unnotated tradition.[42] This viewpoint is supported by the late-fourteenth-century Berkeley treatise author: 'But these are frequently present virtually in BfaBmi although not always notated',[43] as well as several others slightly later. When signs were used, they were the same ones, ♮ and ♭, hard and soft b, that were applied to the tone b. Hard b signified *mi* and soft b *fa*, that is, they indicated where the semitone lies in relation to the sign, even when it occurs in a location other than in the three basic hexachords on C, F and G. By referring to inflected notes in this way, medieval writers revealed that the *ut–la* syllables served as the primary navigational tool for discussing their tonal system. Many scholars today hold that the syllables served the same purpose in practice.[44]

17 Music manuscripts

EMMA DILLON

Unless sounds are remembered by man, they perish, for they cannot be written down.[1]
ISIDORE OF SEVILLE

Of all the evidence we rely on to construct the story of the medieval musical past, the manuscript is the most important, but also the most capricious.[2] Not only are the extant sources just a tiny portion of the original bibliographic picture, but they also transmit repertories that were, in Nino Pirrotta's famous characterization, the 'tip of an iceberg, most of which is submerged and invisible'.[3] Created in a culture sophisticated in practices of memory and improvisation, the written record was one among many technologies for storing music. Moreover, the written record connects to oral practices in numerous ways: notation is a shorthand more than a prescription, assuming the invisible knowledge of a performer. Finally, writers from Isidore of Seville to Ingarden suggest a drastic distinction between inscription and performance: music exists in sound, and writing (on the page, or, in Isidore's case, in the memory) is a representation removed from musical reality.

If music manuscripts are incomplete witnesses to sound, they still have much to tell, particularly when we consider not just what they transmit, but also how they do so. 'Manuscript' is a retrospective designation that, as Peter Stallybrass reminds us, is only possible with the advent of print.[4] No mere truism, this distinction emphasizes the technologies and materials of textual production: manuscripts are made by the hand. From the fingers flow implements of inscription – pen, brush or rastrum; and, from these, ink, paint or the dry marks or prick points that produce a text-line; then to the surface – parchment (also referred to as 'vellum'), cut from the hides of sheep, goats, cows, or pigs. Beyond the writing surfaces are bindings, clasps or seals that encase or endorse the texts. Meanwhile, behind the hand lies a body of producers – scribes, illuminators, parchment makers, binders and compilers. Enfolded in the hand, then, are both the physical properties of written texts and the agency of those who assemble these materials.

'Manus' thus invites contemplation of manuscripts not just as conduits of texts but as objects whose materials inflect the reception of the things they contain. From the economic value of raw materials to the subjective agency of the scribe, production shapes sense; or, as bibliographer Donald

McKenzie has it, 'forms effect meaning'.[5] Two examples can illustrate that dictum. The earliest music books, produced in the monastic foundations of ninth-century Europe, and containing their most sacred liturgies, were not only objects of reverence or reference, but also part of a monastic micro-economy. Parchment production coexisted with provision for housing and slaughtering livestock. The ninth-century statutes of the abbey of Corbie make a rare allusion to a parchment maker, and, in considering his job description, Rosamund McKitterick conjures in flesh-crawling detail the practicalities of production:

> Skins, if they are to be of any use for parchment making, must be fresh and put to soak soon after the animals have been killed . . . Corbie's own livestock included cattle, sheep, goats and pigs, so that there was the potential for a regular supply of skins. Whether skins for parchment making would only have been available at particular killing seasons is not known, but it seems most likely. The season of the year in which the animals are slaughtered determines the fat content, and thus the quality, of the skins. The possibility cannot be excluded, moreover, that some centres imported their parchment from a supplier who was able to work in close proximity to an abattoir, rather than preparing their own skins.[6]

The cost of livestock necessary for usable parchment helps explain why contemporary inventories of monastic treasuries located books alongside precious reliquaries, icons and devotional objects.

Outside the monasteries and royal houses of the early Middle Ages, manuscripts would have been little known. By the thirteenth century, production of manuscripts was increasingly more public and commercial, with university cities such as Paris, Oxford and Cambridge hosting a lively book trade. In Paris, the 'orchard of books',[7] books were evident to anyone who passed through the city gates, literate or illiterate. Some would have known manuscripts only as the stink of parchment shops on Rue neuve Notre Dame, the street running up to the cathedral; for others, books were a geographical marker – Rue des Escrivains, like many Parisian streets, took its name from those who worked there.[8] At a minimum, then, books signified urban commerce.

In what follows, we shall need to keep in mind McKenzie's proposition, and examine ways in which the physical remains of lost sound encode in their very materiality a little of the values and meanings of music in the world beyond their bindings. But there is also a more practical purpose: to examine what makes a music manuscript different from other kinds of manuscripts, and what were the specific technical demands required to position music on the page, and to organize repertories across folios. As we shall see, the look of music could be determined by a host of motivations, from the banally practical to the eloquently expressive. Where possible, manuscripts cited exist in modern facsimile, and readers are directed to the bibliography and New Grove 'Sources' article for full citations.

Reading music manuscripts

Forms

The main form in which medieval music survives is the book, which in the Middle Ages most often took the form of a codex (as distinct from the book roll).[9] Before going further, it will be helpful to describe some of the bare essentials, and essential vocabulary, associated with codices. Closing the covers of a manuscript, and tipping its spine up for scrutiny, the naked eye can usually see an even, clustering pattern of parchment folios, as if into mini-books within the book. These mark the arrangement into gatherings (also known as 'quires'), which, Christopher de Hamel argues, 'is probably the single most important observation that can be made about the making of medieval books'.[10] Produced from large sheets of parchment (treated animal hides), gatherings were made by placing sheets on top of one another, normally with hair side facing hair side, and flesh side facing flesh side (the flesh side of parchment is more velvety to the touch than the waxier, sometimes bristly hair side). These were folded in half, the groove of the fold later being sewn to secure the leaves, and trimmed to size. A gathering normally comprised four bifolia, a total of eight folios (also described as a quatern or quaternion), although three-, five-, six- and even eight-sheet gatherings were also sometimes used.

The gathering was the unit by which scribes and artists operated. Inscribing onto unbound gatherings, it was possible for scribes, notators and illuminators to work simultaneously, with a scribe passing on gatherings he had finished working on to the next in the production line, while moving on to inscribe the next gathering. To keep track, scribes used catchwords (the first word of the following gathering was written at the very end of the gathering preceding), or even numbering or lettering systems, traces of which are often still visible. Sometimes, gatherings never made it to the binders. The texts circulated in individual gatherings, or in gatherings sewn together to form the unit of the libellus, or fascicle. As we shall see, these more ephemeral forms of circulating texts are particularly important in the history of music transmission.

Despite uniformity of design, the same materials, ordered in the same structures of gatherings, and transmitting the same musical texts, could produce radically different effects. Placing a gradual of the ninth century, small enough to fit in the hands, next to a huge, table-top-sized missal of the fifteenth century, so heavy as to need two people to heave it from shelf to library desk or lectern, the sense of how 'forms effect meaning' is never more evident. While the books contain the same melodic material, the visual impression communicates the texts in different ways. One suggests intimacy, privacy, and singular access; the other implies communality and display, designed to be big enough for its notations to be seen by a group standing at some distance.

Size is just one variable. The *cantatorium*, one of the oldest liturgical service books, often took unusual and precious forms. *Cantatoria* had an elevated status, containing some of the most important chants of the liturgy, those sung by the cantor during the mass (graduals, alleluias or tracts; some also contain solo tropes, or the verse portions of chants intended for solo performance). Their form articulates that special role. Early, unnotated examples were inscribed in silver and gold on purple-dyed parchment, colours of economic and symbolic prestige.[11] Others have a distinctively thin, spindly format, and spectacular bindings. *CH-SGs* 359, dating from the early tenth century and the earliest to contain musical notation, has long, delicate ivory covers that are widely accepted to predate the contents by several centuries. Carved with images that have little to do with the sacred contents (scenes of combat), the covers nonetheless appear to have dictated the shape of this codex: the ivories were a precious part of the monastery's treasure, and part of the book's function was to furnish an opportunity both to display that collateral, and also, perhaps, to mingle the earthly value of its exterior with the mystical, liturgical purposes of its contents.

The codex was by no means the only musical form. Music also circulated in unbound units, either of sheets, gatherings or libelli. This is particularly relevant to understanding the transmission of liturgical polyphony and non-liturgical traditions. Medieval compositions do not take up much physical space – a sheet or two at most – and for a composer or singer wanting to copy down a new piece, a sheet or notebook could be an inexpensive solution (and, practically, easier to perform from than a cumbersome book).[12] What is more, these free-floating 'ephemera', as Andrew Wathey designates them, are intricately bound up in book making, their relationship being one of 'interdependence'. The libellus or sheet could contain excerpts of a larger book, and some extant manuscripts are nothing more than bound compilations of once-independent libelli. Missals, for example, which brought together all the texts and chants of the mass, evolved as a consolidation of smaller, discrete books that together had performed that function. The earliest missals from the eleventh and twelfth centuries are little more than a binding together of separate, smaller books – gradual, sacramentary and lectionary. In the thirteenth century, some French chansonniers include once-independent fascicles of songs in their final compilation. Many books, however, cover their tracks, and are the copied consolidation of a process of material assembly and design of assorted ephemera now long gone.

Occasionally, though, books offer a snapshot of that process: the study by Wulf Arlt and Susan Rankin of two early St Gall tropers (*CH-SGs* 484 and 381) illustrates how the books' scribe puzzled over how to transform small, independent written sources for a growing repertory into the finite form of a book.[13]

Another important musical surface was the book roll, or *rotulus*, which, like the codex, had a history dating back to antiquity. Although produced with the same raw parchment material, the roll is read, referred to, and handled in a very different way from a codex, being designed to be scrolled through, rather than flipped back and forth. Made by sewing sheets of parchment together, the blocks of texts in a roll do not, however, correspond to the leaf of a book: texts were copied to be read vertically, with page-like units often spilling over the parchment joins, and with just the face side used (although in the later Middle Ages it was common to use the verso, or dorse side, too). While the codex supplanted the roll as the more popular form around the fourth century, rolls persisted, but in the early Middle Ages their use was often confined to special ceremonial occasions, signifying gravity and prestige. Most musical rolls date from a later period, when the roll had assumed a more practical function; like the sheets and libelli, rolls were an ideal and cheap way to transmit individual or small compilations of music. The fourteenth-century *GB-BER* sel. 55, containing a collection of English polyphony, neatly captures that more practical, disposable quality of the later roll. The music is copied onto the dorse of a roll whose face contains a series of household accounts dating from a couple of decades before the music was added.[14] The roll's double function is vivid illustration of the sheer economy and pragmatism often associated with parchment use. By contrast, the 'exultet' rolls popular in southern Italy from the tenth to the fourteenth centuries illustrate how music could participate in the more solemn function of the early roll.[15] These magnificent objects contained texts and notation for a portion of the Easter Vigil, and their use was thus limited to a one-off ritual appearance each year. Adding to their prestige was the tendency to illuminate them, but in inversion to the liturgical texts: as the deacon or celebrant sang from the roll, with text and music facing him, he unravelled the roll to reveal images upside-down from his perspective, but the right way up for those listening and watching. Conscious of their own innovative technology, some of those images are self-referential, depicting rolls unfurling from the pulpit, complete with their topsy-turvy layout.

Finally, a word about some more unusual sites of music inscription. Notation could serve a decorative function, serving as a kind of musical wallpaper. A much-quoted passage from the early-fourteenth-century *Chroniques de France* states that the great lord and trouvère Thibaut de Champagne composed songs and 'had them inscribed in the chambers of Provins and Troyes' ('les fist escripre en la sale a Provins et en celle de Troyes').[16] Although no physical traces of such wall paintings at either location survive, a romance from roughly the same period, the *Roman de Fauvel*, describes the genres and notational details of the music painted on the palace walls of its fantastical hero, the horse-king Fauvel. Contemporary archaeological evidence relating to the palace of the late Capetian kings, the model for the satire, indicates that wall decorations were part of the decor, suggesting a lost reality behind the *roman*'s fantasy palace.[17] While musical writing on the wall in these examples has a symbolic or heraldic function, making the culture of the court visible to those who visit, there are some later 'sources' that fall between the poles of decoration and use. The Philadelphia Art Museum has a collection of musical knives from the late fifteenth century: each blade is etched with a short line of polyphony which, when the blades are assembled, form the voices of a four-part benediction.

While music manuscripts adapt to the forms of other sorts of texts in the Middle Ages, the technology of musical notation represented unique challenges to the scribes and compilers responsible for the folio-by-folio organization of texts. In the next section I will trace some of the main modes of designing music on the page: far from being exhaustive, my purpose is to select from a range of periods and repertories, to illustrate just how different the look of the musical book could be. It will be helpful to adopt a medieval framework for thinking about the design of the book: this loosely conceived writing at the micro level, according to the layout and order of individual folios (or *ordinatio*), and at the macro level, according to the organization or order of things at the level of the codex (or *compilatio*).[18] As we shall see, both in their different ways have an impact on the meanings of the texts: at the technical level of performance, but also at the hermeneutic level – in determining what the reader understood the text of music to be.

Designing music
Service books

How did the earliest scribes and compilers conceive of a space for music on the page? Like most successful revolutions, the emergence of music writing (in service books of the ninth century) involved a minimum of change. The earliest music scribes were pragmatic in their efforts to make space on the page for notation. Neumatic lines first appeared in places traditionally given over to commentary, afterthought or correction: in between text lines, and, less frequently, in the margins. In some early sources, no provision was made for music in the pricking and ruling of the folios. The layout of text was undisturbed by the presence of simple accent neumes inserted between lines spaced with the same regularity as non-notated books. As notation became more widespread and prescriptive, folios were subject to more systematic preparation for the insertion of melody. Again, though, older, pre-notation systems of page design were barely disrupted by the presence of music.

The text line remained the governing unit of page division, and music was simply assigned lines originally occupied by text. If allocation of space was a relatively simple matter, scribes faced more complicated challenges at the moment of inscription, particularly with regard to the spacing of text to allow for vocal melismas. In *CH-E* 121 (1151), a compilation of graduals, with assorted processional antiphons, texts and proses, dating from the late tenth century, neumes sit comfortably in *campo aperto*, positioned roughly halfway between two lines of text, as if hovering around an invisible text line. However, throughout the book melismas (characteristic in the chants of the gradual) consistently creep out into the margins, as the scribe struggles to make verbal space wide enough to accommodate melodic expanse.

Neumes in these examples make no use of vertical space to indicate pitch relations. With the emergence of diastematic notations, the ghostly text-line (or text-lines) over which music was copied were put to new use as a fixed pitch reference, turning gaps between texted lines into a pitch-sensitive space. Even before systematic use of the staff (as envisioned by Guido of Arezzo around 1030), a number of notational systems deployed the text-line as a basic tonal reference point. From the late tenth century, certain Aquitanian manuscripts ruled lines within the music space in dry-point as pitch reference.[19] The staff's institution thus exploited what was already available in the language of books. Indeed, in two-staff systems like those found in many Beneventan sources, the use of two-colour staves (red and yellow) to mark different pitch points took advantage of another book-ish technology – using ink's expressive capabilities now to communicate musical information (for a sample of Beneventan notations see *I-BV* 34, 38, 39 and 40). What we often perceive as musical-theoretical innovations are thus bound into the broadest context of writing: indeed, we could go so far as to say that the staff is the work of a bibliographer as much as of a theorist.

While developments in notational technology did little more than modify the basic graphic ingredients, the form and order of liturgical books underwent constant change. Although there is not space here to detail the many genres of service book, it will be helpful to make a broad distinction between the function and order of books of the earlier Middle Ages and those more common from the thirteenth century onwards. Many early notated books were defined by highly specialized function, and often by the person using them. The sacramentary mentioned above is a case in point: it was limited to texts and chants relating to the mass and was used exclusively by the celebrant. Likewise, the pontifical, the earliest examples of which date from the tenth century, contained rites relating exclusively to bishops. Although books with a more comprehensive function were also common in the earlier Middle Ages (for example the gradual, containing mass propers), the small format of many implies a fairly limited use, perhaps restricted to the cantor, who would consult the book and then teach its melodies to the choir. However, not all service books were designed for exclusively practical purposes. Examples of manuscripts produced for the abbey of St Gall include some containing not only bibliographic staples like the gradual, but also sequences and writings attributed to the abbey's own Notker the Stammerer (ca840–912). The abbey also produced some of the earliest tropers (such as *CH-SGs* 484), likely composed *in situ*. Such codices are more than just reference tools: they are archives of an erudite and creative musical monastery tradition.

There is significant change both in the format and in the function of service books in the later Middle Ages. Two of the most popular books from the thirteenth century were the missal and the breviary, encyclopaedic and comprehensive compilations of text, chants and instructions relating to the mass and offices. While versions of both had been around since the eleventh century, their importance (and complex design) grows in ensuing centuries. Designed to do the job of several books at once, they often rely heavily on abbreviation, multiple ink colours, and a variety of script sizes to communicate information about texts, chant, ritual movements, and performing forces. With barely a patch of parchment left unfilled, these books reflect broader advances in the complexity of book design in the later Middle Ages; we should situate them in the landscape of the great glossed bibles of the thirteenth century, or the encyclopaedias and *florilegia* that were renowned for their innovative systems of organization and navigating technologies.

Early polyphony

Roughly around the time of Guido's *Micrologus*, another technological challenge emerged: that of how to represent music in more than one voice. Early sources reflect a range of solutions: solutions that, as with chant, often demonstrate a surprising lack of disruption of older writing habits, and that suggest a conceptualization of polyphony not as novelty but as a facet of chant. While theorists had described polyphony well over a century earlier, in texts such as the *Musica enchiriadis*, the earliest written source dates from the first half of the millennium. *GB-Ccc* 473 is one of two manuscripts (the other is *GB-Ob* Bodley 775) containing tropes, proses, sequences and other liturgical chants made for the Benedictine house at Old Minster in Winchester, and known collectively as the Winchester Tropers.[20] *GB-Ccc* 473 also contains 174 organal settings, appearing alongside tropes, proses, sequences and a fascicle of alleluias, all organized according to the order of the liturgical year. Thus, the design programme makes clear that the addition of a new voice, the *vox organalis*, to the older chant voice, the *vox principalis*, was understood within a liturgical framework, as a form of the trope.

Described as 'both a treasure and a tragedy',[21] *GB-Ccc* 473 provides only the *vox organalis*: the chant voices to which the newly created voices were set are all absent. Moreover, the notation is English non-diastematic neumes, typical of the rest of the manuscript, and, at this early stage in the history of notation, devoid of any kind of rhythmic indicators. While difficult for the modern scholar to decipher, early readers would have known the chant and, most likely, the organal voices by heart. The book, then, can be understood as part memory prompt, and part repository for the melodic treasures of the institution.

By the twelfth century, polyphony began to look very different. In the four Aquitanian sources loosely known as the 'St Martial' manuscripts (*F-Pn* fonds lat. 1139, *F-Pn* fonds lat. 3549, *F-Pn* fonds lat. 3791, and *GB-Lbl* add. 36881, also often referred to as *St-M A–D*), the need to notate both voices was inevitable, given that at least half of the roughly seventy pieces extant included versus that had a newly composed *vox principalis*. While polyphony once again shares space with monophonic additions to the liturgy, the sense of 'liturgical' is here considerably looser than in the Winchester manuscript, as liturgical order is abandoned in the organization of the versus.

The two distinct styles of polyphony – note-against-note discant style, and the florid styles that would eventually come to be known as *organum purum* (where the *vox organalis* performed lengthy melismatic flourishes over a static lower voice) – posed practical problems to which scribes responded with a range of solutions. The first important difference when compared to *GB-Ccc* 473 is the score representation. The same dry-point ruling as we saw in the monophonic chant books prevails here, with clefs and in some cases custos marks (small notes at the ends of lines to indicate the first note at the beginning of the next line). Now, though, voices are aligned over one another, and in some cases the distinction between the two parts is made visible by use of a dividing line, often in red ink. But score is just one solution. On one occasion, in *F-Pn* fonds lat. 3791 (*St-M C*), the two voices appear on different parts of the folio. On another, in *F-Pn* fonds lat. 1139 (*St-M A*), two Benedicamus settings have the unusual design of having both voices on one staff. In both instances the polyphony takes the florid, organum purum style, which means that there are only a few notes in the *vox principalis*. The scribe distinguishes them from the *vox organalis* by notating them in red ink in one setting, and marking a circle around the notes of the second setting.

However, the books in this repertory are far from consistent in their presentation of polyphony. It is in the thirteenth century that we witness a systematic, professional method for copying music that was outside the remit of the traditional chant manuscripts. And little wonder. The famous compendia of Notre Dame repertories are contemporary with the establishment of a commercial book trade in Paris, and right at the doors of the very cathedral whose music was inscribed on their folios.

Magnus liber organi

The thirteenth century bears witness to a repertory synonymous with the book. Anonymous IV's celebrated account of the musical tradition of the Paris cathedral characterized it as a 'Magnus liber organi', deploying 'liber' in the sense of 'opus' or repertory, but also perhaps in a material sense. Referring to liturgical polyphony associated with the generation of Leoninus and his successor Perotinus, Anonymous IV's musical descriptions match portions of several extant manuscripts, the earliest dating from the third or fourth decade of the thirteenth century. The main sources of Notre Dame polyphony embody an important change in the history of music manuscripts. Comprehensive – even dogmatically encyclopaedic – in their range of music, these new collections also deploy elaborate and varied new systems of *compilatio* and *ordinatio*. There are also numerous correspondences between manuscripts: not just a high degree of concordance, but also many precise shared features of design and layout, hinting at a tradition of music outside the realms of liturgical chant.

The design of *I-Fl* Plut. 29.1 (commonly referred to as *F*), which dates from the 1240s, illustrates some of the main technological advances in the material life of this repertory. It reflects a summatic attitude to its diverse musical contents, in part via sophisticated systems of ordering: the manuscript is organized in a series of libelli or fascicles within the *liber*, defined by genre and, where appropriate, liturgical function. Beginning with forms with a strictly liturgical context, organum and clausula, it progresses through genres with increasingly tenuous liturgical connections (conductus and motet), concluding with a collection of Latin refrain songs. Each fascicle is subject to careful planning, the earliest shadowing the order of service books – arranging pieces according to liturgical order of the temporale and sanctorale. Within genres, the scribes create order through number of voices: pairing organum with clausulas of the same number of voices, it opens with the great quadrupla setting *Viderunt omnes*, and ends with two-part settings. That the manuscript was regarded as more than purely functional is emphasized by the illuminations. Exquisitely decorated throughout, *F* begins with a statement of purpose, a threefold depiction of Musica, reflecting the threefold Boethian notion of music known through the university curriculum and contemporary music theory. This explicitly theoretical gesture thus frames the collection as 'music' in the sense of the quadrivium, as well as of a practical, singable collection.

While the many different genres in the book may suggest a challenge for the scribe, the mechanics of making *I-Fl* Plut.29.1 (*F*), as other books of this tradition, were not as complex as one might imagine. Although the scribes moved between score format for organum and clausula settings, and successive layout for the texted repertories, folios were ruled throughout according to a simple rule of thumb. In scored sections (organum, clausula and polyphonic conductus), tenor or chant voices were generally ruled with a four-line staff, and all other voice-parts with five lines, with regular amounts of space left between staff blocks to accommodate text underlay (see Figure 17.1); scribes left blocks of space at the end of conductus settings for additional text verses, to be set to the preceding music (see Figure 17.2). Notice also how the decorated capital also serves to beam. In the monophonic and motet sections (where voices were copied successively), pages were ruled up with staffs of five lines, and with uniform space between each for text; chant tenors were tucked in at the end of each motet (see Figure 17.3).

While there is continuity of repertory across the four main sources (*I-Fl* Plut. 29.1, *D-W* 628, *D-W* 1099 and *GB-Lbl* Egerton 2615, also commonly referred to as *F*, *W₁*, *W₂* and *LoA*), there is also consistency – and sometimes interesting change – in the organization. Most of the manuscripts open with four-part organal settings, following the same liturgical sequence witnessed in *F*. However, while the motets in *I-Fl* Plut. 29.1 (*F*) are organized according to the liturgical order of their tenors (reflecting the original status of the motets as clausulae), motets in *D-W* 1099 (*W₂*) are not only more extensive and linguistically diverse, including French-texted works, but are also ordered according to a new priority: they are arranged alphabetically, a shift that suggests a loosening of liturgical associations in this genre. At the same time, certain continuities of page set-up suggest close relations between manuscripts. Mark Everist's in-depth palaeographical study not only of the main sources but also of more fragmentary traces demonstrates precise consistencies down to the very dimensions of the written block, number and proportions of staff lines, pointing not only to the possibility that existing manuscripts were copied from a common exemplar but also, more intriguingly, indicating 'evidence of a systematized, and perhaps professional production of music books in Paris between ca1240 and ca1300'.[22] For the first time outside the main service books of the liturgy, then, we have something approaching a tradition of musical book production.

Contemporary with the multi-genre compendia associated with Notre Dame are other more specialized compilations. I shall deal with vernacular chansonniers presently, but closely related to the Notre Dame repertories are the motet-only collections of the thirteenth century (of which *F-MOf* H. 196, *D-BAs* lit. 115, and *F-Pn* n.a.f. 13521 are classic examples). Although

Figure 17.1 Florence, Biblioteca Medicea Laurenziana, Plut.29.1, fol. 12r

generically independent of the earlier tradition, some motet collections nonetheless gesture to their heritage. The Montpellier Codex (*F-MOf* H. 196), created in the final decades of the thirteenth century, contains a rich assortment of motets at all stages of the genre's development. Organized into eight fascicles, each ordered by voice number and language, and

Figure 17.2 Florence, Biblioteca Medicea Laurenziana, Plut.29.1, fol. 205r

Figure 17.3 Florence, Biblioteca Medicea Laurenziana, Plut.29.1, fol. 411r

moving in a roughly chronological sequence stylistically speaking (old to new), the book begins with a fascicle largely devoted to organum (including pieces transmitted in the Notre Dame manuscripts), a brief retrospective gesture to the musical origins of the motet genre that ensues. Moreover, as Montpellier illustrates, the emergence of new motet forms in as many as four voices inspired new column-format page design, in which different voices were visible simultaneously, not in score, but in parallel-column voice format. Although scribes did not always coordinate voices to correspond with folio turns, the technology of column format in this and other motet compendia marks a significant broadening of the visual vocabulary of medieval music, one that would have far-reaching consequences for the layout of music in the later, choirbook formats of the fifteenth century.

Chansonniers

At the same time that scribes were standardizing the Notre Dame repertories, another repertory was starting to appear in manuscript. The thirteenth century is also the epoch of the chansonnier – retrospective compilations of vernacular lyrics of the troubadours and trouvères in France, and Minnesang of Germany, and the vernacular devotional songs comprising the *Cantigas de Santa Maria* of the Iberian peninsula.

Before examining the forms of the chansonnier, we must consider a startling absence of written evidence: there is a considerable time lag between the moment at which songs were created and their first extant written record. The earliest of the forty chansonniers containing Occitan song all date from the middle of the thirteenth century, with the biggest wave of production occurring in the fourteenth century – well over a century after the period of the earliest troubadour for whom songs survive, Guillaume IX, Duke of Aquitaine (1071–1126), and a good fifty years after the main period of troubadour activity.[23] Although trouvère chansonnier production (the earliest date from ca1250) coincides with the active life of trouvères such as Adam de la Halle, the earliest Northern poets had likewise been dead for almost half a century by the time their songs were written down.[24] How, then, did the repertory survive prior to writing? While memory was undoubtedly a major factor in songs' survival, some scholars speculate that internal evidence of the poems, where the poet-protagonist alludes to notating songs, implies a situation in which songs were written down, most likely on rolls or song-sheets, whose ephemerality may explain their loss.[25]

Chansonniers reflect their temporal distance from the originary moment of their songs in numerous ways: although there are important differences between the transmission of northern and southern French traditions, their creators were united in their awareness of themselves as history makers. As William Burgwinkle writes, chansonniers were not just records for performance but were 'complex and encyclopedic, documenting not just the lyrics but also the lives of the poets, the development of the genres'.[26] Such perspective requires a certain amount of distance. Moreover, in the case of the troubadours, there is an added geographical distance between the chansonnier makers and the Occitan origins of the songs: the majority were produced in northern France and Italy, the Italian chansonniers reflecting a quasi-antique taste for the long-vanished cultures of Occitan in culture-driven courts such as the Visconti.

What of the forms of the chansonniers? Not all are notated: indeed, melodies of troubadour song survive in just four sources, two of which contain predominantly Northern repertories; there are likewise numerous text-only trouvère chansonniers. The absence of melody may again reflect the books' distance from a living performance tradition. Those with melodies are fairly consistent in the format of their music. Songs occupy either one or two columns per folio; the first strophe only is notated, with subsequent strophes copied out beneath, often in prose format, with punctuation and small decorative capitals to mark strophe breaks. Figure 17.4 carries a typical example. Taken from the opening folio of the Chansonnier Cangé (*F-Pn* fonds fr. 846, also referred to as *Trv O*), it begins with the first notated strophe of Thibaut de Champagne's *Ausi com unicorne sui* at top left, followed by unnotated strophes (marked in all but one case with a coloured capital letter); his second song, *Amours me tant comment*, begins at the bottom. It is not uncommon to see gaps left for staves, or simply empty staves: lacunae suggesting that scribes had not yet access to musical exemplars when they inserted texts. We see a vivid example of gaps left for songs in Figures 17.5 and 17.6, from the Chansonnier du Roi (*F-Pn* fonds fr. 844, referred to also as *Trv M*), dating from the 1260s or 1270s. In a section attributed at the head of the folio to '*Vidames de Chartres*', notice the empty parchment following the song *D'amours vient*, spilling over to the top of the verso. Because of the simple syllabic or neumatic style of vernacular song, scribes did not necessarily need access to exemplars to determine text spacing: notice that the text underlay in these two manuscripts is more spacious than for the prose sections, but essentially evenly paced and roomy enough for the style of melodies in this repertory.

Perhaps the most fascinating aspect of chansonniers is their complex systems of organization, which tell a story about the songs – about the poets, about the cultural world of song, and about a tradition (its chronology and genres). In the Occitan tradition, the biographical component of song was heightened by the inclusion of prose vidas and razos, short lives

Figure 17.4 Paris, Bibliothèque nationale de France, fonds français 846 (Chansonnier Cangé), fol. 1

of the poets, and vignettes explaining the real-life scenarios that prompted the creation of a given song (as in *F-Pn* fonds fr. 22543, referred to also as *Trb R*).[27] Authorship is also the guiding principle in many trouvère chansonniers, and extends to the German Minnesang tradition. In many

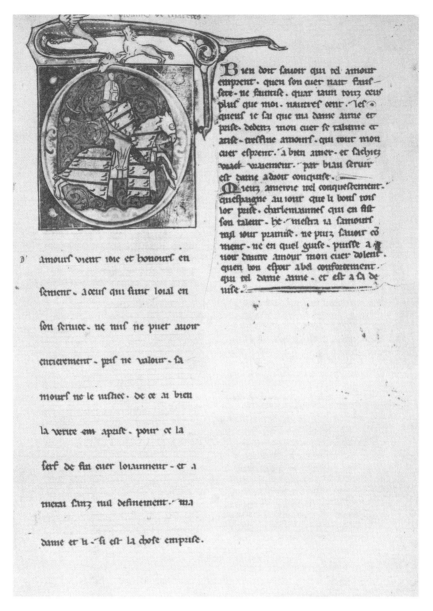

The manuscript text reads:

Bien doit savoir qui tel amour
emprent. quen son cuer nair fauf-
fere. ne faurait. quar iaun touz ceu
pluf que moi. nautref cent. lef
queuf ie fai que ma dame aime et
prife. dedenz mon cuer fe ralime et
arife. treffine amourf. qui tout mon
cuer esprent. a bien amer. et fachiez
vraiement. par biau servir
eft dame adouf conquife.
Mieuz ameroie tel conqueftement.
queffpaigne auiour que li bouf toit
lor puit. charlemaunef qui en fit
fon talent. he mestra la famourf
uil tour pramif. ne puiz fauoir co
ment. ne en quel guife. puiffe a
uoir dame amour mon cuer dolent.
quen bon espoir abel confortement.
qui tel dame aime. et eft a fa de
uife.

D' amourf vient ioie et honourf en
fement. a ceuf qui funt loial en
fon feruice. ne nuf ne puet auoir
entierement. prif ne valour. fa
mourf ne le uftice. de ce ai bien
la verite em aprife. pour ce la
ferf de fin cuer loiaument. et a
merai fanz nul definement. ma
dame et li. fi eft la chofe emprife.

Figure 17.5 Paris, Bibliothèque nationale de France, fonds français 844 (Chansonnier du Roi), fol. 14r

cases, songs are arranged by poet, an arrangement enhanced in some cases by red rubric names and small author portraits to mark the beginnings of each mini collection. Authors are often arranged by social rank, with the noblest poets listed first: trouvère collections invariably begin with Thibaut de Champagne (as in the Cangé example, Figure 17.4), the so-called 'prince' of poets, or Roi de Navarre, and conclude with gatherings of anonymous songs. The Chansonnier du Roi often adds to the sense of social order with

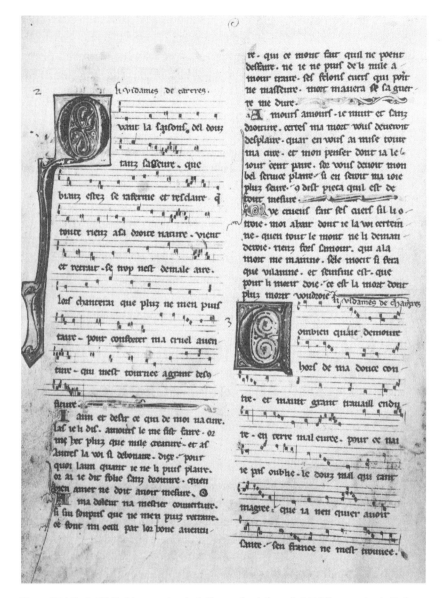

Figure 17.6 Paris, Bibliothèque nationale de France, fonds français 844 (Chansonnier du Roi), fol. 14v

the inclusion of heraldry in its surviving illuminations. Moreover, certain authors may have circulated separately. In the Chansonnier de Noailles (*F-Pn* fonds fr. 12615, also known as *Trv T*), for example, the songs of Thibaut may originally have formed a separate libellus: the dimensions of the layout as well as the foliation set them apart from the rest of the book.

Authorship was not the only compilatory rationale. The Chansonnier Cangé, for example, organizes songs alphabetically, according to the opening incipit of the song. However, within each letter, songs are generally ordered by author. In the example shown in Figure 17.4, for example, the opening collection of Thibaut de Champagne ('Roi de Navarre') begins with songs that start with the letter 'A' (*Ausi, Amours*). A final mode for organizing song was according to genre, an ordering that suggests ways in which book design was theoretical as well as practical: defining genre in the act of writing connected book production to the intellectual enterprise of treatises such as Johannes de Grocheio's *De musica*, from the early fourteenth century, which takes a similarly encyclopaedic look at music, defining it genre by genre.

The chansonnier was just one form of song transmission. Another important context was within the lyric-interpolated romances of northern France, the most famous of which is Jean Renart's *Roman de la Rose*, dating from ca1227, in whose prologue the author declares an intention to notate songs for posterity. The ensuing romance gives incipits for a number of well-known troubadour and trouvère lyrics, but in the only extant source no notational provision is given. Other romances have an interesting means of signalling the presence of a song, often just as an incipit or line, rather than the complete lyric. They are inked in red, or indented, or marked off with capitals; only occasionally are they fully notated. Song's presence, then, may be felt in a number of manuscripts we do not traditionally think of as being musical.

The later Middle Ages

While the fourteenth century is often cited as the start of an Ars Nova, the 'new' often implied no more than a fresh sense of the 'old'. Retrospection and historical awareness in contexts of change shape attitudes not only to notation and musical design, but also towards the material. Chansonniers containing repertories long past their performance life continued to be produced, while older books, secular and sacred, took on new status as collectors' pieces, finding their way into the libraries of the great and the educated. While scribes devised new ways of designing music on the page, there was also continuity, with occasional, self-conscious citation of older systems of organization. One book to embody awareness of past forms in a spirit of innovation is *F-Pn* fonds fr. 146, containing a famous version of the *Roman de Fauvel*. Produced in Paris in the second decade of the fourteenth century, the manuscript contains a range of music from older-repertory chant and conductus to state-of-the-art motets. The encyclopaedic scope also extends to design. As well as the *roman* the book contains a collection of songs, attributed to Jehan de Lescurel, that has a classic alphabetical chansonnier format. Within the *roman*, scribes, working with the constraints of fitting song into written narrative, deployed a range of systems for copying

Figure 17.7 Paris, Bibliothèque nationale de France, fonds français 146, fol. 1r

polyphony. In Figure 17.7, the scribes use familiar column format for presenting three two-part motets, tucking tenors in at the end of each duplum
voice. On the verso, Figure 17.8, we see a design that is by contrast highly
unconventional, responding to the demands of images and text on the page,
and also to the musical style of the motet. The three voices (each marked
by a decorated capital) are copied separately, the triplum beginning lower
left, the motets upper right, and the tenor again at the bottom of the centre

Figure 17.8 Paris, Bibliothèque nationale de France, fonds français 146, fol. 1v

column. The scribe mainly drew staves column by column, each block separate from the next. However, like many motets of the early fourteenth century, the triplum has more words, and also a faster, more note-filled musical line. The resulting, complex spatial problems were resolved by adding an extra line of staves at the very top of the central column, where the triplum continues; and, most dramatically, by ruling four sets of staves across two columns, so the scribe could copy the concluding section of the triplum across the space.

By the middle of the fourteenth century, the composer, poet and *clerc* Guillaume de Machaut was overseeing the compilation of his life's work. Accounting in part for why he is sometimes known as the last trouvère, Machaut's books echo earlier, single-author compilations (such as *F-Pn* fonds fr. 25566, the Adam de la Halle manuscript). At least four of the six main Machaut manuscripts were copied during his lifetime, probably with Machaut's direct involvement. The earliest, *F-Pn* fonds fr. 1586, referred to also as *MachC*, dates from ca1350; *US-KAferrell* (*Mach Vg*) dates from ca1370, while *F-Pn* fonds fr. 1585 (*MachB*), a copy, was made shortly after; *F-Pn* fonds fr. 1584 (*MachA*) dates from just prior to Machaut's death; *F-Pn* fonds fr. 22545–6 (*Mach F–G*) and *F-Pn* fonds fr. 9221 (*MachE*) postdate the composer. There is a *vita*-like quality to the chronological ordering of works in the manuscripts, so that they simultaneously document the history of a creative life. Moreover, recent work by Elizabeth Eva Leach and Anne Walters Robertson suggests that the order within individual lyric units determines and reflects narrative and musical connections between works. There is also a fascinating meshing of authorial and scribal identities. In *F-Pn* fonds fr. 1584 (*MachA*), for instance, the composer assumes scribal authority in the paratextual incipit 'Vesci l'ordenance que G. de Machaut vet qu'il ait en son livre'. Meanwhile, among the numerous author portraits that decorate the books, we see Machaut in a variety of poses, emphasizing that composition is linked to writing: in his atelier, book before him, or in a pastoral setting, quill in hand, roll unfurling over his knee.

Echoes of chansonnier-like forms are heard as late as the fifteenth century. While the troubadours and trouvères were by now a distant memory, a manuscript such as the Squarcialupi Codex (*I-Fl* Palatino 87) illustrates how older systems of manuscript organization still had relevance. The book is organized by composer, in a chronological sequence, beginning with some of the earliest trecento composers and extending to those active at the time of the book's production. Each section begins with an author portrait whose attention to attire communicates information about the author's social or ecclesiastical rank; authors' names run as headers in coloured ink across each opening. The book thus functions as a chronicle of trecento song, while the costume and attires remind the viewer of the specific world from which those song makers come – the order of song reflecting and enhancing with its luxury and coherence the social world of the book's makers and consumers.

The books described thus far are the exception rather than the rule: they are luxury items, demanding a team of artisans to produce, and made with a specific patron in mind. Moreover, their emphasis on order suggests that they were made to an explicit design, probably determined by a compiler, or someone overseeing the whole project. By contrast, many manuscripts of this period are far from luxurious, and far more haphazard in their design. The mid-fourteenth-century Ivrea Codex (*I-IV* 115), containing a collection of Latin and French motets, and a corpus of liturgical polyphony, came together almost by accident. Produced by two scribes, with a third filling in remaining space at a later stage, its gathering structure suggests that it started out as separate libelli, which were only later constructed into a single book.[28] We cannot know who determined its assembly, or why. Yet the story of *I-IV* 115 is indicative of a fluidity and opportunism in the compilation of musical repertories.

Scribes and compilers of the later Middle Ages faced challenges that reflected not just changes in reading habits but also shifting geographical and political identities. In an era of papal schism, war, peace and international treaties, and with expanding trade routes, the world became suddenly more accessible, and culture flowed down its newly opened routes. While many have written of the so-called international style in music of this period, internationalism also has a material correlate. Many of the great trecento sources are truly bilingual in their juxtaposition of French and Italian song traditions, with scribes switching between formats and notations. The Panciatichi Codex (*I-Fn* Panciatichiano 26) is an excellent illustration of these hybridities (along with the Reina Codex, *F-Pn* n.a.f. 6771). Combining repertories that overlap with manuscripts such as the Squarcialupi Codex, and the French-repertory Chantilly Codex (*F-CH* 564), it documents the many musical, notational and visual languages of music, a snapshot of the flexibility of the period. Like the Ivrea Codex, the book was an ongoing project, with numerous scribes participating in its production well after the first main scribe finished work in the 1390s. Its musical contents are, not surprisingly, rather broad, with concordances with some of the oldest trecento manuscripts, including the Rossi Codex (*I-Rvat* Rossi 215); it also contains a large corpus of French polyphony, including ballades by Machaut. Frenchness was present, too, in certain scribes' tendency to translate Italian notational language into French. The shift into different conventions for visual disposition of voices and texts could sometimes lead to visible confusion. For example, the ballade format, particular to the French corpus and visually distinctive on account of its musical reprise, was sometimes taxing to Italian scribes who were unaccustomed to its conventions for underlaying the musical return.[29]

Paradoxically, in an age of hybridity and experimentation, the other lasting achievement of music writers of this period was the creation of a uniform language for the layout of polyphony. By the end of the fourteenth century, the standard procedure was now to distribute one voice per folio, abandoning the older column formats we saw with the thirteenth and early fourteenth-century motet compendia. The legacy of this choirbook format would be far-reaching, extending beyond the culture of parchment and into the era of print.

Traces

Music books, particularly the non-liturgical kind, often had short shelf lives. However, medieval attitudes to books were ferociously economical, and old books were habitually dismembered and reconstituted in service of the new. Among these discards are echoes of lost musical repertories. The recent supplement to the *RISM* (*Répertoire international des sources musicales*) volume of sources of polyphony from the British Isles, a tradition notoriously sparse in its sources, reads like a chronicle of bibliographic massacre, of books systematically torn apart to become binding leaves and spine reinforcers or wrappers, or scraped clean to make surfaces for new texts.[30] Part of manuscript studies, then, is the examination of traces: locating, extracting and scrutinizing history's tattered leftovers, extrapolating from them spectres of books vanished for ever. Yet with the forensic work of palaeography, and with analytical techniques to interpret the musical lines that remain, it is possible to reconstruct forms of lost choirbooks to rival Old Hall (*GB-Lbl* add. 57950),[31] or to trace the movement of French Ars Nova motets to England.

Traces prompt other questions. Why do some books survive and not others? Were books kept for their material value alone, or were certain repertories felt to be 'classic'? Does a book's survival necessarily mean its contents were still performed? In short, can the survival patterns of books tell us anything about the values, meanings and uses of the repertories they contain? In the case of English polyphony, the questions are tricky, given the extraordinary erasing effects of the Reformation on liturgical practice, musical and otherwise. However, evidence can occasionally offer more concrete insights. The scribe of *I-Bc* Q15, an early-fifteenth-century Italian compendium, returned to add to and edit his work over several years: as pieces seemed outdated to his taste, he cannibalized them by excising decorated capitals and pasting these into newer sections.[32]

Other kinds of evidence help in determining value. Like other material goods, manuscripts had a meaning beyond their practical use: the very substance of their production could be accounted for, as prized possession, as practical transaction between patron and producer, and, more often than not, as yet one more item to be inventoried in the goods and chattels of a library or household treasury. This evidence is not only useful for revealing what books were 'worth' (inventories often ascribe to them a monetary value), but can also tell us about circulation and ownership. Once again, such evidence frequently records absence: part of the picture of English polyphony is gleaned from inventories of books that no longer exist.[33] For example, inventories point to the existence of at least one additional notated *Fauvel* text, cautioning us about overemphasizing the uniqueness of *F-PN* fonds fr. 146;[34] in the later fifteenth century, they reveal that the same manuscript was in the hands of none other than the French king, François I.[35]

In the case of the Notre Dame repertory, evidence of lost manuscripts points not only to an international taste for the music, but also an interest in it after it ceased to be performed. Investigations into inventory accounts of organum by Rebecca A. Baltzer and Peter Jeffrey gather evidence for as many as seventeen lost sources for the Parisian repertory in addition to the extant sources.[36] A sense of the repertory's prestige and international reputation may be inferred from those who owned copies: books of organum are mentioned in England in the household of Edward I and in the possession of one William de Ravenstone, who was a schoolmaster at St Paul's, London; elsewhere, copies surface in the library of the popes from Boniface VIII and his successors, and in the library of Charles V of France. As Baltzer points out, mere possession of a book does not necessarily mean the repertory was performed – indeed, in many cases there is no evidence to support such a claim – however, in the case of Edward I's book 'we can only assume that Edward or some member of his family felt that these books were worthwhile to own, whether this feeling was prompted by the manuscripts themselves or by having heard such polyphony performed'.[37] On the other hand, Baltzer's investigation of accounts of two modest books of organum at the Sorbonne in Paris makes the convincing argument for the use of books in performance. Not only are the books themselves cheap by comparison to others in the inventory (and therefore likely to be preserved for purposes of performance rather than material pride), but the bigger picture of the liturgy of the Sorbonne, gleaned from extant liturgical books, points to a shared liturgical usage with the cathedral of Notre Dame. If the Sorbonne shared the main liturgical use, it is all the more likely that, in such close proximity to the cathedral, and within easy reach of its singers and books, the college also adopted its prestigious musical traditions; 'from a liturgical standpoint, Notre Dame organum would have been perfectly appropriate in the Sorbonne chapel'.[38] Finally, evidence of the treasury inventories in Notre Dame itself details where, precisely, books were positioned in the cathedral, allowing us to imagine books back into practical and ceremonial positions within the ritual space.[39]

Future bound

What does the future hold for medieval music manuscripts? After more than a century of cataloguing, describing and editing, what more can they yield? Indeed, the seeming limitations of manuscript studies – bounded by the finite nature of the object's materiality – has become a theme within medieval studies in the past couple of decades, and also in caricatures of medievalism by those outside the discipline. Traditional philological methodologies for contextualizing and editing manuscripts have been described as fetishistic, driven by a 'neurotic obsession' to generate hard facts from the concrete evidence, and as the antithesis to the plurality of meaning advocated in the theoretical and critical climate of the start of the twenty-first century.[40]

While such characterization has of course provoked dispute, the 'philology versus interpretation' debate has nonetheless generated fruitful new directions in manuscript studies. One trajectory has been to look back, not just to medieval contexts for manuscripts, but also to the emergence of philology. Across medieval studies, this historiographical turn has resulted in studies of disciplinary origins, many under the aegis of the so-called New Philology or New Medievalism. Work by Bernard Cerquiglini, Michael Camille, R. Howard Bloch, Hans Gumbrecht and Kathleen Biddick, in particular, historicizes the philological movements of the nineteenth century, suggesting that the 'science' of textual criticism and codicological analysis were part of highly contingent and politicized discourses of the time, and illuminate scholarly formations that continue to shape the questions we ask even today. The afterlife of manuscripts is also a lens through which to view other historical narratives: manuscript sales in the nineteenth and twentieth centuries lead us into the world of bibliophiles such as Pierpont Morgan, the Rothschild family, and more generally into the place of the Middle Ages in the cultural aspirations of early Americans. Music is part of these stories; at the same time, the historiography of music books leads us to the foundations of the entire discipline, as Katherine Bergeron's study of the nineteenth-century chant revival at Solesmes illuminates. There, efforts to resuscitate liturgical rites for practical use via editing and studying chant manuscripts fostered traditions of musical study that endure today.

Reappraisal has also inspired a new kind of hands-on interpretative approach, in which differences between sources of the same text are celebrated as evidence of creative agency rather than of human fallibility in the act of copying. Donald McKenzie's edict, that 'forms effect meaning', has been realized in a number of recent case studies that approach the variance of text, illuminating, design, order and layout of books as expressive. Sylvia

Huot's studies of French literary and lyric repertories exemplify ways of seeing the book as a kind of performance, a theme taken up still further in Ardis Butterfield's recent monograph on French song. Meanwhile, the significance of the compilatory order of Machaut's opus has been newly emphasized by Anne Walters Robertson's work on his motets.

The early years of this century also mark a revolution within more traditional philological methods. No matter how rich the new critical approach to manuscripts may be, practical challenges persist: despite their extraordinary resilience, books are organic objects, and in a constant state of decay. Even with the sophistication of modern restoration techniques, librarians face ethical issues in keeping books available for reading: to read is ultimately to participate in a book's demise. As a result, 'originals' are now less accessible. Yet in another sense manuscripts have never been more visible. In place of originals, there are ever-crisper photographic reproductions, while innovations in digital imaging, computer technology and the internet create a major new forum for consulting manuscripts. In the past decade, research libraries have not only increased the number of books they reproduce digitally, but have turned more and more to the internet as a site of access for their holdings. In the United States, projects such as the Digital Scriptorium are burgeoning: hosted by a consortium of academic institutions and funded by national arts foundations, the Digital Scriptorium, free and accessible to all, brings images and catalogue descriptions of a range of medieval sources to life at the click of a button.[41] In the more specifically musical domain, the Digital Image Archive of Medieval Music aims to make available all sources of English music, and is constantly added to as new discoveries are made.[42] The virtual realm thus makes more efficient traditional kinds of philology: in the space of the screen, leaves and fragments detached from the same book centuries ago, now held in different libraries, sometimes on different continents, can rub shoulders again, while the digital technology permits us to 'see' manuscripts with a clarity that is denied the naked eye or magnifying glass.

Let us conclude by returning to the opening citation of this chapter. Writing at the cusp of a technological transformation of music, Isidore of Seville imagined the unimaginable – a world in which sound did not decay. Despite his seeming denial of a materiality in music, it is possible that he had in fact glimpsed strange, wispy signs hanging over words, the first indicators of vocal sound, and that affirmation of sound's perishability was a resistance to the possibility that inscription could be an aesthetic equivalent to living sounds.[43] Little could he have known how the signs of song would solidify into the range of forms that became the written tradition of music. Perhaps we detect a hint of awe in Isidore's rumination: awe at the incredible notion that music could exist and endure in realms that were more tangible than memory, less fleeting than performance. Perhaps we may relate to that sense of possibility, and feel in our own epoch the insinuation of another conceptual transformation of the stuff of music. As our eyes adjust to the new clarity of the past flickering on our computer screens, we cannot but wonder what lies ahead for musical sound, and wonder (like Isidore) not only at conceptions of sound beyond our experience, but also at new, as yet unthinkable ways to re-vision or experience afresh what has long since passed.

18 The geography of medieval music

CHRISTOPHER PAGE

The space where medieval music happened: the Latin West

In the 1290s an Italian friar travelled through part of what is now Iraq and found a Latin missal on sale in Al-Mawsil, north of Baghdad. The book had undoubtedly been looted from a church in one of the last Crusader possessions, probably from the port city of Acre that fell in 1291. The missal was the token of a failed endeavour to carry the ritual music of the Latin West to the Holy Land and to install it there. By the time the first Crusaders took Jerusalem in 1099, a shared body of Frankish-Roman or Gregorian chant for the mass arose whether it was night or day, and regardless of the normal patterns of sleep and sustenance, from western Spain to Hungary and from Scandinavia to Sicily. The intention had been that conquests in Palestine and Syria should become part of this Latin-Christian territory forever, and when the Crusading enterprise collapsed another Franciscan complained that 'there is only the abominable melody of Saracens where there should only be psalmody'. The muezzin and minaret had silenced the cantor and the bell tower.[1]

The medieval music addressed in the *Cambridge Companion to Medieval Music* is essentially the liturgical and vocal music, both sacred and secular, of this Latin and Western civilization. It was performed in a particular geographical space and shaped by its patterns of communication, by its shifting political configurations and even perhaps by its many and varied ecologies. Figure 18.1 shows the principal territories at issue. Bounded on three sides by water, this space corresponds to the lands where Alexander the Great had no interest in making conquests and where Greek was therefore never imposed as the language of administration and literature. Under the Roman Empire, and indeed long afterwards, Latin was the principal language associated with a functional literacy in this Occidental space and, as a result, Latin was also the only language used for Christian worship, whether for readings or for the massive repertories of sacred song, in contrast to the linguistic pluralism of the Eastern churches.

To a considerable extent, this Latin Occident acquired its medieval form by accident, or rather through major territorial losses. It is easy to forget that one of the richest and most important territories in the Christian West

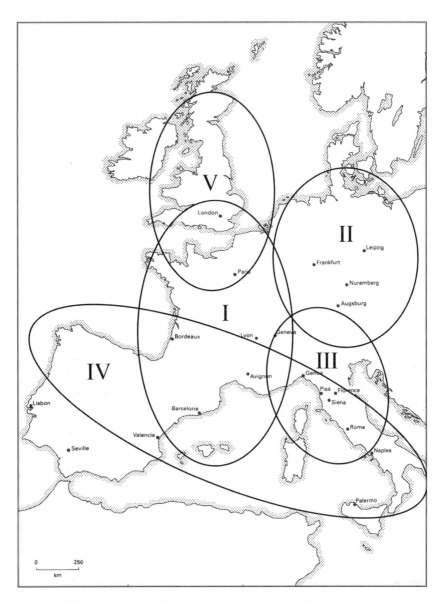

Figure 18.1 The geography of medieval music expressed as circuits of communication and long-term political history (I: West Frankish; II: East Frankish; III: Alpine Gate; IV: Romania south; V: Anglo-Norman)

once bordered the Sahara and vanished in 698. This was the Christian civilization of Roman, Vandal and then Byzantine Africa, strung out along the narrow lowlands from Tunisia westward to Morocco (approximately the part of Africa shown in Figure 18.1). In botanical and ecological terms, this coastal band is unmistakably of a piece with Mediterranean Europe. The significance of Africa's removal from the medieval Mediterranean system can be gauged from the riches that the littoral provided while it was still

Latin and Christian. The earliest reference in any document to the psalmody of the fore-mass, destined to be of capital importance for the evolution of Western musical art, appears just after 200 in the Latin writings of Tertullian and relates to the Catholic liturgy of Carthage. The history of the chant later known as the gradual, in other words, opens in Africa. Examples between the third century and the fifth could be multiplied up to the time of Saint Augustine (bishop of a provincial African city) and beyond. A case might be made that the cradle of the Western and Latin-Christian space lies not in Rome but in Carthage, and therefore in a city whose ruins stand today in Tunisia.[2]

Much of Spain was also lost to the same invaders in 711, marking the western extreme of an expansive wave that saw Islamic armies in Pakistan the following year. The conquest of Spain drove the Latin-Christian civilization of the Visigoths to the north, and when it fell this kingdom was in full flower. Ruled by Catholics from 589, Spain was highly creative in matters of liturgical music (the names of several composers are known) and could produce a scholar such as Isidore of Seville (d. 636) whose *Etymologies* remained a fundamental work of reference for a thousand years. The Visigothic civilization was also remarkably self-contained; its bishops in the 600s undertook far-reaching reforms of liturgy and chant with only the most passing reference to Rome. The kingdom possessed a palace administration, indeed a palatine culture, funded by the land tax and based in the royal capital of Toledo, such as kings elsewhere in the West could only envy. Had Spain not fallen, the musical achievement of the Carolingian Franks (see below) might appear in a very different light.[3]

The circuits

Figure 18.1 shows the principal circuits of communication and long-term political history that shape the surviving medieval music. It cannot be stressed too strongly that this map has been drawn with reference to what survives in notation, with results that reveal a slippage between the notational record and major currents in the social, political and ecclesiastical history of the Middle Ages, to say nothing of musical life in the broader sense of all music making, regardless of whether it has left a deposit in notation or not. The immense contribution of Ireland to the monastic and spiritual history of the medieval West, for example, fails to register on this map because there are virtually no notated remains from medieval Ireland. In the same way, the rich evidence of Irish (or Icelandic) minstrelsy, mentioned in literary sources, does not register, because there is no notational record of medieval date.

These circuits are not geographical in a sense that can be explored with a physical map showing mountains, rivers and coasts. Both the Pyrenees and the Alps are crossed, and it is not the Rhine that separates I from II but a broader zone of overlap approximately corresponding to Lotharingia (> *Lorraine*), a product of Frankish politics with no logic in either nature or the frontier between Romance and Germanic speech. Indeed, these circuits do not follow any linguistic boundaries save in the very approximate sense that I is largely an area of Romance speech and II of Germanic. Nor is there much in these circuits one could trace with a modern political map. They do not follow the boundaries of nation states formed in post-medieval Europe, and therefore pull away from the nineteenth-century tradition of interpreting Western European history in terms of peoples with an ethnicity expressed above all in relationships of language to territorial home, viewed as the foundation for nation states. Circuits I and II, for example, do not define a nascent France or Germany; the 'French' zone reaches too far south and the 'German' zone is inextricably linked to III as the Holy Roman Empire. To some extent, these circuits follow ecological lines more closely than any others. Most of circuit IV corresponds quite well to what botanists and climatologists define as the Mediterranean environment in Western Europe. Circuits I, II and V mostly fall in temperate Europe, and although I has a considerable southern reach its core political name, *France*, was still confined to lands north of Lyon as late as the seventeenth century.

I The West Frankish circuit
Between the sixth century and the ninth, when a new political order of kingship was consolidated in the West, circuits I and II defined the largest and most powerful polity in existence, namely the kingdom of the Franks. Charlemagne's conquest of Lombardy and his acclamation as [Western] Roman Emperor in 800 annexed III and created the Carolingian Empire. The foundational music of the Western musical tradition, namely Gregorian (or, better, 'Frankish-Roman') chant, was developed here between ca750 and ca850 in churches of the Carolingian core such as the cathedral of Rouen on the lower Seine and the abbey of St-Denis near Paris, but more consistently in the eastern reaches of I where the Carolingians were most at home, notably at the cathedral of Metz but also perhaps at heartland monasteries such as Prüm, refounded by Charlemagne's father, Pépin. It is certain that at least one Roman singer came north to teach Frankish pupils. This was at Rouen, a vital port where commodities brought by barge traffic could be unloaded onto sea-going vessels, but there are other reports of ninth-century singers travelling between the Frankish kingdom and Italy using the Alpine Gate (III). The Gregorian music spread into other circuits in ways to be described below, creating a truly Western European repertory whose

melodic idioms and sense of musical line were to saturate the hearing, the artistic imagination and the musical articulacy of Western musicians for centuries to come.

Many new compositions were created here for the liturgy between the ninth and the eleventh centuries. Chant composers can be traced by name at Auxerre, Chartres, Corbie, Fleury, Montier-en-Der, St-Riquier and Sens, among other places, together with centres showing a vigorous northeastern reach such as Gembloux, Liège, Metz, Toul and Trier. The sequence appears to have emerged from circuit I in the earliest layers of this activity, but since music for the mass was otherwise a more or less closed repertory of Gregorian plainsong the aim of these composers was often to compose tropes (verbal and musical additions to an existing Gregorian composition) or to create office chants, antiphons and responsories, for new or revived cults of saints. Their most ambitious project was to create a complete matins service, both the readings and the chants, producing a complex assemblage of music, poetry and prose that was often undertaken in a conscious effort to improve on the quality of older materials. (The sense of wielding a superior Latinity, a gift of the Carolingian Renaissance, was thus a vital spur to composition.) These office chants rarely achieved a wide circulation because the saints honoured were often of little fame elsewhere, but they could make a major contribution in a local context. The city of Mons, for example, grew around the family seat of the counts and the church of St Waudru; a count translated the relics of Saint Veronus there in 1012 and soon afterwards the monk Olbert of Gembloux composed a set of matins chants, at the count's request, for the Feast of the Translation. In gratitude, the count and his wife donated lands to Olbert's abbey. Thus the monastery, the power of the comital family and the nascent settlement of Mons prospered together, and new chants helped to foster all three.[4]

The rise of Gregorian chant in the northerly districts of I, and the sheer density of composers traceable there, firmly establish this as the long-term metropolitan district in the geography of medieval music. The luxuriant twelfth-century developments south of the Loire, including superbly elastic compositions in two parts set to a wide range of devotional and accentual poetry (called versus by the scribes), show Aquitaine joining the old Frankish core as a productive zone yet maintaining an independence in its choice of texts, and in the fluidity of the voices in the two-part texture, which probably owes something to Aquitaine's long geopolitical history as a far-from-compliant dependency of the Frankish (or by now French) kingdom to the north. The metropolitan status of circuit I is sometimes also very evident in developments around its periphery. In 1080, Spanish bishops at the Council of Burgos decided to replace their indigenous Mozarabic liturgy with the Frankish-Roman rite and its Gregorian chant, a decision that reflected mounting pressure from Pope Gregory VII but also from the abbey of Cluny, the massive Benedictine prayer-factory in the centre of circuit I. Several generations later, the same process of conscious assimilation to the metropolitan zone can be seen in the twelfth-century collection now known as the Codex Calixtinus, probably created in central I for use in the cathedral of St James in Galicia. This book contains the *Historia Turpini*, ostensibly a ninth-century account of how Charlemagne crossed the Pyrenees to Galicia and uncovered the relics of Saint James (a fine picture in the manuscript shows him riding out from Aachen to do so). There are also monophonic and polyphonic pieces in the book attributed (by a later hand) to churchmen associated with Vézelay, Bourges, Paris, Troyes and Soissons, among other places evoking Burgundy, Champagne and Picardy. Those territories had defined the principal region of monastic revival in western Europe – the Cistercians, the Cluniacs and the Premonstratensian canons had all begun somewhere there – just as they produced the greatest contribution to the Crusading enterprise. The music of the Codex Calixtinus is not a preamble to later achievements at Notre Dame of Paris. Instead, it sings circuit I, the heartland of the twelfth-century West.[5]

The importance of Paris as a Capetian capital, and as a centre for polyphonic composition after approximately 1150, reveals once more the vigour of circuit I and exposes the region's deep geopolitical roots in the north. Paris is a natural fort, protected to the east by a series of escarpments, able to receive provisions along the Seine, one of the most important fluvial highways of France, and fed by the vast agricultural expanse of La Beauce. Benefactions to the abbey of St Denis, and the distribution of fiscal lands, show that Paris had been important to Frankish kings of Merovingian and Carolingian descent for many hundreds of years before Capetian ascendancy in the city added another layer. (It is salutary to remember that Paris became a centre for masters and students because there was no room for expansion on the Plateau of Laon, a Carolingian heartland city if ever there was one. This is where Charlemagne has his core estate or *cambre* in the *Song of Roland*.) By 1175 Paris was a place of exceptional opportunity with sophisticated arrangements for copying texts and music. Drawing men from all over the Latin world, it was an unparalleled and international clearing-house for musical talent. Music redacted and copied, but not necessarily composed, in Paris could reach the far ends of the Latin West, including St Andrews in Scotland (*D-W* 628, the 'Notre Dame' source W_1) and the chapel of the royal monastery at Burgos (the Las Huelgas manuscript), centres which lie not far short of two thousand miles apart. The importance of Paris as a musical centre continued into the first half of the fourteenth century when the musical interpolations in the Français 146 manuscript of *Le Roman de Fauvel* (*F-Pn* fonds fr. 146), principally comprising monophonic songs and polyphonic motets, give Paris an unrivalled claim to be the centre of notational and stylistic developments associated today with the term Ars Nova. This was once more a function of the city's power to draw men of talent from many miles distant, including Philippe de Vitry who was probably from Champagne.[6]

At this point, with Philippe de Vitry's fellow Champenois Guillaume de Machaut on the horizon, one should look back to review the geographical origins of courtly song in circuit I. Places mentioned in this survey so far, all associated with named composers, include Auxerre, Bourges, Chartres, Corbie, Fleury, Gembloux, Liège, Metz, Montier-en-Der, Paris, St-Riquier, Sens, Soissons, Toul, Trier, Troyes and Vézelay. The majority of these centres lie between the Loire and the Moselle, with a marked concentration in lands east of Paris. These are mostly regions of immense open plains produced by forest clearances (already accomplished by the beginning of the Middle Ages) or of softly undulating mountains. From the eighth century, when they were Carolingian heartland and the probable birthplace of Gregorian chant, these sweeping cornlands continuously produced their crop of musical talent. After a great many chant composers of 900–1150, the period 1150–1300 brings a new harvest with the trouvères who created some two thousand monophonic songs with texts in French (to count only the songs that survive) in an immense arc of territory reaching as far south as Berzé near Cluny in Burgundy but mostly encompassing cities, towns and smaller settlements further north such as Amiens, Arras, Béthune, Cambrai, Chartres, Coucy, Épinal, Soignies, Nesles and St-Quentin. The easterly distribution of the trouvères' art is evident from the relatively small number of them securely connected with Paris, from the almost complete absence of Normans or Bretons among them, and from the quasi-classical status (very apparent in the manuscript record) of songs by Thibaut de Champagne and Gace Brulé, both associated with the Champenois district. In a sense, that tradition continued into the fourteenth century with Philippe de Vitry, but it survives more durably with the 'last of the trouvères', the Champenois Guillaume de Machaut (d. 1377), who was considerably more interested than his older colleague in vernacular song. Although Machaut was a much-travelled man with many court connections, the geographical background to his songs, both monophonic and polyphonic, lies in the great French song-making region of *grands chants*, *ballades*, *rondets de carole*, *pastourelles* and other lyric genres extending east of Paris from approximately the Plateau of Langres to Lille and Arras.

In the final decades of the fourteenth century the legacy of Machaut and other composers from the northerly reaches of circuit I was subjected to a major stylistic and geographical shift. Practised by composers such as Senleches and Solage, the rhythmic refinements of the phase in polyphonic song now commonly called Ars Subtilor were cultivated in southern regions of I at the courts of Foix and Béarn, in Aragon and Catalonia. The composers almost exclusively used texts in French, not in any form of literary language used in Romania south (IV), marking this development as an unexplained southern extrusion of a polyphonic art whose principal elements were developed further north (one of Solage's most exuberant pieces honours Jean of Berry). There is no clear connection between the Ars Subtilior and the monophonic vernacular-song traditions of circuit IV, save perhaps in the composers' fondness for the inherently serious and grandiloquent form of the ballade, arguably their equivalent of the troubadour canso or the northern chanson. Comparable developments in circuit III, with composers such as Matteo da Perugia, also make extensive use of French texts, suggesting once more the predominant influence of the north, partly exerted through the French-dominated papal court at Avignon.

With the fifteenth century, the Seine–Moselle district of circuit I produced a crop of talented musicians all over again. The cities that will figure in the lives (and to some extent the careers) of Ciconia, Du Fay, Binchois, Josquin, Pierre de la Rue and many other Franco-Flemish musicians include Bruges, Cambrai, Ghent, Liège, Mons, St-Quentin and Tournai. This is deep Frankish territory. In the city of Tournai, today just across the Franco-Belgian frontier, Josquin walked over the concealed grave of Childeric, the father of Clovis the first Christian king of the Franks (d. 511), every time he passed the church of St Brice. In Liège, Ciconia sang barely a few kilometres from the birthplace of the first Carolingian king and the instigator of Gregorian chant, Charlemagne's father Pépin (d. 768). For the history of medieval music in its geographical aspects, these connections are the equivalent of aerial photography.

II The East Frankish circuit

Gregorian chant spread eastwards into circuit II from the core Carolingian abbeys and churches of I, and in many different ways. Some of the forces concerned were in operation well before the Treaty of Verdun in 843 that separated the West Frankish and East Frankish kingdoms with a Lotharingian band between them (note the overlap of I and II). Much was achieved by conversion at the point of a sword, especially in Saxony where Charlemagne hammered away for decades and eventually saw Paderborn emerge as a major ecclesiastical centre. The establishment of new bishoprics in the east, such as Würzburg and Salzburg, both of them eighth-century creations, created churches in which the Carolingians had a direct reforming interest, while imperial chapels founded in palaces at Aachen, Worms, Ingelheim and elsewhere established centres where the palatine chaplains, the *palatini*, followed the emperors to sing Gregorian chant for mass and office. The prayer confraternities, predominantly a ninth-century phenomenon, which bound abbeys and churches together throughout circuits I, II and III were of great importance in the work of dissemination, and so were ties of blood and friendship between abbots and bishops; a letter survives in which one Frankish churchman of the ninth century asks another to send a singer trained in 'Roman' (that is to say, Gregorian) chant as a personal favour. As in circuit I, the period 850–1100 brings many composers who created liturgical chant, including the East Frankish repertory of sequences and responsories for the offices for the Sanctorale. Again as in circuit I, these melodies were often composed against the grain of Gregorian style, so to speak, by those who regarded themselves as *moderni* for doing so. Composers mentioned in literary sources were active at the Bavarian abbey of St Emmeram in Regensburg (with a rich musical legacy, and surviving musical remains), Eichstätt, Fulda, Mettlach, Säckingen, St-Gall and Utrecht, to look no further.[7]

Circuit II was home to a vigorous and expansionist Catholic civilization. In the 860s, missionaries directed from frontier sees such as Freising, Salzburg and Passau can be found among the Bulgars and Slavs, trying to prevail over their Byzantine competitors and characteristically insisting, with papal approval, that converts should worship exclusively in a Latin liturgy. A century later, the sheer military and political strength of the Holy Roman Emperors forced a complete reconfiguration of Hungary, shattering the tribal structure and introducing both kingship and Catholicism through German missionaries (facing down Byzantine competitors) under Prince Géza (ca970–97) on the model of realms further west. By 1000, the see of Esztergom was in existence and Hungary, gradually assimilating Gregorian chant, was established as the eastern frontier of the Latin-Christian world. By the thirteenth century, narrative sources show priests singing Latin sequences at mass in the stockade churches of Riga in modern Latvia; charters reveal hospitals, many with chapels for daily chanted masses, in Mecklenburg and Pomerania.[8]

In the polyphonic arts, the contribution of circuit II was minimal, being confined before the fifteenth century almost entirely to oddities such as the polyphonic songs of the Monk of Salzburg. There was no German Machaut to marry the polyphonic techniques of the Ars Nova to an adapted form of the lyric traditions inherited from the thirteenth century. (Something similar may be said for England; the influences of I and IV, with their various traditions, were so strong that no form of vernacular polyphonic song developed in any Germanic language before the fifteenth century). Yet the situation with regard to monophonic song in the vernacular, or Minnesang, was very different. The imperial and aristocratic courts of circuit II yielded nothing in either grandeur or historical importance to their counterparts in I. In the eleventh and twelfth centuries, the Holy Roman Emperors recruited their bishops from the palace chaplains – from specialists in liturgy and chant, in other words – and the candidates for such offices were admired for a wide range of courtly skills including eloquence, decorous bearing and reserve under the stress of court life with its many intrigues. Courtliness, or *curialitas*, is insistently celebrated in the biographies devoted to these men when they became bishops, providing an open window onto the milieu where German courtly song was beginning to emerge by 1150 or so. The range and sophistication of the musical arts that such a milieu could encourage are well illustrated in poems such as the Latin *Ruodlieb* of ca1000 and the thirteenth-century *Tristan* of Gottfried von Strasburg. The celebrated *Carmina Burana* manuscript (*D-Mbs* clm 4660), though using unheighted neumes, also suggests the sophistication of vernacular and Latin song at the German courts and in the monastic or cathedral refectories of the Empire. The musical remains of courtly lyric in various dialects of Middle High German are much less abundant than those in French, but they are enough to reveal an art of song deeply indebted to contacts with circuit I. The earliest German songmakers, for example, who were for most part Rhineland and Westerly poets of the period 1150–1200, seem to have derived their contact with troubador lyric through French intermediaries (that is to say circuit II reached through I into IV). From there the art of German lyric expanded in the thirteenth century to fill the lands of the Holy Roman Empire, embracing all of present-day Germany (including the Low German dialect area of the north), Austria and German-speaking Switzerland.[9]

III The Alpine Gate

There are two principal ways of viewing this circuit. For the period 800–900, it principally figures as the zone that gave elements of the Roman liturgy, including musical materials, to the Franks in circuit I, and which then became the district where the immense cultural achievements of I were gathered and transmitted through transalpine links to northern and central Italy. For the period 900 onwards, circuit III is much more closely linked to circuit II, for the two interlink to form the transalpine polity of the Holy Roman Empire of the German Nation.

Gregorian chant came to northern Italy with Charlemagne's conquest of Lombardy in 774, as witness the magnificent Monza cantatorium, one of the earliest sources for the Gregorian gradual and probably copied in Francia during the ninth century then taken across the Alps to Monza by an emigrant Frankish bishop or abbot. By the ninth century, many churches in circuits I and II were bound in ties of prayer confraternity to houses of III, further establishing lines of transmission. Maritime contact between I and III could be fluent in the warmer months when the sea was open, but the ninth century brought a shift to the transalpine land route. This helps to explain how an abbey in an obscure place like the monastery of St Gall could mature into a wealthy house and become a major centre of Frankish-Roman chant with associated arts composition (including a major contribution to the sequence repertory) and of notation carried to a level of the utmost sophistication. The house chroniclers of St Gall cherished especially vivid (and mostly apocryphal) stories of Roman singers passing northwards through the Alpine Gate and remaining in their abbey to teach pure Roman chant.[10]

There were two principal non-Gregorian liturgies in III, the Ambrosian and the Beneventan, the former reflecting the wealth and independence of what had once been a Western-imperial capital and the latter the long-standing (but precarious) autonomy of the Lombard duchy of Benevento. In the half-century 1050–1100 that produced the First Crusade and the Spanish bishops' decision to suppress the Mozarabic liturgy in favour of the Frankish-Roman, Pope Stephen X (1057–8) demanded the end of Beneventan chant at the great abbey of Monte Cassino and the imposition of the Gregorian. Monte Cassino at this time was a major musical centre, home at various times to composers such as Leo of Ostia, Alfanus (also a physician, a reminder that Salerno and the Greek south of Italy are not far away) and Alberic (a composer and theorist). Stephen IX was a Lotharingian, appointed as part of the Holy Roman Emperors' policy to put trusted northerners on the throne of Saint Peter instead of the scions of feuding Italian families whom the Germans were inclined to regard as deeply untrustworthy. The kind of liturgical change Stephen demanded could not be accomplished overnight, but with the decisions at Monte Cassino and Burgos, only a few decades apart, a little more of the Latin-Christian sound-scape that characterizes the medieval West fell into place.[11]

Soon after 1000, the 'monk' Guido of Arezzo, who spent all or most of his life in III, gathered up existing techniques of notation and created what is arguably the defining technology of the Western musical tradition: the staff with meaningful *spaces* as well as lines. So fluent was the movement of envoys, military retinues, traders and pilgrims through the Alpine Gate in the eleventh century that Guido's new technique was being taught in the distant imperial city of Liège within a generation of his death, perhaps less. The background to this seminal invention lies with the wealth of the Canossa family in the Po valley; enriched by rents from land reclamation and forest clearances, they were effectively Guido's patrons both at the abbey of Pomposa and subsequently at the cathedral of Arezzo where his invention was developed and tested. Equally important was the nearness of southern Italy with its wide contacts in the Arabo-Byzantine Mediterranean and links with Islamic science, manifest in the adoption of Hindu-Arabic numerals, recorded in Italy within Guido's century. (Guido's notation is essentially a form of graph, the earliest known in the Western tradition.) Finally, the context for Guido's invention should be sought in the quickening of monastic and clerical conscience in northern Italy after 1000, often prompted by lay congregations in the new hilltop towns of the *incastellamento* who demanded higher moral and pastoral standards from their priests. This breadth of reference is necessary, for Guido was far from being a simple choirmaster; he was remembered by the Canossa family several generations after his death as a 'blessed hermit', and he probably possessed a conspicuously ascetic temperament that was inseparable, in his judgement, from the highest standards in the performance of chant. He invented his notation to preserve Roman chant in its pure state (that is to say, to disseminate it in his preferred form) and went to Rome where John XIX approved it.[12]

Italian sources of the thirteenth and indeed the fourteenth century contain numerous examples of indigenous polyphony whose techniques stand outside the 'Notre Dame' tradition, although literary records of polyphonic composition (such as the remarkable detailed references to song making by several Franciscans in the Chronicle of Salimbene de Adam, including settings of poems by Philippe the Chancellor of Paris) suggest that Parisian materials were by no means remote; they were probably brought through the Alpine Gate by the well-attested travels of Franciscan scholars attending the university. For vernacular song, including the trecento repertory, see the next section.[13]

IV Romania south

By the twelfth century, Circuit IV can be traced as a large area of southern Romance speech used for a rich and interconnected culture of lyric in Gallego, Catalan, Old Occitan, Sicilian and 'Italian'. The extensive song repertories that survive from this circuit, almost exclusively monophonic, include the massive Alfonsine anthology of the *Cantigas de Santa Maria*, the troubadour corpus and the lauda repertory from Italy. Much material, especially pertaining to lighter-courtly or satirical genres, has been preserved without musical notation, or only in fragments that have serendipitously survived, such as the *Cantigas de amigo* of Martin Codax.

The vernaculars of this circuit, even when cast in artificial literary forms, were probably comprehensible across the whole area. There was also a consensus that they were suitable for different things than the French or *langue d'oïl* used in the northern parts of circuit 1. Soon after 1200, the Catalan poet Raimon Vidal de Besalú wrote that French is best for romances (that is to say for narratives in poetry or prose), for *retronsas* (a refrain form, not well represented) and for *pasturellas* (a lighter-courtly and semi-narrative genre), whereas literary Occitan or Lemozi was most appropriate for high-style love songs and for lyrics of political or satirical comment. About a century later, Dante was so impressed by the long-established tradition of grave and authoritative French prose, represented by works such as the Vulgate Arthurian romances, that he praised French as an especially fit language for 'compilations from the Bible and the histories of Troy and Rome, and the beautiful tales of King Arthur and many other works of history and doctrine'. Old Occitan prose was by no means so assured at this date, for it was not stiffened by the usage of clerics with a background in Paris or some other northern cathedral school. There seems to have been a consciousness throughout this circuit that a central and prized troubadour tradition existed whose language had a richness and dignity that made it especially appropriate for songs of love and ethical instruction: for *amors* and *essenhamen*. There was a widespread conviction that this Occitan was a quintessentially lyric medium, inspiring closely related forms of romance speech to comparable heights of literary eminence from Galicia to Sicily, and correspondingly less appropriate for the august purposes in prose that the *langue d'oïl* served so well. It was the privilege of those using southern romance in this circuit to share in that troubadour tradition, even though long study of the accepted literary language might be necessary to acquire proficiency.[14]

Despite the importance of Gallego (the literary language of Galician-Portuguese, and an Atlantic tongue), IV is a Mediterranean circuit with the area of Occitan speech as its metropolitan district, essentially comprising the Auvergne, Aquitaine, the Limousin, Provence and Languedoc. The primacy of the troubadour material in this circuit seems undeniable, as witness the immense respect in which Dante held the art of the troubadours (while lamenting the lack of a court speech in Italian) at the eastern end of the circuit and the similar reverence shown by the Gallego poets in their imitations of troubadour forms and literary manner at the far west. It was also in this circuit that the art of vernacular song first acquired its own tradition of theory. Handbooks for those wishing to compose troubadour poetry began to appear in Spain, Catalonia, Italy and Occitania during the thirteenth century and continued to be written well into the fifteenth. Some are manuals of grammar or dictionaries; others, like the celebrated *Leys d'Amors*, produced in Toulouse during the early fourteenth century and existing in various versions, adapt the entire apparatus of Latin grammar and rhetoric to create a new art of good judgement in vernacular song based upon literacy, ethical discernment and the acute sensitivity to the sounds of the human voice that was one of the glories of the Greco-Roman education in grammar. Some of these manuals include references to the musical idioms of the songs, even to their mode of performance, and suggest that contemporaries were well aware that the musical language of their lyrics, including its rhythmic aspect, was not the same as that of Ars Nova songs practised in the north of circuit I, just as they regarded the literary languages of IV as essentially different from French. The *Leys d'amors*, in one of the most explicit remarks about musical idiom, inveighs against those who spoil the dansa by assimilating its music to the *redondel* and introducing 'the minims and semibreves of their motets'. Since the compiler of the *Leys d'amors*, Guilhem Molinier, regarded the *redondel* as primarily a French-language form, this is probably a fling at very up-to-date monophonic songs like those in the manuscript of the *Roman de Fauvel* (*F-Pn* fonds fr. 146), whose notation (including unsigned semibreves) is probably to be read in the up-to-date manner codified in the dossier long associated with the name Ars Nova and regarded as a treatise by Philippe de Vitry.[15]

Only in northern Italy did a genre of polyphonic song develop applying music with the 'minims and semibreves' of Ars Nova notation to poetry in a literary language of Romania south. The large and predominantly two-part repertory of trecento lyric with forms such as the madrigale, caccia and ballata is one of the mysteries of medieval music. More or less entirely contained by the fourteenth century, and barely known to traverse the Alps, this often determinedly virtuosic music shows signs of dependency upon earlier, extemporised practices of two-part florid counterpoint, revealing a sense of melody quite unlike anything shown by antecedent monophonic song in IV or the French Ars Nova. By the end of the fourteenth century it was gone, and manuscripts from what is now northern Italy (a zone where French was widely understood and spoken as a court language) begin to reveal extensive traces of transalpine contacts with music from the metropolitan zone, preserving much music by composers such as Binchois, Du Fay, Brassart and others from oblivion. The sheer long-term prestige of that metropolitan district is strikingly apparent in the way musical history during the first half of the fifteenth century runs in the opposite direction to the received narrative of an Italian renaissance feeding the north.

V The Anglo-Norman zone

England between 1066 and 1500 was a country of small account, producing only one pope (suggesting a massive failure of influence at the papal curia) and only one monastic order (the Gilbertines) which was of no interest elsewhere. In some respects, the music that survives unsurprisingly demands that Circuit V be drawn down to northern France. A small but remarkably precocious corpus of courtly songs with Anglo-Norman texts, and of Anglo-Norman motets, shows that there were trouvères and sophisticated polyphonists in the insular reaches of V, and numerous manuscripts (including the Dublin Troper, *GB-Cu* Add. 710) attest to the wealth of Latin songs in circulation, some of them truly 'international' pieces brought in by what has been called the 'Channel culture' of the twelfth and thirteenth centuries. Music redacted in Paris found its way as far north as St Andrews in Scotland. Nonetheless, there is a distinctively insular story to be told. Musicians in England heard the intervals of third and sixth in a fundamentally different way to their Continental counterparts (suggesting the use of Just rather than Pythagorean intonation) and treated them as consonances. English composers in the thirteenth and fourteenth centuries sometimes assembled substantial sections of their pieces from chains of parallel chords with the third present, suggesting the closeness of extemporized techniques, and were even prepared to countenance pieces with the third in the *final* sonority. In other words, the long history of England's inward-looking concern with its own overflowing creativity in musical art had already begun by 1250. The music of the celebrated Old Hall manuscript, however, dating from the first years of the fifteenth century, nonetheless reveals substantial exposure to the late Ars Nova and indeed to the French polyphonic chanson of the Loqueville generation, presumably gained during the residence of household chaplains in Rouen, Paris and elsewhere during various stages of the Hundred Years War. This transplanting of the English musical language to France does much to explain the Continental reception of music by John Dunstaple and other English composers.

By 1400 there were three districts of polyphonic expertise in the West, defined by circuits I, III and V. The musicians of circuits III and V were not often in frequent or close communication (although signs of Italian influence appear in the Old Hall manuscript). For a central and European language of counterpoint to emerge it was necessary for musicians in I, III and V to come into sustained contact – or, in less abstract (and less accurate) language, for English, French and Italian musicians to pool their resources. The Conciliar movement of the fifteenth century provided the means for this to happen with results of far-reaching consequence for the rise of a European language of counterpoint to match the European music of Gregorian plainsong that was already some five hundred years old.[16]

19 Reception

LAWRENCE EARP

The following survey distinguishes three types of music – plainchant, vernacular song, and polyphony – each with a very different reception history. Plainchant enjoyed an active and constantly evolving reception even in the Middle Ages; its modern reception history dates from the efforts, beginning in the early nineteenth century, to restore the medieval shape of the chant, a project that would bear fruit in the early twentieth century. New interest in vernacular song came in the wake of philological and historical research into European languages strongly under way by the eighteenth century. The unaccompanied melodies, free from any religious association, were subject to a variety of adaptations, often tinged by nationalism and ideology. Medieval polyphony was completely lost until isolated fragments came to light in the late eighteenth century, and it was well into the twentieth century before its outlines became clear.

Most medieval music was improvised, and so is lost or only dimly discernible through performance directions in music theory treatises. Works transmitted in musical notations required an active generation-to-generation updating to remain current. Liturgical chant – a repertory not as stable as we might think – was retranslated, sometimes undergoing recomposition. Notations for secular monophony and polyphony tended to fall out of use, since each generation was sufficiently occupied with the cultivation of its own new music. By the time we reach the point when scholars took a modicum of interest in the remnants of medieval music – the mid eighteenth century – no one could read the sources any longer. The problem was particularly acute for polyphony, usually notated in separate parts. All told, it required around a century and a half to crack the various codes and to put the polyphony in score for study. If we add to this the need to reconstruct performance practices in music, we see how difficult and ramified the project has been.

Medieval plainchant

Some of the most interesting yet intractable problems of reception in music history involve plainchant, a development that can be traced over 1,250 years.[1] At times the faithful have adapted liturgical chants to changing tastes and local needs; at other times, the church has taken care to maintain

a venerable sacred tradition, as well as its own central authority. Here I will
epitomize the many issues surrounding the reception of Gregorian chant
in one moment: the legend of Saint Gregory as the codifier of 'Gregorian'
chant. The legend holds out the promise of a repertory bequeathed *in toto*
by a canonized pope, yet at the same time warns of the ease with which the
repertory could be corrupted.

The period of the creation of Gregorian chant in the wake of the alliance
between the Carolingians and the papacy came at a decisive moment in
the emergence of northern and western Europe. For both the papacy and
the Franks, the alliance filled urgent political needs. The papacy gained an
ally against the resurgent Lombards, while the Franks, now defenders of
the faith, gained liturgical uniformity based on the Roman rite to help hold
their far-flung realm together, as well as papal legitimation of their royal
blood line.

All this happened quickly. The Frankish church had reached a lamentable
state of moral and disciplinary turpitude under Charles Martel. His son and
heir Pépin (r. 741–68) was more open to Roman influence, and the pope
immediately dispatched the English Benedictine missionary Saint Boniface,
who consolidated the highly decentralized Gallican church, introducing
archbishops and yearly synods. Through Boniface and later Chrodegang,
who became Archbishop of Metz after the martyrdom of Boniface in 755,
Pépin pushed for the adoption of the Roman rite. The indigenous Gallican
chant either succumbed to Pépin's order, or was absorbed into the new
chant.

Strong ties with Rome also served to legitimize the Carolingian rulers
as kings. Still nominally the mayor of the palace, Pépin ousted the last
Merovingian king and was first anointed king of the Franks by his bishops
in 751. The anointing was repeated in 754 by Pope Stephen II, who had
come to consult Pépin on the matter of the Lombards. Pope Stephen's trip to
Francia, accompanied by Chrodegang, turned out to be decisive for Pépin's
design to institute the Roman usage throughout his realm. Stephen brought
Roman singers and chant books, and Bishop Chrodegang went on to form
a *schola cantorum* at Metz. Meanwhile, Remedius, Bishop of Rouen (and
Pépin's brother) was inculcating the Roman chant there. Pope Paul I (r. 757–
68), who sent an 'antiphonale' and a 'responsale' (gradual and antiphoner?)
to Rouen, indicates in a letter that the monks had not fully mastered the
chant when he had to recall his emissary from the Roman *schola cantorum*,
and so monks from Rouen came to Rome for further instruction. This
incident may be the source of a story embellished in different ways some
125 years later by John the deacon and Notker Balbulus.

The programme of reform continued under Pépin's son Charlemagne
(r. 768–814). Charlemagne's *Admonitio generalis* of 789 to the Frankish

clergy ordered that all clergy should learn and perform the Roman chant that Pépin had directed to be substituted for the Gallican chant, and further urged that books be carefully emended, including both *cantus* and *nota* (chants and signs?).[2] While we should not impugn the spiritual motives behind the Carolingian move to replace diverse Gallican usages with the Roman rite, there were also undeniable political advantages to the religious unification of the realm. Unity was maintained partially through the *missi*, a team of royal inspectors sent far and wide to assure broad-based loyalty and adherence to directives on diverse matters including chant.

The Carolingians introduced several means to establish liturgical fixity. Carolingian scholars were committed to careful verification and emendation of written texts. Not only did the Carolingians revise liturgical texts to conform to the scriptures, but whole services had to be filled in by the Franks, for the books sent from Rome only contained texts used by the pope on special occasions. To help fix music in the memory, chants came to be categorized by the eight modes, a system foreign to Old Italian chant dialects (Old Roman, Beneventan and Ambrosian). Our earliest extant tonary, a book organizing chants in modal order, is the St Riquier tonary (*F-Pn* fonds lat. 13159), datable to the late eighth century. Another means of establishing musical fixity for subsequent transmission was musical notation. Our first extant complete neumed source for the gradual is datable to the late ninth century; for the antiphoner, ca1000. Despite an enormous amount of recent research, there is no agreement on how far back the origin of neumes can be pushed. Were they applied to the chants already in the late eighth century, or did notation grow up piecemeal in the course of the ninth century, at first for special purposes, later systematically applied to the entire repertory?[3] Finally, and I will dwell on it because of its importance to reception, there was a third means of enforcing fixity in the chant: the legend associating the invention of Gregorian chant with Saint Gregory. This story lent a particular authority to the Roman chant, providing spiritual conviction to supplement the royal decree.

The legend of Saint Gregory

Pope Gregory (r. 590–604) was indeed an important pope. Two hundred years before Charlemagne, he reasserted the primacy of Rome at a dangerous juncture in church history. Further, it was Gregory who undertook the conversion of England in 597 by dispatching Saint Augustine, later the first Archbishop of Canterbury. The Venerable Bede maintained favourable memories of Pope Gregory in his *Ecclesiastical History of the English People* (finished 731), and the strong influence of English scholars such as Alcuin of York at the Carolingian court may have been critical in maintaining the prestige of Pope Gregory as the inventor of plainchant.

Late-eighth-century sources indicate that both Rome and the Franks had already attached the authority of Saint Gregory to the chant, and two important narratives linking Gregory to the invention of the chant date from the ninth century.[4] Our principal source is the *Life of Saint Gregory* (ca873–5) by John the deacon of Monte Cassino. John credits Gregory as the founder of the Roman *schola cantorum*, and as the compiler of a 'centonate antiphonary' (presumably texts for mass chants pieced together from Biblical citations). Though John describes Gregory as inspired by the dove of the Holy Spirit, he associates this anecdote with Gregory's writings on theology, not music. John writes that efforts to transmit the Roman chant to Gaul were difficult due to the Gauls' 'natural rusticity' and their horrible voices. Eventually Charlemagne left two clerics in Rome with Pope Hadrian I (r. 772–95) to learn the chant; they returned to teach at Metz, and from there the chant spread throughout Gaul. After their death, Charlemagne once again found the chant of churches outside Metz to be corrupt, whereupon Hadrian sent two more singers.

A further source for the story of the transmission of the chant has an entirely different perspective. According to the *Deeds of Charlemagne* (883–5) by Notker Balbulus of St Gall, Charlemagne obtained twelve singers from the pope. Jealous of the glory of the Franks, they sabotaged the effort by singing poorly. After Charlemagne discovered this, Pope Leo III (r. 795–816) suggested that Charlemagne infiltrate the papal *schola* with two trusted clerics in disguise. They returned to teach the chant, one at the imperial court in Aachen, the other at Metz. Finally, the last step in the formation of the legend of Saint Gregory, the association of the dove of the Holy Spirit with Gregory's dictation of notated music, is first found in an illumination in the Hartker antiphoner (*CH-SGs* 390–391, ca980–1011), the first extant complete neumed manuscript of office chants.[5]

In the end the experiment, strictly speaking, failed. But in another sense, the vision succeeded in forming an enormous body of music that was indeed transmitted whole. We celebrate the Carolingians for their preservation of most of what remains of ancient literature, and we celebrate them for the Carolingian minuscule. Yet it appears that the reception, assimilation and transformation of the Roman chant resulted in the greatest artistic creation of the Carolingians, Gregorian chant. Eventually it drove out all regional chant dialects in Europe except the Ambrosian, which was maintained in Milan because of Saint Ambrose's prestige there. Mozarabic chant survived until the eleventh century in Moorish Spain, and we have full manuscripts with music, unfortunately copied before the palaeographical revolution of heighted neumes. Beneventan chant, practised in south Italy, was finally suppressed in the eleventh century. Rome itself fell before the onslaught of the imported repertory, though not until the thirteenth century. The notion of a uniform music – reproducible and transmissible, and guarded from change – was new, the invention of the Carolingians. It determined as no other single factor the subsequent development of Western music. The very notion of the 'reception' of music depends on it. Despite the long road before the full implications of an *opus perfectum* would be realized in Western music history, Pépin's vision of imposing the Roman chant on the Carolingian realm effectively foreordained the path.

Gregory stands at the centre of a circumpolar history. Succeeding ages, in pruning accumulated abuses, often sought justification in Gregory for the changes, even when they were in no position to consult old manuscripts.[6] When finally the nineteenth century took on the restoration of the chant, the legend of Saint Gregory made it an ideal subject for scholarly investigation in nineteenth-century terms, since it taught that Gregorian chant was a coherent work of genius, the closed oeuvre of a saint and pope inspired by the Holy Spirit. Heeding the lesson of the myth, scholars sought the original state of the core repertory, ignoring decayed and peripheral later forms.

In 1889, with systematic, devastating logic, Gevaert showed that documentary evidence does not support the notion that Pope Gregory invented plainchant.[7] The Benedictine scholars at Solesmes immediately rejected Gevaert's argument, and in the end it took generations of scholars working after 1950 to draw the full implications of this change of view. Just as it had been essential to scholarly progress in the nineteenth century to maintain the Gregory legend, the discarding of the legend was essential to open new avenues of research in the second half of the twentieth century.

That, and the discovery in 1886 of the 'Old Roman' chant, a complete repertory for the mass and office, virtually identical to Gregorian chant in terms of the texts set but utilizing different melodies, or, more precisely, melodies vaguely similar, but usually more florid and less sharply profiled.[8] Initially the Old Roman repertory was dismissed as a corruption of the Gregorian. By the 1950s, however, scholars had begun to confront the fact that our earliest extant chant manuscripts from Rome itself transmit the Old Roman rather than the Gregorian melodies. Further, these Roman manuscripts, which date from 1071 to the early thirteenth century, postdate by nearly 200 years the earliest northern manuscripts transmitting the familiar 'Gregorian' repertory. At first liturgists tried to place both chant dialects in Rome at the same time, associating one or the other with a special chant reserved for the pope. Many musicologists, however, realized that such a scenario, besides ignoring the curious manuscript tradition, also ignored common-sense issues of musical transmission. Until the twentieth century, scholars had assumed that Pope Gregory had fixed the propers in writing around the year 600 by means of a letter notation.⁹ Now, with no direct evidence of chant notation until around the middle of the ninth century, and no fully notated graduals until around 900, the *terra incognita* of a notationless culture loomed. It was simply impossible that two such distinct repertories could have maintained themselves unchanged over centuries.

With the challenge of a Roman chant in a different melodic tradition, fresh scrutiny of the documents surrounding the legend of Saint Gregory took on new urgency. Indeed, the legend's salient point – the difficulty inherent in transmitting a chant dialect from one soil to another – was finally revealed. In a brilliant new synthesis, Helmut Hucke, a German musicologist not yet thirty years old at the time, proposed that what we call 'Gregorian' chant is actually a product of the Frankish reception of the Old Roman chant.¹⁰ Authenticated by a newly concocted imprimatur of the Holy Spirit acting through Saint Gregory, the transformed chant conquered most of Europe, displacing the indigenous chant in Rome itself by the thirteenth century. While there remain quibbles with details of Hucke's theory, the outlines remain the dominant view.¹¹

Through a series of articles starting in 1974, Leo Treitler has been the moving force behind a mode of inquiry hardly conceivable before the second half of the twentieth century, the effort to characterize a musical repertory operating through oral transmission.¹² Studies from the late nineteenth and first half of the twentieth century regarding compositional processes in chant, finding in some genres a restricted number of melody types, or in other genres a process of deploying mosaic-like formulas at beginnings, middles and ends of sections, now found a new context. It is no accident that the deposing of 'Homer' as 'the' poet who composed 'the' *Iliad* and *Odyssey* set the stage for Treitler's line of inquiry, in which the deposing of 'Gregory' as 'the' composer of 'the' Gregorian chant led to the study of oral processes in the early centuries of the church. The challenge has been in determining the constraints under which the Old Roman chant – in the shape it had 200 years before it was fixed in writing – was transformed into Gregorian chant, and how quickly this happened, and when it was written down.

Kenneth Levy has proposed that the Gregorian mass propers were recorded in the course of the late eighth century in Palaeo-Frankish neumes, a no-nonsense style of neumation that directly traces the ups and downs of melody, lacking the beautiful ductus and performance indications of many of the later styles of neumation. By ca800, a complete notated gradual – the 'Carolingian archetype' – was available for transmission throughout the realm.¹³ This hypothesis explains the relative fixity and authority of the corpus as the Gregorian propers were transmitted abroad, and yet allows time for the palaeographical richness of later regional neume families to develop. It argues that the propers were fixed in relatively short order after their transmission from Rome. Unfortunately, we lack unequivocal proof that such a document existed.

In any case, scholars today believe that Roman chant was transmitted to the north in an oral state (the vicissitudes witnessed by the Gregory legend confirm as much), but what connection either the Old Roman chant in its earliest extant written form ca1071 (in pitch-specific neumes) or Gregorian chant in its earliest extant written form ca900 (in unheighted neumes) might have had to what Chrodegang sang to his students at Metz ca775 is still untouchable. Further, there is the question of the Carolingian reception and adaptation of Byzantine modal theory, an aspect foreign to the Old Italian repertories.

When fully notated graduals did finally appear on the scene, it was at a time when there was wholesale new composition of accretions to the core liturgy, including ordinaries with and without tropes, tropes to the core propers, and sequences. Perhaps it was the vast increase of service music that left overly taxed memories in need of notation.[14] It is noteworthy, however, that the accretions do not show the degree of fixity of the old core propers: they are malleable new materials added in and around the propers, which shine like jewels, the legacy of Pépin's bold experiment.

Chant reforms and late plainchant composition

New religious orders, first the Cistercians and later the Dominicans, sought simplicity, pruning accretions to the chant, also calling for the reform of the melodies of the propers themselves.[15] Examination of early manuscripts at Metz proved disappointing in this goal; with melodies shaped by the sophisticated modal theory of the eleventh century in their ears, the Cistercians went about emending the chant according to the modern aesthetic understanding of the twelfth century.

Always in the service of clearing away layers of abuses of previous generations, countless later episodes of chant reform exhibit exactly the same tension, a tension between the allure of a mythical original state – vouchsafed by the divine transmission through Saint Gregory – and practical exigencies, among them the musical aesthetic values of the moment. Battles pitting the allure of an endangered 'Classical' past against the inexorable pull of modernism are nothing new.

From the perspective of the scholars of the late nineteenth century working like archaeologists to recover a mythical original layer of the chant, the reforms of the Cistercians held little interest; variants in a late manuscript represent a level of corruption easy to eliminate on philological grounds.

More recently, however, scholars have begun to historicize later plainchant, taking up repertories formerly considered peripheral. Myriad local idiosyncrasies touching the entire service, concerning saints venerated in newly assembled offices, the selection of accretions performed (tropes, sequences, liturgical drama), not to mention the diverse application of improvised polyphonic performance practices – all of this would have varied over time. Today, ongoing musicological projects are busy organizing and collecting the great corpus of medieval accretions to plainchant. After the Solesmes emphasis on graduals and antiphoners, one is beginning to see the publication of more and more facsimiles of tropers and prosers. Late chant also brings with it developments in rhymed poetry; it is here that the historical narrative links to that of vernacular monophony, which entered on the scene slightly later than rhymed Latin chant.

What had once appeared as a coherent historical development moving from freedom and variety towards schematic order – as in the case of the history of the sequence from Notker to Adam – is now challenged by the rehabilitation of Hildegard of Bingen (1098–1179), a figure previously simply ignored in music history.[16] How the larger narrative will be adjusted to account for Hildegard's music is not yet clear. It may force us finally to acknowledge a vastly more complex narrative, with sharper geographical distinctions and a great richness of local practices.

The Council of Trent

The crisis of the Protestant Reformations in the sixteenth century dealt the biggest blow to the ongoing cultivation of the chant rooted in the Frankish tradition of the Carolingian Empire. The Council of Trent (1545–63) quickly established the texts of a reformed liturgy, stripping off most of the accretions, publishing a Breviary in 1568 and a Missal in 1570. A more difficult task lay ahead, touching the shape of the ancient melodies themselves.

By the late sixteenth century, humanists cultivating a polished Latin style found their sensitivities offended by the ancient Gregorian chant, in which one was apt to find long melismas emphasizing unimportant syllables. The chant was surely corrupt and in need of reform. In 1577 Pope Gregory XIII engaged Pierluigi da Palestrina and Annibale Zoilo to revise the chantbooks for mass and office, which he found 'filled to overflowing with barbarisms, obscurities, contrarieties, and superfluities as a result of the clumsiness or negligence or even wickedness of the composers, scribes, and printers'.[17]

The new Gradual, the so-called Editio Medicaea edited by Anerio and Soriano, finally appeared in 1614 (temporale) and 1615 (sanctorale). It is popularly thought that that was largely the end of the story until the late nineteenth century, when the assiduous work of the Solesmes monks led to the publication of the Editio Vaticana in 1908, approximately restoring the readings of the oldest manuscripts. This view, however, is vastly oversimplified. Theodore Karp has recently catalogued over 650 Graduals printed in the period from about 1590 to 1890. Even his preliminary analysis shows not only that the Medicean Gradual was not universally adopted, but also that its music exerted little influence on subsequent reformed Graduals.[18] In general, post-Tridentine editors, responding to the humanist demands outlined above, made changes to provide clear prosody, but also to sharpen modal focus. Thus a chant already exhibiting good prosody and a strong modal profile, such as *Puer natus est*, introit of the Third Christmas Mass, was typically left with few emendations, but the very next proper chant in the same mass, the gradual *Viderunt omnes*, was subject to much revision. Nothing is systematic; anonymous editors made *ad hoc* decisions, and were even inconsistent in their adjustment of chants that are musically related.

Nineteenth- and twentieth-century chant reforms

Nineteenth-century movements for the restoration of plainchant to its medieval state are so complex that no single study has yet encompassed the broad-based, multinational efforts, each with different coteries and motivations. The amount of space to cover, both from the perspective of scholarship and from the perspective of human consciousness, is enormous. Nostalgia for the Middle Ages and a concomitant Catholic revival were awakened partly in reaction to the anti-religious rationality of the Enlightenment, and, in France, partly by the destruction of religious monuments in the French Revolution. A political component is seen in the support for the revival of medieval chant lent by partisans for the restoration of the monarchy.[19] The project to recover the 'original' state of the chant through the application of the scientific principles of Lachmannian philology received confirmation in the Gregory legend, which promised that there was an original form. Confidence was particularly strong in the wake of the discovery and publication of new sources. In 1851 Lambillotte published the St Gall cantatorium (*CH-SGs* 359), considered to be the antiphoner of Saint Gregory himself, in a diplomatic facsimile (hand-drawn lithography).[20] Though written in unheighted neumes, the identity of neumes and later melodies was evident after the discovery of the 'rosetta stone' for neumatic notation, the tonary of St Bénigne of Dijon (*F-MOf* H.159), discovered in 1847 by Danjou and published by Nisard in 1851.

The inertia of custom, however, was strong, and it took the entire nineteenth century to bring about chant restoration, which occurred in two stages. First, Pope Pius IX (r. 1846–78), after over 250 years of Vatican acquiescence to a variety of chant editions, gave exclusive recognition to the Catholic publisher Pustet in Regensburg to publish the official chant, a monopoly that would last thirty years. The 1871 Pustet Gradual, edited by the German scholar and church musician Franz Xaver Haberl, did not in any sense restore medieval chant, but instead presented the post-Tridentine melodies of the Medicean Gradual of 1614–15, and, since the Medicean lacked ordinaries, Haberl composed new ones. At this stage the pope supported uniformity of practice, but not yet the restoration of medieval melodies.

In the meantime, the scientific musicology of the Solesmes monks, under way since 1856, had borne fruit in Dom Joseph Pothier's *Liber gradualis* (1883), followed by a *Liber antiphonarius* (1891), the first *Liber usualis* (1895), and other books, all displaying a beautiful new typography modelled on thirteenth-century square notation.[21] To support Pothier's readings, Dom André Mocquereau launched in 1889 the *Paléographie musicale*, a series of photographic facsimiles of early chant manuscripts that present the evidence for the essential uniformity of the early readings for all to verify. Looking back from 1921, Mocquereau characterized the *Paléographie musicale* as a 'kind of scientific tank – powerful, invulnerable, and capable of crushing all the enemy's reasoning'.[22] The French team was aiming directly at the German edition and the papal privilege supporting it.

A second stage, the actual restoration of medieval melodies, came early in the new century. In 1901, Pope Leo XIII (r. 1878–1903) let Pustet's privilege lapse. Finally, on 22 November 1903, the famous *motu proprio* of Pope Pius X (r. 1903–14) approved the restoration of Gregorian chant following the principles of the Solesmes research:

> These qualities [of sacred music] are found most perfectly in Gregorian chant, which is therefore the proper chant of the Roman Church, the only chant which she has inherited from the ancient Fathers, which she has jealously kept for so many centuries in her liturgical books, which she offers to the faithful as her own music, which she insists on being used exclusively in some parts of her liturgy, and which, lastly, has been so happily restored to its original perfection and purity by recent study.[23]

In the end, the contentious commission charged with implementing the reforms accepted the earlier work of Dom Pothier over the most recent research of Dom Mocquereau (the commission was particularly dubious about Mocquereau's rhythmic theories and their overly fussy typographical presentation). The hierarchy of the church, not surprisingly, found it impossible to ally itself unconditionally with the forces of scientific research, with the promise (or threat) of rendering its authority obsolete tomorrow.

Despite its shortcomings, the Vatican edition should be recognized as a great achievement, characteristic of the nineteenth century. Yet after a century of effort, the reforms stood for less than sixty years. The Second Vatican Council (1962–5) revised the liturgy again, admitting vernacular languages and popular idioms of sacred song, and leaving the Latin mass and plainchant as a rarity. New service books of Latin plainchant continue to be published, however, and most recently, the church has adopted a new typography and rhythmic principles based on the work of Solesmes scholar Dom Cardine.[24]

Secular monophony

Before secular music of the Middle Ages came into play as an area of scholarly research, Classical antiquity had to make room. Around 1700 a literary debate broke out concerning the relative merits of the ancients and moderns, pitting those who upheld the order, balance and rule-bound models of ancient Greece and Rome against those who argued for originality in form and flexibility of genre. One aspect of the debate – ongoing since Dante – defended the use of the vernacular languages, arguing that native poets in their native language were perfectly capable of rivalling the ancients. In France, the discussion led to the first serious efforts to recover the legacy of the Middle Ages. Medieval literature became a legitimate subject for scholarship, a sign of pride in a French civilization not indebted to the ancients. It was, after all, not Classical antiquity but the French antiquity – the *antiquité françoise* – that had produced the roots of the language and manners that eventually culminated in the refined taste of the eighteenth century.[25]

Such enthusiasm was not universal. To radical Enlightenment *philosophes* such as Voltaire and the Encyclopaedists, the Middle Ages truly were the Dark Ages. It was conservatives, such as the scholars associated with the Académie des Inscriptions et Belles-Lettres, a branch of the French Academy instituted in 1701 specifically for the study of the history and antiquities of France, who saw the Middle Ages as a heroic age of chivalry, as valid as the heroic age of ancient Greece. The historical record of the Middle Ages, preserved not only in charters but also in literature, provided the foundations for kingship, upholding the *ancien régime*. Particularly important were the troubadours, the first important secular culture since antiquity, who produced the first modern poetry, rooted not in ancient poetic metres, but in rhyme scheme and syllable count. Manuscripts of troubadour poetry were culled not only for philological study of the language and its relationship to Old French, but also for historical material on society and customs.

The most important of the eighteenth-century scholars was Jean-Baptiste de La Curne de Sainte-Palaye.[26] Sainte-Palaye's enormous project of a glossary of Old French (left incomplete at his death in 1781 in sixty-one manuscript volumes) was path-breaking in its systematic use of original manuscripts as sources. Work on the dictionary contributed to the *Mémoires sur l'ancienne chevalerie* (1759) and the *Histoire littéraire des troubadours* (1774), well known throughout eighteenth- and nineteenth-century Europe in English and German translations (Herder's knowledge of medieval culture rested on Sainte-Palaye's scholarship).

Sainte-Palaye was also among the popularizers of the Middle Ages, freely translating monuments of Old French and Provençal into modern French. His modernized edition of *Aucassin et Nicolette* (1752) was the source for Sedaine's libretto *Aucassin et Nicolette*, set as an *opéra-comique* by Grétry in 1779. Another collection of popularizations, the *Bibliothèque des romans*, attributed to the marquis de Paulmy, was the source for the story of the rescue of King Richard Lionheart by Blondel de Nesle, set by Grétry as *Richart Coeur-de-Lion* in 1784. Grétry used no medieval sources for the music of either of these *opéras-comiques*.

Attention turned only slowly to the musical aspect of the trouvères and troubadours. A stroke of good fortune led Burney to Gaucelm Faidit's *Fortz causa es*, a lament on the death of Richard Lionheart – of interest to his English readers – in a manuscript at the Vatican. It would remain the only troubadour melody published in the eighteenth century.[27] Music of the trouvères fared much better. The first publication of a chanson was Thibaut de Navarre's *Je me cuidoie partir*, published in 1702 by Crescimbeni, and reprinted by Hawkins in 1776.[28] Several early-eighteenth-century French aristocratic book owners, royal servants and copyists were active as scholars, exchanging chansonniers, comparing readings of texts, even annotating the margins of the manuscripts they owned.[29] The most well known of these was the Châtre de Cangé, who owned three chansonniers, *F-Pn* fonds fr. 845, 846, and 847. Soon quite a lot of trouvère music became available.[30]

There was also much publication of 'romance' – songs evoking the style of the trouvères – for example, Moncrif's *Choix de chansons* (1755–6).[31] Further, Burney and Forkel were willing to supply accompaniments in the style of Moncrif to trouvère songs. By the addition of accompaniments, the songs obtained a form palatable to contemporary readers.[32] Neither Burney nor Forkel could have entertained the notion that he was subject to prejudice, to the limitations of his historical situation. For both, the goal was to master music as natural scientists were mastering the physical world. No eighteenth-century scholar had a true nostalgia for the Middle Ages. It went without saying that Enlightenment culture was superior.

The revival of medieval music in the wake of the French Revolution

A very different feeling for the Middle Ages developed after the French Revolution, when various threads came together leading to the definitive revival of medieval music – chant, vernacular monophony, and, eventually, polyphony. The following points only touch on a few of the issues at play. Reacting to the anti-Christian scepticism of the Enlightenment, many in the early nineteenth century turned to Christianity – particularly to the mysteries of Catholicism. Chateaubriand's popular *Génie du christianisme* (1802) can be considered in this light, as well as the more general anti-intellectual tendencies of Romanticism, which in some circles found solace in the mysticism of the Middle Ages. This, of course, was important for the revival of Gregorian chant, as well as for the Palestrina revival, the first step in the recovery of early polyphony.

Further, the dissolution during the Revolution of the French *maîtrises*, the cathedral schools for the teaching of vocal music, required the founding of new institutions of music pedagogy, of which the Paris Conservatoire, founded in 1796, was the most important. At a time well before the establishment of musicology as an academic subject, the position of librarian at the Paris Conservatoire supplied a chair for many scholars of critical importance to the revival of early music, including Perne, Fétis, Bottée de Toulmon, and later Weckerlin. Fétis went on to head the new Brussels Conservatory and was followed there by Gevaert. Institutional support was still not the rule, however. Some armchair scholars important to the revival of medieval music in the first half of the nineteenth century include Thibaut, a jurist and law professor in Heidelberg, Kiesewetter, a government counsellor in Vienna, and Coussemaker, a lawyer in northern France.

In Germany reaction to the Enlightenment took on a strong anti-French flavour, an aspect of the growing nationalism in response to Napoleon's occupation forces. But even before this, Herder had set the stage with his emphasis on the genius of the common people (*Volk*) as the root of culture, having found the cultural orientation of late-eighteenth-century German princes too Frenchified for his taste. Herder's view strongly shaped a new approach to the reception of secular monophony in the early nineteenth century. He put the troubadours and trouvères in the position of folk singers, and included the texts of two trouvère songs in his collection of *Volkslieder* (Folksongs, 1778–9), thereby feeding the early Romantics' search for quasi-mythical roots of a nation's culture. The attribute of *Volkstümlichkeit* (a quality characteristic of the common people), formerly a liability, was now a positive virtue.[33]

The destruction of cultural monuments lamented by Victor Hugo in the preface to his novel *Notre-Dame de Paris 1482* (1832) was among the factors that fostered the preservation movement in nineteenth-century France, of which Viollet-le-Duc's reconstruction of the cathedral of Paris is the best-known monument. The analogous movement in Germany, which saw the completion of Cologne Cathedral during the years from 1842 to 1880, had a different emphasis. A growing consciousness of the power of a unified national state, awakened by the challenge of France and the Napoleonic wars, brought new interest in medieval German culture to the politically fragmented Germans. Cologne Cathedral thus became a symbol of German nation building.[34]

Long the cosmopolitan consumers of foreign styles, the Germans now focused on authentic German roots. But as with Herder's *Volkstümlichkeit*, early stages of this cultural programme were already in place in the late eighteenth century. Annette Kreutziger-Herr emphasizes the new aesthetic seen in Goethe's hymn to Strasbourg Cathedral (1772) as a watershed moment.[35] Here Goethe found himself unexpectedly awed, even dizzied, by the sheer grandeur of the medieval architectural setting. The new enthusiasm for German medieval ('Gothic') culture saw the publication of some seventy editions of Middle High German and Middle Low German poems between 1760 and 1800, as well as popular collections of folk poetry and fairy tales, the *Des Knaben Wunderhorn* (1805) of Arnim and Brentano, and the *Märchen* (1813–14) of the brothers Grimm. By the end of the nineteenth century, German historical scholarship had outstripped that of all other countries, voraciously gobbling up records of the past and printing great collections of documents. Throughout Europe, the unaffiliated armchair scholar was replaced by research concentrated at universities. There was also an upsurge of French philological research, seen, for example, in the founding of the journal *Romania* in 1872, and the establishment in 1875 of the series of literary monuments published by the Société des Anciens Textes Français, founded, as Gaston Paris put it, so that 'Germany should no longer be the European country where the most monuments of our language and literature are printed'.[36]

Rhythm in secular monophony

We have seen some of the ideological and national issues that attended the rediscovery of medieval monophonic song. Most of these issues were stimulated by the poetry. Musical rhythm, however, remained the sole domain of the music scholar. To eighteenth-century readers, publications of trouvère songs in loose diplomatic facsimile may have implied rhythms something along the lines heard in contemporary performances of plainsong, either an equalist approach or one distinguishing long, breve, and semibreve.[37] In any case, the first scholar to grapple seriously with the problem of transcribing the rhythms of the trouvère sources was François Louis Perne (1772–1832). Perne's study of black mensural notation culminated in a complete transcription of Machaut's Mass presented to the French Institut royal in 1814, but unfortunately these materials never saw publication. Later an opportunity arose to collaborate with the philologist Francisque Michel on an edition of the chansons of the Châtelain de Couci, and Perne applied his mensural rules to an edition of twenty chansons, published in 1830.[38] A few years later, this mensuralist approach was given a firmer grounding by Coussemaker, whose study of the Montpellier Codex (*F-MOf* H.196) led him to identify several trouvères as composers of polyphony – *trouvères-harmonistes*.[39]

The French mensuralist approach had a certain logic because the note shapes used for chansons are the same as those used to notate motets. By contrast, the German sources of Minnesang offer nothing of the sort. Throughout the nineteenth century, there had been little attention to the musical component of Minnesang. Sources for the music of Minnesinger songs are comparatively meagre and very late, beginning over 200 years after the art they transmit. Even single manuscripts display a bewildering variety of notational styles, none of them providing consistent clues to scholars attempting transcription into modern notation.

At the end of the nineteenth century, Riemann seized upon text metre as the key to rhythm in Minnesang, and ranged all medieval secular monophony into an all-encompassing theory of metrical organization in music. The norm prescribed duple metre in regular periods comprising pairs of four-bar phrases, and Riemann adjusted note values as needed to force lines of varying lengths to fall into four- or eight-bar periods.[40]

Not long after Riemann proclaimed his theory as a universal truth, Pierre Aubry, Jean Beck and Friedrich Ludwig began to work on applying the rhythmic modes of Notre Dame polyphony to the problem of rhythm in the trouvères.[41] Music scholars justified the application of the system of the rhythmic modes to secular monophony because they found refrains incorporated into thirteenth-century motets. Refrains are short bits of text, sometimes found with music, that may appear in hybrid narratives or as parts of chansons or dance songs. Thus the refrains were considered crossovers between the trouvère repertory and the modal rhythm of the early motet. Before long, what we now know to be a very problematic link authorized wholesale adaptation of the principles of modal rhythm to all categories of monophonic song.

In the early twentieth century, the question of rhythm in secular monophony took on a life of its own, becoming the overriding issue for any musicologist engaged with this repertory. John Haines has traced the scholarly debate, which became particularly intense in the first decade of the twentieth century, involving Riemann, Aubry, Beck and Ludwig.[42] Nationalist tensions lay close to the surface. Riemann had seen military service in the Franco-Prussian War, while Aubry considered it his mission to restore the glories of French musicology after France's political defeat. Beck was a bilingual Alsatian, a doctoral student at the newly established Friedrich-Wilhelm Universität at Strasbourg working in the high-powered Romance section under Gustav Gröber and studying musicology with Friedrich Ludwig. In the end the battle over credit for the initial formulation of the theory left Aubry shamed and hastened his death in 1910, a likely suicide, and discredited Beck.

Jacques Handschin raised important objections to the modal interpretation in reviewing Carl Appel's path-breaking 1934 edition of Bernart de Ventadorn, which gives the music in black note-heads.[43] But the allure of the fixity of modern notation in metre and barlines has been hard to resist. Hendrick van der Werf was almost alone among musicologists in his call in the 1970s for more refined views of genre and orality in the songs of the troubadours and trouvères, and in his admonitions against the use of refrains in motets as grounds for rhythmicizing the melodies.[44] After the refined work on genre by the French literary scholar Pierre Bec was applied by John Stevens and Christopher Page to musical questions, new views have begun to emerge.[45] Yet the fact that Hans Tischler could still publish fifteen volumes of melodies in 1997 transcribed according to principles of modal rhythm indicates the obstinate nature of the problem.[46]

The twentieth-century story of modal rhythm in monophonic song is a sad chapter in music history, and the question of the nature of rhythm in secular monophony is still unsolved. Unfortunately the nature of the sources precludes a definitive answer to the problem. Of all of the surviving monophonic repertories from the Middle Ages, it is the Minnesang sources that present the question in the bluntest form. It would be easy to belittle the German manuscripts as inadequate to the task of transmitting the art of the Minnesinger. Burkhard Kippenberg states it well when he finds fundamental issues of composition, performance and transmission at stake in Minnesang: 'to what extent was medieval secular monophony in its essence – not considered merely by the level of the notation – notatable at all in its own time?'[47] The question could well be posed regarding any of the surviving monophonic repertories, all of which were arts that resisted writing.[48]

Hearing medieval polyphony in the nineteenth century

The turn to historiography around 1800 strongly affected scholarship on Gregorian chant and secular monophony, as we have seen, and soon these repertories were harnessed for ideological projects that manifested themselves throughout the nineteenth century. There was no urgency to the study of medieval polyphony, however. While chant fulfilled a function within the Catholic church, and secular monophony was adaptable to modern circumstances through the addition of a suitable accompaniment, medieval polyphony had been an embarrassment since Gerbert published examples from the *Musica enchiriadis* in 1774.[49] Despite Herder's appeal that understanding depends on history and cultural context, scholars still assumed the unchanging nature of human hearing, and thus only one of two conclusions was possible: either composers of polyphony were incompetent, or theorists were making up abstractions. Kiesewetter, for example, found it inconceivable that organum of the style described in the *Musica enchiriadis* (ascribed to Hucbald in Gerbert) was ever performed:

> Even Hucbald must have renounced the organum, if he could ever have listened to it with his own ears; but the superior of his monastery would most probably have put an immediate stop to its use after trial of the first couplet, since, among the penances and mortifications in the rules of the order, one of a nature so painful to the senses could never have been inflicted.[50]

Until the twentieth century, scholars lacked a sufficient store of practical monuments to evaluate medieval music theory, tiptoeing around the incomprehensibility of medieval polyphony by evoking the gulf between the good and natural contributions of the folk and the crabbed and unnatural speculations of scholastic theorists. Paradoxically, one and the same composer, such as Adam de la Halle or Guillaume de Machaut, could embody both tendencies, the childlike simplicity of monophony and the 'scholastic rubbish' of polyphony.[51]

Coussemaker had no patience for this sort of thing. Already in 1852, he insisted 'that most of these pieces were conceived according to ideas different from those that prevail today, that it is necessary, in order to appreciate their value, to clear one's mind of the predisposition that one usually brings to the judgment of a piece of modern music'.[52] Coussemaker was a lawyer, and his approach was to adduce enough evidence to overwhelm earlier interpretations. But he only made a start.

Today Helmholtz is credited as the first to assert the variability of factors that go into musical perception, although in fact this insight was a fundamental precept of Fétis's philosophy of music history, which saw scale systems – the qualities and disposition of scale degrees – as the basis for musical expression, a mirror of society itself.[53] But neither Fétis nor Helmholtz immediately affected the historiography of medieval music. The theory of the folk origins of all that is good in music lived on in Riemann's all-encompassing project. He too held to the view of an unchanging human faculty of hearing and put the *Musica enchiriadis* into the realm of an abstract theory reflecting no practice.[54]

Soon the sheer weight of the practical monuments Ludwig adduced provided the evidence to dislodge Riemann's fantastic theories, showing the links between theory and practice. By the 1920s, it is easy to ascertain a change in hearing as well, expressed in the views of Heinrich Besseler and Rudolf Ficker.[55] Karl Dèzes soon expounds a view completely in tune with our own time, and yet not so far from Coussemaker: 'If Machaut, as main representative of the "ars nova", amounts to nothing because he is as yet unable to fulfil the ideals of Palestrina, that is proof you are applying principles that were never valid for his work . . . the reason for the difficulties is not that the composer was incapable of finding the right path, but that we are incapable of following him on his path.'[56]

The Palestrina revival

The modern periodization of music history, with its division between 'medieval' and 'Renaissance' as 'periods' does not fit the slow recovery of medieval polyphony over the course of the nineteenth and twentieth centuries. An accurate account would start not with medieval music, but with the twin peaks of J. S. Bach and Palestrina, demonstrating that the seventeenth and early eighteenth centuries were being reclaimed at around the same time as the sixteenth and late fifteenth centuries. The situation had evolved very little by the late nineteenth century, when Ambros definitively recovered the late fifteenth century, reaching back to Obrecht, Josquin and Pierre de la Rue. He had little sympathy, however, for earlier music, and indeed polyphony of the early fifteenth century and before remained off limits except to the most diehard music historians, who demonstrated at best an impersonal interest; true sympathy for the music itself would have to await the cataclysms of the twentieth century.

Although the Palestrina renaissance of the early nineteenth century was only the first step in the recovery of what we would term 'medieval' polyphony, the historiographical issues raised at this time formed the backdrop as a handful of amateurs undertook the slow and specialized course of research into earlier periods. E. T. A. Hoffmann's essay 'Alte und neue Kirchenmusik' (Old and New Church Music) can stand as a guide. Some of Hoffmann's observations were hardly new as he wrote in 1814; others changed the direction of musical research, while still others remained controversial and have been open to different approaches to this day.[57]

Hoffmann's picture of a decayed state of church music was nothing new, as we have already seen in our consideration of Gregorian chant. But the question specifically of church polyphony had a broader resonance. With actual relics of the Palestrina style largely confined to the Sistine Chapel since the beginning of the seventeenth century, more and more the church style in practical use had become indistinguishable from opera. Historicism answered the practical problem of religious expression at a time when the current art (which at least for Hoffmann was indeed technically superior to the old art) was not a suitable religious art.

What Hoffmann brings to the table is an explicit nationalist dimension. The issue had been latent in Herder. Now, in the wake of the first victory over Napoleon, Hoffmann explicitly blames the Enlightenment, in other words, the French, the enemies of religion, for the frivolousness affecting church music. From now on, nationalist agendas would colour the emerging narrative of medieval music history, as we have seen from the course of the recovery of medieval secular monophony, intimately associated with language. It would be a mistake, however, to overplay the nationalist card at this point in the recovery of medieval polyphony. Polyphony was so powerfully connected with the Italian tradition that it took a long time before even French scholars would acknowledge French contributions to medieval polyphony, mainly because the polyphony itself was not congenial to the nineteenth-century ear. Hoffmann pushed the origins of music back to Gregory the Great, confirming Italy as the traditional leader in music, and now he would draw upon the great Italian polyphonist Palestrina as a foil against the French. What Palestrina had to offer, first and foremost, was myth, the story of Palestrina as the 'saviour of church music'. This single composer now stood as a monumental focal point for writing music history.[58] For Hoffmann, Palestrina was the beginning point for a magnificent 200 years of church music, while for others he stood at the end of the painfully slow development of polyphony since the *Musica enchiriadis*.

Hoffmann's strategy takes on a special twist here, yielding a point critical to the recovery of medieval music: he dismisses the relevance of ancient Greece. Lacking both melody and harmony, the sort of music the Greeks cultivated was simply not music in the modern sense of the word. Murmurings to this effect are already present in Burney, who was not happy about having to rehearse the tedious details of ancient Greek theory, and soon the trend led to histories that omitted the Greeks entirely. Kiesewetter's *History of the Modern Music of Western Europe*, for example, begins with the Middle Ages.

Hoffmann characterizes the *a cappella* Palestrina style as 'simple, truthful, childlike, pious, strong, and powerful . . . Without any ornament, without melodic drive, mostly perfect consonant chords succeed one another, with whose strength and boldness the heart is seized with inexpressible power and raised up on high.'[59] Hoffmann thereby makes Palestrina a new classical antiquity of music, evoking Winckelmann's characterization of ancient art, epitomized in the famous expression 'noble simplicity and serene grandeur'. As James Garratt has noted, Hoffmann, the great admirer of Beethoven's Romantic instrumental music, thereby sets up Palestrina as a composer of absolute music, affirming the spiritual power of music as an autonomous art – texts are unimportant, for the music in and of itself is now an object of aesthetic enjoyment.[60] This brings up two final issues critical to the revival of early music, both still relevant to us today: the problem of the function of early music brought to performance in new contexts, and the problem of the appropriation of old music by composers in a new present. We will return to these questions after surveying some of the important scholars actually involved with research on medieval music in the nineteenth century.

Some nineteenth-century musicologists

No myth comparable to Palestrina could champion the cause of medieval polyphony. The best available, an eighteenth-century invention associating Machaut's Mass with the coronation of Charles V, did not live up to the promise of the small fragment of the Gloria made available at the beginning of the nineteenth century, still found replete with errors in Riemann's 1891 revision of Ambros.[61] Two nineteenth-century transcriptions of the entire mass, one by Perne (ca1810), another by Auguste Bottée de Toulmon (ca1830), never saw publication.[62]

After the deaths of Kiesewetter and Bottée in 1850, Fétis and Coussemaker were left as the most important scholars with interests in medieval music. Twenty-one years older than Coussemaker, Fétis had already staked out positions he was unwilling to alter. In Fétis's history, music up to the time of Palestrina utilized the 'tonality of plainchant', that is, the church modes. Since all but the F modes lack a leading tone, the basic character is perforce one of calm and serenity, a religious demeanour. Palestrina represented perfection in this line of development, the end point of a great historical arch.[63]

Fétis considered the period circa 1480–1590, what we tend to label the Renaissance, sufficiently well outlined in Burney and Forkel; the challenge was to fill the gap from the thirteenth century up to 1450. Schooled in the Winckelmannian organic model of origin, growth, change and decline, Fétis considered it the task of music history to show how early music prepared the high point of Palestrina. Fétis found the minimum number of practical monuments to fill the gap to his satisfaction: a single rondeau of Adam de la Halle at the early end and a single ballata of Landini at the later end.

The section of rondeaux in the Adam de la Halle 'complete works' collection, *F-Pn* fonds fr. 25566, provided ideal material: a series of short three-voice works notated in score, which facilitated vertical alignment of the sonorities despite Fétis's rudimentary knowledge of mensural notation. Fétis printed one example in 1827, the rondeau *Tant con je vivray* (Figure 19.1 gives Fétis's original transcription).[64]

Adam's rondeau stands between parallel organum and fifteenth-century counterpoint. Fétis's transcription generated considerable comment (sparring with Fétis was something of a sport for nineteenth-century musical scholars), and competing transcriptions of *Tant con je vivray* mark stages along the path towards full mastery of the Franconian system of notation by the 1860s.

Just a month after the first publication of *Tant con je vivray*, Fétis closed in on the last part of the gap in the practical sources, offering a transcription of Landini's three-voice ballata *Non avrà ma' pietà*, which he considered another milestone in the history of harmony, the origin of the counterpoint that would be perfected in the sixteenth century.[65] The work confirmed the superior role of the Italian trecento for the progress of music, an idea carried into the twentieth century by Riemann and Wolf. By 1835, when Fétis published his 'Résumé philosophique de l'histoire de musique', the 254-page general history of music prefacing the first volume of the first edition of the *Biographie universelle*, a few additional pieces had assumed supporting roles in his narrative, and from this point on Fétis dismissed all challenges to his views.[66]

Function and appropriation of early music in the nineteenth century

Let us conclude our survey of nineteenth-century historicism by returning to a consideration of the two questions raised by Hoffmann's essay: the function of early music brought to performance, and the appropriation of early music in new compositions. We can distinguish a variety of functions for the performance of early music (not yet encompassing medieval music) in the nineteenth century. For the early Romantics, early music induced a sublime and ineffable *schwärmerei*, a mood expressed in Wackenroder, Tieck and Hoffmann. More or less explicit efforts to reform culture lie behind performances of early music, usually the church style, by musicians in several German-speaking regions, such as Zelter in Berlin, Thibaut in Heidelberg, and Kiesewetter in Vienna. Choron's concerts in Paris were a bit different, because they were public, and therefore cultivated an aesthetic appropriate to entertain the Parisian audience. Fétis's *concerts historiques* in Paris and Brussels had a different focus still, namely pedagogical inculcation,

Figure 19.1 Adam de la Halle, *Tant con je vivray* (rondeau) (transcribed by F.-J. Fétis [ca1827], *B-Bc* X 27.935 [unnumbered folio]). With permission of the Conservative royal – Koninklijk Conservatorium Brussels.

a function to which I will return shortly. None of these instances, of course, is true to the original function of the music.[67]

Hoffmann himself was not in favour of the actual restoration of early church music, believing that young composers should simply find inspiration from the old masterworks. Echoing Herder, Hoffmann considered it impossible for a contemporary composer to write like Palestrina or Handel. His view was an early salvo in a long and continuing debate concerning the degree and manner of incorporating the old into the new.[68]

The same debate occurred in France, and it is this less studied side that I would like to dwell on, for potentially the most promising answer to the problem of reconciling early music and a contemporary compositional style was Fétis's doctrine of eclecticism, which dealt at the same time with both function and appropriation. In essence, Fétis's eclecticism stems from his urge to put historical research in the service of the present, as a way forward for composers facing the many crises that he perceived in the music of his time, such as the exacerbated materialism brought on by the end of the patronage system, the decline of taste as composers catered to a new public, and the end of the reign of tonality as new harmonic possibilities were almost exhausted. The answer to the many crises lay in the selective use of past masters to reinvigorate present-day composition:

> the simplicity and the majesty of the style of Palestrina, the scientific and elegant forms of Scarlatti, the poignant expression of Leo, of Pergolesi, of Majo, and of Jomelli, the dramatic force of Gluck, the incisive harmony of Johann Sebastian Bach, the massed power of Handel, the richness of Haydn, the passionate accents of Mozart, the independent spirit of Beethoven, the suavity of Italian melodies, the energy of German songs, the dramatic decorum of French music, all the combinations of voices, all the systems of instrumentation, all the effects of sonority, all the rhythms, all the forms, in short all resources, will be able to find their place within a single work, and will produce effects all the more penetrating in that they will be employed apropos.[69]

Eclecticism reveals the point behind Fétis's famous *concerts historiques*, practical efforts to demonstrate the palette of genres and affects available to the composer for the purpose of revitalizing music.

The ultimate failure of this plan is symptomatic of one moment in the ongoing historicist debate. Looking back from our vantage point, one might attribute its failure to the fact that the affects Fétis attributes to various early musics are not hard-wired into human consciousness (nor would later research find his characterization of the affects accurate). But in the context of the nineteenth century, the plan failed for ideological reasons.

Fétis saw an ideal representative of his music of the future in Meyerbeer. That composer was eminently suitable to French taste, cosmopolitan and sure of itself after centuries of development. But Meyerbeer horrified the German nation builders, who resisted foreign influence in an effort to forge a national taste. Herder, Hegel and Hoffmann all agreed that form and content must reflect the *Zeitgeist* authentically.[70] Meyerbeer – a German Jew who followed a pan-European career not unlike that of the great Handel or Mozart – was incompatible with the new demands for originality, a fact brutally exposed by the spokesmen Robert Schumann and Richard Wagner. Eventually their view won out over public taste itself.

Following several more years of diligent archaeology, a new medieval world revealed itself once scholars again occupied themselves with forming a narrative. Fétis's research, exposed as factually insufficient by Kiesewetter and especially by Coussemaker, would no longer be cited by musicologists, but by then it had stamped the narrative subliminally.

The twentieth century: Friedrich Ludwig

Already in the 1902–3 volume of the yearbook of the International Musical Society, Friedrich Ludwig sketched out a survey of fourteenth-century music that is the sort of account one still reads, covering sources, genres, major figures and style history.[71] Ludwig's treatment of fourteenth-century music history weighs the significance of national developments according to political history. French music receives pride of place, because it was the most broadly based and most influential musical art of the fourteenth century: 'The world of tones in these masterpieces – at that time experienced as such – had unified the entire western cultural world in common admiration and enjoyment . . . Italian music . . . lacked this sounding board which French art enjoyed throughout the West.'[72] It is clear why Ludwig later began publication of practical monuments with Machaut's works: it was a matter of historical balance. Yet Ludwig is unequivocal in stating that he finds the aesthetic rewards of the Italian trecento superior to the 'clear-headed' French, trusting his ear in this matter:

> We would certainly find among the sonorities sufficient asperities and all manner of progressions whose impossibility and deficiency later belong to the elementary rules of compositional technique and which we no longer encounter from the mid fifteenth century on, but alongside these there is also a wealth of passages that prove how often the Italians dared to follow the ear against the conventions of the school and thereby to obtain effects that we seek in vain among the French.[73]

Having transcribed virtually the entire repertory (almost none of which, incidentally, would have been accessible to his readers), Ludwig saw the possibility of writing a history without drawing on invented influences, 'before we proceed further on shaky ground, going in quest of the influence of so-called folk music and instrumental music, questions that have more frequently led researchers in medieval music astray'.[74] Even simple Latin-texted two-voice polyphony receives an airing in Ludwig's survey, since it is found throughout the Western cultural sphere in that period, even on the periphery.[75] Without evoking the label 'Renaissance', the survey ends with a glance towards the very different circumstances of the fifteenth century, to the 'great invasion' of foreign musicians into Italy, when the national forms cultivated in the fourteenth century disappear in a lively exchange of artists of different nations.

Ludwig's fundamental contribution was his exhaustive knowledge of the sources and repertory of polyphony and secular monophony, from the twelfth to the early fifteenth century. Not relying on music theory treatises to organize medieval historiography, as had been done from Gerbert to Johannes Wolf, Ludwig shifted the balance, seeking his point of departure in the music itself. Ludwig carried out not just the first step of positivist historiography – to ascertain the facts – but also the second, rarely seen at the time – to formulate a general picture based on just that evidence.

Rudolf Ficker and *Geistesgeschichte*

From around the last decade of the nineteenth century through the first third of the twentieth, many German historians in reaction to positivism pursued *Geistesgeschichte* – the history of the intellect – an approach to history that seeks to demonstrate how the *Zeitgeist*, the unifying inner spirit that characterizes an age, manifests itself in the cultural phenomena of that age.[76] The approach was highly influential at the time, and though unfamiliar as a concept today, to some extent it continues to colour music history writing. A sketch of medieval music history by Rudolf Ficker, published in 1925 and dedicated to Guido Adler, can stand as an example.[77] The following extended paraphrase of Ficker's imaginative narrative – a succinct, though complete history of medieval polyphony – is warranted in order to understand other twentieth-century trends in historiography.

Ficker begins by staking out a new point of departure. In the past, he avers, medieval music had been branded as primitive, aesthetically foreign to a nineteenth-century ideal of music imprinted in our ears since childhood. It is now clear, however, that this ideal is only one of many musical and aesthetic possibilities, none of which have universal validity, but which are determined by context: 'today we listen completely differently than we did even ten or twenty years ago, when for example we suddenly hear the monotonous song of a savage South Sea islander from a gramophone. Today the laughter that formerly accompanied our feelings of superiority over such a song has passed.'[78]

In this survey, the developmental stages do not so much trace a progression as they document artistic responses to cultural clashes rooted in deep-seated intellectual propensities of north and south. There are, according to Ficker, only three fundamental driving forces of music: the melodic, the 'sonorous-chordal', and the rhythmic. Melody, a sinuous and sensual microtonal improvised melody that originated in the Orient, epitomizes the culture of the south.[79] Nordic musical culture is epitomized by the 'sonorous-chordal', a dubious concept that Ficker supports by citing the nineteenth-century discovery of the lur, a 3,500-year-old brass instrument found in Denmark.[80] (Writing in the 1920s, Ficker associates the term 'Nordic' as much as he can with the German orbit, but often and somewhat reluctantly it refers to the French – as one would think it must, given the facts of the development of medieval polyphony – and in one instance even to the English.) Since lurs were always found in pairs, this is proof enough, he concludes, that Ur-Germanic peoples practised a polyphony of diatonic overtone combinations.

Under these dialectical circumstances, a first confrontation is not long in coming. It brought about a number of milestones, including diatonicism in the chant, staff notation, the earliest polyphony, and the concept of the cantus firmus. In earlier music histories, singing in parallel fifths or fourths had always been considered an indication of the musical barbarity of 'our Germanic ancestors'.[81] In Ficker's new interpretation, the diatonic chant chafed against the northerners' fundamental musical orientation toward the sonorous, and so they further transformed it, building a fundamental sonority on each pitch, each sonority a world unto itself.

A second conflict between north and south produced the Gothic, and with it rhythm as a third constituent element of music. The most decisive development took place in France, for the Crusaders left from France in the eleventh century, and contact with the 'strange fairy-tale land of the Orient' stimulated a new music. Instead of the weighty chords above chant pitches seen in 'Romanesque' organum, Gothic organum exhibits a lively, freely composed, naturalistic melody, juxtaposed with the intellectual symbol of the supporting cantus firmus.[82]

A comparison of Romanesque and Gothic architecture provides Ficker with numerous analogies to musical practice. While the Romanesque church presents a unified conception of space, weighty and powerful, the Gothic church has a multitude of complementary parts, banishes forces of weight, and places structural elements in full view. Similarly, while Romanesque organum had exhibited spatial and chordal unities, Gothic organum and motet dissolve these into a multiplicity of lines. The new feeling for life expressed in Gothic art transformed music, placing a new structural element in full view: rhythm.

Ficker's stylistic analysis of an early motet is highly charged.[83] The tenor cantus firmus, the symbolic foundation, fragments the melodic sense of the chant, analogous to the visible skeleton of Gothic cathedrals. Different texts gloss the basic idea in the two upper voices, which appear to have been created independently, and later forcibly welded together, resulting in some harsh dissonances at points of overlap. The aesthetic of the French motet is even more difficult for moderns to comprehend, an extreme confrontation of 'unbridled naturalism' in the vernacular texts of the upper voices with 'religious-dogmatic subordination' in the chant tenor.[84] The result resembles a French Gothic cathedral bristling with grotesque gargoyles. Although perplexing to the modern observer, the mixture of the sacred and the secular expresses the Gothic ideal of linking religion to all aspects of the natural world.

Soon intellectual values lose control over secular naturalism, and a third conflict between north and south signals the early Renaissance (ca1300), the first and only time that Ficker posits an initiative from the south. Significantly, it will fizzle out. Italy had already displayed an ambiguous reception of northern Gothic architecture, transferring stylistic elements into a 'more earthbound' spatial conception. Similarly, Italian trecento composers borrowed the outward stylistic forms of instrumentally accompanied French secular vocal music in their madrigals, but the musical results were uniquely Italian. Now divergent forces are reconciled in a more unified complex eschewing religious symbolism. Melody is freely rhythmicized and set in a sonorous harmony exhibiting a sense of progression. Unfortunately, later composers, especially the last great Italian of the fourteenth century, Francesco Landini, yield too much to French influence.

Ficker pauses here in recounting the epoch-making struggles of medieval music history to pick up the late Gothic art of fourteenth-century France. Too little of the Ars Subtilior was known at the time to be of any use to Ficker; for him, the most extreme tension between the old and new, the Gothic and the emerging Renaissance, is found in Burgundy, and it is in this context (drawing upon a new book by Johan Huizinga) that Ficker considers an excerpt from a Machaut motet, *Tous corps / De souspirant / Suspiro.*[85]

> It appears completely senseless to us that a completely unintelligible and free rhythmic scheme, lacking any causal melodic relationship, could determine the structure, and that all harmonic and melodic activity should be completely dependent on this schema, even imputed to mere chance. Nowhere does the purely constructive treatment of form manifest itself with such naked and unjustifiable candour as in the fourteenth-century isorhythmic motet. If we recall the immeasurable rigidity of, say, the Burgundian court ceremony, with its boundless formalism, its extravagance

of class distinctions, and the frequently grotesque pomp of its dress, then we must indeed admit that this *Zeitgeist* found a congenial musical expression in the isorhythmic motet.[86]

The fourth conflict between north and south comes after 1400, when 'the Nordic Gothic attempts to summon all its powers once again to subdue the forces awakened in the south'.[87] Emotionally detached yet exhibiting a kind of mystical rapture, the new musical style resembles the spirit of early Netherlandish painting, like the panel of *a cappella* singers in the Ghent altarpiece, 'filled with secret symbols that are neither audible nor visible'.[88] English composers, and Burgundian masters working from the example of the English, reconciled apparently incompatible demands by joining a flowing melos, sensual and individualistic, with the religious symbolism of the rigid cantus firmus, which is now invisible and inaudible, for the individual pitches fall 'arbitrarily' along the course of a new melody.

A fifth and final confrontation between north and south comes in the second half of the fifteenth century, and this time the Netherlanders obtained a definitive synthesis, settling the two-centuries-long tension between the Renaissance call for individual emotion and the medieval propensity for the intellectual and for musical construction. Here, free or borrowed musical motives are subject to repetition and development throughout the texture, and according to Ficker this principle characterizes music to the present day.

Ficker's survey synthesizes the history of music, art and architecture to distinguish five periods: the Romanesque, the Gothic, the early Renaissance, the later-Gothic, and the Renaissance, each with a logic of its own. His new hearing, aided by art-historical analogies, for the first time affords an essentially positive (if curious) assessment of ninth-century organum. The Gothic is treated most thoroughly in Ficker's account, sympathetically accompanied by numerous vivid analogies from architecture.[89] The placement of a French 'late Gothic' after the discussion of an early Renaissance highlights the perplexity with which a scholar in 1925 greeted the discovery of isorhythm. Tempted by the outrageous images of Huizinga's court of Burgundy, Ficker alters the chronology by about a hundred years in order to call up an analogy between society and art to explain it.

Most troubling to our sensibilities is our knowledge of the future of Ficker's north/south dichotomy. As Leech-Wilkinson puts it, 'Ficker's Nordic reading of so much medieval music ... was itself warped, regardless of how it may later have been used.'[90] Writing in 1936, Collingwood saw the roots of such readings in the proto-anthropology of Herder, attributing different natures to different races, whose individual character depends on geography and environment. There were dire consequences: 'Once Herder's theory of race is accepted, there is no escaping the Nazi marriage laws.'[91] It is ironic that in the nineteenth century Herder's attribution of the diversity of human nature was an essential factor in opening people's minds to other musics, including medieval music.

The density of interrelationships between music and art seen in Ficker's narrative continued to provide a compelling model for large-scale music history. For example, it reappears in the structure and in the detail of Paul Henry Lang's account of the same periods in his *Music in Western Civilization*. Compare the following passage, characterizing the upper voice in trecento polyphony, one example of many close paraphrases of Ficker: 'This melody was a happy medium between Nordic rigidity and the contourlessness of Oriental melismatic flow, and, free from the shackles of modal meter, it obeyed a natural sense of free symmetry and articulation.'[92] In textbooks, Ludwig's drier, more sober account has tended to prevail, one richer in factual material and illustrative examples, but now and again musicologists have found images of the sort Ficker evokes irresistible to provide a splash of cultural context or local colour.

Edward Lowinsky and the historiography of medieval music

As knowledge of early music grew, musicological training beginning around the 1930s tended more and more to produce specialists. Particularly after the Second World War, this usually led to source studies and edition making, biography and style analysis, but some scholars were capable of a broader view. I would like briefly to consider one example, Edward Lowinsky, a specialist in music of the Renaissance. Trained at Heidelberg under Besseler, Lowinsky was one of the many Jewish scholars who found their way to the United States in the wake of Nazi social policy of the 1930s. Although one might not expect to see Lowinsky figuring in a sketch of the historiography and reception of medieval music, the positioning of the Middle Ages in his influential essay 'Music in the Culture of the Renaissance' (1954) is worth reviewing, for Lowinsky's stark formulations continue to frame questions that occupy musicologists.[93] The overall approach shares the concern for cultural context and the long-range perspective of *Geistesgeschichte*, but Lowinsky's specialist's viewpoint finds only one historical moment of any consequence, the one focused on the creation of the Renaissance that he so loved.

The dominant force characterizing the Renaissance for Lowinsky was the ineluctable urge to individual freedom, and he links this cultural force to musical developments. For example, Lowinsky relates the hold of the cantus firmus on the medieval motet to the hold of the church on the individual. The advent of the Renaissance saw emancipation from a whole host of shackles. Critical to the evolution of vocal music, in Lowinsky's estimation, was its delivery from 'ready-made patterns', including the pre-existing melodies of Gregorian chant subject to the old church modes, the straitjacket of the cantus firmus, the fixed forms, and fixed rhythms (the rhythmic modes). Further, medieval music was constructed in layers by successively adding voices over a cantus firmus, while Renaissance composers could think in harmonies and conceive of voices simultaneously. The imitative style developed in vocal music then contributed to the evolution of instrumental music, emancipating it in turn from vocal models, and pointing the way towards the ultimate perfection of absolute music to come. Once again, essential qualities of north (Flanders) and south (Italy) were locked in a struggle, this time between northern polyphony and southern harmony, reaching a first synthesis in Josquin des Prez. The dialectical struggle, always between these two poles – sensuous sound (material, body) and linear counterpoint (intellect, spirit) – sums up the rest of music history, reaching perfect balance in Viennese Classicism (especially in Mozart), only to shift emphasis to the material in the nineteenth century and to the intellect in the twentieth.[94]

Lowinsky devotes a special segment of his argument to the Ars Nova, which he delimits as the period 1300–1450. In Lowinsky's scenario, this period does not merit the term 'Renaissance', though a few of the Renaissance's formative aspects are put in place at this time. For example, the break-up of the rhythmic modes and the new short note values available around 1300 imply a new rhythmic freedom, but composers did not take advantage of their accomplishment: 'As if bewildered and frightened by the onrush of so many novel rhythmic possibilities, the musician of the *ars nova* immediately imposed severe restrictions on them.'[95] In the event, the strict and at the same time arbitrary constraints of isorhythmic periodicity would postpone for a century the realization of full freedom of rhythmic invention.

In my view the most pernicious thread running through the three samples of twentieth-century historiography of medieval polyphony that I have surveyed here is the rigorous propensity to label, expressed as a distinction between 'medieval' and 'Renaissance'. This is the sort of history writing that Collingwood characterized as 'apocalyptic'.[96] Originally an aspect of early Christian historiography in which the birth of Christ was viewed a climactic dividing point between a period of darkness and light, of preparation and revelation, the 'apocalyptic' approach was later applied to all sorts of decisive events, such as the Renaissance or the Enlightenment. It leads to rigorous periodization. It is least present in Ludwig. It essentializes periods in Ficker, reaching a moment of near-religious revelation in Lowinsky, and continues to maintain a hold on historiography today. More recently, however, Reinhard Strohm has realized both a new periodization and new views of musical centres in his history of late-fourteenth- and fifteenth-century music.[97]

Instrumental accompaniment of late medieval song

Daniel Leech-Wilkinson has traced the curious origins of the practice, common through much of the twentieth century, of accompanying voice with instruments in the performance of late medieval songs. His research points to Riemann who, on the basis of a remark in the 1898 Stainer edition of works from *GB-Ob* Can. misc. 213, shifted his view of the late medieval chanson from an *a cappella* conception to one treating the chanson as accompanied melody, a view that conveniently served Riemann's account of a long historical development culminating in the German Lied.[98] Soon Riemann's editions of late medieval chansons strongly encroached on the sources, rearranging texting to set off melismatic segments as instrumental preludes and interludes. Slightly later, Schering offered a hypothesis even more distant from the original sources, proposing that songs in the manuscripts are actually organ pieces embellishing a simple melody, whose original shape is adumbrated by the text underlay of the source.[99] Despite the less dogmatic views of Adler, Kroyer and Handschin, and some half-hearted misgivings of Reaney and Harrison, it was Riemann's view that prevailed, and so performance practice rested on dubious premises for a good seventy-five years before Christopher Page returned to the *a cappella* conception, demonstrating first in 1977 that it was typical medieval practice to perform songs of Machaut and Du Fay with voices on all parts.[100] The circumstances surrounding the origin of the voices-and-instruments hypothesis and the long adherence to it do not, in Leech-Wilkinson's view, paint a favourable picture of the workings of musical scholarship: 'Judgements about history, therefore, depended on assumptions specific to a particular group at a particular time. Evidence (of which there was only a little) played only a small part in the process, and what it meant changed.'[101]

I am a bit less pessimistic in looking back at this episode, one that so effectively sums up the twentieth-century recovery of medieval polyphony. In one sense Riemann did arbitrarily change a prevailing nineteenth-century conception of late medieval song as *a cappella* music. But in another sense he did not, because there was no active performance tradition of late medieval music in the nineteenth century. Riemann in effect prepared the way for the very first serious tries at performing medieval polyphony at all. From his time to the present, the scholarly aspect and an aesthetic aspect would proceed in a more or less reciprocal relationship.

Numerous factors came together to lend support to Riemann's hypothesis. All of them, of course, are explicable given the circumstances and personalities of the early twentieth century. Yet enough of them resonate with the state of the evidence as it stood at the time to make me feel that the approach to performance was not an arbitrary encroachment.

A prerequisite to any aesthetic engagement with early polyphony was the new hearing, the ability to regard non-tonal music with equanimity. Assaults on tonality, either through extreme harmonic instability or through exploitation of non-functional colouristic harmony, as well as exposure to exotic cultures at world expositions and ongoing ethnomusicological research, led to a new openness to give this music a chance that it had never before enjoyed. Harmony had killed the prospects for medieval polyphony from its first rediscovery; now, changes in the musical world offered a new possibility for understanding.

In fact the new understanding came not so much through harmony as through counterpoint. Writing in 1912, Schering explicitly related the contrapuntal complexity of early-twentieth-century music to that of a Machaut ballade: 'the attention is not so much on the sounding together of the voices as on their horizontal stretching-out . . . For at the time of Machaut chords are not bound one to another but rather only "voices", a peculiarity in which the compositional technique of this time in many ways touches that of the present.'[102] The emphasis on linearity (a genuine quality of this music) made the music less strange to the modern ear. Theoretical authorization of this tack lay in the concept of 'successive composition', traced back to Johannes de Garlandia in the mid thirteenth century.[103]

Both literary and iconographical sources seemed to support the use of instruments. Besides vague popular conceptions of the wandering troubadour, some more concrete material justified the notion of instrumental accompaniment, such as the following passage from a letter in Machaut's *Le Livre dou Voir Dit* (1363–5), in which Machaut provides some valuable yet curious indications of performance practice of the ballade *Nes qu'on porroit* (named in the letter by its refrain):

> I am sending you my poem entitled *Morpheus*, also called *The Fountain of Love*, along with 'The Great Desire I Have to See You', on which I have made the music as you have ordered, and in the German style [a la guise d'un rés d'Alemangne[104]]. And by God, it has been a long time since I composed anything good that pleased me this much. And the tenor parts are as sweet as unsalted porridge. And so I beg you to be willing to hear and learn the piece exactly as it has been written without adding to or taking away any part, and it is intended to be recited with a quite long measure, and whoever could arrange [it] for the organ, the bagpipe, or other instruments that is its very nature.[105]

It would be easy to interpret the letter to mean that one performs the work as written, most effectively by assigning instruments to the lower voices. This was the performance practice before the 1980s. Today, however, even in light of our best scholarship, the passage resists interpretation. On the one hand, the composer wants the work to be learned precisely as written, which we believe to mean voices on all three parts; on the other hand, he claims that the work's true nature lies in instrumental arrangement, presumably without voices. In our current view, this does not mean an ensemble of instruments literally playing the written music, but some kind of creative rearrangement, and thus not 'exactly as it has been written', because that segment of the musical practice was carried on in a largely unwritten tradition.

From the beginning of modern performances, performers tended to score pieces with dissimilar instruments. Contrasting sonorities not only highlighted the linear aspect of the music, but also helped to mask unusual vertical combinations.[106] Musicologists justified a piebald instrumentarium with a variety of evidence. Iconography, such as the panel of the Ghent altarpiece showing angel musicians playing different instruments (this time not the panel of *a cappella* angel singers), or, better, Memling's angel musicians of the Najera Triptych, confirmed literary evidence known since the eighteenth century, such as the two long lists of miscellaneous instruments in Machaut.[107] Bottée de Toulmon had imagined in 1832 a large orchestra of instruments (the list in Machaut's *Remede de Fortune*) in unison with voices, and this was the image, supported also by the colourful soundscape implied by Huizinga, that Ficker realized in sound in his 1927 concerts at the Beethoven centenary festival conference in Vienna.[108] In sum, to performers and scholars of the first three-quarters of the twentieth century, iconographical, literary, and historical evidence sufficiently supported then-current practical realizations of medieval polyphony.

At least three new interdisciplinary points of departure of the 1970s contributed to the discarding of the voices-and-instruments approach in favour of the *a cappella* approach. First, a revolution in French studies brought a new focus on late medieval poetry. New literary sources, as well as new interpretations of old literary sources, were brought to bear on the issue of music performance.[109] Second, renewed scrutiny of historical archives sharpened our knowledge of the actual performing forces available to various institutions.[110] Finally, detailed codicological studies of late medieval manuscripts found evidence of scribal practice bearing on text entry and thus indirectly on performance practice.[111]

Some aspects of the new performance practice deserve more attention. For example, highly refined experiments in tuning by the professional voices required for *a cappella* scoring reveal an unsuspected dynamic.[112] The ramifications are enormous, particularly if Page's view of a Pythagorean Continental tuning on the one hand, and a mean-tone English tuning on the other, can be maintained. Now, for example, the degree of instability of the sonorities categorized by Sarah Fuller needs to be evaluated in both tunings, and the actual compositional practice re-examined in this light.[113]

The new sound, utilizing voices alone instead of voice accompanied by contrasting instruments, focuses on uniform sonorities, a chordal flow, instead of counterpoint, a network of lines unfolding linearly. Riemann had already laid out the stark contrast of vertical as against linear construction in 1905, and the two twentieth-century performance practices seem to represent just these two approaches to the music.[114] I hope that my presentations of Ficker's 1925 article and Lowinsky's 1954 article sufficiently warn of the danger of playing one concept against its opposite. To do so makes for a powerful narrative, but runs roughshod over the complexity of the material. Ficker's opposing concepts are oversimplified, and thus his syntheses do not convince. Lowinsky omits synthesis entirely, leaving (in his mind) a set of bad choices and a set of good choices. Unfortunately it is Lowinsky's stark conceptual contrast of 'simultaneous composition' with 'successive composition' that has remained the most common shorthand for these two views, a gross oversimplification in both cases.

Kevin Moll has brought historiographical material to bear on this question, demonstrating that German writings on the question of compositional process in the early fifteenth century are actually more nuanced than Anglo-American writings, which have been too prone to emphasize the polar opposites of 'successive' and 'simultaneous'.[115] Moll's examination of repertory and quibbles with Besseler's anachronistic premises led him to support a new refinement of Ernst Apfel's work, which argues for composers' continuing dependence on a two-voice contrapuntal framework up to ca1500, a view long argued by Margaret Bent as well.[116] If we accept this analysis, we still need to explain a question posed by reception history, namely, what was the sonorous quality in Du Fay that Besseler perceived that led him to explain it in terms of emerging tonality, and by what strategies did composers obtain it?

One might imagine a way forward – or at least some new questions to pose – through the recent emphasis on musical hearing. Citing examples from Ciconia's *Doctorem principem / Melodia suavissima*, and quoting work of Peter M. Lefferts and Julie Cumming, Richard Taruskin characterizes the late medieval motet using terms such as 'monumental' and 'grandiose', music in the service of despots.[117] To my modern ear, the most grandiose moments in several of Ciconia's motets are the passages at the ends of sections, sustained in harmonic rhythm but active in rhythmic and motivic vitality. This texture was initiated about thirty years earlier in another

Example 19.1 Philippe Royllart, end of first *talea* of motet, *Rex Karole / Leticie, pacis / Virgo prius ac posterius*

political motet, Philippe Royllart's widely transmitted *Rex Karole / Leticie, pacis / Virgo prius ac posterius*, which concludes its five *taleae* with rhythmically animated sections of a style directly analogous to those in Ciconia (Example 19.1).[118]

It would seem that Royllart's purpose was the sonically monumental, a visceral effect that moves the listener on a grand scale. Composers continued to cultivate Royllart's procedure for a period of about fifty years in motets and mass ordinaries. At some point however, this awesome sonority gave way to a different awesome sonority, that of comparatively unanimated, ringing chords. Were the harmonic asperities occasioned by overlapping motifs now old-fashioned, or was hyperanimation not suitable to the acoustics of certain architectural surroundings, or did English pieces heard at church councils in a different tuning demonstrate the effectiveness of chordal sonorities? This is the new sound that Besseler heard, although he was unable to find a suitable analytical model to express it appropriately.

For our part, in moving ahead, we must learn to separate a potentially useful insight from its presentation, the baggage of a particular moment in history. After all, our present views are subject to the same strictures, and they too will be found wanting. I agree with Dahlhaus that 'not all insights into the past are possible at all times', but by now it ought to be possible to cumulate insights, even if we must concede that we will always have only a partial answer.[119]

Notes

1 Plainsong

1 Peter Jeffery, 'Rome and Jerusalem: From Oral Tradition to Written Repertory in Two Ancient Liturgical Centers', in Graeme Boone, ed., *Essays on Medieval Music: In Honor of David G. Hughes* (Cambridge, MA, Harvard University Press, 1995), pp. 207–47.

2 Jeffery, 'Rome and Jerusalem', and James McKinnon, 'Liturgical Psalmody in the Sermons of St Augustine: An Introduction', in Peter Jeffery, ed., *The Study of Medieval Chant: Paths and Bridges, East and West, in Honor of Kenneth Levy* (Woodbridge: Boydell, 2001), pp. 7–24.

3 Joseph Dyer, 'The Desert, the City, and Psalmody in the Late Fourth Century', in Sean Gallagher, James Haar, John Nádas and Timothy Striplin, eds., *Western Plainchant in the First Millennium: Studies in the Medieval Liturgy and Its Music* (Aldershot: Ashgate, 2003), pp. 11–43; Peter Jeffery, 'Monastic Reading and the Emerging Roman Chant Repertory', in Gallagher et al., eds., *Western Plainchant in the First Millennium*, pp. 45–103; James McKinnon, 'Desert Monasticism and the Later Fourth-Century Psalmodic Movement', *Music and Letters*, 75 (1994), pp. 505–21.

4 Margot Fassler, 'Sermons, Sacramentaries, and Early Sources for the Office in the Latin West: The Example of Advent', in Margot Fassler and Rebecca A. Baltzer, eds., *The Divine Office in the Latin Middle Ages: Methodology and Source Studies, Regional Developments, Hagiography* (Oxford University Press, 2000), pp. 15–47.

5 On gospel tones see David Hiley, *Western Plainchant: A Handbook* (Oxford: Clarendon Press, 1993), pp. 55–7.

6 For an outline of this system see John Harper, *The Forms and Orders of Western Liturgy from the Tenth to the Eighteenth Century: A Historical Introduction and Guide for Students and Musicians* (Oxford University Press, 1991), pp. 243–50.

7 Joseph Dyer, 'The Singing of Psalms in the Early-Medieval Office', *Speculum* 64 (1989), pp. 535–78.

8 Joseph Dyer, 'Monastic Psalmody of the Middle Ages', *Revue bénédictine* 99 (1989), pp. 41–74.

9 The Te Deum, which concluded matins, was sung to a melody that somewhat resembled a psalm tone.

10 See Michel Huglo, 'Tonary', *Grove Music Online*, www.oxfordmusiconline.com.

11 For an edition of mode 1 antiphons, see László Dobszay and Janka Szendrei, eds., *Antiphonen*, Monumenta Monodica Medii Aevi 5, vol. I (Kassel and New York: Bärenreiter, 1991).

12 From the ninth to the eleventh century, hymns were sung primarily in the monastic office.

13 Susan Boynton, 'Orality, Literacy and the Early Notation of the Office Hymns', *Journal of the American Musicological Society* 56 (2003), pp. 99–168.

14 A great responsory could also be performed at vespers.

15 In the monastic office of matins, the third nocturn had canticles rather than psalms.

16 James Grier, 'The Divine Office at Saint-Martial in the Early Eleventh Century: Paris, BNF lat. 1085', in Fassler and Baltzer, eds., *Divine Office*, pp. 179–204, describes an unusual manuscript that indicates the performance of the entire doxology at the conclusion of every responsory, which the compiler would have thought reflected Roman (rather than Frankish) practice.

17 The ceremonial of the mass described here reflects the state of the liturgy in the central Middle Ages.

18 On the Kyrie see Hiley, *Western Plainchant*, pp. 150–6.

19 David Bjork, *The Aquitanian Kyrie Repertory of the Tenth and Eleventh Centuries*, ed. Richard L. Crocker (Aldershot: Ashgate, 2003).

20 Emma Hornby, *Gregorian and Old-Roman Eighth-Mode Tracts: A Case Study in the Transmission of Western Chant* (Aldershot: Ashgate, 2002); Edward Nowacki, 'Text Declamation as a Determinant of Melodic Form in the Old Roman Eighth-Mode Tracts', *Early Music History* 6 (1986), pp. 193–226.

21 Joseph Dyer, '*Tropis semper variantibus:* Compositional Strategies in the Offertories of Old Roman Chant', *Early Music History* 17 (1998), pp. 1–60; Rebecca Maloy, 'The Word–Music Relationship in the Gregorian and

Old Roman Offertories', *Studia musicologica* 45 (2004), pp. 131–48.

22 *Regula benedicti* 43: 'nihil operi dei praeponatur' ('may nothing be placed before the work of God').

23 *Regula benedicti* 19: 'Ergo consideremus qualiter oporteat in conspectu Divinitatis et angelorum eius esse, et sic stemus ad psallendum, ut mens nostra concordet voci nostrae.'

24 James McKinnon, *The Advent Project: the Later Seventh-Century Creation of the Roman Mass Proper* (Berkeley and Los Angeles: University of California Press 2000), and the important review by Joseph Dyer in *Early Music History* 20 (2001), pp. 279–309; Peter Jeffery, 'The Lost Chant Tradition of Early Christian Jerusalem: Some Possible Melodic Survivals in the Byzantine and Latin Chant Repertories', *Early Music History* 11 (1992), pp. 151–90; and Jeffery, 'The Earliest Christian Chant Repertory Recovered: The Georgian Witnesses to Jerusalem Chant', *Journal of the American Musicological Society* 47 (1994), pp. 1–39.

25 Susan Rankin, 'Ways of Telling Stories', in Boone, ed., *Essays on Medieval Music*, pp. 371–94.

26 For both mass and office chants, however, manuscripts from central and eastern Europe exhibit an avoidance of the melodic half-step that is known as the 'Germanic chant dialect'; see Alexander Blachly, 'Some Observations on the "Germanic" Plainchant Tradition', in Peter M. Lefferts and Brian Seirup, eds., *Studies in Medieval Music: Festschrift for Ernest H. Sanders* (New York: Department of Music, Columbia University, 1990), pp. 85–117.

27 This is a very brief summary of a much larger debate regarding the function and origins of Western notation in the transmission of Gregorian chant. For representative statements of three points of view see David Hughes, 'Evidence for the Traditional View of the History of Gregorian Chant', *Journal of the American Musicological Society* 40 (1987), pp. 377–404; Kenneth Levy, *Gregorian Chant and the Carolingians* (Princeton University Press, 1998) and Leo Treitler, *With Voice and Pen: Coming to Know Medieval Song and How It Was Made* (Oxford and New York: Oxford University Press, 2003).

28 The character of the Gallican chant can only be surmised from its purported survivals in some Gregorian melodies. See Michel Huglo with Jane Bellingham and Marcel Zijlstra, 'Gallican Chant', *Grove Music Online*, www.oxfordmusiconline.com.

29 A list of sources of the Roman liturgy before the fourteenth century appears in Joseph Dyer, 'Prolegomena to a History of Music and Liturgy at Rome in the Middle Ages', in Boone, ed., *Essays on Medieval Music*, pp. 87–115.

30 See Kenneth Levy, 'A New Look at Old Roman Chant I', *Early Music History* 19 (2000), pp. 81–104; Kenneth Levy, 'A New Look at Old Roman Chant II', *Early Music History*, 20 (2001), pp. 173–98; Hornby, *Gregorian and Old-Roman Eighth-Mode Tracts*; Andreas Pfisterer, *Cantilena Romana: Untersuchungen zur Überlieferung des gregorianischen Chorals* (Paderborn: Schöningh, 2002).

31 Peter Jeffery, 'The Earliest Oktōēchoi: The Role of Jerusalem and Palestine in the Beginnings of Modal Ordering', in Jeffery, ed., *The Study of Medieval Chant*, pp. 147–209.

32 Thomas Forrest Kelly, *The Beneventan Chant* (Cambridge University Press, 1989).

33 Thomas Forrest Kelly, *The Exultet in Southern Italy* (Oxford University Press, 1996).

34 The use of letter notation in some manuscripts and theoretical writings also facilitates transcription.

35 See especially James Grier, *The Musical World of a Medieval Monk: Adémar de Chabannes in Eleventh-Century Aquitaine* (Cambridge University Press, 2006).

36 Thirteen editions of offices have been published thus far in the Historiae series (Ottawa: Institute of Mediaeval Music, 1995–). For a study and electronic edition of many compositions see Andrew Hughes, *Late Medieval Liturgical Offices*, Subsidia Mediaevalia 23–24 (Toronto: Pontifical Institute of Mediaeval Studies, 1994–6).

37 An important study of this phenomenon is Andrew Hughes, 'Modal Order and Disorder in the Rhymed Office', *Musica Disciplina* 37 (1983), pp. 29–51.

38 Hartmut Möller, 'Office Compositions from St Gall: Saints Gallus and Otmar', in Fassler and Baltzer, eds., *The Divine Office*, pp. 255–6, suggests that this innovation could have originated around the same time at St Gall, during the reign of Abbot-Bishop Salomo III (890–920), as attested by the office of St Otmar.

39 For studies of 'post-Gregorian' office chant see David Hiley, 'The *Historia* of St Julian of Le Mans by Létald of Micy: Some Comments and Questions about a North French Office of the Early Eleventh Century', in Fassler and Baltzer, eds., *The Divine Office*, pp. 444–62; and Hiley, 'Style and Structure in Early Offices of the Sanctorale', in Gallagher et al., eds., *Western Plainchant in the First Millennium*, pp. 157–79.

40 Andrew Hughes, 'Late Medieval Plainchant for the Divine Office', in Reinhard Strohm and Bonnie Blackburn, eds., *Music as Concept and Practice in the Late Middle Ages* (Oxford University Press, 2001), pp. 31–96; Eyolf Østrem, *The Office of Saint Olav: A Study in Chant Transmission* (Uppsala Universitet, 2001); Kay Slocum, *Liturgies in Honour of Thomas Becket* (University of Toronto Press, 2003).

41 James John Boyce, 'The Carmelite Feast of the Presentation of the Virgin: A Study in Musical Adaptation', in Fassler and Baltzer, eds., *The Divine Office*, pp. 485–518.

42 See Manuel Pedro Ferreira, 'Music at Cluny, The Tradition of Gregorian Chant for the Proper of the Mass – Melodic Variants and Microtonal Nuances', PhD diss. (Princeton University Press, 1993); Hiley, *Western Plainchant*, pp. 574–8.

43 See particularly Chrysogonus Waddell, 'The Origin and Early Evolution of the Cistercian Antiphonary: Reflections on Two Cistercian Chant Reforms', in M. Basil Pennington, ed., *The Cistercian Spirit: A Symposium: In Memory of Thomas Merton*, Cistercian Studies 3 (Washington, DC: Cistercian Press, 1970), pp. 190–223.

44 James Boyce, *Praising God in Carmel: Studies in Carmelite Liturgy* (Washington: Carmelite Institute, 1999).

45 Leonard E. Boyle, Pierre-Marie Gy and Paweł Krupa, eds., *Aux origines de la liturgie dominicaine: le manuscrit Santa Sabina XIV L 1*, Collection de l'École Française de Rome 327, Documents, études et répertoires publiés par l'IRHT 67 (Paris: CNRS Éditions and Rome: École Française de Rome, 2004).

46 Andrew Mitchell, 'The Chant of the Earliest Franciscan Liturgy', PhD diss. (University of Western Ontario, 2003); Stephen J. P. van Dijk and Joan Hazelden Walker, *The Origins of the Modern Roman Liturgy: The Liturgy of the Papal Court and the Franciscan Order in the Thirteenth Century* (London: Westminster, 1960).

47 Barbara Haggh, 'Reconstructing the Plainchant Repertory of Brussels and Its Chronology', in *Musicology and Archival Research: Proceedings of the Colloquium held at the Algemeen Rijksarchief, Brussel, 22–23 April 1993*, Archief- en Bibliotheekwezen in België, Extranummer 46 (Brussels: Archives Générales du Royaume, 1994), pp. 177–213; Marica Tacconi, *Cathedral and Civic Ritual in Late Medieval and Renaissance Florence: The Service Books of Santa Maria del Fiore* (Cambridge University Press, 2006); Michael Noone and Graeme Skinner, 'Toledo Cathedral's Collection of Manuscript Plainsong Choirbooks: A Preliminary Report and Checklist', *Notes* 63 (2006), pp. 289–328.

48 Jaroslav Kolár, Anežka Vidmanová and Hana Vlhová-Wörner, eds., *Jistebnický kancionál, MS Praha, Knihovna Národniho muzea, II C 7, Kritická edice/Jistebnice Kancionál, MS Prague, National Museum Library II C 7, critical edition*, vol. I, *Graduale*, Monumenta Liturgica Bohemica 2 (Brno: LuBos Marek, 2005)

49 Barbara Haggh, 'The Celebration of the "Recollectio Festorum Beatae Mariae Virginis", 1457–1987', *Studia Musicologica Academiae Scientiarum Hungaricae* 30 (1988), pp. 361–73.

50 Barbara Haggh, 'Nonconformity in the Use of Cambrai Cathedral: Guillaume Du Fay's Foundations', in Fassler and Baltzer, eds., *The Divine Office*, pp. 372–97; see also her 'Foundations or Institutions? On Bringing the Middle Ages into the History of Medieval Music', *Acta Musicologica* 68 (1996), pp. 87–128.

51 For a recent study of eighteenth-century chant see Xavier Bisaro, *Une nation de fidèles: L'Église et la liturgie parisienne au XVIIIe siècle* (Turnhout: Brepols, 2006).

2 Enriching the Gregorian heritage

1 The adoption of the Roman rite was never comprehensive or universal. See James W. McKinnon, *The Advent Project: The Later Seventh-Century Creation of the Roman Mass Proper* (Berkeley and Los Angeles: University of California Press, 2000), pp. 375–403; for the incorporation of non-Roman elements see Kenneth Levy, 'Toledo, Rome, and the Legacy of Gaul', *Early Music History* 4 (1984), pp. 49–99; 'A New Look at Old Roman Chant I', *Early Music History* 19 (2000), pp. 81–104; 'A New Look at Old Roman Chant II', *Early Music History* 20 (2001), pp. 173–198.

2 See for example Lori Kruckenberg-Goldenstein, 'The Sequence from 1050–1150: Study of a Genre in Change', PhD diss., University of Iowa, 1997, pp. 137–9, 155–60 and 176–184; and Klaus Rönnau, *Die Tropen zum Gloria in excelsis Deo. Unter besonderer Berücksichtigung des Repertoires der St Martial-Handschriften* (Wiesbaden: Breitkopf & Härtel, 1967), pp. 5 and 76–82.

3 See, for example, Richard Crocker and David Hiley, eds., *The New Oxford History of Music*, vol. II, *The Early Middle Ages to 1300* (Oxford and New York: Oxford University Press, 1990), p. 225.

4 For studies of these sources see Paul Evans, *The Early Trope Repertory of Saint Martial de Limoges* (Princeton University Press, 1970);

Richard Crocker, *The Early Medieval Sequence* (Berkeley and Los Angeles: University of California Press, 1977); and Susan Rankin, 'From Tuotilo to the First Manuscripts: The Shaping of a Trope Repertory at Saint Gall', in Wulf Arlt and Gunilla Björkvall, eds., *Recherches nouvelles sur les tropes liturgiques*, Studia Latina Stockholmiensia 36 (Stockholm: Almqvist and Wiksell International, 1993), pp. 395–413.

5 Wolfenbüttel, Herzog August Bibliothek: Cod. Guelf. 1062 Helmst., fol. 219r; Wilfried Hartmann, ed., *Die Konzilien der Karolingischen Teilreiche 843–859*, Monumenta Germaniae Historica, Concilia III (Hanover: Hahn, 1984), p. 129.

6 Brussels, Bibliothèque Royale, 10127–10144.

7 The chants are *Alleluia / Beatus vir, Alleluia / Dominus regnavit decorem, Alleluia / Iubilate deo, Alleluia / Te decet hymnus*, and the extra verses *Laudamini in nomine* and *Notum fecit dominus*. See Brussels, Bibliothèque Royale, 10127–10144, fols. 114v–115 and René-Jean Hesbert, *Antiphonale missarum sextuplex* (Brussels: Vromant, 1935), p. 198.

8 For a transcription of the *neuma triplex* see Richard Taruskin, *The Oxford History of Western Music*, vol. I, *The Earliest Notations to the Sixteenth Century* (Oxford University Press, 2005), p. 38. For Amalrius's comments see David Hiley, *Western Plainchant: A Handbook* (Oxford: Clarendon Press, 1993), pp. 200–1 and 569–71. See also Johannes M. Hanssens, *Amalarii episcopi opera liturgica omnia* (Vatican City: Biblioteca apostolica vaticana, 1948–50); for the *sequentia* see *Liber officialis* 3.16 (vol. III, p. 304); for the *neuma triplex* see *Liber de ordine antiphonarii* 18.2 (vol. III, p. 54).

9 St Gall, Stiftsbibliothek 484, pp. 185–86.

10 Munich, Bayerische Staatsbibliothek, clm 9543, fol. 119v. For a facsimile see Hartmut Möller and Rudolf Stephan, *Neues Handbuch der Musikwissenschaft*, vol. II, *Die Musik des Mittelalters* (Laaber: Laaber-Verlag, 1991), p. 190 for a facsimile; for a transcription see *Dictionary of the Middle Ages*, 13 vols. (New York: Scribner, 1982–2003), under 'Tropes to the proper of the mass'.

11 For a transcription see 'Plainchant', section 6 (ii): 'Expansion of the Liturgy: Prosula', *The New Grove Dictionary of Music and Musicians*, 2nd edn.

12 Richard L. Crocker, 'The Troping Hypothesis', *Musical Quarterly* 52 (1966), pp. 183–203; see also Paul Evans, *The Early Trope Repertory of Saint Martial de Limoges* (Princeton University Press, 1970), pp. 1–15.

13 Hiley, *Western Plainchant*, p. 196.

14 Evans, *Early Trope Repertory*, p. 3.

15 David Bjork, 'The Kyrie Trope', *Journal of the American Musicological Society* 33 (1980), pp. 1–41.

16 St Gall, Stiftsbibliothek 381, p. 288.

17 For the sources of this terminology see Ritva Jonsson, 'Corpus troporum,' *Journal of the Plainsong and Medieval Music Society* 1 (1978), pp. 98–115.

18 An introduction to the melodic style of tropes appears in Hiley, *Western Plainchant*, pp. 215–23.

19 For a discussion of this shift see James Grier, 'A New Voice in the Monastery: Tropes and Versus from Eleventh and Twelfth Century Aquitania', *Speculum* 69 (1994), pp. 1024–69, esp. 1027–8.

20 See Leo Treitler, 'The Polyphony of Saint Martial', *Journal of the American Musicological Society* 17 (1964), pp. 29–42, esp. 35–39.

21 An analysis of a versus appears in Leo Treitler, 'Medieval Lyric', in Mark Everist, ed., *Models of Musical Analysis: Music before 1600* (Oxford: Basil Blackwell, 1992), pp. 1–19.

22 For the complete text of Notker's preface, see Piero Weiss and Richard Taruskin, eds., *Music in the Western World: A History in Documents* (New York: Schirmer, 1984), pp. 46–7.

23 Susan Rankin, 'The Earliest Sources of Notker's Sequences: St Gallen Vadiana 317, and Paris, Bibliothèque Nationale Lat. 10587', *Early Music History* 10 (1991), pp. 201–33.

24 The details of the two traditions are beautifully surveyed and discussed in Kruckenberg-Goldenstein, 'The Sequence from 1050–1150', pp. 86–139. Richard Crocker sees greater unity in the eastern and western traditions. See his *Early Medieval Sequence*, pp. 1–14.

25 See Henry Marriot Bannister, *Anglo French Sequelae* (London: Plainsong and Medieval Music Society, 1934); and Bruno Stäblein, 'Zur Frühgeschichte der Sequenz', *Archiv für Musikwissenschaft* 18 (1961), pp. 1–33.

26 Kruckenberg-Goldenstein, 'The Sequence from 1050–1150', pp. 111–13 and 137–9.

27 Translation from David Hiley, 'The Sequence Melodies Sung at Cluny and Elsewhere', in Peter Cahn and Ann-Katrin Heimer, eds., *De musica et cantu: Studien zur Geschichte der Kirchenmusik und der Oper: Helmut Hucke zum 60. Geburtstag* (Hildesheim: G. Olms, 1993), p. 139.

28 A thorough discussion of this composition appears in Crocker, *The Early Medieval Sequence*, pp. 189–203.

29 Translations of this sequence by Leofranc Holford-Strevens. See liner notes for *Musique et*

poésie à Saint-Gall. Séquences et tropes du IXe siècle, Harmonia Mundi France 905239, p. 40.
30 Kruckenberg-Goldstein, 'The Sequence from 1050–1150', pp. 273–9.
31 Ibid., pp. 160–6.
32 Text and translation in Margot Fassler, *Gothic Song: Victorine Sequences and Augustinian Reform in Twelfth-Century Paris* (Cambridge University Press, 1993), p. 331.
33 Fassler, *Gothic Song*, pp. 64–70.
34 Ibid., p. 70.
35 For Adam's life see ibid., pp. 209–19.
36 Ibid., pp. 209–10.
37 Ibid., pp. 267–320.
38 Margot E. Fassler, 'The Role of the Parisian Sequence in the Evolution of Notre-Dame Polyphony', *Speculum* 62 (1987): 345–74.
39 Fassler, *Gothic Song*, pp. 321–43, esp. pp. 330–34.
40 More than six hundred texts are preserved in Karl Young's *The Drama of the Medieval Church*, 2 vols. (Oxford: Clarendon Press, 1933); nearly four hundred of these are examples of the Easter play. The Easter plays alone are edited in Walther Lipphardt, *Lateinische Osterfeiern und Osterspiele*, 6 vols. (Berlin and New York: Walter De Gruyter, 1975–81). The term 'liturgical drama' was coined by Félix Clément in the mid nineteenth century.
41 Susan Rankin, 'Liturgical Drama', in R. Crocker and D. Hiley, eds., *The Early Middle Ages to 1300*, vol. II of *The New Oxford History of Music* (Oxford and New York: Oxford University Press), 1990, p. 313.
42 The version in Mark is the only one to mention three women explicitly. The scene is also found in Matthew 28:1–7 and Luke 24:1–9.
43 As in St Gall, Stiftsbibliothek, MS 484, p. 111. The oldest version, preserved in Paris, Bibliothèque nationale fonds lat. 1240, is slightly more elaborate than this.
44 The chronology of the early sources is a complex matter. See David A. Bjork, 'On the Dissemination of *Quem queritis* and the *Visitatio Sepulchri* and the Chronology of Their Early Sources', *Comparative Drama* 14 (1980), pp. 60. Bjork makes a convincing argument that the geographic pattern of preservation tells us more about the early history of *Quem queritis* than the chronology of the sources.
45 Timothy J. McGee, 'The Liturgical Placements of the "Quem Queritis" Dialogue', *Journal of the American Musicological Society* 29 (1976), pp. 1–29.
46 Rankin, 'Liturgical Drama', p. 320, fn 25.
47 Thomas Symons, ed. and trans., *Regularis Concordia Anglicae Nationis Monachorum Sanctimonialiumque. The Monastic Agreement of the Monks and Nuns of the English Nation* (London and New York: Nelson, 1953), section 51.
48 For a survey see C. Clifford Flanigan, 'The Fleury Playbook, the Traditions of Medieval Latin Drama, and Modern Scholarship', in Thomas P. Campbell and Clifford Davidson, eds., *The Fleury Playbook: Essays and Studies* (Kalamazoo, MI: Medieval Institute Publications, 1985), pp. 1–25.
49 Norma Kroll explores this feature and frames it in Augustinian terms in her 'Power and Conflict in Medieval Ritual and Plays: The Re-Invention of Drama', *Modern Philology* 102 (2005), pp. 452–83.
50 For a discussion of Herod's anger and Rachel's sorrow see John Stevens, *Words and Music in the Middle Ages: Song, Narrative, Dance and Drama, 1050–1350* (Cambridge University Press, 1986), pp. 348–71.
51 Young, *Drama of the Medieval Church*, vol. II, pp. 411–14.
52 For a glimpse of the type of behaviour that disturbed and alarmed Gerhoh and Herrad see Margot Fassler, 'The Feast of Fools and the *Danielis Ludus*: Popular Tradition in a Medieval Cathedral Play', in Thomas Forrest Kelly, ed., *Plainsong in the Age of Polyphony* (Cambridge University Press, 1992), pp. 66–99.
53 See, for example, Anne Walters Robertson, *The Service-Books of the Royal Abbey of Saint-Denis: Images of Ritual and Music in the Middle Ages* (Oxford University Press, 1991), pp. 235–71.
54 Jean-Baptiste Pelt, *Études sur la cathédrale de Metz*, vol. IV, *La liturgie 1: Ve–XIIIe siècle* (Metz: Imprimerie du Journal le Lorrain, 1937), p. 378; Metz, Bibliothèque municipale 82, fol. 96v. The manuscript was destroyed in World War Two and survives only on microfilm.
55 Pelt, *Études*, p. 286; Metz, Bibliothèque municipale 82, fol. 27r.
56 Pelt, *Études*, p. 425; Metz, Bibliothèque municipale 82, fol. 129v.
57 Pelt, *Études*, p. 425; Metz, Bibliothèque municipale 82, fol. 129r.
58 Pelt, *Études*, p. 283; Metz, Bibliothèque municipale 82, fol. 25v.
59 Pelt, *Études*, p. 294; Metz, Bibliothèque municipale 82, fol. 32v.
60 Lanfranc, *Decreta Lanfranci monachis Cantuariensibus transmissa*, ed. David Knowles, Corpus Consuetudinum Monasticarum 3 (Siegburg: F. Schmitt, 1967), p. 50; J. B. L. Tolhurst and the Abbess of Stanbrook, eds., *The Ordinal and Customary of the Abbey of Saint Mary, York* (St John's College, Cambridge, ms. D. 27), vol. II, Henry Bradshaw Society

Publications 75 (London: Henry Bradshaw
Society, 1936), p. 187; Antonia Gransden, ed.,
*The Customary of the Benedictine Abbey of Bury
St Edmunds in Suffolk (from Harleian MS. 1005
in the British Museum)*, Henry Bradshaw Society
99 (London: Henry Bradshaw Society, 1973),
p. 93.

3 Early polyphony to circa 1200

1 'Superficies quaedam artis musicae pro
ornatu ecclesiasticorum carminum utcumque in
his designata sit.' *Musica Enchiriadis*, Chapter
18, ca850. H. Schmid, ed., *Musica et Scolica
Enchiriadis una cum aliquibus tractatulis
adiunctis*, Bayerische Akademie der
Wissenschaften Veröffentlichung der
Musikhistorischen Kommission 3 (Munich:
Verlag der Bayerischen Akademie der
Wissenschaften, 1981), p. 56. There is a slightly
different English translation in C. V. Palisca, ed.,
Musica enchiriadis and Scolica enchiriadis, trans.,
R. Erickson (New Haven: Yale University Press,
1995), p. 30.
2 'Incipiunt melliflua organorum modulamina
super dulcissima celeste preconia', *GB-Ccc* 473,
fol. 135r, ca1000.
3 'Sed quocumque modo fiat . . . [*MS
illegible*] . . . sic faciendo precentori conveniat et
creatori laudem diaphonia concinat.' *I-PCd* 65,
fol. 268r, ca1142. Facsimile in B. M. Jensen, ed.,
Il Libro del Maestro Codice 65 (Piacenza: Tip. Le.
Co. editore, 1997).
4 On important and complex aspects of
improvisation and intersections between oral
and written practices, see L. Treitler, *With Voice
and Pen: Coming to Know Medieval Song and
How It Was Made* (Oxford University Press,
2003), pp. 1–67. Treitler's views include, but are
not limited to, polyphony: 'The production of
music as the actualization of both written and
unwritten composition is a premiss for the
understanding of medieval music cultures',
p. 11.
5 *Musica Enchiriadis*, Chapter 13, Schmid
edition, p. 37; Erickson translation, p. 21.
6 'Diaphonia vocum disjunctio sonat, quam
nos organum vocamus, cum disjunctae ab
invicem voces et concorditer dissonant et
dissonanter concordant.' Guido of Arezzo,
Micrologus, ed., J. Smits van Waesberghe,
Corpus Scriptorum de Musica 4 (American
Institute of Musicology, 1955), pp. 196–7. There
is a slightly different translation in C. V. Palisca,
ed., *Hucbald, Guido, and John on Music: Three
Medieval Treatises*, trans. W. Babb (New Haven,
CT: Yale University Press, 1995), p. 77. Latin *vox*
is multivalent as used by early medieval
theorists and can denote a pitch, a melodic line,

or the human voice. Here, the sense
appropriately embraces both 'pitch' and 'line'.
Dissonare is here used not in its later, cognate
sense, but simply to indicate separation or
distinction in sound. Guido's statement is itself
indebted to the formulation in *Musica
Enchiriadis*, Chapter 13.
7 See the remarks by Susan Rankin in
'Winchester Polyphony: The Early Theory and
Practice of Organum', in S. Rankin and D. Hiley,
eds., *Music in the Medieval English Liturgy:
Plainsong and Medieval Music Centennial Essays*
(Oxford: Clarendon Press, 1993), pp. 65, 70–8.
8 Individual notions of 'how the music
went' also play a substantial role in modern
reconstructions, a situation evident in
widely divergent editions and recorded
interpretations of Aquitanian and Compostelan
polyphony.
9 See the *Quatuor Principalia Musicae* written
by an anonymous English monk and dated
1351, Book 4:2; L. F. Aluaş, ed. and trans., 'The
Quatuor Principalia Musicae: A Critical Edition
and Translation, with Introduction and
Commentary', PhD diss., Indiana University
(1996), pp. 746–7. Susan Rankin discusses
retrospective Italian polyphony in 'Between
Oral and Written: Thirteenth-Century Italian
Sources of Polyphony', in G. Cattin and F. A.
Gallo, eds., *Un millennio di polifonia liturgica tra
oralità e scrittura*, Quaderni di *Musica e storia* 3
(Bologna: Il Mulino, 2002), pp. 75–98. An
important study of the persistence of early
organum teaching is F. Reckow, 'Guido's Theory
of Organum after Guido: Transmission –
Adaptation – Transformation', in G. M. Boone,
ed., *Essays on Medieval Music in Honor of David
G. Hughes* (Cambridge, MA: Harvard University
Press, 1995), pp. 395–413.
10 Both Guido of Arezzo and John [of
Afflighem] refer to their local 'use' rather
than claiming a monolithic, standard
practice. See *Micrologus*, Chapter 18, Palisca,
ed., *Hucbald, Guido and John on Music*,
pp. 77–8 and John, *De Musica*, Chapter 23, in
ibid., p. 160.
11 'Que omnia melius usu organizatorum
quam regulis declarantur.' H. H. Eggebrecht and
F. Zaminer, eds., *Ad Organum Faciendum:
Lehrschriften der Mehrstimmigkeit in
nachguidonischer Zeit* (Mainz: B. Schott's Söhne,
1970), p. 160. This treatise, designated as Berlin
B within the 'new organum teaching' orbit, is a
descendant of *Ad organum faciendum*. For the
Musica Enchiriadis statement, see note 1.
12 Andreas Holschneider suggests that
Wulfstan, Cantor at Winchester, was responsible
for the Winchester organum repertory, notated

in the first quarter of the eleventh century. See Holschneider's *Die Organa von Winchester: Studien zum ältesten Repertoire polyphoner Musik* (Hildesheim: Georg Olms Verlagsbuchhandlung, 1968), pp. 76–81. The repertory evidences a concentration on chants in which soloists already took a leading role.

13 The thirteen polyphonic proses in this repertory exhibit no coherent liturgical ordering, and most are incomplete, the polyphony ceasing after the first few text couplets.

14 The variety in strands of teaching signals that theorists were trying to fix through written precepts and plausible rationales what was essentially an informal practice. On those strands, see S. Fuller, 'Early Polyphony', in R. Crocker and D. Hiley, eds., *The New Oxford History of Music*, vol. II, *The Early Middle Ages to 1300* (Oxford University Press, 1990), pp. 497–502.

15 Guido of Arezzo, *Micrologus*, Chapter 18, Palisca, ed., *Hucbald, Guido and John on Music*, pp. 77–8. Guido stands apart in giving a strict example in parallel fourths rather than fifths.

16 The text of the formulaic psalm tone in Example 3.1a is verse 31 of Psalm 103. Nancy Phillips identified the melody and proposed an elegant solution to a notational error in the sources, a solution followed here. See N. Phillips, '"Musica" and "Scolica Enchiriadis": The Literary, Theoretical, and Musical Sources', PhD diss., New York University, 1984, pp. 459–60.

17 *Ipsi soli* is an antiphon from the Matins of St Agnes. Its text units are: 'To him alone / I keep faith / to him all [my] / devotion I commit.' Lack of occursus in Guido's third phrase reflects the ongoing syntax of the text at that point, 'tota devotione'. C and F, the two diatonic tones with a half-step interval below, are the tritus boundaries. The *Musica Enchiriadis* formulates its boundary tone theory in a different way consistent with the daseian scale.

18 See the significant digest and reworking of *Musica Enchiriadis* designated the 'Paris Elaboration' by H. Schmid: see Schmid, ed., *Musica et Scolica Enchiriadis*, p. 206.

19 'Verumtamen modesta morositate edita, quod suum est maxime proprium, et concordi diligentia procurata honestissima erit cantionis suavitas.' H. Schmid, ed., *Musica et Scolica Enchiriadis*, p. 97. There is a slightly different translation in Palisca, *Musica enchiriadis and Scolica enchiriadis*, p. 58.

20 See the rubrics edited in Holschneider, *Die Organa von Winchester*, pp. 41–55.

21 See the studies of Holschneider, *Die Organa von Winchester* and Rankin, 'Winchester Polyphony', pp. 59–99. Facsimiles of the notation are published at the end of Holschneider's book.

22 See Rankin, 'Winchester Polyphony', for an excellent overview.

23 The transcription of this excerpt is based on the full realization by Holschneider in *Die Organa von Winchester*, pp. 165–7. The notes in the principal voice have here been numbered for ease in reference. Because the notation is not pitch-specific, the reconstruction is conjectural, based on properties of the neumes in conjunction with theoretical precepts of the epoch.

24 The *x*s in the transcription suggest alternate readings that generally increase the proportion of fourths.

25 See W. Arlt, 'Stylistic Layers in Eleventh-Century Polyphony: How Can the Continental Sources Contribute to Our Understanding of the Winchester Organa?' in Rankin and Hiley, eds., *Music in the Medieval English Liturgy*, pp. 101–41.

26 Eggebrecht and Zaminer, eds., *Ad Organum Faciendum*, p. 46. *Ad Organum Faciendum* is a pivotal document for the start of this phase; its teachings are often paraphrased and modified in subsequent redactions.

27 For a facsimile of the original alphabetic notation, and staff transcriptions of Examples 3.3a and 3.3b, see Eggebrecht and Zaminer, eds., *Ad Organum Faciendum*, plate 5 and pp. 48–9, 52–3.

28 An excellent recording of this polyphonic Alleluia can be found on *Aquitania Christmas Music from Aquitanian Monasteries (12th Century)*, Sequentia, B. Bagby and B. Thornton, dirs., Deutsche Harmonia Mundi / BMG Music 05472–77383-2 (1997), track 8.

29 Eggebrecht and Zaminer, eds., *Ad Organum Faciendum*, p. 111. On the significance of the notion of 'affinity' within early organum theory, see S. Fuller, 'Theoretical Foundations of Early Organum Theory', *Acta Musicologica* 53 (1981), pp. 62–6.

30 Eggebrecht and Zaminer, eds., *Ad Organum Faciendum*, p. 115. This celebration of a dominant organal voice is not taken up in later treatises.

31 Ibid., pp. 113, 115.

32 Chapter 23, 'Caeterum hic facillimus eius usus est, si motuum varietas diligenter consideretur; ut ubi in recta modulatione est elevatio, ibi in organica fiat depositio et e converso.' J. Smits van Waesberghe, ed., *Johannis Affligemensis: De musica cum tonario*,

Corpus Scriptorum de Musica 1 (Rome: American Institute of Musicology, 1950), pp. 159–60. English translation, in Palisca, ed., *Hucbald, Guido, and John On Music*, p. 160.

33 For the Latin, see the Smits van Waesberghe edition, p. 160; English translation, Palisca, ed., *Hucbald, Guido, and John On Music*, p. 161. The Latin verb indicating multiplication of notes is *conglobare*.

34 The prevalent German term, often adopted in English-language studies, is 'Klangschritt-Lehre'. The classic study of these texts is K.-J. Sachs, 'Zur Tradition der Klangschritt-Lehre: Die Texte mit der Formel "Si cantus ascendit . . ." und ihre Verwandten', *Archiv für Musikwissenschaft* 28 (1971), pp. 233–70.

35 On the important role of memorization in medieval music training, see A. M. Busse Berger, *Medieval Music and the Art of Memory* (Berkeley: University of California Press, 2005), especially Chapter 4 on counterpoint.

36 While largely promoting contrary motion, the much-perused Vatican Organum Treatise includes some examples of parallel motion; see the conspectus of progressions in M. Bernhard, 'Eine neue Quelle für den Vatikanischen Organum-Traktat', in Bernhard, ed., *Quellen und Studien zur Musiktheorie des Mittelalters*, vol. III, Bayerische Akademie der Wissenschaften, Veröffentlichungen der Musikhistorischen Kommission 15 (Munich: C. H. Beck, 2001), pp. 178–83. A study of late medieval singing in fifths is S. Fuller, 'Discant and the Theory of Fifthing', *Acta Musicologica* 50 (1978), pp. 241–75.

37 For a map showing the area in which Aquitanian notation flourished see *Le Graduel Romain* II, *édition critique par les moines de Solesmes*, Abbaye Saint-Pierre de Solesmes, 1957, p. 231. The older designator for this repertory, Saint-Martial (still preserved in the *New Grove Dictionary of Music and Musicians*, 2nd edn), was based on a mistaken impression that the sources originated at the monastery of St-Martial of Limoges, the locale where many of them were collected by the early thirteenth century.

38 For text topics and possible contexts see R. G. Carlson, 'Striking Ornaments: Complexities of Sense and Song in Aquitanian "Versus"', *Music and Letters* 84 (2003), pp. 527–56 and S. Fuller, 'Aquitanian Polyphony of the Eleventh and Twelfth Centuries', PhD diss., University of California, Berkeley, 1969, pp. 16–22. The northern European term for versus was

conductus. The Codex Calixtinus offices for St James and some thirteenth-century Circumcision offices indicate how versus were incorporated in church rituals.

39 Some of the libelli were bound together in the thirteenth century. On the separate sources and on concordances, see Sarah Fuller, 'The Myth of Saint-Martial Polyphony: A Study of the Sources', *Musica Disciplina* 33 (1979), pp. 5–26. The exact tally of polyphonic works is uncertain, due to some notational ambiguities and differing judgements about whether some apparently monophonic songs are actually polyphonic, inscribed in successive notation.

40 Treatises of this period shift their terminology from 'principal' and 'organal' voices to 'cantus' and 'organum'.

41 On approaches to medieval lyric, including two monophonic Aquitanian versus, see L. Treitler. 'Medieval Lyric', in M. Everist, ed., *Models of Musical Analysis: Music Before 1600* (Oxford: Basil Blackwell, 1992), pp. 1–19. R. G. Carlson analyses two versus (one monophonic, one polyphonic), giving particular attention to text, in 'Striking Ornaments', pp. 541–55.

42 Transmitted in three sources, *Per partum virginis* is among the more widely circulated of the polyphonic versus.

43 The transcription given here of couplets 1, 4 and line 5 respects the rhythmic indeterminacy of the original notations. Editorial alignments in indeterminate passages are suggested on the basis of vertical consonance. For the complete versus in a striking variety of rhythmic realizations see B. Gillingham, *Saint-Martial Mehrstimmigkeit / Saint-Martial Polyphony*, Musicological Studies 44 (Henryville, PA: Institute of Medieval Music, 1984), pp. 71–4, 102–6, 144–9; T. Karp, *The Polyphony of Saint Martial and Santiago de Compostela*, vol. II, (Berkeley and Los Angeles: University of California Press, 1992), pp. 8–11, 50–4, 117–20; and H. van der Werf, *The Oldest Extant Part Music and the Origin of Western Polyphony* (Rochester, NY: the author, 1993), vol. II, pp. 17–31. Each editor presents the three versions separately. Noteworthy recorded interpretations are *Shining Light: Music from Aquitanian Monasteries*, Sequentia, B. Bagby and B. Thornton, dirs., Deutsche Harmonia Mundi / BMG Music 05472 77370 2 (1996), track 10 and *The Fire and the Rose: Aquitanian Chant*, Heliotrope, J. Todd, dir., Koch International Classics, 3–7356-2H1 (1998), track 3.

44 Many versus settings have a greater degree of musical repetition, often a simple strophic design or the same music for both lines in a couplet, as Examples 3.4a, 3.4b here.

45 These terminal melismas are ancestors of Parisian conductus caudae.

46 See, for example, *clausit*, line 1b, *est clemencia*, line 4a, *Immortalis*, line 5 (Examples 3.4a, 3.4b), and the reduction of line 1a given in Example 3.5a.

47 Example 3.4a, verse 1a, *hominis sunt*, 1b *tribuitur*.

48 The binary progressions shown in the reduction relate well to the teaching methods of the interval-progression manuals.

49 Facsimiles of the notated versions of *Per partum virginis* may be found in B. Gillingham, ed., *Paris, Bibliothèque Nationale, fonds Latin 3549 and London, British Library 36881*, Publications of Musical Manuscripts No. 16 (Ottawa: Institute of Medieval Music, ca1987); fol. 150v (*F-Pn* fonds lat. 3549, 'B') and fol. 4r (*GB-Lbl* add. 36881, 'D'). The version in *F-Pn* fonds lat. 3719, fol. 64r closely resembles the 'B' version.

50 The 'B' version as I interpret it increases the similarity to the parallel moment on *virginis*.

51 Facsimile edition in *Codex Calixtinus de la Catedral de Santiago de Compostela* (Madrid: Kaydeda Ediciones, 1993). A plausible dating for the manuscript is ca1150–60. E. Roesner summarizes divergent opinions on the dating in 'The *Codex Calixtinus* and the *Magnus Liber Organi*: Some Preliminary Observations', in J. López-Calo and C. Villanueva, eds., *El Códice Calixtino y la Música de su Tiempo* (La Coruña: Fundación Pedro Barrié da la Maza, 2001), pp. 146–7.

52 Despite its codicological status as a supplement, the polyphonic section is an integral component of the Codex Calixtinus in terms of relationships to the music of Book I and notational traits. See S. Fuller, 'Perspectives on Musical Notation in the *Codex Calixtinus*', in López-Calo and Villanueva, eds., *El Códice Calixtino*, p. 188.

53 On the origins of the codex, see M. Díaz y Díaz, *El Codice Calixtino de la Catedral de Santiago: Estudio Codicológico y de contenido*, Monografias de Compostellanum 2 (Santiago de Compostela: Centro de Estudios Jacobeos, 1988), pp. 90–1, 310–14. Most of the music is attributed (probably spuriously) to clerics from northern cities, such as Bourges or Troyes.

54 *Ad superni regis decus* is a version of *Noster cetus psallat letus* (copied in three Aquitanian sources, including the earliest), while *Gratulantes celebremus festum* is cognate with the Aquitanian *Ad honorem sempiterni regis*. For notational and musical comparisons between these pieces, see Fuller, 'Perspectives on Musical Notation in the *Codex Calixtinus*', pp. 211–14.

55 An exception is the mass gradual 'Misit Herodes', where the elaborative voice dips below the cantus several times.

56 The transcription of *O adjutor* presented here uses perfect consonances and scribal neume groupings as guides to a contingent but not implausible alignment between the voices. For other transcriptions see Karp, *The Polyphony of Saint Martial and Santiago de Compostela*, vol. II, pp. 219–22; van der Werf, *The Oldest Extant Part Music*, vol. II, pp. 202–3; and J. López-Calo, *La musica en la Catedral de Santiago*, vol. V (La Edad Media, La Coruña: Diputación Provincial de La Coruña, 1994), pp. 378–85. For a performed interpretation, see *Miracles of Sant'Iago Music from the Codex Calixtinus*, Anonymous 4, Harmonia Mundi France, HMU 907156 (1995), track 18. For the original notation, see the facsimile cited in note 51 above, fols. 217r–217v.

57 On these resemblances see Fuller, 'Perspectives on Musical Notation in the *Codex Calixtinus*', pp. 218–19. The *porrectus praepunctis* figure common in the treatise and in the repertory occurs in the second and sixth segments of the *O adjutor* verse. These similarities bring a slightly different perspective to the Vatican Organum Treatise, which is chiefly linked with Parisian organum traditions.

4 The thirteenth century

1 The cartoon was published in the syndicated press on 20 March 1987 and is available at www.mycomicspage.com/feature/doonesbury/?date=19870320.

2 The word *conductus* is found in medieval sources in both the second and fourth declensions with the plural in *conducti* and *conductus* respectively.

3 The conductus repertory has been inventoried no less than three times. See Eduard Gröninger, *Repertoire-Untersuchungen zum mehrstimmigen Notre-Dame Conductus*, Kölner Beiträge zur Musikforschung 2 (Regensburg: Gustav Bosse Verlag, 1939); Gordon Anderson, 'Notre-Dame and Related Conductus: A Catalogue Raisonné', *Miscellanea musicologica* 6 (1972), pp. 153–229; 7 (1975), pp. 1–81; Robert Falck, *The Notre Dame Conductus: A Study of the Repertory*, Musicological Studies 33 (Henryville, Ottawa, and Binningen: Institute of Mediaeval Music, 1981). Although published after Anderson's catalogue, Falck's was based on a doctoral dissertation finished in 1970, and although Anderson's work is more complete, Falck's is the more accessible.

4 There is a facsimile of *I-Fl* Plut. 29.1 in Luther Dittmer, ed., *Facsimile Reproduction of the Manuscript Firenze, Biblioteca Mediceo-Laurenziana Pluteo 29.1,* 2 vols., Publications of Mediaeval Musical Manuscripts 10–11 (Brooklyn, NY: Institute of Mediaeval Music, [1966]–7).

5 A complete edition of the conductus repertory is in Gordon Anderson, ed., *Notre-Dame and Related Conductus: Opera omnia*, 10 vols., [Institute of Mediaeval Music] Collected Works 10 (Henryville, Ottawa, and Binningen: Institute of Mediaeval Music, 1979–) (all but vol. VII have appeared). A smaller but useful edition is in Janet Knapp, ed., *Thirty-Five Conductus for Two and Three Voices*, Collegium Musicum 6 (New Haven: Yale University Department of Music Graduate School, 1965). Both editions attempt to present the rhythm of the *cum littera* (texted) sections of the conductus in a metrical, if not modal, form, in contrast to the examples provided here.

6 For thoroughgoing studies on the chronology of the conductus, see Ernest H. Sanders, 'Style and Technique in Datable Polyphonic Notre-Dame Conductus', in Luther Dittmer, ed., *Gordon Athol Anderson (1929–1981) In memoriam von seinen Studenten, Freunden und Kollegen*, 2 vols., Musicological Studies 49 (Henryville, Ottawa, and Binningen: Institute of Mediaeval Music, 1984), vol. II, pp. 505–30, and Thomas B. Payne, 'Datable "Notre Dame" Conductus: New Historical Observations on Style and Technique', *Current Musicology* 64 (2001), pp. 104–51.

7 A useful analysis of the subject matter of conductus texts (but restricted to those in *I-Fl* Plut. 29.1 and including liturgical and motet texts) is in Massimo Masani Ricci, *Codice Pluteo 29.1 della Biblioteca Laurenziana di Firenze: storia e catalogo comparato*, Studi musicali toscani 8 (Pisa: ETS, 2002), pp. 513–46.

8 The literature on the genre's function is enormous. The current views are represented by the following texts: Frank Ll. Harrison, 'Benedicamus, Conductus, Carol', *Acta Musicologica* 37 (1965), pp. 35–48; Bryan Gillingham, 'A New Etymology and Etiology for the Conductus', in Bryan Gillingham and Paul Merkley, eds., *Beyond the Moon: Festschrift Luther Dittmer*, Musicological Studies 53 (Ottawa: Institute of Mediaeval Music, 1990), pp. 100–17; Nancy van Deusen, '*Ductus, Tractus, Conductus*: The Intellectual Context of a Musical Genre', *Theology and Music at the Early University: The Case of Robert Grosseteste and*

Anonymous IV, Brill Studies in Intellectual History 57 (Leiden: Brill, 1995), pp. 37–53.

9 For a wider discussion on the terms *cum* and *sine caudis*, see Ernest H. Sanders, '*Sine littera* and *Cum littera* in Medieval Polyphony', in Edmond Strainchamps, Maria Rika Maniates and Christopher Hatch, eds., *Music and Civilisation: Essays in Honor of Paul Henry Lang* (New York and London: W. W. Norton, 1984), pp. 215–31.

10 *I-Fl* Plut. 29.1, fols. 322r–322v.

11 The text of *Virtus moritur* is a trenchant attack on the place of money at the papal curia. The translation of the text of Example 4.1 is 'Virtue is dying / Sin lives / Faith is cast out / into Exile.'

12 *I-Fl* Plut. 29.1, fols. 359v–360. The versions presented here may be compared with the metrical transcriptions in Anderson, *Notre Dame and Related Conductus*, vol. V, pp. 71–2 and 20–1.

13 The repertory of Parisian organum is edited from *I-Fl* Plut. 29.1 in Mark Everist, ed., *Les Organa à deux voix du manuscrit de Florence, Biblioteca Medicea-Laurenziana, Plut. 29.1*, 3 vols., Le Magnus liber organi de Notre Dame de Paris 2–4 (Monaco: Éditions de l'Oiseau-Lyre, 2001–3); the repertory from *D-W 1099* is edited in Thomas B. Payne, ed., *Les Organa à deux voix du manuscrit de Wolfenbüttel, Hertzog [sic] August Bibliothek, Cod. Guelf. 1099 Helmst.*, 2 vols., Le Magnus liber organi de Notre-Dame de Paris 6A-6B (Monaco: Éditions de l'Oiseau-Lyre, 1996).

14 For the three- and four-part organa, see Edward H. Roesner, ed., *Les Quadrupla et tripla de Paris*, Le Magnus liber organi de Notre-Dame de Paris 1 (Monaco: Éditions de l'Oiseau-Lyre, 1993).

15 Fritz Reckow, ed., *Der Musiktraktat des Anonymus 4*, 2 vols., Beihefte zum Archiv für Musikwissenschaft 4–5 (Wiesbaden: Franz Steiner Verlag, 1967), vol. I, pp. 46, translated in Jeremy Yudkin, *The Music Treatise of Anonymous IV: A New Translation*, Musicological Studies and Documents 41 (Neuhausen-Stuttgart: American Institute of Musicology, 1985), p. 39.

16 See Mark Everist, *Polyphonic Music in Thirteenth-Century France: Aspects of Sources and Distribution* (New York: Garland, 1989), pp. 1–6 and the sources cited there.

17 For the date of *D-W 628* (known as W_1 in older literature), see Mark Everist, 'From Paris to St Andrews: The Origins of W_1', *Journal of the American Musicological Society* 43 (1990), pp. 1–42; Rebecca A. Baltzer, 'The Manuscript Makers of W1: Further Evidence for an Early Date', in *Quomodo cantabimus canticum? Studies*

in Honor of Edward H. Roesner, ed. David Butler Cannata, Gabriela Ilnitchi Currie, Rena Charnin Mueller and John Louis Nádas (Middleton, WI: American Institute of Musicology, 2008), pp. 103–20. For *I-Fl* Plut. 29.1, see Rebecca A. Baltzer, 'Thirteenth-Century Illuminated Miniatures and the Date of the Florence Manuscript', *Journal of the American Musicological Society* 25 (1972), pp. 1–18.

18 For a broader view of the liturgical dimension of Parisian organum, see Craig Wright, *Music and Ceremony at Notre Dame of Paris 500–1550* (Cambridge University Press, 1989), pp. 258–67.

19 *I-Fl* Plut. 29.1, fols. 121v–122r; *D-W* 1099, fols. 81r–82r. It is edited in Everist, ed., *Les Organa à deux voix du manuscrit de Florence*, vol. III, pp. 190–200.

20 See, for example, the older editions of this repertory that transcribe *organum per se* according to the principles of the rhythmic modes: William Waite, ed., *The Rhythm of Twelfth-Century Polyphony: Its Theory and Practice*, Yale Studies in the History of Music 2 (New Haven: Yale University Press; London: Geoffrey Cumberledge and Oxford University Press, 1954), and Hans Tischler, ed., *The Parisian Two-Part Organa: Complete Comparative Edition*, 2 vols. (New York: Pendragon, 1988).

21 There is an important variant in the two cursus of the tenor here: the pitch is *g* at 32 but *a* at 47, and the manuscript is clear in both cases. However, the plainsong preserves an *a* (the second of the two choices) which could point to an error in pitch in *I-Fl* Plut. 29.1 at 32.

22 Although the discussion of *copula* in theoretical sources is extensive – and hotly debated – its identification in sources such as *I-Fl* Plut. 29.1 or *D-W* 628 and 1099 is much less clear. See Fritz Reckow, *Die Copula: Über einige Zusammenhänge zwischen Setzweise, Formbildung, Rhythmus und Vortragstil in der Mehrstimmigkeit von Notre-Dame*, Abhandlungen der Geistes- und Sozialwissenschaftlichen Klasse der Akademie der Wissenschaften und der Literatur 13 (Wiesbaden: Steiner, 1972), pp. 609–70; Jeremy Yudkin, 'The Copula according to Johannes de Garlandia', *Musica disciplina* 34 (1980), pp. 67–84; and his 'The Anonymous of St Emmeram and Anonymous IV on the Copula', *Musical Quarterly* 70 (1984), pp. 1–22.

23 With nearly 100 organa some of which are in three sources, the permutations of clausulae become truly staggering. This aspect of the repertory is controlled in Friedrich Ludwig, *Repertorium organorum recentioris et motetorum vetustissimi stili*, 2 vols (1/1 – Halle: Verlag von

Max Niemeyer, 1910; *R* [ed. Luther A. Dittmer, Musicological Studies 7] Brooklyn, NY: Institute of Mediaeval Music; Hildesheim: Georg Olms, 1964; 1/2 – [345–456 ed. Friedrich Gennrich including *R* of 'Die Quellen der Motetten altesten Stils', *Archiv für Musikwissenschaft* 5 (1923), pp. 185–222 and 273–315, Summa Musicae Medii Aevi 7] Langen bei Frankfürt: n.p., 1961; *R* [345–456] [457–783, ed. Luther A. Dittmer, Musicological Studies 26] [Binningen]: Institute of Mediaeval Music, 1978; 2 – [1–71 ed. Friedrich Gennrich, Summa Musicae Medii Aevi 8 – 65–71 in page proof only] Langen bei Frankfürt: n.p., 1962; *R* [1–64, 65–71 corrected] [72–155 ed. Luther A. Dittmer, Musicological Studies 17] Brooklyn, NY: Institute of Mediaeval Music, n.d.; Hildesheim: Georg Olms, 1972).

24 Mark Everist, *French Motets in the Thirteenth Century: Music, Poetry and Genre*, Cambridge Studies in Medieval and Renaissance Music (Cambridge University Press, 1994), pp. 15–42.

25 For views on chronology, see Everist, *Polyphonic Music in Thirteenth-Century France*, pp. 6–27.

26 The clausula is found in *I-Fl* Plut. 29.1, fol. 158r and edited in Rebecca A. Baltzer, ed., *Les clausules à deux voix du manuscrit de Florence, Biblioteca Medicea-Laurenziana, Pluteus 29.1, fascicule V*, Le Magnus liber organi de Notre-Dame de Paris 5 (Monaco: Éditions de l'Oiseau-Lyre, 1995), p. 82. The motet is in *I-Fl* Plut. 29.1, fols. 411r–411v, and edited in Hans Tischler, ed., *The Earliest Motets (to circa 1270): A Complete Comparative Edition*, 3 vols. (New Haven and London: Yale University Press, 1982) vol. II, p. 490. There is a single exception to the exact congruity of the two tenors: at 33–5 the notation of the clausula tenor has a descending *conjunctura* (three lozenges, indicated in the example by a broken slur) whereas the motet has a straightforward ligature.

27 For a fuller account of *Immolata paschali victima / Latus*, and of a large number of analogous motet–clausula pairs, see Norman E. Smith, 'The Earliest Motets: Music and Words', *Journal of the Royal Musical Association* 114 (1989), pp. 141–63, especially 160–3.

28 See Rebecca A. Baltzer, 'Aspects of Trope in the Earliest Motets for the Assumption of the Virgin', in Peter M. Lefferts, and Brian Seirup, eds., *Festschrift for Ernest Sanders* (New York: Trustees of Columbia University, 1991), pp. 7–42.

29 In this context, the list of functions for the motets in *I-Fl* Plut 29.1 in Ricci, *Codice Pluteo 29.1*, is valuable.

30 Anderson, 'Notre Dame Bilingual Motets: A Study in the History of Music, c.1215–1245', *Miscellanea musicologica* 3 (1968), pp. 50–144.

31 Ludwig's *Repertorium* not only explains how organa and clausulae interrelate, but also links the motet repertory into the same bibliographical tool. That part of his work that deals with the motets was updated in Friedrich Gennrich, *Bibliographie der ältesten französischen und lateinischen Motetten*, Summa Musicae Medii Aevi 2 (Darmstadt: author, 1957).

32 *D-W* 1099, fol. 181v–182r.

33 *F-Pn* fr. 12615, fols. 186r–186v; *F-Pn* fr. 844, p. 200.

34 *D-W* 1099, fols. 198v–199v; *F-Pn* n.a.f. 13521, pp. 738–9; *F-MOf* H.196, fols. 126v–127r.

35 *D-BAs* Lit. 115, fol. 55r.

36 Gordon Anderson, 'Notre Dame Latin Double Motets ca.1215–1250', *Musica disciplina* 25 (1971), pp. 35–92.

37 The standard bibliography for the texts of *refrains* is Nico H. J. van den Boogaard, *Rondeaux et refrains du xiie siècle au début du xive: collationnement, introduction, et notes*, Bibliothèque française et romane, D:3 (Paris: Éditions Klincksieck, 1969). For the music, see Anne Ibos-Augé, 'La fonction des insertions lyriques dans des oeuvres narratives et didactiques aux xiiième et xivème siècles', 4 vols. (PhD diss., Université Michel de Montaigne-Bordeaux III, 2000).

38 The motet '*Amis, vostre demoree / Pro patribus* is unique in *F-MOf* H.196, fol. 249r and edited in Hans Tischler, ed., *The Montpellier Codex*, 4 vols. [vol. IV ed. and trans. Susan Stakel and Joel C. Relihan], Recent Researches in the Music of the Middle Ages and Early Renaissance 2–8 (Madison, WI: A. R. Editions, 1978–85), vol. III, p. 28.

39 The *Quinque incitamenta* are edited in André Wilmart, 'Gérard de Liège: *Quinque incitamenta ad Deum amandum ardenter*', *Analecta reginensia*, Studi e testi 59 (Vatican City: Biblioteca Apostolica Vaticana, 1933), pp. 205–47; see also Nico van den Boogaard, 'Les insertions en français dans un traité de Gérard de Liège', in Rita Lejeune, ed., *Marche romane: mélanges de philologie et de littératures romanes offerts à Jeanne Wathelet-Willem* (Liège: Cahiers de l'A. R. U. Lg., 1978), pp. 679–97.

40 The song is found in *F-Pn* fr. 844, fol.118v; *F-Pn* fr. 12615, fol. 118r; *I-Rvat* Reg. Lat. 1490, fol. 44r.

41 See the editions of the *refrain* in Ibos-Augé, 'La fonction des insertions lyriques', vol. II, pp. 145–6.

42 The range of functions of the *refrain* within the motet is outlined in Everist, *French Motets in the Thirteenth Century*, pp. 54–66.

43 See the listing and discussion in Thomas Walker, 'Sui Tenor Francesi nei motetti del "200" ', *Schede medievali: rassegna dell' officina di studi medievali* 3 (1982), pp. 309–36.

44 Everist, 'Motets, French Tenors and the Polyphonic Chanson ca. 1300', *Journal of Musicology* 24 (2007), pp. 365–406.

45 *F-MOf* H.196, fols. 273r–275r; *I-Tr* vari 42, fols. 14r–15v; edited in Tischler, *Montpellier Codex*, vol. III, pp. 65–7.

46 The innovations found in 'Aucun ont trouvé chant par usage' were attributed to Petrus de Cruce in the thirteenth century. A full list of these works, together with the evidence for his authorship, is in Ernest H. Sanders and Peter M. Lefferts, 'Petrus de Cruce', *Grove Music Online*, www.oxfordmusiconline.com.

47 Albert Seay, trans., *Johannes de Grocheo: Concerning Music (De musica)*, Colorado College Music Press Translations 1 (Colorado Springs: Colorado College Music Press, 1967–74), p. 26.

48 Christopher Page, *The Owl and the Nightingale: Musical Life and Ideas in France 1100–1300* (London: Dent, 1989), pp. 144–54.

49 See, among others, Jeremy Yudkin, 'The Rhythm of Organum Purum', *Journal of Musicology* 2 (1983), pp. 355–76.

50 For the conductus around 1300 see Mark Everist, 'Reception and Recomposition in the Polyphonic *Conductus cum cauda*: The Metz Fragment', *Journal of the Royal Musical Association* 125 (2000), pp. 135–63 and the sources cited there. The key sources for the recasting of organum are the first fascicle of *F-MOf* H.196, *D-B* Lat. 4° 523; and *DK-Kk* 1810 4°. For the former, see Kurt von Fischer, 'Neue Quellen zur Musik des 13., 14., und 15. Jahrhunderts', *Acta Musicologica* 36 (1964), pp. 80–3, and for the latter John Bergsagel, 'The Transmission of Notre-Dame Organa in Some Newly-Discovered "Magnus liber organi" Fragments in Copenhagen', in Angelo Pompilio, ed., *Atti del XIV Congresso della Società Internazionale di Musicologia: Trasmissione e recezione delle forme di cultura musicale*, 3 vols. (Turin: EDT, 1990), vol. III, pp. 629–36.

5 The fourteenth century

1 Barbara Wertheim Tuchman, *A Distant Mirror: The Calamitous Fourteenth Century* (New York: Knopf, 1978).

2 See Andrew Tomasello, *Music and Ritual at Papal Avignon 1309–1403*, Studies in Musicology 75, ed. George J. Buelow (Ann Arbor and Epping: Bowker Publishing, 1983); Yolanda Plumley, 'An "Episode in the South"? Ars Subtilior and the Patronage of French Princes', *Early Music History* 22 (2003), pp. 103–68; Margaret Bent, 'Early Papal Motets', in Richard Sherr, ed., *Papal Music and Musicians in Late Medieval and Renaissance Rome* (Oxford: Clarendon Press, 1998).

3 See Lawrence Earp, 'Lyrics for Reading and Lyrics for Singing in Late Medieval France: The Development of the Dance Lyric from Adam de la Halle to Guillaume de Machaut', in Rebecca A. Baltzer, Thomas Cable and James I. Wimsatt, eds., *The Union of Words and Music in Medieval Poetry*, (Austin: University of Texas Press, 1991). Philippe de Vitry was later elected Bishop of Meaux; see 'Vitry, Philippe de', *New Grove Dictionary of Music and Musicians*, 2nd edn.

4 Andrew Wathey, 'The Motets of Philippe de Vitry and the Fourteenth-Century Renaissance', *Early Music History* 12 (1993), pp. 133–5. On Clement VI in general see Diana Wood, *Clement VI: The Pontificate and Ideas of an Avignon Pope* (Cambridge University Press, 1989).

5 It should be noted that Clement VII was also the name used by Ippolito Aldobrandini, elected Pope in 1592.

6 See Christopher Allmand, *The Hundred Years War: England and France at War* (Cambridge University Press, rev. edn 2001).

7 Andrew Wathey, 'The Peace of 1360–1369 and Anglo-French Musical Relations', *Early Music History* 9 (1989).

8 See William Chester Jordan, *The Great Famine: Northern Europe in the Early Fourteenth Century* (Princeton University Press, 1996); Gregory Clark, 'The Economics of Exhaustion, the Postan Thesis, and the Agricultural Revolution', *Journal of Economic History* 52 (1992).

9 The Black Death has been believed by many to have been the bubonic plague (*yersinia pestis*) spread by fleas from infected rodents; modern epidemiologists dispute both the microbiological agent and the means of transmission. See Ole Benedictow, *The Black Death 1346–1353: The Complete History* (Woodbridge: Boydell and Brewer, 2004).

10 Malcolm Vale, *The Princely Court: Medieval Courts and Culture in North-West Europe 1270–1380* (Oxford University Press, 2001).

11 M. T. Clanchy, *From Memory to Written Record: England 1066–1307*, 2nd edn, (Oxford: Blackwell, 1993); Peter Spufford, *Money and Its Use in Medieval Europe* (Cambridge University Press, 1988).

12 See Frank Hentschel, *Sinnlichkeit und Vernunft in der mittelalterlichen Musiktheorie: Strategien der Konsonanzwertung und der Gegenstand der 'musica sonora' um 1300* (Stuttgart: Steiner, 2000); Nan Cooke Carpenter, *Music in the Medieval and Renaissance Universities* (Norman: University of Oklahoma Press, 1958).

13 While this might seem rather abstract it has been argued that this 'mania for measurement' (sometimes the rather intangible quantification of qualities such as God's mercy) was a direct result of the engagement by academics in the busy monetarized marketplaces of Oxford, Paris and other university towns, their management of college accounts, and their practical understanding of the functioning of money in the newly monetarized economy. See Joel Kaye, *Economy and Nature in the Fourteenth Century: Money, Market Exchange, and the Emergence of Scientific Thought* (Cambridge University Press, 1998). Artistic creation (especially poetry – an oral performance art in this period) was often compared metaphorically to coin. This period sees it, like coin, being commoditized within the emerging market economy.

14 See the arguments in Dorit Esther Tanay, *Noting Music, Marking Culture* (Holzerlingen: Hänssler, 1999). See also 'Muris, Johannes de', *New Grove*.

15 Albert Douglas Menut, *Maistre Nicole Oresme: Le livre de politiques d'Aristote* (Philadelphia: American Philosophical Society, 1970).

16 See 'Versified Office', *New Grove*.

17 See the comments in Anna Maria Busse Berger, *Medieval Music and the Art of Memory* (Berkeley: University of California Press, 2005), Chapter 1.

18 A summary of, and bibliography for, these developments can be found in 'Motet', *New Grove*.

19 The terms *color* and *talea* are used here as commonly applied in modern scholarship; their medieval use was less clearly distinct. Overlapping *taleae* are more common in the later motets of Vitry and widely used by Machaut.

20 On the meaning provided by number in specific examples of fourteenth-century motets see Margaret Bent, 'Deception, Exegesis and Sounding Number in Machaut's Motet 15', *Early Music History* 10 (1991); David Howlett, '*Apollinis eclipsatur*: Foundation of the "Collegium musicorum"', in Suzannah Clark and Elizabeth Eva Leach, eds., Auctoritas *in*

Medieval and Renaissance Musical Culture: Learning from the Learned (Woodbridge: Boydell Press, 2005).

21 See 'Motet', New Grove.

22 For this point and for reasons behind his choice, see the analysis in Anne Walters Robertson, Guillaume de Machaut and Reims: Context and Meaning in His Musical Works (Cambridge University Press, 2002).

23 See Jacques Boogaart, '"O Series Summe Rata." De Motetten van Guillaume de Machaut. De Ordening van het Corpus en de Samenhang van Tekst en Muziek', PhD diss., Utrecht, 2001; Thomas Brown, 'Another Mirror of Lovers? Order, Structure and Allusion in Machaut's Motets', Plainsong and Medieval Music 10 (2001); Robertson, Guillaume de Machaut and Reims.

24 See Peter M. Lefferts, The Motet in England in the Fourteenth Century (Ann Arbor: UMI, 1986). However, pieces from the international repertory of French motets circulated in francophone England as well as elsewhere in Europe.

25 See Earp, 'Lyrics for Reading and Lyrics for Singing'.

26 One balade by Vitry survives, without music, in F-Pn lat. 3343. James I. Wimsatt, Chaucer and the Poems of 'Ch' in University of Pennsylvania MS French 15 (Cambridge: Brewer, 1982), pp. 56–7 dates this between 1340 and 1361, most likely after 1346. F. N. M. Diekstra, 'The Poetic Exchange between Philippe de Vitry and Jean de le Mote', Neophilologus 70 (1986) suggests it could be earlier.

27 Christopher Page, 'Tradition and Innovation in BN fr. 146: The Background to the Ballades', in Margaret Bent and Andrew Wathey, eds., Fauvel Studies: Allegory, Chronicle, Music, and Image in Paris, Bibliothèque Nationale de France, MS français 146 (Oxford: Clarendon Press, 1998).

28 Texts edited in Georg Steffens, 'Die altfranzösische Liederhandschrift der Bodleiana in Oxford, Douce 308', Archiv für das Studium der neueren Sprachen und Litteraturen 99 (1897).

29 The picture is on fol. 51r of F-Pn fr. 1586 and is reproduced in colour as plate 24 in François Avril, Manuscript Painting at the Court of France: The Fourteenth Century (1320–1380) (London: Chatto and Windus, 1978), p. 87. Low-definition copies can be viewed online by entering 'Machaut' as a search term into an image search engine and following the links.

30 See Virginia Newes, 'Chace, Caccia, Fuga: The Convergence of French and Italian Traditions', Musica Disciplina 41 (1987); Elizabeth Eva Leach, Sung Birds: Music, Nature,

and Poetry in the Later Middle Ages (Ithaca: Cornell University Press, 2007).

31 See 'Lai', New Grove.

32 Ibid.

33 Gilbert Reaney, 'Concerning the Origin of the Medieval Lai', Music and Letters 39 (1958).

34 'Lai', New Grove.

35 The poet Eustache Deschamps reports of the lai 'c'est une chose longue et malaisiee a faire et trouver' ('it is long and difficult to do and to invent'). Deborah M. Sinnreich-Levi, ed., Eustache Deschamps L'Art de dictier (East Lansing: Colleagues Press, 1994), p. 94.

36 'Madrigal', New Grove.

37 'Mass', section II, 3–4, New Grove.

38 The Ivrea and Tremoïlle manuscripts; see ibid.

39 Janet Knapp, 'Polyphony at Notre Dame of Paris', in Richard Crocker and David Hiley, eds., The New Oxford History of Music, vol. II, The Early Middle Ages to 1300, (Oxford University Press, 1990); Mark Everist, French Motets in the Thirteenth Century: Music, Poetry and Genre (Cambridge University Press, 1994); Rebecca A. Baltzer, 'Aspects of Trope in the Earliest Motets for the Assumption of the Virgin', Current Musicology 45–7 (1990) (Festschrift for Ernest Sanders, ed. Peter M. Lefferts and Brian Seirup); Gerald R. Hoekstra, 'The French Motet as Trope: Multiple Levels of Meaning in Quant florist la violete / El mois de mai / Et Gaudebit', Speculum 73 (1998).

40 'Mass', section II, 4, 'Toulouse Mass', and 'Barcelona Mass', New Grove.

41 Andrew Kirkman, 'The Invention of the Cyclic Mass', Journal of the American Musicological Society 54 (2001).

42 Roger Bowers, 'Guillaume de Machaut and His Canonry of Reims, 1338–1377', Early Music History 23 (2004); Robertson, Guillaume de Machaut and Reims, Chapter 9.

43 Margaret Bent, 'Fauvel and Marigny: Which Came First?' in Bent and Wathey, eds., Fauvel Studies, p. 52.

44 Passerose and Roses et lis, both in the Chantilly Codex; see Gilbert Reaney, 'The Manuscript Chantilly, Musée Condé 1047', Musica Disciplina 8 (1954), pp. 76–7.

45 Robertson argues that M18 was adapted for later reuse; Robertson, Guillaume de Machaut and Reims, Chapter 2, especially p. 60. However, given that its use as the initial triplum rhyme (Guillerme / inerme) locks the name of this specific archbishop tightly into the work, it might be better to view it as serving an ongoing warning to later incumbents rather than as something that could be substituted.

46 See Robertson, *Guillaume de Machaut and Reims.*

47 Kevin Brownlee, 'Machaut's Motet 15 and the *Roman de la Rose*: The Literary Context of *Amours qui a le pouoir / Faus samblant m'a deceü / Vidi Dominum*', *Early Music History* 10 (1991).

48 See Sylvia Huot, 'Guillaume de Machaut and the Consolation of Poetry', *Modern Philology* 100 (2002).

49 See Christopher Page, *The Owl and the Nightingale: Musical Life and Ideas in France 1100–1300* (London: Dent, 1989), pp. 33–40.

50 Saint Augustine, 'On Music', in *Writings of Saint Augustine*, vol. II, trans. and ed. Robert Catesby Taliaferro (Washington, DC: Catholic University of America, 1977), p. 171, explains that noblemen properly use music to relax from their labours. Isidore, *Etymologies* III: 17 mentions that 'music soothes the mind so that it can endure toil, and song assuages the weariness encountered in any task' (trans. in James McKinnon, ed., *The Early Christian Period and the Latin Middle Ages*, vol. II [New York: W. W. Norton, 1998], p. 40). Later, Peter the Chanter admits the morality of paying for music so long as it is designed either to relieve sadness and tedium ('tristia et taedium amoveantur'), or to excite devotion (the latter also an Augustinian rationale mentioned in the *Confessions*). Peter's views were developed throughout the thirteenth century by Thomas Chobham (*Penetential*, 1216), Robert Courson (*Summa*, 1208–1212/13), and the Franciscan Thomas Docking (*Commentary on Galatians*, 1265). In general, thirteenth-century preachers recognized a division between entertainers who were primarily acrobats, actors etc. and those professionals who sang with instrumental accompaniment of exploits to give relaxation (*recreationem*) or instruction (*informationem*). See Page, *The Owl and the Nightingale*, pp. 20–2, citing J. Baldwin, *Masters, Princes and Merchants: The Social Views of Peter the Chanter and His Circle* (Princeton University Press, 1970).

51 See Mary B. Schoen-Nazzaro, 'Plato and Aristotle on the Ends of Music', *Laval Théologique et Philosophique* 34 (1978).

52 Full exposition in Leach, *Sung Birds*, Chapter 4.

53 See 'Performing Practice', section I, 2–3, *New Grove*.

54 See the summary in Daniel Leech-Wilkinson, *The Modern Invention of Medieval Music: Scholarship, Ideology, Performance* (Cambridge University Press, 2002).

55 See the arguments in Margaret Bent, 'The Grammar of Early Music: Preconditions for Analysis', in Cristle Collins Judd, ed., *Tonal Structures in Early Music* (New York: Garland, 1998).

56 See the bibliography supporting 'Notation', section III, 3, *New Grove*.

57 See, for example, the essays in Margaret Bent, *Counterpoint, Composition, and Musica Ficta* (London and New York: Routledge, 2002) compared with the differing views in Karol Berger, *Musica Ficta: Theories of Accidental Inflections in Vocal Polyphony from Marchetto da Padova to Gioseffo Zarlino* (Cambridge University Press, 1987) and Thomas Brothers, *Chromatic Beauty in the Late Medieval Chanson: An Interpretation of Manuscript Accidentals* (Cambridge University Press, 1997).

58 Sarah Fuller, 'Tendencies and Resolutions: The Directed Progression in Ars Nova Music', *Journal of Music Theory* 36 (1992).

59 See entries for 'Ars Antiqua', 'Ars Nova', and 'Ars Subtilior', *New Grove*.

60 *US-BEm* 744, p. 62. See Richard Crocker, 'A New Source for Medieval Music Theory', *Acta Musicologica* 39 (1967), and Figure 5.1 on p. 101 below.

61 See, for example, the arguments made in James Webster, 'The Concept of Beethoven's "Early" Period in the Context of Periodizations in General', *Beethoven Forum* 3 (1994).

62 Sarah Fuller, 'A Phantom Treatise of the Fourteenth Century? The *Ars Nova*', *Journal of Musicology* 30 (1985–6).

63 Elizabeth Randell Upton, 'The Chantilly Codex (*F-CH* 564): The Manuscript, Its Music, Its Scholarly Reception', PhD diss., University of North Carolina at Chapel Hill, 2001.

64 M. T. Clanchy, '*Moderni* in Education and Government in England', *Speculum* 50 (1975).

65 MS 0744, fol. 31v, Jean Gray Hargrove Music Library, University of California, Berkeley.

66 Craig Wright, *The Maze and the Warrior: Symbols in Architecture, Theology, and Music* (Cambridge, MA: Harvard University Press, 2001), pp. 239–42.

67 Anne Stone, 'Self-Reflexive Songs and their Readers in the Late 14th Century', *Early Music* 31/2 (2003); Stone, 'The Composer's Voice in the Late-Medieval Song: Four Case Studies', in Philippe Vendrix, ed., *Johannes Ciconia: musicien de la transition* (Turnhout: Brepols, 2003); and Stone, 'Music Writing and Poetic Voice in Machaut: Some Remarks on B12 and B14', in Elizabeth Eva Leach, ed., *Machaut's Music: New Interpretations* (Woodbridge: Boydell and Brewer, 2003).

68 See Elizabeth Eva Leach, 'Death of a Lover and the Birth of the Polyphonic Balade: Machaut's Notated Balades 1–5', *Journal of Musicology* 19 (2002); Robertson, *Guillaume de Machaut and Reims*.
69 Reinhard Strohm, *The Rise of European Music* 1380–1500 (Cambridge University Press, 1993).
70 Daniel Poirion, *Le poète et le prince: l'évolution du lyrisme courtois de Guillaume de Machaut à Charles d'Orléans* (Grenoble: Allier, 1965).
71 See the arguments about *Soiez liez* in Earp, 'Lyrics for Reading and Lyrics for Singing', pp. 106–9.
72 Wathey, 'The Motets of Philippe de Vitry and the Fourteenth-Century Renaissance'.
73 See Lawrence Earp, *Guillaume de Machaut: A Guide to Research* (New York and London: Garland, 1995), Chapter 2.
74 Christopher Page, *Discarding Images: Reflections on Music and Culture in Medieval France* (Oxford University Press, 1993), 200.
75 Jessie Ann Owens, 'Music Historiography and the Definition of "Renaissance"', *Notes* 47 (1990).

6 England
1 Recommended surveys and general resources include John Caldwell, *The Oxford History of English Music*, vol. I, *From the Beginnings to c.1715* (Oxford: Clarendon Press, 1991); Frank Ll. Harrison, *Music in Medieval Britain* (London: Routledge & Kegan Paul, 1958; 2nd edn 1963, repr. Buren: Fritz Knuf, 1980); Peter M. Lefferts, 'Medieval England, 950–1450', in James McKinnon, ed., *Antiquity and the Middle Ages: From Ancient Greece to the Fifteenth Century*, Music and Society 1 (London: Macmillan, 1990), pp. 170–96; Christopher Page, 'Music', in Boris Ford, ed., *The Cambridge Guide to the Arts in Britain*, vol. I, *Prehistoric, Roman, and Early Medieval* (Cambridge University Press, 1988), pp. 247–53; Nick Sandon and Christopher Page, 'Music', in Boris Ford, ed., *The Cambridge Guide to the Arts in Britain*, vol. II, *The Middle Ages* (Cambridge University Press, 1988), pp. 214–50; and Paul Szarmach, M. Teresa Tavormina and Joel T. Rosenthal, eds., *Medieval England: An Encyclopedia* (London: Garland, 1998).
2 The album *An English Ladymass* (Harmonia Mundi France HMU 907080), recorded by the singing ensemble Anonymous 4, was at or near the top of the classical music charts for the better part of two years in 1993–4.
3 On Ledrede's lyrics, see Edmund Colledge, *The Latin Poems of Richard Ledrede, OFM*

(Toronto: Pontifical Institute, 1974); for vernacular motet tenors, see Peter M. Lefferts, *The Motet in England in the Fourteenth Century* (Ann Arbor: UMI, 1986).
4 For the polyphonic songs, see Ernest H. Sanders, ed., *English Music of the Thirteenth and Early Fourteenth Centuries*, Polyphonic Music of the Fourteenth Century 14 (Paris and Monaco: Éditions de l'Oiseau-Lyre, 1979). For the dances, see Timothy J. McGee, ed., *Medieval Instumental Dances* (Bloomington: Indiana University Press, 1989).
5 See Peter M. Lefferts and David Fallows, 'Songs', in *Medieval England: An Encyclopedia*, and David Fallows, *A Catalogue of Polyphonic Songs, 1415–1480* (Oxford: Clarendon Press, 1999).
6 For more on narrative melodies, see John Stevens, *Words and Music in the Middle Ages: Song, Narrative, Dance and Drama, 1050–1350* (Cambridge University Press, 1986).
7 See Peter M. Lefferts and Richard Rastall, 'Minstrels and Minstrelsy', in *Medieval England: An Encyclopedia*, and John Southworth, *The English Medieval Minstrel* (Woodbridge: Boydell, 1989).
8 The extant later medieval English-language songs have been edited by Eric J. Dobson and Frank Ll. Harrison in *Medieval English Songs* (London: Faber, 1979). The Anglo-Norman songs are anticipated in a forthcoming edition from the estate of the late John Stevens; for now, see John Stevens, 'Alphabetical Check-list of Anglo-Norman Songs', *Plainsong and Medieval Music* 3 (1994), pp. 1–22.
9 For an overview of these later songs, see Fallows, *Catalogue of Polyphonic Songs*. On the carols see Richard L. Greene, *The Early English Carols*, 2nd edn (Oxford: Clarendon Press, 1977), John Stevens, ed., *Mediaeval Carols*, Musica Britannica 4 (London: Stainer & Bell, 1958) and Stevens, ed., *Early Tudor Songs and Carols*, Musica Britannica 36 (London: Stainer & Bell, 1952; 2nd rev. edn, 1975).
10 The best short survey of the medieval church and its music in England is Nick Sandon, 'Liturgy and Church Music, History of', in *Medieval England: An Encyclopedia*.
11 Alejandro E. Planchart, *The Repertory of Tropes at Winchester*, 2 vols. (Princeton University Press, 1977).
12 See Richard W. Pfaff, *New Liturgical Feasts in Later Medieval England* (Oxford: Clarendon Press, 1970), and Andrew Hughes, 'British Rhymed Offices: A Catalogue and Commentary', in Susan Rankin and David Hiley, eds., *Music in the Medieval English Liturgy; Plainsong and Medieval Music Centennial*

Essays (Oxford: Clarendon Press, 1993), pp. 239–84.

13 See Susan Rankin, 'Winchester Polyphony: The Early Theory and Practice of Organum', in Rankin and Hiley, eds., *Music in the Medieval English Liturgy*, pp. 59–99, and Susan Rankin, ed., *The Winchester Troper: Facsimile Edition*, Early English Church Music 50 (London: Stainer & Bell, 2007).

14 See Nick Sandon, 'Salisbury (Sarum), Use of', in *Medieval England: An Encyclopedia*.

15 See Terence Bailey, *The Processions of Sarum and the Western Church* (Toronto: Pontifical Institute of Mediaeval Studies, 1971), and Peter M. Lefferts, 'Holy Week and Easter, Music for', in *Medieval England: An Encyclopedia*.

16 See Peter M. Lefferts, 'Cantilena and Antiphon: Music for Marian Services in Late Medieval England', in *Studies in Medieval Music: Festschrift for Ernest H. Sanders*, ed. Peter M. Lefferts and Brian Seirup as *Current Musicology* 45–7 (1990), pp. 247–82, and Sally E. Roper, *Medieval English Benedictine Liturgy: Studies in the Formation, Structure, and Content of the Monastic Votive Office, c. 950–1540* (New York: Garland, 1993).

17 See Roger D. Bowers, 'Choirs, Choral Establishments', in *Medieval England: An Encyclopedia*, and Andrew Wathey, *Music in the Royal and Noble Households in Late Medieval England: Studies of Sources and Patronage* (New York: Garland, 1989).

18 For all these repertories, see Sanders, ed., *English Music of the Thirteenth and Early Fourteenth Centuries*.

19 For English notations of the thirteenth century, see Lefferts, *The Motet in England*, pp. 104–24, and for the next century see also Peter M. Lefferts, 'Some Aspects of Musical Notation in Fourteenth-Century England', in Maria Caraci Vela, Daniele Sabaino and Stefano Aresi, eds., *Le notazioni della polifonia vocale dei secoli ix–xvii, Antologia parte prima secoli ix–xiv* (Pisa: Edizioni ETS, 2007), pp. 263–75.

20 For the style, context, and influence of English sacred music of the later fourteenth and fifteenth centuries, see Reinhard Strohm, *The Rise of European Music 1380–1500* (Cambridge University Press, 1993).

7 Italy to 1300

1 On this topic see the enlightening pages of Varvaro: Alberto Varvaro, *Letterature romanze del medioevo* (Bologna: Il Mulino, 1985), pp. 9–82.

2 Giulio Cattin, '"Secundare" e "succinere". Polifonia a Padova e Pistoia nel Duecento', *Musica e storia* 3 (1995), pp. 41–120.

3 Cattin, '"Secundare" e "succinere"', p. 119.

4 The two important sources are quoted in B. Baroffio and C. Antonelli, 'La passione nella liturgia della Chiesa cattolica fino all'epoca di Johann Sebastian Bach', in E. Povellato, ed., *Ritorno a Bach. Dramma e ritualità delle passioni* (Venice: Marsilio, 1986), p. 16, and in Giacomo Baroffio, 'Le polifonie primitive nella tradizione manoscritta italiana. Appunti di ricerca', in Giulio Cattin and F. Alberto Gallo, eds., *Un millennio di polifonia liturgica tra oralità e scrittura* (Bologna: Il Mulino, 2002), pp. 201–5: 201.

5 See Guido Milanese, *Paraphonia-paraphonista dalla lessicografia greca alla tarda antichità romana*, in Enrico Menesto, Antonio Island, Alessandra Di Pilla and Ubaldo Pizzani *Curiositas. Studi di cultura classica e medievale in onore di Ubaldo Pizzani* (Naples: ESI, 2002), pp. 407–21.

6 A first list of Italian sources of sacred polyphony up to ca1300 is in Susan Rankin, 'Between Oral and Written: Thirteenth-Century Italian Sources of Polyphony', in G. Cattin and F. A. Gallo, eds., *Un millennio di polifonia liturgica tra oralità e scrittura* (Bologna: Il Mulino, 2002), pp. 75–98: 93–5.

7 Adam de Salimbene, *Cronica*, ed. Giuseppe Scalia, 2 vols. (Bari: Laterza, 1966), vol. I, pp. 264–5.

8 F. Alberto Gallo, 'The Practice of "Cantus planus binatim" in Italy from the Beginning of the Fourteenth to the Beginning of the Sixteenth Century', in C. Corsi and P. Petrobelli, eds., *Le polifonie primitive in Friuli e in Europa* (Rome: Torre d'Orfeo, 1989), pp. 13–30.

9 Tadeusz Miazga, *Die Melodien des einstimmigen Credo der römisch-katholischen lateinischen Kirche: Eine Untersuchung der Melodien im den handschriftlichen Überlieferungen mit besonderer Berücksichtigung der polnischen Handschriften* (Graz: Akademische Druck- und Verlagsanstalt, 1976), p. 81, no. 319.

10 Photographed by Romina Sani Brenelli for the project *Raphael*.

11 Carla Vivarelli, '"Di una pretesa scuola napoletana": Sowing the Seeds of the Ars Nova at the Court of Robert of Anjou', *Journal of Musicology* 24/2 (2007), pp. 272–96.

12 Arezzo, Museo Diocesano, s.n., C.216; Cividale del Friuli, Museo Archeologico Nazionale, Biblioteca 35, fol. 202; Cividale del Fruili, Museo Archeologico Nazionale, Biblioteca 58, fol. 344r; Gorizia, Biblioteca Seminario Teologico Centrale H, c. 274; Gubbio, Archivio di Stato, Fondo S. Domenico, Corale O, fols. 109v–112r; Lucca, Biblioteca Statale

1061, fol. 19; Modena, Biblioteca Estense, α.R.I.6, fols. 193v–194v; Monza, Basilica di S. Giovanni Battista, Biblioteca Capitolare e Tesoro L 12, fol. 3v; Monza, Basilica di S. Giovanni Battista, Biblioteca Capitolare e Tesoro L 13, fol. 141; Padua, Duomo, Biblioteca Capitolare E 46, fols. 249v–253r; Padua, Biblioteca Capitolare, Curia Vescovile A.20, fol. 83v; Parma, Duomo Archivio Capitolare con Archivio della Fabbriceria F-09, fols. 136v–140r; Piacenza, Biblioteca e Archivio Capitolare 65, fol. 449; Piacenza, Biblioteca e Archivio Capitolare, D, fol. 285; Piacenza, Biblioteca e Archivio Capitolare, D, fol. 302; Rome, Bibl. Ap. Vaticana, Barb. lat. 657, fol. 419v; Rome, Bibl. Ap. Vaticana, Vat. lat. 10654, fol. 29; Todi, Biblioteca Comunale Lorenzo Leonj 73, fols. 6v–8r; Trento, Biblioteca S. Bernardino 310, fol. 48r; Udine, Duomo, Archivio Capitolare 10, fol. 398; Udine, Duomo, Archivio Capitolare 27, fol. 83.

13 For transcriptions of first and last of these see Kurt von Fischer and F. Alberto Gallo, *Italian Sacred Music*, Polyphonic Music of the Fourteenth Century 12 (Monaco: Éditions de l'Oiseau-Lyre 1976), nos. 11a and 11b.

14 On the adaptation of books of chant to the official editions of the Breviary and of the Missal, see Marco Gozzi, 'Le edizioni liturgico-musicali dopo il Concilio', in Danilo Curti and Marco Gozzi, eds., *Musica e liturgia nella riforma tridentina* (Trento: Provincia autonoma di Trento – Servizio Beni Librari e Archivistici, 1995), pp. 39–55.

15 Giacomo Baroffio, 'I libri con musica sono libri di musica?' in Giulio Cattin, Danilo Curti and Marco Gozzi, eds., *Il canto piano nell'era della stampa* (Trento: Provincia autonoma di Trento, 1999), pp. 9–12.

16 Frank D'Accone, *The Civic Muse: Music and Musicians in Siena during the Middle Ages and the Renaissance* (Chicago and London: University of Chicago Press, 1997).

17 Giulio Cattin tackles the problem in his 'Studio sulle melodie cortonesi', in Giorgio Varanini, Luigi Banfi and Anna Ceruti Burgio, eds., *Laude cortonesi dal secolo 13° al 15°* (Florence: Olschki, 1981).

18 Timothy McGee, '*Dança amorosa*: A Newly-Discovered Medieval Dance Pair', in Brian Gillingham and Paul Merkley, eds., *Beyond the Moon: Festschrift Luther Dittmer* (Ottawa: Institute of Mediaeval Music, 1990), pp. 295–306.

19 Marco Gozzi, 'La notazione del codice Add. 29987 di Londra', in Bianca Maria Antolini, Teresa M. Gialdroni and Annunzìato Pugliese, eds., '*Et facciam dolçi canti*'. *Studi in onore di*

Agostino Ziino in occasione del suo 65° compleanno (Lucca: LIM, 2004), pp. 207–61: 253.

8 The trecento

1 On fourteenth-century Italian motets, see Margaret Bent, 'The Fourteenth-Century Italian Motet', in Giulio Cattin and Patrizia Dalla Vecchia, eds., *L'ars nova italiana del Trecento VI: Atti del congresso internazionale 'L'Europa e la musica del Trecento', Certaldo, 19–21 luglio 1984* (Certaldo: Polis, 1992), pp. 85–125. For liturgical music see Marco Gozzi, 'Liturgia e musica mensurale nel Trecento italiano: i canti dell'Ordinarium', in Oliver Huck, ed., *Kontinuität und Transformation der italienischen Vokalmusik zwischen Due- und Quattrocento* (Hildesheim: Olms, 2006), pp. 53–98.

2 About the five pieces see Oliver Huck, *Die Musik des frühen Trecento* (Hildesheim: Olms, 2005), pp. 262–4; Billy Jim Layton, 'Italian Music for the Ordinary of the Mass 1300–1450' (PhD diss., Harvard University, 1960), pp. 77–115, and Kurt von Fischer, 'Il ciclo dell'Ordinarium missae del ms F-Pn568 (Pit)', in Agostino Ziino, ed., *L'ars nova italiana del Trecento V* (Palermo: Enchiridion, 1985), pp. 123–37.

3 Kurt von Fischer, 'Musica e società nel Trecento Italiano', in F. Alberto Gallo, ed., *L'Ars nova italiana del Trecento III* (Certaldo: Centro di Studi sull'Ars Nova Italiana del Trecento, 1970), pp. 11–28 at 21–2.

4 About the phenomenon of the composition on *cantus prius factus* derived from Gregorian chant and with equal values, see Marco Gozzi, '"Cantus firmus per notulas plani cantus": alcune testimonianze quattrocentesche', in Francesco Facchin, ed., *Il cantus firmus nella polifonia: Atti del convegno internazionale di studi, Arezzo, 27–29 dicembre 2002* (Arezzo: Fondazione Guido d'Arezzo, 2005), pp. 45–88; available on line at www.polifonico. org/edizioni/QUADERNI/Quad 3.htm.

9 The Iberian peninsula

1 See I. Fernández de la Cuesta, *Historia de la música española*, vol. I, *Desde los orígenes hasta el 'ars nova'* (Madrid: Alianza Editorial, 1983), pp. 15–84.

2 W. M. Lindsay, ed., *Isidori hispalensis episcopi Etymologiarum sive originum libri xx*, 2 vols. (Oxford: Clarendon Press, 1911); a new edition is in progress (*Étymologies*, 20 vols., Paris: Les Belles Lettres, 1981–).

3 C. M. Lawson, ed., *Sancti Isidori episcopi hispalensis De ecclesiasticis officiis*, Corpus

Christianorum Series Latina 113 (Turnhout: Brepols, 1989).

4 See L. Brou, 'Liturgie "mozarabe" ou liturgie "hispanique"?' *Ephemerides liturgicae* 63 (1949), pp. 66–70.

5 See S. Corbin, *Essai sur la musique religieuse portugaise au Moyen Âge (1100–1385)* (Paris: Les Belles Lettres, 1952), pp. 137–40; M. P. Ferreira, *Antologia de música em Portugal na Idade Média e no Renascimento*, 2 vols (Lisbon: CESEM / Arte das Musas, 2008), vol. I, pp. 9–22: the two surviving Portuguese fragments of Old Spanish chant are reproduced as plates 1–3.

6 Now Verona, Biblioteca Capitolare, MS 89.

7 The major sources are described by J. M. Pinell, 'Los textos de la antigua liturgia hispánica: fuentes para su estudio', in J. F. Rivera, ed., *Estudios sobre la liturgia mozárabe* (Toledo: Diputación Provincial, 1965), pp. 165–87. A list of all known chants is provided in D. M. Randel, *An Index to the Chant of the Mozarabic Rite* (Princeton University Press, 1973). All sources with musical notation are illustrated in colour and described in S. Zapke, ed., *Hispania Vetus: Musical-Liturgical Manuscripts from Visigothic Origins to the Franco-Roman Transition (9th–12th Centuries)* (Bilbao: Fundación BBVA, 2007).

8 L. Brou, 'Notes de paléographie musicale mozarabe', *Anuario musical* 7 (1952), pp. 51–77 and 10 (1955), pp. 23–44; S. Zapke, 'Notation Systems in the Iberian Peninsula: From Spanish Notations to Aquitanian Notation (9th–12th Centuries)', in Zapke, *Hispania Vetus*, pp. 189–243.

9 This *Liber ordinum* is preserved as Madrid, Real Academia de la Historia, Aemil. 56.

10 The first major study of this repertory was C. Rojo and G. Prado, *El canto mozárabe* (Barcelona: Diputación provincial, 1929). A fuller understanding has been enabled by C. W. Brockett, *Antiphons, Responsories, and Other Chants of the Mozarabic Rite* (Brooklyn: Institute of Mediaeval Music, 1968) and D. M. Randel, *The Responsorial Psalm Tones for the Mozarabic Office* (Princeton University Press, 1969).

11 For an example of the former, see S. Zapke, *Das Antiphonar von Sta. Cruz de la Serós, XII. Jh.* (Neuried: Ars Una, 1996); for the latter see I. Fernández de la Cuesta, ed., *Antiphonale silense: British Library Mss. Add. 30.850* (Madrid: Sociedad Española de Musicología, 1985). See also Zapke, *Hispania Vetus* for all other sources from the time of transition.

12 See C. J. Gutiérrez, 'The Hymnodic Tradition in Spain', in A. Haug, C. März and L. Welker, eds., *Der lateinische Hymnus im*

Mittelalter: Überlieferung, Ästhetik, Ausstrahlung, Monumenta Monodica Medii Aevi, Subsidia 4 (Kassel: Bärenreiter, 2004), pp. 215–43. An edition of this repertory is forthcoming.

13 L. Brou, 'Séquences et tropes dans la liturgie mozarabe', *Hispania sacra* 4 (1951), pp. 27–41, gives examples of tropes and sequences in Visigothic notation, but these were nevertheless sung in the context of the Roman rite.

14 M. S. Gros i Pujol, *Els tropers prosers de la Catedral de Vic: estudi i edició*, Biblioteca litúrgica Catalana 2 (Barcelona: Institut d'Estudis Catalans, 1999).

15 See E. Castro Caridad, *Tropos y troparios hispánicos* (Universidade de Santiago de Compostela, 1991); G. Iversen, 'Osanna vox laudabilia: Vocabulary and Compositional Forms in Sanctus Tropes in Iberian Liturgical Manuscripts', in Zapke, *Hispania Vetus*, pp. 141–57; A. Tello Ruiz-Pérez, 'Transferencias del canto medieval: los tropos del *ordinarium missae* en los manuscritos españoles', PhD diss., Universidad Complutense de Madrid, 2006, 2 vols. P. Peláez Bilbao is currently undertaking a complementary study of Iberian sequence repertories.

16 R. B. Donovan, *The Liturgical Drama in Medieval Spain* (Toronto: Pontifical Institute of Mediaeval Studies, 1958); see also H. Anglès, *La música a Catalunya fins al segle XIII* (Barcelona: Institut d'Estudis Catalans, 1935), pp. 267–311, and M.-C. Gómez, 'El drama litúrgico', in Gómez, ed., *Historia de la música en España e Hispanoamérica*, vol. I, *De los orígenes hasta c. 1470* (Madrid: Fondo de Cultura Económica, 2009), pp. 77–124.

17 See H. Anglès, 'Epistola farcida del martiri de Sant Esteve', *Vida Cristiana* 9 (1922), pp. 69–75.

18 See Anglès, *La música a Catalunya*, pp. 288–302 and tables 1–3; M.-C. Gómez, *El canto de la Sibila*, 2 vols. (Madrid: Alpuerto, 1996–7).

19 The manuscript remains in the cathedral archives at Santiago, without pressmark. A complete colour facsimile has been published: *Iacobus: Codex Calixtinus de la Catedral de Santiago de Compostela* (Madrid: Kaydeda, 1993). The two principal studies and editions of the polyphony are J. López-Calo, *La música medieval en Galicia* (La Coruña: Fundación Pedro Barrié de la Maza, 1982) and T. Karp, *The Polyphony of Saint Martial and Santiago de Compostela*, 2 vols. (Oxford: Clarendon Press, 1992); see also J. Williams and A. Stones, eds., *The Codex Calixtinus and the Shrine of St James* (Tübingen: Narr, 1992), and J. López-Calo and

C. Villanueva, eds., *El Códice Calixtino y la música de su tiempo* (La Coruña: Fundación Pedro Barrié de la Maza, 2001).

20 See M.-C. Gómez, 'El *ars antiqua* en Cataluña', *Revista de musicología* 2 (1979), pp. 197–255 and 3 (1980), pp. 279–84, and K. Nelson, *Medieval Liturgical Music of Zamora* (Ottawa: Institute of Mediaeval Music, 1996).

21 See L. Dittmer, ed., *Faksimile-Ausgabe der Handschrift Madrid 20486*, Veröffentlichungen mittelalterlicher Musikhandschriften 1 (New York: Institute of Mediaeval Music, 1957); the edition made by J. C. Asensio, J. Paz and V. Puego, *El códice de Madrid, Biblioteca nacional, MSS. 20486*, Patrimonio musical español 3 (Madrid: Alpuerto, 1997); and the study of the manuscript by J. Pumpe, *Die Motetten der Madrider Notre-Dame-Handschrift* (Tutzing: Schneider, 1991).

22 MS 9. The principal study of this manuscript, including a complete black-and-white facsimile and transcription, is H. Anglès, *El còdex musical de Las Huelgas: música a veus dels segles XIII–XIV*, 3 vols. (Barcelona: Institut d'Estudis Catalans, 1931). A colour facsimile edition has been published more recently (Madrid: Testimonio, 1997; companion study by N. Bell, 2003), as well as two further editions of the music: G. A. Anderson, ed., *The Las Huelgas Manuscript*, 2 vols., Corpus Mensurabilis Musicae 79 (Neuhausen: American Institute of Musicology, 1982) and J. C. Asensio, *El códice de las Huelgas*, Patrimonio musical español 8 (Madrid: Alpuerto, 2001).

23 A black-and-white facsimile and edition of the musical pages of the Llibre Vermell is given in M.-C. Gómez, *El Llibre Vermell de Montserrat: cantos y danzas s. XIV* (Sant Cugat del Vallès: Los libros de la Frontera, 1990); for a colour facsimile see F. X. Altés i Aguiló, *Llibre Vermell de Montserrat: edició facsímil parcial del manuscrit núm. 1 de la Biblioteca de l'Abadia de Montserrat* (Barcelona: Publicacions de l'Abadia de Montserrat, 1989).

24 See M.-C. Gómez, *La música en la casa real catalano-aragonesa durante los años 1336–1432* (Barcelona: Bosch, 1979); J. Ruiz, *La librería de canto de organo: creación y pervivencia del repertorio del Renacimiento en la actividad musical de la catedral de Sevilla* (Granada: Junta de Andalucía, Consejería de Cultura, 2007), and both authors' contributions to Gómez, *Historia de la música en España*.

25 R. Perales de la Cal, ed., *Cancionero de la Catedral de Segovia: edición facsimilar del Códice de la Santa Iglesia Catedral de Segovia* (Segovia: Caja de Ahorros y Monte de Piedad de Segovia, 1977).

26 The classic study of this period is R. Stevenson, *Spanish Music in the Age of Columbus* (The Hague: Nijhoff, 1960); see also K. Kreitner, *The Church Music of Fifteenth-Century Spain* (Woodbridge: Boydell, 2004).

27 Codex of Azagra, Madrid, Biblioteca Nacional, MS 10029. The texts are edited by L. Traube, *Poetae Latini aevi Carolini*, Monumenta Germaniae Historica, Poetae III (Berlin: Weidmann, 1896), pp. 122–42; for an illustration, see M.-C. Gómez, *La música medieval en España* (Kassel: Reichenberger, 2001), p. 157.

28 On this later period see especially D. Fallows, 'A Glimpse of the Lost Years: Spanish Polyphonic Song, 1450–1470', in J. Wright and S. A. Floyd, eds., *New Perspectives in Music: Essays in Honor of Eileen Southern* (Warren, MI: Harmonie Park Press, 1992), pp. 19–36.

29 New York, Pierpont Morgan Library, M979; the most recent of various editions and facsimiles is M. P. Ferreira, *O som de Martin Codax* (Lisbon: Unisys, 1986).

30 These are edited by M. P. Ferreira, *Cantus coronatus: 7 cantigas d'El-Rei D. Dinis* (Kassel: Reichenberger, 2005).

31 Facsimile, edition and commentary in H. Anglès, *La música de las cantigas de Santa María del rey Alfonso el Sabio*, 3 vols. in 4 (Barcelona: Biblioteca Central, 1943–65). The other manuscripts are El Escorial, T.j.I (facsimile: *Cantigas de Santa María: edición facsímil del códice rico T.I.1 de la Biblioteca de San Lorenzo el Real de El Escorial, siglo XIII*, 2 vols. [Madrid: Edilán, 1979]); Madrid, Biblioteca Nacional, 10069, a manuscript without illustrations from Toledo (facsimile: *Cantigas de Santa María: edición facsímil do códice de Toledo (To), Biblioteca Nacional de Madrid (ms. 10.069)* [Santiago de Compostela: Consello da Cultura Galega, 2003]); and Florence, Biblioteca Nazionale Centrale, Banco rari 20, which lacks musical notation (facsimile: *Cantigas de Santa María: edición facsímil del códice B.R.20 de la Biblioteca Nazionale di Florencia, siglo XIII*, 2 vols. [Madrid: Edilán, 1989]).

32 Claims of an Arabic origin were first outlined by J. Ribera, *La música de las cantigas: estudio sobre su origen y naturaleza* (Madrid: Tipografía de la Revista de Archivos, 1922); see also two articles by M. P. Ferreira: 'Andalusian music and the *Cantigas de Santa Maria*', in S. Parkinson, ed., *Cobras e son: Papers on the Text, Music and Manuscripts of the 'Cantigas de Santa Maria'* (Oxford: Legenda, 2000), pp. 7–19 and 'Rondeau and Virelai: The Music of Andalus

and the *Cantigas de Santa Maria*', *Plainsong and Medieval Music*, 13 (2004), pp. 127–40.

33 Many such accounts are surveyed in Ribera, *La música de las cantigas*, pp. 53–85. See also R. de Zayas, 'Musicology and the Cultural Heritage of the Spanish Moors', in C. E. Robertson, ed., *Musical Repercussions of 1492: Encounters in Text and Performance* (Washington: Smithsonian Institution Press, 1992), pp. 129–48, and Gómez, *La música medieval*, pp. 325–43. Attempts have also been made to recover medieval songs from modern oral traditions in northern Africa: see B. M. Liu and J. T. Monroe, *Ten Hispano-Arabic Strophic Songs in the Modern Tradition* (Berkeley: University of California Press, 1989).

34 These Arabic sources are catalogued in A. Shiloah, *The Theory of Music in Arabic Writings (c. 900–1900)*, 2 vols., RISM B X (Munich: Henle, 1979, 2003).

35 For a discussion of a specific example, see D. M. Randel, 'Al-Fārābī and the Role of Arabic Music Theory in the Latin Middle Ages', *Journal of the American Musicological Society* 29 (1976), pp. 173–88.

36 A picture of the Iberian dissemination of music theory treatises may be gleaned from *The Theory of Music*, RISM B III 5 (Munich: Henle, 1997), pp. 57–134. A survey of fifteenth-century Spanish music theory is provided in R. Stevenson, *Spanish Music*, pp. 50–101.

37 For a bibliography, see 'Jewish Music', *The New Grove Dictionary of Music and Musicians*, 2nd edn, esp. Bibliography, C.iii, D.v.

38 See I. J. Katz, 'The Music of Sephardic Spain: An Exploratory View', in Robertson, ed., *Musical Repercussions of 1492*, pp. 97–128; S. G. Armistead, J. H. Silverman and I. J. Katz, *Judeo-Spanish Ballads from Oral Tradition*, 3 vols. to date (Berkeley: University of California Press; Newark, DE: Juan de la Cuesta; 1986–).

10 Music east of the Rhine

1 Paul Robert Magocsi, *Historical Atlas of East Central Europe*, A History of East Central Europe 1 (Seattle and London: University of Washington Press, 1993), maps 7b, 8, 10 and 14.

2 Jean W. Sedlar, *East Central Europe in the Middle Ages, 1000–1500*, A History of East Central Europe 3 (Seattle and London: University of Washington Press, 1994); Piotr Wandycz, *The Price of Freedom: A History of East Central Europe from the Middle Ages to the Present* (London and New York: Routledge, 1992); Oscar Halecki, *Borderlands of Western Civilization: A History of East Central Europe* (New York: Ronald Press, 1952); and Jerzy Kłoczowski, *Europa słowiańska w XIV–XV wieku* (Warsaw: Państwowy Instytut Wydawniczy, 1984).

3 *A History of Music in Poland*, ed. Stefan Sutkowski, trans. John Comber, 7 vols. (Warsaw: Sutkowski Edition, 2001–4). The best synoptic coverage of medieval music in Bohemia is Jaromír Černý, 'Středověk (800–1420)', in Jaromír Černý et al., eds., *Hudba v českých dějinách od středověku do nové doby* (Prague: Editio Supraphon, 1983), pp. 11–77. Two articles by László Dobszay cover medieval music in Hungary: 'Plainchant in Medieval Hungary', *Journal of the Plainsong & Mediaeval Music Society* 13 (1990), pp. 49–78; and 'Liturgical Polyphony in Medieval Hungary', in Giulio Cattin and F. Alberto Gallo, eds., *Un millennio di polifonia liturgica tra oralità e scrittura*, Quaderni di 'Musica e storia' 3 (Bologna and Venice: Società Editrice II Mulino / Fondazione Ugo e Olga Levi, 2002), pp. 173–85. For Slovakia (northern Hungary in the Middle Ages) see also Ladislav Kačic, 'From the Middle Ages to the Renaissance', in Oskár Elschek, ed., *A History of Slovak Music From the Earliest Time to the Present*, trans. Martin Styan (Bratislava: Veda, 2003), pp. 54–79.

4 Velehrad (Staré Město) in Moravia was the site of the first metropolitan. The first bishop of Hungary was an Orthodox monk, Hierotheus, ordained by Patriarch Theophylactus (d. 956).

5 Hieronim Feicht, 'Św. Cyril i Methody w polskich księgach chorałowych i śpiewnikach', in *Studia nad muzyką polskiego średniowiecza*, Opera Musicologica Hieronymi Feicht 1 (Cracow: Polskie Wydawnictwo Muzyczne, 1975), pp. 244–9; Černý, 'Středověk', pp. 26–29, 37.

6 Jerzy Morawski, ed., *Musica Medii Aevi*, 8 vols. (Cracow: Polskie Wydawnictwo Muzyczne, 1965–91); includes 250 black-and-white plates of Polish manuscripts. Eva Veselovská, *Mittelalterliche liturgische Kodizes mit Notation in den Archivbeständen von Bratislava*, Musaeum Musicum (Bratislava: Slovenské národné múzeum – Hudobné múzeum, 2002); Hana Vlhová-Wörner, 'Středověké liturgické rukopisy z katedrály sv. Víta na Pražském hradě' (PhD diss., Prague: Univerzita Karlova, 2000).

7 Recently discovered and now available in facsimile is *The Istanbul Antiphonal c.1360* (Topkapi Sarayi Müzesi. Deissmann 42), Musicalia Danubiana 18, ed. Janka Szendrei and Mária Czigler (Budapest: Akadémiai Kiadó, 2002). This is the most complete extant book of offices for Hungarian saints. See also *Corpus Antiphonarium Officii – Ecclesiarum Centralis*

Europae. Hungarian Academy of Sciences, Institute of Musicology. www.zti.hu/earlymusic/cao-ece.html. For Bohemian chant manuscripts, see http://dig.vkol.cz (Digitální knihovna historických fondů Vědecké knihovny v Olomouci), and http://cantica.kh.cz/grad/muzeum/ (Kutnohorské hudební rukopisy).

8 For Polish manuscripts, see Tadeusz Maciejewski, 'Elementy systemu menzuralnego w monodii chorałowej XIII–XVI wieku', in Elżbieta Witkowska-Zaremba, ed., *Notae musicae artis. Notacja muzyczna w źródłach polskich XI–XVI wieku,* (Cracow: Musica Iagellonica, 1999), pp. 283–347. For Bohemian manuscripts, see Charles E. Brewer, 'The Mensural Significance of Bohemian Chant Notation and Its Origins', in László Dobszay, Agnes Papp and Ferenc Sebő, eds., *Cantus planus: IMS Study Group, Papers Read at the Fourth Meeting, Pécs, Hungary, 3–8 September 1990* (Budapest: Hungarian Academy of Science, Institute of Musicology, 1992), pp. 55–68.

9 Richard Taruskin, *The Oxford History of Western Music,* vol. I, *The Earliest Notations to the Sixteenth Century* (Oxford University Press, 2005), p. 62.

10 Jerzy Morawski, 'Recherches sur les variantes régionales dans le chant grégorien', *Studia Musicologica Academiae Scientiarum Hungaricae* 30 (1988), pp. 412–13.

11 Barbara Haggh, *Two Offices for St Elizabeth of Hungary: Gaudeat Hungaria and Letare Germania* (Ottawa: Institute of Mediaeval Music, 1995); Jerzy Morawski, ed., *Historia rymowana o św. Wojciechu* (Cracow: Polskie Wydawnictwo Muzyczne, 1979).

12 Jerzy Morawski, *The Middle Ages, Part 1: Up to 1320,* trans. John Comber, Historia muzyki polskiej, I/1 (Warsaw: Edition Sutkowski, 2003), p. 564. Idem, *Historia rymowana o św. Jadwidze* (Cracow: Polskie Wydawnictwo Muzyczne, 1977).

13 Zoltán Falvy, 'Die Weisen des König Stephan-Reimoffiziums', *Studia Musicologica Academiae Scientiarum Hungaricae* 6 (1964), pp. 207–69. Jerzy Pikulik, 'Polskie oficja rymowane o św. Wojciechu / Les offices polonais de saint Adalbert', in Pikulik, ed., *Stan badań nad muzyką religijną w kulturze polskiej* (Warsaw: Akademia Teologii Katolickiej, 1973), pp. 279–341.

14 Andrew Hughes, 'Chants in the Offices of Thomas of Canterbury and Stanislaus of Poland', *Musica Antiqua Europae Orientalis* 6 (1982), pp. 267–77.

15 On the offices of Ludmila and Procopius, see Dominique Patier, 'Les éléments locaux dans les offices rythmiques composés en Bohême aux XIIIème et XIVème siècles', *Studia Musicologica Academiae Scientiarum Hungaricae* 26, nos. 1–4 (1985), pp. 109–15.

16 Hana Vlhová-Wörner, '*Fama crescit eundo.* Der Fall: Domazlaus predicator, der älteste bekannte böhmische Sequenzendichter', *Hudební věda* 39, no. 4 (2002), pp. 311–30.

17 Zsuzsa Czagány, 'Bemerkungen zum Prager Offizium', *Miscellanea Musicologica* 37 (2003), p. 105.

18 László Dobszay, 'The System of the Hungarian Plainsong Sources', *Studia Musicologica Academiae Scientiarum Hungaricae* 27 (1985), pp. 44ff. Janka Szendrei, *Medieval Notated Codex Fragments from Hungary,* trans. Erzsébet Mészáros (Budapest: Hungarian Academy of Sciences, 2000).

19 Janka Szendrei, 'Gibt es ein ungarisches Gregorianum? Über das Problem des Nationalcharakters der Gregorianik im Licht der ungarischen Choralquellen', in Stefan Fricke et al. eds., *Zwischen Volks- und Kunstmusik: Aspekte der ungarischen Musik* (Saarbrücken: Pfau-Verlag, 1999), pp. 28–42.

20 Henryk Kowalewicz and Jerzy Morawski, eds., 'Hymny polskie', *Musica Medii Aevi* 8 (1991), pp. 10–138; Henryk Kowalewicz, *Cantica Medii Aevi Polono-Latina,* vol. I, *Sequentiae,* Biblioteca Latina Medii et Recentioris Aevi 14 (Warsaw: Państwowe Wydawnictwo Naukowe, 1964); Jerzy Pikulik, 'Sekwencje polskie', *Musica Medii Aevi* 4 (1973), pp. 7–126.

21 Pikulik, 'Sekwencje polskie', pp. 63–4.

22 Antoni Reginek, 'Repertuar hymnów diecezji krakowskiej', *Musica Medii Aevi* 8 (1991), p. 321. Paul Crossley, '"*Ara Patriae*" Saint Stanislaus, the Jagiellonians and the Coronation Ordinal for Cracow Cathedral', in Jiří Fajt and Markus Hörsch, eds., *Kunstlerische Wechselwirkungen in Mitteleuropa,* Studia Jagiellonica Lipsiensia 1 (Ostfildern: Jan Thorbecke Verlag, 2006), pp. 103–21.

23 Arnold Geering, *Die Organa und mehrstimmigen Conductus in den Handschriften des deutschen Sprachgebietes vom 13. bis 16. Jahrhundert,* Publikationen der Schweizerischen Musikforschenden Gesellschaft, II/1 (Bern: Verlag Paul Haupt, 1952); Theodor Göllner, *Die mehrstimmigen liturgischen Lesungen,* Münchner Veröffentlichungen zur Musikgeschichte 15 (Tutzing: Hans Schneider Verlag, 1969). More recent studies include Paweł Gancarczyk, 'Cantus *planus multiplex* in Polen: von einer

mündlichen Tradition zur Notenschrift', in László Dobszay, ed., *The Past in the Present: Papers Read at the IMS Intercongressional Symposium and the 10th Meeting of the Cantus Planus, Budapest and Visegrád, 2000* (Budapest: Liszt Ferenc Academy of Music, 2003), pp. 483–95; and Giulio Cattin and F. Alberto Gallo, eds., *Un millennio di polifonia liturgica tra oralità e scrittura* (Bologna: Il Mulino, 2002).

24 Jaromír Černý, 'Das retrospektive Organum oder Neo-organum', *Hudební věda* 38, nos. 1–2 (2001), pp. 3–31. Paweł Gancarczyk, 'Polifonia w Polsce do około 1500 roku: źródła i problemy ich interpretacji', *Muzyka* 51, nos. 1–2 (2006), pp. 85–103.

25 The Philip de Vitry fragment, *PL-WRu* Akc.1955/195, is described in Fritz Feldmann, *Musik und Musikpflege in mittelalterlichen Schlesien*, Darstellungen und Quellen zur schlesischen Geschichte 37 (Breslau: Trewendt & Granier, 1938), pp. 126–7. It was lost during the Second World War and rediscovered in 1970 by Mirosław Perz. For a colour plate, see Elżbieta Zwolińska, 'Musica mensuralis w polskich źródłach muzycznych do 1600 roku', in Elżbieta Witkowska-Zaremba, ed., *Notae musicae artis. Notacja muzyczna w źródłach polskich XI–XVI wieku* (Cracow: Musica Iagellonica, 1999), pp. 428.

26 Guillaume de Machaut, *La Prise d'Alexandre – ou Chronique de Roi Pierre I de Lusignan*, ed. M. L. de Mas Latrie (Geneva, 1877), lines 1268–88.

27 Charles E. Brewer, 'The Introduction of the "ars nova" into East Central Europe: A Study of the Late Medieval Polish Sources' (PhD diss., City University of New York, 1984), pp. 163–232.

28 Robert Curry, 'Fragments of *Ars antiqua* Music at Stary Sącz and the Evolution of the Clarist Order in Central Europe in the Thirteenth Century' (PhD diss., Monash University, Melbourne, 2003).

29 Robert Curry, 'Lost and Found in Stary Sącz', in Tomasz Jeż, ed., *Complexus effectuum musicologiae. Studia Miroslao Perz septuagenario dedicata*, Studia et Dissertationes Instituti Musicologiae Universitatis Varsoviensis, B/13 (Cracow: Rabid, 2003), pp. 31–42.

30 Katarzyna Morawska, *The Middle Ages, Part 2: 1320–1500*, trans. John Comber, Historia muzyki polskiej, I/2 (Warsaw: Sutkowski Edition, 2001), pp. 117–21.

31 Charles E. Brewer, ed., *Collectio cantilenarum saeculi XV: rękopis Biblioteki Jagiellońskiej Kj 2464*, music score and facsimiles, Latin poetry revised by Anna Sobańska, Źródła do historii muzyki polskiej 30 (Cracow: Polskie Wydawnictwo Muzyczne, 1990).

32 Jaromír Černý, 'Cantio', in Ludwig Finscher, ed., *Die Musik in Geschichte und Gegenwart: allgemeine Enzyklopädie der Musik* (Kassel and Stuttgart: Bärenreiter & Metzler, 1994), pp. 392–3.

33 *CZ-VB* 42 (Hohenfurt Cantionale)

34 Reinhard Strohm, *The Rise of European Music 1380–1500* (Cambridge University Press, 1993), pp. 331–2.

35 Paweł Gancarczyk, 'Petrus Wilhelm de Grudencz (b. 1392) – A Central European Composer', *De musica disserenda* 2, no. 1 (2006), pp. 103–12. Jaromír Černý, ed., *Petrus Wilhelmi de Grudencz Magister Cracoviensis Opera Musica*, music score with introduction and critical commentary, foreword by Mirosław Perz (Cracow: Polskie Wydawnictwo Muzyczne, 1993).

36 Martin Staehelin, 'Uwagi o wzajemnych związkach biografii, twórczości i dokumentacji dzieł Piotra Wilhelmiego z Grudziądza', *Muzyka* 49, no. 2 (2004), pp. 9–18. The composer identified his compositions using an acrostic of his name: for example, in his cantio: ***P**residiorum **e**rogatrix **t**utris **r**ei **v**irens **s**atrix.*

37 Martin Horyna, 'Utwory Piotra Wilhelmiego z Grudziądza w tradycji polifonii późnośredniowiecznej w Europie Środkowej, a zwłaszcza w Czechach XV i XVI wieku', *Muzyka* 49 (2004), pp. 21–54. Horyna draws on unpublished sections of the treatise by Paulus Paulirini (Pavel Žídek), *Liber viginti artium* (Plzeň, ca1460 [*PL-Kj* 257, fols.153–62]), where Paulus recommends what type and how many pieces befit specific liturgical occasions.

38 Gustave Reese, *Music in the Renaissance*, rev. edn (New York: W. W. Norton, 1959), p. 732.

39 Jistebnický Kancionál, *CZ-Pnm* II C 7. A new edition of the gradual has recently appeared, *Jistebnický kancionál. 1. svazek – Graduale*, edited by Jaroslav Kolár, Anežka Vidmanová and Hana Vlhová-Wörner, Monumenta Liturgica Bohemica 2 (Brno: Luboš Marek, 2005).

40 The royal chapel did not follow the Esztergom rite, the most characteristic feature of Catholic liturgy in Hungary.

41 Corvinus's library, second only to the Vatican's, numbered some 3,000 volumes. Csaba Csapodi, et al., comps., *Biblioteca Corviniana: The Library of King Matthias Corvinus of Hungary*, trans. Zsuzsanna Horn (New York: Praeger, 1969).

42 Dobszay, 'Liturgical Polyphony', pp. 173–85. Dobszay concludes that major churches, unlike in the West, seem to have

played little role in the cultivation of liturgical polyphony above the level of *cantus planus binatim*. See also Charles E. Brewer, 'The Historical Context of Polyphony in Medieval Hungary: An Examination of Four Fragmentary Sources', *Studia Musicologica Academiae Scientiarum Hungariae* 32 (1990), pp. 5–21.

43 Leeman L. Perkins and Howard Garey, eds., *The Mellon Chansonnier*: vol. I, *The Edition*; vol. II, *Commentary* (New Haven and London: Yale University Press, 1979), vol. I, p. 30.

44 Košice Fragments (Fragmenty koszyckie, Kassa-Fragmente), ca1465, SK-*Brm* 33, SK-*Bru* 318.

45 Glogauer Liederbuch (Śpiewnik głogowski), 1475–85, PL-*Kj* 40098.

46 By 1469 Hungary had acquired Moravia, Silesia, Upper and Lower Lusatia and Habsburg Lower Austria including Vienna.

47 Paweł Gancarczyk, *Musica scripto. Kodeksy menzuralne II połowy XV wieku na wschodzie Europy Łacińskiej* (Warsaw: Instytut Sztuki PAN, 2001), pp. 71–110.

48 The archbishopric sided with the Catholic king of Hungary, Matthias Corvinus, against the Utraquist king of Bohemia, George of Poděbrady. Corvinus was symbolically crowned king of Bohemia in Olomouc in 1469; he had to wait another five years before he acceded in fact to the Bohemian throne.

49 Codex Speciálník, CZ-*HK* II A 7.

50 Lenka Mráčková, 'Kodex Speciálník. Eine kleine Folio-Handschrift böhmischer Provenenz', *Hudební věda* 39, nos. 2–3 (2002), pp. 163–84.

51 In large measure the same holds true for the important Lviv Fragments (Fragmenty lwowskie), 1485–90, PL-*Pu* 7022. Lwów was the seat of Poland's second metropolitan. Primate Gregory of Sanok (1451–77) maintained contacts with singers at the Florentine court of Pope Eugenius IV.

52 Given Mikotaj Radomski's up-to-date musical style, it seems likely that he is the musician Nicolai Geraldi de Radom whose name appears in documents from the Roman *curia* of Pope Boniface IX (r. 1389–1404). His music is found in two manuscripts both of unknown provenance: PL-*Wn* 8054 and PL-*Wn* 378.

53 Strohm, *Rise of European Music*, p. 262; Katarzyna Grochowska, 'Motet as Propaganda: The Historigraphi aciem's Embellishment of the Jagellonian Dynasty', in *Early Music – Context and Ideas: International Conference in Musicology, Kraków, 18–21 September 2003* (Cracow: Institute of Musicology, Jagellonian University, 2003), pp. 359–70.

11 Music and liturgy

1 J. McKinnon, ed., *Music in Early Christian Literature* (Cambridge University Press, 1987), no. 25, p. 20.

2 E. G. C. F. Atchley, ed. and trans., *Ordo Romanus primus* (London: Moring, 1905), pp. 127–9. For the Latin texts of the *Ordines romani* as a whole, see M. Andrieu, *Les Ordines romani du haut moyen âge*, 5 vols. (Louvain: Spicilegium Sacrum Lovaniense, 1931–61); an introduction to this resource is provided in C. Vogel, *Medieval Liturgy: An Introduction to the Sources*, trans. W. Storey and N. Rasmussen, assisted by J. Brooks-Leonard (Washington, DC: Pastoral Press, 1986), pp. 135–224.

3 On the problems of reading early documents concerning Christian liturgy, see P. Bradshaw, *The Search for the Origins of Christian Worship: Sources and Methods for the Study of Early Liturgy* (London: SPCK, 2002; rev. edn.); for a summary introduction to the era that pays due attention to these problems, see P. Bradshaw, *Early Christian Worship: A Basic Introduction to Ideas and Practice* (London: SPCK, 1996).

4 Given the concentration on select sources in this chapter, attention should be drawn at this point to studies providing a more comprehensive overview. The most wide-ranging single-volume history of Christian worship is now G. Wainwright and K. B. Westerfield Tucker, eds., *The Oxford History of Christian Worship* (hereafter, *OHCW*) (Oxford University Press, 2006), replacing the still useful C. Jones, E. Yarnold, G. Wainwright and P. Bradshaw, eds., *The Study of the Liturgy* (London: SPCK and New York: Oxford University Press, 1992; rev. edn). The most informative single-volume dictionary remains F. L. Cross and E. A. Livingstone, eds., *The Oxford Dictionary of the Christian Church*, rev. edn (Oxford University Press, 1983). As for liturgy in particular, T. Klauser, *A Short History of the Western Liturgy: An Account and Some Reflections*, trans. J. Halliburton (London: Oxford University Press, 1969), is still usable, but needs to be read in the light of more recent specialist studies. The best introduction to medieval liturgical sources is Vogel, *Medieval Liturgy*; a less dense introduction to this area is provided by E. Palazzo, *A History of Liturgical Books from the Beginning to the Thirteenth Century*, trans. M. Beaumont (Collegeville: Liturgical Press, 1998). An eminently practical introduction to medieval liturgy for those with a special interest in music is J. Harper, *The Forms and Orders of Western Liturgy from the Tenth to the Eighteenth Century: A Historical Introduction*

and Guide for Students and Musicians (Oxford University Press, 1991).

5 The column summarizing the account provided by Justin Martyr also draws on the earlier description in his *First Apology* (ch. 65), hence the inclusion of a kiss of greeting or peace; for the earlier account, see T. B. Falls, trans., *Saint Justin Martyr* (Washington DC: Catholic University of America Press, 1948), p. 105. The prayer by the celebrant over the offerings after their presentation is not mentioned in *Ordo Romanus* I, but it has been included since it is found in the earliest sacramentaries.

6 Here, I follow J. McKinnon, *The Advent Project: The Later Seventh-Century Creation of the Roman Mass Proper* (Berkeley and Los Angeles: University of California Press, 2000), pp. 35–48.

7 For further details, see R. Taft, 'The Structural Analysis of Liturgical Units: An Essay in Methodology', *Worship* 52 (1978), pp. 314–29.

8 For further detail than can be presented here concerning the formalization of Christian worship focusing on the fourth through to the seventh centuries, see most recently J. Baldovin, 'The Empire Baptized', *OHCW*, pp. 77–130.

9 On the new basilican style of architecture in Rome and related developments in liturgy, see J. Baldovin, *The Urban Character of Christian Worship: The Origins, Development, and Meaning of Stational Liturgy* (Rome: Pontifical Oriental Institute, 1987), pp. 106–18 and 147–66.

10 On the later-fourth-century psalmodic movement, see J. McKinnon, 'Desert Monasticism and the Later Fourth-Century Psalmodic Movement', *Music and Letters* 75 (1994), pp. 505–21, and J. Dyer, 'The Desert, the City and Psalmody in the Late Fourth Century', in S. Gallagher, J. Haar, J. Nádas and T. Striplin, eds., *Western Plainchant in the First Millennium: Studies in the Medieval Liturgy and Its Music* (Aldershot: Ashgate, 2003), pp. 11–43.

11 R. Taft, *The Liturgy of the Hours in East and West: The Origins of the Divine Office and Its Meaning for Today* (Collegeville: Liturgical Press, 1993; rev. edn), p. 139.

12 See J. McKinnon, 'Lector Chant versus Schola Chant: A Question of Historical Plausibility', in J. Szendrei and D. Hiley, eds., *Laborare fratres in unum: Festschrift Lázló Dobszay zum 60. Geburtstag* (Hildesheim: Weidmann, 1995); pp. 201–11.

13 On the dating of the Roman *schola cantorum*, see J. Dyer, 'The Schola Cantorum and Its Roman Milieu in the Early Middle Ages', in P. Cahn and A.-K. Heimer, eds., *De musica et cantu: Studien zur Geschichte der Kirchenmusik und der Oper. Helmut Hucke zum 60. Geburtstag* (Hildesheim: Olms, 1993), pp. 19–40 (at pp. 38–9); for the development of a cycle of mass propers in the seventh century, see McKinnon, *The Advent Project*, pp. 101–91.

14 To appreciate this association on a broader canvas, recourse is needed to the classic study of the mass, J. Jungmann, *The Mass of the Roman Rite*, trans. F. A. Brunner, 2 vols. (New York: Benzinger Brothers, 1951–5); for a briefer overview, see J. D. Crichton, *A Short History of the Mass* (London: Incorporated Catholic Truth Society, 1983).

15 Paul the Deacon, *Deeds of the Bishops of Metz*, ed. G. H. Pertz, Monumenta Germaniae Historica, Scriptores II (Hanover: Hahn, 1829), p. 268.

16 On the achievements of Bishop Chrodegang, and his successor Angilram with respect to the introduction of Roman practices, see, most recently, M. A. Claussen, *The Reform of the Frankish Church: Chrodegang of Metz and the 'Regula canonicorum' in the Eighth Century* (Cambridge University Press, 2004), esp. Chapter 6 ('Hagiopolis').

17 For a facsimile of this manuscript, one of the most highly decorated sacramentaries of the Middle Ages, see F. Mütherich, ed., *Drogo-Sakramentar: manuscrit latin 9428, Bibliothèque nationale, Paris*, 2 vols. (Graz: Akademische Druck- u. Verlagsanstalt, 1974).

18 Information about the early development of the annual liturgical cycle is taken from the now standard work on the subject: T. Talley, *The Origins of the Liturgical Year* (Collegeville: Liturgical Press, 1991; 2nd edn).

19 On the Metz stational list, see, with further references, Claussen, *The Reform of the Frankish Church*, pp. 276–89; for stational liturgy at Rome, see Baldovin, *The Urban Character of Christian Worship*, pp. 106–66; on the adaptation of Roman stational liturgy to Frankish cloisters in general, see A. A. Häussling, *Mönchskonvent und Eucharistiefeier* (Münster: Aschendorff, 1973).

20 For the contents of the Hadrianum and its supplement, see J. Deshusses, *Le sacramentaire grégorien: Ses principales formes d'après les plus anciens manuscrits*, 2 vols. (Freiburg: Éditions Universitaires Fribourg Suisse, vol. I, 1971 and 1979 [2nd edn]; vol. II, 1979).

21 For an overview of the history of the office concentrating on its early history, see Taft, *The Liturgy of the Hours in East and West*; on the current state of research on the music of the medieval office in particular, see most recently M. E. Fassler and R. A. Baltzer, eds., *The Divine*

Office in the Latin Middle Ages (Oxford University Press, 2000).

22 This fundamental distinction between 'cathedral' and 'monastic' practice was first noted by Anton Baumstark; see A. Baumstark, *Comparative Liturgy*, rev. B. Botte, trans. F. L. Cross, (London: A. R. Mowbray, 1958), pp. 111–20.

23 The structure of the offices can be abstracted from several chapters in Amalarius's *Liber officialis* and *Liber de ordine antiphonarii:* see J.-M. Hanssens, ed., *Amalarii episcopi opera liturgica omnia*, 3 vols. (Rome: Bibliotheca Apostolica Vaticana, 1948–50), vol. II, pp. 403–65, and vol. III, pp. 13–17. For discussion and summary see P. Salmon, *L'office divin au moyen âge: histoire de la formation du bréviaire du IXe au XVIe siècle* (Paris: Éditions du Cerf, 1967), pp. 33–43; this provides additional information from *Ordo Romanus XII.*

24 Amalarius, Prologue to the *Liber de ordine antiphonarii:* see Hanssens, ed., *Amalarii episcopi opera*, vol. I, pp. 361–2.

25 With reference in particular to saints' offices in the Middle Ages, see A. Hughes, 'Late Medieval Plainchant for the Divine Office', in R. Strohm and B. J. Blackburn, eds. *Music as Concept and Practice in the Late Middle Ages* (Oxford University Press, 2001), pp. 31–9; on festal offices, see most recently W. Arlt, 'The Office for the Feast of the Circumcision from Le Puy', in Fassler and Baltzer, eds., *The Divine Office*, pp. 324–41.

26 For an introduction to tropes, see A. Haug, 'Tropus', in *Musik in Geschichte und Gegenwart* (henceforth *MGG*), vol. IX, cols. 897–921; for a complementary introduction to sequences, see L. Kruckenberg, 'Sequenz', *MGG*, vol. VIII, cols. 1254–86.

27 On the significance of trope texts, see G. Iversen, '"Pax et sapientia": A Thematic Study on Tropes from Different Traditions', in R. Jacobsson, ed., *Pax et Sapientia: Studies in Text and Music of Liturgical Sequences in Memory of Gordon Anderson* (Stockholm: Almquist & Wiksell International, 1986), pp. 23–58. For medieval commentaries on sequence texts, see E. Kihlman, *Expositiones sequentiarum: Medieval Sequence Commentaries and Prologues. Editions with Introductions* (Stockholm: Almquist & Wiksell International, 2006).

28 D. Hiley, 'Cluny, Sequences and Tropes', in C. Leonardi and E. Menestò eds., *La tradizione dei tropi liturgici* (Spoleto: Centro Italiano di Studi sull' Alto Medioevo, 1990), pp. 125–38.

29 On the role of Gorze in relation to the dissemination of tropes, see L. Kruckenberg-Goldstein, 'The Lotharingian

Axis and Monastic Reforms: Towards the Recovery of an Early Messine Trope Tradition', *Cantus Planus – Study Group of the International Musicological Society: Papers Read at the Twelfth Meeting, Lillafüred, Hungary. 23–28 August 2004.* Edited by L. Dobszay et al. (Budapest: Hungarian Academy of Sciences, 2006), pp. 723–52.

30 C. Maître, *La réforme cistercienne du plain-chant. Étude d'un traité théorique* (Brecht: Commentarii Cistercienses, 1995), pp. 42–52.

31 On private masses, see Vogel, *Medieval Liturgy*, pp. 156–9.

32 See, in general, C. W. Bynum, *Jesus as Mother: Studies in the Spirituality of the High Middle Ages* (Berkeley: University of California Press, 1982).

33 *Musica enchiriadis*; see R. Erickson, *Musica enchiriadis and Scolica enchiriadis*, trans. and ed. C. V. Palisca, (New Haven: Yale University Press, 1995).

34 C. Wright, *Music and Ceremony at Notre Dame of Paris, 500–1550* (Cambridge University Press, 1989), p. 267.

35 For full details, see S. J. P. van Dijk and J. H. Walker, *The Origins of the Modern Roman Liturgy: The Liturgy of the Papal Court and the Franciscan Order in the Thirteenth Century* (London: Darton, Longman & Todd and Westminster, MD: Newman Press, 1960); on the music of the Franciscan order, see H. Hüschen (rev. H. Schmidt), 'Franziskaner', in *MGG*, vol. III, cols. 819–43.

36 See S. J. P van Dijk (completed by J. H. Walker), *The Ordinal of the Papal Court from Innocent III to Boniface VIII, and Related Documents* (Fribourg University Press, 1975).

37 William Durandus, *Rationale divinorum officiorum* (ca1292–6) as quoted and translated in T. Thibodeau, 'Western Christendom', *OHCW*, p. 230.

38 For a brief and accessible introduction to the sources and modern editions of Salisbury Use, see Harper, *Forms and Orders*, pp. 202–16.

39 The generalized description of Salisbury Use is based on the summary provided in Harper, *Forms and Orders*, pp. 122–4, with additional material from W. H. Frere, ed., *The Use of Sarum I Consuetudinary and Customary* (Cambridge University Press, 1898), pp. 52–68; the summary of Sunday processions is provided in T. W. Bailey, *The Processions of Sarum and the Western Church* (Toronto: Pontifical Institute of Mediaeval Studies, 1971), pp. 13–16. The Use of the Papal Chapel is reconstructed using the Franciscan order and ceremonial as edited by Haymo of Faversham ca1250: for full details, see S. J. P. van Dijk, *Sources of the Roman Liturgy*, 2

vols. (Leiden: E. J. Brill, 1963), vol. I, pp. 50–67, 95–109, vol. II, pp. 3–14 and 352–5. Items in brackets are only alluded to in Haymo's texts, thus 'the epistle, gradual and others' are to be declaimed before the gospel (vol. II, p. 8). Clear directions for the performance of sung items are not given in Haymo's instructions, but since a choir is repeatedly mentioned it would seem safe to assume that all items customarily sung were performed in this way.

40 Bede, *A History of the English Church and People*, I. 27, trans. L. Sherley-Price, rev. R. E. Latham (London: Penguin, 1968), p. 73.

41 For an introduction to Islamic and Jewish music in the Middle Ages, see A. Shiloah, 'Muslim and Jewish Musical Traditions of the Middle Ages', in R. Strohm and B. J. Blackburn *Music as Concept and Practice in the Late Middle Ages* (Oxford University Press, 2001). pp. 1–30.

42 For a recent revisionist account of early medieval liturgy with reference to music, see Y. Hen, *The Royal Patronage of Liturgy in Frankish Gaul to the Death of Charles the Bald (877)* (London: Henry Bradshaw Society, 2001).

43 On the word 'liturgy', see P.-M. Gy, 'Rites et cérémonies, liturgie, culte: Les noms de la liturgie dans l'Occident moderne', in P.-M. Gy, *La liturgie dans l'histoire* (Paris: Éditions Saint Paul and Éditions du Cerf, 1990), pp. 177–84.

44 McKinnon, ed., *Music in Early Christian Literature*, no. 352, p. 155.

12 Vernacular poetry and music

1 For a useful, concise summary, see Elizabeth Aubrey, *The Music of the Troubadours* (Bloomington: Indiana University Press, 1996), pp. 240–54, referred to henceforth in the text as Aubrey.

2 For discussion and facsimile reproductions of this song, see, respectively, Margaret L. Switten, *Music and Poetry in the Middle Ages: A Guide to Research on French and Occitan Song, 1100–1400* (New York and London: Garland, 1995), pp. 4–5, and John Haines, *Eight Centuries of Troubadours and Trouvères: The Changing Identity of Medieval Music* (Cambridge University Press, 2004), p. 16.

3 Aubrey, *Music of the Troubadours*, p. 26; William Burgwinkle, 'The Chansonniers as Books', in Simon Gaunt and Sarah Kay, eds., *The Troubadours: An Introduction* (Cambridge University Press, 1999), pp. 246–62 (p. 246).

4 See Switten, *Music and Poetry*; Aubrey, *Music of the Troubadours*; Ardis Butterfield, *Poetry and Music in Medieval France: From Jean Renart to Guillaume de Machaut* (Cambridge University Press, 2002); Haines, *Eight Centuries*.

5 Aubrey gives 315 'discrete musical settings' for 246 poems (*Music of the Troubadours*, p. xvi; Haines gives 322 'different melodic readings' for 253 poems (*Eight Centuries*, pp. 20 and 41, n. 32).

6 Anglica Rieger, *Trobairitz. Der Beitrag der Frau in der altokzitanischen höfischen Lyrik: Edition des Gesamtkorpus* (Tübingen: Niemeyer, 1991), pp. 585–626.

7 Aubrey, *Music of the Troubadours*, pp. 15–16.

8 See, for instance, the vidas of Giraut de Borneill, Gaucelm Faidit and Cadenet (Margarita Egan, *The Vidas of the Troubadours* [New York and London: Garland, 1984], nos. 41, 37 and 22).

9 Ardis Butterfield, 'Le tradizioni della canzone cortese medievale', in Jean-Jacques Nattiez, gen. ed., *Enciclopedia della musica (The Einaudi Encyclopedia of Music)*, 4 vols, vol. IV, *Storia della musica europea* (Turin: Einaudi, 2004), pp. 130–51.

10 See Gaston Paris's two articles, 'Études sur les romans de la Table Ronde: *Lancelot du Lac*, II: *Le conte de la charrette*', *Romania* 10 (1881), pp. 465–96 and 'Études sur les romans de la Table Ronde: *Lancelot du Lac*', *Romania* 12 (1883), pp. 459–534.

11 Switten, *Music and Poetry*, p. xi.

12 The term *vers* used before this date may have referred to Aquitanian versus.

13 Christopher Page, *The Owl and the Nightingale: Musical Life and Ideas in France 1100–1300* (London: Dent, 1989), Chapter 5; Walter Salmen, 'Dances and Dance Music, c.1300–1530', in Reinhard Strohm and Bonnie J. Blackburn, eds., *Music as Concept and Practice in the Late Middle Ages*, vol. III, part I of *The New Oxford History of Music* (Oxford University Press, 2001), pp. 162–90.

14 Aubrey, *Music of the Troubadours*, pp. 136–7.

15 Text and translation taken from L. T. Topsfield, *Troubadours and Love* (Cambridge University Press, 1975), pp. 128–9; Topsfield is using the edition by C. Appel, *Bernart von Ventadorn: seine Lieder mit Einleitung und Glossar* (Halle: Niemeyer, 1915), pp. 1–24. It differs from the text in Example 12.1, which is taken by van der Werf and Bond from Paris, Bibliothèque nationale de France, fonds français 1591.

16 See, for instance, the arguments of Amelia E. Van Vleck, *Memory and Re-Creation in Troubadour Lyric* (Berkeley: University of California Press, 1991).

17 This order is printed by Aubrey, *Music of the Troubadours*, pp. 90–92, with music from MS G (Milan, Biblioteca Ambrosiana, S.P.4).

18 Simon Gaunt, 'Orality and Writing: The Text of the Troubadour Poem', in Simon Gaunt and Sarah Kay, eds., *The Troubadours: An Introduction* (Cambridge University Press, 1999), pp. 228–45 (at 236).

19 This is argued by Aubrey, *Music of the Troubadours*, p. 92.

20 The latter two terms are the modern editor's (F. Lecoy, ed., *Le Roman de la Rose ou de Guillaume de Dole*, CFMA 91 (Paris: Champion, 1962).

21 See Butterfield, *Poetry and Music*, Appendix, pp. 303–13, where 231 manuscripts from Renart's *Rose* to the early fourteenth century are listed.

22 The canso as a style moved across Europe as the *Minnelied* in German, the chanson in Anglo-Norman, the cantio in Latin, the canzone in Italian and, without surviving music, the *cantigas de amigo* in Spain. It also prompted religious rewriting in the *chanson pieuse* (of which the pioneer was Gautier de Coinci [1177/8–1236]), certain monophonic conductus, the Italian *laude spirituali*, and the Spanish *Cantigas de Santa Maria* (which do survive with music) (John Stevens, 'Medieval Song', in Richard Crocker and David Hiley, eds., *The Early Middle Ages to 1300*, *The New Oxford History of Music*, vol. II, 2nd edn (Oxford University Press, 1990), pp. 357–451).

23 On the refrain, see Nico H. J. van den Boogaard, ed., *Rondeaux et refrains du XIIe siècle au début du XIVe* (Paris: Éditions Klincksieck, 1969), hereafter vdB; E. Doss-Quinby, *Les refrains chez les trouvères du XIIe siècle au début du XIVe* (New York: Peter Lang, 1984); Butterfield, *Poetry and Music*, pp. 75–102.

24 For a convenient edition, see Samuel N. Rosenberg and Hans Tischler, eds., with Marie-Geneviève Grossel, *Chansons des trouvères: Chanter m'estuet* (Paris: Le Livre de Poche, 1995), no. 97, pp. 388–92.

25 Refrain no. 17 in the *Tournoi*. See Table 1.

26 Hans Tischler, ed., *The Montpellier Codex*, 4 vols. (vol. IV ed. and trans. Susan Stakel and Joel C. Relihan), Recent Researches in the Music of the Middle Ages and Early Renaissance 2–8 (Madison, WI: A. R. Editions, 1978–85), hereafter *Mo*.

27 *F-Pn* fonds fr. 847, R1700 (R = G. Raynauds *Bibliographie des altfranzösischen Liedes, neu bearbeitet und ergänzt von Hans Spanke*, I, ed. Hans Spanke [Leiden, 1955; repr. with index, 1980]).

28 Edward H. Roesner, ed., *Le Roman de Fauvel in the Edition of Mesire Chaillou de Pesstain: A Reproduction in Facsimile of the Complete Manuscript, Paris, Bibliothèque nationale, fonds français 146* (New York: Broude Brothers, 1990).

29 Mary Atchison, ed., *The Chansonnier of Oxford Bodleian MS Douce 308: Essays and Complete Edition of Texts* (Aldershot: Ashgate, 2005); Eglal Doss-Quinby and Samuel N. Rosenberg, eds., with Elizabeth Aubrey, *The Old French Ballette: Oxford Bodleian Library, MS Douce 308* (Geneva: Droz, 2006). See Butterfield, *Poetry and Music*, Chapter 16; M. Everist, 'Motets, French Tenors, and the Polyphonic Chanson ca1300', *Journal of Musicology* 24 (2007), pp. 365–406 and ' "Souspirant en terre estrainge": The Polyphonic Rondeau from Adam de la Halle to Guillaume de Machaut', *Early Music History* 26 (2007), pp. 1–42.

30 Butterfield, *Poetry and Music*, pp. 57–63, 87–102.

31 *Par ci va la mignotise / Par ci ou je vois!* ('Along here goes graciousness, along here where I go') (vdB, refr.1473).

32 Jacques Boogaart, 'Encompassing Past and Present: Quotations and Their Function in Machaut's Motets, *Early Music History* 20 (2001), pp. 1–86. A project entitled 'Citation and Allusion in Fourteenth-Century French Lyric and Song' led by Yolanda Plumley is currently under way at the Centre for Medieval Studies at the University of Exeter (funded by the Arts and Humanities Research Council).

13 Latin poetry and music

1 See in general Dag Ludvig Norberg, *An Introduction to the Study of Medieval Latin Versification*, trans. Grant C. Roti and Jacqueline de La Chapelle Skulby, ed. Jan Ziolkowski (Washington DC: Catholic University of America Press, 2004).

2 Cf. Friedrich Leo, *Venanti Honori Clementiani Fortunati presbyteri Italici opera poetica*, Monumenta Germaniae Historica, Auctores antiquissimi IV/1 (Berlin: Weidmann, 1881), 'Index rei metricae', p. 326.

3 *Analecta Hymnica medii aevi*, ed. C. Blune and G. M. Dreves, 55 vols. (Leipzig: Fues's Verlag [R. Reisland], 1886–1922; repr. Frankfurt am Main: Minerva, 1961), vol. XIX, pp. 260–1, no. 472; pp. 146–7, no. 126; pp. 192–3, no. 171. Henceforth *AH*.

4 Jan M. Ziolkowski, *Nota Bene: Reading Classics and Writing Melodies in the Early Middle Ages*, Publications of the Journal of Medieval Latin 7 (Turnhout: Brepols, 2007); Alma Colk Santosuosso, 'Music in Bede's *De temporum ratione*: An 11th-Century Addition to MS London, British Library, Cotton Vespasian B. VI', *Scriptorium* 43 (1989), pp. 255–9; Silvia

Wälli, *Melodien aus mittelalterlichen Horaz-Handschriften: Edition und Interpretation der Quellen*, Monumenta Monodica Medii Aevi, Subsidia 3 (Kassel: Bärenreiter, 2002), p. 55.
5 See e.g. Wälli, *Melodien*, pp. 253–89; for elision, contrast, for example, p. 189 (*miserarum est, lavere aut* elided) with pp. 189, 200 (*pulverem Olympicum, presidium et* prised apart).
6 *AH*, vol. L, pp. 317–18, no. 244; for one version of the medieval chant see *The Liber Usualis, with Introduction and Rubrics in English* (Tournai and New York: Desclée, 1961), p. 273.
7 Owen Rees, ed., *Aires Fernandez (fl. ca. 1550): Alma Redemptoris Mater, Asperges me, Lumen ad revelationem*, Mapa Mundi Renaissance Performing Scores, Series A: Spanish and Portuguese Church Music 182 (Lochs [Isle of Lewis]: Mapa Mundi, 2002), pp. 2–4.
8 See Victorinus, *Ars Palaemonis de metrica institutione, Grammatici Latini*, ed. Heinrich Keil, 8 vols. (Leipzig: B. G. Teubner, 1855–80; repr. Hildesheim: Olms, 1961), vol. VI, p. 206 (henceforth GLK), and Audax, *De metro*, GLK, vol. VII, p. 331, who are thought to draw on the same fourth-century source.
9 *AH*, vol. LI, pp. 340–6, no. 252. Fifteen lines in this verse-form are found appended to the trochaic tetrameters of Venantius's *Pange lingua*; see *AH*, vol. XXVII, p. 96.
10 *AH*, vol. LI, pp. 140–2, no. 123, stanza 4, v. 1.
11 For sources see Christopher Page, *Latin Poetry and Conductus Rhythm in Medieval France*, RMA Monographs 8 (London: Royal Musical Association, 1997), pp. 49–53.
12 Janet Knapp, ed., *Thirty-Five Conductus for Two and Three Voices*, Collegium Musicum 6 (New Haven, CT: Yale University Department of Music Graduate School, 1965), p. 46, verses 4, 10 = bars 8–10, 21–3, from F (= MS Florence, Biblioteca Medicea Laurenziana, Plut. 29. 1), fols. 239v–240r.
13 *AH*, vol. LI, pp. 61–3, no. 61; for stress on the second syllable see stanza 7, l. 1 *tu nobis dona fontem lacrimarum.*
14 For a (?)sixth-century approximation to the rhythm, though without rhyme or stanzaic form, see David Howlett, *Cambro-Latin Compositions: Their Competence and Cratfsmanship* (Dublin: Four Courts Press, 1998), pp. 26–7.
15 See Paul Gerhard Schmidt, 'The Quotation in Goliardic Poetry: The Feast of Fools and the Goliardic Strophe cum auctoritate', in Peter Godman and Oswyn Murray, eds., *Latin Poetry and the Classical Tradition: Essays in Medieval and Renaissance Literature* (Oxford University Press, 1990), pp. 39–55.

16 Knapp, *Thirty-Five Conductus*, pp. 40–1, from F, fol. 230r–v, cf. Ma = MS Madrid, Biblioteca Nacional 20846, fols. 139r–v, Hu = MS Burgos, Monasterio de Las Huelgas 9, fol. 101v.
17 *AH*, vol. L, pp. 602–16, no. 398.
18 Knapp, *Thirty-Five Conductus*, pp. 98–100, from F, fols. 327r–v; W_1 = MS Wolfenbüttel, Herzog August Bibliothek 628 (677), fol. 111(102)r, Ma, fol. 101r.
19 Ed. Otto Schumann, in Alfons Hilka and Otto Schumann, eds., *Carmina Burana*, 2 vols. in 4 (Heidelberg: Carl Winters Universitätsbuchhandlung, 1930–70), vol. I/2, pp. 298–301, no. 179, stanza 8, l. 1, from Munich, Bayerische Staatsbibliothek, clm 4660, fol. 70v.
20 Ibid., pp. 53–8, no. 77 (fols. 31v–33v), stanzas 1. 1, 2. 1, 8. 1–4 = fols. 31v, 32r.
21 On the origins of the motet, and discussion of some Latin texts, see Mark Everist, *French Motets in the Thirteenth Century: Music, Poetry and Genre*, Cambridge Studies in Medieval and Renaissance Music (Cambridge University Press, 1994), pp. 15–42.
22 F, fols. 405r–v, Wolfenbüttel, Herzog August Bibliothek 1099 (1206) fols. 174v–175r, Hu MS, fols. 92r–93r; Higini Anglès, ed., fols. *El còdex musical de Las Huelgas (música a veus dels segles XIII–XIV): introducció, facsímil i transcripció*, 3 vols., Biblioteca de Catalunya, Publicacions del Departament de Música 6 (Barcelona Institut d'Estudis Catalans, 1931), no. 90: vol. I; pp. 249–50, vol. III, pp. 151–5.
23 Anglès's edition includes the clausula (from F, fol. 174v) and the vernacular texts.
24 MS Bamberg, Staatsbibliothek, Lit. 115 (*olim* Ed. IV. 6), fol. 8r–v (no. 14 in the editions of Aubry and Anderson), triplum, vv. 4–5.
25 Text ed. Emile Dahnk, *L'Hérésie de Fauvel*, Leipziger romanische Studien II, Literaturwissenschaftliche Reihe 4 (Leipzig and Paris: C. & E. Vogel, 1935), pp. 67–8, pièce musicale 33, triplum, vv. 15–16, from MS Bibliothèque nationale de France, f. fr. 146, fol. 10r. On the dispute over whether this or the version addressed to 'Ludowice' in MS f. fr. 571, fol. 144r is the original see contributions to Margaret Bent and Andrew Wathey, *Fauvel Studies: Allegory, Chronicle, Music, and Image in Paris, Bibliothèque nationale de France, MS français 146* (Oxford: Clarendon Press, 1998).
26 *Primum argumentum*, vv. 5–6, ed. Heinrich Besseler, rev. David Fallows, *Guillelmi Dufay opera omnia*, vol. VI, *Cantiones*, Corpus Mensurabilis Musicae 1 (Stuttgart: American Institute of Musicology, 1995), no. 9.
27 *Solutio primi argumenti*, vv. 3–4; *secundum argumentum*, even lines.

28 Leo Schrade, ed., *Guillaume de Machaut: Œuvres complètes*, vol. II, *Les Motets* (Monaco: Éditions de l'Oiseau-Lyre, 1977), no. 23, pp. 82–9, triplum, bars 53–63, 194–8. In the motetus *génitrix* rhymes with *víctrix* (the *c* was probably silent), *íter* with *viríliter* (bars 16–17, 22–4; 113, 119–21).

29 See *Les Fleurs du mal*, 67 (60), 'Franciscae meae laudes'.

30 Aosta, Biblioteca del Seminario Maggiore, Cod. 15 (*olim* A^1 D 19), fols. 4v–7r; Kurt von Fischer and F. Alberto Gallo, eds., *Polyphonic Music of the Fourteenth Century*, vol. XIII, *Italian Sacred and Ceremonial Music* (Monaco: Éditions de l'Oiseau-Lyre, 1987), no. 49, pp. 220–7, motetus, bars 152–61.

31 Ursula Günther, ed., *The Motets of the Manuscripts Chantilly, Musée Condé, 564 (olim 1047) and Modena, Biblioteca Estense, α. M. 5, 25 (olim lat. 568)*, Corpus Mensurabilis Musicae 39 (Rome: American Institute of Musicology, 1965), no. 3, pp. xxiv–xxvii, 8–13.

32 Andrew Wathey, 'The Motets of Philippe de Vitry and the Fourteenth-Century Renaissance', *Early Music History* 12 (1993), 119–50.

33 Frank Ll. Harrison, ed., *Musicorum collegio: Fourteenth-Century Musicians' Motets* (Monaco: Éditions de l'Oiseau-Lyre, 1986), no. 2, pp. 7–10.

34 Ibid., no. 1, pp. 1–6, bars 1–3.

35 Gordon A. Anderson, ed., *Motets of the Manuscript La Clayette, Paris, Bibliothèque nationale, nouv. acq. f. fr. 13521*, Corpus Scriptorum de Musica 68 (Rome: American Institute of Musicology 1975), no. 11, pp. 14–15.

36 Leo Schrade, ed., *Philippe de Vitry: Complete Works* (Monaco: Éditions de l'Oiseau-Lyre, 1984), no. 7, pp. 20–5, at p. 23, bars 102–4. (In the triplum incipit *qui* is corrupt for *quid*.)

37 Ibid., no. 14, pp. 50–3.

38 Günther, *Motets*, no. 2, pp. xxi–xxiii, 4–7.

39 Ibid., no. 15, pp. lxii–lxv, 66–70.

40 Margaret Bent and Anne Hallmark, eds., *The Works of Johannes Ciconia* (Monaco: Éditions de l'Oiseau-Lyre, 1985), no. 19, pp. 103–7, 224–5.

41 For detailed discussion see Leofranc Holford-Strevens, 'Du Fay the Poet? Problems in the Texts of His Motets', *Early Music History* 16 (1997), pp. 97–160.

42 See Jeffrey Dean, 'Okeghem's Valediction? The Meaning of *Intemerata Dei mater*', in Philippe Vendrix, ed., *Johannes Ockeghem: Actes du XLe Colloque international d'études humanistes, Tours, 3–8 février 1997* (Paris: Klincksieck, 1998), pp. 521–70; cf. Heinz-Jürgen Winkler, 'Zur Vertonung von Mariendichtung in antiken Versmaßen bei Johannes Ockeghem und Johannes Regis', in Vendrix, *Ockeghem*, pp. 571–93.

43 *Magnanimae gentis / Nexus amicitiae / Haec est vera fraternitas*, triplum, bars 77–88, in Heinrich Besseler, ed., *Guillelmi Dufay Opera omnia*, vol. I, Corpus Mensurabilis Musicae 1 (Rome: American Institute of Musicology, 1966), no. 17, pp. xxii, 76–80 at 77–8, from ModB = Modena, Biblioteca Estense, α. X. 1. 11 (Lat. 37, *olim* VI. H. 15), fols. 63v–64r.

44 But even the great humanist Politian can write accentual Ambrosians (*O virgo prudentissima, Ecce ancilla Domini*) and a lament for Lorenzo de' Medici (*Quis dabit capiti meo*) in pure syllabic verse (8, 8, 8, 5, 5) without regard to accent; however, these poems are unrhymed and respect elision except in the phrase *ecce | ancilla* (Luke 1:38), heard in church with hiatus.

14 Compositional trajectories

1 The possibility of microtones in early chant is controversial, but is given less credence now than formerly. See David Hiley, *Western Plainchant: A Handbook* (Oxford: Clarendon Press, 1993), pp. 361 and 388.

2 Example 14.1, the anonymous respond (refrain) of *Exsurge domine*, a Gregorian gradual of ca800, is adapted from *The Liber Usualis* (Tournai: Desclée, 1956), pp. 553–4.

3 On third- and fourth-mode graduals, see Willi Apel, *Gregorian Chant* (Bloomington: Indiana University Press, 1958), pp. 351–4. On third-mode graduals and *Exsurge domine* in particular, see Richard Crocker, 'Chants of the Roman Mass,' in Richard Crocker and David Hiley, eds., The New Oxford History of Music, vol. II, *The Early Middle Ages to 1300*, new edn (Oxford University Press, 1990), pp. 174–222.

4 Psalms were sung in the liturgy by rising to, encircling, and falling from a reciting tone (the pitch to which most syllables were set), in a kind of inflected monotone. As psalm singing became elaborated with refrains (the responds of responsorial psalmody and the antiphons of antiphonal psalmody), the refrains tended to retain the feature of an important and reiterated secondary pitch above the final. This pitch correlated with mode; refrain melodies with final on E in third mode, F in fifth mode and G in eighth mode mostly feature a prominent secondary tone, or reciting tone, on the C above.

5 Example 14.2, the beginning of Hildegard's chorus *In principio*, is adapted from Claude Palisca, ed., *Norton Anthology of Western Music*, vol. I; *Ancient to Baroque*, 4th edn (New York: Norton, 2001), pp. 35–7.

6 Example 14.3, the sequence *Fulgens preclara*, is adapted from W. Thomas Marrocco and Nicholas Sandon, *Medieval Music*, Oxford

Anthology of Music I (London: Oxford University Press, 1977), pp. 34–5, no. 11h. They transcribe it from London, British Library, Lansdowne 462, fols. 50v–51v. Another version is available in Sarah Fuller, *The European Musical Heritage 800–1750* (New York: Knopf, 1987), pp. 11–13, no. 1g, which has been transcribed from Paris, Bibliothèque nationale, fonds latin 1112, fols. 11v–12; it differs significantly in the level of transposition of individual phrases. Neither version fits comfortably into the eight-mode scheme (see the comment in Fuller, p. 22).

7 Example 14.4, the versus *Ortum floris*, is edited here from Cambridge, University Library, Hh.vi.11, fols. 69v–70; for additional bibliography, see Gordon A. Anderson, 'Notre Dame and Related Conductus – a Catalogue Raisonné', *Miscellanea Musicologica* 6 (1972), pp. 153–229 at p. 214, no. L81.

8 John Stevens, *Words and Music in the Middle Ages: Song, Narrative, Dance and Drama, 1050–1350* (Cambridge University Press, 1986), pp. 119–55.

9 Contrary motion, rather than parallel motion, is championed in the theory and practice of elite French polyphony of the later Middle Ages. But a quotidian style of discanting in parallel perfect fifths above the given part (fifthing, also referred to as *diapentizare, quintare, quintizans*) is still in evidence in both theory and practice; see Sarah Fuller, 'Discant and the Theory of Fifthing', *Acta Musicologica* 50 (1978), pp. 241–75.

Example 14.5a, *Ipsi soli*, an organum from Guido's *Micrologus*, Chapter XIX, ca1025, is adapted from Fuller, *The European Musical Heritage*, p. 33.

Example 14.5b is an anonymous polyphonic version of a Christmas Matins lesson tone from London, British Library, Additional 28598, fol. 14v; the present example is adapted from Theodor Göllner, *Die mehrstimmigen liturgischen Lesungen*, 2 vols. (Tutzing: Hans Schneider, 1969), vol. I, p. 11, no. A4.

Example 14.5c is from a polyphonic setting of the sequence *Victime paschali laudes* in Burgos, Monasterio de Las Huelgas 9, fol. 54v; it is adapted from the edition in Higini Anglès, ed., *El còdex musical de Las Huelgas*, 3 vols. (Barcelona: Institut d'Estudis Catalans and Biblioteca de Catalunya, 1931), vol. III, p. 92, no. 63.

Example 14.5d is from a polyphonic setting of the hymn *Conditor alme siderum* in London, British Library, Additional 16975, fol. 166r.

10 Example 14.6a is from a polyphonic hymn for Saint Magnus, *Nobilis humilis*, from Uppsala, Universitetsbiblioteket, C.233, fols. 19v–20r; this example is adapted from Archibald Davison and Willi Apel, eds., *Historical Anthology of Music*, rev. edn, 2 vols. (Cambridge, MA: Harvard University Press, 1964), vol. I, p. 22, no. 25c.

Example 14.6b, *Laudes deo*, is from London, British Library, Harley 3965, fol. 137; this example is adapted from Frank Ll. Harrison, Ernest H. Sanders and Peter M. Lefferts, eds., *English Music for Mass and Offices*, vol. I, Polyphonic Music of the Fourteenth Century 16 (Paris and Monaco: Éditions de l'Oiseau-Lyre, 1983), pp. 191–4, no. 82.

Example 14.6c, *Ave celi regina virginum*, is from Cambridge, Gonville and Caius College, 512/543, fols. 258v–259; a three-voice concordance is edited in Frank Ll. Harrison, Ernest H. Sanders and Peter M. Lefferts, eds., *English Music for Mass and Offices*, vol. II, Polyphonic Music of the Fourteenth Century, vol. XVII (Paris and Monaco: Éditions de l'Oiseau-Lyre, 1986), pp. 82–6, no. 38.

11 Discussed with example in Franchino Gaffurio, *Practica musice* (Milan, 1496), Book III, Chapter 14.

12 Example 14.7, a clausula on *Nostrum*, is adapted from Rebecca A. Baltzer, ed., *Les clausulas à deux voix du manuscrit de Florence, Biblioteca Medicea-Laurenziana, Pluteus 29.1, fascicule V*, Le Magnus liber organi de Notre-Dame de Paris 5 (Monaco: Éditions de l'Oiseau-Lyre, 1995), p. 78, no. 97.

13 See Peter M. Lefferts, 'Signature-systems and tonal types in the fourteenth-century French chanson', *Plainsong and Medieval Music* 4 (1995), pp. 117–47, and Lefferts, 'Machaut's B-flat Balade *Honte, Paour* (B25)', in Elizabeth Eva Leach, ed., *Machaut's Music: New Interpretations* (Woodbridge: Boydell & Brewer, 2003), pp. 161–74.

14 Example 14.8, from Machaut's virelai *Se je souspir*, is adapted from Leo Schrade, ed., *The Works of Guillaume de Machaut*, Polyphonic Music of the Fourteenth Century, vol. III (Monaco: Éditions de l'Oiseau-Lyre, 1956), p. 189.

15 Machaut ballades B2, B5, B9 and B24 (using Leo Schrade's numeration) are excellent examples of such underfifth harmonization. For a fuller discussion and more examples, see Lefferts, 'Signature-systems and tonal types', pp. 118–22 and Table 1.

16 Example 14.9, from Giovanni da Firenze's madrigal *Nel meço*, is adapted from the edition by W. Thomas Marrocco in *Italian Secular Music by Magister Piero, Giovanni da Firenze, Jacopo da Bologna*, Polyphonic Music of the Fourteenth Century, vol. VI (Monaco: Éditions de l'Oiseau-Lyre, 1967), pp. 48–9.

17   Example 14.10, the versus *Soli nitorem*, is
found in Florence, Biblioteca Medicea
Laurenziana, Plut.29.1, fols. 327v–328v and
Burgos, Monasterio de Las Huelgas 9, fols.
138r–193v. For other modern editions, see
Anglès, ed., *El còdex musical de Las Huelgas*, vol.
III, pp. 324–7, no. 149; Richard H. Hoppin, ed.,
Anthology of Medieval Music (New York:
Norton, 1978), pp. 69–71, no. 37; and Gordon
A. Anderson, ed. *Notre Dame and Related
Conductus: Opera Omnia*, vol. V (Henryville,
Ottawa and Binningen: Institute of Mediaeval
Music, 1979), pp. xi, 23–5, 114, no. J15.

15 Ecclesiastical foundations and secular institutions

1   Rosamond McKitterick, by a careful and
judicious sifting of the evidence, finds support
for a somewhat broader literacy than my
statement might imply; see her *The Carolingians
and the Written Word* (Cambridge University
Press, 1989), especially pp. 211–70 on the
literacy of the laity.
2   A significant anticipation of and impetus for
the Carolingian reforms came from Bishop
Chrodegang of Metz, who took office in the
740s and died in 766. For an excellent discussion
of his role see M. A. Claussen, *The Reform of the
Frankish Church: Chrodegang of Metz and the
'Regula canonicorum' in the Eighth Century*
(Cambridge University Press, 2004). See also the
comprehensive study by Yitzhak Hen, *The Royal
Patronage of Liturgy in Frankish Gaul to the
Death of Charles the Bald (877)* (London: Henry
Bradshaw Society, 2001).
3   Excerpts quoted in English are from *Einhard:
The Life of Charlemagne*, trans. Samuel Epes
Turner (New York: Harper & Brothers, 1880.)
For a more recent translation, see Paul Edward
Dutton, ed. and trans., *Charlemagne's Courtier:
The Complete Einhard* (Peterborough, Ont.:
Broadview Press, 1998).
4   The Latin word here translated as 'music' is
acroama –atis, a noun meaning an
entertainment, especially musical, or an
entertainer, that is, reader, actor, or singer.
5   *Einhard*, Chapter 24.
6   Ibid., Chapter 29.
7   Ibid., Chapter 25.
8   Charlemagne's two-storey octagonal church
at Aachen took as its model the two-storey
octagonal church of San Vitale in Ravenna, built
by the powerful Emperor Justinian two
centuries earlier. This was a conscious
Carolingian attempt to connect with past
imperial splendour.
9   *Einhard*, Chapter 26.

10   For a good overview see Giles Brown,
'Introduction: The Carolingian Renaissance', in
Rosamond McKitterick, ed., *Carolingian
Culture: Emulation and Innovation* (Cambridge
University Press, 1994), pp. 1–51.
11   Hartmut Möller, 'Zur Frage der
musikgeschichtlichen Bedeutung der Academia
am Hofe Karls des Grossen: Die Musica Albini',
in Wolf Frobenius, et al., eds., *Akademie und
Musik: Erscheinungsweisen und Wirkungen des
Akademiegedankens in Kultur- und
Musikgeschichte – Institutionen, Veranstaltungen,
Schriften. Festschrift für Werner Braun zum 65.
Geburtstag* (Saarbrücken: Saarbrücken
Druckerei und Verlag, 1993), pp. 269–88.
12   The Latin text is accessible online through
the Thesaurus Musicarum Latinarum (TML)
housed at the Indiana University School of
Music. (Go to 6th–8th-century files, ALCMUS.)
13   See Michel Huglo, 'Un tonaire du Graduel
de la fin du VIIIe siècle (Bibliothèque Nationale
lat.13159)', *Revue grégorienne* 31 (1952), pp.
176–86, 224–33, and his *Les tonaires: inventaire,
analyse, comparaison* (Paris: Société française de
musicologie, 1971), pp. 26–8.
14   The Latin edition of Charlemagne's
Admonitio generalis is in Monumenta
Germaniae Historica, Capitularia I/22
(Hanover: Hahn, 1883), pp. 52–62; an English
translation in P. D. King, *Charlemagne:
Translated Sources* (Kendal, Cumbria: author,
1987); see the discussion in Rosamond
McKitterick, *The Frankish Church and the
Carolingian Reforms, 789–895* (London: Royal
Historical Society, 1977), and Brown,
'Carolingian Renaissance', pp. 17–21.
15   A useful collection of essays is James C. King
and Werner Vogler, eds., *The Culture of the
Abbey of St Gall: An Overview*, translated from
the German (*Die Kultur der Abtei Sankt Gallen*)
by James C. King (Stuttgart: Belser, 1991).
16   St Gall codices can be found at CESG
(Codices Electronici Sangallenses),
www.cesg.unifr.ch/de/index.htm.
17   A facsimile of Stiftsbibliothek MS 359 is in
Paléographie Musicale, 2nd series, vol. II,
*Cantatorium, IXe siècle: no. 359 de la
Bibliothèque de Saint-Gall* (Solesmes: Atelier de
Paléographie Musicale de Solesmes, 1924).
18   See the following Publications by Susan
Rankin: 'Notker und Tuotilo: Schöpferische
Gestalter in einer neuen Zeit', *Schweizer Jahrbuch
für Musikwissenschaft* 11 (1991), pp. 17–42; 'The
Earliest Sources of Notker's Sequences: St Gallen
Vadiana 317, and Paris, Bibliothèque Nationale
lat. 10587', *Early Music History* 10 (1991), pp.
201–33; and 'From Tuotilo to the First
Manuscripts: The Shaping of a Trope Repertory

at Saint Gall', in Wulf Arlt and Gunilla Björkvall, eds., *Recherches nouvelles sur les tropes liturgiques*, Studia Latina Stockholmiensia 36, (Stockholm: Almqvist & Wiksell International, 1993), pp. 395–413. MS 381 is available in facsimile in Wulf Arlt and Susan Rankin, eds., *Stiftsbibliothek Sankt Gallen Codices 484 & 381*, (Winterthur: Amadeus, 1996).

19 The Old Minster was replaced by the current cathedral after the Norman conquest of 1066. Winchester was one of many English cathedrals run by monastics rather than secular canons, but this form of monastic organization was almost unknown among cathedrals on the Continent.

20 The English translation of Ethelwold's account by E. K. Chambers in *The Medieval Stage*, vol. II (1903), pp. 14ff., is widely reprinted – for example, in *Music and Letters* 27 (1946), pp. 5–6.

21 Useful are Richard L. Crocker, *The Early Medieval Sequence* (Berkeley and Los Angeles: University of California Press, 1977), and Alejandro E. Planchart, *The Repertory of Tropes at Winchester* (Princeton University Press, 1977).

22 See Andreas Holschneider, *Die Organa von Winchester* (Hildesheim: Georg Olms, 1968), and Susan Rankin, 'Winchester Polyphony: The Early Theory and Practice of Organum', in Susan Rankin and David Hiley, eds., *Music in the Medieval English Liturgy* (Oxford: Clarendon Press, 1993), pp. 59–99.

23 See, most recently, the essays in Bonnie Wheeler and John Carmi Parsons, eds., *Eleanor of Aquitaine, Lord and Lady* (New York: Palgrave Macmillan, 2002), and, with specific reference to music, Rebecca A. Baltzer, 'Music in the Life and Times of Eleanor of Aquitaine', in William W. Kibler, ed., *Eleanor of Aquitaine: Patron and Politician* (Austin: University of Texas Press, 1976), pp. 61–80.

24 See Margarita Egan, trans., *The Vidas of the Troubadours* (New York and London: Garland, 1984).

25 Chrétien de Troyes, *Erec et Enide*, in Mario Roques, ed., *Les romans de Chrétien de Troyes*, vol. I (Paris: Champion, 1953), lines 1983–2000. The translation is my adaptation of W. W. Comfort, *Chrétien de Troyes, Arthurian Romances* (London: Everyman's Library, 1914), p. 27.

26 *Erec et Enide*, lines 6330–33; compare the translation in Comfort, *Crétien de Troyes*, p. 82. It quickly becomes a *topos* in medieval romances to list as many musical instruments as the author can name when he wishes to show the importance of an occasion and indicate that no expense was spared. Such lists should not imply a sort of twelfth-century Poitou Philharmonic.

27 Chansonniers that begin with a collection of Thibaut's songs include Paris, Bibliothèque de l'Arsenal 5198 (the Chansonnier de l'Arsenal, MS *K*); Paris, *F-Pn* fonds fr. 845 (MS *N*): Paris, *F-Pn* fonds fr. 12615 (the Chansonnier de Noailles, MS *T*); and Paris, *F-Pn* n.a.f. 1050 (Chansonnier de Clairambault, MS *X*). See Kathleen J. Brahney, ed. and trans., *The Lyrics of Thibaut de Champagne* (New York: Garland, 1989), and Hendrik van der Werf, ed., *Trouvères-Melodien*, II, Monumenta Monodica Medii Aevi 12 (Kassel: Bärenreiter, 1979).

28 A colour facsimile is in *El 'Códice Rico' de las Cantigas de Alfonso el Sabio: Ms. T.I.1 de la Biblioteca de El Escorial* (Madrid, 1979); there is also a sepia facsimile and edition with commentary of El Escorial, Biblioteca del Real Monasterio, b.I.2 (also known as j.b.2) by Higini Anglès, ed., *La música de las cantigas de Santa María del rey Alfonso el Sabio*, 3 vols. in 4 (Barcelona: Biblioteca Central, 1943–64).

29 See Barbara Newman, ed., *Saint Hildegard of Bingen: Symphonia: A Critical Edition of the 'Symphonia armonie celestium revelationum'* (Ithaca, NY: Cornell University Press, vol. I 1988, vol. II 1998), with translations but only four musical transcriptions; W. Berschin and H. Schipperges, eds., *Hildegard von Bingen: Symphonia: Gedichte und Gesänge* (Gerlingen: Lambert Schneider, 1995). Both manuscripts, Dendermonde (Sint-Pieter- en Paulusabdij Codex 9, and Wiesbaden, Hessische Landesbibliothek, MS 2 ('Riesenkodex'), have been issued in facsimile.

30 Audrey E. Davidson, ed., *The 'Ordo virtutum' of Hildegard of Bingen* (Kalamazoo: Western Michigan University, 1985; performance edition); see also Peter Dronke, ed. and trans. 'Play of the Virtues', in Dronke, ed. and trans. *Nine Medieval Plays* (Cambridge University Press, 1994), pp. 161–81.

31 See Benjamin Guérard, ed., *Cartulaire de l'église Notre-Dame de Paris* (4 vols., Paris: Crapelet, 1850), introduction to vol. I, pp. xcix–cviii.

32 Craig Wright, *Music and Ceremony at Notre Dame of Paris 500–1550* (Cambridge University Press, 1989), pp. 18–27.

33 The medieval Parisian monetary system was based on 12 deniers to a sou and 20 sous to a livre, or pound; thus, it was the ultimate ancestor of the former British system of pence, shillings, and pounds that lasted through much of the twentieth century.

34 See Patricia Stirnemann, 'Les bibliothèques princières et privées au XIIe et XIIIe siècles', in André Vernet, ed., *Les bibliothèques médiévales: Du VIe siècle à 1530*, Histoire des bibliothèques

françaises 1 (Paris: Éditions du Cercle de la Librairie / Promodès, 1989), pp. 173–91.

35 Barbara Haggh and Michel Huglo, '*Magnus liber – Maius munus:* Origine et destinée du manuscrit F', *Revue de musicologie* 90 (2004), pp. 193–230.

36 Catherine Parsoneault, 'The Montpellier Codex: Royal Influence and Musical Taste in Late Thirteenth-Century Paris', PhD diss., University of Texas at Austin, 2001, especially pp. 153–226.

37 See Margaret Bent and Andrew Wathey, eds., *Fauvel Studies: Allegory, Chronicle, Music, and Image in Paris, Bibliothèque nationale de France, MS français 146* (Oxford: Clarendon Press, 1998).

38 An edition and translation of the *Remede*, including the music and photographs of all the miniatures from MS 'C', is in James I. Wimsatt and William W. Kibler, eds., *Guillaume de Machaut: Le Jugement du roy de Behaigne and Remede de Fortune*, music edited by Rebecca A. Baltzer (Athens, GA, University of Georgia Press, 1988).

39 For the most important material concerning Machaut, see the indispensable *Guillaume de Machaut: A Guide to Research*, by Lawrence Earp (New York and London: Garland, 1995), and Anne Walters Robertson, *Guillaume de Machaut and Reims: Context and Meaning in His Musical Works* (Cambridge University Press, 2002).

40 See Earp, *Guillaume de Machaut, passim.*

41 See Pierre Tucoo-Chala, *Gaston Fébus, un grand prince d'occident au XIVe siècle* (Pau: Marrimpouey, 1976); Jean-Jacques Casteret, 'Musique et musiciens à la cour de Gaston Fébus', PhD diss., Université de Paris IV, 1992; and Alice V. Clark, 'Vernacular Dedicatory Motets in Fourteenth-Century France', *Journal of Musicological Research* 20 (2000), pp. 41–69.

42 See Beth Anne Lee-De Amici, '*Ad Sustentacionem Fidei Christiani:* Sacred Music and Ceremony in Medieval Oxford', PhD diss., University of Pennsylvania, 1999.

43 Anne Bagnall Yardley, '"Ful weel she soong the service dyvyne": The Cloistered Musician in the Middle Ages', in Jane Bowers and Judith Tick, eds., *Women Making Music: The Western Art Tradition, 1150–1950* (Urbana: University of Illinois, 1986), pp. 26–7, for a table of polyphony in Continental nunneries. For the evidence in English nunneries, see Yardley, *Performing Piety: Musical Culture in Medieval English Nunneries* (New York: Palgrave Press, 2006), pp. 109–11.

16 Theory and notation

1 C. V. Palisca, 'Theory, theorists', *Grove Music Online*, www.oxfordmusiconline.com.

2 G. Friedlein, ed., *Anicii Manlii Torquati Severini Boetii De institutione arithmetica libri duo. De institutione musica libri quinque. Accedit Geometria quae fertur Boetii* (Leipzig: B. G. Teubner, 1867/R); Boethius, *Fundamentals of Music*, trans., C. M. Bower (New Haven: Yale University Press, 1989); M. Bernhard and C. M. Bower, eds., *Glossa maior in institutionem musicam Boethii* (Munich: Verlag der Bayerischen Akademie der Wissenschaft, 1993–6); G. Marzi, ed., *An.M.T. Severini Boethii de institutione musica* (Rome: Istituto italiano per la storia della musica, 1990).

3 J. Willis, ed., *Martianus Capella: De nuptiis Philologiae et Mercurii* (Leipzig: B. G. Teubner, 1983).

4 R. A. B. Mynors, ed., *Cassiodori Senatoris Institutiones* (Oxford: Clarendon Press, 1937); partial English translation in Oliver Strunk, *Source Readings in Music History* (New York: W. W. Norton & Co., 1950) (henceforth, StrunkSR1), pp. 87–92, and O. Strunk, *Source Readings in Music History*, rev. edn, ed. Leo Treitler (New York: W. W. Norton & Co., 1998) (henceforth, StrunkSR2), pp. 143–8; M. Adriaen, ed., *Cassiodorus: Expositio psalmorum* (Turnhout: Brepols, 1958).

5 F. Arévalo, ed., *S. Isidori hispalensis episcopi opera omnia* (Rome: Typis A. Fulgonii, 1797–1803); also in *Patrologiae cursus completus, Series Latina*, ed. J.-P. Migne, 221 vols. (Paris: Garnier, 1844–1864), vols. LXXXI–LXXXIV; Isidore of Seville, *Isidori hispalensis episcopi Etymologiarum sive originum libri xx*, ed. W. M. Lindsay, 2 vols. (Oxford: Clarendon Press, 1911); English translation of book III, chapters 15–23 in StrunkSR1, pp. 93–100, SR2, pp. 149–55; J. Oroz Reta and M.-A. Marcos Casquero, eds., *Etimologías*, 2 vols. (Madrid: Editorial Católica, vol. I 1982–3, vol. II 1993–4) (parallel Latin and Spanish trans.); P. K. Marshall, ed., *Etymologies*, book II (Paris: Les Belles Lettres, 1983); C. M. Lawson, ed., *Sancti Isidori episcopi hispalensis De ecclesiasticis officiis*, Corpus Christianorum, Series Latina 113 (Turnhout: Brepols, 1989).

6 Scholars generally refer to the chant that is transmitted in early manuscripts as Frankish-Roman chant since it most likely represents an amalgamation of what had been sung in the Frankish kingdom before Charlemagne's reforms and the Roman version. See L. Treitler, 'Homer and Gregory: The Transmission of Epic Poetry and Plainchant', *Musical Quarterly* 60, (1974), pp. 333–72; H. Hucke, 'Toward a New Historical View of Gregorian Chant', *Journal of the American Musicological Society* 33 (1980), pp. 437–67; H.

van der Werf, *The Emergence of Gregorian Chant* (Rochester, NY: author, 1983); D. Hughes, 'Evidence for the Traditional View of the Transmission of Gregorian Chant', *Journal of the American Musicological Society* 40 (1987), pp. 377–404; K. Levy, 'Charlemagne's Archetype of Gregorian Chant', *Journal of the American Musicological Society* 40 (1987), pp. 1–30; J. McKinnon, 'The Emergence of Gregorian Chant in the Carolingian Era', in J. McKinnon, ed., *Antiquity and the Middle Ages* (London: Macmillan, 1990), pp. 88–119; D. Hiley, *Western Plainchant: A Handbook* (Oxford: Clarendon Press, 1993).

7 L. Gushee, ed., *Aurelianus Reomensis: Musica disciplina*, Corpus Scriptorum de Musica (henceforth CSM) 21 ([Rome]: American Institute of Musicology, 1975); *The Discipline of Music (ca. 843) by Aurelian of Réôme*, trans. J. Ponte (Colorado Springs: Colorado College Music Press, 1968).

8 J. Chailley, ed., *Alia musica: traité de musique du IXe siècle* (Paris: Centre de Documentation Universitaire et Société d'Édition d'Enseignement Supérieur Réunis, 1965); E. B. Heard, '"Alia musica": A Chapter in the History of Music Theory' (PhD diss., University of Wisconsin, 1966) (edn and Eng. trans.); partial English translation in StrunkSR2, pp. 196–8.

9 A. Traub, ed. and trans.,'Hucbald von Saint-Amand: De harmonica institutione', *Beiträge zur Gregorianik* 7 (1989), pp. 3–101; Y. Chartier, ed., *L'oeuvre musicale d'Hucbald de Saint-Amand: les compositions et le traité de musique* ([Saint-Laurent, Québec]: Bellarmin, 1995) (critical edition of musical works and the *Musica*, with French translation and commentary); C. V. Palisca, ed., *Hucbald, Guido, and John on Music: Three Medieval Treatises*, trans. W. Babb (New Haven, CT: Yale University Press, 1978), pp. 13–44.

10 H. Schmid, ed., *Musica et Scolica Enchiriadis, una cum aliquibus tractatulis adjunctis* (Munich: Verlag der Bayerischen Akademie der Wissenschaften, 1981); C. V. Palisca, ed., *Musica enchiriadis and Scolica enchiriadis*, trans. R. Erickson (New Haven, CT: Yale University Press, 1995).

11 M. Gerbert, *Scriptores ecclesiastici de musica sacra potissimum*, 3 vols. (Sankt Blasien: Typis San-Blasianis 1784; repr. Hildesheim: Olms, 1963), vol. I, pp. 251–64; K.-W. Gümpel, ed., *Pseudo-Odo: Dialogus de musica* (forthcoming); partial English translation in StrunkSR1, pp. 103–16, SR2, pp. 198–210.

12 Joseph Smits van Waesberghe, ed., *Guidonis Aretini Micrologus*, CSM 4 ([Nijmegen]:

American Institute of Musicology, 1955); Palisca, ed., *Hucbald, Guido, and John on Music*, pp. 57–83; D. Pesce, *Guido d'Arezzo's 'Regulae rhythmicae', 'Prologus in antiphonarium', and 'Epistola ad Michaelem': A Critical Text and Translation with an Introduction, Annotations, Indices and New Manuscript Inventories* (Ottawa: Institute of Mediaeval Music, 1999).

13 See D. Pesce, *The Affinities and Medieval Transposition* (Bloomington: Indiana University Press, 1987), Chapter 3, 'Hexachords: Seats of the Modes'.

14 L. Ellinwood, ed., *Musica Hermanni Contracti* (Rochester, NY: Eastman School of Music, 1936) (ed. and Eng. trans.).

15 J. Smits van Waesberghe, ed., *Johannes Afflighemensis: De musica cum tonario*, CSM 1 (Rome: American Institute of Musicology, 1950); Palisca, ed., *Hucbald, Guido, and John on Music*, pp. 101–87.

16 W_1 = Wolfenbüttel, Herzog August Bibliothek 628; F = Florence, Biblioteca Medicea Laurenziana, Plut. 29.1; W_2 = Wolfenbüttel, Herzog August Bibliothek 1099. Edward H. Roesner has undertaken the supervision of an edition of the Notre Dame repertory: *Le Magnus liber organi de Notre-Dame de Paris* (Monaco: Éditions de l'Oiseau-Lyre, ca1993–).

17 *De plana musica* exists in four versions: no. 1 is in G. Reaney, A. Gilles and J. Maillard, eds., *Philippi de Vitriaco Ars nova*, CSM 8 ([Rome]: American Institute of Musicology, 1964), pp. 13–21; English translation in L. Plantinga, 'Philippe de Vitry's Ars Nova: A Translation', *Journal of Music Theory* 5 (1961), pp. 204–23; all four are in C. Meyer, ed., *Musica plana Johannis de Garlandia* (Baden-Baden: V. Koerner, 1998), pp. 3–62. *De mensurabili musica* is in Charles Edmond Henri de Coussemaker, *Scriptorum de musica medii aevi novam seriem a Gerbertina alteram*, 4 vols. (Paris: Durand, 1864–76; repr. Hildesheim: Olms, 1963) (henceforth CoussemakerS), vol. I, pp. 175–82, and E. Reimer, ed., *Johannes de Garlandia: De mensurabili musica* (Wiesbaden: F. Steiner, 1972); Eng. trans. S. Birnbaum, *Johannes de Garlandia: Concerning Measured Music (De mensurabili musica)*, Colorado College Music Press Translations 9 (Colorado Springs: Colorado College Music Press, 1978); partial English translation in StrunkSR2, pp. 223–6.

18 See summary by R. A. Baltzer, 'Johannes de Garlandia,' in *Grove Music Online*.

19 The tendency to propose modal schemata that reached beyond practice continued into the third quarter of the century: Magister Lambertus, writing circa 1265–75, advocated a

system of nine rhythmic modes instead of six. See Lambertus, *Tractatus de musica*, ed. in CoussemakerS, vol. I, pp. 251–81; ed. in CSM, forthcoming.

20 1=single note; 2=2-note ligature; 3=3-note ligature.

21 G. Reaney and A. Gilles, eds., *Franconis de Colonia Ars cantus mensurabilis*, CSM 18 ([Rome]: American Institute of Musicology, 1974); StrunkSR1, pp. 139–59. SR2, pp. 226–45.

22 Montpellier, Bibliothèque Inter-Universitaire, Section Médecine, H.196: H. Tischler, ed., *The Montpellier Codex*, 4 vols. (Madison, WI: A. R. Editions, 1978–85); Bamberg, Staatsbibliothek, lit.115 (formerly Ed.IV.6): *Compositions of the Bamberg Manuscript: Bamberg Staatsbibliothek, lit. 115 (olim Ed.IV, 6)*, ed. Gordon A. Anderson, Corpus mensurabilis musicae (henceforth CMM) 75. (Neuhausen-stuttgart: American Institute of Musicology, 1977); Paris, Bibliothèque Nationale de France, n.a.fr.13521: *Motets of the manuscript La Clayette: Paris, Bibliothèque nationale, nouv. acq. f. fr. 13521*, ed. Gordon A. Anderson, CMM 68 ([Rome]: American Institute of Musicology, 1975); Burgos, Monasterio de Las Huelgas: *The Las Huelgas manuscript: Burgos, Monasterio de Las Huelgas*, ed. Gordon A. Anderson, CMM 79 (Neuhausen-Stuttgart: American Institute of Musicology, 1982).

23 J. Yudkin, ed., *De musica mensurata: The Anonymous of St Emmeram* (Bloomington: Indiana University Press, 1990) (complete critical edn, trans., and commentary).

24 Petrus is likely to have studied at the University of Paris as a member of the Picard nation, earning there the title Magister. No major treatise by Petrus survives, but he is cited by later theorists for his innovations. See E. H. Sanders and P. M. Lefferts, 'Petrus de Cruce', *Grove Music Online*.

25 CoussemakerS, i, pp. 1–155; S. M. Cserba, ed., *Der Musiktraktat des Hieronymus Moravia OP* (Regensburg: Friedrich Pustet, 1935).

26 Reaney et al., eds., *Philippi de Vitriaco Ars nova*, CSM 8; Plantinga, 'Philippe de Vitry's Ars Nova'.

27 U. Michels, ed., *Johannis de Muris Notitia artis musicae et Compendium musicae practicae: Tractatus de musica*, CSM 17 ([Rome]: American Institute of Musicology, 1972), pp. 47–107; partial English translation in StrunkSR1, pp. 172–9, SR2, pp. 261–9.

28 F. F. Hammond, ed., *Walteri Odington: Summa de speculatione musicae*, CSM 14 ([Rome]: American Institute of Musicology, 1970); J. A. Huff, trans., *De speculatione musicae.*

Part VI, Musicological Studies and Documents 31 ([Rome]: American Institute of Musicology, 1973).

29 R. Bragard, ed., *Speculum musice*, CSM 3 [Rome]: American Institute of Musicology, 1955–73); partial English translation in StrunkSR1, pp. 180–90, SR2, pp. 269–78.

30 E. Rohloff, ed., *Die Quellenhandschriften zum Musiktraktat des Johannes de Grocheio* (Leipzig: Deutscher Verlag für Musik,1972); A. Seay, ed. and trans., *Johannes de Grocheo: Concerning Music (De musica)*, Colorado College Music Press Translations 1 (Colorado Springs: Colorado College Music Press, 1967; 2nd edn 1973).

31 C. Page, 'Johannes de Grocheio', *Grove Music Online*.

32 *Lucidarium in arte musice plane*: Gerbert, *Scriptores*, vol. III, pp. 64–121; J. Herlinger, ed. and trans., *The Lucidarium of Marchetto of Padua* (University of Chicago Press, 1985). *Pomerium in arte musice mensurate*: Gerbert, *Scriptores*, vol. III, pp. 121–87; J. Vecchi, *Marcheti de Padua Pomerium*, CSM 6 ([Rome]: American Institute of Musicology, 1961); partial English trans. in StrunkSR1, pp. 160–71, SR2, pp. 251–61.

33 Vatican City, Biblioteca Apostolica Vaticana, Rossi 215 [Rs; R; VR] and Ostiglia, Opera Pia G. Greggiati, Biblioteca Musicale, s.s. ('Ostiglia fragment'): two fragments belonging to one source (dated mid to late fourteenth century); editions: Nino Pirrotta, ed., *The Music of Fourteenth-Century Italy*, CMM 8/2 (Amsterdam: American Institute of Musicology, 1960), pp. 15–46 (excluding OS); G. Vecchi, ed., *Il canzoniere musicale del codice Vaticano Rossi 215*, Monumenta Lyrica Medii Aevi Italica 3/2 (Università degli Studi di Bologna, 1966) (facs. of the two sources together); V. Guaitamacchi, ed., *Madrigali trecenteschi del frammento 'Greggiati' di Ostiglia* (Bologna: [s.n.], 1970); *Italian Secular Music: Anonymous Madrigals and Cacce and the Works of Niccolò da Perugia*, ed. W. Thomas Marrocco, Polyphonic Music of the Fourteenth Century (henceforth PMFC) 8 (Monaco: Éditions de l'Oiseau-Lyre, 1972); *Italian Secular Music: Bartolino da Padova, Egidius de Francia, Guilielmus de Francia, Don Paolo da Firenze*, ed. W. Thomas Marrocco, PMFC 9 (Monaco: Éditions de l'Oiseau-Lyre,1975); N. Pirrotta, ed., *Il codice Rossi 215* (Lucca: Libreria Musicale Italiana, 1992) (facs. with introduction). Florence, Biblioteca Nazionale Centrale, Panciatichiano 26 (main corpus dated 1380–90 by Fischer and Campagnolo, ca1400 by Pirrotta and Nádas); editions: *The works of Francesco Landini*, ed. Leo

Schrade, PMFC 4 (Monaco: Éditions de l'Oiseau-Lyre, 1958), uses *I-Fn* 26 as primary source; F. A. Gallo, ed., *Il Codice musicale Panciatichi 26 della Biblioteca Nazionale di Firenze* (Florence: Olschki, 1981) (facs. with introduction).

34 *Tractatus figurarum* (or *Tractatus de diversis figuris*): CoussemakerS, III, pp. 118–24; P. E. Schreur, ed., *Tractatus figurarum: Treatise on Noteshapes* (Lincoln: University of Nebraska Press, 1989).

35 CoussemakerS, III, pp. 124–8; partial critical edn in D. Leech-Wilkinson, *Compositional Techniques in the Four-Part Isorhythmic Motets of Philippe de Vitry and His Contemporaries*, 2 vols. (New York: Garland, 1989), vol. I, pp. 18–20.

36 Chantilly, Musée Condé, 564 (formerly 1047); editions: *The Motets of the Manuscripts Chantilly, Musée Condé, 564 (olim 1047) and Modena, Biblioteca Estense, α. M. 5, 24 (olim lat. 568)*, ed. Ursula Günther, CMM 39 ([Rome]: American Institute of Musicology, 1965) (all motets); *Motets of French Provenance*, ed. Frank Ll. Harrison, French texts edited by Elizabeth Rutson, notes on the Latin texts by A. G. Rigg, PMFC 5 (Monaco, Éditions de l'Oiseau-Lyre, 1968) (all motets); *French Secular Compositions of the Fourteenth Century*, ed. Willi Apel, edition of the literary texts by Samuel N. Rosenberg, 3 vols., CMM 53 ([Rome]: American Institute of Musicology, 1970–2) (all chansons of basic corpus); *Early Fifteenth-Century Music*, ed. Gilbert Reaney, CMM 11 ([Rome]: American Institute of Musicology, 1955–[83]), part 1 (1955) (pieces by Cordier); part 2/2 (1959) (songs by Hasprois and Johannes Haucourt); *Aus der Frühzeit der Motette*, ed. Friedrich Gennrich, Musikwissenschaftliche Studien-Bibliothek 22–3 (Frankfurt: Langen, 1963) (16 facs. pages); *Manuscript Chantilly, Musée Condé 564*, ed. Gordon K. Greene, literary texts by Terence Scully, PMFC 18–19 (Monaco: Éditions de l'Oiseau-Lyre, 1981–2) (all chansons); *Virelais*, ed. Gordon K. Greene, literary texts by Terence Scully, PMFC 21 (Monaco: Éditions de l'Oiseau-Lyre, 1987) (appendix with new four-voice version of no. 100); *Codex Chantilly: Bibliothèque du château de Chantilly, Ms. 564: Fac-similé*, ed. Yolanda Plumley and Anne Stone (Turnhout: Brepols, 2008). Modena, Biblioteca Estense e Universitaria, α.M.5.24 (olim lat.568); editions: F. Fano, ed., *La cappella musicale del Duomo di Milano: le origini e il primo maestro di cappella, Matteo da Perugia* (Milan: Ricordi, 1956) (all mass movts and most songs by Matteo, incl. some doubtful works and facs.); CMM 11/2

(two songs by Hasprois); CMM 39 (nos. 3, 11, 13); N. S. Josephson, AMw, xxvii (1970), 41–58, esp. 56–8 (no. 30); CMM 53 (1970–72) (all French and Latin songs); *French Secular Music Ballads and Canons*, ed. Gordon K. Greene, literary texts by Terence Scully, PMFC 20 (Monaco: Éditions de l'Oiseau-Lyre, 1982) (23 ballades, 1 canon); *The Works of Johannes Ciconia*, ed. Margaret Bent and Anne Hallmark, Latin texts edited by M. J. Connolly, PMFC 24 (Monaco: Éditions de l'Oiseau-Lyre, 1985) (nos. 45–6); PMFC 24 (1987) (17 virelais); *Rondeaux and Miscellaneous Pieces*, ed. Gordon K. Greene, literary texts by Terence Scully, PMFC 22 (Monaco: Éditions de l'Oiseau-Lyre, 1989) (12 rondeaux).

37 *Liber de natura et proprietate tonorum*; A. Seay, ed., *Opera theoretica Johannis Tinctoris*, 2 vols. in 3, CSM 22 ([Rome]: American Institute of Musicology, 1975–8); A. Seay, trans., *Concerning the Nature and Propriety of Tones. De natura et proprietate tonorum* (Colorado Springs: Colorado College Music Press, 1967, 2nd edn 1976).

38 D. Pesce, 'A Case for Coherent Pitch Organization in the Thirteenth-Century Double Motet', *Music Analysis* 9/3 (October 1990), pp. 287–318.

39 S. Fuller, 'Modal Tenors and Tonal Orientation in Motets of Guillaume de Machaut', *Current Musicology*, 45–7 (1990), pp. 199–245 and S. Fuller, 'Tendencies and Resolutions: The Directed Progression in Ars Nova Music', *Journal of Music Theory* 36 (1992), pp. 229–58.

40 Despite the infrequent usage of these expressions by medieval theorists, modern scholars use them because they encapsulate so well the reasons for ficta.

41 A major study that summarizes and elaborates the points just made is K. Berger, *Musica ficta: Theories of Accidental Inflections in Vocal Polyphony from Marchetto da Padova to Gioseffo Zarlino* (Cambridge University Press, 1987).

42 A summary of currently held viewpoints regarding application of ficta is given by M. Bent in 'Music ficta' in *Grove Music Online*.

43 O. Ellsworth, ed., *The Berkeley Manuscript: University of California Music Library, ms. 744 (olim Phillipps 4450)* (Lincoln: University of Nebraska Press, ca1984) (critical text and trans.).

44 An overview of solmization is found in A. Hughes, 'Solmisation' in *Grove Music Online*. Bent in 'Musica ficta', section 1.i, discusses musica ficta as having its basis in solmization.

17 Music manuscripts

1 'Nisi enim ab homine memoria teneantur soni, pereunt, quia scribi non possunt'. W. M. Lindsay, ed. *Isidori hispalensis episcopi. Etymologiarum sive Originum libri xx* (Oxford: Clarendon Press, 1911), lib. III, xv, p. 2.

2 Manuscripts are referred to by their sigla throughout this chapter. A complete list of manuscripts and their sigla is given on pages xxii–xxxii.

3 N. Pirrotta, 'The Oral and Written Traditions of Music', in his *Music and Culture in Italy from the Middle Ages to the Baroque: A Collection of Essays* (Cambridge, MA: Harvard University Press, 1984), pp. 72–9, at p. 72.

4 P. Stallybrass in the first of his 2006 Rosenbach Lectures in Bibliography, 'Writing after Printing, or How Printing Invents Manuscript', University of Pennsylvania, forthcoming with University of Pennsylvania Press.

5 D. McKenzie, *The Panizzi Lectures 1985: Bibliography and the Sociology of Texts* (London: British Library, 1986), p. 4.

6 R. McKitterick, *The Carolingians and the Written Word* (Cambridge University Press, 1989), p. 139.

7 Richard of Bury, *The Love of Books: The Philobiblon of Richard of Bury*, trans. E. C. Thomas, ed. with a foreword by Michael Maclagan (Oxford: Blackwell, 1960), p. 56.

8 R. Rouse and M. Rouse, *Manuscripts and Their Makers: Commercial Book Producers in Medieval Paris, 1200–1500*, 2 vols. (Turnhout: Harvey Miller Publishers, 2000).

9 The terminology associated with books is notoriously complex and often inconsistent. Here, I follow the oldest (antique) definition of *liber*, which includes both codex and book roll, but which could also be used in the sense of 'opus', or to mark sections of a large work. For a helpful and comprehensive account of the terminology of manuscripts, see B. Bischoff, *Latin Palaeography: Antiquity and the Middle Ages*, trans. D. Ó Cróinín and D. Ganz (Cambridge University Press, 1991). My thanks to Shane Butler for help on the classical context for terminology associated with the book.

10 A helpful account of the process of making a book, from parchment preparation through to binding, occurs in C. de Hamel, *Medieval Craftsmen: Scribes and Illuminators* (London: British Museum Press, 1992), quoting from p. 18.

11 P. Siffrin, 'Eine Schwesterhandschrift des Graduale von Monza', *Ephemerides liturgicae* 64 (1950), pp. 53–80.

12 For an example of the significant role sheets and libelli can play in the transmission of polyphony, see A. Wathey, 'The Production of Books of Liturgical Polyphony', in J. Griffiths and D. Pearsall, eds., *Book Production and Publishing in Britain, 1375–1475* (Cambridge University Press, 1989), pp. 143–61, esp. 146–8.

13 W. Arlt and S. Rankin, eds., *Stiftsbibliothek Sankt Gallen Codices 484 & 381* (Winterthur: Amadeus, 1996).

14 GB-BER select roll 55 is described in A. Wathey, ed., *Manuscripts of Polyphonic Music: The British Isles, 1100–1400. Supplement to RISM B IV 1–2* (Munich: G. Henle, 1993), pp. 8–10.

15 T. Forrest Kelly, *The Exultet in Southern Italy* (Oxford University Press, 1996).

16 J. Haines, *Eight Centuries of the Troubadours and Trouvères: The Changing Identity of Medieval Music* (Cambridge University Press, 2004), pp. 34–5, 104–6, 299–304.

17 E. Dillon, *Medieval Music-Making and the Roman de Fauvel* (Cambridge University Press, 2002), pp. 113–19.

18 The *compilatio–ordinatio* distinction articulated by Bonaventure is now commonplace among medievalists, in part owing to the seminal article of M. Parkes, 'The Influence of the Concepts of *Ordinatio* and *Compilatio* on the Development of the Book', in J. Alexander and M. Gibson, eds., *Medieval Learning and Literature: Essays Presented to Richard William Hunt* (Oxford: Clarendon Press, 1976), pp. 115–41. A recent example of how the differentiation has been applied by musicologists is M. Everist, 'Le fonti della musica polifonica, ca. 1170–1330', in C. Fiore, ed., *Il Libro di musica: per una storia materiale delle fonti musicali in Europa* (Palermo: L'Epos, 2004), pp. 43–64.

19 For sample plates of Aquitanian notation, see *Pal. Mus.* 1st ser., ii., plates 83–103.

20 S. Rankin, 'Winchester Polyphony: The Early Theory and Practice of Organum', in S. Rankin and D. Hiley, eds., *Music in the Medieval English Liturgy* (Oxford University Press, 1993), pp. 55–99.

21 H. van der Werf, 'Early Western Polyphony', in T. Knighton and D. Fallows, eds., *Companion to Medieval and Renaissance Music* (London: Dent, 1992), p. 107.

22 M. Everist, *Polyphonic Music in Thirteenth-Century France: Aspects of Sources and Distribution* (New York: Garland, 1989), p. 170.

23 Two excellent introductions to troubadour manuscripts are W. Burgwinkle, 'The

Chansonniers as Books', in S. Gaunt and S. Kay, eds., *The Troubadours: An Introduction* (Cambridge University Press, 1999), pp. 246–62, and W. Paden, 'Manuscripts', in F. Akehurst and J. Butler, eds., *A Handbook of the Troubadours* (Berkeley: University of California Press, 1995), pp. 307–33.

24 See M. O'Neill, *Courtly Love Songs of Medieval France: Transmission and Style in the Trouvère Repertoire* (Oxford University Press, 2006), esp. pp. 13–52 which gives a comprehensive overview of the sources.

25 Amelia E. Van Vleck, *Memory and Re-Creation in Troubadour Lyric* (Berkeley: University of California Press, 1991), pp. 56–68.

26 Burgwinkle, 'The *Chansonniers*', p. 247.

27 For an excellent account of these paratextual components, see O. Holmes, *Assembling the Lyric Self: Authorship from Troubadour Song to Italian Poetry Book* (Minneapolis: University of Minnesota Press, 2000).

28 See K. Kügle, *The Manuscript Ivrea, Biblioteca Capitolare 115: Studies in the Transmission and Composition of Ars Nova Polyphony* (Ottawa: Institute of Mediaeval Music, 1997) and A. Tomasello, 'Scribal Design in the compilation of Ivrea Ms. 115', *Musica Disciplina* 42 (1988), pp. 73–100.

29 One example of such confusion occurs in the layout of Machaut's *De toute flors* on folio 99v.

30 Wathey, B IV 1–2 Suppl. I.

31 See M. Bent, 'The Progeny of Old Hall: More Leaves from a Royal English Choirbook', *Gordon Athol Anderson (1929–1981): In Memoriam von seinen Studenten, Freunden und Kollegen*, Musicological Studies 49, 2 vols. (Henryville: Institute of Mediaeval Music, 1984), vol. I, pp. 1–54.

32 M. Bent, 'A Contemporary Perception of Early Fifteenth-Century Style: Bologna Q 15 as a Document of Scribal Editorial Initiative', *Musica Disciplina* 41 (1987), pp. 183–201.

33 A. Wathey, 'Lost Books of Polyphony in Medieval England: A List to 1500', *Royal Musical Association: Research Chronicle* 21 (1988), pp. 1–19.

34 See the Introduction to E. Roesner, F. Avril and N. Freeman Regalado, eds., *Le Roman de Fauvel in the Edition of Mesire Chaillou de Pesstain: A Reproduction in Facsimile of the Complete Manuscript, Paris, Bibliothèque Nationale, fonds français 146* (New York: Broude Brothers, 1990), pp. 4–5.

35 M. Meneghetti, 'Il Manuscritto fr. 146 della Bibliothèque Nationale di Parigi, Tommaso di Saluzzo e gli affreschi della Manta', *Romania* 110 (1989), pp. 511–35.

36 P. Jeffery, 'Notre Dame Polyphony in the Library of Pope Boniface VIII', *Journal of the American Musicological Society* 32 (1979), pp. 118–24, and R. A. Baltzer, 'Notre Dame Manuscripts and Their Owners: Lost and Found', *Journal of Musicology* 5 (1987), pp. 380–99.

37 Baltzer, 'Notre Dame Manuscripts', p. 383.

38 Ibid., 392–5, quoting from p. 394.

39 C. Wright, *Music and Ceremony at Notre Dame of Paris 500–1500* (Cambridge University Press, 1989), pp. 329–35.

40 A. Taylor, *Textual Situations: Three Medieval Manuscripts and Their Readers* (Philadelphia: University of Pennsylvania Press, 2002), p. 197.

41 http://sunsite.berkeley.edu/Scriptorium.

42 www.diamm.ac.uk. See, too, A. Wathey, M. Bent and J. Craig-McFeely, 'The Art of Virtual Restoration: Creating the Digital Image Archive of Medieval Music (DIAMM)', in *The Virtual Score: Representation, Retrieval, Restoration*, special volume of *Computing in Musicology* 12 (1999–2000), pp. 227–40.

43 B. Sullivan, 'The Unwritable Sound of Music: The Origins and Implications of Isidore's Memorial Metaphor', *Viator* 30 (1999), pp. 1–13.

18 The geography of medieval music

1 For the missal, see S. Schein, *Fideles Crucis: The Papacy, the West and the Recovery of the Holy Land 1274–1314* (Oxford: Clarendon Press, 1991), p. 125, and for the psalmody vanished from the Holy Land, see C. Kohler, 'Traité du recouvrement de la Terre Sainte adressé, vers l'an 1295, à Philippe le Bel par Galvano de Levanto, médécin génois', *Revue de l'orient latin*, 6 (1898), pp. 367–8: 'ubi cultus Jhesu Christi deberet et psalmodia, ibi fit a Saracenis abominabilis melodia'. Foundational works for the concerns of this chapter include J. L. Abu-Lughod, *Before European Hegemony: The World System AD 1250–1350* (Oxford University Press, 1989); R. Bartlett, *The Making of Europe: Conquest, Colonization and Cultural Change 950–1350* (Princeton University Press, 1993); M. McCormick, *Origins of the European Economy: Communications and Commerce AD 300–900* (Cambridge University Press, 2001), and C. Wickham, *Framing the Early Middle Ages: Europe and the Mediterranean 400–800* (Oxford University Press, 2005).

2 For the fore-mass psalm in Tertullian, see *De anima*, 9:4. James McKinnon (*The Temple, the Church Fathers and Early-Western Chant* [Aldershot: Variorum, 1998], Essay IX) makes an admirably balanced, but in my view unsuccessful, attempt to limit the implications

of Tertullian's evidence. For a survey of Christian Africa, see C. Briand-Ponsart and C. Hugoniot, *L'Afrique romaine* (Paris: Armand Colin, 2005), and for the ecology of the littoral where it lay, W. M. Adams, A. S. Goudie and A. R. Orme, eds., *The Physical Geography of Africa* (Oxford University Press, 1996), pp. 169–70 and 307–25.

3 On culture and territory in Visigothic Spain, see C. Martin, *La géographie du pouvoir dans l'Espagne visigothique* (Lille: Presses Universitaires du Septentrion, 2003), and Wickham, *Framing the Early Middle Ages, passim*. Most of the crucial documents for the liturgical reform of the 600s are conciliar and edited (with Spanish translation) in J. Vives, ed., *Concilios Visigóticos y Hispano-romanos* (Barcelona: Consejo Superior de Investigaciones Científicas, 1963).

4 For Olbert, see Sigebert of Gembloux, *Gesta abbatum Gemblacensium*, in *Patrologiae cursus completus, Series Latina*, ed. J.-P. Migne, 221 vols. (Paris: Garnier, 1844–64), vol. CLX, p. 25.

5 Spanish developments from the eleventh century on, including relations with the north, are neatly summarized and discussed in A. MacKay, *Spain in the Middle Ages: From Frontier to Empire 1000–1500* (London: Macmillan, 1977). The Frankish-Roman liturgy began to make headway in Spain as Alfonso VI of Castile and León strove to expand and repopulate the territories of his kingdom. Gregory VII, in his letters to the king, presented a sweeping vision of Spain's Christian history from apostolic times, a profound expression of Gregory's own convictions but also very well calculated to accord with the more fervent and long-term aspirations of the king. See H. E. J. Cowdrey, *The Register of Pope Gregory VII, 1073–1085: An English Translation* (Oxford University Press, 2002), pp. 67–9, a letter of 19 March 1074, and for the king, A. Gambra, *Alfonso VI: Cancillería, Curia e Imperio*, 2 vols. (León: Cajade Ahorros y Monte de Piedad, 1997–8), especially the king's letter of July 1077 (vol. II, document 47). See also R. Walker, *Views of Transition: Liturgy and Illumination in Medieval Spain* (London: British Library and University of Toronto Press, 1998).

6 For the Parisian milieu, A. Murray, *Reason and Society in the Middle Ages* (Oxford: Clarendon Press, 1985) and J. Baldwin, *Masters, Princes, and Merchants: The Social Views of Peter the Chanter and His Circle*, 2 vols. (Princeton University Press, 1970), have yet to be bettered. On the book trade, R. Rouse and M. Rouse, *Manuscripts and Their Makers: Commercial Book Production in Medieval Paris, 1200–1500* (Turnhout: Harvey Miller Publishers, 2000) also remains unsurpassed.

7 For an example of work by a *modernus* from St Emmeram, see D. Hiley, ed., *Historia Sancti Emmerammi Arnoldi Vohburgensis circa 1030* (Ottawa: Institute of Mediaeval Music, 1996).

8 The fundamental study in English on Hungary is now N. Berend, *At the Gate of Christendom: Jews, Muslims and 'Pagans' in Medieval Hungary c.1000–c.1300* (Cambridge University Press, 2001). For some of the longer-term musical consequences of Hungary's westward leanings (still evident in the title of the article about to be cited) see J. Szendrei, 'The Introduction of Staff Notation into Middle Europe', *Studia Musicologica* 28 (1986), pp. 303–319. The primary sources for Livonia are available as J. A. Brundage, *The Chronicle of Henry of Livonia* (Madison: Columbia University Press, 1961) and J. C. Smith and W. C. Urban, *The Livonian Rhymed Chronicle* (Bloomington: Indiana University Press, 1977).

9 For courtliness in circuit II the outstanding studies are both by C. Stephen Jaeger: *The Origins of Courtliness: Civilizing Trends and the Formation of Courtly Ideals 939–1210* (Pennsylvania University Press, 1985) and Stephen Jaeger, *Scholars and Courtiers: Intellectuals and Society in the Medieval West* (Aldershot: Ashgate, 2002).

10 The ninth-century move to the land route is discussed in McCormick, *Origins of the European Economy*, 79.

11 For Stephen IX and chant, there is full discussion and context in T. F. Kelly, *The Beneventan Chant* (Cambridge University Press, 1989), p. 39, *et passim*.

12 For Guido's papal visit, see D. Pesce, ed., *Guido d'Arezzo's 'Regulae Rhythmicae', 'Prologus in Antiphonarium' and 'Epistola ad Michaelem': A Critical Text and Translation* (Ottawa: Institute of Mediaeval Music, 1999), pp. 448–55. See also the essays in A. Rusconi, ed., *Guido d'Arezzo monaco pomposiano: atti dei convegni di studio, Codigoro (Ferrara), Abbazia di Pomposa, 3 ottobre 1997* (Florence: Olschk: 2000).

13 Salimbene's material is readily accessible in J. L. Baird, G. Baglivi and J. R. Kane, *The Chronicle of Salimbene de Adam* (Binghamton: Center for Medieval and Early Renaissance Studies, University Center at Binghamton, 1986), pp. 172–5.

14 For Raimon Vidal, see J. H. Marshall, *The 'Razos de Trobar' and Associated Texts* (Oxford University Press, 1972), pp. 6 and 7. For Dante's comments, S. Botterill, *Dante: De Vulgari Eloquentia* (Cambridge University Press, 1996), pp. 22–3, gives Latin text and translation.

15 The standard edition of the *Leys* is still M. Gatien-Arnoult, *Monumens de la littérature romane*, 3 vols. (Toulouse: J.-B. Paya, 1841–3), I, pp. 342 and 350.

16 R. Strohm, *The Rise of European Music 1380–1500* (Cambridge University Press, 1993).

19 Reception

1 For a fully documented survey of all aspects of medieval chant, see D. Hiley, *Western Plainchant: A Handbook* (Oxford: Clarendon Press, 1993).

2 Ibid., p. 364.

3 See ibid., pp. 361–73 and 520–1 for a bibliography.

4 See ibid., pp. 503–18 for details and a bibliography.

5 An image in the Gradual of Monza (*I-MZ* CIX) from the mid ninth century probably conveys the same intent, but it is not clear that Gregory is dictating music. An oft-reproduced Gregory leaf by the Master of the Registrum Gregorii, an Ottonian illuminator (984), depicts Gregory dictating theological tracts.

6 On anonymous editors of printed editions, see T. Karp, *An Introduction to the Post-Tridentine Mass Proper*, 2 vols. (Middleton, WI: American Institute of Musicology, 2005, vol. I, p. 3.

7 F.-A. Gevaert, *Les origines du chant liturgique de l'église latine: étude d'histoire musicale* (Ghent: Hoste, 1890; repr. Hildesheim and New York: Olms, 1971); and F.-A. Gevaert, *La melopée antique dans le chant de l'église latine* (Ghent: Hoste, 1895; repr. Osnabrück: Zeller, 1967), pp. ix–xxxvi. Gevaert supported a thesis that put the composition of the chant in the Roman *schola cantorum* especially under Sergius I (r. 687–701), a project brought to completion under Gregory II (r. 715–31). J. McKinnon fleshed out Gevaert's thesis in *The Advent Project: The Later-Seventh-Century Creation of the Roman Mass Proper* (Berkeley and Los Angeles: University of California Press, 2000).

8 F. X. Haberl, 'Die römische "schola cantorum" und die päpstlichen Kapellsänger bis zur Mitte des 16. Jahrhunderts', *Vierteljahrsschrift für Musikwissenschaft* 3 (1887), p. 199 n. 1. Dom Mocquereau independently discovered the Old Roman graduals in 1890; see Dom P. Combe, *The Restoration of Gregorian Chant: Solesmes and the Vatican Edition*, trans. T. N. Marier and W. Skinner (Washington, DC: Catholic University of America Press, 2003), pp. 132–3.

9 See, for example, C. Burney, *A General History of Music from the Earliest Ages to the Present* (4 vols., London, 1776–89; 2nd edn with notes by F. Mercer, 2 vols., New York: Harcourt Brace, 1935; repr. New York: Dover, 1957), vol. I, p. 430. Gevaert also assumed notation, though he had removed the composition of the chant to the late seventh century.

10 H. Hucke, 'Die Einführung des gregorianischen Gesangs im Frankenreich', *Römische Quartalschrift* 49 (1954), pp. 172–87, and H. Hucke, 'Gregorianischer Gesang in altrömischer und fränkischer Überlieferung', *Archiv für Musikwissenschaft* 12 (1955), pp. 74–87.

11 McKinnon (*The Advent Project*, p. 377) proposed that what was known as Gregorian chant is actually very close to what the Roman singers came with, because there was not much time to alter it, but Hiley (*Western Plainchant*, p. 549) noted that other Old Italian chant repertories (Ambrosian and Beneventan) share the essentially florid profile seen in what we know as Old Roman chant.

12 L. Treitler, 'Homer and Gregory: The Transmission of Epic Poetry and Plainchant', *Musical Quarterly* 60 (1974), pp. 333–72. A. M. Busse Berger, *Medieval Music and the Art of Memory* (Berkeley, Los Angeles and London: University of California Press, 2005), has recently broadened the study of oral practice and memory in medieval music, including aspects of polyphony.

13 K. Levy, 'Charlemagne's Archetype of Gregorian Chant', *Journal of the American Musicological Society* 40 (1987), pp. 1–30, and K. Levy, 'On the Origin of Neumes', *Early Music History* 7 (1987), pp. 59–90. Both articles are reprinted in K. Levy, *Gregorian Chant and the Carolingians* (Princeton University Press, 1998), pp. 82–108 and 109–40.

14 Hiley, *Western Plainchant*, pp. 520–1.

15 Ibid., pp. 608–13.

16 For example, there is no mention of Hildegard in G. Reese, *Music in the Middle Ages, with an Introduction on the Music of Ancient Times* (New York: Norton, 1940); or in R. H. Hoppin, *Medieval Music* (New York: Norton, 1978).

17 O. Strunk, ed., *Source Readings in Music History*. rev. edn L. Treitler (New York: Norton, 1998), p. 375.

18 Karp, *An Introduction*, vol. I, 202.

19 J. Pasler outlines the political aspect in her review of Bergeron (see note 20) in *Journal of the American Musicological Society* 52 (1999), pp. 370–83.

20 For an illustration of Lambillotte's facsimile compared with that in *Paléographie musicale*, see K. Bergeron, *Decadent Enchantments: The*

Revival of Gregorian Chant at Solesmes (Berkeley: University of California Press, 1998), pp. 78–9.

21 See facsimiles and discussion in P. M. Pfaff, 'Die liturgische Einstimmigkeit in ihren Editionen nach 1600', in T. G. Georgiades, ed., *Musikalische Edition im Wandel des historischen Bewusstseins* (Kassel, Basel, Tours and London: Bärenreiter, 1971), pp. 50–61, and Bergeron, *Decadent Enchantments*, pp. 25–62.

22 Combe, *The Restoration of Gregorian Chant*, p. 106.

23 R. F. Hayburn, *Papal Legislation on Sacred Music 95 AD to 1977 AD* (Collegeville, MN: Liturgical Press, 1979), p. 224.

24 P. Jeffery, 'The New Vatican Chant Editions', *Notes*, 2nd ser., 47/4 (1991), pp. 1039–63.

25 On the term *antiquité françoise*, see J. Haines, *Eight Centuries of Troubadours and Trouvères: The Changing Identity of Medieval Music*, Musical Performance and Reception (Cambridge University Press, 2004), pp. 49–52. Haines covers all aspects of the reception of the art of the troubadours and trouvères to the present day. See also the historiographical overview in M. L. Switten, *Music and Poetry in the Middle Ages: A Guide to Research on French and Occitan Song, 1100–1400*, Garland Medieval Bibliographies 19 (New York and London: Garland, 1995), pp. 1–59.

26 L. Gossman, *Medievalism and the Ideologies of the Enlightenment: The World and Work of La Curne de Sainte-Palaye* (Baltimore, MD: Johns Hopkins University Press, 1968).

27 Burney, *A General History*, vol. I, pp. 574–7; see Haines, *Eight Centuries of Troubadours and Trouvères*, pp. 89–91 and 118–19.

28 J. Hawkins, *A General History of the Science and Practice of Music* (London: Novello 1776; 2nd edn, London: Novello, 1853), vol. I, p. 186.

29 E. Aubrey, 'Medieval Melodies in the Hands of Bibliophiles of the *Ancien Régime*', in Barbara Haggh, ed., *Essays on Music and Culture in Honor of Herbert Kellman*, Collection Epitome musicale 8 (Paris: Minerve, 2001), pp. 17–34; and Haines, *Eight Centuries of Troubadours and Trouvères*, pp. 120–5.

30 On eighteenth-century editions, see Haines, *Eight Centuries of Troubadours and Trouvères*, pp. 108–18.

31 Ibid., pp. 125–41.

32 On arrangements of troubadour and trouvère song from the eighteenth century to the present, see Haines, *Eight Centuries of Troubadours and Trouvères*, *passim*; concerning techniques of a practising musician in the late twentieth century, see T. Binkley, 'Zur Aufführungspraxis der einstimmigen Musik des Mittelalters – Ein Werkstattbericht', *Basler Jahrbuch für historische Musikpraxis* 1 (1977), pp. 19–76.

33 A. Kreutziger-Herr, *Ein Traum vom Mittelalter: Die Wiederentdeckung mittelalterlicher Musik in der Neuzeit* (Cologne, Weimar and Vienna: Böhlau, 2003), pp. 105–10.

34 Ibid., p. 55 n. 91.

35 Ibid., pp. 19–41 and 66–77.

36 E. Emery, 'The "Truth" about the Middle Ages: *La Revue des Deux Mondes* and Late Nineteenth-Century French Medievalism', in C. A. Simmons, ed., *Medievalism and the Quest for the 'Real' Middle Ages* (London and Portland, OR: Cass, 2001), p. 109.

37 Haines, *Eight Centuries of Troubadours and Trouvères*, pp. 108–25.

38 The edition forms an appendix to F. Michel, *Chansons du Châtelain de Coucy: Revues sur tous les manuscrits* (Paris: Crapelet, 1830).

39 Coussemaker, *L'art harmonique aux XIIe et XIIIe siècles* (Paris: Durand, 1865; repr. Hildesheim: Olms, 1964), pp. 180–208. Haines, *Eight Centuries of Troubadours and Trouvères*, pp. 174–8, includes a list of Coussemaker's thirteen *trouvères-harmonistes* with discussion.

40 H. Riemann, *Handbuch der Musikgeschichte*, vol. I, part 2, *Die Musik des Mittelalters (bis 1450)*, 2nd edn (Leipzig: Breitkopf & Härtel, 1920), pp. 224–93.

41 More details on the application of the rhythmic modes to songs are found in G. Reese, *Music in the Middle Ages*, pp. 206–10.

42 Haines, *Eight Centuries of Troubadours and Trouvères*, pp. 210–34 and the bibliography cited there.

43 J. Handschin, 'Die Modaltheorie und Carl Appels Ausgabe der Gesaenge von Bernart de Ventadorn', *Medium Ævum* 4 (1955), 69–82, discussed in Reese, *Music in the Middle Ages*, pp. 210–11.

44 H. van der Werf, *The Chansons of the Troubadours and Trouvères: A Study of the Melodies and Their Relation to the Poems* (Utrecht: Oosthoek, 1972); H. van der Werf, review of S. N. Rosenberg and H. Tischler, eds., *Chanter m'estuet: Songs of the Trouvères*, in *Journal of the American Musicological Society* 35 (1982), pp. 539–54; see also the overview of research in E. Aubrey, *The Music of the Troubadours* (Bloomington: Indiana University Press, 1996), pp. 240–54.

45 P. Bec, *La lyrique française au Moyen Âge (XIIe–XIIIe siècles): Contribution à une typologie des genres poétiques médiévaux*, 2 vols. (Paris: Picard, 1977–8); J. Stevens, *Words and Music in the Middle Ages: Song, Narrative, Dance and Drama, 1050–1350*, Cambridge Studies in Music

(Cambridge University Press, 1986); C. Page, *Voices and Instruments of the Middle Ages: Instrumental Practice and Songs in France 1100–1300* (Berkeley and Los Angeles: University of California Press, 1986); there is a helpful overview of research in Switten, *Music and Poetry in the Middle Ages*, pp. 59–152.

46 H. Tischler, ed., *Trouvère Lyrics with Melodies: Complete Comparative Edition*, Corpus Mensurabilis Musicae 107 (Neuhausen: American Institute of Musicology, 1997), and H. Tischler, ed., *Trouvère Lyrics with Melodies: Complete Comparative Edition, Revisited* (Ottawa: Institute of Mediaeval Music, 2006).

47 B. Kippenberg, 'Die Melodien des Minnesangs', in T. G. Georgiades, ed., *Musikalische Edition im Wandel des historischen Bewusstseins* (Kassel, Basel, Tours and London: Bärenreiter, 1971), p. 92. Here and elsewhere, translation is by the author of this chapter, unless otherwise noted.

48 For a consideration of this question in light of the French sources, see A. Butterfield, *Poetry and Music in Medieval France: From Jean Renart to Guillaume de Machaut*, Cambridge Studies in Medieval Literature (Cambridge University Press, 2002), pp. 171–90.

49 M. Gerbert, *De cantu et musica sacra a prima ecclesiae aetate usque ad praesens tempus*, 2 vols. (Sankt Blasien: Typis San-Blasianis, 1774; repr. O. Wessely, ed., Die grossen Darstellungen der Musikgeschichte in Barok und Aufklärung 4, Graz: Akademische Druck- u. Verlagsanstalt, 1968), vol. II, pp. 112–16.

50 R. G. Kiesewetter, *History of the Modern Music of Western Europe from the First Century of the Christian Era to the Present Day*, trans. Robert Müller (London: Newby, 1848), repr. with new introduction by F. Harrison (New York: Da Capo, 1973), pp. 45–6. It would be very easy to multiply such quotations; see D. Leech-Wilkinson, *The Modern Invention of Medieval Music: Scholarship, Ideology, Performance*, Musical Performance and Reception (Cambridge University Press, 2002), pp. 158–61, and Kreutziger-Herr, *Ein Traum vom Mittelalter*, pp. 103–5.

51 R. G. Kiesewetter, *Die Verdienste der Niederländer um die Tonkunst* (Amsterdam: Muller, 1829), p. 48. Riemann expressed essentially the same view as late as 1888; see Leech-Wilkinson, *The Modern Invention*, p. 265 n. 50.

52 E. de Coussemaker, *Histoire de l'harmonie au Moyen Âge* (Paris: Didron, 1852; repr. Hildesheim: Olms, 1966), p. x. On the question

of hearing and the *Musica enchiriadis*, see ibid., pp. 18–19 and 72.

53 H. L. F. Helmholtz, *On the Sensations of Tone as a Physiological Basis for the Theory of Music*, trans. A. J. Ellis, with a new introduction by H. Margenau (New York: Dover, 1954). For context, see L. Botstein, 'Time and Memory: Concert Life, Science, and Music in Brahms's Vienna', in Walter Frisch, ed., *Brahms and His World* (Princeton University Press, 1990), pp. 3–22. For Fétis, see Earp, 'Machaut's Music in the Early Nineteenth Century: The Work of Perne, Bottée de Toulmon, and Fétis', in J. Cerquiglini-Toulet and N. Wilkins, eds., *Guillaume de Machaut 1300–2000* (Paris: Presses de l'Université de Paris-Sorbonne, 2002), pp. 23–4.

54 Riemann, *Handbuch der Musikgeschichte*, cited in Kreutziger-Herr, *Ein Traum vom Mittelalter*, pp. 86 and 154–5; and R. C. Wegman, '"Das musikalische Hören" in the Middle Ages and Renaissance: Perspectives from Pre-War Germany', *Musical Quarterly* 82 (1998), p. 438.

55 See Kreutziger-Herr, *Ein Traum vom Mittelalter*, pp. 154–5 and 197–9; and Wegman, '"Das musikalische Hören"'.

56 K. Dèzes, review of van den Borren, *Dufay* (1927), quoted in Kreutziger-Herr, *Ein Traum vom Mittelalter*, p. 198.

57 E. T. A. Hoffmann, 'Alte und neue Kirchenmusik', *Allgemeine musikalische Zeitung* 16 (1814), cols. 577–84, 593–603 and 611–19; cf. *E. T. A. Hoffmann's Musical Writings: 'Kreisleriana', 'The Poet and the Composer', Music Criticism*, ed. D. Charlton, trans. M. Clarke (Cambridge University Press, 1989), pp. 351–76. For further discussion, see J. Garratt, *Palestrina and the German Romantic Imagination*, Musical Performance and Reception (Cambridge University Press, 2002), Chapter 2.

58 The myth dates at least to Agazzari (1607); see L. Lockwood, ed., *Palestrina: Pope Marcellus Mass: An Authoritative Score, Backgrounds and Sources, History and Analysis, Views and Comments* (New York: Norton, 1975), pp. 28–9.

59 Hoffmann, 'Alte und neue Kirchenmusik', cols. 583 and 582 (cf. the translation in Hoffmann, *E. T. A. Hoffmann's Musical Writings*, pp. 358 and 357).

60 Garratt, *Palestrina*, pp. 52–7.

61 L. Earp, *Guillaume de Machaut: A Guide to Research*, Garland Composer Resource Manuals 36 (New York and London: Garland, 1995), p. 344. For the following, see also Earp, 'Machaut's Music', pp. 14–23 and Kreutziger-Herr, *Ein Traum vom Mittelalter*, pp. 122–6.

62 For a facsimile of some pages of Bottée's transcription, see B. Gagnepain, 'A la recherche du temps passé: du rôle de quelques précurseurs dans la renaissance du patrimoine musical français', in M.-C. Mussat, J. Mongrédien and J.-M. Nectous, eds., *Échos de France et d'Italie: Liber amicorum Yves Gérard* (Paris: Buchet/Chastel Société française de musicologie, 1997), pp. 119–28.

63 F.-J. Fétis, 'De la nécessité de considérer la musique dans son histoire, soit pour en étudier les principes, soit pour ajouter à ses progrès', *Revue musicale*, 5e année (1831), p. 278.

64 F.-J. Fétis, 'Découverte de plusieurs manuscrits intéressans pour l'histoire de la musique', *Revue musicale* 1, prospectus (1827), pp. 3–11; see Earp, 'Machaut's Music', p. 26; and Haines, *Eight Centuries of Troubadours and Trouvères*, pp. 168–73.

65 F.-J. Fétis, 'Découverte de manuscrits intéressans pour l'histoire de la musique (deuxième article)', *Revue musicale* 1 (1827), pp. 106–13; see Earp, 'Machaut's Music', pp. 26–7.

66 See Earp, 'Machaut's Music', pp. 27–30 for details of this last stage.

67 On Zelter and Thibaut, see Garratt, *Palestrina*, pp. 62–8; on Kiesewetter, see H. Kier, 'Kiesewetters historische Hauskonzerte: zur Geschichte der kirchenmusikalische Restauration in Wien', *Kirchenmusikalisches Jahrbuch* 52 (1968), pp. 95–119; on Choron, see W. Kahl, 'Zur musikalischen Renaissancebewegung in Frankreich während der ersten Hälfte des 19. Jahrhunderts', in D. Weise, ed., *Festschrift Joseph Schmidt-Görg zum 60. Geburtstag* (Bonn: Beethovenhaus, 1957), pp. 156–74; on Fétis, see Earp, 'Machaut's Music', pp. 33–4.

68 See Garratt, *Palestrina*, Chapter 1.

69 F.-J. Fétis, 'Du sort futur de la musique', *Revue musicale* 9 (1830), pp. 225–9, at pp. 228–9; for more on Fétis's eclecticism, see K. Ellis, *Music Criticism in Nineteenth-Century France: 'La Revue et Gazette musicale de Paris', 1834–80* (Cambridge University Press, 1995), pp. 33–45.

70 Cf. Garratt, *Palestrina*, p. 33, and the discussion, pp. 28–35.

71 F. Ludwig, 'Die mehrstimmige Musik des 14. Jahrhunderts', *Sammelbände der Internationalen Musik-Gesellschaft* 4 (1902–3), pp. 16–69. At this stage, Ludwig knew fewer English sources than he later would; nor had he examined the trecento source *GB-LBl* add. 29987. The account of sacred music would expand in later surveys in light of the subsequent discovery of the Ivrea Codex (*I-IV* 115) and Spanish fragments.

72 Ibid., p. 45.

73 Ibid., pp. 61–2.

74 Ibid., p. 67.

75 Such traditions are treated in context in R. Strohm, *The Rise of European Music 1380–1500* (Cambridge University Press, 1993), pp. 267–374.

76 For some background on *Geistesgeschichte*, see P. Potter, *Most German of the Arts: Musicology and Society from the Weimar Republic to the End of Hitler's Reich* (New Haven and London: Yale University Press, 1998), pp. 166–72; and Kreutziger-Herr, *Ein Traum vom Mittelalter*, pp. 196–7.

77 R. Ficker, 'Die Musik des Mittelalters und ihre Beziehungen zum Geistesleben', *Deutsche Vierteljahrschrift für Literaturwissenschaft und Geistesgeschichte* 3 (1925), pp. 501–35. Parts of this and another of Ficker's early essays are discussed in Leech-Wilkinson, *The Modern Invention*, pp. 167–9 and 248. An essay in English has some similar points; see R. Ficker, 'Polyphonic Music of the Gothic Period', trans. T. Baker, *Musical Quarterly* 15 (1929), pp. 483–505.

78 Ficker, 'Die Musik des Mittelalters', p. 503; discussed in Kreutziger-Herr, *Ein Traum vom Mittelalter*, p. 197.

79 For more on this Oriental hypothesis and its later ramifications for instrumental performance, see Leech-Wilkinson, *The Modern Invention*, pp. 64–6 and 98; and J. Haines, 'The Arabic Style of Performing Medieval Music', *Early Music* 29 (2001), pp. 369–78.

80 See A. Rehding, 'The Quest for the Origins of Music in Germany circa 1900', *Journal of the American Musicological Society* 53 (2000), pp. 345–85. For further discussion of nationalist sentiments circa 1900, see Leech-Wilkinson, *The Modern Invention*, pp. 28–35.

81 Ficker, 'Die Musik des Mittelalters', p. 511.

82 Ficker's example, the two-voice alleluia *Pascha nostrum*, had been performed in 1922 by Gurlitt at Karlsruhe from an edition supplied by Ludwig. See F. Ludwig, 'Musik des Mittelalters in der Badischen Kunsthalle Karlsruhe, 24.–26. September 1922', *Zeitschrift für Musikwissenschaft* 5 (1922–3), pp. 434–60. Kreutziger-Herr, *Ein Traum vom Mittelalter*, pp. 355–66, prints the complete programme booklet.

83 Ficker, 'Die Musik des Mittelalters', pp. 516–23. Ludwig had identified Ficker's example, *Homo luge / Homo miserabilis / Brumas e mors*, as a motet possibly composed in Germany. It had already been performed on two occasions, at a 1921 Dante celebration in Freiburg and in

Gurlitt's 1922 concert at Karlsruhe; see Ludwig, 'Musik des Mittelalters', pp. 438–40.

84 Ficker, 'Die Musik des Mittelalters', p. 524.

85 Note the allusions to J. Huizinga, *Herbst des Mittelalters: Studien über Lebens- und Geistesformen des 14. und 15. Jahrhunderts in Frankreich und in den Niederlanden* (Munich: Drei Masken, 1924 [original Dutch edn 1919]; published in English as *The Autumn of the Middle Ages*, trans. R. J. Payton and U. Mammitzsch (University of Chicago Press, 1996).

86 Ficker, 'Die Musik des Mittelalters', p. 531.

87 Ibid., p. 532.

88 Ibid., p. 533. A colour reproduction of the Ghent altarpiece is in R. Wangermée, *Flemish Music and Society in the Fifteenth and Sixteenth Centuries*, trans. R. E. Wolf (New York, Washington and London: Praeger, 1968), Pl. 3.

89 Cf. C. Page, *Discarding Images: Reflections of Music and Culture in Medieval France* (Oxford University Press, 1993); see also Kreutziger-Herr, *Ein Traum vom Mittelalter*, pp. 19–25, 161–2 and 268–74.

90 Leech-Wilkinson, *The Modern Invention*, p. 251; see also Kreutziger-Herr, *Ein Traum vom Mittelalter*, pp. 163–7. On a Nordic Leoninus and Perotinus, see Potter, *Most German of the Arts*, p. 179; and Leech-Wilkinson, *The Modern Invention*, pp. 168, 249 and 270 n. 163.

91 R. G. Collingwood, *The Idea of History*, rev. edn by Jan van der Dussen (Oxford University Press, 1993), p. 92.

92 P. H. Lang, *Music in Western Civilization* (New York: Norton, 1941), p. 150; see especially pp. 122–81.

93 E. E. Lowinsky, 'Music in the Culture of the Renaissance', in B. J. Blackburn, ed., *Music in the Culture of the Renaissance and Other Essays*, 2 vols. (University of Chicago Press, 1989), vol. I, pp. 19–39, with some footnote additions. First published in *Journal of the History of Ideas*, 15 (1954), pp. 509–53.

94 Lowinsky, 'Music in the Culture of the Renaissance', vol. I, p. 31.

95 Ibid., p. 35.

96 Collingwood, *Idea of History*, pp. 49–52.

97 Strohm, *The Rise of European Music*, with comments on periodization, pp. 540–42; see also R. Taruskin, *The Oxford History of Western Music*, vol. I, *The Earliest Notations to the Sixteenth Century* (Oxford University Press, 2005), pp. 380–5.

98 Leech-Wilkinson, *The Modern Invention*, Chapter 1.

99 See ibid., pp. 44–7; Kreutziger-Herr, *Ein Traum vom Mittelalter*, p. 204; and Earp, 'Machaut's Music', p. 38 n. 99.

100 C. Page, 'Machaut's "Pupil" Deschamps on the Performance of Music', *Early Music* 5 (1977), pp. 484–91.

101 Leech-Wilkinson, *The Modern Invention*, p. 225.

102 Translation taken from ibid., p. 165.

103 Ibid., pp. 182–4.

104 On interpretations of the term 'res d'Alemangne', see the works cited in Earp, *Guillaume de Machaut*, p. 350; and J. Bain, 'Balades 32 and 33 and the "Res Dalemangne"', in E. E. Leach, ed., *Machaut's Music: New Interpretations*, Studies in Medieval and Renaissance Music (Woodbridge: Boydell & Brewer, 2003), pp. 205–19.

105 G. de Machaut, *Le Livre dou Voir Dit (The Book of the True Poem)*, ed. D. Leech-Wilkinson, trans. R. B. Palmer, Garland Library of Medieval Literature (New York and London: Garland, 1998), p. 125.

106 Leech-Wilkinson, *The Modern Invention*, pp. 70–6.

107 J. I. Wimsatt, W. W. Kibler, and R. A. Baltzer, eds., *G. de Machaut, Le Jugement du roy de Behaigne and Remede de Fortune* (Athens, GA: University of Georgia Press, 1988), ll. 3962–88; and R. B. Palmer, ed. and trans. *G. de Machaut, La Prise d'Alexandre (The Taking of Alexandria)* (New York: Routledge, 2002), ll. 1139–67. See references in Earp, *Guillaume de Machaut*, pp. 214 and 233. On the Ghent altarpiece, see n. 88 above. On Memling's Najera Triptych, see the colour reproduction in Wangermée, *Flemish Music*, Plates 68 and 69.

108 On Bottée, see Leech-Wilkinson, *The Modern Invention*, p. 263 n. 18. For the Beethoven conference performances, see Kreutziger-Herr, *Ein Traum vom Mittelalter*, pp. 177–8. On Huizinga in Ficker, Schering and Pirro, see Leech-Wilkinson, *The Modern Invention*, p. 72. Page considered Huizinga a deleterious influence on performance practice; see Leech-Wilkinson, *The Modern Invention*, pp. 55–8, 99, 106 and 122; and as a deleterious influence on late medieval historiography; see Page, *Discarding Images*, Chapter 5.

109 See works cited in n. 45, and Earp, *Guillaume de Machaut*, pp. 389–92.

110 See C. Wright, 'Voices and Instruments in the Art Music of Northern France during the 15th Century: A Conspectus', in D. Heartz and B. Wade, eds., *International Musicological Society: Report of the Twelfth Congress Berkeley 1977* (Kassel: Bärenreiter, 1981), pp. 643–9; D. Fallows, 'Specific Information on the Ensembles for Composed Polyphony, 1400–1474', in Stanley Boorman, ed., *Studies in the Performance of Late Mediaeval Music* (Cambridge University

Press, 1983), pp. 109–59; and R. Bowers, 'The Performing Ensemble for English Church Polyphony, c.1320–c.1390', in ibid., pp. 161–92.

111 Among these are Margaret Bent's dissertation on Old Hall (1969), with material on texting in M. Bent, 'Text Setting in Sacred Music of the Early 15th Century: Evidence and Implications', in U. Günther and L. Finscher, eds., *Musik und Text in der Mehrstimmigkeit des 14. und 15. Jahrhunderts: Vorträge des Gastsymposions in der Herzog August Bibliothek Wolfenbüttel, 8. bis 12. September 1980*, Göttinger musikwissenschaftliche Arbeiten 10 (Kassel: Bärenreiter, 1984), pp. 291–326; my dissertation on Machaut (1983), with material on texting in L. Earp, 'Texting in 15th-century French Chansons: A Look Ahead from the 14th Century', *Early Music* 19 (1991), pp. 195–210; and Dennis Slavin's dissertation on Binchois (1988), with material on texting in D. Slavin, 'In Support of "Heresy": Manuscript Evidence for the *a cappella* Performance of Early 15th-Century Songs', *Early Music* 19 (1991), pp. 179–90.

112 C. Page, 'Polyphony before 1400', in H. M. Brown and S. Sadie, eds., *Performance Practice: Music Before 1600*, Norton/Grove Handbooks in Music (New York and London: Norton, 1990), pp. 79–84.

113 S. Fuller, 'On Sonority in Fourteenth-Century Polyphony: Some Preliminary Reflections', *Journal of Music Theory* 30 (1986), pp. 35–70.

114 See Leech-Wilkinson, *The Modern Invention*, p. 164; and K. Moll, ed. and trans., *Counterpoint and Compositional Process in the Time of Dufay: Perspectives from German Musicology*, Criticism and Analysis of Early Music (New York and London: Garland, 1997), p. 9.

115 Moll, *Counterpoint and Compositional Process*, pp. 3–64, provides a historiographical overview and explication of terminologies; see also Leech-Wilkinson, *The Modern Invention*, pp. 174–7.

116 See M. Bent, 'The Grammar of Early Music: Preconditions for Analysis', in C. C. Judd, ed., *Tonal Structures in Early Music*, Criticism and Analysis of Early Music (New York and London: Garland, 1998), pp. 15–59.

117 R. Taruskin, *Oxford History*, pp. 277–81.

118 This is not the only musical aspect of this motet that was received well; see J. M. Allsen, 'Style and Intertextuality in the Isorhythmic Motet 1400–1440', PhD diss., University of Wisconsin-Madison (1992), pp. 33–5, and Strohm, *The Rise of European Music*, pp. 41 and 67.

119 C. Dahlhaus, *Foundations of Music History*, trans. J. B. Robinson (Cambridge University Press, 1983 [original German edn 1977]), p. 107.

Bibliography

Abu-Lughod, Janet L., *Before European Hegemony: The World System AD 1250–1350* (Oxford University Press, 1989)

Adams, William, Goudie, Andrew and Orme, Antony, eds., *The Physical Geography of Africa* (Oxford University Press, 1996)

Adriaen, Marcus, ed., *Cassiodorus: Expositio psalmorum* (Turnhout: Brepols, 1958; English trans. 1990)

Albarosa, Nino and Turco, Alberto, eds., *Benevento, Biblioteca capitolare 40, Graduale* (Padua: Linea Editrice, 1991)

Alexander, Jonathan, *Medieval Illuminators and Their Methods of Work* (New Haven: Yale University Press, 1992)

Allmand, Christopher, *The Hundred Years War: England and France at War* (Cambridge University Press, rev. edn, 2001)

Allsen, J. Michael, 'Style and Intertextuality in the Isorhythmic Motet 1400–1440' (PhD diss., University of Wisconsin-Madison, 1992)

Altés i Aguiló, Francesc Xavier, ed., *Llibre Vermell de Montserrat: edició facsímil parcial del manuscrit núm. 1 de la Biblioteca de l'Abadia de Montserrat* (Barcelona: Publicacions de l'Abadia de Montserrat, 1989)

Aluaş, Luminiṭa Florea, ed. and trans., 'The *Quatuor Principalia Musicae*: A Critical Edition and Translation, with Introduction and Commentary' (PhD diss., Indiana University, 1996)

An Old St. Andrews Music Book (Cod. Helmst, 628), with an introduction by James Baxter (London: Oxford University Press; Paris: Honoré Champion, 1931)

Analecta Hymnica medii aevi, ed. C. Blume and G. M. Dreves, 55 vols. (Leipzig: Fues's Verlag [R. Reisland], 1886–1922; repr. Frankfurt am Main: Minerva, 1961)

Anderson, Gordon, 'Notre Dame Bilingual Motets: A Study in the History of Music c.1215–1245', *Miscellanea musicologica* 3 (1968), pp. 50–144

'Notre Dame Latin Double Motets ca.1215–1250', *Musica disciplina* 25 (1971), pp. 35–92

'Notre-Dame and Related Conductus: A Catalogue Raisonné', *Miscellanea musicologica* 6 (1972), pp. 153–229, and 7 (1975), pp. 1–81

ed., *Compositions of the Bamberg Manuscript: Bamberg, Staatsbibliothek, lit. 115 (olim Ed. IV. 6)*, Corpus Mensurabilis Musicae 75 (Neuhausen-Stuttgart: American Institute of Musicology, 1977)

ed., *Motets of the Manuscript La Clayette, Paris, Bibliothèque nationale, nouv. acq. f. fr. 13521*, Corpus Mensurabilis Musicae 68 ([Rome]: American Institute of Musicology, 1975)

ed., *Notre-Dame and Related Conductus: Opera omnia*, 10 vols., [Institute of Mediaeval Music] Collected Works 10 (Henryville, Ottawa, and Binningen: Institute of Mediaeval Music, 1979–)

ed., *The Las Huelgas Manuscript*, 2 vols., Corpus Mensurabilis Musicae 79 (Neuhausen-Stuttgart: American Institute of Musicology, 1982)

Andrieu, Michel, *Les Ordines romani du haut moyen âge*, 5 vols. (Louvain: Spicilegium Sacrum Lovaniense, 1931–61)

Anglès, Higini, 'Epistola farcida del martiri de Sant Esteve', *Vida Cristiana* 9 (1922), pp. 69–75

La música a Catalunya fins al segle XIII (Barcelona: Institut d'estudis catalans, 1935)

La música de las cantigas de Santa María del rey Alfonso el Sabio, 3 vols. in 4 (Barcelona: Biblioteca Central, 1943–64)

ed., *El còdex musical de Las Huelgas*, 3 vols. (Barcelona: Institut d'Estudis Catalans and Biblioteca de Catalunya, 1931)

Apel, Willi, *Gregorian Chant* (Bloomington: Indiana University Press, 1958)

ed., *French Secular Compositions of the Fourteenth Century*, edition of the literary texts by Samuel N. Rosenberg, 3 vols., CMM 53 ([Rome]: American Institute of Musicology, 1970–2)

Appel, Carl, *Bernart von Ventadorn: seine Lieder mit Einleitung und Glossar* (Halle: Niemeyer, 1915)

Arévalo, Faustino, ed., *S. Isidori hispalensis episcopi opera omnia* (Rome: Typis A. Fulgonii, 1797–1803)

Arlt, Wulf, 'Stylistic Layers in Eleventh-Century Polyphony: How Can the Continental Sources Contribute to Our Understanding of the Winchester Organa?' in Susan Rankin and David Hiley, eds., *Music in the Medieval English Liturgy: Plainsong and Medieval Music Centennial Essays* (Oxford: Clarendon Press, 1993), pp. 101–44

'The Office for the Feast of the Circumcision from Le Puy' in Margot Fassler and Rebecca A. Baltzer, eds., *The Divine Office in the Latin Middle Ages* (Oxford University Press, 2000), pp. 324–41

and Rankin, Susan, eds., *Stiftsbibliothek Sankt Gallen Codices 484 & 381* (Winterthur: Amadeus, 1996)

Armistead, Samuel, Silverman, Joseph and Katz, Israel, *Judeo-Spanish Ballads from Oral Tradition*, 3 vols. to date (Berkeley: University of California Press; Newark, DE: Juan de la Cuesta; 1986–)

Asensio, Juan Carlos, *El códice de las Huelgas*, Patrimonio musical español 8 (Madrid: Alpuerto, 2001)

Paz, Julián and Pliego, Victor, *El códice de Madrid, Biblioteca nacional, MSS. 20486*, Patrimonio musical español 3 (Madrid: Alpuerto, 1997)

Atchison, Mary, ed., *The Chansonnier of Oxford Bodleian MS Douce 308: Essays and Complete Edition of Texts* (Aldershot: Ashgate, 2005)

Atchley, Edward Godfrey Cuthbert Frederick, ed. and trans., *Ordo Romanus primus* (London: Moring, 1905)

Aubrey, Elizabeth, 'Medieval Melodies in the Hands of Bibliophiles of the *Ancien Régime*', in Barbara Haggh, ed., *Essays on Music and Culture in Honor of Herbert Kellman*, Collection Épitome musicale 8 (Paris: Minerve, 2001), pp. 17–34

The Music of the Troubadours (Bloomington: Indiana University Press, 1996)

Aubry, Pierre, *Cent motets du XIIIe siècle, publiés d'après le manuscrit Ed. IV. 6 de Bamberg*, 3 vols. (Paris: A. Rouart, Lerolle, 1908)

Augustine, Saint, 'On Music', in Robert Catesby Taliaferro, trans. and ed., *Writings of Saint Augustine*, vols. II, IV. The Fathers of the Church: A New Translation (Washington, DC: Catholic University of America Press in association with Consortium Books, 1977)

Avril, François, *Manuscript Painting at the Court of France: The Fourteenth Century (1320–1380)* (London: Chatto and Windus, 1978)

Bailey, Terence W., *The Processions of Sarum and the Western Church* (Toronto: Pontifical Institute of Mediaeval Studies, 1971)

Bain, Jennifer, 'Balades 32 and 33 and the "Res Dalemagne"', in Elizabeth Eva Leach, ed., *Machaut's Music: New Interpretations*, Studies in Medieval and Renaissance Music (Woodbridge: Boydell & Brewer, 2003), pp. 205–19

Baird, Joseph, Baglivi, Giuseppe and Kane, John Robert, trans., *The Chronicle of Salimbene de Adam* (Binghamton: Center for Medieval and Early Renaissance Studies, University Center at Binghamton, 1986)

Baldovin, John, *The Urban Character of Christian Worship: The Origins, Development, and Meaning of Stational Liturgy* (Rome: Pontifical Oriental Institute, 1987)

Baldwin, John, *Masters, Princes and Merchants: The Social Views of Peter the Chanter and His Circle* (Princeton University Press, 1970)

Baltzer, Rebecca A., 'Aspects of Trope in the Earliest Motets for the Assumption of the Virgin', *Current Musicology* 45–7 (1990), pp. 5–42 (*Festschrift for Ernest Sanders*, ed. Peter M. Lefferts and Brian Seirup)

 'How Long Was Notre-Dame Organum Performed?' in Bryan Gillingham and Paul Merkley, eds., *Beyond the Moon: Festschrift Luther Dittmer*, Musicological Studies 53 (Ottawa: Institute of Mediaeval Music, 1990)

 'Johannes de Garlandia', in *Grove Music Online*. www.oxfordmusiconline.com

 'Music in the Life and Times of Eleanor of Aquitaine', in William W. Kibler, ed., *Eleanor of Aquitaine: Patron and Politician* (Austin: University of Texas Press, 1976)

 'Notre Dame Manuscripts and Their Owners: Lost and Found', *Journal of Musicology* 5 (1987), pp. 380–99

 'The Manuscript Makers of W1: Further Evidence for an Early Date', in *Quomodo cantabimus canticum? Studies in Honor of Edward H. Roesner*, ed. David Butler Cannata, Currie, Gabriela Ilnitchi, Mueller, Rena Charnin and Nádas, John Louis (Middleton, WI: American Institute of Musicology, 2008), pp. 103–20

 'Thirteenth-Century Illuminated Miniatures and the Date of the Florence Manuscript', *Journal of the American Musicological Society* 25 (1972), pp. 1–18

 ed., *Les clausules à deux voix du manuscrit de Florence, Biblioteca Medicea-Laurenziana, Pluteus 29.1, fascicule V*, Le Magnus liber organi de Notre-Dame de Paris 5 (Monaco: Éditions de l'Oiseau-Lyre, 1995)

Bannister, Henry Marriot, *Anglo French Sequelae* (London: Plainsong and Medieval Music Society, 1934)

Baroffio, Giacomo, 'I libri con musica sono libri di musica?' in Giulio Cattin, Danilo
    Curti and Marco Gozzi, eds., *Il canto piano nell'era della stampa: Atti del
    Convegno internazionale di studi sul canto liturgico nei secoli XV–XVIII, Trento –
    Castello del Buonconsiglio, Venezia – Fondazione Ugo e Olga Levi, 9–11 ottobre
    1998* (Trento: Provincia autonoma di Trento, 1999), pp. 9–12
    Iter Liturgicum Italicum (Padua: CLEUP, 1999)
    'Le polifonie primitive nella tradizione manoscritta italiana. Appunti di ricerca', in
        Giulio Cattin and F. Alberto Gallo, eds., *Un millennio di polifonia liturgica tra
        oralità e scrittura* (Bologna: Il Mulino, 2002), pp. 201–5
    and Antonelli, Cristiana, 'La passione nella liturgia della Chiesa cattolica fino
        all'epoca di Johann Sebastian Bach', in Elena Povellato, ed., *Ritorno a Bach:
        Dramma e ritualità delle passioni* (Venice: Marsilio, 1986), pp. 11–33
Bartlett, Robert, *The Making of Europe: Conquest, Colonization and Cultural Change
    950–1350* (Princeton University Press, 1993)
Baumstark, Anton, *Comparative Liturgy*, rev. Bernard Botte, trans. F. L. Cross
    (London: A. R. Mowbray, 1958)
Bec, Pierre, *La lyrique française au Moyen Âge (XIIe–XIIIe siècles): Contribution à une
    typologie des genres poétiques médiévaux*, 2 vols., Publications du Centre d'Études
    Supérieures de Civilisation Médiévale de l'Université de Poitiers, 6–7 (Paris:
    Picard, 1977–8)
Beck, Jean, ed., *Les chansonniers des troubadours et des trouvères*, vol. I, *Reproduction
    phototypique du Chansonnier Cangé* (Philadelphia: University of Pennsylvania
    Press; Paris: Honoré Champion, 1927)
    ed., *Les chansonniers des troubadours et des trouvères*, vol. II, *Le manuscrit du roi*
        (Philadelphia: University of Pennsylvania Press; Paris: Honoré Champion,
        1927)
Bede, *A History of the English Church and People*, trans. Leo Sherley-Price, rev.
    Ronald E. Latham (London: Penguin, 1968)
Bell, Nicolas, *Music in Medieval Manuscripts* (London: British Library, 2001)
    The Las Huelgas Music Codex: A Companion Study to the Facsimile (Madrid:
        Testimonio, 2003)
Benedictow, Ole, *The Black Death 1346–1353: The Complete History* (Woodbridge:
    Boydell & Brewer, 2004)
Bent, Margaret, 'A Contemporary Perception of Early Fifteenth-Century Style:
    Bologna Q 15 as a Document of Scribal Editorial Initiative', *Musica Disciplina* 41
    (1987), pp. 183–201
    Counterpoint, Composition, and Musica Ficta (London and New York: Routledge,
        2002)
    'Deception, Exegesis and Sounding Number in Machaut's Motet 15', *Early Music
        History* 10 (1991), pp. 15–27
    'Early Papal Motets', in Richard Sherr, ed., *Papal Music and Musicians in Late
        Medieval and Renaissance Rome* (Oxford: Clarendon Press, 1998)
    'Editing Early Music: The Dilemma of Translation', *Early Music* 22 (1994),
        pp. 373–94
    'Musica ficta', in *Grove Music Online*. www.oxfordmusiconline.com

'Text Setting in Sacred Music of the Early 15th Century: Evidence and
    Implications', in Ursula Günther and Ludwig Finscher, eds., *Musik und Text in
    der Mehrstimmigkeit des 14. und 15. Jahrhunderts: Vorträge des Gastsymposions in
    der Herzog August Bibliothek Wolfenbüttel, 8. bis 12. September 1980*, Göttinger
    musikwissenschaftliche Arbeiten 10 (Kassel: Bärenreiter, 1984), pp. 291–326
'The Fourteenth-Century Italian Motet', in Giulio Cattin and Patrizia Dalla
    Vecchia, eds., *L'ars nova italiana del Trecento VI: Atti del Congresso internazionale
    'L'Europa e la musica del Trecento'*, Certaldo, 19–21 luglio 1984 (Certaldo: Polis,
    1992) pp. 85–125
'The Grammar of Early Music: Preconditions for Analysis', in Cristle Collins Judd,
    ed., *Tonal Structures in Early Music* (New York and London: Garland, 1998),
    pp. 15–59
'The Machaut Manuscripts Vg, B and E', *Musica Disciplina* 37 (1983), pp. 53–82
'The Progeny of Old Hall: More Leaves from a Royal English Choirbook', in
    Gordon Athol Anderson (1929–1981) in Memoriam von seinen Studenten,
    Freunden und Kollegen, 2 vols., Musicological Studies 49 (Henryville: Institute
    of Mediaeval Music, 1984), pp. 1–54
    ed., *Bologna Q 15: The Making and Remaking of a Musical Manuscript: Introductory
    Study and Facsimile*, 2 vols., Ars Nova, nuova seria 2 (Lucca: LIM Editrice, 2008)
    and Hallmark, Anne, eds., *The Works of Johannes Ciconia*, Polyphonic Music of
    the Fourteenth Century 14 (Monaco: Éditions de l'Oiseau-Lyre, 1985)
    and Wathey, Andrew, eds., *Fauvel Studies: Allegory, Chronicle, Music, and Image in
    Paris, Bibliothèque Nationale de France, MS français 146* (Oxford: Clarendon
    Press, 1998)
Berend, Nora, *At the Gate of Christendom: Jews, Muslims and 'Pagans' in Medieval
    Hungary c.1000–c.1300* (Cambridge University Press, 2001)
Berger, Anna Maria Busse, *Medieval Music and the Art of Memory* (Berkeley:
    University of California Press, 2005)
Berger, Karol, *Musica Ficta: Theories of Accidental Inflections in Vocal Polyphony
    from Marchetto da Padova to Gioseffo Zarlino* (Cambridge University Press,
    1987)
Bergeron, Katherine, *Decadent Enchantments: The Revival of Gregorian Chant at
    Solesmes*, California Studies in 19th-Century Music 10 (Berkeley: University of
    California Press, 1998)
Bergsagel, John, 'The Transmission of Notre-Dame Organa in Some
    Newly-Discovered "Magnus liber organi" Fragments in Copenhagen', in Angelo
    Pomilio et al., eds., *Atti del XIV Congresso della Società Internazionale di
    Musicologia: Trasmissione e recezione delle forme di cultura musicale*, 3 vols.
    (Turin: EDT, 1990), pp. 629–36
Bernhard, Michael, 'Eine neue Quelle für den Vatikanischen Organum-Traktat', in
    Bernhard, ed., *Quellen und Studien zur Musiktheorie des Mittelalters*, vol. III,
    Bayerische Akademie der Wissenschaften, Veröffentlichungen der
    Musikhistorischen Kommission 15 (Munich: C. H. Beck, 2001), pp. 175–90
    and Bower, Calvin M., eds., *Glossa maior in institutionem musicam Boethii*
    (Munich: Verlag der Bayerischen Akademie der Wissenschaft, 1993–6)

Berschin, Walter and Schipperges, Heinrich, eds., *Hildegard von Bingen: Symphonia: Gedichte und Gesänge* (Gerlingen: Lambert Schneider, 1995)

Besseler, Heinrich, *Schriftbild der mehrstimmigen Musik*, Musikgeschichte in Bildern 3/5 (Leipzig: Deutscher Verlag für Musik, 1973)

ed., *Guillelmi Dufay opera omnia*, 6 vols., Corpus Mensurabilis Musicae 1 (Rome: American Institute of Musicology, 1951–66)

Biddick, Kathleen, *The Shock of Medievalism* (Durham, NC: Duke University Press, 1998)

Binkley, Thomas, 'Zur Aufführungspraxis der einstimmigen Musik des Mittelalters – ein Werkstattbericht', *Basler Jahrbuch für historische Musikpraxis* 1 (1977), pp. 19–76

Birnbaum, Stanley, trans., *Johannes de Garlandia: Concerning Measured Music (De mensurabili musica)*, Colorado College Music Press Translations 9 (Colorado Springs: Colorado College Music Press, 1978)

Bisaro, Xavier, *Une nation de fidèles: L'Église et la liturgie parisienne au XVIIIe siècle* (Turnhout: Brepols, 2006)

Bischoff, Bernhard, *Latin Palaeography: Antiquity and the Middle Ages*, trans. Dáibhí Ó Cróinín and David Ganz (Cambridge University Press, 1991)

Bjork, David, 'On the Dissemination of Quem queritis and the Visitatio Sepulchri and the Chronology of Their Early Sources', *Comparative Drama* 14 (1980), pp. 46–69

The Aquitanian Kyrie Repertory of the Tenth and Eleventh Centuries, ed. Richard L. Crocker (Aldershot: Ashgate 2003)

'The Kyrie Trope', *Journal of the American Musicological Society* 33 (1980), pp. 1–41

Blachly, Alexander, 'Some Observations on the "Germanic" Plainchant Tradition', in Peter M. Lefferts and Brian Seirup, eds., *Studies in Medieval Music: Festschrift for Ernest H. Sanders* (New York: Department of Music, Columbia University, 1990)

Bloch, R. Howard and Nichols, Stephen, eds., *Medievalism and the Modernist Temper* (Baltimore: Johns Hopkins University Press, 1996)

Boethius, *Fundamentals of Music*, trans. Calvin M. Bower (New Haven: Yale University Press, 1989)

Boogaart, Jacques, 'Encompassing Past and Present: Quotations and Their Function in Machaut's Motets', *Early Music History* 20 (2001), pp. 1–86

'"O Series Summe Rata". De Motetten van Guillaume de Machaut. De Ordening van het Corpus en de Samenhang van Tekst en Muziek' (PhD diss., Utrecht, 2001)

Boorman, Stanley, et al., 'Sources, MS', in *Grove Music Online*. www.oxfordmusiconline.com

Botstein, Leon, 'Time and Memory: Concert Life, Science, and Music in Brahms's Vienna', in Walter Frisch, ed., *Brahms and His World* (Princeton University Press, 1990), pp. 3–22

Botterill, Steven, *Dante: 'De Vulgari Eloquentia'* (Cambridge University Press, 1996)

Bowers, Roger D., "Choirs, Choral Establishments", in *Medieval England: An Encyclopedia*

'Guillaume de Machaut and His Canonry of Reims, 1338–1377', *Early Music History* 23 (2004), pp. 1–48

'The Performing Ensemble for English Church Polyphony, c.1320–c.1390', in Stanley Boorman, ed., *Studies in the Performance of Late Mediaeval Music* (Cambridge University Press, 1983), pp. 161–92

Boyce, James, *Praising God in Carmel: Studies in Carmelite Liturgy* (Washington: Carmelite Institute, 1999)

Boyle, Leonard E., Gy, Pierre-Marie, and Krupa, Paweł, eds., *Aux origines de la liturgie dominicaine: le manuscrit Santa Sabina XIV L 1*, Collection de l'École Française de Rome 327, Documents, études et répertoires publiés par l'IRHT 67 (Paris: CNRS Éditions and Rome: École Française de Rome, 2004)

Boynton, Susan, 'Orality, Literacy and the Early Notation of the Office Hymns', *Journal of the American Musicological Society* 56 (2003), pp. 99–168

Bradshaw, Paul, *Early Christian Worship: A Basic Introduction to Ideas and Practice* (London: Society for Promoting Christian Knowledge, 1996)

The Search for the Origins of Christian Worship: Sources and Methods for the Study of Early Liturgy (London: SPCK, 2002) (rev. edn)

Bragard, Roger, ed., *Speculum musice*, Corpus Scriptorum de Musica 3 ([Rome]: American Institute of Musicology, 1955–73)

Brahney, Kathleen J., ed. and trans., *The Lyrics of Thibaut de Champagne* (New York: Garland, 1989)

Brewer, Charles, 'The Historical Context of Polyphony in Medieval Hungary: An Examination of Four Fragmentary Sources', *Studia Musicologica Academiae Scientiarum Hungaricae* 32 (1990), pp. 5–21

'The Introduction of the "ars nova" into East Central Europe: A Study of the Late Medieval Polish Sources' (PhD diss., City University of New York, 1984)

'The Mensural Significance of Bohemian Chant Notation and Its Origins', in László Dobszay, Ágnes Papp and Ferenc Sebő, eds., *Cantus planus: IMS Study Group, Papers Read at the Fourth Meeting, Pécs, Hungary, 3–8 September 1990* (Budapest: Hungarian Academy of Science, Institute of Musicology, 1992), pp. 55–68

ed. *Collectio cantilenarum saeculi XV: rękopis Biblioteki Jagiellońskiej Kj 2464* (music score and facsimiles). Źródła do historii muzyki polskiej 30 (Cracow: Polskie Wydawnictwo Myzyczne, 1990)

Briand-Ponsart, Claude and Hugoniot, Christophe, *L'Afrique romaine* (Paris: Armand Colin, 2005)

Brockett, Clyde Waring, *Antiphons, Responsories, and Other Chants of the Mozarabic Rite* (Brooklyn: Institute of Mediaeval Music, 1968)

Brothers, Thomas, *Chromatic Beauty in the Late Medieval Chanson: An Interpretation of Manuscript Accidentals* (Cambridge University Press, 1997)

Brou, Louis, 'Liturgie "mozarabe" ou liturgie "hispanique"?' *Ephemerides liturgicae* 63 (1949), pp. 66–70

'Notes de paléographie musicale mozarabe', *Anuario musical* 7 (1952), pp. 51–77 and 10 (1955), pp. 23–44

'Séquences et tropes dans la liturgie mozarabe', *Hispania sacra* 4 (1951), pp. 27–41

Brown, Giles, 'Introduction: The Carolingian Renaissance', in Rosamond McKitterick, ed., *Carolingian Culture: Emulation and Innovation* (Cambridge University Press, 1994)

Brown, Thomas, 'Another Mirror of Lovers? Order, Structure and Allusion in
    Machaut's Motets', *Plainsong and Medieval Music* 10 (2001), pp. 121–34
Brownlee, Kevin, 'Machaut's Motet 15 and the *Roman de la Rose*: The Literary
    Context of *Amours qui a le pouoir/Faus samblant m'a deceü/Vidi Dominum*', *Early
    Music History* 10 (1991), pp. 1–14
Brownlee, Marina, Brownlee, Kevin and Nichols, Stephen, eds., *The New
    Medievalism* (Baltimore: Johns Hopkins University Press, 1991)
Brownrigg, Linda, ed., *Making the Medieval Book: Techniques of Production* (Los
    Altos Hills: Red Gull Press, 1995)
  ed., *Medieval Book Production: Assessing the Evidence* (Los Altos Hills: Red Gull
    Press, 1990)
Brundage, James A., *The Chronicle of Henry of Livonia* (Madison: Columbia
    University Press, 1961)
Burgwinkle, William, 'The Chansonniers as Books', in Simon Gaunt and Sarah Kay,
    eds., *The Troubadours: An Introduction* (Cambridge University Press, 1999),
    pp. 246–62
Burney, Charles, *A General History of Music from the Earliest Ages to the Present*, 4
    vols. (London, 1776–89; 2nd edn with notes by Frank Mercer, 2 vols., New York:
    Harcourt Brace, 1935; repr. New York: Dover, 1957)
Busse Berger, Anna Maria, *Medieval Music and the Art of Memory* (Berkeley, Los
    Angeles and London: University of California Press, 2005)
Butterfield, Ardis, 'Le tradizioni della canzone cortese medievale', in Jean-Jacques
    Nattiez, gen. ed., *Enciclopedia della musica (The Einaudi Encyclopedia of Music)*,
    vol. IV, *Storia della musica europea* (Turin: Einaudi, 2004), pp. 130–51
  Poetry and Music in Medieval France: From Jean Renart to Guillaume de Machaut
    (Cambridge University Press, 2002)
  'The Art of Repetition: Machaut's Ballade 33 "Nes qu'on porroit"', in Tess
    Knighton and John Milsom, eds., *Close Readings: Essays in Honour of John
    Stevens and Philip Brett*, Special Issue of *Early Music*, 31 (2003), pp. 346–60
Bynum, Caroline Walker, *Jesus as Mother: Studies in the Spirituality of the High
    Middle Ages* (Berkeley: University of California Press, 1982)
Caldwell, John, *The Oxford History of English Music*, vol. I, *From the Beginnings to
    c.1715* (Oxford: Clarendon Press, 1991)
Camille, Michael, *Mirror in Parchment: The Luttrell Psalter and the Making of
    Medieval England* (London: Reaktion Books, 1998)
Carapetyan, Armen, *An Early Fifteenth-Century Italian Source of Keyboard Music:
    The Codex Faenza, Biblioteca Comunale 117* (n.p.: American Institute of
    Musicology, 1961)
Carlson, Rachel Golden, 'Striking Ornaments: Complexities of Sense and Song in
    Aquitanian "Versus"', *Music and Letters* 84 (2003), pp. 527–56
Carmina Burana, ed. Alfons Hilka and Otto Schumann, 2 vols. in 4 (Heidelberg:
    Carl Winters Universitätsbuchhandlung, 1930–70)
Carpenter, Nan Cooke, *Music in the Medieval and Renaissance Universities* (Norman:
    University of Oklahoma Press, 1958)
Casteret, Jean-Jacques, *Musique et musiciens à la cour de Gaston Fébus* (PhD diss.,
    Université de Paris IV, 1992)

Castro Caridad, Eva Maria, *Tropos y troparios hispánicos* (Universidade de Santiago de Compostela, 1991)

Cattin, Giulio, *La monodia nel Medioevo*, Storia della musica, Società Italiana di Musicologia 2 (Turin: Edizioni de Torino, 1991)

'"Secundare" e "succinere": Polifonia a Padova e Pistoia nel Duecento', *Musica e Storia* 3 (1995), pp. 41–120

'Studio sulle melodie cortonesi', in Giorgio Varanini, Luigi Banfi and Anna Ceruti Burgio, eds., *Laude cortonesi dal secolo 13° al 15°* (Florence: Olschki, 1981)

and Gallo, F. Alberto, eds., *Un millennio di polifonia liturgica tra oralità e scrittura* (Bologna: Il Mulino, 2002)

Černý, Jaromír, 'Cantio', in *Die Musik in Geschichte und Gegenwart*

'Das retrospektive Organum oder Neo-organum', *Hudební věda* 38 (2001), pp. 3–31

'Knejstarším dějinám moteta v českých zemích', *Miscellanea Musicologica* 24 (1971), pp. 7–90

'Středověk (800–1420)', in Jaromír Černý et al., eds., *Hudba v českých dějinách od středověku do nové doby* (Prague: Editio Supraphon, 1983)

'Vícehlasé písně konduktového typu v českých pramenech 15. století', *Miscellanea Musicologica* 31 (1984), pp. 39–142

ed., *Petrus Wilhelmi de Grudencz Magister Cracoviensis Opera Musica* (Cracow: Polskie Wydawnictwo Muzyczne, 1993)

Cerquiglini, Bernard, *Éloge de la variante: histoire critique de la philologie* (Paris: Éditions du Seuil, 1989), trans. Betsy Wing as *In Praise of the Variant: A Critical History of Philology* (Baltimore: Johns Hopkins University Press, 1999)

Chailley, Jacques, ed., *Alia musica: traité de musique du IXe siècle* (Paris: Centre de Documentation Universitaire et Société d'Édition d'Enseignement Supérieur Réunis, 1965)

Chartier, Roger, *The Order of Books: Readers, Authors, and Libraries in Europe between the Fourteenth and Eighteenth Centuries*, trans. Lydia Cochrane (Stanford University Press, 1994)

Chartier, Yves, ed., *L'oeuvre musicale d'Hucbald de Saint-Amand: les compositions et le traité de musique* ([Saint-Laurent, Quebec]: Bellarmin, 1995)

Chrétien de Troyes, 'Erec et Enide', in Mario Roques, ed., *Les Romans de Chrétien de Troyes*, vol. I (Paris: Champion, 1953)

Clanchy, Michael T., *From Memory to Written Record: England 1066–1307* (London: Edward Arnold, 1979; 2nd edn, Oxford: Blackwell, 1993)

'Moderni in Education and Government in England', *Speculum* 50 (1975), pp. 671–88

Clark, Alice V., 'Vernacular Dedicatory Motets in Fourteenth-Century France', *Journal of Musicological Research* 20 (2000), pp. 41–69

Clark, Gregory, 'The Economics of Exhaustion, the Postan Thesis, and the Agricultural Revolution', *Journal of Economic History* 52 (1992), pp. 61–84

Claussen, Martin A., *The Reform of the Frankish Church: Chrodegang of Metz and the 'Regula canonicorum' in the Eighth Century* (Cambridge University Press, 2004)

Codex Calixtinus de la Catedral de Santiago de Compostela (Madrid: Kaydeda Ediciones, 1993)

Codex 121 Einsiedeln: Graduale und Sequenzen Notkers von St. Gallen, with a commentary by Odo Lang (Weinheim: VCH Acta Humaniora, 1991)

Códice de canto polifónico [de Las Huelgas] (Madrid: Testimonio, 1997)

Colledge, Edmund, *The Latin Poems of Richard Ledrede, OFM* (Toronto: Pontifical Institute, 1974)

Collingwood, Robin George, *The Idea of History*, rev. edn by Jan van der Dussen (Oxford University Press, 1993)

Combe, Dom Pierre *The Restoration of Gregorian Chant: Solesmes and the Vatican Edition*, trans. Theodore N. Marier and William Skinner (Washington, DC: Catholic University of America Press, 2003)

Comfort, William W., *Chrétien de Troyes: Arthurian Romances* (London: Everyman's Library, 1914)

Corbin, Solange, *Essai sur la musique religieuse portugaise au Moyen Âge (1100–1385)* (Paris: Les Belles Lettres, 1952)

Corpus Antiphonarium Officii – Ecclesiarum Centralis Europae. Hungarian Academy of Sciences. Institute of Musicology www.zti.hu/earlymusic/cao-ece/cao-ece.html

Corsi, Cesare and Petrobelli, Pierlugi, eds., *Le polifonie primitive in Friuli e in Europa* (Rome: Torre d'Orfeo, 1989)

Corsi, Giuseppe, *Poesie musicali del Trecento* (Bologna: Commissione per i testi di lingua, 1970)

Coussemaker, Charles Edmond Henri de, *Histoire de l'harmonie au Moyen Âge* (Paris: Didron, 1852; repr. Hildesheim: Olms, 1966)

  L'art harmonique aux XIIe et XIIIe siècles (Paris: Durand, 1865, repr. Hildesheim: Olms, 1964)

  Scriptorum de musica medii aevi novam seriem a Gerbertina alteram, 4 vols. (Paris: Durand, 1864–76; repr. Hildesheim: Olms, 1963)

Cowdrey, Herbert, *The Register of Pope Gregory VII, 1073–1085: An English Translation* (Oxford University Press, 2002)

Crichton, James Dunlop, *A Short History of the Mass* (London: Incorporated Catholic Truth Society, 1983)

Crocker, Richard, 'A New Source for Medieval Music Theory', *Acta Musicologica* 39 (1967), pp. 161–71

  The Early Medieval Sequence (Berkeley and Los Angeles: University of California Press, 1977)

  'The Troping Hypothesis', *Musical Quarterly* 52 (1966), pp. 183–203

  and Hiley, David, eds., *The New Oxford History of Music*, vol. II, *The Early Middle Ages to 1300* (Oxford and New York: Oxford University Press, 1990)

Cross, Frank and Livingstone, Elizabeth A., eds., *The Oxford Dictionary of the Christian Church*, rev. edn (Oxford University Press, 1983)

Crossley, Paul, 'Ara Patriae: Saint Stanislaus, the Jagiellonians and the Coronation Ordinal for Cracow Cathedral', in Jiří Fajt and Markus Hörsch, eds., *Kunstlerische Wechselwirkungen in Mitteleuropa*, Studia Jagiellonica Lipsiensia 1 (Ostfildern: Jan Thorbecke Verlag, 2006), pp. 103–21

Csapodi, Csaba, Csapodiné Gárdonyi, Klára, and Szántó, Tibor, comps., *Biblioteca Corviniana: The Library of King Matthias Corvinus of Hungary*, trans. Zsuzsanna Horn (New York: Praeger, 1969)

Cserba, Simon M., ed., *Der Musiktraktat des Hieronymus de Moravia OP* (Regensburg: Friedrich Pustet, 1935)

Cullin, Olivier, *L'image musique* (Paris: Fayard, 2006)

Curry, Robert, 'Fragments of *Ars antiqua* at Stary Sącz and the Evolution of the Clarist Order in Central Europe in the Thirteenth Century' (PhD diss., Monash University, Melbourne, 2003)

'Lost and Found in Stary Sącz', in Tomasz Jeż, ed., *Complexus effectuum musicologiae. Studia Miroslao Perz septuagenario dedicata*, Studia et Dissertationes Instituti Musicologiae Universitatis Varsoviensis B/13 (Cracow: Rabid, 2003)

Czagány, Zsuzsa, 'Bemerkungen zum Prager Offizium', *Miscellanea Musicologica* 37 (2003), pp. 105–10

D'Accone, Frank, *The Civic Muse: Music and Musicians in Siena during the Middle Ages and the Renaissance* (Chicago and London: University of Chicago Press, 1997)

Dahlhaus, Carl, *Foundations of Music History*, trans. J. Bradford Robinson (Cambridge University Press, 1983)

Dahnk, Emilie, *L'Hérésie de Fauvel*, Leipziger romanistische Studien II, Literaturwissenschaftliche Reihe 4 (Leipzig: C. & E. Vogel, 1935)

Davidson, Audrey E., ed., *The 'Ordo virtutum' of Hildegard of Bingen* (Kalamazoo: Western Michigan University, 1985)

Davies, Norman, *Europe. A History* (Oxford and New York: Oxford University Press, 1996)

God's Playground. A History of Poland (New York: Columbia University Press, 1982)

Davison, Archibold and Apel, Willi, eds., *Historical Anthology of Music*, rev. edn, 2 vols. (Cambridge, MA: Harvard University Press, 1964)

Dean, Jeffrey, 'Okeghem's Valediction? The Meaning of *Intemerata Dei mater*', in Philippe Vendrix, ed., *Johannes Ockeghem: Actes du XLᵉ Colloque international d'études humanistes, Tours, 3–8 février 1997* (Paris: Klincksieck, 1998), pp. 521–70

Deshusses, Jean, *Le sacramentaire grégorien: Ses principales formes d'après les plus anciens manuscrits*, 2 vols. (Fribourg: Éditions Universitaires Fribourg Suisse, vol. I, 1971 and vol. II, 1979)

Díaz y Díaz, Manuel, *El Códice Calixtino de la Catedral de Santiago: Estudio Codicológico y de contenido* (Santiago de Compostela: Centro de Estudios Jacobeas, 1988)

Dictionary of the Middle Ages, 13 vols. (New York: Scribner, 1982–2003)

Die mittelalterliche Musikhandschrift W₁: vollständige Reproduktion des 'Notre Dame'-Manuskrits der Herzog August Bibliothek Wolfenbüttel Cod. Guelf. 628 Helmst., with a forward by Martin Staehelin (Wiesbaden: Harrassowitz, 1995)

Diekstra, Franciscus Nicolaas Maria, 'The Poetic Exchange between Philippe de Vitry and Jean de le Mote', *Neophilologus* 70 (1986), pp. 504–19

Digital Image Archive of Medieval Music, www.diamm.ac.uk/index.html

Dillon, Emma, *Medieval Music-Making and the Roman de Fauvel* (Cambridge University Press, 2002)

Dittmer, Luther A., ed., *Facsimile Reproduction of the Manuscript Wolfenbüttel 1099 (1206)*, Publications of Mediaeval Musical Manuscripts 2 (Brooklyn: Institute of Mediaeval Music, ca1960)

　ed., *Facsimile Reproduction of the Manuscript Firenze, Biblioteca Mediceo-Laurenziana, Pluteo 29.1*, 2 vols., Publications of Mediaeval Musical Manuscripts 10–11 (Brooklyn: Institute of Mediaeval Music, 1966–7)

　ed., *Faksimile-Ausgabe der Handschrift Madrid 20486*, Veröffentlichungen mittelalterlicher Musikhandschriften 1 (New York: Institute of Mediaeval Music, 1957)

　ed., *Paris 13521 and 11411: Facsimile, Index, and Transcription from the mss. Paris, Bibl. Nat. nouv. acq. 13521 (La Clayette) and Lat. 11411*, Publications of Mediaeval Musical Manuscripts 4 (Brooklyn, Institute of Mediaeval Music, ca1959)

Dobson, Eric J., and Harrison, Frank Ll., *Medieval English Songs* (London: Faber, 1979)

Dobszay, László, 'Plainchant in Medieval Hungary', *Journal of the Plainsong & Mediaeval Music Society* 13 (1990), pp. 49–78

　'The System of the Hungarian Plainsong Sources', *Studia Musicologica Academiae Scientiarum Hungaricae* 27 (1985), pp. 37–65

　and Szendrei, Janka, eds., *Antiphonen*, Monumenta Monodica Medii Aevi 5, vol. I (Kassel and New York: Bärenreiter, 1991)

Donovan, Richard B., *The Liturgical Drama in Medieval Spain* (Toronto: Pontifical Institute of Mediaeval Studies, 1958)

Doss-Quinby, Eglal, *Les refrains chez les trouvères du XIIe siècle au début du XIVe* (New York: Peter Lang, 1984)

　The Lyrics of the Trouvères: A Research Guide (1970–90) (New York: Garland, 1994)

　and Rosenberg, Samuel N., eds., with Elizabeth Aubrey, *The Old French Ballette: Oxford Bodleian Library, MS Douce 308* (Geneva: Droz, 2006)

　et al., eds., *Songs of the Women Trouvères* (New Haven and London: Yale University Press, 2001)

Drogin, Marc, *Medieval Calligraphy: Its History and Technique* (Montclair: Allanheld and Schram, 1980)

Dronke, Peter, *The Medieval Lyric*, 2nd edn (London: Hutchinson, 1978)

　ed. and trans., 'Play of the Virtues', in Dronke, ed. and trans., *Nine Medieval Plays* (Cambridge: Cambridge University Press, 1994)

Durling, Nancy Vine, ed., *Jean Renart and the Art of Romance: Essays on Guillaume de Dole* (Gainesville: University Press of Florida, 1997)

Dürrer, Martin, *Altitalienische Laudenmelodien: das einstimmige Repertoire der Handschriften Cortona und Florenz* (Kassel: Bärenreiter, 1996)

Dutton, Paul Edward, ed. and trans., *Charlemagne's Courtier: The Complete Einhard* (Peterborough, Ont.: Broadview Press, 1998)

Duys, Kathryn, 'Books Shaped by Song: Early Literacy in the *Miracles de Nostre Dame* of Gautier de Coinci' (PhD diss., New York University, 1997)

Dyer, Joseph, 'Monastic Psalmody of the Middle Ages', *Revue bénédictine* 99 (1989), pp. 41–74

'Prolegomena to a History of Music and Liturgy at Rome in the Middle Ages', in Graeme Boone, ed., *Essays on Medieval Music: In Honor of David G. Hughes* (Cambridge, MA: Harvard University Press, 1995), pp. 87–115

'The Desert, the City and Psalmody in the Late Fourth Century', in Sean Gallagher, James Haar, John Nádas and Timothy Striplin, eds., *Western Plainchant in the First Millennium: Studies in the Medieval Liturgy and Its Music* (Aldershot: Ashgate, 2003), pp. 11–43

'The Schola Cantorum and Its Roman Milieu in the Early Middle Ages', in Peter Cahn and Ann-Katrin Heimer, eds., *De musica et cantu: Studien zur Geschichte der Kirchenmusik und der Oper. Helmut Hucke zum 60. Geburtstag* (Hildesheim: Olms 1993), pp. 19–40

'The Singing of Psalms in the Early-Medieval Office', *Speculum* 64 (1989), pp. 535–78

'*Tropis semper variantibus*: Compositional Strategies in the Offertories of Old Roman Chant', *Early Music History* 17 (1998), pp. 1–60

Earp, Lawrence, *Guillaume de Machaut: A Guide to Research*, Garland Composer Resource Manuals 36 (New York and London: Garland, 1995)

'Lyrics for Reading and Lyrics for Singing in Late Medieval France: The Development of the Dance Lyric from Adam de la Halle to Guillaume de Machaut', in Rebecca A. Baltzer, Thomas Cable and James Wimsatt, eds., *The Union of Words and Music in Medieval Poetry* (Austin: University of Texas Press, 1991), pp. 101–31

'Machaut's Music in the Early Nineteenth Century: The Work of Perne, Bottée de Toulmon, and Fétis', in Jacqueline Cerquiglini-Toulet and Nigel Wilkins, eds., *Guillaume de Machaut 1300–2000* (Paris: Presses de l'Université de Paris-Sorbonne, 2002), pp. 9–40

'Scribal Practice, Manuscript Production and the Transmission of Music in Late Medieval France: The Manuscripts of Guillaume de Machaut' (PhD diss., Princeton University, 1983)

'Texting in 15th-Century French Chansons: A Look Ahead from the 14th Century', *Early Music* 19 (1991), pp. 195–210

Eben, David, 'Tradice gregoránského chorálu v Čechách – minulost a současnost', in Marie Novaková, ed., *Kirchenmusikalisches Symposium. Verpflichtungen und Möglichkeiten in Ausbildung und Praxis der Musica Sacra im Licht der Weisungen des II. Vatikanischen Konzils*, Musicae Sacrae Ministerium, 31/1–2 (Rome: Consociatio Internationalis Musicae Sacrae, 1994), pp. 47–60

Egan, Margarita, trans., *The Vidas of the Troubadours*, Garland Library of Medieval Literature, ser. B., 6 (New York and London: Garland, 1984)

Eggebrecht, Hans Heinrich and Zaminer, Frieder, *Ad Organum Faciendum: Lehrschriften der Mehrstimmigkeit in nachguidonischer Zeit* (Mainz: B. Schott's Söhne, 1970)

Ellinwood, Leonard, ed., *Musica Hermanni Contracti* (Rochester, NY: Eastman School of Music, 1936)

Ellis, Katharine, *Music Criticism in Nineteenth-Century France: 'La Revue et Gazette musicale de Paris', 1834–80* (Cambridge University Press, 1995)

Ellsworth, Oliver, ed., *The Berkeley Manuscript: University of California Music Library, ms. 744 (olim Phillipps 4450)* (Lincoln: University of Nebraska Press, 1984)

Emery, Elizabeth, 'The "Truth" about the Middle Ages: *La Revue des Deux Mondes* and Late Nineteenth-Century French Medievalism', in Clare A. Simmons, ed., *Medievalism and the Quest for the 'Real' Middle Ages* (London and Portland, OR: Cass, 2001), pp. 99–114

Erickson, Raymond, trans. *Musica enchiriadis and Scolica enchiriadis*, ed. Claude V. Palisca (New Haven: Yale University Press, 1995)

Evans, Paul, *The Early Trope Repertory of Saint Martial de Limoges* (Princeton University Press, 1970)

Everist, Mark, *French Motets in the Thirteenth Century: Music, Poetry and Genre*, Cambridge Studies in Medieval and Renaissance Music (Cambridge University Press, 1994)

'From Paris to St Andrews: The Origins of W1', *Journal of the American Musicological Society* 43 (1990), pp. 1–42

'Le fonti della musica polifonica, ca. 1170–1330', in Carlo Fiore, ed., *Il Libro di musica: per una storia materiale delle fonti musicali in Europa* (Palermo: L'Epos, 2004), pp. 43–64

'Motets, French Tenors and the Polyphonic Chanson ca. 1300', *Journal of Musicology* 24 (2007), pp. 365–406

Polyphonic Music in Thirteenth-Century France: Aspects of Sources and Distribution (New York: Garland, 1989)

'Reception and Recomposition in the Polyphonic *Conductus cum cauda*: The Metz Fragment', *Journal of the Royal Musical Association* 125 (2000), pp. 135–63

'Souspirant en terre estrainge': The Polyphonic Rondeau from Adam de la Halle to Guillaume de Machaut', *Early Music History* 26 (2007), pp. 1–42

ed., *French 13th-Century Polyphony in the British Library: A Facsimile Edition of the Manuscripts Additional 30091 and Egerton 2615 (folios 79–94v)* (London: Plainsong and Mediaeval Music Society, 1988)

ed., *Les Organa à deux voix du manuscrit de Florence, Biblioteca Medicea-Laurenziana, Plut. 29.1*, 3 vols., Le Magnus liber organi de Notre Dame de Paris 2–4 (Monaco: Éditions de l'Oiseau-Lyre, 2001–3)

Fabbri, Mario and Nádas, John, 'A Newly Discovered Trecento Fragment: Scribal Concordances in Late-Medieval Florentine Manuscripts', *Early Music History* 3 (1983), pp. 67–81

Facchin, Francesco, ed., *Polifonie semplici: atti del convegno internazionale di studi, Arezzo, 28–30 dicembre 2001* (Arezzo: Fondazione Guido d'Arezzo, 2003)

Falck, Robert, *The Notre Dame Conductus: A Study of the Repertory*, Musicological Studies 33 (Henryville, Ottawa, and Binningen: Institute of Mediaeval Music, 1981)

Fallows, David, *A Catalogue of Polyphonic Songs, 1415–1480* (Oxford: Clarendon Press, 1999)

'A Glimpse of the Lost Years: Spanish Polyphonic Song, 1450–1470', in Josephine Wright and Samuel, Floyd, eds., *New Perspectives in Music: Essays in Honor of Eileen Southern* (Warren, MI: Harmonie Park Press, 1992)

'Specific Information on the Ensembles for Composed Polyphony, 1400–1474', in Stanley Boorman, ed., *Studies in the Performance of Late Mediaeval Music* (Cambridge University Press, 1983), pp. 109–59

Falls, Thomas B., trans., *Saint Justin Martyr* (Washington, DC: Catholic University of America Press, 1948)

Falvy, Zoltán, 'Die Weisen des König Stephan-Reimoffiziums', *Studia Musicologica Academiae Scientiarum Hungaricae* 6 (1964), pp. 207–69

Fano, Fabio, ed., *La cappella musicale del Duomo di Milano: le origini e il primo maestro di cappella, Matteo da Perugia* (Milan: Ricordi, 1956)

Fassler, Margot, *Gothic Song: Victorine Sequences and Augustinian Reform in Twelfth-Century Paris* (Cambridge University Press, 1993)

'Sermons, Sacramentaries, and Early Sources for the Office in the Latin West: The Example of Advent', in Margot Fassler and Rebecca A. Baltzer, eds., *The Divine Office in the Latin Middle Ages: Methodology and Source Studies, Regional Developments, Hagiography* (Oxford University Press, 2000), pp. 15–47

'The Feast of Fools and the *Danielis Ludus*: Popular Tradition in a Medieval Cathedral Play', in Thomas Forrest Kelly, ed., *Plainsong in the Age of Polyphony* (Cambridge University Press, 1992), pp. 66–99

'The Role of the Parisian Sequence in the Evolution of Notre-Dame Polyphony', *Speculum* 62 (1987), pp. 345–74

and Baltzer, Rebecca A., eds., *The Divine Office in the Latin Middle Ages: Methodology and Source Studies, Regional Developments, Hagiography* (Oxford University Press, 2000)

Feicht, Hieronym, 'Muzyka liturgiczna w polskim średniowieczu', in *Studia nad muzyką polskiego średniowiecza*, Opera Omnia Musicologica Hieronymi Feicht 1 (Cracow: Polskie Wydawnictwo Muzyczne, 1975), pp. 244–9

"Św. Cyril i Methody w polskich księgach chorałowych i śpiewnikach', in *Studia nad muzyką polskiego średniowiecza*, Opera Musicologica Hieronymi Feicht 1 (Cracow: Polskie Wydawnictwo Muzyczne, 1975), pp. 244–9

Feldmann, Fritz, *Musik und Musikpflege in mittelalterlichen Schlesien*, Darstellungen und Quellen zur schlesischen Geschichte 37 (Breslau: Trewendt & Granier, 1938)

Fernández de la Cuesta, Ismael, *Historia de la música española*, vol. I, *Desde los orígenes hasta el 'ars nova'* (Madrid: Alianza Editorial, 1983)

ed., *Antiphonale silense: British Library Mss. Add. 30.850* (Madrid: Sociedad Española de Musicología, 1985)

Ferreira, Manuel Pedro, 'Andalusian Music and the *Cantigas de Santa Maria*', in Stephen Parkinson, ed., *Cobras e son: Papers on the Text, Music and Manuscripts of the 'Cantigas de Santa Maria'* (Oxford: Legenda, 2000), pp. 7–19

Cantus coronatus: 7 cantigas d'El-Rei D. Dinis (Kassel: Reichenberger, 2005)

'Music at Cluny: The Tradition of Gregorian Chant for the Proper of the Mass – Melodic Variants and Microtonal Nuances' (PhD diss., Princeton University, 1993)

O som de Martin Codax (Lisbon: Unisys, 1986)

'Rondeau and Virelai: The Music of Andalus and the *Cantigas de Santa Maria*',
   Plainsong and Medieval Music 13 (2004), pp. 127–40

Fétis, François-Joseph, 'De la nécessité de considérer la musique dans son histoire,
   soit pour en étudier les principes, soit pour ajouter à ses progrès', *Revue musicale*
   5 (1831), pp. 277–80

'Découverte de manuscrits intéressans pour l'histoire de la musique (deuxième
   article)', *Revue musicale*, 1 (1827), pp. 106–13

'Découverte de plusieurs manuscrits intéressans pour l'histoire de la musique',
   Revue musicale 1, prospectus (1827), pp. 3–11

'Du sort futur de la musique', *Revue musicale* 9 (1830), pp. 225–9

Ficker, Rudolf, 'Die Musik des Mittelalters und ihre Beziehungen zum Geistesleben',
   Deutsche Vierteljahrschrift für Literaturwissenschaft und Geistesgeschichte 3
   (1925), pp. 501–35

'Polyphonic Music of the Gothic Period', trans. Theodore Baker, *Musical Quarterly*
   15 (1929), pp. 483–505

Flanigan, C. Clifford, 'The Fleury Playbook, the Traditions of Medieval Latin
   Drama, and Modern Scholarship', in Thomas P. Campbell and Clifford
   Davidson, eds., *The Fleury Playbook: Essays and Studies* (Kalamazoo, MI:
   Medieval Institute Publications, 1985), pp. 1–25

Frere, Walter Howard, ed., *The Use of Sarum I Consuetudinary and Customary*
   (Cambridge University Press, 1898)

Friedlein, Godofredus, ed., *Anicii Manlii Torquati Severini Boetii De institutione
   arithmetica libri duo. De institutione musica libri quinque. Accedit Geometria quae
   fertur Boetii* (Leipzig: B. G. Teubner, 1867)

Fuller, Sarah, 'A Phantom Treatise of the Fourteenth Century? The *Ars Nova*',
   Journal of Musicology 30 (1985–6), pp. 23–50

'Aquitanian Polyphony of the Eleventh and Twelfth Centuries' (PhD diss.,
   University of California, Berkeley 1969)

'Discant and the Theory of Fifthing', *Acta Musicologica* 50 (1978), pp. 241–75

'Early Polyphony', in Richard Crocker and David Hiley, eds., *The New Oxford
   History of Music*, vol. II, *The Early Middle Ages to 1300* (Oxford University Press,
   1990), pp. 485–556

'Modal Tenors and Tonal Orientation in Motets of Guillaume de Machaut',
   Current Musicology 45–7 (1990), pp. 199–245

'On Sonority in Fourteenth-Century Polyphony: Some Preliminary Reflections',
   Journal of Music Theory 30 (1986), pp. 35–70

'Perspectives on Musical Notation in the *Codex Calixtinus*', in José López-Calo and
   Carlos Villanueva Abelairas, eds., *El Códice Calixtino y la Música de su Tiempo*
   (La Coruña: Fundación Pedro Barrié da la Maza, 2001), pp. 183–234

'Tendencies and Resolutions: The Directed Progression in Ars Nova Music',
   Journal of Music Theory 36 (1992), pp. 229–58

The European Musical Heritage 800–1750 (New York: Knopf, 1987)

'The Myth of Saint-Martial Polyphony: A Study of the Sources', *Musica Disciplina*
   33 (1979), pp. 5–26

'Theoretical Foundations of Early Organum Theory', *Acta Musicologica* 53 (1981), pp. 52–84

Gaffurio, Franchino, *Practica musice* (Milan, 1496)

Gagnepain, Bernard, 'A la recherche du temps passé: du rôle de quelques précurseurs dans la renaissance du patrimoine musical français', in Marie-Claire Mussat, Jean Mongrédien and Jean-Michel Nectoux, eds., *Échos de France et d'Italie: Liber amicorum Yves Gérard* (Paris: Buchet/Chastel Société française de musicologie, 1997), pp. 119–28

Gallo, F. Alberto, *La polifonia nel Medioevo*, Storia della musica, Società Italiana di Musicologia 3 (Turin: EDT, 1991)

'The practice of "Cantus planus binatim" in Italy from the beginning of the fourteenth to the beginning of the sixteenth century', in Cesare Corsi and Pierlugi Petrobelli, eds., *Le polifonie primitive in Friuli e in Europa* (Rome: Torre d'Orfeo, 1989)

ed., *Il Codice musicale Panciatichi 26 della Biblioteca nazionale di Firenze* (Florence: Olschki, 1981)

ed., *Il Codice Squarcialupi* (Lucca: Libreria Musicale Italiana Editrice, 1992)

Gambra, Andrés, *Alfonso VI: Cancillería, Curia e Imperio*, 2 vols. (León: Caja de Ahorros y Monte de Piedad, 1997–8)

Gancarczyk, Paweł, '*Cantus planus multiplex* in Polen: von einer mündlichen Tradition zur Notenschrift', in László Dobszay, ed., *The Past in the Present: Papers Read at the IMS Intercongressional Symposium and the 10th Meeting of the Cantus Planus, Budapest and Visegrád, 2000* (Budapest: Liszt Ferenc Academy of Music, 2003), pp. 483–95

Musica scripto. Kodeksy menzuralne II połowy XV wieku na wschodzie Europy Łacińskiej (Warsaw: Instytut Sztuki PAN, 2001)

'Petrus Wilhelm de Grudencz (b. 1392): A Central European Composer', *De musica disserenda* 2, no. 1 (2006), pp. 103–12

'Polifonia w Polsce do około 1500 roku: źródła i problemy ich interpretacji', *Muzyka* 51, nos. 1–2 (2006), pp. 85–103

Garratt, James, *Palestrina and the German Romantic Imagination: Interpreting Historicism in Nineteenth-Century Music*, Musical Performance and Reception (Cambridge University Press, 2002)

Gatien-Arnoult, Adolphe, *Monumens de la littérature romane*, 3 vols. (Toulouse: J.-B. Paya, 1841–3)

Gaunt, Simon and Kay, Sarah, eds., *The Troubadours: An Introduction* (Cambridge University Press, 1999)

Geering, Arnold, *Die Organa und mehrstimmigen Conductus in den Handschriften des deutschen Sprachgebietes vom 13. bis 16. Jahrhundert*, Publikationen der Schweizerischen Musikforschenden Gesellschaft II/1 (Bern: Verlag Paul Haupt, 1952)

Gellrich, Jesse, *The Idea of the Book in the Middle Ages: Language Theory, Mythology, and Fiction* (Ithaca, NY: Cornell University Press, 1985)

Gennrich, Friedrich, *Aus der Frühzeit der Motette*, Musikwissenschaftliche Studien-Bibliothek 22–3 (Frankfurt: Langen, 1963)

Bibliographie der ältesten französischen und lateinischen Motetten, Summa Musicae
    Medii Aevi 2 (Darmstadt: author, 1957)

Gerbert, Martin, *De cantu et musica sacra a prima ecclesiae aetate usque ad praesens
    tempus*, 2 vols. (Sankt-Blasianis: Typis San-Blasianis, 1774; repr. Othmar Wessely,
    ed., Die grossen Darstellungen der Musikgeschichte in Barok und Aufklärung 4,
    Graz: Akademische Druck- u. Verlagsanstalt, 1968)

    Scriptores ecclesiastici de musica sacra potissimum, 3 vols. (Sankt Blasien: Typis
    San-Blasianis, 1784; repr. Hildesheim: Olms, 1963)

Gevaert, François-Auguste, *La mélopée antique dans le chant de l'église latine*,
    (Ghent: Hoste, 1895, repr. Osnabrück: Zeller, 1967)

    Les origines du chant liturgique de l'église latine: étude d'histoire musicale (Ghent:
    Hoste, 1890; repr. Hildesheim and New York: Olms, 1971)

Gillingham, Bryan, 'A New Etymology and Etiology for the Conductus', in
    Bryan Gillingham and Paul Merkley, eds., *Beyond the Moon: Festschrift Luther
    Dittmer*, Musicological Studies 53 (Ottawa: Institute of Mediaeval Music, 1990)

    Saint-Martial Mehrstimmigkeit/Saint-Martial Polyphony, Musicological Studies 44
    (Henryville, PA: Institute of Mediaeval Music, 1984)

    ed., *Paris, Bibliothèque Nationale, fonds Latin 1139*, Publications of Musical
    Manuscripts 14 (Ottawa: Institute of Mediaeval Music, 1987)

    ed., *Paris, Bibliothèque Nationale, fonds Latin 3549 and London, British Library
    36881*, Publications of Musical Manuscripts 16 (Ottawa: Institute of Mediaeval
    Music, 1987)

    ed., *Paris, Bibliothèque Nationale, fonds Latin 3719*, Publications of Musical
    Manuscripts 15 (Ottawa: Institute of Mediaeval Music, 1987)

Göllner, Theodor, *Die mehrstimmigen liturgischen Lesungen*, 2 vols. (Tutzing: Hans
    Schneider, 1969)

Gómez , M.-C., 'El ars antiqua en Cataluña', *Revista de musicología* 2 (1979),
    pp. 197–255 and 3 (1980), pp. 279–84

    El canto de la Sibila, 2 vols. (Madrid: Alpuerto, 1996–7)

    El Llibre Vermell de Montserrat: cantos y danzas s. XIV (Sant Cugat del Vallès: Los
    libros de la Frontera, 1990)

    La música en la casa real catalano-aragonesa durante los años 1336–1432
    (Barcelona: Bosch, 1979)

    La música medieval en España (Kassel: Reichenberger, 2001)

Gossman, Lionel, *Medievalism and the Ideologies of the Enlightenment: The World
    and Work of La Curne de Sainte-Palaye* (Baltimore: Johns Hopkins University
    Press, 1968)

Gozzi, Marco, ' "Cantus firmus per notulas plani cantus": alcune testimonianze
    quattrocentesche', in Francesco Facchin, ed., *Il cantus firmus nella polifonia: Atti
    del convegno internazionale di studi, Arezzo, 27–29 dicembre 2002* (Arezzo:
    Fondazione Guido d'Arezzo, 2005), pp. 45–88

    'La notazione del codice Add. 29987 di Londra', in Bianca Maria Antolini, Teresa
    M. Gialdroni and Annunziato Pugliese, eds., '*Et facciam dolçi canti': Studi in
    onore di Agostino Ziino in occasione del suo 65° compleanno* (Lucca: Libreria
    Musicale Italiana, 2004), pp. 207–61

'Le edizioni liturgico-musicali dopo il Concilio', in Danilo Curti and Marco Gozzi, eds., *Musica e liturgia nella Riforma tridentina* (Trento: Provincia autonoma di Trento – Servizio Beni Librari e Archivistici, 1995), pp. 39–55

'Liturgia e musica mensurale nel Trecento italiano: i canti dell'Ordinarium', in Oliver Huck, ed., *Kontinuität und Transformation der italienischen Vokalmusik zwischen Due- und Quattrocento* (Hildesheim: Olms, 2006), pp. 53–98

'On the Text–Music Relationship in the Italian Trecento: The Case of the Petrarchan Madrigal "Non al so amante" Set by Jacopo da Bologna', *Polifonie* 4/3 (2004), pp. 197–222

and Luisi, Francesco, eds., *Il canto fratto: l'altro gregoriano. Atti del convegno internazionale di studi, Parma – Arezzo, 3–6 dicembre 2003* (Rome: Torre d'Orfeo, 2005)

Gransden, Antonia, *The Customary of the Benedictine Abbey of Bury St Edmunds in Suffolk (from Harleian MS 1005 in the British Museum)* Henry Bradshaw Society Publications 99 (London: Henry Bradshaw Society, 1973)

Greene, Gordon K., ed., *French Secular Music: Ballads and Canons*, literary texts by Terence Scully, PMFC 20 (Monaco: Éditions de L'Oiseau-Lyre, 1982)

ed., *Manuscript Chantilly, Musée Condé 564*, literary texts by Terence Scully, PMFC 18–19 (Monaco: Éditions de L'Oiseau-Lyre, 1981–2)

ed., *Rondeaux and Miscellaneous Pieces*, literary texts by Terence Scully, PMFC 22 (Monaco: Éditions de L'Oiseau-Lyre, 1989)

ed., *Virelais*, literary texts by Terence Scully, PMFC 21 (Monaco: Éditions de L'Oiseau-Lyre, 1987)

Greene, Richard L., *The Early English Carols*, 2nd edn (Oxford: Clarendon Press, 1977)

Grier, James, 'A New Voice in the Monastery: Tropes and Versus from Eleventh and Twelfth Century Aquitania', *Speculum* 6 (1994), pp. 1024–69

'The Divine Office at Saint-Martial in the Early Eleventh Century: Paris, BNF lat. 1085', in Margot Fassler and Rebecca A. Baltzer, eds., *The Divine Office in the Latin Middle Ages: Methodology and Source Studies, Regional Developments, Hagiography; Written in Honor of Professor Ruth Steiner* (Oxford University Press, 2000), pp. 179–204

The Musical World of a Medieval Monk: Adémar de Chabannes in Eleventh-Century Aquitaine (Cambridge University Press, 2006)

Grochowska, Katarzyna, 'Motet as Propaganda: The Historigraphi aciem's Embellishment of the Jagellonian Dynasty', in *Early Music – Context and Ideas: International Conference in Musicology, Kraków, 18–21 September 2003* (Cracow: Institute of Musicology, Jagellonian University, 2003), pp. 359–70

Gröninger, Eduard, *Repertoire-Untersuchungen zum mehrstimmigen Notre-Dame Conductus*, Kölner Beiträge zur Musikforschung 2 (Regensburg: Gustav Bosse, 1939)

Gros i Pujol, Miquel S., *Els tropers prosers de la Catedral de Vic: estudi i edició*, Biblioteca litúrgica Catalana 2 (Barcelona: Institut d'Estudis Catalans, 1999)

Guaitamacchi, Valeria, ed., *Madrigali trecenteschi del frammento 'Greggiati' di Ostiglia* (Bologna: [s.n.], 1970)

Guérard, Benjamin, ed., *Cartulaire de l'église Notre-Dame de Paris*, 4 vols. (Paris: Crapelet, 1850)

Guido of Arezzo, *Micrologus*, ed. Joseph Smits van Waesberghe, Corpus Scriptorum de Musica 4 ([Nijmegen]: American Institute of Musicology, 1955). English translation by Warren Babb in Claude Palisca, ed., *Hucbald, Guido, and John on Music* (New Haven and London: Yale University Press, 1995)

Gumbrecht, Hans, '*Un souffle d'Allemagne ayant passé*: Friedrich Diez, Gaston Paris, and the Genesis of National Philologies', *Romance Philology* 40 (1986–7), pp. 1–37

Gümpel, Karl-Werner, ed., *Pseudo-Odo: Dialogus de musica* (forthcoming)

Günther, Ursula, *The Motets of the Manuscripts Chantilly, Musée Condé, 564 (olim 1047) and Modena, Biblioteca Estense, α. M. 5, 25 (olim lat. 568)*, Corpus Mensurabilis Musicae 39 ([Rome]: American Institute of Musicology, 1965)

Gushee, Lawrence, ed., *Aurelianus Reomensis: Musica disciplina*, Corpus Scriptorum de Musica 21 ([Rome]: American Institute of Musicology, 1975)

Gutiérrez, Carmen Julia, 'The Hymnodic Tradition in Spain', trans. Yolanda Acker, in Andreas Haug, Christoph März and Lorenz Welker, eds., *Der lateinische Hymnus im Mittelalter: Überlieferung, Ästhetik, Ausstrahlung*, Monumenta Monodica Medii Aevi, subsidia 4 (Kassel: Bärenreiter, 2004), pp. 215–43

Gy, Pierre-Marie, *La liturgie dans l'histoire* (Paris: Éditions Saint Paul and Éditions du Cerf, 1990)

Haberl, Franz Xaver, 'Die römische "schola cantorum" und die päpstlichen Kapellsänger bis zur Mitte des 16. Jahrhunderts', *Vierteljahrschrift für Musikwissenschaft* 3 (1887), pp. 189–296

Haggh, Barbara, 'Foundations or Institutions? On Bringing the Middle Ages into the History of Medieval Music', *Acta Musicologica* 68 (1996), pp. 87–128

'Nonconformity in the Use of Cambrai Cathedral: Guillaume Du Fay's Foundations', in Margot Fassler and Rebecca A. Baltzer, eds., *The Divine Office in the Latin Middle Ages: Methodology and Source Studies, Regional Developments, Hagiography* (Oxford University Press, 2000), pp. 372–97

'Reconstructing the Plainchant Repertory of Brussels and Its Chronology', in Barbara Haggh, Frank Daelemans and André Vanrie, eds., *Musicology and Archival Research: Proceedings of the Colloquium held at the Algemeen Rijksarchief, Brussel, 22–23 April 1993*, Archief- en Bibliotheekwezen in België, Extranummer 46 (Brussels: Archives Générales du Royaume, 1994), pp. 177–213

'The Celebration of the "Recollectio Festorum Beatae Mariae Virginis", 1457–1987', *Studia Musicologica Academiae Scientiarum Hungaricae* 30 (1988), pp. 361–73

Two Offices for St Elizabeth of Hungary: Gaudeat Hungaria and Letare Germania (Ottawa: Institute of Mediaeval Music, 1995)

and Huglo, Michel, '*Magnus liber – Maius munus*: Origine et destinée du manuscrit F', *Revue de musicologie* 90 (2004), pp. 193–230

Haines, John, *Eight Centuries of the Troubadours and Trouvères: The Changing Identity of Medieval Music* (Cambridge University Press, 2004)

'The Arabic Style of Performing Medieval Music', *Early Music* 29 (2001),
pp. 369–78

and Rosenfeld, Randall, eds., *Music and Medieval Manuscripts: Paleography and
Performance. Essays Dedicated to Andrew Hughes* (Aldershot: Ashgate, 2004)

Halecki, Oscar, *Borderlands of Western Civilization: A History of East Central Europe*
(New York: Ronald Press, 1952)

Halle, Adam de la, *Le Jeu de Robin et Marion*, ed. and trans. Jean Dufournet (Paris:
Flammarion, 1989)

Le Jeu de Robin et Marion, ed. and trans. Shira I. Schwam-Baird; music ed. Milton
G. Scheuermann, Jr., Garland Library of Medieval Literature 94A (New York:
Garland, 1994)

The Lyrics and Melodies of Adam de la Halle, lyrics trans. and ed. Deborah Nelson;
melodies ed. Hendrik van der Werf, Garland Library of Medieval Literature 24
(New York: Garland, 1985)

Hamel, Christopher de, *Medieval Craftsmen: Scribes and Illuminators* (London:
British Museum Press, 1992)

The Rothschilds and their Collection of Illuminated Manuscripts (London: British
Library, 2005)

Hammond, Frederick F., ed., *Walteri Odington: Summa de speculatione musicae*,
Corpus Scriptorum de Musica 14 ([Rome]: American Institute of Musicology,
1970)

Handschin, Jacques, 'Die Modaltheorie und Carl Appels Ausgabe der Gesaenge von
Bernart de Ventadorn', *Medium Ævum* 4 (1955), pp. 69–82

Hanssens, Jean-Michel [Johannes M.], ed., *Amalarii episcopi opera liturgica omnia*, 3
vols. (Vatican City: Biblioteca Apostolica Vaticana, 1948–50)

Harper, John, *The Forms and Orders of Western Liturgy from the Tenth to the
Eighteenth Century: A Historical Introduction and Guide for Students and
Musicians* (Oxford University Press, 1991)

Harrison, Frank Ll., 'Benedicamus, Conductus, Carol', *Acta Musicologica* 37 (1965),
pp. 35–48

Music in Medieval Britain (London: Routledge & Kegan Paul, 1958; 2nd edn 1963;
repr. Buren: Fritz Knuf, 1980)

ed., *Motets of French Provenance*, French texts edited by Elizabeth Rutson, notes on
the Latin texts by A. G. Rigg, Polyphonic Music of the Fourteenth Century 5
(Monaco: Éditions de L'Oiseau-Lyre, 1968)

ed., *Musicorum collegio: Fourteenth-Century Musicians' Motets* (Monaco: Éditions
de l'Oiseau-Lyre, 1986)

Sanders, Ernest H. and Lefferts, Peter M., eds., *English Music for Mass and Offices*,
2 vols., Polyphonic Music of the Fourteenth Century 16 (Paris and Monaco:
Éditions de l'Oiseau-Lyre, 1983–6)

Hartmann, Wilfried, ed., *Die Konzilien der Karolingischen Teireiche 843–859*,
Monumenta Germaniae Historica, Concilia III (Hanover: Hahn, 1984)

Haug, Andreas, 'Tropus', *MGG IX*, cols. 897–921 (Kassel: Bärenreiter-Metzler, 1998)

Häussling, Angelus A., *Mönchskonvent und Eucharistiefeier. Eine Studie über die
Messe in der abendländischen Klosterliturgie des frühen Mittelalters und zur
Geschichte der Messhäufigkeit* (Münster: Aschendorff, 1973)

Hawkins, Sir John, *A General History of the Science and Practice of Music* (London, Novello: 1776; 2nd edn, London: Novello, 1853)

Hayburn, Robert F. *Papal Legislation on Sacred Music 95 AD to 1977 AD* (Collegeville, MN.: Liturgical Press, 1979)

Heard, Edmund Brooks, '"Alia musica": A Chapter in the History of Music Theory' (PhD diss., University of Wisconsin, 1966)

Heisler, Maria-Elisabeth, 'Die Problematik des "germanischen" oder "deutschen" Choraldialekts', *Studia Musicologica Academiae Scientiarum Hungaricae* 27 (1985), pp. 67–82

Helmholtz, Hermann von, *On the Sensations of Tone as a Physiological Basis for the Theory of Music*, trans. Alexander John Ellis, with new introduction by Henry Margenau (New York: Dover, 1954)

Hen, Yitzhak, *The Royal Patronage of Liturgy in Frankish Gaul to the Death of Charles the Bald (877)* (London: Henry Bradshaw Society, 2001)

Hentschel, Frank, *Sinnlichkeit und Vernunft in der mittelalterlichen Musiktheorie: Strategien der Konsonanzwertung und der Gegenstand der 'musica sonora' um 1300*, Beihefte zum Archiv für Musikwissenschaft 47 (Stuttgart: Steiner, 2000)

Herlinger, Jan, ed. and trans., *The Lucidarium of Marchetto of Padua* (University of Chicago Press, 1985)

Hesbert, René-Jean, *Antiphonale missarum sextuplex* (Brussels: Vromant, 1935)

Hiley, David, 'Cluny, Sequences and Tropes', in Claudio Leonardi and Enrico Menestò, eds., *La tradizione dei tropi liturgici* (Spoleto: Centro Italiano di Studi sull'Alto Medioevo, 1990), pp. 125–38

'Style and Structure in Early Offices of the Sanctorale', in Sean Gallagher, James Haar, John Nádas and Timothy Striplin, eds., *Western Plainchant in the First Millennium: Studies in the Medieval Liturgy and Its Music* (Aldershot: Ashgate, 2003)

'The Historia of St Julian of Le Mans by Létald of Micy: Some Comments and Questions about a North French Office of the Early Eleventh Century', in Margot Fassler and Rebecca A. Baltzer, eds., *The Divine Office in the Latin Middle Ages: Methodology and Source Studies, Regional Developments, Hagiography* (Oxford University Press, 2000), pp. 444–62

'The Sequence Melodies Sung at Cluny and Elsewhere', in Peter Cahn and Ann-Katrin Heimer, eds., *De musica et cantu: Studien zur Geschichte der Kirchenmusik und der Oper: Helmut Hucke zum 60. Geburtstag* (Hildesheim: G. Olms, 1993)

Western Plainchant: A Handbook (Oxford: Clarendon Press, 1993)

ed., *Historia Sancti Emmerammi Arnoldi Vohburgensis circa 1030* (Ottawa: Institute of Mediaeval Music, 1996)

Hilka, Alfons, and Schumann, Otto, eds., *Carmina Burana*, 2 vols. (Heidelberg: Carl Winters Universitätsbuchhandlung, 1930–70)

A History of Music in Poland, ed. Stefan Sutkowski, trans. John Comber, 7 vols. (Warsaw: Sutowski Edition, 2001–4)

Hoekstra, Gerald R., 'The French Motet as Trope: Multiple Levels of Meaning in *Quant florist la violete / El mois de mai / Et Gaudebit*', *Speculum* 73 (1998), pp. 32–57

Hoffmann, Ernst Theodor Amadeus, 'Alte und neue Kirchenmusik', *Allgemeine musikalische Zeitung*, 16 (1814), cols. 577–84, 593–603 and 611–19

'Old and New Church Music', in *E. T. A. Hoffman's Musical Writings: 'Kreisleriana', 'The Poet and the Composer', Music Criticism*, ed. David Charlton, trans. Martyn Clarke (Cambridge University Press, 1989)

Holford-Strevens, Leofranc, 'Du Fay the Poet? Problems in the Texts of His Motets', *Early Music History* 16 (1997), pp. 97–160

Holmes, Olivia, *Assembling the Lyric Self: Authorship from Troubadour Song to Italian Poetry Book*, Medieval Cultures 21 (Minneapolis: University of Minnesota Press, 2000)

Holschneider, Andreas, *Die Organa von Winchester: Studien zum ältesten Repertoire polyphoner Musik* (Hildesheim: Georg Olms, 1968)

Hoppin, Richard H., *Anthology of Medieval Music* (New York: Norton, 1978)
Medieval Music (New York: Norton, 1978)

Hornby, Emma, *Gregorian and Old-Roman Eighth-Mode Tracts: A Case Study in the Transmission of Western Chant* (Aldershot: Ashgate, 2002)

Horyna, Martin, 'Utwory Piotra Wilhelmiego z Grudziądza w tradycji polifonii późnośredniowiecznej w Europie środkowej, a zwłaszcza w Czechach XV i XVI wieku' *Muzyka* 49, no. 2 (2004), pp. 21–54

Howlett, David, '*Apollinis eclipsatur*: Foundation of the "Collegium musicorum"', in Suzannah Clark and Elizabeth Eva Leach, eds., *Auctoritas in Medieval and Renaissance Musical Culture: Learning from the Learned* (Woodbridge: Boydell Press, 2005)

Cambro-Latin Compositions: Their Competence and Craftsmanship (Dublin: Four Courts Press, 1998)

Huck, Oliver, *Die Musik des frühen Trecento* (Hildesheim: Olms, 2005)

ed., *Kontinuität und Transformation der italienischen Vokalmusik zwischen Due- und Quattrocento* (Hildesheim: Olms, 2006)

and Dieckmann, Sandra, with Evelyn Arnrich and Julia Gehring in association with Marco Gozzi, *Die mehrfach überlieferten Kompositionen des frühen Trecento*, Musica Mensurabilis 2 (Hildesheim, Zürich and New York: Olms, 2007)

Hucke, Helmut, 'Die Einführung des gregorianischen Gesangs im Frankenreich', *Römische Quartalschrift* 49 (1954), pp. 172–87

'Gregorianischer Gesang in altrömischer und fränkischer Überlieferung', *Archiv für Musikwissenschaft* 12 (1955), pp. 74–87

'Toward a New Historical View of Gregorian Chant', *Journal of the American Musicological Society* 33 (1980), pp. 437–67

Huff, Jay A., trans., *De speculatione musicae. Part VI*, Musicological Studies and Documents 31 ([Rome]: American Institute of Musicology, 1973)

Hughes, Andrew, 'British Rhymed Offices: A Catalogue and Commentary', in Susan Rankin and David Hiley, eds., *Music in the Medieval English Liturgy: Plainsong and Medieval Music Centennial Essays* (Oxford: Clarendon Press, 1993), pp. 239–84

'Chants in the Offices of Thomas of Canterbury and Stanislaus of Poland', *Musica Antiqua Europae Orientalis* 6 (1982), pp. 267–77

Late Medieval Liturgical Offices, Subsidia Mediaevalia 23–4 (Toronto: Pontifical Institute of Mediaeval Studies, 1994–6)

'Late Medieval Plainchant for the Divine Office', in Reinhard Strohm and Bonnie J. Blackburn, eds., *Music as Concept and Practice in the Late Middle Ages* (Oxford University Press, 2001), pp. 31–96

Medieval Manuscripts for Mass and Office: A Guide to Their Organization and Terminology (University of Toronto Press, 1982)

'Modal Order and Disorder in the Rhymed Office', *Musica Disciplina* 37 (1983), pp. 29–51

Hughes, David, 'Evidence for the Traditional View of the Transmission of Gregorian Chant', *Journal of the American Musicological Society* 40 (1987), pp. 377–404

Huglo, Michel, *Les livres de chant liturgique*, Typologie des sources du Moyen Âge occidental 52 (Turnhout: Brepols, 1988)

Les tonaires: inventaire, analyse, comparaison (Paris: Société française de musicologie, 1971)

'Tonary', in *Grove Music Online*. www.oxfordmusiconline.com

'Un tonaire du Graduel de la fin du VIIIe siècle (Bibliothèque Nationale lat. 13159)', *Revue grégorienne* 31 (1952), pp. 176–86, 224–33

et al., 'Gallican chant', in *Grove Music Online*. www.oxfordmusiconline.com

Huizinga, Johan, *Herbst des Mittelalters: Studien über Lebens- und Geistesformen des 14. und 15. Jahrhunderts in Frankreich und in den Niederlanden* (Munich: Drei Masken, 1924; original Dutch edn 1919); trans. as *The Autumn of the Middle Ages* by Rodney J. Payton and Ulrich Mammitzsch (University of Chicago Press, 1996)

Hult, David, 'Reading It Right: The Ideology of Text Editing', in Marina Brownlee, Kevin Brownlee and Stephen Nichols, eds., *The New Medievalism* (Baltimore: Johns Hopkins University Press, 1991)

Huot, Sylvia, *Allegorical Play in the Old French Motet: The Sacred and Profane in Thirteenth-Century Polyphony* (Stanford University Press, 1997)

From Song to Book: The Poetics of Writing in Old French Lyric and Lyrical Narrative Poetry (Ithaca, NY: Cornell University Press, 1987)

'Guillaume de Machaut and the Consolation of Poetry', *Modern Philology* 100 (2002), pp. 169–95

The Romance of the Rose and Its Medieval Readers: Interpretation, Reception, Manuscript Tradition, Cambridge Studies in Medieval Literature 16 (Cambridge University Press, 1993)

Hüschen, Heinrich, 'Franziskaner', rev. Hans Schmidt, in *Musik in Geschichte und Gegenwart*, vol. III (Kassel: Bärenreiter-Metzler, 1954)

Iacobus: Codex Calixtinus de la Catedral de Santiago de Compostela (Madrid: Kaydeda, 1993)

Ibos-Augé, Anne, 'La fonction des insertions lyriques dans des œuvres narratives et didactiques aux XIIIème et XIVème siècles', 4 vols. (PhD diss., Université Michel de Montaigne-Bordeaux III, 2000)

Ingarden, Roman, *The Work of Music and the Problem of Its Identity*, trans. Adam Czerniawski (Berkeley: University of California Press, 1986)

Isidore of Seville, *Étymologies*, 20 vols. (Paris: Les Belles Lettres, 1981–)

Isidori hispalensis episcopi Etymologiarum sive originum libri xx, ed. W. M. Lindsay, 2 vols. (Oxford: Clarendon Press, 1911)

Iversen, Gunilla, '"Pax et sapientia": A Thematic Study on Tropes from Different Traditions', in Ritva Jacobsson, ed., *Pax et Sapientia: Studies in Text and Music of Liturgical Sequences in Memory of Gordon Anderson* (Stockholm: Almqvist & Wiksell International, 1986), pp. 23–58

Jaeger, C. Stephen, *Scholars and Courtiers: Intellectuals and Society in the Medieval West* (Aldershot: Ashgate, 2002)

> *The Origins of Courtliness: Civilizing Trends and the Formation of Courtly Ideals 939–1210* (Philadelphia: University of Pennsylvania Press, 1985)

Jager, Eric, *The Book of the Heart* (University of Chicago Press, 2000)

Jeffery, Peter, 'Monastic Reading and the Emerging Roman Chant Repertory', in Sean Gallagher, James Haar, John Nádas and Timothy Striplin, eds., *Western Plainchant in the First Millennium: Studies in the Medieval Liturgy and Its Music* (Aldershot: Ashgate Publishing, 2003), pp. 45–103

> 'Notre Dame Polyphony in the Library of Pope Boniface VIII', *Journal of the American Musicological Society* 32 (1979), pp. 118–24

> 'Rome and Jerusalem: From Oral Tradition to Written Repertory in Two Ancient Liturgical Centers', in Graeme Boone, ed., *Essays on Medieval Music: In Honor of David G. Hughes* (Cambridge, MA: Harvard University Press, 1995), pp. 207–47

> 'The Earliest Christian Chant Repertory Recovered: The Georgian Witnesses to Jerusalem Chant', *Journal of the American Musicological Society* 47 (1994), pp. 1–39

> 'The Earliest Oktōēchoi: The Role of Jerusalem and Palestine in the Beginnings of Modal Ordering', in Peter Jeffery, ed., *The Study of Medieval Chant: Paths and Bridges, East and West – In Honor of Kenneth Levy* (Woodbridge: Boydell and Brewer, 2001), pp. 147–209

> 'The Lost Chant Tradition of Early Christian Jerusalem: Some Possible Melodic Survivals in the Byzantine and Latin Chant Repertories', *Early Music History* 11 (1992), pp. 151–90

> 'The New Vatican Chant Editions', *Notes*, 2nd ser., 47/4 (1991), pp. 1039–63

Jensen, Brian Møller, ed., *Il Libro del Maestro Codice 65* (Piacenza: Tip. Le. Co. editore, 1997)

John [of Afflighem], *Johannis Affligemensis De musica cum Tonario*, ed. Joseph Smits van Waesberghe, Corpus Scriptorum de Musica 1 (Rome: American Institute of Musicology, 1950). English translation by Warren Babb, in Claude V. Palisca, ed., *Hucbald, Guido, and John on Music* (New Haven and London: Yale University Press, 1978)

Johnson, Lonnie R., *Central Europe: Enemies, Neighbours, Friends*, 2nd edn (New York: Oxford University Press, 2002)

Jones, Cheslyn, Yarnold, Edward, Wainwright, Geoffrey and Bradshaw, Paul, eds., *The Study of the Liturgy* (London: SPCK and New York: Oxford University Press, 1992; rev. edn)

Jonsson, Ritva, 'Corpus troporum', *Journal of the Plainsong and Medieval Music Society* 1 (1978), pp. 98–115

Jordan, William Chester, *The Great Famine: Northern Europe in the Early Fourteenth Century* (Princeton University Press, 1996)

Jungmann, Joseph, *The Mass of the Roman Rite*, trans. Francis Brunner, 2 vols. (New York: Benzinger Brothers, 1951–5)

Justin Martyr, Saint, 'First Apology', in Leslie William Barnard, trans., *Ancient Christian Writers: The First and Second Apologies* (New York and Mahwah, NJ: Paulist Press, 1997), pp. 23–73

Kačic, Ladislav, 'From the Middle Ages to the Renaissance', in *A History of Slovak Music from the Earliest Time to the Present*, ed. Oskár Elschek, trans. Martin Styan (Bratislava: Veda, 2003), pp. 54–79

Kahl, Willi, 'Zur musikalischen Renaissancebewegung in Frankreich während der ersten Hälfte des 19. Jahrhunderts', in Dagmar Weise, ed., *Festschrift Joseph Schmidt-Görg zum 60. Geburtstag* (Bonn: Beethovenhaus, 1957), pp. 156–74

Karp, Theodore, *An Introduction to the Post-Tridentine Mass Proper*, 2 vols. (Middleton, WI: American Institute of Musicology, 2005)

   The Polyphony of Saint Martial and Santiago de Compostela, 2 vols. (Oxford: Clarendon Press, 1992)

Katz, Israel J., 'The Music of Sephardic Spain: An Exploratory View', in Carol E. Robertson, ed., *Musical Repercussions of 1492: Encounters in Text and Performance* (Washington, DC: Smithsonian Institution Press, 1992), pp. 101–28

Kaye, Joel, *Economy and Nature in the Fourteenth Century: Money, Market Exchange, and the Emergence of Scientific Thought* (Cambridge University Press, 1998)

Kelly, Thomas Forrest, *The Beneventan Chant* (Cambridge University Press, 1989)

   The Exultet in Southern Italy (Oxford University Press, 1996)

Kier, Herfrid, 'Kiesewetters historische Hauskonzerte: zur Geschichte der kirchenmusikalische Restauration in Wien', *Kirchenmusikalisches Jahrbuch* 52 (1968), pp. 95–119

Kiesewetter, Raphael Georg, *Die Verdienste der Niederländer um die Tonkunst* (Amsterdam: Muller, 1829)

   Geschichte der europäisch-abendländischen oder unserer heutigen Musik (Leipzig: Breitkopf und Härtel, 1834), trans. Robert Müller as *History of the Modern Music of Western Europe from the First Century of the Christian Era to the Present Day* (London: Newby, 1848); rept. with new introduction by F. Harrison (New York: Da Capo, 1973

Kihlman, Erika, *Expositiones sequentiarum: Medieval Sequence Commentaries and Prologues. Editions with Introductions*, Studia Latina Stockholmiensia 53 (Stockholm: Almquist & Wiksell International, 2006)

King, James C. and Vogler, Werner, eds., *The Culture of the Abbey of St Gall: An Overview*, trans. James C. King (Stuttgart: Belser, 1991)

King, P. D., *Charlemagne: Translated Sources* (Kendal: author, 1987)

Kippenberg, Burkhard, 'Die Melodien des Minnesangs', in Thrasybulos G. Georgiades, ed., *Musikalische Edition im Wandel des historischen Bewusstseins* (Kassel, Basle, Tours and London: Bärenreiter, 1971), pp. 62–92

Kirkman, Andrew, 'The Invention of the Cyclic Mass', *Journal of the American Musicological Society* 54 (2001), pp. 1–47

Klauser, Theodore, *A Short History of the Western Liturgy: An Account and Some Reflections*, trans. John Halliburton (London: Oxford University Press, 1969)

Kłoczowski, Jerzy, *Europa słowiańska w XIV–XV wieku* (Warsaw: Państwowy Instytut Wydawniczy, 1984)

Knapp, Janet, 'Polyphony at Notre Dame of Paris', in Richard Crocker and David Hiley, eds., *The New Oxford History of Music: The Early Middle Ages to 1300* (Oxford University Press, 1990), pp. 632–5

  ed., *Thirty-Five Conductus for Two and Three Voices*, Collegium Musicum 6 (New Haven: Yale University Department of Music Graduate School, 1965)

Kohler, Charles, 'Traité du recouvrement de la Terre Sainte adressé, vers l'an 1295, à Philippe le Bel par Galvano de Levanto, médécin génois', *Revue de l'orient latin* 6 (1898), pp. 367–8

Kolár, Jaroslav, Vidmanová-Schmidtová, Anežka and Vlhová-Wörner, Hana, eds., *Jistebnický kancionál, MS Praha, Knihovna Národního muzea, II C 7, Kritická edice/Jistebnice Kancionál, MS Prague, National Museum Library II C 7, critical edition*, vol. I, *Graduale*, Monumenta Liturgica Bohemica 2 (Brno: Luboš Marek, 2005)

Kowalewicz, Henryk, *Cantica Medii Aevi Polono-Latina*, vol. I, *Sequentiae*, Biblioteca Latina Medii et Recentioris Aevi 14 (Warsaw: Państwowe Wydawnictwo Naukowe, 1964)

  and Morawski, Jerzy, eds., 'Hymny polskie', *Musica Medii Aevi* 8 (1991), pp. 10–138

Kreitner, Kenneth, *The Church Music of Fifteenth-Century Spain* (Woodbridge: Boydell, 2004)

Kreutziger-Herr, Annette, *Ein Traum vom Mittelalter: Die Wiederentdeckung mittelalterlicher Musik in der Neuzeit* (Cologne, Weimar and Vienna: Böhlau, 2003)

Kroll, Norma, 'Power and Conflict in Medieval Ritual and Plays: The Re-Invention of Drama', *Modern Philology* 102 (2005), pp. 452–83

Kruckenberg, Lori, 'Sequenz', in *MGG VIII* (Kassel: Bärenreiter-Metzler, 1994), cols. 1254–86

  'The Sequence from 1050–1150: Study of a Genre in Change' (PhD diss., University of Iowa, 1997)

Kruckenberg-Goldenstein, Lori, 'The Lotharingian Axis and Monastic Reforms: Towards the Recovery of an Early Messine Trope Tradition', in *Cantus Planus – Study Group of the International Musicological Society: Papers Read at the Twelfth Meeting, Lillafüred, Hungary. 23–28 August 2004*, edited by László Dobszay et al. (Budapest: Hungarian Academy of Sciences, 2006), pp. 723–52

Kügle, Karl, *The Manuscript Ivrea, Biblioteca Capitolare 115: Studies in the Transmission and Composition of Ars Nova Polyphony* (Ottawa: Institute of Mediaeval Music, 1997)

Lanfranc, *Decreta Lanfranci monachis Cantuariensibus transmissa*, ed. David Knowles, Corpus Consuetudinum Monasticarum 3 (Siegburg: F. Schmitt, 1967)

Lang, Paul Henry, *Music in Western Civilization* (New York: Norton, 1941)

Lannutti, Maria Sofia and Locanto, Massimiliano, eds., *Tracce di una tradizione sommersa: i primi testi lirici italiani tra poesia e musica* (Florence: Sismel, 2005)

Lawson, Christopher M., *Sancti Isidori episcopi hispalensis De ecclesiasticis officiis*,
  Corpus Christianorum Series Latina 113 (Turnhout: Brepols, 1989)
Layton, Billy Jim, 'Italian Music for the Ordinary of the Mass 1300–1450' (PhD diss.,
  Harvard University, 1960)
*Le Codex 121 de la Bibliothèque d'Einsiedeln (Xe–XIe siècle): Antiphonale missarum
  sancti Gregorii*, Paléographie musicale 4 (Berne: Herbert Lang, 1974)
*Le Codex VI.34 de la Bibliothèque capitulaire de Bénévent (XIe–XIIe siècle): Graduel de
  Bénévent, avec prosaire et tropaire*, Paléographie musicale 15 (Berne: Herbert
  Lang, 1971)
Leach, Elizabeth Eva, 'Death of a Lover and the Birth of the Polyphonic Balade:
  Machaut's Notated Balades 1–5', *Journal of Musicology* 19 (2002), pp. 461–502
  Sung Birds: Music, Poetry, and Nature in the Later Middle Ages (Ithaca, NY: Cornell
  University Press, 2007)
Lecoy, Felix, ed., *Le Roman de la Rose ou de Guillaume de Dole*, CFMA 91 (Paris:
  Champion, 1962)
Lee-De Amici, Beth Anne, '*Ad Sustentacionem Fidei Christiani*: Sacred Music and
  Ceremony in Medieval Oxford' (PhD diss., University of Pennsylvania, 1999)
Leech-Wilkinson, Daniel, *Compositional Techniques in the Four-Part Isorhythmic
  Motets of Philippe de Vitry and his Contemporaries*, 2 vols. (New York: Garland,
  1989)
  The Modern Invention of Medieval Music: Scholarship, Ideology, Performance,
  Musical Performance and Reception (Cambridge University Press, 2002)
Lefferts, Peter M., 'Machaut's B-flat Balade *Honte, Paour* (B25)', in Elizabeth Eva
  Leach, ed., *Machaut's Music: New Interpretations* (Woodbridge: Boydell &
  Brewer, 2003)
  'Medieval England, 950–1450', in James McKinnon, ed., *Antiquity and the Middle
  Ages: From Ancient Greece to the Fifteenth Century*, Music and Society 1 (London:
  Macmillan, 1990), pp. 170–96
  The Motet in England in the Fourteenth Century, Studies in Musicology 94 (Ann
  Arbor: UMI, 1986)
  'Signature-Systems and Tonal Types in the Fourteenth-Century French Chanson',
  Plainsong and Medieval Music 4 (1995), pp. 117–47
  and Rastall, Richard, 'Minstrels and Minstrelsy', in *Medieval England: An
  Encyclopedia*
Leo, Friedrich, *Venanti Honori Clementiani Fortunati presbyteri Italici opera poetica*,
  Monumenta Germaniae Historica, Auctores antiquissimi IV/1 (Berlin:
  Weidmann, 1881)
Levy, Kenneth, 'A New Look at Old Roman Chant I', *Early Music History* 19 (2000),
  pp. 81–104
  'A New Look at Old Roman Chant II', *Early Music History* 20 (2001), pp. 173–98
  'Charlemagne's Archetype of Gregorian Chant', *Journal of the American
  Musicological Society* 40 (1987), pp. 1–30
  Gregorian Chant and the Carolingians (Princeton University Press, 1998)
  'On the Origin of Neumes', *Early Music History* 7 (1987), pp. 59–90; repr. in
  Kenneth Levy, *Gregorian Chant and the Carolingians* (Princeton University Press,
  1998), pp. 109–40

'Toledo, Rome, and the Legacy of Gaul', *Early Music History* 4 (1984), pp. 49–99

Liber Usualis (Tournai: Desclée, 1956)

Lindsay, W. M., ed., *Isidori hispalensis episcopi Etymologiarum sive originum libri xx*, 2 vols. (Oxford: Clarendon Press, 1911)

Lipphardt, Walther, *Lateinische Osterfeiern und Osterspiele*, 6 vols. (Berlin and New York: Walter De Gruyter, 1975–81)

Liu, Benjamin M. and Monroe, James T., *Ten Hispano-Arabic Strophic Songs in the Modern Tradition* (Berkeley: University of California Press, 1989)

Liuzzi, Fernando, *La lauda e i primordi della melodia italiana*, 2 vols. (Rome: Libreria dello Stato, 1934)

Lockwood, Lewis, ed., *Palestrina: Pope Marcellus Mass: An Authoritative Score, Backgrounds and Sources, History and Analysis, Views and Comments* (New York: Norton, 1975)

López-Calo, José, *La musica en la Catedral de Santiago*, vol. V (La Coruña: Diputación Provincial de La Coruña, 1994)

La música medieval en Galicia (La Coruña: Fundación Pedro Barrié de la Maza, 1982)

and Villanueva, Carlos, eds., *El Códice Calixtino y la música de su tiempo* (La Coruña: Fundación Pedro Barrié de la Maza, 2001)

López Serrano, Matilde, et al., eds., *Cantigas de Santa María: edición facsímil del códice B.R.20 de la Biblioteca Nazionale de Florencia, siglo XIII*, 2 vols. (Madrid: Edilán, 1979)

Lowinsky, Edward E., 'Music in the Culture of the Renaissance', in Bonnie J. Blackburn, ed., *Music in the Culture of the Renaissance and Other Essays*, 2 vols. (University of Chicago Press, 1989), vol. I, pp. 19–39. First published in *Journal of the History of Ideas* 15 (1954), pp. 509–53

Ludwig, Friedrich, 'Die mehrstimmige Musik des 14. Jahrhunderts', *Sammelbände der Internationalen Musik-Gesellschaft* 4 (1902–3), pp. 16–69

'Musik des Mittelalters in der Badischen Kunsthalle Karlsruhe, 24.–26. September 1922', *Zeitschrift für Musikwissenschaft* 5 (1922–3), pp. 434–60

Repertorium organorum recentioris et motetorum vetustissimi stili, 2 vols. (1/1 – Halle: Verlag von Max Niemeyer, 1910; R [ed. Luther A. Dittmer, Musicological Studies 7] Brooklyn, NY: Institute of Mediaeval Music; Hildesheim: Georg Olms, 1964; 1/2 – [345–456 ed. Friedrich Gennrich including R of 'Die Quellen der Motetten altesten Stils', *Archiv für Musikwissenschaft* 5 (1923), pp. 185–222 and 273–315, Summa Musicae Medii Aevi 7] Langen bei Frankfürt: n.p., 1961; R [345–456] [457–783, ed. Luther A. Dittmer, Musicological Studies 26] [Binningen]: Institute of Mediaeval Music,1978; 2 – [1–71 ed. Friedrich Gennrich, Summa Musicae Medii Aevi 8 – 65–71 in page proof only] Langen bei Frankfürt: n.p., 1962; R [1–64, 65–71 corrected] [72–155 ed. Luther A. Dittmer, Musicological Studies 17] Brooklyn, NY: Institute of Mediaeval Music, n.d.; Hildesheim: Georg Olms, 1972)

Machaut, Guillaume de, *La prise d'Alexandrie ou chronique du roi Pierre Ier de Lusignan par Guillaume de Machaut*, ed. [Jacques Marie Joseph] Louis de Mas Latrie, Publications de la Société de l'Orient latin, série historique 1 (Geneva: Fick, 1877; repr. Osnabrück: Zeller, 1968); new edn, ed. and trans. R. Barton

Palmer, *Guillaume de Machaut: La prise d'Alixandre* (The Taking of Alexandria) (New York: Routledge, 2002)

Le Livre dou Voir Dit (The Book of the True Poem), ed. Daniel Leech-Wilkinson, trans. R. Barton Palmer, Garland Library of Medieval Literature (New York and London: Garland, 1998)

Maciejewski, Tadeusz, 'Elementy systemu menzuralnego w monodii chorałowej XIII–XVI wieku', in Elżbieta Witkowska-Zaremba, ed., *Notae musicae artis. Notacja muzyczna w źródłach polskich XI–XVI wieku* (Cracow: Musica Iagellonica, 1999)

MacKay, Angus, *Spain in the Middle Ages: From Frontier to Empire 1000–1500* (London: Macmillan, 1977)

Magocsi, Paul Robert, *Historical Atlas of East Central Europe*, A History of East Central Europe 1 (Seattle and London: University of Washington Press, 1993)

Maître, Claire, *La réforme cistercienne du plain-chant: Étude d'un traité théorique* (Brecht: Commentarii Cistercienses, 1995)

Maloy, Rebecca, 'The Word–Music Relationship in the Gregorian and Old Roman Offertories', *Studia musicologica* 45 (2004), pp. 131–48

Marrocco, W. Thomas, ed., *Italian Secular Music*, Polyphonic Music of the Fourteenth Century 6–11 (Monaco: Éditions de l'Oiseau-Lyre, 1971–8)

Marshall, John H., *The 'Razos de Trobar' and Associated Texts* 6 and 7 (London: Oxford University Press, 1972)

Marshall, Peter K., ed., *Etymologies*, book II (Paris: Les Belles Lettres, 1983)

Martin, Céline, *La géographie du pouvoir dans l'Espagne visigothique* (Lille: Presses Universitaires du Septentrion, 2003)

Marzi, Giovanni, ed., *An.M.T. Severini Boethii de institutione musica* (Rome: Istituto italiano per la storia della musica, 1990)

McCormick, Michael, *Origins of the European Economy: Communications and Commerce AD 300–900* (Cambridge University Press, 2001)

McGann, Jerome, *The Beauty of Inflections: Literary Investigations in Historical Method and Theory* (Oxford: Clarendon Press, 1985)

McGee, Timothy, '*Dança amorosa*: A Newly-Discovered Medieval Dance Pair', in Bryan Gillingham and Paul Merkley, eds., *Beyond the Moon: Festschrift Luther Dittmer* (Ottawa: Institute of Mediaeval Music, 1990), pp. 295–306

Medieval Instrumental Dances (Bloomington: Indiana University Press, 1989)

'The Liturgical Placements of the "Quem Queritis" Dialogue', *Journal of the American Musicological Society* 29 (1976), pp. 1–29

McKenzie, Donald, *The Panizzi Lectures 1985: Bibliography and the Sociology of Texts* (London: British Library, 1986)

McKinnon, James, 'Desert Monasticism and the Later Fourth-Century Psalmodic Movement', *Music and Letters* 75 (1994), pp. 505–21

'Lector Chant versus Schola Chant: A Question of Historical Plausibility', in Janka Szendrei and David Hiley, eds., *Laborare fratres in unum: Festschrift László Dobszay zum 60. Geburtstag* (Hildesheim: Weidmann, 1995), pp. 201–11

'Liturgical Psalmody in the Sermons of St Augustine: An Introduction', in Peter Jeffery, ed., *The Study of Medieval Chant: Paths and Bridges, East and West, in Honor of Kenneth Levy* (Woodbridge: Boydell, 2001), pp. 7–24

The Advent Project: The Later Seventh-Century Creation of the Roman Mass Proper
  (Berkeley and Los Angeles: University of California Press, 2000)

'The Emergence of Gregorian Chant in the Carolingian Era', in James McKinnon,
  ed., *Antiquity and the Middle Ages* (London: Macmillan, 1990), pp. 88–119

The Temple, the Church Fathers and Early-Western Chant (Aldershot: Variorum,
  1998)

ed., *Music in Early Christian Literature*, Cambridge Readings in the Literature of
  Music 25 and 352 (Cambridge University Press, 1987)

ed., *The Early Christian Period and the Latin Middle Ages* 2 (New York and
  London: Norton, 1998)

McKitterick, Rosamond, *The Carolingians and the Written Word* (Cambridge
  University Press, 1989)

The Frankish Church and the Carolingian Reforms, 789–895 (London: Royal
  Historical Society, 1977)

Meneghetti, Maria, 'Il Manuscritto fr. 146 della Bibliothèque Nationale di Parigi,
  Tommaso di Saluzzo e gli affreschi della Manta', *Romania* 110 (1989), pp. 511–35

Menut, Albert Douglas, *Maistre Nicole Oresme: Le livre de politiques d'Aristote*,
  Transactions of the American Philosophical Society, New Series 60, part 6
  (Philadelphia: American Philosophical Society, 1970)

Meyer, Christian, *Musica plana Johannis de Garlandia* (Baden-Baden: V. Koerner,
  1998)

Miazga, Tadeusz, *Die Melodien des einstimmigen Credo der römisch-katholischen
  lateinischen Kirche: Eine Untersuchung der Melodien im den handschriftlichen
  Überlieferungen mit besonderer Berücksichtigung der polnischen Handschriften*
  (Graz: Akademische Druck- und Verlagsanstalt, 1976)

Michel, Francisque, *Chansons du Châtelain de Coucy: Revues sur tous les manuscrits*
  (Paris: Crapelet, 1830)

Michels, Ulrich, ed., *Johannis de Muris Notitia artis musicae et Compendium musicae
  practicae: Tractatus de musica*, Corpus Scriptorum de Musica 17 ([Rome]:
  American Institute of Musicology, 1972)

Migne, Jacques-Paul, ed., *Patrologiae cursus completus, Series Latina*, 221 vols. (Paris:
  Garnier, 1844–64)

Milanese, Guido, 'Paraphonia-paraphonista dalla lessicografia greca alla tarda
  antichità romana', in Enrico Menesto, Antonio Island, Alessandra Di Pilla and
  Ubaldo Pizzani, eds., *Curiositas: Studi di cultura classica e medievale in onore di
  Ubaldo Pizzani* (Naples: ESI, 2002), pp. 407–21

Minnis, Alastair, 'Late Medieval Discussions of *compilatio* and the Role of the
  compilator', *Beiträge zur Geschichte der deutschen Sprache und Literatur* 101
  (1979), pp. 385–421

Mitchell, Andrew, 'The Chant of the Earliest Franciscan Liturgy' (PhD diss.,
  University of Western Ontario, 2003)

Moll, Kevin, ed. and trans., *Counterpoint and Compositional Process in the Time of
  Dufay: Perspectives from German Musicology*, Criticism and Analysis of Early
  Music (New York and London: Garland, 1997)

Möller, Hartmut, 'Office Compositions from St Gall: Saints Gallus and Otmar', in
  Margot Fassler and Rebecca A. Baltzer, eds., *The Divine Office in the Latin Middle*

Ages: Methodology and Source Studies, Regional Developments, Hagiography (Oxford University Press, 2000), pp. 237–56

'Zur Frage der musikgeschichtlichen Bedeutung der Academia am Hofe Karls des Grossen: Die Musica Albini', in Wolf Frobenius et al., eds., *Akademie und Musik: Erscheinungsweisen und Wirkungen des Akademiegedankens in Kultur- und Musikgeschichte – Institutionen, Veranstaltungen, Schriften. Festschrift für Werner Braun zum 65. Geburtstag* (Saarbrücken: Saarbrücker Druckerei und Verlag, 1993), pp. 269–88

and Rudolf, Stephan, eds., *Neues Handbuch der Musikwissenschaft*, vol. II, *Die Musik des Mittelalters* (Laaber: Laaber-Verlag, 1991)

Monumenta Germaniae Historica, Capitularia I/22 (Hanover: Hahn, 1883)

Morawska, Katarzyna, *The Middle Ages*, Part 2, *1320–1500*, trans. John Comber, Historia muzyki polskiej I/2 (Warsaw: Sutkowski Edition, 2001)

Morawski, Jerzy, 'Recherches sur les variantes régionales dans le chant grégorien', *Studia Musicologica Academiae Scientiarum Hungaricae* 30 (1988), pp. 403–14

The Middle Ages, Part 1, *Up to 1320*, trans. John Comber, Historia muzyki polskiej I/1 (Warsaw: Edition Sutkowski, 2003)

ed., *Historia rymowana o św. Jadwidze* (Cracow: Polskie Wydawnictwo Muzyczne, 1977)

ed., *Historia rymowana o św. Wojciechu* (Cracow: Polskie Wydawnictwo Muzyczne, 1979)

ed., *Musica Medii Aevi*, 8 vols. (Cracow: Polskie Wydawnictwo Muzyczne, 1965–91)

Mráčková, Lenka, 'Kodex Speciálník: Eine kleine Folio-Handschrift böhmischer Provenienz', *Hudební věda* 39, nos. 2–3 (2002), pp. 163–84

Murray, Alexander, *Reason and Society in the Middle Ages* (Oxford: Clarendon Press, 1985)

Musik in Geschichte und Gegenwart: Allgemeine Enzyklopädie der Musik, ed. Ludwig Finscher (Kassel: Bärenreiter, 1949–86; new edn 1994)

Mütherich, Florentine, ed., *Drogo-Sakramentar: manuscrit latin 9428, Bibliothèque nationale, Paris*, 2 vols. (Graz: Akademische Druck- u. Verlagsanstalt, 1974)

Mynors, Roger Aubrey Baskerville, ed., *Cassiodori Senatoris Institutiones* (Oxford: Clarendon Press, 1937)

Nádas, John, 'The Structure of Ms Panciatichi 26 and the Transmission of Trecento Polyphony', *Journal of the American Musicological Society* 34 (1981), pp. 393–427

and Di Bacco, Giuliano, 'The Papal Chapels and Italian Sources of Polyphony during the Great Schism', in Richard Sherr, ed., *Papal Music and Musicians in Late Medieval and Renaissance Rome* (Oxford: Clarendon Press, 1998), pp. 44–92

and Ziino, Agostino, eds., *The Lucca Codex* (Lucca: Libreria Musicale Italiana, 1990)

Needham, Paul, *Twelve Centuries of Bookbinding, 400–1600* (New York: Pierpont Morgan Library, 1979)

Nelson, Kathleen, *Medieval Liturgical Music of Zamora* (Ottawa: Institute of Mediaeval Music, 1996)

New Grove Dictionary of Music and Musicians, 2nd edn (Oxford University Press, 2001)

Newes, Virginia, 'Chace, Caccia, Fuga: The Convergence of French and Italian Traditions', *Musica Disciplina* 41 (1987), pp. 27–57

Newman, Barbara, ed., *Saint Hildegard of Bingen: Symphonia: A Critical Edition of the 'Symphonia armonie celestium revelationum'* (Ithaca, NY: Cornell University Press, 1988)

Nichols, Stephen, 'Philology and Its Discontents', in William Paden, ed., *The Future of the Middle Ages: Medieval Literature in the 1990s* (Gainesville: University Press of Florida, 1994), pp. 113–41

  ed., *The New Philology*, *Speculum* 65 (special edn) (1990)

Noone, Michael and Skinner, Graeme, 'Toledo Cathedral's Collection of Manuscript Plainsong Choirbooks: A Preliminary Report and Checklist', *Notes* 63 (2006), pp. 289–328

Norberg, Dag Ludvig, *An Introduction to the Study of Medieval Latin Versification*, trans. Grant C. Roti and Jacqueline de La Chapelle Skulby, ed. Jan Ziolkowski (Washington, DC: Catholic University of America Press, 2004)

Nowacki, Edward, 'Text Declamation as a Determinant of Melodic Form in the Old Roman Eighth-Mode Tracts', *Early Music History* 6 (1986), pp. 193–226

O'Neill, Mary, *Courtly Love Songs of Medieval France: Transmission and Style in the Trouvère Repertoire* (Oxford University Press, 2006)

Oroz Reta, José and Marcos Casquero, Manuel-A., eds., *Etimologías*, 2 vols. (Madrid: Editorial Católica, 1/1982–3, 2/1993–4)

Østrem, Eyolf, *The Office of Saint Olav: A Study in Chant Transmission* (Uppsala Universitet, 2001)

Owens, Jessie Ann, 'Music Historiography and the Definition of "Renaissance"', *Notes* 47 (1990), pp. 305–30

Paden, William, 'Manuscripts', in F. R. P. Akehurst and Judith M. Davis, eds., *A Handbook of the Troubadours* (Berkeley: University of California Press, 1995), pp. 307–33

Page, Christopher, *Discarding Images: Reflections on Music and Culture in Medieval France* (Oxford University Press, 1993)

  "Grocheio, Johannes de", in *Grove Music Online.* www.oxfordmusiconline.com

  Latin Poetry and Conductus Rhythm in Medieval France, RMA Monographs 8 (London: Royal Musical Association, 1997)

  'Machaut's "Pupil" Deschamps on the Performance of Music', *Early Music* 5 (1977), pp. 484–91

  'Music', in Boris Ford, ed., *The Cambridge Guide to the Arts in Britain*, vol. I, *Prehistoric, Roman, and Early Medieval* (Cambridge University Press, 1988), pp. 247–53

  'Polyphony before 1400', in Howard Mayer Brown and Stanley Sadie, eds., *Performance Practice: Music Before 1600*, Norton/Grove Handbooks in Music (New York and London: Norton, 1990), pp. 79–104

  The Owl and the Nightingale: Musical Life and Ideas in France 1100–1300 (London: Dent, 1989)

  Voices and Instruments of the Middle Ages: Instrumental Practice and Songs in France 1100–1300 (Berkeley and Los Angeles: University of California Press, 1986)

Palazzo, Eric, *A History of Liturgical Books from the Beginning to the Thirteenth Century*, trans. Madeleine Beaumont (Collegeville: Liturgical Press, 1998)

Paléographie Musicale, 2nd series, vol. II, *Cantatorium, IXe siècle: no. 359 de la Bibliothèque de Saint-Gall* (Solesmes: Atelier de Paléographie Musicale de Solesmes, 1924)

Palisca, Claude V., ed., *Hucbald, Guido, and John on Music: Three Medieval Treatises*, trans. Warren Babb (New Haven, CT: Yale University Press, 1978)

ed., *Musica enchiriadis and Scolica enchiriadis*, trans. Raymond Erickson (New Haven, CT: Yale University Press, 1995)

ed., *Norton Anthology of Western Music*, vol. I, *Ancient to Baroque*, 4th edn (New York: Norton, 2001)

and Bent, Ian D., 'Theory, theorists', in *Grove Music Online*. www.oxfordmusiconline.com

Palmer, R. Barton, ed. and trans., *G. de Machaut, La Prise d'Alexandre (The Taking of Alexandria)* (New York: Routledge, 2002)

Paris, Gaston, 'Études sur les romans de la Table Ronde: *Lancelot du Lac*', *Romania* 12 (1883), pp. 459–534

'Études sur les romans de la Table Ronde: *Lancelot du Lac*, II: *Le conte de la charrette*', *Romania* 10 (1881), pp. 465–96

Parkes, Malcolm, 'Folia librorum quaerere: Medieval Experience of the Problems of Hypertext and the Index', in Claudio Leonardi, Marcello Morelli and Francesco Santi, eds., *Fabula in tabula: una storia degli indici dal manoscritto al testo elettronico: atti del Convegno di studio della Fondazione Ezio Franceschini e della Fondazione IBM Italia, Certosa del Galluzzo, 21–22 ottobre 1994* (Spoleto: Centro Italiano di Studi sull' Alto Medioevo, 1995), pp. 23–41

Scribes, Scripts and Readers: Studies in the Communication, Presentation, and Dissemination of Medieval Texts (London: Hambledon Press, 1991)

'The Influence of the Concepts of *Ordinatio* and *Compilatio* on the Development of the Book', in Jonathan Alexander and Margaret Gibson, eds., *Medieval Learning and Literature: Essays Presented to Richard William Hunt* (Oxford: Clarendon Press, 1976), pp. 115–41

and Watson, Andrew, eds., *Medieval Scribes, Manuscripts and Libraries: Essays Presented to N. R. Ker* (London: Scolar Press, 1978)

Parkinson, Stephen, ed., *Cobras e son: Papers on the Text, Music and Manuscripts of the 'Cantigas de Santa Maria'* (Oxford: Legenda, 2000)

Parsoneault, Catherine, 'The Montpellier Codex: Royal Influence and Musical Taste in Late Thirteenth-Century Paris' (PhD diss., University of Texas at Austin, 2001)

Pasler, Jann, review of Katherine Bergeron, *Decadent Enchantments: The Revival of Gregorian Chant at Solesmes*, California Studies in 19th-Century Music 10 (Berkeley: University of California Press, 1998), in *Journal of the American Musicological Society* 52 (1999), pp. 370–83

Patier, Dominique, 'Les éléments locaux dans les offices rythmiques composés en Bohême aux XIIIème et XIVème siècles', *Studia Musicologica Academiae Scientiarum Hungaricae* 26, nos. 1–4 (1985), pp. 109–15

Paul the Deacon, *Deeds of the Bishops of Metz*, ed. Georg Heinrich Pertz, Monumenta Germaniae Historica, Scriptores II (Hanover: Hahn, 1829)

Payne, Thomas B., 'Datable "Notre Dame" Conductus: New Historical Observations on Style and Technique', *Current Musicology* 64 (2001), pp. 104–51

   ed., *Les Organa à deux voix du manuscrit de Wolfenbüttel, Hertzog [sic] August Bibiliothek, Cod. Guelf. 1099 Helmst.*, 2 vols, Le Magnus liber organi de Notre-Dame de Paris 6A–6B (Monaco: Éditions de l'Oiseau-Lyre, 1996)

Pelt, Jean-Baptiste, *Études sur la cathédrale de Metz*, vol. IV, *La liturgie 1 (Ve–XIIIe siècle)* (Metz: Imprimerie du Journal le Lorrain, 1937)

Perales de la Cal, Ramón, ed., *Cancionero de la Catedral de Segovia: edición facsimilar del Códice de la Santa Iglesia Catedral de Segovia* (Segovia: Caja de Ahorros y Monte de Piedad de Segovia, 1977)

Perkins, Leeman L., and Garey, Howard, eds., *The Mellon Chansonnier.* vol. I, *The Edition*, vol. II, *Commentary* (New Haven and London: Yale University Press, 1979)

Perz, Mirosław, 'Fragmenty lwowskie. Źródło Dzieł Dufaya, Josquina, Piotra de Domarto i Piotra z Grudziądza w Polsce XV wieku', *Muzyka* 34 (1989), pp. 3–46

   ed., *Sources of Polyphony up to c.1500 (Facsimiles)*, Antiquitates Musicae in Polonia 13 (Graz and Warsaw: Akademische Druck- und Verlagsanstalt and PWN – Polish Scientific Publishers, 1973)

   ed., *Sources of Polyphony up to c.1500 (Transcriptions)*, trans. Henryk Kowalewicz, Antiquitates Musicae in Polonia 14 (Graz and Warsaw: Akademische Druck- und Verlagsanstalt, and PWN – Polish Scientific Publishers, 1976)

Pesce, Dolores, 'A Case for Coherent Pitch Organization in the Thirteenth-Century Double Motet', *Music Analysis* 9/3 (1990), pp. 287–318

   Guido d'Arezzo's 'Regulae rhythmicae', 'Prologus in antiphonarium', and 'Epistola ad Michaelem': A Critical Text and Translation with an Introduction, Annotations, Indices and New Manuscript Inventories (Ottawa: Institute of Mediaeval Music, 1999)

   The Affinities and Medieval Transposition (Bloomington, IN: Indiana University Press, 1987)

Pfaff, Maurus, 'Die liturgische Einstimmigkeit in ihren Editionen nach 1600', in Thrasybulos G. Georgiades, ed., *Musikalische Edition im Wandel des historischen Bewusstseins* (Kassel, Basel, Tours and London: Bärenreiter, 1971), pp. 50–61

Pfaff, Richard W., *New Liturgical Feasts in Later Medieval England* (Oxford: Clarendon Press, 1970)

Pfisterer, Andreas, *Cantilena Romana: Untersuchungen zur Überlieferung des gregorianischen Chorals* (Paderborn: Schöningh, 2002)

Phillips, Nancy, '"Musica" and "Scolica Enchiriadis": The Literary, Theoretical, and Musical Sources' (PhD diss., New York University, 1984)

Pikulik, Jerzy, 'Polskie oficja rymowane o św. Wojciechu / Les offices polonais de saint Adalbert', in Pikulik, ed., *Stan badań nad muzyką religijną w kulturze polskiej / État des recherches sur la musique religieuse dans la culture polonaise* (Warsaw: Akademia Teologii Katolickiej, 1973)

   'Sekwencje polskie', *Musica Medii Aevi* 4 (1973), pp. 7–126

Pinell, Jordi, 'Los textos de la antigua liturgia hispánica: fuentes para su estudio', in Juan Rivera, *Estudios sobre la liturgia mozárabe* (Toledo: Diputación Provincial, 1965), pp. 165–87

Pirrotta, Nino, 'The Oral and Written Traditions of Music', in Nino Pirrotta, *Music and Culture in Italy from the Middle Ages to the Baroque: A Collection of Essays* (Cambridge, MA: Harvard University Press, 1984), pp. 72–9

ed., *Il Codice Rossi 215: Roma, Biblioteca apostolica vaticana; Ostiglia, Fondazione Opera pia Don Giuseppe Greggiati* (Lucca: Libreria Musicale Italiana, 1992)

ed., *The Music of Fourteenth-Century Italy*, 5 vols., Corpus Mensurabilis Musicae 8 (Amsterdam: American Institute of Musicology, 1954–64)

Plamenac, Dragan, *Keyboard Music of the Late Middle Ages in Codex Faenza 117*, Corpus Mensurabilis Musicae 57 (Rome: American Institute of Musicology, 1972)

Planchart, Alejandro E., *The Repertory of Tropes at Winchester*, 2 vols. (Princeton University Press, 1977)

Plantinga, Leo, 'Philippe de Vitry's Ars Nova: A Translation', *Journal of Music Theory* 5 (1961), pp. 204–23

Plumley, Yolanda, 'An "Episode in the South"? Ars Subtilior and the Patronage of French Princes', *Early Music History* 22 (2003), pp. 103–68

and Stone, Anne, eds., *Codex Chantilly: Bibliothèque du château de Chantilly, Ms. 564: Fac-similé* (Turnhout: Brepols, 2008)

Poe, Elizabeth, 'The *Vidas* and *razos*', in F. R. P. Akehurst and Judith M. Davis, eds., *A Handbook of the Troubadours* (Berkeley: University of California Press, 1995)

Poirion, Daniel, *Le poète et le prince: l'évolution du lyrisme courtois de Guillaume de Machaut à Charles d'Orléans* (Grenoble: Allier, 1965)

Ponte, Joseph, trans., *The Discipline of Music (ca. 843) by Aurelian of Réôme* (Colorado Springs: Colorado College Music Press, 1968)

Potter, Pamela, *Most German of the Arts: Musicology and Society from the Weimar Republic to the End of Hitler's Reich* (New Haven and London: Yale University Press, 1998)

Pumpe, Jutta, *Die Motetten der Madrider Notre-Dame-Handschrift* (Tutzing: Schneider, 1991)

Randel, Don Michael, 'Al-Fārābī and the Role of Arabic Music Theory in the Latin Middle Ages', *Journal of the American Musicological Society* 29 (1976), pp. 173–88

An Index to the Chant of the Mozarabic Rite (Princeton University Press, 1973)

The Responsorial Psalm Tones for the Mozarabic Office (Princeton University Press, 1969)

Rankin, Susan, 'Between Oral and Written: Thirteenth-Century Italian Sources of Polyphony', in Giulio Cattin and F. Alberto Gallo, eds., *Un millennio di polifonia liturgica tra oralità e scrittura*, Quarderni di Musica e Storia 3 (Bologna: Il Mulino, 2002), pp. 75–98

'From Tuotilo to the First Manuscripts: The Shaping of a Trope Repertory at Saint Gall', in Wulf Arlt and Gunilla Björkvall, eds., *Recherches nouvelles sur les tropes liturgique*, Studia Latina Stockholmiensia 36 (Stockholm: Almqvist and Wiksell International, 1993), pp. 395–413

'Liturgical Drama', Richard Crocker and David Hiley, eds., *The Early Middle Ages to 1300*, vol. II of *The New Oxford History of Music* (Oxford and New York: Oxford University Press, 1990), pp. 310–56

'Notker und Tuotilo: Schöpferische Gestalter in einer neuen Zeit', *Schweizer Jahrbuch für Musikwissenschaft* 11 (1991), pp. 17–42

'The Earliest Sources of Notker's Sequences: St Gallen Vadiana 317, and Paris, Bibliothèque Nationale Lat. 10587', *Early Music History* 10 (1991), pp. 201–33

The Music of the Medieval Liturgical Drama in France and in England (New York: Garland, 1989)

'Ways of Telling Stories', in Graeme Boone, ed., *Essays on Medieval Music in Honor of David G. Hughes* (Cambridge, MA: Harvard University Press, 1995), pp. 371–94

'Winchester Polyphony: The Early Theory and Practice of Organum', in Susan Rankin and David Hiley, eds., *Music in the Medieval English Liturgy: Plainsong and Medieval Music Centennial Essays* (Oxford: Clarendon Press, 1993), pp. 59–100

ed., *The Winchester Troper: Facsimile Edition*, Early English Church Music 50 (London: Stainer & Bell, 2007)

Reaney, Gilbert, 'Concerning the Origin of the Medieval Lai', *Music and Letters* 39 (1958), pp. 343–6

'The Manuscript Chantilly, Musée Condé 1047', *Musica Disciplina* 8 (1954), pp. 59–113

ed., *Early Fifteenth-Century Music*, CMM 11 ([Rome]: American Institute of Musicology, 1955–83)

ed., *The Manuscript London, British Museum, Additional 29987*, Musicological Studies and Documents 13 (Rome: American Institute of Musicology, 1965)

and Gilles, André, eds., *Franconis de Colonia Ars cantus mensurabilis*, Corpus Scriptorum de Musica 18 ([Rome]: American Institute of Musicology, 1974)

Gilles, André and Maillard, Jean, eds., *Philippi de Vitriaco Ars nova*, Corpus Scriptorum de Musica 8 ([Rome]: American Institute of Musicology, 1964)

Reckow, Fritz, *Die Copula: Über einige Zusammenhänge zwischen Setzweise, Formbildung, Rhythmus und Vortragstil in der Mehrstimmigkeit von Notre-Dame*, Abhandlungen der Geistes- und Sozialwissenschaftlichen Klasse der Akademie der Wissenschaften und der Literatur 13 (Wiesbaden: Steiner, 1972)

'Guido's Theory of Organum after Guido: Transmission – Adaptation – Transformation', in Graeme Boone, ed., *Essays on Medieval Music in Honor of David G. Hughes* (Cambridge, MA: Harvard University Press, 1995), pp. 395–413

ed., *Der Musiktraktat des Anonymus 4*, 2 vols., Beihefte zum Archiv für Musikwissenschaft 4–5 (Wiesbaden: Franz Steiner, 1967), translated in Jeremy Yudkin, *The Music Treatise of Anonymous IV: A New Translation*, Musicological Studies and Documents 41 (Neuhausen-Stuttgart: American Institute of Musicology, 1985)

Rees, Owen, ed., *Aires Fernandez (fl. ca. 1550): Alma Redemptoris Mater, Asperges me, Lumen ad revelationem*, Mapa Mundi Renaissance Performing Scores, Series A: Spanish and Portuguese Church Music 182 (Lochs [Isle of Lewis]: Mapa Mundi, 2002)

Reese, Gustave, *Music in the Middle Ages, with an Introduction on the Music of Ancient Times* (New York: Norton, 1940)

Music in the Renaissance (rev. edn) (New York: Norton, 1959)

Reginek, Antoni, 'Repertuar hymnów diecezji krakowskiej', *Musica Medii Aevi* 8 (1991), pp. 142–371

Rehding, Alexander, 'The Quest for the Origins of Music in Germany circa 1900', *Journal of the American Musicological Society* 53 (2000), pp. 345–85

Reimer, Erich, *Johannes de Garlandia: De mensurabili musica* (Wiesbaden: F. Steiner, 1972)

Ribera, Julian, *La música de las cantigas: estudio sobre su origen y naturaleza* (Madrid: Tipografía de la Revista de Archivos, 1922)

Ricci, Massimo Masani, *Codice Pluteo 29.1 della Biblioteca Laurenziana di Firenze: storia e catalogo comparato*, Studi musicali toscani 8 (Pisa: ETS, 2002)

Rieger, Angelica, *Trobairitz. Der Beitrag der Frau in der altokzitanischen höfischen Lyrik: Edition des Gesamtkorpus* (Tübingen: Niemeyer, 1991)

Riemann, Hugo, *Handbuch der Musikgeschichte*, vol. I, part 2, *Die Musik des Mittelalters* (*bis 1450*), 2nd edn (Leipzig: Breitkopf & Härtel, 1920)

Rivera, Juan Francisco, *Estudios sobre la liturgia mozárabe* (Toledo: Diputación Provincial, 1965)

Robertson, Anne Walters, *Guillaume de Machaut and Reims: Context and Meaning in His Musical Works* (Cambridge University Press, 2002)

The Service-Books of the Royal Abbey of Saint-Denis: Images of Ritual and Music in the Middle Ages (Oxford University Press, 1991)

Robertson, Carol E., ed., *Musical Repercussions of 1492: Encounters in Text and Performance* (Washington: Smithsonian Institution Press, 1992)

Roesner, Edward H., 'The *Codex Calixtinus* and the *Magnus Liber Organi*: Some Preliminary Observations', in José López-Calo and Carlos Villanueva, eds., *El Códice Calixtino y la música de su tiempo* (La Coruña: Fundación Pedro Barrié da la Maza, 2001), pp. 135–61

ed., *Antiphonarium, seu, magnus liber organi de gradali et antiphonario: Color Microfiche Edition of the Manuscript Firenze, Biblioteca Medicea Laurenziana, Pluteus 29.1*, Codices Illuminati Medii Aevi 45 (Munich: Helga Lengenfelder, 1996)

ed., *Les quadrupla et tripla de Paris*, Le Magnus liber organi de Notre-Dame de Paris 1 (Monaco: Éditions de l'Oiseau-Lyre, 1993)

François Avril and Nancy Freeman Regalado, eds., *Le Roman de Fauvel in the Edition of Mesire Chaillou de Pesstain: A Reproduction in Facsimile of the Complete Manuscript, Paris, Bibliothèque nationale, fonds français 146* (New York: Broude Brothers, 1990)

Rohloff, Ernst, ed., *Die Quellenhandschriften zum Musiktraktat des Johannes de Grocheio* (Leipzig: Deutscher Verlag für Musik, 1972)

Rojo, Casiano and Prado, German, *El canto mozárabe* (Barcelona: Diputación Provincial, 1929)

Rönnau, Klaus, *Die Tropen zum Gloria in excelsis Deo: Unter besonderer Berücksichtigung des Repertoires der St Martial-Handschriften* (Wiesbaden: Breitkopf & Härtel, 1967)

Rosenberg, Samuel N. and Tischler, Hans, eds., with Marie-Geneviève Grossel, *Chansons des trouvères: Chanter m'estuet* (Paris: Livre de Poche, 1995)

Rokseth, Yvonne, ed., *Polyphonies du XIIIe siècle: Le manuscrit H 196 de la Faculté de Médecine de Montpellier*, 4 vols. (Paris: Oiseau Lyre, 1935).

Rouse, Richard and Rouse, Mary, *Manuscripts and Their Makers: Commercial Book Producers in Medieval Paris, 1200–1500*, 2 vols. (Turnhout: Harvey Miller Publishers, 2000)

  'Statim invenire: Schools, Preachers, and New Attitudes to the Page', in Robert Benson and Giles Constable, eds., *Renaissance and Renewal in the Twelfth Century* (Cambridge, MA: Harvard University Press, 1982), pp. 201–29

Ruiz, Juan, *La librería de canto de organo: creación y pervivencia del repertorio del Renacimiento en la actividad musical de la catedral de Sevilla* (Granada: Junta de Andalucía, Consejería de Cultura, 2007)

Rusconi, Angelo, *Guido d'Arezzo monaco pomposiano: atti dei convegni di studio, Codigoro (Ferrara), Abbazia di Pomposa, 3 ottobre 1997* (Florence: Olschki, 2000)

Sachs, Klaus-Jürgen, 'Zur Tradition der Klangschritt-Lehre: Die Texte mit der Formel "Si cantus ascendit . . . " und ihre Verwandten', *Archiv für Musikwissenschaft* 28 (1971), pp. 233–70

Saenger, Paul, 'Reading in the Later Middle Ages', in Guglielmo Cavallo and Roger Chartier, eds., *A History of Reading in the West* (Amherst: University of Massachusetts, 1999), pp. 120–48

  Space between Words: The Origins of Silent Reading (Stanford University Press, 1997)

Salimbene of Parma, *Cronica*, ed. Giuseppe Scalia, 2 vols. (Bari: Laterza, 1966)

Salmen, Walter, 'Dances and Dance Music, c.1300–1530', in Reinhard Strohm and Bonnie J. Blackburn, eds., *Music as Concept and Practice in the Late Middle Ages*, vol. III, part 1 of *The New Oxford History of Music* (Oxford University Press, 2001), pp. 162–90

Salmon, Pierre, *L'office divin au moyen âge: histoire de la formation du bréviaire du IXe au XVIe siècle* (Paris: Éditions du Cerf, 1967)

Sanders, Ernest H., ed., *English Music of the Thirteenth and Fourteenth Centuries*, Polyphonic Music of the Fourteenth Century 14 (Paris and Monaco: Éditions de l'Oiseau-Lyre, 1979)

  '*Sine littera* and *Cum littera* in Medieval Polyphony', in Edmond Strainchamps, Maria Rika Maniates and Christopher Hatch, eds., *Music and Civilisation: Essays in Honor of Paul Henry Lang*, (New York and London: W. W. Norton, 1984), pp. 215–31

  'Style and Technique in Datable Polyphonic Notre-Dame Conductus', in Luther Dittmer, ed., *Gordon Athol Anderson (1929–1981): In memoriam von seinen Studenten, Freunden und Kollegen*, 2 vols., Musicological Studies 49 (Henryville, Ottawa, and Binningen: Institute of Mediaeval Music, 1984), pp. 505–30

  and Lefferts, Peter M., 'Petrus de Cruce', in *Grove Music Online*. www.oxfordmusiconline.com

Sandon, Nick, 'Liturgy and Church Music, History of', in *Medieval England: An Encyclopedia*

  'Salisbury (Sarum), Use of', in *Medieval England: An Encyclopedia*.

and Page, Christopher, 'Music', in Boris Ford, ed., *The Cambridge Guide to the Arts in Britain*, vol. II, *The Middle Ages* (Cambridge University Press, 1988), pp. 214–50

Santosuosso, Alma Colk, 'Music in Bede's *De temporum ratione*; An 11th-Century Addition to MS London, British Library, Cotton Vespasian B. VI', *Scriptorium* 43 (1989), pp. 255–9

Schein, Sylvia, *Fideles Crucis: The Papacy, the West and the Recovery of the Holy Land 1274–1314* (Oxford: Clarendon Press, 1991)

Schmid, Hans, ed., *Musica et Scolica Enchiriadis, una cum aliquibus tractatulis adiunctis*, Bayerische Akademie der Wissenschaften Veröffentlichung der Musikhistorischen Kommission 3 (Munich: Verlag der Bayerischen Akademie der Wissenschaften, 1981). Translated by Raymond Erickson, in Claude Palisca, ed., *Musica enchiriadis and Scolica enchiriadis* (New Haven: Yale University Press, 1995)

Schmidt, Paul Gerhard, 'The Quotation in Goliardic Poetry: The Feast of Fools and the Goliardic Strophe cum auctoritate', in Peter Godman and Oswyn Murray, eds., *Latin Poetry and the Classical Tradition: Essays in Medieval and Renaissance Literature* (Oxford University Press, 1990), pp. 39–55

Schoen-Nazzaro, Mary B., 'Plato and Aristotle on the Ends of Music', *Laval Théologique et Philosophique* 34/3 (1978), pp. 261–73

Schrade, Leo, ed., *The Works of Guillaume de Machaut*, 2 vols., Polyphonic Music of the Fourteenth Century 2 and 3 (Monaco: Éditions de l'Oisean-Lyre, 1956. Repr. in 5 vols. as *Guillaume de Machaut: Œuvres complètes*, 1977)
   Philippe de Vitry: Complete Works (Monaco: Éditions de l'Oiseau-Lyre, 1984)
   The Works of Francesco Landini, Polyphonic Music of the Fourteenth Century 4 (Monaco: Éditions de l'Oiseau-Lyre, 1958)

Schreur, Philip E., ed., *Tractatus figurarum = Treatise on Noteshapes* (Lincoln: University of Nebraska Press, 1989)

Seay, Albert, ed. and trans., *Johannes de Grocheo: Concerning Music (De musica)*, Colorado College Music Press Translations 1 (Colorado Springs: Colorado College Music Press, 1967; 2nd edn 1973)

Sedlar, Jean W., *East Central Europe in the Middle Ages, 1000–1500*, A History of East Central Europe 3 (Seattle and London: University of Washington Press, 1994)

Shiloah, Amnon, 'Muslim and Jewish Musical Traditions of the Middle Ages', in Reinhard Strohm and Bonnie J. Blackburn, eds., *Music as Concept and Practice in the Late Middle Ages*, New Oxford History of Music, vol. III, part 1, new edn (Oxford University Press, 2001), pp. 1–30
   The Theory of Music in Arabic writings (c. 900–1900), 2 vols., RISM B X (Munich: Henle, 1979, 2003)

Siffrin, Petrus, 'Eine Schwesterhandschrift des Graduale von Monza', *Ephemerides liturgicae* 64 (1950), pp. 53–80

Sigebert of Gembloux, *Gesta abbatum Gemblacensium*, in *Patrologiae cursus completus, Series Latina*, ed. J.-P. Migne, 221 vols. (Paris: Garnier, 1844–64), vol. CLX

Sinnreich-Levi, Deborah M., ed., *Eustache Deschamps: L'Art de dictier* (East Lansing: Colleagues Press, 1994)

Slavin, Dennis, 'In Support of "Heresy": Manuscript Evidence for the *a cappella*
    Performance of Early 15th-Century Songs', *Early Music* 19 (1991), pp. 179–90
Slocum, Kay, *Liturgies in Honour of Thomas Becket* (University of Toronto Press,
    2003)
Smith, Jerry C. and Urban, W. C., *The Livonian Rhymed Chronicle* (Bloomington,
    IN: University of Indiana Publications, 1977)
Smith, Norman E., 'The Earliest Motets: Music and Words', *Journal of the Royal
    Musical Association* 114 (1989), pp. 141–63
Smits van Waesberghe, Joseph, ed., *Guidonis Aretini Micrologus*, Corpus Scriptorum
    de Musica 4 ([Nijmegen]: American Institute of Musicology, 1955)
Southworth, John, *The English Medieval Minstrel* (Woodbridge: Boydell, 1989)
Spufford, Peter, *Money and Its Use in Medieval Europe* (Cambridge University Press,
    1988)
Stäblein, Bruno, 'Zur Frühgeschichte der Sequenz', *Archiv für Musikwissenschaft* 18
    (1961), pp. 1–33
Staehelin, Martin, 'Uwagi o wzajemnych związkach biografii, twórczości i
    dokumentacji dzieł Piotra Wilhelmiego z Grudziądza', *Muzyka* 49, no. 2 (2004),
    pp. 9–18
Stallybrass, P., 'Writing after Printing, or How Printing Invents Manuscript',
    Rosenbach Lecture in Bibliography, delivered at the University of Pennsylvania
    in 2006
Steffens, Georg, 'Die altfranzösische Liederhandschrift der Bodleiana in Oxford,
    Douce 308 [Balettes]', *Archiv für das Studium der neueren Sprachen und
    Litteraturen* 99 (1897), pp. 339–88
Stevens, John, 'Alphabetical Check-List of Anglo-Norman Songs', *Plainsong and
    Medieval Music* 3 (1994), pp. 1–22
  'Medieval Song', in Richard Crocker and David Hiley, eds., *The Early Middle Ages
    to 1300*, vol. II of *The New Oxford History of Music*, 2nd edn (Oxford University
    Press, 1990), pp. 357–51
  *Words and Music in the Middle Ages: Song, Narrative, Dance and Drama,
    1050–1350*, Cambridge Studies in Music (Cambridge University Press, 1986)
  ed., *Early Tudor Songs and Carols*, Musica Britannica 36 (London: Stainer & Bell,
    1975)
  ed., *Mediaeval Carols*, Musica Britannica 4 (London: Stainer & Bell, 1952; 2nd rev.
    edn, 1958)
  and Butterfield, Ardis, 'Troubadours, Trouvères', *New Grove Dictionary of Music
    and Musicians*, 2nd edn (Oxford University Press, 2001)
Stevenson, Robert, *Spanish Music in the Age of Columbus* (The Hague: Nijhoff,
    1960)
Stirnemann, Patricia, 'Les bibliothèques princières et privées aux XIIᵉ et XIIIᵉ
    siècles', in André Vernet, ed., *Les bibliothèques médiévales: Du VIᵉ siècle à 1530*,
    Histoire des bibliothèques françaises 1 (Paris: Éditions du Cercle de la Librairie /
    Promodès, 1989), pp. 173–91
Stone, Anne, 'Music Writing and Poetic Voice in Machaut: Some Remarks on B12
    and R14', in Elizabeth Eva Leach, ed., *Machaut's Music: New Interpretations*
    (Woodbridge: Boydell & Brewer, 2003), pp. 125–38

'Self-Reflexive Songs and Their Readers in the Late 14th Century', *Early Music* 31/2 (2003), pp. 180–94

'The Composer's Voice in the Late-Medieval Song: Four Case Studies', in Philippe Vendrix, ed., *Johannes Ciconia: musicien de la transition* (Turnhout: Brepols, 2003), pp. 169–94

ed., *Il manoscritto alpha.M.5.24 della Biblioteca Estense* (Lucca: Libreria Musicale Italiana, 2004)

Strayer, Joseph, ed., *Dictionary of the Middle Ages* (New York: Scribner, 1982–2003)

Strohm, Reinhard, *The Rise of European Music 1380–1500* (Cambridge University Press, 1993)

Strunk, Oliver, *Source Readings in Music History* (New York: Norton, 1950)

  Source Readings in Music History, rev. edn., ed. Leo Treitler (New York: Norton, 1998)

Sullivan, Blair, 'The Unwritable Sound of Music: The Origins and Implications of Isidore's Memorial Metaphor', *Viator* 30 (1999), pp. 1–13

Switten, Margaret L., *Music and Poetry in the Middle Ages: A Guide to Research on French and Occitan Song, 1100–1400* (New York and London: Garland, 1995)

Symons, Thomas, ed. and trans., *Regularis Concordia Anglicae Nationis Monachorum Sanctimonialiumque. The Monastic Agreement of the Monks and Nuns of the English Nation* (London and New York: Nelson, 1953)

Szarmach, Paul, Tavormina, M. Teresa and Rosenthal, Joel T., eds., *Medieval England: An Encyclopedia* (London: Garland, 1998)

Szendrei, Janka, 'Gibt es ein ungarisches Gregorianum? Über das Problem des Nationalcharakters der Gregorianik im Licht der ungarischen Choralquellen', in Stefan Fricke, Wolf Frobenius, Sigrid Konrad and Theo Schmitt, eds., *Zwischen Volks- und Kunstmusik: Aspekte der ungarischen Musik* (Saarbrücken: Pfau-Verlag, 1999), pp. 28–42

  Medieval Notated Codex Fragments from Hungary, trans. E. Mészáros (Budapest: Hungarian Academy of Sciences, 2000)

  'The Introduction of Staff Notation into Middle Europe', *Studia Musicologica* 28 (1986), pp. 303–19

  and Mária Czigler, eds., *The Istanbul Antiphonal c.1360*, Musicalia Danubiana 18 (Budapest: Akadémiai Kiadó, 2002)

Tacconi, Marica, *Cathedral and Civic Ritual in Late Medieval and Renaissance Florence: The Service Books of Santa Maria del Fiore* (Cambridge University Press, 2006)

Taft, Robert, 'The Structural Analysis of Liturgical Units: An Essay in Methodology', *Worship* 52 (1978), pp. 314–29

  The Liturgy of the Hours in East and West: The Origins of the Divine Office and Its Meaning for Today, rev. edn (Collegeville: Liturgical Press, 1993)

Talley, Thomas, *The Origins of the Liturgical Year*, 2nd edn (Collegeville: Liturgical Press, 1991)

Tanay, Dorit Esther, *Noting Music, Marking Culture*, Musicological Studies and Documents 46 (Holzerlingen: Hänssler, 1999)

Tanselle, George Thomas, *A Rationale of Textual Criticism* (Philadelphia: University of Pennsylvania Press, 1989)

Taruskin, Richard, *The Oxford History of Western Music*, vol. I: *The Earliest Notations to the Sixteenth Century* (Oxford University Press, 2005)

Taylor, Andrew, *Textual Situations: Three Medieval Manuscripts and Their Readers* (Philadelphia: University of Pennsylvania Press, 2002)

Tertullian, *L'anima (De anima)* ed. and trans. Martino Menghi (Venice: Marsilio, 1988)

Tischler, Hans, ed., *The Earliest Motets (to circa 1270): A Complete Comparative Edition*, 3 vols. (New Haven and London: Yale University Press, 1982)

  The Montpellier Codex, 4 vols. (vol. IV edited and translated by Susan Stakel and Joel C. Relihan), Recent Researches in the Music of the Middle Ages and Early Renaissance 2–8 (Madison, WI: A-R Editions, 1978–85)

  The Parisian Two-Part Organa: Complete Comparative Edition, 2 vols. (New York: Pendragon, 1988)

  Trouvère Lyrics with Melodies: Complete Comparative Edition, Corpus Mensurabilis Musicae 107 (Neuhausen: American Institute of Musicology, 1997)

  Trouvère Lyrics with Melodies: Complete Comparative Edition, Revisited (Ottawa: Institute of Mediaeval Music, 2006)

Tolhurst, John Basil Lowder, and the Abbess of Stanbrook [Laurentia McLachlan], *The Ordinal and Customary of the Abbey of Saint Mary, York (Saint John's College, Cambridge, ms d. 27)*, Henry Bradshaw Publications 75 (London: Henry Bradshaw Society, 1936)

Tomasello, Andrew, *Music and Ritual at Papal Avignon 1309–1403*, Studies in Musicology 75 (Ann Arbor and Epping: Bowker Publishing, 1983)

  'Scribal Design in the Compilation of Ivrea Ms. 115', *Musica Disciplina* 42 (1988), pp. 73–100

Traub, Andreas, ed. and trans., 'Hucbald von Saint-Amand: De harmonica institutione', *Beiträge zur Gregorianik* 7 (1989), pp. 3–101

Traube, Ludwig, ed., *Poetae Latini aevi Carolini*, Monumenta Germaniae Historica, Poetae III (Berlin: Weidmann, 1896)

Treitler, Leo, 'Homer and Gregory: The Transmission of Epic Poetry and Plainchant', *Musical Quarterly* 60 (1974), pp. 333–72

  'Medieval Lyric', in Mark Everist, ed., *Models of Musical Analysis: Music before 1600* (Oxford: Basil Blackwell, 1992), pp. 1–19

  'The Polyphony of Saint Martial', *Journal of the American Musicological Society* 17 (1964), pp. 29–42

  With Voice and Pen: Coming to Know Medieval Song and How It Was Made (Oxford and New York: Oxford University Press, 2003)

Tuchman, Barbara Wertheim, *A Distant Mirror: The Calamitous Fourteenth Century* (New York: Knopf, 1978)

Tucoo-Chala, Pierre, *Gaston Fébus, un grand prince d'occident au XIVᵉ siècle* (Pau: Marrimpouey, 1976)

Turner, Samuel Epes, trans., *Einhard: The Life of Charlemagne* (New York: Harper & Brothers, 1880)

Upton, Elizabeth Randell, 'The Chantilly Codex (F-Ch 564): The Manuscript, Its Music, Its Scholarly Reception' (PhD diss., University of North Carolina at Chapel Hill, 2001)

Vale, Malcolm, *The Princely Court: Medieval Courts and Culture in North-West Europe 1270–1380* (Oxford University Press, 2001)

van den Boogaard, Nico, 'Les insertions en français dans un traité de Gérard de Liège', in Rita Lejeune, ed., *Marche romane: mélanges de philologie et de littératures romanes offerts à Jeanne Wathelet-Willem* (Liège: Cahiers de l'A. R. U. Lg., 1978), pp. 679–97

    Rondeaux et refrains du XIIe siècle au début du XIVe: collationnement, introduction, et notes, Bibliothèque française et romane D:3 (Paris: Éditions Klincksieck, 1969)

van Deusen, Nancy, '*Ductus, Tractus, Conductus*: The Intellectual Context of a Musical Genre', in *Theology and Music at the Early University: The Case of Robert Grosseteste and Anonymous IV*, Brill Studies in Intellectual History 57 (Leiden: Brill, 1995)

van Dijk, Stephen J. P., *Sources of the Roman Liturgy*, 2 vols. (Leiden: E. J. Brill, 1963)

    (completed by Joan Hazelden Walker), *The Ordinal of the Papal Court from Innocent III to Boniface VIII, and Related Documents*, Spicilegium Friburgense 22 (Fribourg University Press, 1975)

    and Walker, Joan Hazelden, *The Origins of the Modern Roman Liturgy: The Liturgy of the Papal Court and the Franciscan Order in the Thirteenth Century* (London: Darton, Longmann & Todd; and Westminster, MD: Newman Press, 1960)

Van Vleck, Amelia E., *Memory and Re-creation in Troubador Lyric* (Berkeley: University of California Press, 1991)

Varvaro, Alberto, *Letterature romanze del medioevo* (Bologna: Il Mulino, 1985)

Vecchi, Giuseppe, ed., *Il canzoniere musicale del codice Vaticano Rossi 215*, Monumenta Lyrica Medii Aevi Italica 3/2 (Bologna: Università degli Studi di Bologna, 1966)

Vecchi, Joseph, *Marcheti de Padua Pomerium*, Corpus Scriptorum de Musica 6 ([Rome]: American Institute of Musicology, 1961)

Veselovská, Eva, *Mittelalterliche liturgische Kodizes mit Notation in den Archivbeständen von Bratislava*, Musaeum Musicum (Bratislava: Slovenské národné múzeum – Hudobné múzeum, 2002)

Vivarelli, Carla, '"Di una pretesa scuola napoletana": Sowing the Seeds of the Ars nova at the Court of Robert of Anjon', *Journal of Musicology* 24 (2007), pp. 272–96

Vives, José, ed., *Concilios Visigóticos e Hispano-romanos* (Barcelona: Consejo Superior de Investigaciones Científicas, 1963)

Vlhová-Wörner, Hana, '*Fama crescit eundo*. Der Fall: Domazlaus predicator, der älteste bekannte böhmische Sequenzendichter', *Hudební věda* 39 (2002), pp. 311–30

    Repertorium troporum Bohemiae Medii Aevi, I, *Tropi proprii missae* (Prague: Bärenreiter, 2004)

    Repertorium troporum Bohemiae Medii Aevi, II: Tropi ad Kyrie et Gloria in excelsis Deo (Prague: Bärenreiter, 2006)

    'Středověké liturgické rukopisy z katedrály sv. Víta na Pražském hradě' (PhD diss., Prague: Univerzita Karlova, 2000)

Hana, Jiří Matl and Brodský, Pavel, *Officium sancti Ieronimi. Editio critica.* CD-ROM (Prague: Koniasch Latin Press, 1999)

Vogel, Cyrille, *Medieval Liturgy: An Introduction to the Sources*, trans. William Storey and Niels Rasmussen, assisted by John Brooks-Leonard (Washington, DC: Pastoral Press, 1986)

von Fischer, Kurt, 'Il ciclo dell'Ordinarium missae del ms F-Pn568 (Pit)', in Agostino Ziino, ed., *L'ars nova italiana del Trecento V* (Palermo: Enchiridion, 1985), pp. 123–37

'Musica e società nel Trecento Italiano', in F. Alberto Gallo, ed., *L'Ars nova italiana del Trecento III* (Certaldo: Centro di Studi sull' Ars Nova Italiana del Trecento, 1970), pp. 11–28

'Neue Quellen zur Musik des 13., 14., und 15. Jahrhunderts', *Acta Musicologica* 36 (1964), pp. 79–97

Studien zur italienischen Musik des Trecento und frühen Quattrocento (Bern: Haupt, 1956)

and Gallo, F. Alberto, eds., *Italian Sacred Music*, Polyphonic Music of the Fourteenth Century 12 (Monaco: Éditions de l'Oiseau-Lyre, 1976)

and Gallo, F. Alberto, eds., *Italian Sacred and Ceremonial Music*, Polyphonic Music of the Fourteenth Century 13 (Monaco: Éditions de l'Oiseau-Lyre, 1987)

Waddell, Chrysogonus, 'The Origin and Early Evolution of the Cistercian Antiphonary: Reflections on Two Cistercian Chant Reforms', in M. Basil Pennington, ed., *The Cistercian Spirit: A Symposium: In Memory of Thomas Merton*, Cistercian Studies 3 (Washington, DC: Cistercian Press, 1970), pp. 190–223

Wainwright, Geoffrey and Westerfield Tucker, Karen B., eds., *The Oxford History of Christian Worship* (Oxford University Press, 2006)

Waite, William, ed., *The Rhythm of Twelfth-Century Polyphony: Its Theory and Practice*, Yale Studies in the History of Music 2 (New Haven: Yale University Press; London: Geoffrey Cumberledge and Oxford University Press, 1954)

Walker, Rose, *Views of Transition: Liturgy and Illumination in Medieval Spain* (London: British Library and University of Toronto Press, 1998)

Walker, Thomas, 'Sui Tenor Francesi nei motetti del '200', *Schede medievali: rassegna dell'officina di studi medievali* 3 (1982), 309–36

Wälli, Silvia, *Melodien aus mittelalterlichen Horaz-Handschriften: Edition und Interpretation der Quellen*, Monumenta Monodica Medii Aevi, Subsidia 3 (Kassel: Bärenreiter, 2002)

Wandycz, Piotr, *The Price of Freedom: A History of East Central Europe from the Middle Ages to the Present* (London and New York: Routledge, 1992)

Wangermée, Robert, *Flemish Music and Society in the Fifteenth and Sixteenth Centuries*, trans. Robert Erich Wolf (New York, Washington and London: Praeger, 1968)

Ward, Tom R., 'Polyphonic Music in Central Europe, c.1300–c.1520', in Reinhard Strohm and Bonnie Blackburn, eds., *Music as Concept and Practice in the Late Middle Ages* (Oxford University Press, 2001), pp. 191–243

Wathey, Andrew, 'Lost Books of Polyphony in Medieval England: A List to 1500', *Royal Musical Association: Research Chronicle* 21 (1988), pp. 1–19

   Music in the Royal and Noble Households in Late Medieval England: Studies of Sources and Patronage (New York: Garland, 1989)

   'The Motets of Philippe de Vitry and the Fourteenth-Century Renaissance', *Early Music History* 12 (1993), pp. 119–50

   'The Peace of 1360–1369 and Anglo-French Musical Relations', *Early Music History* 9 (1989), pp. 129–74

   'The Production of Books of Liturgical Polyphony', in Jeremy Griffiths and Derek Pearsall, eds., *Book Production and Publishing in Britain 1375–1475* (Cambridge University Press, 1989), pp. 143–161

   ed., *Berkeley Castle, Select Roll 55: Motets and Sequences from the Early Fourteenth Century* (Newton Abbott: Antico Church Music, 1991)

   ed., *Manuscripts of Polyphonic Music: The British Isles, 1100–1400: Supplement 1 to RISM B IV 1–2* (Munich: G. Henle, 1993)

   Bent, Margaret and Craig-McFeely, Julia, 'The Art of Virtual Restoration: Creating the Digital Image Archive of Medieval Music (DIAMM)', in *The Virtual Score: Representation, Retrieval, Restoration*, special volume of *Computing in Musicology* 12 (1999–2000), pp. 227–40

Webster, James, 'The Concept of Beethoven's "Early" Period in the Context of Periodizations in General', *Beethoven Forum* 3 (1994), pp. 1–27

Wegman, Rob C., '"Das musikalische Hören" in the Middle Ages and Renaissance: Perspectives from Pre-War Germany', *Musical Quarterly* 82 (1998), pp. 434–53

Weiss, Piero and Taruskin, Richard, eds., *Music in the Western World: A History in Documents* (New York: Schirmer Books, 1984)

Werf, Hendrik van der, 'Early Western Polyphony', in Tess Knighton and David Fallows, eds., *Companion to Medieval and Renaissance Music* (London: Dent, 1992), pp. 107–13

   'Jean Renart and Medieval Song', in Nancy Vine During, ed., *Jean Renart and the Art of Romance: Essays on Guillaume de Dole* (Gainesville: University Press of Florida, 1997), pp. 157–88

   review of Samuel N. Rosenberg and Hans Tischler, eds., *Chanter m' estuet: Songs of the Trouvères*, in *Journal of the American Musicological Society* 35 (1982), pp. 539–54

   The Chansons of the Troubadours and Trouvères: A Study of the Melodies and Their Relation to the Poems (Utrecht: Oesthoek, 1972)

   The Emergence of Gregorian Chant: A Comparative Study of Ambrosian, Roman, and Gregorian Chant (Rochester, NY: author, 1983)

   The Oldest Extant Part Music and the Origin of Western Polyphony, 2 vols. (Rochester, NY: author, 1993)

   ed., *Trouvères-Melodien* I and II, Monumenta Monodica Medii Aevi 10–12 (Kassel: Bärenreiter, 1979)

   and Bond, Gerald A., eds., *The Extant Troubadour Melodies: Transcriptions and Essays for Performers and Scholars* (Rochester, NY: author, 1984)

Wheeler, Bonnie and Parsons, John Carmi, eds., *Eleanor of Aquitaine, Lord and Lady* (New York: Palgrave Macmillan, 2002)

Wickham, Chris, *Framing the Early Middle Ages: Europe and the Mediterranean 400–800* (Oxford University Press, 2005)

Williams, John and Stones, Alison, eds., *The Codex Calixtinus and the Shrine of St James* (Tübingen: Narr, 1992)

Willis, James, ed., *Martianus Capella: De nuptiis Philologiae et Mercurii* (Leipzig: B. G. Teubner, 1983)

Wilmart, André, 'Gérard de Liège: *Quinque incitamenta ad Deum amandum ardenter*', in *Analecta reginensia*, Studi e testi 59 (Vatican City: Biblioteca Apostolica Vaticana, 1933), pp. 205–47

Wilson, Blake, *Music and Merchants: The Laudesi Companies of Republican Florence* (Oxford: Clarendon Press, 1992)

    The Florence Laudario: An Edition of Florence, Biblioteca Nazionale Centrale, Banco rari 18, Recent Researches in the Music of the Middle Ages and Early Renaissance 29 (Madison, WI: A-R Editions, 1995)

Wimsatt, James I., *Chaucer and the Poems of 'Ch' in University of Pennsylvania MS French 15*, Chaucer Studies 9 (Cambridge: Brewer, 1982)

    Kibler, William W., and Rebecca A. Baltzer eds., *Guillaume de Machaut: Le Jugement du roy de Behaigne and Remede de Fortune* (Athens, GA: University of Georgia Press, 1988)

Winkler, Heinz-Jürgen, 'Zur Vertonung von Mariendichtung in antiken Versmaßen bei Johannes Ockeghem und Johannes Regis', in Philippe Vendrix, ed., *Johannes Ockeghem: Actes du XLᵉ Colloque international d'études humanistes, Tours, 3–8 février 1997* (Paris: Klincksieck, 1998), pp. 571–93

Wolinski, Mary, 'The Compilation of the Montpellier Codex', *Early Music History* 11 (1992), pp. 263–301

Wood, Diana, *Clement VI: The Pontificate and Ideas of an Avignon Pope*, Cambridge Studies in Medieval Life and Thought: Fourth Series 13 (Cambridge University Press, 1989)

Wright, Craig, *Music and Ceremony at Notre Dame of Paris 500–1500* (Cambridge University Press, 1989)

    The Maze and the Warrior: Symbols in Architecture, Theology, and Music (Cambridge, MA: Harvard University Press, 2001)

    'Voices and Instruments in the Art Music of Northern France during the 15th Century: A Conspectus', in Daniel Heartz and Bonnie Wade, eds., *International Musicological Society: Report of the Twelfth Congress, Berkeley 1977* (Kassel: Bärenreiter, 1981), pp. 643–49

Yardley, Anne Bagnall, '"Ful weel she soong the service dyvyne": The Cloistered Musician in the Middle Ages', in Jane Bowers and Judith Tick, eds., *Women Making Music: The Western Art Tradition, 1150–1950* (Urbana: University of Illinois, 1986), pp. 15–39

    Performing Piety: Musical Culture in Medieval English Nunneries (New York: Palgrave Press, 2006)

Young, Karl, *The Drama of the Medieval Church*, 2 vols. (Oxford: Clarendon Press, 1933)

Yudkin, Jeremy, 'The Anonymous of St. Emmeram and Anonymous IV on the Copula', *Musical Quarterly* 70 (1984), pp. 1–22

    'The Copula According to Johannes de Garlandia', *Musica disciplina* 34 (1980), pp. 67–84

'The Rhythm of Organum Purum', *Journal of Musicology* 2 (1983), pp. 355–76

  ed., *De musica mensurata: The Anonymous of St. Emmeram* (Bloomington, IN: Indiana University Press, 1990)

Zaminer, Frieder, et al., eds., *Geschichte der Musiktheorie*, vols. I and II (Darmstadt: Wissenschaftliche Buchgesellschaft, 2000)

Zapke, Susana, *Das Antiphonar von Sta. Cruz de la Serós, XII. Jh.* (Neuried: Ars Una, 1996)

  ed., *Hispania Vetus: Musical-Liturgical Manuscripts from Visigothic Origins to the Franco-Roman Transition* (*9th–12th Centuries*) (Bilbao: Fundación BBVA, 2007)

Zayas, Rodrigo de, 'Musicology and the Cultural Heritage of the Spanish Moors', in Carol E. Robertson, ed., *Musical Repercussions of 1492: Encounters in Text and Performance* (Washington: Smithsonian Institution Press, 1992), pp. 129–48

Ziino, Agostino, ed., *Il Codice T.III.2 Torino, Biblioteca Nazionale Universitaria* (Lucca: Libreria Musicale Italiana, 1994)

Zimei, Francesco, ed., *Antonio Zacara da Teramo e il suo tempo* (Lucca: Libreria Musicale Italiana, 2004)

Ziolkowski, Jan M., *Nota Bene: Reading Classics and Writing Melodies in the Early Middle Ages*, Publications of the Journal of Medieval Latin 7 (Turnhout: Brepols, 2007)

Zwolińska, Elżbieta, 'Musica mensuralis w polskich źródłach muzycznych do 1600 roku', in Elżbieta Witkowska-Zaremba, ed., *Notae musicae artis. Notacja muzyczna w źródłach polskich XI–XVI wieku* (Cracow: Musica Iagellonica, 1999)

Index

Cambridge Companions to Music